WORKSHOPS IN COMPUTING
Series edited by C. J. van Rijsbergen

Also in this series

continued on back page...

Norman W. Paton and M. Howard Williams (Eds.)

Rules in Database Systems

Proceedings of the 1st International
Workshop on Rules in Database Systems,
Edinburgh, Scotland, 30 August–
1 September 1993

Published in collaboration with the
British Computer Society

Springer-Verlag
London Berlin Heidelberg New York
Paris Tokyo Hong Kong
Barcelona Budapest

Norman W. Paton, BSc, PhD

M. Howard Williams, BSc, PhD, FRSA, FBCS, CEng

Department of Computing and Electrical Engineering,
Heriot-Watt University, Riccarton, Edinburgh, EH14 4AS
Scotland

ISBN-13: 978-3-540-19846-8   e-ISBN-13: 978-1-4471-3225-7
DOI: 10.1007/978-1-4471-3225-7

British Library Cataloguing in Publication Data
Rules in Database Systems : Proceedings of the 1st International Workshop on
Rules in Database Systems, Edinburgh, Scotland, 30 August–1 September 1993. –
(Workshops in Computing Series)
   I.   Paton, Norman W.   II.   Williams, M.H.   III.   Series
   005.74

Library of Congress Cataloging-in-Publication Data
International Workshop on Rules in Database Systems (1st : 1993 : Edinburgh,
Scotland)
   Rules in database systems : proceedings of the 1st International Workshop on
Rules in Database Systems, Edinburgh, Scotland, 30 August–1 September 1993/
Norman W. Paton and M. Howard Williams, (eds).
      p. cm. – (Workshops in computing)
   "Published in collaboration with the British Computer Society."
   Includes bibliographical references and index.

   1.   Data base management–Congresses.   2.   Rule-based programming–
Congresses.   I.   Paton, Norman W.   II.   Williams, M. Howard.
III.   British Computer Society.   IV.   Title.   V.   Series.
QA76.9.D3I594 1993   93–27566
005.74–dc20   CIP

Typesetting: Camera ready by contributors

34/3830-543210 Printed on acid-free paper

Preface

This book is the proceedings of a workshop held at Heriot-Watt University in Edinburgh in August 1993. The central theme of the workshop was *rules in database systems*, and the papers presented covered a range of different aspects of database rule systems. These aspects are reflected in the sessions of the workshop, which are the same as the sections in this proceedings:

Active Databases
Architectures Incorporating Temporal Rules
Rules and Transactions
Analysis and Debugging of Active Rules
Integrating Graphs/Objects with Deduction
Integrating Deductive and Active Rules
Integrity Constraints
Deductive Databases

The incorporation of rules into database systems is an important area of research, as it is a major component in the integration of behavioural information with the structural data with which commercial databases have traditionally been associated. This integration of the behavioural aspects of an application with the data to which it applies in database systems leads to more straightforward application development and more efficient processing of data. Many novel applications seem to need database systems in which structural and behavioural information are fully integrated.

Rules are only one means of expressing behavioural information, but it is clear that different types of rule can be used to capture directly different properties of an application which are cumbersome to support using conventional database architectures.

In recent years there has been a surge of research activity focusing upon active database systems, and this volume opens with a collection of papers devoted specifically to this topic. In the first of these, **Lockemann and Walter** argue that the mechanism provided by active databases is too general and too low-level for handling many applications, such as those which arise in Computer Integrated Manufacturing. To overcome this they propose the notion of an activity, an idea borrowed from tele-communication protocols. An activity provides a means of controlling relationships among active objects by defining constraints which participating objects must conform to. These constraints are specified by means of event-action rules. A prototype for a subset of this model has been implemented.

Gatziu and Dittrich are concerned with the problems of specification, detection and management of events in an object-oriented database system called SAMOS (Swiss Active Mechanism-based Object-oriented database System). For the specification of events a simple but powerful set of constructs is introduced in which events are detected using an approach based upon petri nets.

The paper by **Paton** *et al*, "Dimensions of Active Behaviour", identifies a number of aspects which affect the behaviour of a set of rules at execution time. These aspects, referred to as dimensions, provide a means of characterising and comparing the behaviour of individual active rule systems and the applications to which they can be applied.

The topic of rule management within an active database system is the subject addressed by **Naqvi and Ibrahim**. They describe an active database research prototype called REFLEX, which is designed as an extension to existing database systems. The paper presents the architecture of REFLEX and considers example applications.

By their nature, active database systems are concerned with the notion of time, and it is therefore natural to include some discussion of temporal issues. Two papers deal with architectures which incorporate temporal rules.

Su and Chen put forward a model OSAM*/T in which the definitions of temporal rules are included within the specifications of object classes and object instances. They also describe a language based on this model in which temporal rules are classified into state rules, deductive rules and operational rules. These rules are treated as first class objects and can be managed uniformly as temporal data by the KBMS.

In the paper by **Etzion, Gal and Segev**, the PARDES model is described as a model for maintaining data driven rules. The effects of introducing a temporal dimension to this model are discussed, including the notions of transaction time, valid time and decision time. The types of temporal operations which are required to support transaction processing are also described.

A related issue is that of transactions. **Branding** *et al* describe an active object system called REACH (REal-time ACtive Heterogeneous system) which can be used to control heterogeneous database systems under real-time conditions. Boundaries are defined between controlling and controlled systems, and a rule system defined which includes events and actions in each. Two new coupling modes are identified for handling irreversible actions in external systems and contingency plans.

Geppert and Dittrich are concerned with the development of a construction methodology for DBMS. They consider the problem of specifying transaction models in the context of such a methodology. A mechanism is proposed in which a DBMS is considered to be made up of a set of brokers, each of which comprises a set of production rules. Specifications of transaction models can be expressed in terms of rules which can be transformed into production rules describing the behaviour of the transaction management broker.

The design of a transaction management system which is geared to the integration of database production rule systems is described in the paper by **Danner and Ranft**. This is part of the Joker system (JCF Object-oriented Knowledge Representation and Management Component) which is being developed as part of an Esprit project. This paper discusses the relationship between the object management system, which integrates several different inference mechanisms, and the nested transaction management component in such a way as to support efficient rule evaluation.

As interest in active rule systems grows, there is increasing activity in trying to understand models underlying such systems and in improving the tools for using them. The next group of papers is concerned with facilities for analysis and debugging of active rules.

One of the problems of rule-based systems is that of ensuring that any given set of rules is guaranteed to terminate. **Baralis, Ceri and Widom** consider the problem of termination analysis for active database rules by syntactic analysis. They present an algebraic model for a class of rules together with a theory which determines when rules may activate each other. This forms the basis of an approach to termination analysis for active databases which is less conservative than earlier proposals.

Another problem with active rule systems is the difficulty in understanding the effects of large sets of interacting active rules. Tools are needed to assist users by providing debugging and explanation facilities. **Díaz, Jaime and Paton** describe an approach which they have implemented in a rule debugger for the EXACT rule system for the object-oriented database system ADAM.

Rules can be used for the enforcement of constraints and the maintenance of views, provided that the rule set displays confluent and terminating behaviour. **Van der Voort and Siebes** discuss the enforcement of confluence in the case of a terminating, dependent rule set. An ordering mechanism is defined for the enforcement of confluence without redefinition of dependent rules, together with a means for transforming dependent to independent rules.

Over the last 15 years there has been considerable research into deductive rules for inferring new information from stored facts. This is an important topic of research, and a number of papers on deductive rules are included in this volume. The first group of these focuses on the integration of graphs and objects with deductive systems.

Paredaens, Peelman and Tanca consider the merging of the pattern matching computation paradigm for graph-based languages with the fixpoint computation paradigm for deductive databases. These two paradigms are combined in the query language G-log. A sublanguage of G-log, called Generative G-log, is described which is the graphical equivalent of Datalog, and which can be implemented using a more efficient backtracking fixpoint algorithm than is possible for G-log.

Fernandes, Paton and Williams describe work done on combining the deductive and object-oriented paradigms for databases. They describe an approach to doing this which is similar to that used to extend relational databases with deduction in the last decade. The work is focused on a logical query language called ROLL (Rule Object Logic Language), and

describes the underlying data model and issues relating to its implementation in a prototype.

Benkerimi and Poulovassilis report on work done on a graph-based
declarative language called Hyperlog. After defining the semantics of the
language in terms of a naive bottom-up evaluation strategy, they show
that the semi-naive evaluation strategy developed for relational languages
can be adapted to evaluate Hyperlog programs efficiently.

A topic of particular relevance to this collection of papers is that of the
integration of deductive and active rules. The paper by **Zaniolo** discusses
the problems of integrating these two paradigms and, in particular, the
lack of a unified underlying semantics. He then shows how an extended
model for stratification can be used to unify the two, and outlines the
design of a new rule language based on this approach.

Harrison and Dietrich describe how active and deductive rules can
be integrated through extension and optimisations to a Propagation/
Filtration algorithm which enables events to be detected which affect
both stored and derived relations. An event detector and condition
evaluator have been developed on this basis for an active deductive
database.

Widom approaches the problem by asking whether deductive and
active databases are indeed two separate paradigms, or merely two ends
of a spectrum corresponding to a single paradigm. She argues that the
latter is the case, and that this spectrum can be used to classify proposals
according to how 'declarative' they are.

Bayer and Jonker propose a framework for introducing triggers into
deductive databases. This focuses on a definition of events and event
occurrences (including composite events), and on how this can be applied
to deductive databases. This approach contrasts with that of **Zaniolo**, in
that the semantics of the active rules are not built so directly on the
semantics of the deductive language.

Another important type of rule in database systems is the integrity
constraint, and this is the topic of the next three papers.

Research on the enforcement of integrity constraints in database
systems is reviewed by **Fraternali and Paraboschi**. They describe the
problem of enforcing constraints in general, describe several recent
contributions in this area, and compare them from the point of view of a
number of characterising features.

The SORAC project (Semantic Objects, Relationships And
Constraints) is the subject of a paper by **Doherty, Peckham and Wolfe**.
This project extends an object-oriented model by adding active semantic
relationships. These can be used to express and enforce constraints on an
object. The DDL of SORAC (OIL – Object Interaction Language) can be
automatically mapped to a database implementation using ONTOS.

Embury, Gray and Bassiliades consider how code-generated methods
in Prolog can be used as a flexible and efficient way of implementing
complex semantic constraints in an OODB. The approach has been
implemented in P/FDM using a syntax derived from that of DAPLEX in
a manner which allows querying of constraint descriptions.

The final two papers are devoted to problems within deductive
databases *per se*. The problem of allocating data to different sites in a

distributed database is well known. **Mohania and Sarda** consider the related problem of allocating rules to sites in a distributed deductive database system, and propose an efficient heuristic algorithm for achieving this. The paper presents the results of experimental evaluation of the algorithm using both random hierarchies and hierarchies with varying heights.

Since query languages such as Datalog do not permit the user to query information regarding the schema of the database, the language HiLog (and a restriction of this language called DataHiLog) has been developed which permits a mixture of schema-level and instance-level queries. **Wood** demonstrates how the techniques for evaluating Datalog can be extended to provide a bottom-up evaluation mechanism for DataHiLog.

In conclusion, the proceedings of this workshop present a snapshot of research into different aspects of the use of rules within database systems, and integrate in a single volume papers on a variety of ways in which such systems can contribute to enhancing the next generation of commercial systems.

October 1993   Norman Paton
                                                                          Howard Williams

Contents

Integrating Graphs/Objects with Deduction

Integrating Deductive and Active Rules

Integrity Constraints

Deductive Databases

Acknowledgements

We are particularly indebted to the programme committee for their invaluable assistance in evaluating the 52 papers submitted to the workshop, to yield the 24 which are included in this proceedings. The programme committee consisted of:

J.B. Bocca (Birmingham Uni., UK)
M. Bouzeghoub (Uni. M. Curie, France)
F. Bry (ECRC, Germany)
A. Buchmann (Tech. Uni. Darmstadt, Germany)
G. von Bueltzingsloewen (FZI, Karlsruhe, Germany)
S. Chakravarthy (Uni. Florida, USA)
O. Díaz (Uni. Pais Vasco, Spain)
K.R. Dittrich (Uni. Zurich, Switzerland)
P.M.D. Gray (Aberdeen Uni., UK)
K.G. Jeffery (Rutherford Labs., UK)
R. Manthey (Uni. Bonn, Germany)
N.W. Paton (Heriot-Watt Uni., UK)
T. Sellis (Nat. Tech. Uni. Athens, Greece)
M.H. Williams (Heriot-Watt Uni., UK)
K.F. Wong (Chinese Uni., Hong-Kong)

We are also grateful to the following who helped with reviews: P. Stamatopoulos (U. of Athens, Greece), J. Harrison (U. of Queensland, Australia), S. Bressan (ECRC, Germany), B. Bayer (ECRC, Germany), P. Massey (BIM, Belgium), J. Campin (Heriot-Watt), A. Dinn (Heriot-Watt), R.H. Davis (Heriot-Watt), A. Fernandes (Heriot-Watt) and H. Taylor (Heriot-Watt).

The organising committee consisted of the editors, plus Andrew Dinn and Alvaro Fernandes. We are extremely thankful for the systematic and efficient manner in which Andrew and Alvaro contributed to the smooth running of the workshop.

We would also like to express our thanks to a number of people who helped to publicise the workshop, including R. Anderson, B. Lundberg, A. Pitotte, C. Thanos, Y. Vassiliou, M. Orlowska, S. Nishio, S. Sa, K.-C. Lee, C. Tan, J. Fong, L. Tucherman, R. Carapuca, M. Kersten, R. Anderson and K. Jeffery.

The impetus behind this workshop emerged, at least in part, from the European Community Human Capital and Mobility Network ACT-NET.

Active Databases

Activities in Object Bases†

Peter C. Lockemann
Hans-Dirk Walter

Fakultät für Informatik, Universität Karlsruhe,
Karlsruhe, Germany

Abstract

Objects are collected into an object base because of a presumed need for cooperation among them. In classical object bases the cooperation is based on synchronous, preplanned message exchange. Many of the modern application scenarios such as industrial and office automation with their high volume of concurrent, interleaved, and iterative actions defy preplanning and require the support of a highly dynamic relationships among the objects.

It is the central hypothesis of this paper that the dynamics within such an object base is best covered by the metaphor of communications protocol taken from the telecommunications world. Active objects with their individual threads-of-control establish temporary communication links via a medium which we refer to as activities. Active objects and activity cooperate via a protocol. The main benefit of such an approach is a clear separation of object-local and cooperative aspects of a common task.

The paper augments an existing strongly-typed object-oriented language by active objects with an underlying event processing model based on incoming messages, and by activities with an event processing model based on interfering messages. The interplay between them is demonstrated by an implementation of the classical Two-Phase-Commit protocol as a generic example for negotiations among objects.

1 Introduction

Dynamic cooperation strategies Objects are collected into an object base because of a presumed need for cooperation among them. In classical object bases the cooperation is initiated by synchronous calls to methods of other objects. Such a strategy presupposes a clear a-priori understanding of how cooperation between objects contributes to the problem solution. If such an understanding does not exist — for example because the cooperation is influenced by unpredictable events outside the object base — a more dynamic cooperation strategy is required that allows to respond directly to a spontaneously observed situation. Active objects seem a suitable basis for such a dynamic strategy.

A typical application area where the importance of dynamic strategies seems to grow is Computer Integrated Manufacturing (CIM). Technical artifacts such as mechanical parts, VLSI circuits follow a life cycle model that ranges from

---

†This work was partly supported by the German Research Council (Deutsche Forschungsgemeinschaft DFG) under grant SFB346 Project A1.

early conception through all production phases to their delivery or, finally, recycling and disposal. As it passes along the life cycle, the artifact involves a large number of people, machines, storage facilities and transport vehicles at a wide spectrum of geographic locations.

Internally those artifacts are represented in the object base as a whole set of tightly interrelated objects. Interrelationship invokes interdependence to a certain degree: If during maintenance the construction must be modified, objects reflecting earlier phases must undergo concomitant changes or spawn new versions.

In today's manufacturing world these interdependencies seem to grow. Even in a strictly sequential life cycle model some iterations are unavoidable. However, with a tendency towards simultaneous engineering the interrelationships between the objects of the various phases will become much tighter. Not only will the mutual interactions between objects become more numerous, they also seem to become unplanned and unpredictable, or technically speaking, they seem to take place highly asynchronously.

Activities among active objects Interaction between objects in such an environment will have to follow a metaphor that is particularly suited to asynchronity. Such a metaphor should include two aspects:

1. Objects must seemingly spring to life on their own, take by themselves the initiative to raise or observe events, or to establish communication links to other objects.

2. Once established, a communication link must follow a procedure that is both calculated enough to attain the objective of the cooperation, and flexible enough to do so in light of indeterministic behavior of the participating objects or of disturbances in the communication media.

The first aspect seems to be well-covered by some sort of event-rule mechanism. The second aspect has its traditional counterpart in the notion of telecommunication protocol. Consequently, as a foundation for dynamic cooperation strategies among objects we propose to merge mechanisms for both aspects into a single framework. Within this framework we refer to the first as *active objects*, to the second as *activities*.

Objectives of the paper Today's object-oriented database models fail to distinguish between the two mechanisms and, hence, permit little control over either of them. In the classical, synchronous models the flow of control between cooperating objects is distributed across several object definitions and hidden in the method implementations. Active object-oriented database systems (e.g. [4, 11]) support active objects by means of rules and triggers. However, communication control is still spread across the objects by making all events — such as the invocation of a method from an application or from another object — globally visible to all objects, thus forcing all of them to evaluate the rules. More progressive are methods of object-oriented analysis and design [20]. They provide an object model which follows the traditional approach of object-orientation, and a dynamic model which employs events, scenarios, and state diagrams. Unfortunately, the two models lead a separate life in [20].

To overcome these shortcomings, we propose an object model where active objects communicate by (asynchronously) exchanging messages. Each object has its own thread-of-control in order to schedule the processing of incoming messages. Cooperation relationships between active objects can be expressed by activities which constrain the communications between participating objects and define actions to compensate for protocol violations. These constraints are only supervised as long as the activity exists. Thus, an application programmer will be able to flexibly control the dynamic constraints which normally depend on the task that shall be accomplished by the objects which cooperate in an activity. This approach helps to make a clear distinction between those parts of the code which exclusively relate to an individual object, and those parts of the code that focus on the mutual obligations of cooperating objects.

In this paper we present the concepts and a language that enhance the (conventional) object paradigm towards object activity and cooperation. The organization of the paper is as follows. In the next section we present an example which we will use to illustrate our ideas. Section 3 introduces the object model — an existing, strongly-typed object-oriented database programming language. Section 4 adds to this model the first dynamics mechanism, active objects. Section 5 augments it by the second mechanism, activities. In section 6 we demonstrate how active objects and activities interplay with each other. Section 7 relates our approach to the substantial work done elsewhere in order to identify our major contributions. Section 8 concludes the paper.

2   Scenario: Negotiation

A typical scenario involving a high degree of dynamicity is negotiation. Suppose a warehouse stocking large quantities of items, with clients ordering items and suppliers providing items. Suppose further an unusual-size order from a client which cannot be met with the current inventory. Hence, the warehouse will start to bargain with its suppliers on who will be able to deliver the item in sufficient quantity and quality at the best price within a given time period. The warehouse will ultimately settle on one or more suppliers. After ordering the item the warehouse will have to negotiate with the client whether under the conditions obtained from the suppliers the offer will be acceptable to him or not; the client eventually may accept the offer or revoke his order.

The scenario can be automated to a certain degree so that it makes sense to have warehouse, clients, suppliers, and orders reflected by objects of an object base. There is a large degree of communication between the objects, with one object initiating the communication and others forced to respond, or at liberty to respond or to ignore the request. The response may be delayed so that an outsider may not even be able to establish a clear connection to an earlier communication: the object seems to become active on its own initiative, generating a spontaneous event. The same is true when external actions such as the invocation of an order takes place. Several objects may have to coordinate their responses, particularly in m:n situations. On the other hand, a certain regimen must be imposed on all that interaction such that a commonly agreed objective can be attained.

In an object-oriented database which satisfies this scenario each or at least a certain spectrum of objects in the database ought to have their own thread-of-control like their real-world counterparts. Further, we need to identify tasks that a group of cooperating objects shall accomplish, and specify for them communication protocols which constrain the communication patterns (e.g., sequences of messages), and the actions to take when those constraints are violated by one of the participating objects. Also, objects should coordinate those of their actions that they execute in the scope of several activities they participate in at the same time.

In general, negotiation patterns are highly idiosyncratic. For reasons of economy generic patterns are desirable, though. For example, the well-known Two-Phase Commit Protocol (2PC) could be regarded as such a generic pattern. Consequently, we shall employ a simple 2PC variant as a running example for the remainder of the paper. It works as follows. Initially, the coordinator writes a *begin_commit* record in its log, sends a *prepare* message to all agent sites, and enters the *WAIT* state. When an agent receives a *prepare* message, it checks if it can commit the transaction. If so, the agent writes a *ready* record to its log, sends a *vote_commit* message to the coordinator, and enters the *READY* state; otherwise, the agent writes an *abort* record and sends a *vote_abort* message to the coordinator. If the decision of the agent is to abort, it can forget about that transaction, since an abort decision serves as a veto (i.e., *unilateral abort*). Each agent has only one vote. After the coordinator received a reply from every agent, it decides whether to commit or to abort the transaction. If even a single agent had registered a negative vote, the coordinator has to abort the transaction globally. So it writes an *abort* record, sends an *abort* message to all agent sites save those that voted in the negative, and enters the *ABORT* state; otherwise, it writes a *commit* record, sends a *commit* message to all agents, and enters the *COMMIT* state. Each agent either commits or aborts the transaction according to the coordinator's instructions, and sends back an acknowledgement (it is not allowed to alter its vote). After all these have come in the coordinator terminates the transaction by writing an *end_of_transaction* record to its log.

3   The Object Model GOM

In this section the basic concepts of the object-oriented data model GOM are described — on an intuitive, somewhat informal basis by way of our example. In essence, GOM provides all the compulsory features identified in [3] in one orthogonal syntactical framework. We restrict ourselves to those aspects needed for the discussions of this paper. Readers interested in more details are referred to [15].

Types   Objects incorporate a *structural* and a *behavioral* description. Objects with similar properties, i.e., structure and behavior, are classified into types. A new object type is introduced using an *object type definition frame* for which an example is shown in figure 1.

A newly defined type has a unique type name. The **body** clause precedes the definition of the structural representation of the type. We distinguish tuple-structured types and collection types (see below). The behavior of objects (of a type) is specified by a set of type-associated operations. The **operations** clause contains the abstract signatures of these operations, each consisting of

```
object type Site is
    body [ otherSites: {Site}; log: <Record>; state: State;
           votes: {VoteEntry}; actDC: DC; ]
    operations
        declare initiateCommit:  → void;
        declare prepare: DC  → Vote;
        declare voted: Vote, Site  → void;
        declare globalCommit:  → void;
        declare globalAbort:  → void;
        declare commit:  → void;
        declare abort:  → void;
        declare terminate: bool  → void;
    implementation ...
end object type Site;
```

Figure 1: The object type definition of *Site*

an operation name, a list of input parameter types and the result type. The implementation of these operations is supplied under the **implementation** clause. Operations can be implemented in a C-like syntax offering all control constructs that are usual in "normal" programming languages (e.g., assignment, conditional statements, loops, etc.). Due to space limitations we will not discuss this language in further detail. The state of an instance of an object type may only be accessed by invoking its type-associated operations.

Structural description   Object type *Site* of figure 1 unifies coordinator and agents into a single concept. Such an object is tuple-structured. A tuple consists of a collection of typed attributes. In addition to the tuple constructor, GOM offers type constructors to define *set-* and a *list-structured* types. The structure of a *Site* object contains a set-valued attribute in which identifiers of other known sites — and thus potential partners — can be stored (*otherSites*), a list-valued attribute for the log records, an attribute for storing the actual state which the site is in during a 2PC, and a set where it can store the votes of other sites. The last attribute *actDC* will be explained in section 5. We omit the exact definitions of the types *Record*, *State*, and *VoteEntry*.

Objects are instantiated by using the predefined *create* operation. This operation returns the system-wide unique object identifier of the new object.

Behavioral decription and its shortcomings   Note that the definition of object type *Site* is such that a site may elect to act as either a coordinator or an agent. Now remember that our discussion in section 2 of the 2PC was in terms of the initiatives taken by an object. Unfortunately, in a traditional object model we have to take a complementary approach: Association of operations is with the recipient of the messages, i.e., with the passive communication partner. According to section 2, *Site* accepts the following messages (see figure 1):

In its role as a coordinator: initiateCommit (external request to start the 2PC); *vote* (commit or abort voted by an agent identified by its site); *terminate* (final acknowledgement from the agent); *globalCommit* and *globalAbort* (external request to globally commit or abort a distributed transaction).

In its role as an agent: prepare (request for a vote from the coordinator); *commit* and *abort* (final disposition of the local transaction as requested by the coordinator).

This specification of *Site* sounds kind of unnatural and indeed is difficult to extract from the scenario of section 2. For example, the two messages *globalCommit* and *globalAbort* are only required because the coordinator *Site* is passive, thus forcing the application (an outsider) to check whether all votes have come in — e.g. by polling the database — in order to give the final disposition of the transaction according to the given vote. This is a first clue to the need for a more natural description of the dynamics. Keeping track of all the past, e.g. the votes, and responding on its own once all have come in is one aspect. Events may be the means to do so. Reflecting initiatives rather than receptions is, as mentioned before, a second aspect.

Further, each object has the potential for being a coordinator or an agent, and in fact may be both as in the case of a hierarchical 2PC (see, e.g., CCR [5]). It is also conceivable that some objects may be prohibited from ever becoming coordinators or agents. Consequently, it makes sense to relocate the 2PC somewhere outside the objects and let them deal with just their local transactions and status.

4 Active Objects

4.1 Types and Computation Model

Object Type Definition Frame We turn to our first proposition: to add events. In order to do so we extend the object type definition frame by an event clause. Since active objects may wish to observe their environment for events, and then respond to them, we should also include (event-action) rules [11]. Consequently, we further extend the definition frame by a rules section. The extended specification of a *Site* is shown in figure 2. Before we discuss the events and rules in detail we give a brief overview how an active *Site* object "works".

Event Model In the traditional event models, events are raised by someone, and taken care of by someone else, perhaps conditionally, according to event-condition-action rules (e.g., [4, 7, 11, 17]). In a way, events establish a loose connection since they give the observers a certain degree of latitude on how to react. On the other hand, messages establish a much tighter connection: They address themselves directly to a recipient and prescribe the particular operations to be invoked; they also imply a return message to the sender. Since we wish to embed both, events and messages, within a uniform framework, we establish the following model.

Each active object has a mailbox where incoming messages can be buffered sequentially. The set of messages an object can "understand", i.e., is able to process, is determined by its type. Every time a message arrives at an object an event of the corresponding type is raised.

An object may defer action. For example, an object may wait until a set of certain messages has arrived before it starts processing, and may then decide to ignore some messages. One may consider the materialization of a

```
object type Site is
    body [ !! as before; see figure 1 ]
    operations !! as before; see figure 1
    events
        declare prepareOrder: DC;
        declare commitOrder;
        declare abortOrder;
        declare globalCommit;
        declare globalAbort;
        declare hasVoted: Vote, Site;
        declare endOfDC: bool;
    rules
        on initiateCommit do self.initiateCommit;
        on prepareOrder(dc: DC) do self.prepare(dc);
        on commitOrder do self.commit;
        on abortOrder do self.abort;
        on hasVoted(v: Vote, s: Site) do self.vote(v, s);
        on globalCommit do self.globalCommit;
        on globalAbort do self.globalAbort;
        on endOfDC(b: bool) do self.terminate(b);
    implementation ...
end object type Site;
```

Figure 2: The extended type definition of *Site*

corresponding condition as an event by itself. As a consequence, we distinguish between basic events which are associated with messages, and composite events which are associated with event configurations. Clearly, basic events are raised from outside an object whereas composite events are raised from within an object. (Incidentally, messages need not all come from other objects but may also arrive from the outside world, e.g., a sensor.)

Active objects communicate asynchronously. This means, that after an object has sent a message to another object it is not blocked until the recipient object has processed the message and returned with a result — if some is expected. The return — again a message — raises an event with the original sender.

4.2   Events

Basic Events   Basic events are related to messages. And these are closely related to type-specific operations. Due to the asynchronous communication, with each exchange of messages two events will be associated. Suppose two object types t and t', with an operation $op : t\|t_1,\ldots,t_n \rightarrow t_{n+1}$ declared on t. Suppose further that the implementation of some method in t' contains the statement $o.op(p_1,\ldots,p_n)$ for some variable o of type t. Then objects of type t receive messages $op(t\|t_1,\ldots,t_n \rightarrow t_{n+1})$, and objects of type t' receive result messages $op(t\|t_1,\ldots,t_n).return(t_{n+1})$. With the reception of these messages we associate events labelled like the messages.

In our example, a *Site* can receive the messages *initiateCommit(Site ‖)*, *ini-*

*tiateCommit(Site ||).return, prepare(Site || DC), prepare(Site || DC).return(Vote),
..., terminate(Site || bool), terminate(Site || bool).return.*

Consequently, these are also (the names of) the events that are implicitly defined from operations of *Site* and are raised by the incoming messages which correspond to the operations.

Composite Events Composite events must be explicitly declared in the events section and defined in the implementation section — like operations. As shown in figure 2 an event signature consists of a user-defined event-name and — optionally — a list of parameter types.

The precise composition of the event from other (basic or composite) events must be specified by means of an event definition language. Several such languages have lately been proposed. We base our event definition language on [12]. The main "ingredients" of composite events are basic events, connectors of events and predicates on input parameters of messages and the internal state of the object. Since we are not concerned with event specification in this paper, we skip the details of the event definition language and refer the reader to [12].

In figure 2 composite events for a *Site* have been declared. They have the following meaning:

A *prepareOrder* event is raised whenever the agent receives a "prepare" message. (We will explain the parameter of this message in section 5). The vote of an agent raises with the coordinator the event *hasVoted*, with the voting site and the value of the vote as parameters. The events *globalCommit* and *globalAbort* indicate that the coordinator site has received a "global commit" or "global abort" message, respectively. But as we will see later these messages do not originate with an application but are automatically sent by a special object, wich is referenced by **self**.*actDC* and which we will learn about in section 5. The messages which contain the decision of the coordinator, i.e., "abort" or "commit" messages, raise with the agents *abortOrder* and *commitOrder* events, respectively. Finally, an *endOfDC* event indicates to the coordinator that the distributed commit has been completed. The parameter contains a boolean value whose value depends on whether the commit was sucessful or not.

These events are composite and not — as one may intuitively suspect — basic events. This is demonstrated by the implementation of the event *prepare-Order*:

> **define event** prepareOrder(dc) **is**
> prepare(dc) **from** s: Site **and self**.otherSites.member(s);

It is not sufficient to receive a *prepare* message in order to raise a *prepareOrder* event. Rather, the message must be verified to originate with a site which is contained in the set-valued attribute *otherSites*, e.g., which is accepted as an authorized site.

4.3   Event-Action-Rules

Rules The specification of what action a *Site* shall take upon occurrence of one of the identified events is done via *Event-Action-Rules* (see, e.g., in [11]). An event-action-rule consists of two parts:

1. An event expression which identifies a relevant event or a set of relevant events.

2. A call of a local operation which defines the reaction to the event.

In our example the rules are a simple mapping from the messages to the operations the messages refer to (cf. figure 2). In more complex cases an active object may participate in more than one activity, and the rules can be used to coordinate these activities and, thus, would be more complex.

Refinement of the Event Model We now are in a position to complete our event model. Whenever a message arrives from the outside it does not directly invoke the corresponding operation but raises an event, and it is this event which gets queued in the mailbox. This is in contrast to a call to an operation from inside the object, i.e., self.(operation), which is immediately executed. Hence, contrary to current object models, a clear distinction is made between external and internal messages. The event may in turn cause one or more composite events to be raised and, hence, to be added to the mailbox.

The basic notion is the evaluation cycle. In one cycle the object evaluates all rules in a system-defined order. For a given rule, the mailbox is inspected for its underlying event. If one is found, the rule fires. The object executes the associated operation immediately. After that, the next rule is evaluated. During one evaluation cycle newly incoming messages and, hence, newly raised events as well as modifications of the object state are ignored. Thus, during one cycle, each rule sees the same state and the same contents of the mailbox. Since new events may have been raised during one evaluation cycle due to either new incoming messages or changes in the object state that satisfy conditions of composite events, the object must perform further evaluation cycles until a cycle has been completed without any rule firing. Then the object waits, e.g., a predetermined period of time or until a new message arrives.

Note that the programmer can impose an ordering on the rules by defining appropriate composite events.

5 Activities

5.1 The Notion of Activity

Protocol Model We introduced activities as dynamic relationships between objects, which regulate the communication behavior between objects which cooperate in order to perform a given task. Traditionally, regulating communication behavior has been the province of telecommunication protocols. Figure 3 gives an abstract view of these protocols between two sites. Both sites cooperate on some common task by individually taking certain actions. Cooperation is done by exchanging messages and reacting to them according a certain protocol. Consequently, each site includes a local protocol engine that enforces the protocol. Message exchange is via an (abstract) transport medium. In fact, in a multi-layered architecture such as ISO/OSI [5] the abstract medium is further broken down into lower-level protocol engines and media. For the purpose of our discussion it suffices to assume some abstract medium.

12

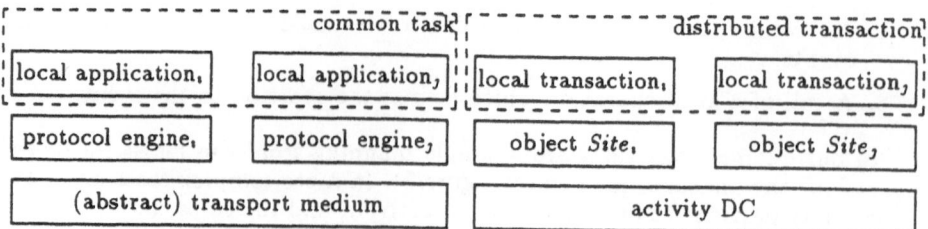

Figure 3: Abstract view of the components of a telecommunications protocol

Figure 4: Sites and activity in a protocol metaphor

The telecommunications protocol serves us as a metaphor. Figure 4 translates figure 3 into a structure consisting of the joint task of completing a distributed transaction, the site objects taking care of the local aspects of the protocol, and — in place of the abstract medium — a concept which we shall refer to as an *activity*.

One of the design decisions in telecommunication protocols is how to divide the functionality among local sites, i.e., the protocol engines, and the medium. (For example, in ISO/OSI there is a definite shift towards more powerful media functionality, viz. the difference between CCR and TP-ASE [5]). This is also true for our context of figure 4.

Characteristics   Like communication protocols that define a certain pattern which must be obeyed in numerous communications between arbitrary partners, it makes sense to classify activities into activity types. Any dynamic relationship set up between given objects is then an instance of some activity type which supervises the communication between objects that participate in that activity, and performs actions on certain events that are deemed relevant. By introducing activities as a special language construct we allow the programmer to specify in just one place all the communication rules which serve as a basis for cooperation between objects.

Activities have much in common with objects since activities with similar properties are classified into types, instances have a unique activity identifier, a structure and operations. On the other hand, they are also similar to operations — and thus differ from objects — because they must be invoked like an operation due to their high dynamicity. As such they can have input parameters and may return a result. Unlike methods of database objects, activities may sometimes be of long and perhaps infinite duration.

One object may participate in more than one activity at the same time. If this is the case the object processes incoming messages which are related to different activities in an interleaved manner.

True to the metaphor, the activity is a passive participant in the common task: it accepts a message from the sender and delivers it to the recipient — with certain guarantees concerning reliability, correctness, coordination, and the like. Activities cannot be directly addressed as recipients of messages, but may initiate messages on their own.

We use the following execution model. Once an activity is invoked, i.e., an activity instance has been created, it observes all messages that are directed to objects that participate in it, i.e., that play a role in it. It may just pass them on to the recipient object. But more often, in order to live up to its guarantees, the activity may have to take actions on its own. Consequently, activities also need an event mechanism with the same power as the one for objects. Observing messages may then raise an event, and the activity may initiate a predefined operation to react to this event. Thus, activities can be used to detect and react upon protocol violations and communication failures, or to multicast messages. Participants in an activity may leave the activity before it is finished, i.e., has been deleted; or they may join an activity after the activity has already lived for a while.

5.2 Activity Types

Activities incorporate the description of objects that can play a role in them, and a set of relevant events and actions that must be performed on the occurrence of an event. Activities with similiar properties, i.e., role-playing objects, events, and rules are classified into *activity types*. A new activity type is introduced using the activity type definition frame for which an example is shown in figure 5.

An activity type has a unique type name. The **role** clause determines which objects can play which role in the activity, where a role is defined by a role name and a type expression. The activity type structure after the **body** clause — for which the same type constructors hold as for object types — specifies the state information about the activity. The **result** clause identifies a result type. The operations given in the **operations** and **implementation** clauses are all internal to the activity and invoked by events, with the singular exception of the operation invoking the activity as a whole. The **event** clause declares events that are deemed relevant for the activity. Their definition is also supplied unter the **implementation** clause. The **rules** clause lists the (event-action) rules.

5.3 Example

Roles, internal state, and operations We now develop the specification for the activity type *DC*. The complete definition is shown in figure 5.

The first thing we have to do is to decide which kind of objects take part in our activity and which role they play in it. In our example all participants are of type *Site*. One site takes the part of the coordinator, the others are the agents. Thus, we start with the definition of the roles. Rather than assigning a role name to every single participant, a role may be defined for a set or list of participating objects. In this way the number of participants in an activity may vary during the lifetime of the activity. The consequence of the role specification is that the activity observes only those messages that are directed to objects whose identifiers are stored in the roles.

When an activity terminates it may return a result value to one or more participants. In our case the result clause specifies return of a boolean value to indicate whether the distributed transaction committed successfully or not.

No internal state needs to be maintained for our activity, so we omit the **body** clause. Also, only a single operation is needed for the 2PC variant, just

```
activity type DC is
   roles
      [ coordinator: Site; agents: {Site}; ]
   result bool;
   operations
      declare DC: Site, {Site}  → void;
   events
      declare allPrepare;
      declare voted: Site, Vote;
      declare allVoted;
      declare allVotedCommit;
      declare oneVotedAbort;
      declare doneCommit: Site;
      declare allDoneCommit;
      declare doneAbort: Site;
      declare allDoneAbort;
      declare protocol;
   rules
      on not protocol do self.coordinator.return (FALSE);
      on allVotedCommit do self.coordinator.globalCommit;
      on oneVotedAbort do self.coordinator.globalAbort;
      on allDoneCommit or allDoneAbort do
         self.coordinator.return (TRUE);
   implementation ...
end activity type DC
```

Figure 5: The activity type definition of *DC*

an initializer with the code in the **implementation** clause:

```
define operation DC (coord, agents) is begin
   self.coordinator:= coord; self.agents:= agents;
end define operation DC;
```

We use the initializer to instantiate the roles of the activity. For instance, object *Site* may contain the following statement for starting an activity:

```
self.actDC:= DC(coordSite, regularSites);
```

In our example the initializer has parameters which one may interpret as input parameters of the activity.

Events   The previous section seems to indicate that it must be the events that are the central aspect of an activity. As before events on activities can be either *basic* or *composite*.

The — implicitly declared — set of basic events can be derived from the types of the roles. Every message that is defined on at least one object type included in a role defines a basic event for that activity. Since only *Site* objects participate in a *DC* activity the set of basic events is — roughly — the same as for a *Site*. The exceptions are two additional events *start* and *return(t)* which are predefined on every activity: *start* indicates the creation of the activity, *return(t)* the termination of the activity and the return of a value of type *t*. In our example this basic event is *return(bool)*.

Following the protocol metaphor there is a difference to the way basic events are raised: Whereas in an object the event is raised upon receipt of a message (in telecommunications parlance: "indication"), in an activity it is raised concurrent with the sending of the message by the sender object ("request"). Incidentally, this way we meet our second proposition of section 3, to reflect initiatives.

Composite events are defined and declared in the same way as for objects. Figure 5 shows such events for our activity type *DC*.

Whenever a "prepare" message has been sent to all agents, an *allPrepare* event is raised. Each vote of an agent, i.e., the agent has returned from its local prepare operation, as well as the fact that all agents have given their vote cause some events: *voted* and *allVoted*, respectively. The parameters of *voted* contain the identifier of the voting agent and the actual value of the vote. In order to identify the two possible results of the vote, the events *allVotedCommit* and *oneVotedAbort* are specified. A *doneCommit* (*doneAbort*) event is raised when an agent, specified as parameter, has returned from its local commit (abort) operation after it received a "commit" ("abort") message. An *allDoneCommit* (*allDoneAbort*) event indicates that all agents have returned from their local commit (abort) operation.

We skip for the most part the implementations and give just an example. An interesting event is *protocol* which we have not explained so far, since it specifies the sequences of allowed messages. There, we may specify, e.g., that a relevant event may occur when an agent aborts a local transaction *before* the coordinator has sent a "prepare" message to this agent; or that an agent aborts a local transaction although all agents had voted for commit.

define event protocol is prefix(start; allPrepare; allVoted;
(allGlobalCommit **or** allGlobalAbort);
(allDoneCommit **or** allDoneAbort))
or self.coordinator.return(bool);

Rules The rules we need for the specification of a *DC* activity are also shown in figure 5. The first rule terminates a *DC* activity if the sequence of messages is illegal. In this case "FALSE" is returned to the coordinator. The second and third rules define the *commit* rule of the 2PC protocol: If all sites voted for commit a *globalCommit* message is sent to the coordinator; if one site has voted for abort a *globalAbort* message is sent to the coordinator. The last rule terminates the activity if all sites either committed or aborted their local transactions, and notified the activity that they did so. Note that none of the basic events and not all of the declared events appear in rules. The missing ones are part of the implementations of the four events used in the rules.

We allow infinite activities. Very high-level activities such as, e.g., an activity *production*, or activities that define the communication with sensors which continuously produce data, may be candidates. Infinite activities may also be due to failures, e.g., when the connection to a site has been broken or an operation loops infinitely. This points to a need for events that are not (directly or indirectly) bound to messages, such as a timer.

Like for objects, event processing is based on evaluation cycles. In particular, hence, messages that are observed during one evaluation cycle (more precisely the events they raise) are not considered until the next evaluation cycle, but are rather buffered until they are evaluated. In addition, activities may delay the deliverance of messages. Consequently, activities resemble — as desired — communication media. By the end of an evaluation cycle the original message and all messages that have been triggered have been delivered. If there is more than one activity that is "interested" in a certain message it must be guaranteed that this message is only delivered once.

Activity Instances Due to the dynamic nature of activities, we do not treat their creation and activitation as separate operations [11, 17] but collapse both into a single action. Likewise, the termination of an activity leads to its deletion from the database.

At invocation time the initializer of the activity is executed, and the rules become activated. A unique *activity identifier* is returned on creation, and may then be used, e.g,. as a message parameter or for assignment to a variable or attribute. In our example, the *prepare* message contains the identifier of the newly created *DC* activity as parameter. Each *Site* can memorize it in its attribute *actDC* (cf. figure 1).

Both objects and activities can start new activities. For instance, the coordinator *Site* may invoke an activity *DC* during the execution of the *initiate-Commit* operation.

Activities cannot be deleted from outside. Like operations they are terminated and deleted when they send a *return* message. In our example this happens on the detection of a protocol violation or on a successful completion of a distributed commit.

Using the terminology of [11] all rules (or triggers) are *perpetual* throughout the lifetime of an activity.

6   Interplay of Objects and Activities

In telecommunications, protocols are a highly indeterministic affair. They are specified by state transition diagrams or by sets of exemplary space-time diagrams. To validate and verify a protocol is a cumbersome affair [18]. To obtain an intuitive feeling, space-time-diagrams can serve as an illustrative tool.

We have to expect that similar problems arise with the active object/activity approach. To convince ourselves that the preceding declarations of object type *Site* and activity type *DC* seem to meet the 2PC characteristics we use an approach similar to space-time diagrams, called an event trace [20].

Figure 6 shows a successful 2PC in which three sites and an activity are involved: one coordinator, two agents, and a *DC* activity. The distributed commit is initiated by an outside message *initiateCommit* directed to the coordinator. The coordinator reacts to this message by invoking a *DC* activity and sending a *prepare* message to all agents. This would be specified in the implementation of the *initiateCommit* operation. The activity remains a passive messenger because none of its rules fire on a *prepare* message. All agents return through *DC* with a commit vote. The coordinator registers each vote. At precisely the moment all agents have voted the activity becomes active again, and

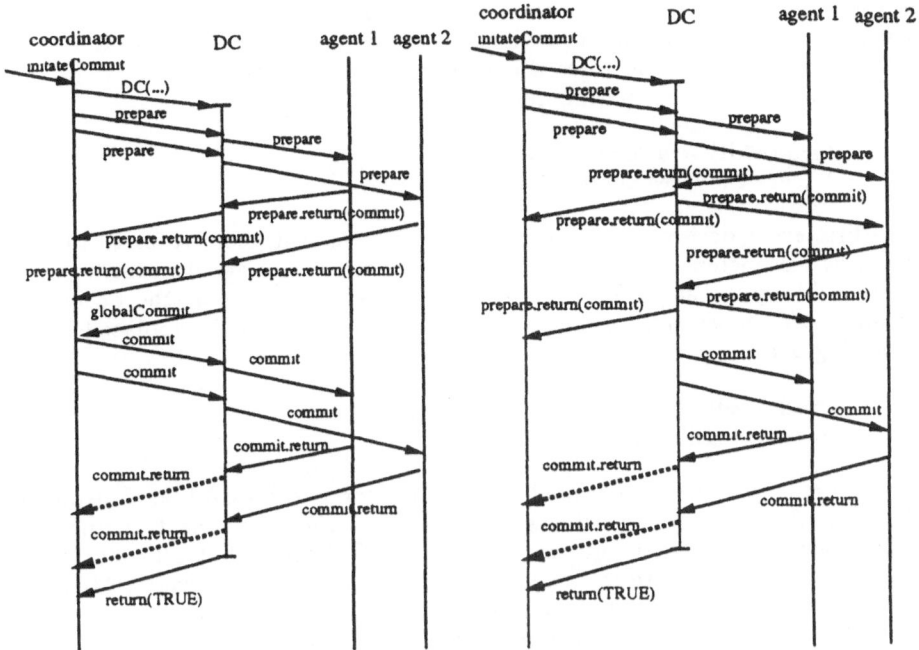

Figure 6: Event trace of a successful 2PC

Figure 7: Event trace of a successful 2PC using the distributed variant

sends a *globalCommit* message to the coordinator. The coordinator reacts to this message by executing its *globalCommit* operation which results in a *commit* message to all agents. Again, the activity remains passive because no rule fires. The coordinator ignores the return messages from the agents. We indicate this by using dashed arrows. When all agents have returned from their *commit* operations the activity sends its own *return* message with a success indicator to the coordinator and terminates.

Activities go beyond objects in that they permit multicast of messages. In order to demonstrate this we slightly modify the 2PC protocol. Instead of the centralized variant we choose a distributed variant. There the vote is not only returned to the coordinator but also to all other agents. Thus, each agent can decide on its own whether it must commit or abort its local transaction.

To do so, we entrust *DC* with the notification of all participants, and add a second operation *notifyAll* to our *DC* activity, which multicasts the vote of each agent to all others. Second, we add a rule to *DC*, which triggers this operation on the detection of the *prepare.return(Vote)* message:

on vote (s: Site, v: Vote) **do** self.notifyAll(v, s);

Remember that the event *voted(v: Vote, s: Site)* occurs if the *prepare.return(v)* message is sent from agent *s* to the coordinator.

In essence, what we have done is to shift some of the coordinator functionality to *DC*. To complete the shift we have also to modify the specification of the events *allVotedCommit* and *oneVotedAbort*. Using the centralized 2PC variant we had only to observe which votes are sent to the coordinator. Now *DC* must take care of the votes which are sent to each single agent. We provide both events with a *Site* parameter.

> **declare** allVotedCommit: Site;
> **declare** oneVotedAbort: Site;

The first event occurs when all other agents have sent their votes to the *Site* given as parameter. The second event occurs when one agent votes for abort at the *Site* given as parameter. The old rules that fire on the occurrence of *allVotedCommit* and *oneVotedAbort*, respectively, must be replaced by the following ones:

> **on** allVotedCommit(s: Site) **do** s.commit;
> **on** oneVotedAbort(s: Site) **do** s.abort;

Figure 7 shows the modified event trace for a successful 2PC using the distributed variant. The *DC* activity forwards the *prepare.return* messages immediately to all other agents. Whenever *DC* detects that all other agents have sent a commit-vote to one site it sends a "commit" message to this site. Note that there is no "global commit" message to the coordinator.

As a last case study we look at what may happen if in our first, centralized variant of the 2PC one participant of the activity violates the rules. Consider, e.g., that an agent aborts its local transaction although all agents have already voted for commit. Note that the termination rule

> **on** allDoneCommit **or** allDoneAbort **do** self.coordinator.**return**(TRUE);

relies on all agents to acknowledge that they all either committed or aborted the transaction. If one of the agents had to change its mind the rule will never fire, and the activity never terminates. This is, of course, not a satisfying situation. In order to react in an appropriate way it would be useful to specify a distinct event that describes such a situation, e.g,.

> **declare event** oneAbortedOnCommit: Site;

The parameter identifies the bad agent. By defining an additional rule we could now cope with such a situation. Note that the rule would not resolve the situation where the acknowledgement is not given at all. Again, a timer solution would be needed.

7   Related Work

Relationships   Relationships between objects have long been identified as an important though often missing concept for modeling [6, 20]. The model proposed here is a generalization of system-supported relationships with a distinct semantics, e.g., system-supported binary relationships as, e.g., in O_2 [9], or part-of and version-of relationships as proposed in many works, such as Ithasca (Orion) [16]. Our main contribution is towards dynamic relationships.

Behavior Modeling The dynamic aspects of systems have long been an issue of intensive research, too. But most approaches are not "object-oriented", as e.g., Petri nets, process algebras. High-level conceptual models which integrate object-orientation and behavior modeling are [19, 21]. They use first-order temporal logic to specify dynamic constraints. Our approach is closer to the implementation level and can be seen on the logical rather than the conceptual level of database design. Hence, some of the interesting aspects of [19, 21] are of lesser importance to us. *Oblog* [21] tries to capture the dynamics of systems in a completely declarative manner. Up to now it remains to be shown how these concepts can be implemented. The *Activity Model* of Liu and Meersman [19] mainly focuses on the object communications and the relationships between communications. Actions that are triggered by messages or composite events are not considered.

Active Rules (ECA-Rules) There are numerous publications that propose active rules as parts of a database system, e.g., [4, 7, 8, 10, 11, 13, 17].

Mostly ECA-rules are intended as a means to keep the database consistent. Consequently, events can be specified which are related to method calls or transactions. The invocation of some method may — or may not — raise some events which may trigger certain actions. Those actions are scheduled according to certain coupling modes [8]. Eventually the invoked method is executed. By contrast, our main focus is not on consistency but on the communication behavior of objects.

Many authors specify ECA rules or triggers globally in the database [8, 17]. This is a contradiction to the object-oriented paradigm. All rules are treated in an equal fashion. The relationship between rules and objects is not explicitly specified. As a consequence, it is cumbersome to decide which rules must be evaluated when an object is accessed. We claim to overcome this weakness.

Rules that currently are not needed should not be evaluated at all. Further, not all rules are valid throughout the whole lifetime of a database. Both issues are often addressed by allowing a user to explicitly activate or deactivate predefined triggers, as, e.g., in [10, 11, 17]. This must individually be done for each single rule in the database. Whereas [11] allows to structure the rules in accordance with the object structure of the database there is no way to structure the rules according to a task that is currently to be performed. Our approach solves — though in a somewhat compromisal manner — both issues: Dynamic establishment of activities can be seen both as a form of activation/deactivation and as a task-specific grouping.

Distributed Programming Languages The need for the language support of concurrent computing in distributed systems has also long been identified by the programming language community [2]. Numerous proposals for *distributed* or *concurrent programming languages* exist. A survey of concepts are given in [1]. Those languages offer comparatively low-level constructs to express communication among objects. By comparison, we specify communication in a declarative manner using rules. Moreover, in distributed object-oriented languages and in object-oriented database languages there is no way to specify communication rules for cooperating objects in one place. Instead those rules are normally hidden inside several object type definitions or implicit in certain sequences of method calls.

Our objective was to overcome these drawbacks. Altogether, communication between objects should be easier to specify and to grasp in our approach. Finally, none of the classical approaches seems to have noticed the close relationship to telecommunication protocols.

8   Conclusions and Outlook

We have proposed an object model that is primarily intended to support database applications like CIM where numerous tasks are executed in a cooperative manner. By basing our approach on the metaphor of communication protocols we developed a model comprising active objects and activities. In this model active objects communicate by asynchronously sending messages. They schedule incoming messages by means of event-action-rules. The cooperation between active objects is supervised by activities. They define constraints on the communication behavior of cooperating objects. These constraints are again specified by means of event-action-rules. Activities are also a means to structure rules according to the actual task to performed.

In order to gain first experiences, a subset of the proposed model has been built as a cross-compiler to Lisp using the Flavors package and the Lucid Lisp multitasking facilities as a first experimental prototype. The prototype is restricted to active objects and basic events. Obviously, such a programming environment is less than ideal to achieve high performance. It is still interesting to note that even under these circumstances and using a single-processor environment of a SUN 3/60 workstation running under UNIX close to 50 active objects could operate before the system became thrashed. This seems to indicate that with proper environments and optimization techniques it should be possible to build systems that easily incorporate several hundred active objects.

Although we briefly demonstrated that our model allows to organize complex distributed algorithms like the *Two-Phase-Commit* protocol in a modular and flexible manner, many issues have been left open. We will sketch some which are related to the implementation of the model and extensions.

First, from our prototype it seems unreasonable to model *all* objects as active objects. Instead we need both — a few active, probably "big" objects — and a large number of "small" conventional passive objects. We then have to define special relationships between these objects. We have already identified one in [14] which we have called *location-of* relationship. This relation allows to specify that some object is co-located with another object. This relation is particulary valuable in a distributed environment.

Our execution model makes a number of fundamental assumptions: messages are sent asynchronously; actions triggered on the evaluation of rules are executed atomically (but not as normal transactions, since they cannot be rolled back because communications are externalized at once) in a system-defined order. Consequently, we should examine the model in the light of the various transaction models. Further, more control should be exerted on the order in which messages are delivered to objects. For instance, it is often necessary to ensure that messages which are causally related to one another are delivered in the correct order. Up to now it seems impossible to ensure this kind of synchronicity in large distributed systems globally because this would cause an exorbitant overhead. Activities may overcome part of the problems if one can assume that only messages which are related to one activity may be in some way causally related.

Activities may not terminate if some active object does not send an expected message. Hence, our model should include the possibility to specify time events.

Due to its closeness to the telecommunications metaphor, activities should also be an ideal means for incorporating (communications between) distributed objects into the model. We plan to explore this issue in detail.

Due to space limitations, we completely left out the issue of persistence in this paper. Since GOM is a database programming language, GOM objects can be made persistent, i.e., they are stored on durable storage media. The same must be possible for activities because they may be long-living.

Acknowledgements

A. Kemper and G. Moerkotte, the originators of the conventional object model GOM, proposed first extensions towards object activity. We would also like to acknowledge helpful discussions with our colleagues A. Zachmann and C. Kilger. Our student E. Appel helped in implementing the experimental prototype.

References

[1] G. Agha. Concurrent object-oriented programming. *Communications of the ACM*, 33(9):125–141, Sep 1990.

[2] G. A. Agha. *ACTORS: A Model of Concurrent Computation in Distributed Systems*. The MIT Press, Cambridge, Ma, 1986.

[3] M. Atkinson, F. Bancilhon, D. J. DeWitt, K. R. Dittrich, D. Maier, and S. Zdonik. The object-oriented database system manifesto. In *Proc. Int. Conf on Deductive and Object-Oriented Databases*, pages 40–57, Kyoto, Japan, Dec 1989.

[4] C. Beeri and T. Milo. A model for active object oriented database. In *Proc. of The Conf. on Very Large Data Bases (VLDB)*, pages 337–349, Barcelona, Spain, 1991.

[5] U. Black. *OSI: A Model for Computer Communications Standards*. Prentice Hall, 1991.

[6] P. P. S. Chen. The Entity Relationship model: Toward a unified view of data. *ACM Trans. Database Syst.*, 1(1):9–36, Mar 1976.

[7] U. Dayal. Active database management systems. In *Proc. of the Third Intl. Conf. on Data and Knowledge Bases: Improving Usability and Responsiveness*, pages 150–170, Jerusalem, Israel, Jun 1988. Morgan-Kaufman.

[8] U. Dayal, M. Hsu, and R. Ladin. Organizing long-running activities with triggers and transactions. In *Proc. of the ACM SIGMOD Intl. Conf. on Management of Data*, pages 204–214, Atlantic City, NJ, May 90.

[9] O. Deux et al. The O$_2$ system. *Communications of the ACM*, 34(10):34–48, Oct 1991.

[10] O. Diaz, N. Paton, and P. Gray. Rule management in object oriented databases: A uniform approach. In *Proc. of The Conf. on Very Large Data Bases (VLDB)*, Barcelona, Spain, 1991.

[11] N. H. Gehani and H. V. Jagadish. Ode as an active database: Constraints and triggers. In *Proc. of The Conf. on Very Large Data Bases (VLDB)*, 1991.

[12] N. H. Gehani, H. V. Jagadish, and O. Shmueli. Composite event specification in active databases: Model and implementation. In *Proc. of the 18th Int. Conf. on Very Large Data Bases (VLDB)*, pages 327–338, Vancouver, British Columbia, Canada, 1992.

[13] N.H. Gehani, H.V. Jagadish, and O. Shmueli. Event specification in an active object-oriented database. In M. Stonebraker, editor, *Proc. of the ACM SIGMOD Intl. Conf. on Management of Data*, pages 81–90, San Diego, California, June 1992.

[14] A. Kemper, G. Moerkotte, and H.-D. Walter. Structuring the distributed object-world of CIM. In *INCOM'92 – 7th IFAC/IFIP/IFORS/IMACS/-ISPE Symposium on Information Control Problems in Manufacturing Technology*, Toronto, Canada, May 1992.

[15] A. Kemper, G. Moerkotte, H.-D. Walter, and A. Zachmann. GOM: a strongly typed, persistent object model with polymorphism. In *Proc. of the German Conf. on Databases in Office, Engineering and Science (BTW)*, pages 198–217, Kaiserslautern, Mar 1991. Springer-Verlag, Informatik Fachberichte Nr. 270.

[16] W. Kim, E. Bertino, and J. F. Garza. Composite objects revisited. In *Proc. of the ACM SIGMOD Intl. Conf. on Management of Data*, pages 337–347, Portland, OR, May 1989.

[17] A. M. Kotz, K. R. Dittrich, and J. A. Mülle. Supporting semantic rules by a generalized event-trigger mechanism. In *Proc. Intl. Conf. Extending Database Technology (EDBT)*, Venice, Italy, Mar 1988.

[18] H. Krumm. *Funktionelle Analyse von Kommunikationsprotokollen*, volume 247 of *Informatik-Fachberichte*. Springer-Verlag, 1990.

[19] L. Liu and R. Meersman. Activity model: Declarative approach for capturing communication behaviour in object-oriented databases. In *18th International Conference on Very Large Data Bases*, Vancouver, British Columbia, Canada, 1992.

[20] J. Rumbaugh, M. Blaha, W. Premerlani, F. Eddy, and W. Lorensen. *Object-Oriented Modeling and Design*. Prentice Hall, Englewood Cliffs, NJ, 1991.

[21] G. Saake. Descriptive specification of database object behavior. *Data & Knowledge Engineering*, 6(1), Jan 1991.

Events in an Active Object-Oriented Database System

Stella Gatziu
Klaus R. Dittrich
Institut für Informatik, Universität Zürich
Zürich, Switzerland

Abstract

In this paper we investigate the definition, detection, and management of events in the active object-oriented database system SAMOS. First, we present various event specification facilities based on simple but nevertheless powerful constructs which support the modelling of time aspects as well. Second we show how events can be detected in an efficient way. Finally, we deal with the internal representation of events using the benefits of the underlying data model.

1 Introduction

Most new developments in database technology aim at representing more real-world semantics in the database which would otherwise be hidden in applications. *Active* database systems (aDBS) are able to recognize specific situations (in the database and beyond) and to react to them without immediate, explicit user or application requests. In addition to the functionalities supported by a passive DBS, an aDBS registers *events, conditions, actions* and the association between them by means of *ECA-rules* (Event-Condition-Action) introduced in [3]. An event indicates a point in time when the DBMS has to react, and a condition relates to a database state; it has to be evaluated when the occurrence of the corresponding event is *signalled*. If the condition holds, the associated action has to be executed. An action can be any executable program including database operations.

Events are one of the most essential issue in an aDBS, and thus, their definition, their detection and their (internal) representation address a main research area in active database systems. Looking at existing work, many questions still remain open or are not yet answered satisfactorily:

- An event can always be regarded as a specific point in time [6]. Because only some points in time for which a reaction is required are of interest, we have to specify them in some way, e.g., as an explicit time definition (at 18:00) or as the beginning or the end of a database operation. Events may be defined in even more complex ways, e.g., as the point in time when the last of a set of events has occurred (*complex events*). Thus, an aDBS has to provide various constructs for the specification of interesting events. Most of the existing systems are restricted to "simple" event definitions; only recent work in ODE [11] and Sentinel [2] deals with advanced event specification. Nevertheless, no simple but powerful constructs exist for the specification of events. An additional open question is how time aspects can be integrated into event definitions.

- An aDBS has to detect the occurrence of all defined events in order to be able to react to them. The so-called *event detector* is responsible for that task, and therefore, one of the main system components of an aDBS. The support of various constructs for modelling a wide range of real-world situations as events requires a mechanism for the detection of *all* these events in an efficient way.
- Defined events have to be represented in the system such that information about them can be retrieved and accessed in an efficient way. The event management may benefit from the underlying data model in that concepts already offered by the data model are used, i.e., data and events are represented using the same constructs. In the recent past, several proposals take into account object-oriented features [1, 4, 5, 10]. Additionally, the user should not be concerned with the way events are represented in the system.

In this paper we elaborate on these aspects in the context of SAMOS (Swiss Active Mechanism-Based Object-Oriented Database System). The combination of active and object-oriented characteristics within one, coherent system is the overall goal of SAMOS. It addresses the three principal problems of an aDBS, namely rule specification, rule execution, and rule management. Rule specification is concerned with the nature of events, conditions and actions and their relationships to the data model. Rule execution refers to the processing of rules, which has to be carried out in the context of the general transaction model supported by the database system (some aspects are presented in [7]). Rule management incorporates tasks for the internal representation of rules and events, for the event detection and the selection of all rules that have to be executed. A short general description of SAMOS can be found in [8].

In this paper, we focus on rule specification and rule management. In particular, we introduce powerful yet rather simple constructs for the specification of events based on an event algebra. Furthermore, we integrate time specification facilities into event definitions. We show that even complex defined events can be detected in a relatively easy way using Petri nets. Lastly, we use the benefits of the object-oriented environment for the internal representation of events, e.g., by exploiting inheritance hierarchies.

The remainder of this paper is organized as follows. Section 2 presents the way a rule or an event is defined, and section 3 discusses the various kinds of events supported by SAMOS. In section 4 we deal generally with implementation aspects and in particular with those aspects concerning events, e.g., the event detectors.

2 Rule Definition Language

In analogy to the data definition language (DDL) which supports the modelling of data structures (and behavior), SAMOS supports a *rule definition language* as a means to specify ECA-rules. The syntax[1] of the definition of a rule is:

---

1. We use the following conventions: "|" denotes alternatives and an expression enclosed in square brackets is optional. Terminal symbols are printed in capital letter.

```
DEFINE RULE rule_name
     ON event_clause IF condition_clause DO action_clause
```

In this rule definition, events are defined as a part of a rule. However, events will often be used in multiple rules. As a matter of reusability and convenience, it is often undesirable to describe the same event (especially a complex one) in each rule. Therefore, events may be named and defined separately (outside the rule definition):

```
DEFINE EVENT event_name event_clause
```

Corresponding rules can then refer to the event via its name:

```
DEFINE RULE rule_name
     ON event_name IF condition_clause DO action_clause
```

The event specification part of the rule definition language includes all constructs that can be used for the specification of events. Actually, we use the notion of "event" as the point in time when the system has to react to an occurrence within the database or its environment. Those occurrences are described within the event definition. In order to distinguish between event occurrence and event definition, we use the notion of *event pattern* to denote the definition of an event. Then, an *event* corresponds to an actual *occurrence* of an event pattern, and more than one event can relate to one event pattern. In the sequel, we will simply talk about events whenever the distinction is clear from the context.

Rule and event definitions have to be "understood" by SAMOS; they are thus analyzed and transformed into an internal form by means of a rule compiler. Compiled rules and events are made a persistent part of the database and build the *rule-* and the *eventbase*, respectively. Of course, like the database the rule- and the eventbase may change over time. In an object-oriented environment, the rule- and the eventbase are represented in an object-oriented way. Thus, events and rules are treated as objects and every user-defined event can be represented as an instance of a system-defined class *event_pattern*.

One important aspect of our approach is that the user is not concerned with the way events are represented by the system, e.g., whether they are objects or class attributes, whereas he has to care for these issues in Sentinel [1] and in ODE [10]. The user only defines event patterns using a high level specification language and the system translates the event definitions and stores them into event objects. In the sequel, we present in turn the way the user defines event patterns, and the way the system deals with those information.

3 Event Specification

A specific contribution of SAMOS is its extensive collection of event specification features. Events can be subdivided into two categories: *primitive* events which correspond to elementary occurrences, and *composite* events (read: events that are described as *compositions* of others) that are described by an *event algebra*. An expression of the event algebra is composed out of other composite or primitive events based on *event constructors*. In this section, we introduce the event specification part of the rule language and present the choices offered to users for the definition of primitive and composite event patterns.

3.1 Primitive Events

A primitive event describes a point in time specified by an occurrence in the database (*method* events), in the DBMS (*transaction* events), or in its environment (*time* and *abstract* events).

3.1.1 Time Events

First of all, an event can be specified as an explicit point in time. These events are called *time* events. They can be defined as absolute (e.g., `93.06.28,22:00`)[2] or as periodically reappearing points in time. The syntax of the latter is:

```
EVERY frequency (YEAR|MONTH|WEEKDAY|HOUR|MINUTE) time WITHIN interval
```

The use of the repeating factor *frequency* is demonstrated by the example of the time event `EVERY 5 DAY 20:00` which is signalled only every fifth day. The optional part *interval* represents the time interval in which the periodical time event should occur. For example, the time event `EVERY 5 DAY 20:00 WITHIN [05.01-05.31]` is signalled every fifth day in May.

In some cases, a time event cannot be defined as an absolute point in time but only in relation to an *implicit* one that represents the point in time when a system activity is performed. To that end, we provide *relative time events (t+x)*, where t is an implicit time point and x is a relative time (e.g., `1 min`). The possibilities for the definition of time intervals and of implicit time points are presented in subsection 3.4.

3.1.2 Method Events

In an object-oriented environment, users manipulate and access objects by sending messages to them. Thus, each message sent to an object requiring the execution of a method gives rise for two events (*method* events): the points in time when the object begins, and when it has finished the execution of the method. Method events are defined according to the syntax

```
(BEFORE|AFTER)"."(class_name|object_name|"*")"."method_name
```

A method event can be related either
- to one class, if a class name is given; it is signalled before or after the execution of the appropriate method on any arbitrary object of this class
- to a particular object, if an object name is given (we assume that unique names are assigned to objects); it is signalled before or after the execution of the appropriate method on this object
- to multiple classes, in case of a "*"; it is signalled when the method is executed on any arbitrary object of any class that has a method with the specified method name (this situation may occur due to the inheritance of methods).

3.1.3 Transaction Events

Transaction events are defined by the start or the termination time of (user-defined) transactions. Assuming that transaction programs are named, a transaction event can

---

2. Within the definition of absolute time points, default values are supported if some parts of a concrete time specification are missing. For example, without giving the year, the actual year is assumed.

be restricted to transactions executing this particular transaction program. Transaction events are defined according to the syntax:

```
(BOT|EOT|ABORT)[transaction_name]
```

3.1.4   Abstract Events

Up to now, we have introduced several kinds of events which are conveying specific semantics known by SAMOS such that their occurrence can be detected by the system itself. However, users and applications may need other events according to their specific semantics as well (*abstract* events). They are defined and named by users:

```
DEFINE EVENT event_name
```

and can be used in rules like any other event. They are not detected by SAMOS, but users/applications have to notify the system about their occurrence by issuing the explicit operation:

```
RAISE EVENT event_name
```

3.2   Composite Events

Primitive events as presented above describe only elementary occurrences. In order to model even complex occurrences as events, we support composite events built from others by means of six event constructors. The *disjunction* of events (E1|E2) occurs whenever either E1 or E2 happens (i.e., the composite event corresponds to the point in time when the respective component event occurs). The *conjunction* of events (E1,E2) occurs when both E1 and E2 have occurred, regardless of order (i.e., the composite event corresponds to the point in time when the second component event happens). In contrast, the *sequence* of events (E1;E2) requires that the component events E1 and E2 occur in that order. E1 and E2 can be any primitive event discussed above as well as any composite event.

Composite events defined with the following three constructors occur depending on how many events of a specific event pattern have occurred during a predefined time interval. A *history* event (TIMES(n,E) IN I) is the point in time when the n-th occurrence of E during the time interval I happens. More precisely, *each time* n occurrences of E have happened, the history event occurs. Furthermore, we provide a modification of the TIMES constructor which now specifies a range of occurrences instead of a definite number, e.g., TIMES([n1-n2],E) IN I which is signalled at the end point of the interval I if the event E has occurred between n1 and n2 times during the interval. If only the lower limit of the range is given, e.g. TIMES([n1],E) IN I, the history event is again signalled at the end point of I if E has occurred more than n1 times during the interval.

A *negative* event (NOT E IN I) corresponds to the end point of I if E has *not* happened during the interval. A composite event with the "*"-constructor (*E IN I) will be signalled at most once during I (at the first occurrence of E), even if E occurs more than once during the time interval I. Negative events and history events with a range frequency factor always require the explicit definition of a time interval. For all other events with no time interval specification, we assume the time between the event definition and infinity as monitoring interval.

3.3 Event Parameters

Event patterns can be parameterized such that information can be passed to the condition or action parts, if necessary. The actual parameters are bound to the formal ones of an event pattern during the signalling of the event. The set of formal parameters is fixed (except for abstract events), i.e., the user cannot define event parameters themselves. We distinguish between *environment* parameters and parameters depending on the kind of the event. Environment parameters are:

- *occ_point*(E): the point in time of the occurrence of an event E,
- *occ_tid*(E): the identifier of the transaction in which event E has occurred (*occurring transaction*),
- *user_id*(E): the identifier of the user who has started the occurring transaction of E.

Occ_point is defined for composite events only, while for primitive events, all environment parameter apply.

Concerning parameters depending on the event kind, method events have in addition the parameters of the method and the object identifier of the object executing the method. A disjunction has the parameters of the event that causes the signalling of the composite one. Events with the "*"-operator have the parameters of the first occurring event. A sequence or a conjunction has the union of the parameters of their components, while history events have the union of the parameters of the *n* occurring events. Note that time and negative events have no parameters.

Influence of Event Parameters on the Definition of Composite Events

The definition of composite events can be extended with the keyword *same* to denote that the component events have the same value of a particular parameter. In case of negation and disjunction, none or only one component event can occur and hence, a comparison of parameters would be meaningless. For all other compositions, we can define the *same* keyword in relation to the environment parameter *occ_tid* and *user_tid*. For example, the sequence (E1;E2):same transaction is signalled when E1 and afterwards E2 have occurred within the same transaction (the occurring transaction of E1). The history event TIMES(5,E):same user occurs if 5 events of the event pattern E have occurred in transactions started by the same user.

Concerning method events (in any composition), we may require that the appropriate methods are executed on the same object. For example, assume the sequence (E1;E2):same object where E1 and E2 are method events related to a class x. Then the sequence is signalled only if the corresponding methods are executed on the same object of class x.

For composite events defined with history and "*"-constructors, it makes sense also to monitor the repeated occurrence of events of a specific event pattern, in case of events having the same parameter. For example, the event definition *E:same parameter means that all occurrences of E having all of their parameters apart from *occ_point* identical to the parameters of the first occurrence of E are ignored, but no E-occurrences with different parameters.

Checking of parameters may also take place in the condition of a rule. Such a rule definition is however semantically different from a definition of a rule with a composite event with the *same* keyword. For example, assume the order of event occurrences

$\text{E1}^1\text{(x)}$ $\text{E2}^1\text{(y)}$ $\text{E1}^2\text{(z)}$ $\text{E2}^2\text{(x)}$ where the parameter in brackets refers to the *user_id* and the index relates to the first or second occurrence of an event of a specific event pattern, and consider the following two rule definitions:

```
DEFINE RULE R1 ON (E1;E2):same user DO A1

DEFINE RULE R2 ON (E1;E2) IF <user_id is the same> DO A1
```

Rule R1 is executed (which corresponds to the execution of the action A1) after E2^2. Rule R2 is executed twice: first after E1^1 and E2^1 and second after E1^2 and E2^2. But, in both cases the condition would not hold, i.e., the action A1 is never executed. For that matter, the two rule definitions model a different real-world semantics.

3.4 Monitoring Intervals

Sometimes it is required that a (primitive or composite) event E is signalled only in case it has occurred during a specific time interval I. Especially, negative events require a time interval, while for events defined by means of the history and the "*"-constructor a time interval is usually at least desirable. Therefore, *monitoring intervals* are introduced for those time intervals during which the event has to occur in order to be considered relevant. Before we present the monitoring intervals, we show how a time interval in general is defined in SAMOS.

3.4.1 Defining Time Intervals

Generally, a time interval is specified by two points in time, a *start_time* and an *end_-time*. Furthermore, time intervals can be defined to reappear periodically, e.g., EVERY MONTH [15.,18:00-15.,24:00]. They can also be computed from other time intervals: we provide operators *overlap* and *extend* to represent the intersection and the union of intervals, respectively.

Start_time and end_time can be defined explicitly as absolute points in time, e.g., 93.10.15, 12:15. The keywords "now" and "infinite" in definitions like [now-93.06.30] or [93.02.01-infinite] express the actual time (i.e., the point in time when the interval is defined) and the infinity, respectively. Note that for negative events the definition of the *end_point* as infinite is not allowed.

Still, the desired points in time may not be known at definition of the time interval. In this case, they can often be defined as the point in time denoting the occurrence of some other event (i.e., according to its *occ_point*) or the completion of the execution of a rule (i.e, according to the *occ_point* of an abstract event which models the point in time when the last statement of the rule's action is successfully executed). In these cases, we refer to *implicit* points in time. They can be used for the definition of time intervals and for the definition of relative events (see subsection 3.1) as well. For example, the time event occ_point(E1)+00:10 is signalled 10 minutes after the occurrence of E1.

3.4.2 Defining Monitoring Intervals

A monitoring interval can now be defined during event definitions, e.g.,

```
DEFINE EVENT E1 AFTER.*.UpdateSalary IN [93.05.01-93.08.30]
```

```
DEFINE RULE R1
    ON E1 IF ...
```

or

```
DEFINE RULE R2
    ON BOT(Program_test) IN EVERY WEEK [Sa-So] IF ...
```

In the first case, the monitoring interval has to be considered for the execution of all rules that refer to the method event E1 and for all composite events that contain this event. In the second case, the monitoring interval concerns only rule R2 and has no influence on composite events.

3.4.3 Examples

- E muss not occur again during two days in August after its first occurrence:
  ```
  NOT E IN overlap([93.08.01-93.08.31],[occ_point(E)+2DAYS])
  ```
- E2 has to occur within one hour after the occurrence of E1:
  ```
  (E1 ; E2 IN [occ_point(E1)+01:00])
  ```
- only the first occurrence of E3 during the interval specified by the occurrences of the events E1 and E2 has to be signalled:
  ```
  *E3 IN [occ_point(E1) - occ_point(E2)]
  ```

3.4.4 Monitoring Intervals and (De)Activate Operations

As discussed above, monitoring intervals enable the timely restriction of event signalling with regard to rule execution, i.e., a rule is not always executed even if the appropriate event has occurred. An additional mechanism to make rules eligible or ineligible to be executed are the operations *activate* and *deactivate* on rules. They can be called in programs and inside the action part of another rule. In SAMOS, we provide both monitoring intervals and the operations *(de)activate* in order to achieve the dynamical change of the behavior of a rule inside the action of another rule. Now we give an example to show how these two mechanisms work together:

```
DEFINE EVENT E1 Program_test IN [93.05.01-93.05.31]
DEFINE RULE R1
    ON E1 IF ...


DEFINE RULE R2
    ON E2 IF ... DO deactivate R1
```

We assume that R1 is in an active state. Then it can be executed when the event E1 is signalled in May and the rule R2 has not yet been executed.

4 Implementation Issues

In addition to the usual functionalities of (passive) DBMS, an active DBMS has to perform tasks like the analyzation and management of rules and the efficient detection of events. Thus, the implementation of an aDBS requires an answer to the following questions:

a. what happens after the definition of a rule or an event pattern?
b. what happens after a primitive event occurs?

Figure 1 illustrates how SAMOS answers these two questions. The left side of the figure shows what kind of structures are created for handling the information gained from the rule or event definition. The right side of the figure shows how these information is used in order to react to the occurrence of a primitive event. We discuss details in the sequel.

After a rule (or an event pattern) is defined, the *analyzer* sends the information about the correct rule and event definitions to the *rule* and *event manager*, respectively. They have to store these information such that it can be retrieved and accessed efficiently. Furthermore, for each defined event the *event detector* has to be "programmed" (see section 4.1 for details).

After the event detector signals the occurrence of a primitive event, whether this event is used in an event composition, the component responsible for the detection of composite events has to be informed. Furthermore, it has to be checked whether at least one rule is defined for the appropriate event pattern; because events occur frequently this search is required frequently as well, thus it has be done efficiently. If such a rule exists, this event is inserted into the *event register* which includes all "events of interest", i.e., all events whose patterns are used in a rule. Based on the (updated) information in the event register, the *rule execution component* has to determine the appropriate rule(s) to be executed. Afterwards, in cooperation with the transaction manager of the underlying DBMS, the rule execution begins (condition evaluation and action execution).

Therefore, in order to implement an aDBS, the architecture of a (passive) DBMS has to be augmented by new components like an analyzer, a rule and an event manager, an event detector for primitive and composite events and a rule execution component. The prototype implementation of SAMOS is based on the commercial ooDBS ObjectStore. Since ObjectStore is a "black box" for our implementation, the new components are located on top of it. In this paper, we concentrate on the detection and the internal representation of events.

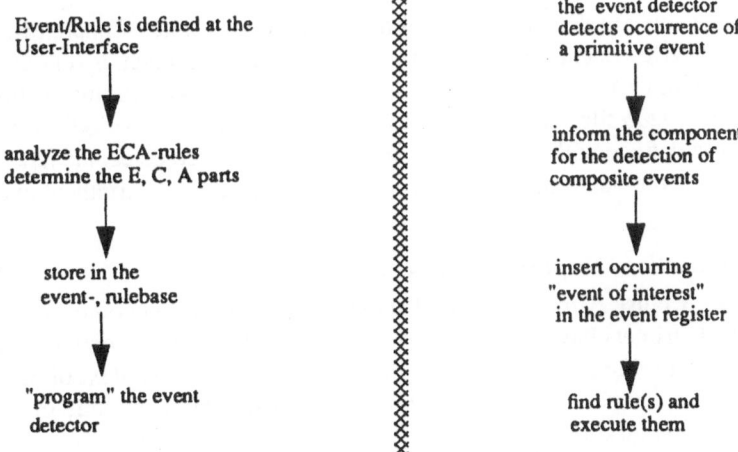

Figure 1. Control flow of tasks in SAMOS

4.1 Event Detection

The system (e.g., the event register) "knows" about the occurrence of an event only when it has received the message *raise event*. This message is sent from the event detector except for abstract events where it is sent directly by users, applications or action parts of a rule. Consequently, all other primitive events and all composite ones have to be detected by the system.

4.1.1 Detecting Primitive Events

Each kind of the primitive events requires a different way to detect it. For method events, one possible approach is to replace the original method (internally) by a new one that contains a call of the operation *raise event* and a call of the original method (the order depends on the kind of the method event relating to BEFORE or AFTER keywords). The new method is called a *method wrapper*. This approach is feasible in Smalltalk-based DBMS (e.g., Gemstone) where the method wrapper can be compiled and then replace the original method *at runtime* [13].

Nevertheless, ObjectStore is based on C++ and, therefore, does not support modification and recompilation of methods at runtime. Hence, we choose the following approach to signal method events without user intervention: the body of these methods for which a method event is defined is modified by inserting a call of the operation *raise event*; i.e., the method implementation has to be parsed, modified and then recompiled.

In ObjectStore, all transactions in progress are instances of the class *os_transaction*. The operations *abort*, *commit* and *begin* on transactions are implemented as methods of this class. Thus, the detection of the appropriate transaction events can be done by overriding those methods in order to include a call of the *raise event* operation for the appropriate transaction events.

Time events are detected by monitoring the system clock. Concretely, we make use of the UNIX system command *cron* which executes commands (in our case calls of the operation *raise event*) at specified dates and times according to instructions found in a *crontab* file. This applies to the absolute and to the periodical time events except those defined with a frequency and a time interval. To detect the latter ones, we have to insert the next one into the *crontab* file every time a periodical event is signalled.

4.1.2 Detecting Composite Events Using Petri Nets

In SAMOS, we use *Petri nets* (PN) [15] to model and to detect composite events. Incidentally, Petri nets have been used for active databases for the modelling of the active behavior during the database design process [14]. In the context of SAMOS, we define a PN as a tuple (N, M_0) where N represents the (static) structure of the PN and M_0 is the *initial marking* of the PN.

N is a 5-tuple (P, T, A, P_s, P_e) where P is a finite set of *places*, T is a finite set of *transitions*, and $A \subset (P \times T \cup T \times P)$ is a finite set of *arcs* denoting the connection between places and transitions. For each transition t we define its *input places* ${}^\bullet t = \{p \mid (p,t) \in A\}$ and its *output places* $t^\bullet = \{p \mid (t,p) \in A\}$. $P_s \subset P$ is the set of all *input places* of the PN that model event patterns and are marked as soon as the corresponding event has occurred. All other places can only be marked upon the firing of transitions. $P_e \subseteq P$ is the finite set of all *output places* of the PN that model composite event patterns. Their marking denotes the occurrence of an event of the corresponding composite event pattern.

In an actual state, a PN has a non-negative number of *tokens* assigned to places. The number of tokens per place is defined by a *marking* M, i.e., a mapping $M : P \rightarrow N \cup \{0\}$. M_0 is the *initial marking* of the PN; it defines the number of tokens for auxiliary places. Every time an input place of the PN is marked it has to be checked whether the corresponding transition(s) can fire. Let M be a marking. Then, a transition t can *fire* if (and only if) $\forall p \in {}^{\bullet}t : M(p) \geq 1$, i.e., all of its input places are marked. The firing of a transition leads to the marking of all its output places. Thus, when t fires, the subsequent marking M′ satisfies the following equation:

$$M'(p) = \begin{cases} M(p) + 1 & \forall p \in t^{\bullet} \\ M(p) - 1 & \forall p \in {}^{\bullet}t \\ M(p) & \text{otherwise} \end{cases} \qquad \text{(Equation 1)}$$

Event patterns can have parameters, and thus, the information about actual parameters has to be treated as a property of places. To that end, *individual tokens* are used to represent actual parameters and can be assigned to places. After the firing of a transition t all output places have to be marked, i.e. the value of the tokens of all input places of t flow into the (individual) tokens of the output places of t. This means that the information about the actual parameter of an event flows through the PN. These aspects can be found in [9].

A Petri net pattern is defined for each constructor of the event algebra. As an example, figure 2 shows the Petri net pattern for a sequence. Note that in this case $E1 \in P_s$ and $E2 \in P_s$ holds, while $(E1;E2) \in P_e$. The firing of t3 leads to the marking of the place $(E1;E2)$ which corresponds to the signalling of the sequence event. The place H is an auxiliary place and serves to ignore all occurrences of E2 before the occurrence of E1.

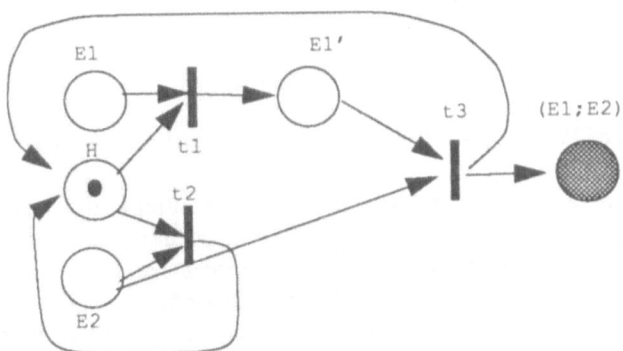

Figure 2. The Petri net pattern for a sequence

Every time the user defines a composite event pattern using one of the event constructors, the system has to create an appropriate Petri net. For that matter, it retrieves the corresponding Petri net pattern and instantiates a new PN that uses the structure of the pattern. The names of the places of the new PN denote the components of the composite event. If these components in turn are composite events the retrieval and in-

34

stantiation process continues recursively. The entire event detector for composite events is a *combination Petri net* (cPN) which consists of all Petri nets.

Instead of modelling all composite events by independent PNs, we combine them into one PN whenever possible. Such a combination is applied in the following cases:

1. An event participates in *more than one* composition, e.g., E1 in E=(E1;E2) and in EE=(E1,E3). Then the place E1 is duplicated into E1' and E1''. The Petri net parts for the two composite events E and EE use the input places E1' and E1'', respectively. In this way, for the event E1 only one place exists while in the independent existence of Petri nets, more places (one for each composition) are required. Thus, every time E1 occurs, only one place has to be marked.

2. A composite event takes part in *further* composite events, e.g., E=(E1,E2) and EE=(E|E3). Then, the output place modelling the composite event E is an input place for the Petri net modelling the composite event EE.

As soon as the event detector signals the occurrence of a primitive event, the corresponding input place of the Petri net is marked. Then, the Petri net possibly fires transitions and an output place of the PN can be marked. In this case, the composite event (signalled by marking this output place) is inserted into the event register, together with the information (actual parameters) included in the respective (individual) token.

The example in Figure 3 shows how a specific Petri net for a sequence works. It shows which places are marked and which transitions fire when an event occurs.

	E1	E2	H	E1'	(E1;E2)
E2 occurs :	–	*	*	–	–
t2 fires	–	–	*	–	–
E1 occurs :	*	–	*	–	–
t1 fires	–	–	–	*	–
E1 occurs :	*	–	–	*	–
E2 occurs :	*	*	–	*	–
t3 fires	*	–	*	–	*
t1 fires	–	–	–	*	–
E2 occurs :	–	*	–	*	–
t3 fires	–	–	*	–	*

Figure 3. An Example

The use of Petri nets for the detection of composite events has several advantages:

- Composite events can be detected step by step, after each occurrence of a primitive event, and, hence, do not require the inspection of a large set of (primitive) events stored in the event register whenever new events are inserted there.
- Petri nets allow the modelling of the semantics of the event constructors in an abstract way and, at the same time, the implementation of the event detector for all defined event patterns as well.
- Petri nets allow for modelling the semantics of *all* constructors used for the specification of events, though some slight extensions are needed (more details can be found in [9]):
    I. Because an event E with the monitoring interval [s-e] can be transformed into the sequence (TS;(NOT TE;E)), where TS and TE are time events denoting the *start_point* s and *end_point* e of the monitoring interval, respectively, events with monitoring intervals can also be modelled as Petri nets.

II. Composite events with the *same* keyword can be modelled as Petri nets as well. To that end we have to compare the parameters, i.e, the value of the corresponding individual tokens, before the fire of a transition.

4.1.3   Internal Representation of Petri Nets

The system maintains a data structure for the internal representation of Petri nets including a *connection matrix* (places **x** transitions) and a *place vector*. The matrix is used for the representation of the connections between places and transitions. For a connection between an input place p_i and a transition t_j, the (i, j) element of the connection matrix has the value 1. For a connection between a transition t_l and an output place p_k, the $(k, 1)$-element of the matrix has the value -1. All other elements of the matrix have the value 0. Each element of the place vector relates to a place of the connection matrix and contains the number of tokens and possibly the value of individual tokens. For the sake of simplicity, the algorithm described below (which is actually implemented in our current prototype) does not consider individual tokens.

Based on the data structure

```
N : ARRAY[1..P,1..T]
m : ARRAY[1..P]
```

the algorithm implementing the firing rules of Petri nets in SAMOS after the occurrence of the event E is as following:

```
firing:=FALSE
mplace:=find(E)   /* find the element of the vector m representing the place
                       modelling this event E */
m[mplace]:=m[mplace]+1 /* increase the number of tokens */
REPEAT
FOR j:=1 TO T DO
       IF N[mplace,j] < 0 THEN     /* find all transitions which have as input
                                       place the mplace */
          IF   N[ ,j] + m > 0 THEN /* try to fire each transition with mplace as
                                       input place by adding the j-th column of
                                       N to the vector m. If all input
                                       places are marked, the vector-addition
                                       results in a vector with positive elements */

             m:=m + N[ ,j]
             firing:=TRUE
          FOR k:=1 to S DO
             IF N[k,j] > 0 /* find the output place of the fired transition */
             THEN mplace:=k
             ELSE firing:=FALSE
UNTIL NOT firing
```

4.2   Event Manager

The event manager has to represent the information gained from the analysis of event definitions, i.e, it is responsible for managing the eventbase which consists of all defined events patterns. The structure of the eventbase is described by the *event schema*. In accordance to the idea "to stay in the same world and exploit its advantages", we built the event schema by means of object-oriented features.

Event patterns are represented as objects and therefore for such an object, all object-oriented characteristics are available. For example, event patterns have an identity and can be manipulated and accessed like any other object by means of methods. Especially, taking inheritance into account, the event schema is described by the class

36

hierarchy illustrated in figure 4, where subclasses of a "general" class *event_pattern* exist for groups of event patterns with the same kind (e.g., for method events). Thus, each defined event pattern is internally represented as an instance of the appropriate subclass. We point out some classes to give further explanations. Note that in this paper we restrict ourselves only to the structure and do not present the behavior of the event hierarchy.

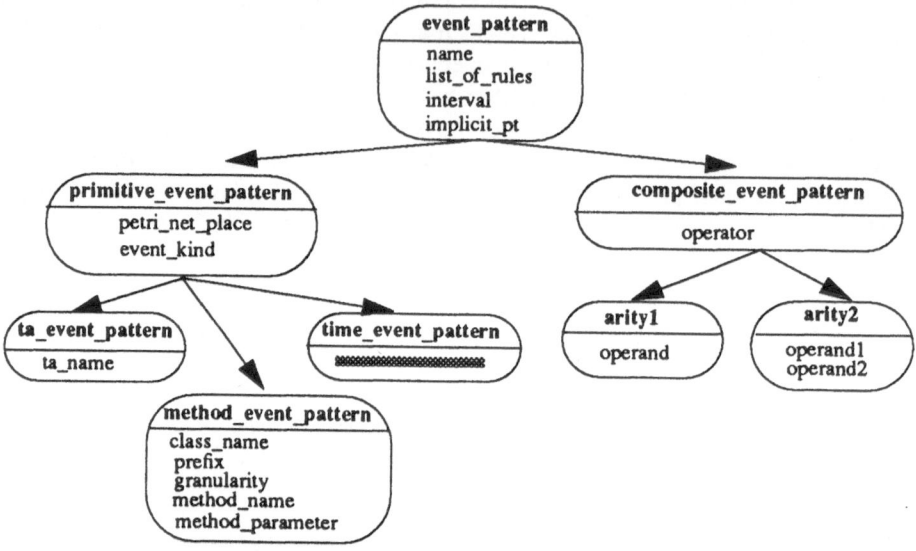

Figure 4. Event-Hierachy

The *event_pattern* superclass provides the common structure shared by all kinds of events and comprises attributes like *name* as the event name (user or system given) and the *list_of_rules* as the list of rules (i.e., references to objects of the class *rule*) which refer to the appropriate event and have to be executed after this event has occurred. The list of rules is split into activated and deactivated rules (according to *activate* and *deactivate* operations). To denote the connection between an event pattern and a monitoring interval, we make use of the attribute *interval* which represents a reference to an object of the class *interval*[3], which has all defined time intervals as instances. Points in time can be defined implicitly in relation to the occurrence of an event. Therefore, the attribute *implicit_pt* is a reference to an object of the class *interval* which is defined implicitly in relation to this event pattern.

The subclass *primitive_event_pattern* has additional attributes *event_kind* ("method", "time", "transaction" or "abstract")[4] and *petri_net_place*. The latter contains the index of the field of the place vector which contains the tokens of the place modelling this primitive event. In this way, after the primitive event occurred, we find the place of the Petri net that has to be marked on the basis of the value of the attribute

---

3. The structure of the class *interval* and the subclass *time events* is rather complex and is not described in this paper.
4. The kind of a primitive event can be determined after analyzing the event definition. For the sake of simplicity, however, it can also be given as part of the event definition. We have chosen the second approach.

petri_net_place (i.e., the implementation of the `find` operation of the firing algorithm is easy).

The subclass *method_event_pattern* has as attribute a list of the name of the classes for which this method is applicable (a method event can be related to one or multiple classes) and a *prefix* ("before" or "after") depending on the kind of the method event relating to BEFORE or AFTER keywords. Because a method event relates to either a class or to an object, the attribute *granularity* determines which case applies and has as its value either "all" or the object name. Note that for abstract events we do not need to create a separate subclass of the class *event_pattern* because they are represented as instances of the class *primitive_event_pattern* itself.

The subclass *composite_event_pattern* has an attribute *operator* to represent the event constructor. The component events are represented as attributes of the subclasses *arity1* and *arity2* which contains references to the appropriate events.

Finally, figure 5 shows the evaluation of tasks in SAMOS. This figure applies figure 1 by using the knowledge introduced in the previous subsections.

5   Conclusions

In this paper, we have investigated how events are defined, detected and managed in the context of the active object-oriented database system SAMOS we are currently implementing.

Rules and events are defined using a rule definition language. For the sake of ease of use, the event specification part of the language is simple, but nevertheless powerful. We achieved this goal by supporting only *six* event constructors for the definition of composite events. These constructs are *orthogonal*:

- to the modelling of time using monitoring intervals, in order to support the timely restriction of (composite or primitive) events which are signalled only within the specified interval and, in order to provide the signalling of an event with regard to a performed system activity (defined by implicit points in time).
- to the support of a fixed set of event parameters which, e.g., can be used in the definition of composite events on the basis of the keyword *same*.

In these aspects, our work differs from work done on other event languages (in ODE [11, 12] and Sentinel [2]). Furthermore, we presented how SAMOS detects the occurrences of events (primitive or composite). The detection of composite events based on Petri nets shows that even complex events can be detected in a relatively simple way. By using Petri nets, we are able to model and to detect the exact semantics of all the event constructors.

Finally, we have shown how the system represents and manages information about events so that it can be retrieved and accessed efficiently. For that matter, we specified an event schema that describes the structure of the eventbase using the benefits of the underlying object-oriented environment. In our approach, it is also important that the user is not required to know the internal representation and the handling of events.

Our current research focuses on the refinement of the event detector for time events and on so-called *value events* (as introduced in [7]). Our future research concerns the investigation of the strengths and possible problems of the rule language in concrete

38

applications environments, e.g., in stock applications. In the longer term we plan to provide (design) tools for active database systems. In detail a graphic editor, a debugger and tools analyzing interrelationships among various rules (e.g., to detect cycles) can help the user to overcome the complexity of applying an active database system.

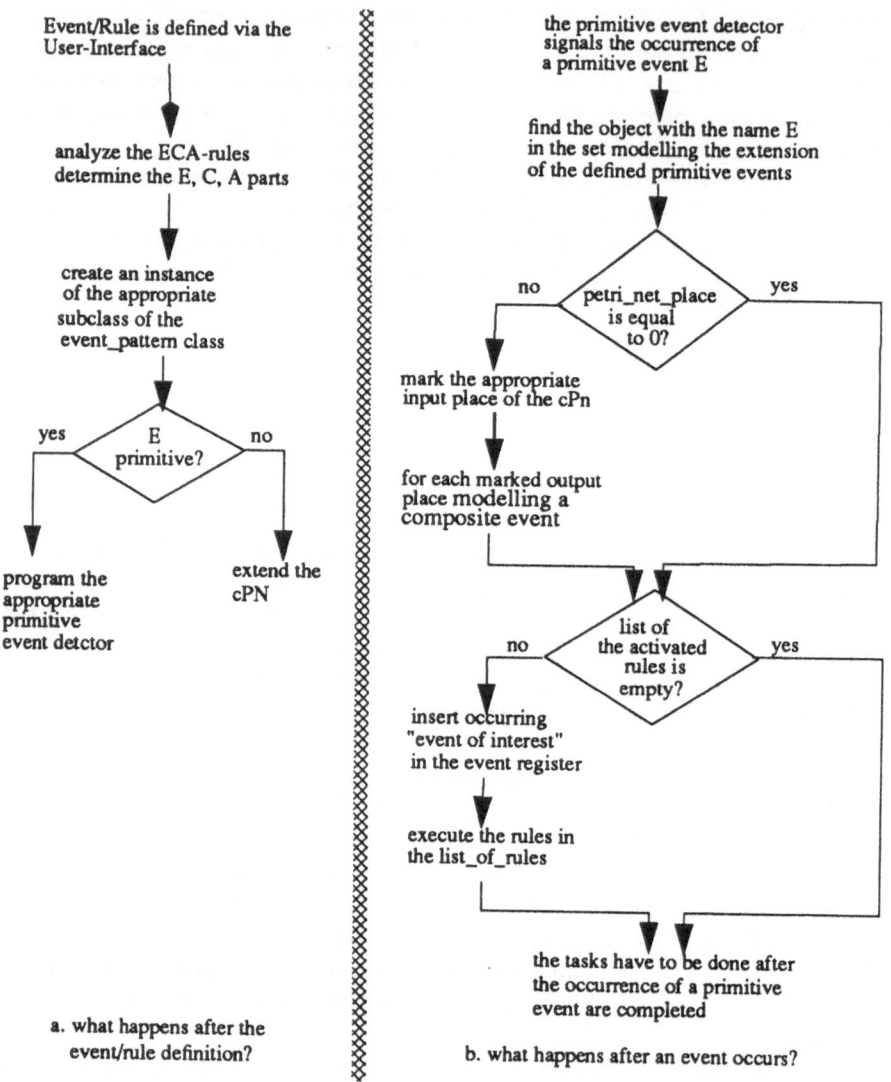

Figure 5. Control flow of tasks in SAMOS

Acknowledgment

The work of S. Gatziu is supported by the UBILAB, the Informatics Laboratorium Union Bank of Switzerland (UBS). Furthermore, we would like to thank all our colleagues, especially Andreas Geppert, who read earlier drafts of this paper.

References

1. Anwar E, Maugis L, Chakravarthy S. A New Perspective on Rule Support for Object-Oriented Databases. Proc. ACM SIGMOD, Washington, May 93

2. Chakravarthy S, Mishra D. An Event Specification Language (Snoop) For Active Databases and its Detection. Techn. Report UF-CIS-TR-91-23, University of Florida, September 91

3. Dayal U, et al. The HiPAC Project: Combining Active Databases and Timing Constraints. ACM Sigmod Record, 17(1), March 88

4. Dayal U, Buchmann A, McCarthy D. Rules Are Objects Too: A Knowledge Model For An Active, Object-Oriented Database System. In: K. R. Dittrich (ed.). Proc. 2nd Intl. Workshop on Object-Oriented Database Systems. (Lecture notes in computer science no. 334)

5. Diaz O, Paton N, Gray P. Rule Management in Object-Oriented Databases: A Uniform Approach. Proc. 17th Intl. Conf. on Very Large Data Bases, Barcelona, September 91

6. Dittrich K.R, Gatziu S. Time Issues in Active Database Systems. Proc. Intl. Workshop on an Infrastucture for Temporal Databases, Arlington, Texas, June 93

7. Gatziu S, Geppert A, Dittrich K.R. Integrating Active Concepts into an Object-Oriented Database System. Proc. of the 3. Intl. Workshop on Database Programming Languages, Nafplion, August 91

8. Gatziu S, Dittrich K.R. SAMOS: an Active Object-Oriented Database System. IEEE Bulletin of the TC on Data Engineering, 15(1-4), Special Issue on Active Databases, December 92

9. Gatziu S, Dittrich K.R. Detecting Composite Events in Active Database Systems Using Petri Nets. To appear in: Proc. of the 4th Intl. Workshop on Research Issues in Data Engineering: Active Database Systems, Houston, Februar 94

10. Gehani N.H, Jagadish H.V. Ode as an Active Database: Constraints and Triggers. Proc. 17th Intl. Conf. on Very Large Data Bases, Barcelona, September 91

11. Gehani N.H, Jagadish H.V, Shmueli O. Event Specification in an Active Object-Oriented Database. Proc. ACM SIGMOD, June 92

12. Gehani N.H, Jagadish H.V, Shmueli O. Composite Event Specification in Active Databases: Model & Implementation. Proc. 18th Intl. Conf. on Very Large Data Bases, Vancouver, August 92

13. Kotz-Dittrich A. Adding Active Functionality on an Object-Oriented Database System: A Layered Approach. Proc. GI Conf. Datenbanksysteme in Büro, Technik und Wissenschaft, Braunschweig, März 93

14. Navathe S.B, Tanaka A, Chakravarthy S. Active Database Modelling and Design Tools: Issues, Approach, and Architecture. IEEE Bulletin of the TC on Data Engineering, 15(1-4), Special Issue on Active Databases, December 92

15. Reisig W. A Primer in Petri Net Design. Springer Verlag, October 91

Dimensions Of Active Behaviour

Norman W. Paton†, Oscar Díaz‡, M. Howard Williams†,
Jack Campin†, Andrew Dinn†and Arturo Jaime‡

Department of Computing and Electrical Engineering,†
Heriot-Watt University, Riccarton
Edinburgh, Scotland.
e-mail: < norm,howard,jack,andrew>@cee.hw.ac.uk

Departamento de Lenguajes y Sistemas Informaticos,
University of the Basque Country,‡
San Sebastián, Spain.
e-mail: < diaz,arturo >@si.ehu.es

Abstract

This paper introduces a number of dimensions of active rule system behaviour which can be used both to highlight differences between proposals for active rule systems, and to identify the requirements of different applications. These dimensions relate to the structure, execution model and management of active rules, and enable the concise expression of what facilities a system supports and what features an application requires.

1   Introduction

The extension of conventional passive databases with features which support automatic responses to particular circumstances has been recognised as a worthwhile endeavour by database researchers. The resulting active database systems not only ease the implementation of time-constrained applications, but can be readily extended with enhanced data modelling facilities. The perceived desirability of active mechanisms has led to a number of detailed proposals for the introduction of active behaviour to new or existing database systems [5, 22, 25, 10, 16]. However, such proposals differ in a number of aspects which significantly affect the behaviour of a set of rules at run-time. In order to aid understanding of active databases, this paper seeks to identify a number of such aspects, referred to here as *dimensions*, which can be used to characterise the behaviour of individual active rule systems.

The variability of proposed systems along the dimensions considered in this paper has a significant bearing upon the applications in which a rule system can be employed. Indeed, it is shown that potential applications can be classified using the same dimensions as the different rule systems, thereby highlighting which proposals for rule systems are most appropriate for different applications.

The classification of applications according to the different dimensions of rule behaviour suggests that a single, inflexible model for rule behaviour is unlikely to be appropriate for a wide range of tasks. This suggests that either rule systems must be sophisticated enough to anticipate the needs of different applications, or must be tailorable to suit different requirements.

The paper is structured as follows. Section 2 introduces the dimensions of active behaviour considered later in the paper. Section 3 indicates how a number of existing systems support the different dimensions, and section 4 relates the dimensions to a number of typical applications. Conclusions are presented in section 5.

2   Dimensions Of Active Behaviour

This section introduces a number of dimensions of active behaviour. This process makes explicit the decision space within which the designers of active rule systems work, without endeavouring to provide any formal description of the semantics of specific rule systems – the actual behaviour of a rule system is also influenced by the environment of which the rule system is part, specifically the data model, query language, update language, etc. However, the fact that the dimensions discussed in this section abstract over certain details of rule system functionality which affect more than 'look and feel' does not significantly detract from the overall aim of providing a framework which highlights key differences between existing systems and applications.

The concepts considered in this section as dimensions are clearly not new – they are supported within a range of proposals for rule systems, and thus the terminology used below should be familiar to the readers of [5, 25, 22]. However, we are not aware of any other attempt to identify generic concepts which can then be used in the comparison of rule systems or applications. The dimensions of rule functionality considered in this paper are presented in Table 1, and are discussed further in the following subsections. In the table the symbol $\subset$ is used to indicate that the particular dimension can take on more than one of the values given, whereas $\in$ indicates a list of alternatives.

An active rule is considered to have (up to) three principal components, an *event*, a *condition* and an *action*. When the event takes place, the condition is evaluated to examine the context in which the event took place, and if true then the action is executed to enact some suitable response to the event.

2.1   Event

The **Type** of an event can be:

Primitive, in which case the event is raised by a single, low-level occurrence, which belongs to one of the categories described in **Source** below.

Composite, in which case the event is raised by some combination of primitive events [5, 14]. A composite event is constructed from a number of other primitive or composite events using a range of operators which vary from system to system, but which may include conjunction, disjunction,

Table 1 – Dimensions of Active Behaviour	
Event	Type ⊂ {Primitive, Composite } Source ⊂ {Structure Operation, Behaviour Invocation, Transaction, Clock, Error, External} Level ⊂ {Instance, Collection} Role ∈ {Mandatory, Optional, None}
Condition	Mode ⊂ {Immediate, Deferred, Detached} Role ∈ {Mandatory, Optional}
Action	Mode ⊂ {Immediate, Deferred, Detached Dependent, Detached Independent} Options ⊂ {Update-Db, Update-Rules, Inform, Abort, Do Instead }
Execution Model	Transition Granularity ∈ {Instance, Set} Binding Model ⊂ {Instance, Set, Prior} Constraints ⊂ {Timing, Alternatives} Scheduling ∈ {All Fired, Some Fired} Priorities ∈ {Numerical, Relative, None}
Management	Operations ⊂ {Activate, Deactivate} Description ⊂ {Programming Language, Extended Query Language, Objects} Adaptability ∈ {Compile Time, Run Time} Data Model ∈ {Relational, Extended Relational, Deductive, Object-Oriented}

sequence and negation. The semantics of composite events are complicated by the need to maintain a *history* of events which have taken place over some timespan (e.g. during a transaction) [15].

The **Source** of an event can be:

Structure Operation, in which case the event is raised by an operation on some piece of structure (e.g. *insert* a tuple, *update* an attribute, *access* a tuple).

Behaviour Invocation, in which case the event is raised by the execution of some user-defined operation [10] (e.g. the message *display* is sent to an object of type *widget*). In the case of behaviour invocation, there is also the issue of *when* the event is raised relative to the invocation of the operation – for example, it is possible for the event to be raised *before* or *after* the execution of the operation.

Transaction, in which case the event is raised at some specific point in a transaction (e.g. before *abort*, start of transaction).

Clock, in which case the event is raised at some particular point in time [5, 14] (e.g. it is 23:00 hours, it is 4 hours since some other event). Furthermore, clock events can be used to specify the time limit within which composite events should take place [14].

Error, in which case some error has occurred within the database.

External, in which case the event is raised by a happening outside the database [5] (e.g. the temperature reading goes above 30 degrees).

The **Level** of an event indicates whether an event is defined for every object in a collection (e.g. every instance of a class), or for specific instance objects (e.g. to prevent unauthorised access to specific instances, or to enable the update of the specific widget objects which are presently on screen).

The **Role** of an event indicates whether events must always be given for active rules, or whether the explicit naming of an event is not necessary. If the **Role** is **Optional**, then when no event is specified *condition-action* rules are supported, which have significantly different functionality and implementations from event-condition-action (ECA) rules [21, 16]. If the **Role** is **None** then events cannot be specified, and all rules are *condition-action* rules. If the **Role** is **Mandatory** then only ECA-rules are supported.

2.2 Condition

The **Mode** of a condition indicates when the condition is to be evaluated relative to the event which triggers the rule [5]. The **Mode** of a condition can be:

Immediate, in which case the condition is evaluated immediately after the event which triggers the rule.

Deferred, in which case the condition is evaluated within the same transaction as the event which triggers the rule, but not necessarily at the earliest opportunity after the event. For example, the condition may not be evaluated until the end of the transaction [25], or may be forced to evaluate at a specific point in time by a *fire rules* command in an application program [25].

Detached, in which case the condition is evaluated within a different transaction from the one in which the event took place.

The **Role** of a condition indicates whether or not it must be given. In ECA-rules, the condition is invariably **Optional**. When no condition is given for an ECA-rule, an *event-action* rule results, which is similar to the notion of a *trigger* supported by some commercial relational database systems. In systems in which both the event and the condition are optional, it is always the case that at least one is given.

2.3 Action

The **Mode** of an action indicates when the action is evaluated relative to the condition of the rule [5]. The **Mode** of an action can be:

Immediate, in which case the action is executed immediately after the condition of the rule.

Deferred, in which case the action is executed within the same transaction as the condition of the rule, but not necessarily at the earliest opportunity.

Detached Dependent, in which case the action is executed within a different transaction from the one in which the condition was evaluated. The execution of the action is **Dependent** upon the transaction in which the event took place committing.

Detached Independent, in which case the action is executed within a different transaction from the one in which the condition was evaluated. The execution of the action is **Independent** of the committing of the transaction in which the event took place.

The range of tasks which can be performed by an action is specified as its **Options**. Actions may **Update** the database or rule set, **Inform** the user or system administrator, **Abort** a transaction or take some alternative course of action using **Do Instead**[22]. As an example of **Do Instead**, if an event was an inappropriate update, then a more appropriate alternative update could be used *instead of* rather than *as well as* the operation which raised the event.

2.4 Execution Model

The execution model specifies how a collection of rules is treated at run-time. The **Transition Granularity** indicates how regularly events are raised, and thus the amount of intermediate information associated with each event. The **Transition Granularity** can be:

Instance, in which case an event can be raised every time an operation is performed on a single data item. For example, if an event is defined on *deletions* to the *student* relation, then an event is raised every time an individual student is deleted. Thus an event is associated with a single *current tuple*.

Set, in which case an event can be raised at a point subsequent to operations which could have modified multiple data items. For example, if an event is defined on *deletions* to the *student* relation, then an event could be raised every time an operation completes which deletes students. Such an operation may delete many students (e.g. delete from student where age > 30), and thus an event is associated with a set of *current tuples*. A further possibility is that events are raised at the end of a transaction. For example, if an event is defined on *deletions* to the *student* relation, then an event is raised at the end of the transaction if any statement has deleted tuples from the student relation. There may have been a number of such operations during the transaction. Indeed, different operations during the transaction may have inserted and then deleted a student tuple. In this case, the *net effect* [25] of a sequence of operations is normally used to associate a set of *current tuples* with an event, and thus rules have the effect of accumulating changes which have taken place during the transaction for processing at commit time.

The **Binding Model** indicates what information on the context of the rule is available to the condition or action of the rule. Clearly it is possible for a rule condition to query the database, but it is often necessary for the condition or action to be able to retrieve details on the nature/effect of the event which has triggered the rule. It is normal for the same binding operations to be supported by the condition and the action, although if an action does not take place immediately after the condition is evaluated then the condition and action may access different data. There are sometimes also mechanisms available to allow information which is retrieved by the condition to be passed on directly to the action. The **Binding Model** can be:

Instance, in which case particular instances associated with an event can be referred to by the condition/action, e.g. a window close event could establish a binding for the variable *Window*.

Set, in which case the accumulation of instances associated with events of a given type could be stored in a collection referred to by the rule condition/action. For example, tuple updates for a given relation could be accumulated to establish a binding for the variable *Updated-People*. Note that **Set** binding can only occur where the **Transition Granularity** is **Set**.

Prior, in which case the value of an instance or collection before an update operation can be explicitly accessed in a condition.

The **Constraints** associated with the execution model relate in particular to *time constrained applications* [5]. These indicate if it is possible to suggest to the system the **Time** within which a rule must be processed to completion, and also some **Alternative** to the standard rule action which is to be carried out if it proves to be impossible to satisfy the time constraint.

The **Scheduling** dimension indicates what is to happen if multiple rules are triggered at the same time – either every rule must be fired (**All Fired**) or only some of the activated rules are processed to completion (**Some Fired**). The actual semantics may be complex. For example, in the case of Starburst [25] a rule may be triggered by some update event which is then subsequently undone by another update, and thus the action of the rule will not be executed, even though Starburst operates an **All Fired** strategy. Where only some of the triggered rules are fired, it is possible that only the *first* is fired (chosen at random, or using a priority scheme), or that rules are fired until one fails [10].

A rule is selected from a collection of simultaneously fired rules for execution using a **Priority** mechanism. Rules can be placed in order using a **Numerical** scheme in which each rule is given an absolute value which is its priority [22], or by indicating the **Relative** priorities of rules, by stating explicitly that a given rule must be fired before another when triggered at the same time [1].

2.5 Management

The above dimensions of rule functionality relate principally to the run-time behaviour of rules. This section considers the facilities provided by the system for managing rules – specifically what operations can be applied to rules, and how rules are themselves represented.

Besides creation and deletion, which are taken to be mandatory, the following **Operations** can be supported on rules:

Activate, which enables a deactivated rule to respond to events.

Deactivate, which prevents a rule from being triggered – a rule will not respond to events while deactivated.

Rules themselves are normally expressed using a database **Programming Language** [15], an **Extended Query Language** [25, 22], or sets of **Objects** [5, 10] in an object-oriented database. These categories are not exclusive. For example, it is possible for an extended query language facility in an object-oriented database to arrange for rules to be stored as objects.

Another key issue relating to the definition and management of rules is the level of **Adaptability** supported. In some systems it is only possible to change the rules associated with an application by recompiling the application code, and thus the rules can only be modified at **Compile Time**. Others support more dynamic **Run Time** rule modification, including the ability of rule actions to modify the rule base. Clearly there is a sliding scale of degrees of **Adaptability** – in the context of dimensions, any system which allows rules to be created after the database has been populated can be considered to support **Run Time** adaptability.

There is an extent to which the **Data Model** with which an active rule system is associated is independent of the other dimensions of rule system functionality. However the data model does have a significant influence on the nature of the resulting system, and is thus included as a dimension.

3 Systems and Dimensions

The previous section has introduced the dimensions of active rule behaviour. This section shows how these dimensions can be used to highlight both the similarities and differences between existing active rule systems. Where it is not clear from the papers what a dimension should be, this is indicated by inserting *??* in the table.

3.1 Starburst

The Starburst active rule system is a set-oriented rule system developed for an extensible relational database system [25]. The system has been used to add a number of features to the underlying database, including integrity constraints [2] and materialised views [3]. The way in which the dimensions are supported in Starburst is depicted in Table 2.

The Starburst rule system derives certain of its characteristics from the relational data model with which it is associated – events are raised by structure operations because user-defined operations are not stored in the database directly; the rule system operates on transitions which consist of sets of values because the relational operations act on sets of tuples; the definition and management of rules is related to the definition and management of queries, reflecting the central role of the query language. The **Binding Model** in Starburst is slightly unusual, in that the action operates over the bindings established by the condition, rather than using the set bindings directly. Furthermore, when a rule is fired multiple times within a single transaction, the changes it has access to are those which have taken place since the last firing of the rule. Within

Table 2 – Dimensions in Starburst	
Event	Type ⊂ {Primitive, Composite } Source ⊂ {Structure Operation} Level ⊂ {Collection} Role ∈ {Mandatory}
Condition	Mode ⊂ {Deferred} Role ∈ {Optional}
Action	Mode ⊂ {Immediate} Options ⊂ {Update-Db, Update-Rules, Abort}
Execution Model	Transition Granularity ∈ {Set} Binding Model ⊂ {Set, Prior} Constraints ⊂ {} Scheduling ∈ {All Fired} Priorities ∈ {Relative}
Management	Operations ⊂ {Activate, Deactivate} Description ∈ {Extended Query Language} Adaptability ∈ {Run-Time} Data Model ∈ {Relational}

these changes, the system considers the *net effect*, e.g. the insertion of a tuple is not considered if this tuple is subsequently deleted within the transaction.

The Starburst rule system can be considered to be conservative in its design – a modest and fixed set of facilities are supported. However, the semantics of rule execution in Starburst are still quite complex [25], and it could be argued that supporting many more facilities would lead to rule sets which are difficult to understand and maintain.

3.2 POSTGRES

The POSTGRES rule system [22], like Starburst, acts on a data model which is based upon the relational model, although this has been extended with certain object-oriented features in the case of POSTGRES [23]. The rule system has been utilised for supporting derived data, integrity checking and authorisation [22]. The way in which the dimensions are supported in POSTGRES is depicted in Table 3.

The POSTGRES rule system, like that of Starburst, can be considered to be quite conservative, although a key distinction is that the POSTGRES rule system is tuple-oriented. Thus, unlike in Starburst, the consequences of an event being triggered take effect immediately, and are not deferred until the end of the transaction. The utility of set and tuple oriented evaluation strategies is considered in section 4.

3.3 Ariel

Ariel [16], like Starburst and POSTGRES, is an active database system utilising the relational data model. However, Ariel is principally a *database production system*, in that while ECA rules are supported, the event is optional. Thus Ariel is based upon a *recognise-act* cycle which is similar to that supported by main-memory forward-chaining expert systems, such as OPS5 [12]. This

Table 3 – Dimensions in POSTGRES	
Event	Type ⊂ {Primitive} Source ⊂ {Structure Operation} Level ⊂ {Collection} Role ∈ {Mandatory}
Condition	Mode ⊂ {Immediate} Role ∈ {Optional}
Action	Mode ⊂ {Immediate} Options ⊂ {Update-Db, Do Instead, Abort }
Execution Model	Transition Granularity ∈ {Tuple} Binding Model ⊂ {Instance, Prior} Constraints ⊂ {} Scheduling ∈ {All Fired} Priorities ∈ {}
Management	Operations ⊂ {} Description ∈ {Extended Query Language} Adaptability ∈ {Run Time} Data Model ∈ {Extended Relational}

approach has been considered by some authors to impose too high an overhead to be practical for use with large database systems, although recent research has sought to overcome the performance problems [21, 16]. The way in which the dimensions are supported in Ariel is depicted in Table 4.

The crucial features of the dimensions in Ariel are the optionality of the event, and the nature of the **Mode** and **Scheduling** dimensions. The **Mode** of a rule condition is normally **Immediate**, but can be **Deferred** by enclosing a sequence of operations in a block – the entire contents of a block are evaluated before the next cycle of the recognise-act loop. As in main-memory production systems, a single rule is considered for firing each time round the recognise-act loop, which leads to some rules being triggered but never fired.

3.4 SAMOS

SAMOS is an acive rule system based upon an object-oriented data model [14, 13], which supports the dimensions as described in Table 5. At time of writing, not all of SAMOS has been implemented.

Noteworthy features of SAMOS include an event language in which composite events can be constructed using the operations *disjunction*, *conjunction*, *sequence* and *negation* (which occur when a given event does not happen during a given time interval). Further, the event *$*E$* is raised once when the event E occurs one or more times in a given time interval, and the event *$TIMES(n,E)$* is raised when the event E has occurred n times during a given time interval.

As well as supporting **Clock** events, composite events can be specified to have taken place within a given time interval. **Clock** events can be described in terms of *absolute, periodic* and *relative* points in time. Events can also be parameterised [13].

A rule can be defined either as a property of a class or as an independent entity. The former, known as *class-internal* rules, can be associated with the encapsulated structure of a class. Rules defined independently of classes are

Table 4 – Dimensions in Ariel	
Event	Type ⊂ {Primitive} Source ⊂ {Structure Operation} Level ⊂ {Collection} Role ∈ {Optional}
Condition	Mode ⊂ {Immediate, Deferred} Role ∈ {Optional}
Action	Mode ⊂ {Immediate} Options ⊂ {Update-Db}
Execution Model	Transition Granularity ∈ {Set} Binding Model ⊂ {Instance, Prior} Constraints ⊂ {} Scheduling ∈ {Some Fired} Priorities ∈ {Numerical}
Management	Operations ⊂ {??} Description ∈ {Extended Query Language} Adaptability ∈ {Compile Time} Data Model ∈ {Relational}

known as *class-external*, and cannot be associated with operations on encapsulated structure.

3.5 HiPAC

HiPAC [5] is a prototype rule system for the PROBE object-oriented data model, in which rules are supported as first-class objects. Table 6 shows the dimensions supported by HiPAC:

In HiPAC, **Clock** events can be defined which are *absolute*, *relative* or *periodic*. Operations supported for constructing **Composite** events include *disjunction*, *sequence* and *closure* (the event closure of an event E is signaled after the event E has been signaled one or more times in a transaction).

The HiPAC execution model is supported using nested transactions, in which multiple rules may be executed in parallel with different levels of nesting [6].

3.6 EXACT

EXACT [9, 7], an EXtensible ACTive rule manager, enhances the object-oriented database system ADAM [19] with active capabilities. The main rationale behind this system is to provide support for rules as normal database objects, and to enable smooth evolution of the functionality of the rule system. Such evolution implies the introduction of new features to the rule manager, as well as redefinition or tuning of characteristics already provided by the system. However, no drastic changes should be involved – the basic model should be retained, but extensions made to the core to cater for new requirements. Therefore, the dimensions given in Table 7 below are those provided by the current system, and can be enlarged or customised by the user to fulfil special needs.

Table 5 – Dimensions in SAMOS	
Event	Type $\subset$ {Primitive, Composite} Source $\subset$ {Structure Operation, Behaviour Invocation, External, Clock, Transaction} Level $\subset$ {Instance, Collection} Role $\in$ {Mandatory}
Condition	Mode $\subset$ {Immediate, Deferred, Detached} Role $\in$ {Optional}
Action	Mode $\subset$ {Immediate, Deferred, Detached Independent} Options $\subset$ {Update-Db, Inform, Abort Transaction}
Execution Model	Transition Granularity $\in$ {Tuple} Binding Model $\subset$ {Instance} Constraints $\subset$ {} Scheduling $\in$ {All Fired} Priorities $\in$ {Relative}
Management	Operations $\subset$ {Activate, Deactivate} Description $\in$ {Extended Query Language} Adaptability $\in$ {Compile-Time} Data Model $\in$ {Object-Oriented}

4 Applications and Dimensions

This section outlines how the dimensions introduced in the previous section can also be used to classify applications, thereby answering the question *Which dimensions are necessary for which applications?*. The use of dimensions when answering the question also helps to highlight the key requirements of rule systems for specific applications.

In the case of dimensions which can take on multiple values, there is the question whether *any* of the values in the set can be used or *all* are required. This is represented in the following tables by using $\subset$ or $\in$ to indicate that any of the stated values will do, and $=$ to indicate that all must be supported. In the case where $\subset$ is used, it may be that system support for several of the options listed would improve the flexibility or performance of the resulting system.

4.1 Composite Objects

Rule systems have been used widely to implement modelling constructs which are not directly supported by a given data model. This section considers support for composite objects using active rules, in which the run-time consequences of the existence of a *part-of* hierarchy are supported using ECA-rules [20].

The model for composite objects to be supported is that of [17], in which a composite part can reference its component parts using references which may be:

1. *Exclusive* and *dependent*,

2. *Exclusive* and *independent*,

3. *Shared* and *dependent*, or

Table 6 – Dimensions in HiPAC	
Event	Type ⊂ {Primitive, Composite} Source ⊂ {Structure Operation, External, Clock, Transaction} Level ⊂ {Instance, Collection} Role ∈ {Mandatory}
Condition	Mode ⊂ {Immediate, Deferred, Detached Dependent, Detached Independent} Role ∈ {Optional}
Action	Mode ⊂ {Immediate, Deferred, Detached Dependent, Detached Independent} Options ⊂ {Update-Db, Update-Rules, Inform, Abort }
Execution Model	Transition Granularity ∈ {Tuple, Set} Binding Model ∈ {Instance, Set, Prior} Constraints ⊂ {Timing, Alternatives} Scheduling ∈ {All Fired} Priorities ∈ {Relative}
Management	Operations ⊂ {Activate, Deactivate} Description ∈ {Objects} Adaptability ∈ {Run Time} Data Model ∈ {Object-Oriented}

4. *Shared* and *independent.*

To give a flavour of these semantics, consider the case where the *engine* of a *car* is referenced using an *exclusive* and *dependent* reference. The engine is referenced by *only* that *car*, and when the *car* is deleted from the database, then so is the *engine*. If the reference was *shared* and *independent*, then the *engine* could be referenced by any number of *cars*, the deletion of which would not result in deletion of the *engine*.

The presence of such additional reference semantics imposes some constraints on legal networks of database objects. Certain update operations must be *forbidden* from taking place, and others must be *extended* with additional functionalities. For example, in the *exclusive-dependent* case above, the system must *forbid* an engine from being attached to multiple *car* objects, and the deletion process must be *extended* to delete the *engine* whenever a *car* is deleted.

Composite objects seem to be most naturally supported by the immediate execution of rules on the detection of events which affect the *part-of* hierarchy. To defer the execution of such rules would be to partition the implementation of primitive operations on composite objects, so that part of an update occurs immediately, and the consequences of the update are addressed at a later date. This would be likely to be counter-intuitive to users of such a composite object scheme, and could easily lead to incorrect assumptions being made about the state of a database in the period after an update has been executed, but before its consequences have been worked out. Thus the following dimensions can be considered appropriate for supporting composite objects using active rules:

Where a dimension is left empty, there is no particular requirement imposed

Table 7 – Dimensions in **EXACT**	
Event	Type ⊂ {Primitive, Composite} Source ⊂ {Structure Operation, Behaviour Invocation, Transaction, Clock} Level ⊂ {Instance, Collection} Role ∈ {Mandatory}
Condition	Mode ⊂ {Immediate} Role ∈ {Mandatory }
Action	Mode ⊂ {Immediate } Options ⊂ {Update-Db, Update-Rules, Inform, Abort Transaction}
Execution Model	Transition Granularity ∈ {Tuple} Binding Model ⊂ {Instance, Prior} Constraints ⊂ { } Scheduling ∈ {Some Fired} Priorities ∈ {Relative}
Management	Operations ⊂ {Activate, Deactivate} Description ∈ {Objects} Adaptability ∈ {Run Time} Data Model ∈ {Object-Oriented}

by the application – for example, the composite objects application does not seem to require a particular priority mechanism. The fact that the **Condition** is **Optional** should not be taken to mean that the rule system need not support conditions, but rather that a rule system should optionally support conditions if it is to be appropriate for supporting composite objects.

4.2 Integrity Constraints

There is no model-independent notion of integrity constraint; most proposals for or implementations of them are built on the relational model, although [8] considers constraints in an object-oriented model based upon an approach developed by Morgenstern [18] called constraint equations. Hence constraints in the relational model are considered as the paradigm example. Constraints in the sort of object-oriented models intended for design databases may be more flexible and expressive, but do not as yet fit into a descriptive framework as comprehensive as the relational one.

There are a variety of integrity constraints defined over the relational model, as described in (for example) [24], [4]:

key constraints: These specify that a group of attributes forms a key for a relation, that is, they may not have multiple or null occurrences. They can be violated by insertions or modifications but not by deletions.

domain constraints: These require that the value of a specified field be of a specified type or lie within a specified range. They subsume *non-null constraints*, which prevent an attribute taking on a null value, which is particularly important for keys.

Table 8 – Dimensions for Composite Objects	
Event	Type $\subset$ {Primitive} Source $\subset$ {Structure Operation} Level $\subset$ {Collection} Role $\in$ {Mandatory}
Condition	Mode $\subset$ {Immediate} Role $\in$ {Optional}
Action	Mode $\subset$ {Immediate} Options $\subset$ {Update-Db, Abort}
Execution Model	Transition Granularity $\in$ {Tuple} Binding Model $\subset$ {Instance} Constraints $\subset$ {} Scheduling $\in$ {All Fired} Priorities $\in$ {}
Management	Operations $\subset$ {} Description $\in$ {} Adaptability $\in$ {Run Time} Data Model $\subset$ {Object-Oriented}

inclusion dependencies: These require one or more columns of a relation to be included in another relation. The most important category of these is *referential integrity constraints* which require part of a key in one relation to be the key of another relation. Enforcing these may require cascaded rule execution.

aggregate dependencies: These restrict the allowable values of aggregate functions on a relation. They may require that the condition compute over the entire relation rather than only the modified tuples.

functional dependencies: These require that a "result" attribute of a relation should be uniquely determined by "argument" attributes, and thus only need to be checked on insertions or modifications; deletions cannot violate them.

more general dependencies: These include multivalued dependencies and join dependencies. They subsume some of the other constraints but add no new requirements to an active rule support mechanism except for increasing the complexity of condition checking.

In the framework of this model, almost all proposals for database integrity enforcement require rule mechanisms lying close to the same point in the classification space, as detailed in the following table.

Constraint rules are triggered by structure operations: insertions, deletions or modifications of tuples. The **Role** of the events is invariably **Mandatory**; rules can only be triggered in response to such operations. The **Level** of events is **Collection**; all tuples in a relation are treated alike by the event mechanism. Composite events will rarely be required.

The **Mode** of the condition that checks one of the above constraints will generally have to be **Deferred** to the end of the transaction (as in Ullman's QBE example), although very simple constraints (like domain constraints) could be

Table 9 – Dimensions for Integrity Constraints	
Event	Type ⊂ {Primitive} Source ⊂ {Structure Operation} Level ⊂ {Collection} Role ∈ {Mandatory}
Condition	Mode ⊂ {Immediate, Deferred} Role ∈ {Mandatory}
Action	Mode ⊂ {Immediate} Options = {Update-Db, Abort, Do Instead }
Execution Model	Transition Granularity ⊂ {Tuple, Set} Binding Model ⊂ {Instance, Set, Prior} Constraints ⊂ {} Scheduling ∈ {SomeFired} Priorities ∈ {Numerical, Relative}
Management	Operations ⊂ {Activate, Deactivate} Description ∈ {Extended Query Language} Adaptability ∈ {Run Time} Data Model ⊂ {Extended Relational}

checked immediately. The **Role** of the condition is **Mandatory**; no violation can be detected without at least an expression evaluation taking place.

The **Mode** of actions will usually be **Immediate**. Since constraint violations should be resolved within the transaction that creates them, the **Detached** modes are semantically ruled out.

The **Transition Granularity** of an integrity support mechanism could be either **Tuple** or **Set** depending on the data manipulation language and the specific type of constraint. Similarly either **Instance** or **Set** binding models could be appropriate. **Prior** binding may also be needed e.g for a constraint that the value of an attribute (like a sequentially allocated accession number for a library) may not decrease. Timeout **Constraints** are irrelevant to integrity.

Support for conflict resolution implies the ability to 'untrigger' a rule. If a single proposed modification violates several constraints and accordingly triggers several rules, it is unlikely that all their actions will need to be executed (an update only need be prevented once). This suggests a **Some Fired** scheduling policy with some sort of **Priority** mechanism.

The **Management** of rules for integrity constraints can be quite simply compared with other applications of active rules; creation of rules at arbitrary points during execution will not generally be needed. Creation of rules may be required independently of the definition of the database schemas although such an option has complications associated with it – how does the system guarantee that the current state of the database satisfies the constraints being inserted?

4.3 Derived data

The term *derived data* can be defined as data which is obtained from other data (i.e. the derivers) through calculations, but which looks as if it is stored. Derived data has been used to support multiple views, capture data semantics or hide database evolution. Recently some authors have proposed active rules as a mechanism for supporting derived data [11, 3]. Active rules provide a means to express how derived data is obtained from its derivers. In [11] it is claimed that a data-driven rather than an event-driven approach is more appropriate for expressing the derivation relationship. However, this section focuses on the requirements posed for rule management regardless of whether a data-driven or event-driven approach is used.

A first issue is whether the derived data is obtained on demand or is materialised (i.e. stored) and updated when any of its derivers is modified. The latter can be motivated by efficiency considerations due to having many retrieval operations and few updates. If derived data is stored, the question is when it should be updated relative to a update to its deriver. The answer can influence the action mode associated with the corresponding rules. The options are:

- the derived data is updated immediately after the modification of the deriver and within the same transaction. This can be supported by an *immediate* mode. This option always ensures a database state consistent with the derivation relationship.

- the update of the derived data is postponed. Two different action modes can be used here, these being:

  - *deferred mode:* the derived data is calculated once at the end of the transaction regardless of the number of updates in its derivers.

  - *detached dependent mode:* the update is performed in a different transaction.

Another requirement is the need for a priority mechanism to avoid non-deterministic results in case more than one derivation rule is available [11].

Finally, composite events can be utilised here, as re-calculation of the materialised derived data can be triggered by updates on any of the derivers.

Table 10 – Dimensions for Derived Data	
Event	Type $\subset$ {Primitive, Composite} Source $\subset$ {Structure Operation} Level $\subset$ {Collection} Role $\in$ {Mandatory, Optional}
Condition	Mode $\subset$ {Immediate} Role $\in$ {Optional}
Action	Mode $\subset$ {Immediate, Deferred, Detached Dependent} Options $\subset$ {Update-Db}
Execution Model	Transition Granularity $\in$ {Tuple} Binding Model $\subset$ {Instance, Set, Prior} Constraints $\subset$ {None} Scheduling $\in$ {Only One Fired} Priorities $\in$ {Numerical, Relative}
Management	Operations $\subset$ {} Description $\in$ {} Adaptability $\in$ {Run-Time} Data Model $\in$ {Object-Oriented, Deductive}

5 Conclusions

Research into active databases has proceeded along similar lines to research into object-oriented databases – there has been considerable experimentation, but little work on standardisation or theory. In the early stages of research into an area this situation need not be seen as a major drawback, in that such research does lead to exploration of alternative approaches driven by the needs of different applications. However, there is also a need to be able to compare and contrast both active rule systems and the applications which it is suggested they should be able to support. This paper has presented a framework within which different systems and applications can be compared by identifying a number of dimensions which highlight principal areas of overlap or difference. This process indicates that major proposals differ in their support for such dimensions, and that different applications have different requirements in terms of such dimensions. The framework should thus prove useful both for designers and users of active rule systems in deciding which facilities they should support or are likely to need.

Acknowledgements We are pleased to acknowledge the support of the UK Science and Engineering Research Council (grant GR/H43847) and the European Community Human Capital and Mobility (ACT-NET) programme in the funding of this research. We are also grateful to Alex Buchmann, Opher Etzion, Stella Gatziu and Jennifer Widom for their comments on how the dimensions relate to their specific systems/interests.

References

[1] R. Agrawal, R. Cochrane, and B. Lindsay. On maintaining priorities in a production rule system. In R. Camps G.M. Lohman, A. Sernadis, editor, *Proceedings of 17th VLDB*, pages 479–488. Morgan-Kaufmann, 1991. ISBN 3-540-50345-5, ISBN 0-387-50345-5.

[2] S. Ceri and J. Widom. Deriving production rules for constraint maintenence. In *Proceedings of 16th VLDB*, pages 566–577. Morgan-Kaufmann, 1990.

[3] S. Ceri and J. Widom. Deriving production rules for incremental view maintenance. In R. Camps G.M. Lohman, A. Sernadis, editor, *Proceedings of 17th VLDB*, pages 577–589. Morgan-Kaufmann, 1991. ISBN 3-540-50345-5, ISBN 0-387-50345-5.

[4] C.J. Date. *Introduction to Database Systems, 5th edition*. Addison-Wesley, 1990.

[5] U. Dayal, A.P. Buchmann, and D.R. McCarthy. Rules are Objects Too. In K.R. Dittrich, editor, *Proceedings of the 2nd International Workshop on Object-Oriented Databases*, LNCS 334, pages 129–143. Springer-Verlag, 1988. ISBN 3-540-50345-5, ISBN 0-387-50345-5.

[6] U. Dayal, M. Hsu, and R. Landin. Organising long-running activities with triggers and transactions. In *SIGMOD Conference*, pages 204–214. ACM, 1990.

[7] O. Diaz and A. Jaime. EXACT: an EXtensible approach to ACTive object-oriented databases. *Submitted for publication*, 1993.

[8] Oscar Diaz. Deriving Active Rules for Constraint Maintenance in an Object-Oriented Database. In A M Tjoa and I Ramos, editors, *Proc. Database and Expert Systems Applications (DEXA)*, pages 332–337. Springer-Verlag, 1992.

[9] Oscar Diaz and Norman W. Paton. Sharing Behaviour in an Object-Oriented Database Using a Rule-Based Mechanism. In M.S. Jackson and A.E. Robinson, editors, *Aspects of Databases: The Proceedings of the Ninth British National Conference on Databases*, pages 17–37, Wolverhampton, July 1991. Butterworth-Heinemann Ltd.

[10] Oscar Diaz, Norman W. Paton, and Peter M.D. Gray. Rule Management in Object-Oriented Databases: A Uniform Approach. In R. Camps G.M. Lohman, A. Sernadis, editor, *Proceedings of 17th VLDB*, pages 317–326. Morgan-Kaufmann, 1991.

[11] Opher Etzion. *PARDES* -a data-driven oriented active database model. *SIGMOD RECORD*, 22(1):7–14, 1993.

[12] C.L. Forgy. Rete: A fast algorithm for the many pattern/many object pattern match problem. *Artificial Intelligence*, 19:17–37, 1982.

[13] S. Gatziu and K.R. Dittrich. Samos: an active object-oriented database system. *IEEE Quartely Bulletin on Data Engineering*, January 1993.

[14] S. Gatziu, A. Geppert, and K.R. Dittrich. Integrating active concepts into an object-oriented database system. In *Proc. of the 3rd Int. Workshop on Database Programming Languages*, pages 399–415, August 1991.

[15] N.H. Gehani, H.V. Jagadish, and O. Shmueli. Event specification in an object-oriented database. In *Proceedings of SIGMOD*, pages 81–90. ACM Press, 1992.

[16] E.N. Hanson. Rule Execution Testing and Action Execution in Ariel. In *Proceedings of SIGMOD*, pages 49–58. ACM, 1992.

[17] Won Kim, Elisa Bertino, and Jorge F. Garza. Composite Objects Revisited. In James Clifford, Bruce Lindsay, and David Maier, editors, *Proceedings of the 1989 ACM SIGMOD International Conference on the Management of Data*, pages 337–347, Portland,OR, June 1989. ACM Press.

[18] M. Morgenstern. Constraint equations: declarative expression of constraints with automatic enforcement. In *Proc. VLDB*. Morgan-Kaufmann, 1984.

[19] Norman W. Paton. ADAM: An Object-Oriented Database System Implemented in Prolog. In M. H. Williams, editor, *Proceedings of the Seventh British National Conference on Databases (BNCOD 7)*, pages 147–161, Edinburgh, July 1989. Cambridge University Press.

[20] N.W. Paton, O. Diaz, and M.L. Barja. Combining active rules and metaclasses for enhanced extensibility in object-oriented databases. *Data and Knowledge Engineering*, 10:45–63, 1993.

[21] T. Sellis, C-C Lin, and L. Raschild. Data intensive production systems: The dips approach. *SIGMOD RECORD*, 18(3):52–53, September 1989.

[22] M. Stonebraker, A.J. Jhingran, J. Goh, and S. Potamianos. On Rules, Procedures, Caching and Views in Data Base Systems. In *Proceedings of SIGMOD*, pages 281–290. ACM Press, 1990.

[23] Michael Stonebraker and Greg Kemnitz. The POSTGRES Next-generation Database Management System. *Communications of the ACM*, 34(10):78–92, October 1991.

[24] J.D. Ullman. *Principles of Database Systems, 2nd edition*. Pitman, 1982.

[25] J. Widom and S.J. Finkelstein. Set Oriented Production Rules in Relational Database Systems. In *Proceedings of SIGMOD*, pages 259–270. ACM Press, 1990.

Rule and Knowledge Management in an Active Database System

Waseem Naqvi
Mohamed T. Ibrahim

Database Systems Research Laboratory
University of Greenwich, London, SE18 6PF, U.K.
{w.naqvi, m.ibrahim}@greenwich.ac.uk

Abstract. Todays new applications require that reasonable inferences be made on the data within the database i.e. knowledge of the application domain is required. Knowledge is a higher level abstraction than the data or facts alone. Active databases strive to encapsulate an application domain's knowledge within the database. REFLEX is an active database research prototype. It's main tenet is that it provides knowledge management facilities for traditional existing database management systems. This short paper discusses the knowledge management facilities and the unique features that REFLEX provides such as its novel *concurrency mechanism*, *self-activity*, its *non-destructive knowledge* model, and its *graphical user-interface*.

Key words: active database, object-oriented, knowledge management, real-time systems

1.   Introduction

There is a growing interest in moving knowledge from an application into a database or knowledge base. This has been attempted by knowledge bases, deductive databases and lately by active databases. In an active database the enterprise's domain knowledge has been encapsulated within the system. The knowledge is centralized in one place, i.e. within the database management system itself, as opposed to being scattered across many application programs. Thus avoiding the problems this may cause, e.g. replication of knowledge, effort and possible inconsistencies.

Typically, most active prototype systems have the notions of event-condition-action (ECA) [2, 3] triples. They include three components: knowledge, event and transaction models. Even though some of these components are common with other types of systems e.g. knowledge and deductive database systems, there are important differences namely, the ability to encode richer and more diverse application logic which is triggerable automatically by the occurance of events in the database. The *coupling modes* between transactions also being major variation.

REFLEX, is a research prototype of an active database system. It is designed for implementation as an extension for existing organisational databases. It builds on and extends notions and concepts from other related research prototypes along a number of dimensions. The philosophy of the REFLEX architecture and design encompasses the provision of a flexible, adaptive and *active* capability to an organisation's existing database. The benefit of such an approach, in addition to the aforementioned features, is that it preserves an organisation's investment in legacy systems, resources and training. REFLEX provides an easy to use, graphic driven, but very powerful active rule system, which may be augmented to an existing database.

The paper is organised as follows, section 2 examines the knowledge management scheme within REFLEX and includes sub-sections on how rules are added to the database, the distribution scheme, the self-activity features. Section 3 looks at related research. Finally section 4 concludes and highlights future directions. Candidate working prototypes of active applications are introduced in the appendices.

2. Knowledge in REFLEX

Active database systems must be able to manage knowledge as well as data. The REFLEX knowledge model combines two schemes of knowledge representation, namely *production-rules* and *frames* [11, 19]. Reflex is thus able to support the cause/effect and deep knowledge reasoning by the provision of these two types of knowledge representation.

REFLEX has been designed and implemented using object-oriented technology, to provide activity to traditional databases. REFLEX differs from other research prototypes [20, 1, 10, 6, 4], as it has a Transparent Interface Manager (TIM), a *gateway*. It is TIM that provides the flexible and adaptive features of REFLEX. A block diagram of the architecture can be found in figure 1. For a more indepth discussion of the model and architecture of REFLEX please see [15].

All access to the DBMS is routed through TIM. All existing applications work as normal, but if any applications require activity, TIM manages the activity. TIM allows internal events to be

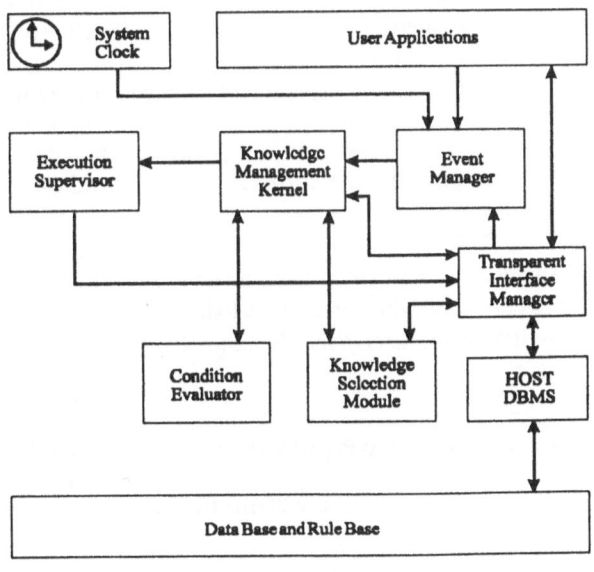

Figure 1   REFLEX Architecture

detected, such as database or transaction requests, mentioned later. TIM couples REFLEX to the underlying technology using *'wrapper'* technology, as host database calls are wrapped with a guard layer of code providing REFLEX information.

2.1. Structure of Knowledge

The structure of the rules in REFLEX have the following main attributes; Knowledge Management Kernel (the neucleus of the system), the list of objects a rule can act upon (class and instances), exempt objects, list of applicable events, event algebra clause, condition clause, action clause, coupling modes (event-condition, condition-action), rule priority, isActive (rule enabled or not). For a more extensive description, please refer to [15, 16].

The following sections describe the event specifications and rule syntax of REFLEX knowledge.

Event Specification

The *ON* or *event* specification clause of the rule allows both *primitive* (simple) or *complex* (compound) events to be specified. The event clause is expressed using an event algebra. The event algebra expresses the temporal relationship between component events. Event chronologies or histories need to be maintained in order to satisfy the event clause. This is the primary purpose of the *temporal log* [15]. The time model employed is based on *interval logic*, with all events having a before/after granularity. All internal events (described later) are preceded by either a *before* or *after* statement. If no mention is made, then *after* is assumed.

A list of the different types of events follow: (i) Internal: *Object events*: before/after create, get, put, delete. *Transaction events*: before/after start, commit, abort (ii) Temporal events: at (specific-time), periodic (repeat-after-period), after (duration), sequential (iii) External events: These events are application defined and hence cannot be listed.

The algebra contains several logical and temporal keywords. The logical keywords are AND, OR, XOR and NOT. The temporal keywords are BEFORE, AFTER, PRECEDES, SUCCEEDS, AT, BETWEEN, ON, WITHIN HOUR/MIN/SEC, EVERY HOUR/MIN/SEC, MIN, MAX, DATE, TIME. Parenthesis are used to override operator precedence.

Events are augmented with the concept of *validity*. An event is only a valid event if it occurred within a certain period. The temporality of events can be quite diverse. Examples of the *user-friendly natural english* event clause syntax are:

Event$_1$	simple single event of any valid type
Event$_1$ AND Event$_2$ WITHIN MIN 30	both Event$_1$ and Event$_2$ must occur within thirty minutes of each other
Event$_1$ PRECEDES Event$_2$ WITHIN HOUR 24	as above, but in sequence
AT TIME 17:00	

Events are totally *user-definable*. Internal events are provided by REFLEX, as are clock-based events. External (application based) and any other types of event, are defined by the user or designer of the active application. All events are detected by the Event Manager/Detector. On detection, the events are first logged in the temporal log, and then the Knowledge Management Kernel is informed of their occurance.

Rule Syntax

Being an adaptive and portable data model, REFLEX allows its condition or action clauses to be expressed in either generic Object SQL or in the proprietary language of the host DBMS. For purposes of illustration, the syntax for REFLEX rules is as follows:

```
ON      event-algebra
IF      either   i) no condition      ii) Object SQL query      iii) proprietary lang. query
THEN    either   i) call user module  ii) Object SQL query      iii) proprietary lang. query
```

Each clause is further exemplified:

i) *event algebra clause*. As described earlier in the section on Event Specification, the clause may be complex or primitive. The clause is subject to our event algebra. e.g.

update(table/class/object name)   on a update or modification of a table, class, or instance object

update(table/class/object name) AND TIME 5.00pm

The event algebra expression provides for a powerful mechanism for testing that certain events have taken place, or are likely to take place, without sacrificing effiency by testing the rules condition clause.

ii) *condition clause*. The clause may be set to TRUE (i.e. no condition), or expressed in either Object SQL or the host DBMS's proprietary language. e.g.

TRUE   i.e. no condition, just an Event-Action pair.

or

class_name.attribute (=, <, <=, >, >=, !=) expression

```
IF    SELECT   a.Name(), a.Salary(), b.Name(), b.Salary()
      FROM     employee a, employee b
      WHERE    a.Name() = OBJECT1
      AND      a.salary > b.manager.salary
```

The above encodes the familiar constraint that an employee cannot earn more than his/her manager. A generic Object-SQL dialect has been employed, for the IF or condition clause, to allow for portability between platforms.

iii) *action clause*. The clause may *call* an object module or as, with the condition clause, a more complete query may be expressed in either Object SQL or the host DBMS's proprietary language. e.g.

call   program module <argument list>

or

delete object

Some examples rules follow:

```
ON    update account                      ON    update stock
IF    select   c Name()                    IF    select   s.itemNo()
      from     account a, customer c             from     stock s
      where    a.customer.name = OBJECT1         where    s.itemName() = OBJECT1
               and a.customer.name = 'Fred Bloggs'        and s.itemQty <= s.reorderQty
               and account.credit_limit = 0
THEN call Alert_No_Credit                  THEN  insert(onorder) itemNo,
                                                 reorder_qty
```

Adding Rules to the System

The user or developer of an active application, using the REFLEX active extension, is presented with a fully object-oriented graphical user interface (GUI), the **REFLEX Visual Supervisor** (VIS). At present rules and events are added and declared to the REFLEX system by means of the VIS. The user interface and access

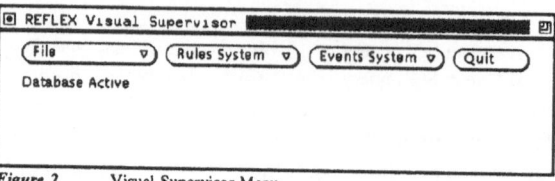

Figure 2   Visual Supervisor Menu

methods of REFLEX are the subject of another paper, currently under preparation. A brief introduction to the prototype is presented.

The user is presented with the simple *REFLEX Visual Supervisor* menu. If the user wishes to perform system administration functions i.e. add new rules or events, or to interrogate the system, they are all completed using this module.

When a user wishes to add a new rule, the *New Rule* option is selected from the Rule System menu. The user is presented with a *New Rule Dialogue Window*. The name and description of the new rule are entered. Following this, the user is presented with a *Class List Window*. This window shows all the classes or tables that are available to the user's application. From this list the user drags the class or classes from the window, onto the Rule Dialogue Window, that the rule will affect. A further window is presented, with the instances of all the classes selected. The user is then able to select particular instances as targets for the rule's action or the user is able to highlight any exemptions from the rule's action.

After the classes have been selected, the event algebra clause must be specified. This is accomplished in much the same fashion as the class selection, except that when the required events have been selected from the *Event List Window*, the user is able to select the logical and temporal operators, to complete the event algebra.

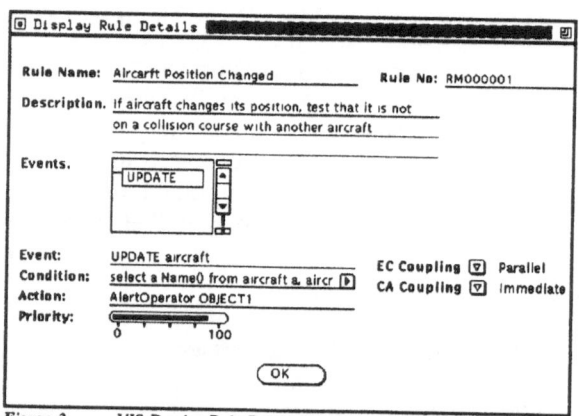

Figure 3   VIS Display Rule Details Window

The condition clause is completed semi-automatically, as the user is presented with windows of all classes, with sub-windows showing the attributes and/or methods of the classes (if any). The user must (with our current prototype), enter the remainder of the query. The system checks for syntactical and existence errors at this stage.

The action clause is completed in the same way as the condition clause, but using windows, which list the available programs and objects which may be selected for the program calls. More extended query language statements are available for the action statement than are available for the condition clause. This is because the action clause may include query operations such as insert or delete.

Both the Condition and Action clauses can access the object that raised the event by using the keyword *OBJECT* followed by its occurance number in the event algebra expression. In the figure above, the action clause calls a user defined operator window called *AlertOperator* and passes the *OBJECT1* as an argument, which in this case will be the actual aircraft object that has been updated.

The same type of approach is used for event management, i.e. decalration of new events etc. The VIS system also provides a rule browser.

2.2. Distributed Systems

The design of REFLEX using object-oriented technology makes it possible to adopt a *distributed* and *parallel* implementation model. This is possible as the modules within REFLEX are modelled as objects. The objects are *autonomous* and communicate with each other using *messages*. Thus the objects can execute on separate processors independently of other processes, on the same multi-processor machine, or as processes on a client-server distributed system. Thus *objects are natural models of concurrency* and exhibit *client-server* communication.

The REFLEX architecture is implemented as a parallel and distributed system i.e. all the modules are executing concurrently. There are areas of difficulty which may be subject to parallelisation. An example of such a tentative concurrent execution could be as follows. If an event has been raised, both the Knowledge Selection Module (KSM) and Condition Evaluation Module (CEM) execute simultaneously trying to satisfy their event algebra and condition clauses respectively for the same rule, see figure 4. As a result, the condition clause is evaluated (by the CEM) and possibly satisfied by the time the event clause has been evaluated (by the KSM). Normally, the condition clause is not evaluated

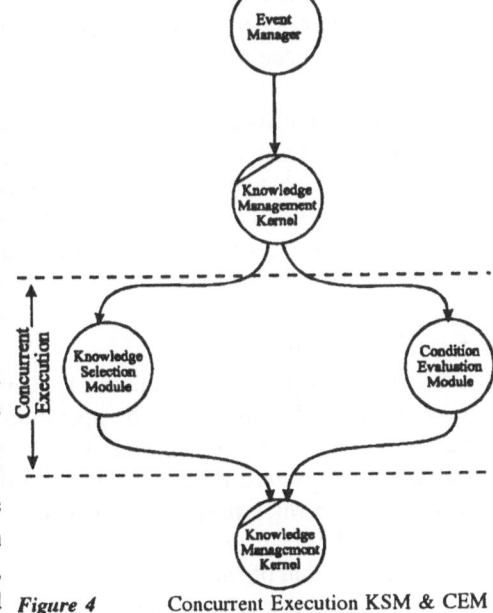

Figure 4   Concurrent Execution KSM & CEM

until the rule has a state of *event-clause-satisfied* i.e. until the event clause has been satisfied.

This feature is desirable in *critical real-time* situations. It may only take place for high priority *trap* rules, at the application designers discretion. However this feature may not always be desirable as efficiency of the database may be adversely affected.

But by using the parallelism only for critical, high-priority periods, it could improve the response time of the overall system without overloading the system performance at normal periods by causing unnecessary condition clause evaluation. However, this, as indicated above, is an efficiency decision made by the designer.

Thus it enables the construction and implementation of high performance systems, capable of modelling real-time critical applications.

2.3. Employing Activity

An active database provides a very fast reaction to any changes within the database's state or the applications environment i.e. *imparting* active capability into the application domain. REFLEX, unlike any other active database research prototypes as far as we are aware, *employs* the active capability itself i.e. it is *self-active*. The knowledge base (KB) as well as an application database are stored within the REFLEX system. Thus the maintenance of the KB can also be subject to the notion of activity. As an example, the rule's state is monitored *actively* by the REFLEX system. Rules have three components: events, conditions and actions. The clauses for each of these components are compiled, translated or recompiled at the point of rule creation or on rule modification. The re-compilation process being automatically triggered on a rule change.

2.4. Non-Destructive Knowledge

REFLEX introduces the concept of *Non-Destructive Knowledge*. By this we mean that if a rule has been declared, and it has not been used, it may be subject to change or amendment. But if the rule has been fired, or linked, it may no-longer be subject to change. It is in effect, locked. This concept allows us to audit our knowledgebase and evaluate why certain events occured. It also allows the provision of *knowledge versioning*. If a change in the rule's definition is required, a new rule must be declared, which the old rule references. The rules even if deactivated, still maintain references to objects that they refered to, thus providing a browsing system of the previous database knowledge state.

2.5. Rule Contention

A conflict resolution mechanism has been implemented as a task of the KMK as part of its scheduling process. The operation of rule conflict resolution depends on the assignment at knowledge capture time of priorities to the object rules. By default, a rule's priority is zero unless it is given a different value by the designer or user. The priority for rules may take any values the designer wishes, but a default is between 0 and 100. If two rules have the same priority, the first to be detected and hence obtain a state of *'in context'*, is actioned first. If the rules have a *trap* priority, then they are executed in parallel.

As explained earlier and as a further example of the *'self-active'* notion mentioned above, when the rule's priority changes, the system will automatically recompile the rules actively. This is a useful and desirable feature since it makes for a flexible system that can easily respond to change of knowledge or rule by the end-user without a need for a developer's intervention.

3. Related Research

Research into active database systems is intense. There are many research groups building research prototypes around the globe. The major research in active databases includes the following prototypes: POSTGRES [20, 21], STARBURST [10], HiPAC [1, D1, 3], ADAM [18, 4] and ODE [6]. REFLEX differs from these research prototypes by its *loose-coupling* to the underlying model in contrast to the high degree of coupling the other models employ. A more in-depth survey can be found in [13]. Another major area that is novel, is that the REFLEX model is designed to function concurrently with the host DBMS. Its design encompasses a multi-processor distributed architecture.

4. Conclusions

REFLEX has proven to be a very effective research prototype. We have implemented the REFLEX extension onto ONTOS [17], on Sun Solaris[23], using AT&T's C++ v2.1[22]. The REFLEX system *has been demonstrated* at various venues, using a graphical simulation of an Air Traffic Control System (see appendix). We are now using REFLEX to generate data on how a *real active applications behave*. We are currently implementing REFLEX onto POET [9], under Microsoft (MS) Windows v3.1 using MS C++ v7.0[12]. This will demonstrate the adaptability and portability features of the model. As REFLEX has been implemented to assertain its viability, performance whilst a major issue, was not a priority for the first prototype. Performance enhancements have been designed in the model, but have not been realised at this early stage. REFLEX has introduced a number of novel features such as its non-destructive knowledge model, its critical concurrency appoach and its self-activity to name a few.

The use of object technology has allowed the construction of a model that closely resembles the real world scenario. Major benefits of object technology have been utilised in terms of distributing the executing processes of REFLEX to both multi-processor and client-server architectures. The fact that the objects can very easily be mapped to independent processors as they exhibit autonomous behaviour via encapsulation, have well defined interfaces, and communicate with each other via messages; they have proved themselves as *natural models for concurrency*.

The knowledge representation schemes of both production-rules and frames together allow REFLEX to support cause/effect and deep knowledge reasoning. The productions providing the cause/effect knowledge and the objects the deeper knowledge about the application domain.

REFLEX is designed as a general purpose active database extension, but its operating tolerances cover the spectrum from critical real-time systems where immediacy is a major concern, and other systems such as stock control, where immediacy of response is important but not critical. For systems where safety, is a major concern, the system must have been carefully validated and verified so as to guarantee a high degree of safety. We are presently working on validation and verification of the REFLEX model and architecture, using petri-nets. We are developing a case tool PETENG which will allow the automatic verification of any petri-net structure, against a number of dimensions. Currently REFLEX utilises the rule-set concept to minimally validate and control its knowledge content. We are currently working to provide a much safer method of rule-set construction, using both static and some novel dynamic analysis techniques.

We intend to make REFLEX available on the public-domain, via ftp. It will initially be released for the ONTOS DBMS system. Please contact the authors for further details.

5. References

[1]   Chakravarthy S., Blaustein B., et al, "HiPAC: A Research Project in Active, Time-Constrained Database Management", Final Technical Report, Xerox Advanced Information Technology Division, July 1989

[2]   Dayal U., Blaustein B., et al, "The HiPAC Project: Combining Active Databases and Timing Constraints", ACM Sigmod Record, Vol. 17, No. 1, March 1988

[3]   Dayal U., "Active Database Management Systems", Sigmod Record, Vol. 18, No. 3, 1989

[4]   Diaz O. and Paton N. W., "Sharing behaviour in an object-oriented database using a rule-based mechanism", Proc. 9th British National Conference On Databases, 1991

[5]   Dittrich K. and Dayal U., "Active Database Systems", Tutorial Notes, VLDB 91, Barcelona, Spain, September 1991

[6]   Gehani N.H. and Jagadish H.V., "Ode an as Active Database: Constraints and Triggers", Proc. 17th Int. Conf. Very Large Data Bases, Barcelona, September 91

[7]   Gehani N.H., Jagadish H.V. and Shmueli O., "Event Specification in an Active Object-Oriented Database", Proc. 1992 ACM SIGMOD Intl. Conf. on Management of Data

[8]   Gehani N.H., Jagadish H.V. and Shmueli O., "Composite Event Specification in Active Databases: Model & Implementation", Proceedings of the 18th Int. Conf. on Very Large Data Bases, Vancouver, Canada, 1992

[9]   Gwb, "P.O.E.T. Reference Manual v.1"

[10]   Lohman G. M., Lindsay B., Pirahesh H. and Schiefer K. B., "Extensions To STARBURST: Objects, Types, Functions, and Rules", CACM October 1991, Vol 34, No 10

[11]   Minsky M., "A Framework for Representing Knowledge", The Psycology of Computer Vision, McGraw-Hill, 1975, pp. 211-277

[12]   Microsoft, "MS C/C++ v7.0 Programmers Manual", MicroSoft, 1992

[13]   Naqvi W. and Ibrahim M.T., "The REFLEX Active Database System", Database Systems Research Laboratory, Technical Report TR-CIT-DB0692, University of Greenwich, 1992

[14]   Naqvi W. and Ibrahim M.T., "REFLEX: An Active Database Extension", Poster at the 11th British National Conference on Databases, July, 1993

[15]   Naqvi W. and Ibrahim M.T., "REFLEX Active Database Model: Application of Petri-Nets", Proc. of the 4th Int. Conf. on Database and Expert Systems Applications, Prague, September 1993

[16]   Naqvi W. and Ibrahim M.T., "REFLEX: An Active Object-Oriented Database Model", sumitted for publication, April 1993

[17]   "ONTOS Reference Manual", ONTOS Inc, 1991

[18]   Paton N.W., "ADAM: An Object-Oriented Database System Implemented In Prolog", Proc. 7th British National Conference On Databases, 1989

[19]   Ringland G., "Structured Object Representation - Schemata and Frames", Approaches to Knowledge Representation, Ed. Ringland and Duce, 1987, pp 81-99

[20]   Stonebraker M., Hearst M. and Potamianos S., "A Commentary on the POSTGRES Rules System", Sigmod Record, Vol. 18, No. 3, September 1989

[21]   Stonebraker M. and Kemnitz G., "The POSTGRES Next-Generation Database Management System", CACM October 1991, Vol 34, No 10

[22]   Stroustrup B., "The C++ Programming Language", Addison Wesley, 1986

[23]   Sun Systems, "Solaris 1.1. User Manaual", 1992

[24]   Widom J., Cochrane R. J. and Lindsay B. G., "Implementing Set-Oriented Production Rules as an Extension to Starburst", Proc. of the 17th Int. Conf. on Very Large Data Bases, Barcelona, Spain 1991

APPENDICES

A.1. Air Traffic Control

An Air Traffic Control System (ATCS) consists of a number of sub-systems: the controller, the radar, the aircraft and its environment, and the ATCS itself. These subsystems exhibit independent behaviour and concurrently interact with each other. The aim of the simulation of the ATCS is to illustrate the operation of such systems under the control of a prototype REFLEX system.

In an air traffic control system, the operators need to know when an aircraft enters their airspace. When an operator manning a radar, observes an aircraft entering the airspace, the operator

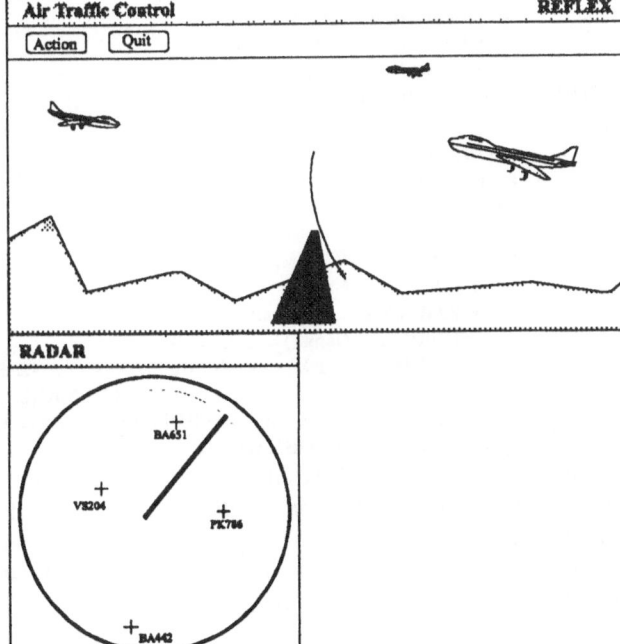

Figure 5   Air Traffic Control Simulation

makes contact with the aircraft, and requests certain details from the pilot. These details are noted down on cards. The details or attributes for the aircraft would be, for example: the aircraft registration number, the flight number, the exact location latitude and longitude, its altitude, its destination, its bearing, its ETA. Similarly for aircrafts that are taking-off or landing within the airspace, but out of scope of the radar; the aircrafts details need to be recorded. The operators would then have to track the aircrafts, making sure that the aircrafts adhered to their prescribed flight-paths.

This task can be automated, whereby the radar, feeds signals direct to the database of current airspace. Application programs would then update information, and other monitoring programs would then poll the database to ensure that the aircrafts are on their prescribed flight-paths. Application programs would also periodically *poll* the database to ensure that aircrafts do not get too close to one-another.

Using REFLEX, when a plane enters the airspace, the radar will produce a pulse. REFLEX, on receipt of the radar signal (external event), will open a dialogue screen with the operator, requesting that the operator make voice contact with the aircraft. Before this stage, the ATCS active application will try to read the aircrafts transponder signal. If successful, will inform the operator via the dialogue screen. Once the aircraft's details have been entered, the object class of aircraft, may have rules attached. Such as:

```
ON      <radar.aircraft_moved>
IF      aircraft.location does not approx.
        equal prescribed flight-plan
THEN    CALL alert operator


ON      <radar.aircraft_moved>          (event)
IF      aircraft in vicinity of another aircraft   (condition)
THEN    CALL alert operator             (action)


            ON AFTER UPDATE aircraft
            IF  SELECT    a.Name()
                FROM  aircraft a, aircraft b
                WHERE     a.Name() = OBJECT1
                    AND   (a.CurX - b.CurX) BETWEEN -5 AND 5
                    AND   (a.CurY - b.CurY) BETWEEN -5 AND 5
                    AND   (a.CurZ - b.CurZ) BETWEEN -5 AND 5;
            THEN   AlertOperator OBJECT1
```

Thus, the database itself would keep the aircraft's position updated in real-time, on radar events such as *aircraft position changed*. The database would monitor the aircrafts position and those of any other aircraft in the vicinity. Informing the operator of the current status in the airspace and altering the operator if an unforeseen or hazardous situation arises.

A.2.   Stock Control

A more conventional example could be that of a stock control system. The system would be required to reorder items when their quantity on hand falls below a pre-set threshold. Admittedly, in a conventional system, the reordering of items can be coded or hard-wired in the application programs. This approach opens to draw to design drawbacks, i) the processing logic is frequently replicated in many application programs and this can cause maintenance problems, ii) the logic, for the item quantity on hand program, could be included in a single specially built application programs which would poll the database at appropriate periods. This has advantages over the first approach in that the logic would probably be concentrated in the one special purpose application program, and hence not distributed over the application programs, across the system. The polling however, still has to be tuned. The polling might occur infrequently. This might cause the polling program to just miss the data, or there may be frequent polling, and this could be excessive in terms of database response time as the system spends time in servicing its polling requests.

An active database system would allow part of the processing logic to be stored alongside the data which it operates upon. In the stock control example, for items such as 'widgets', a rule could be declared that checks whether quantity on hand is below a reorder quantity level and, if the condition is satisfied, the system automatically generates a reorder request. That is, on the event, update widgets, the database determines if there is a rule on the widget's class. If so, the rules condition is evaluated, and if satisfied, its action clause executed i.e. reorder new widgets.

Architectures Incorporating Temporal Rules

Temporal Rule Specification and Management in Object-oriented Knowledge Bases*

Stanley Y. W. Su and Hsin-Hsing M. Chen

Database Systems Research & Development Center
Department of Computer and Information Sciences
Department of Electrical Engineering
University of Florida
Gainesville, FL32611
E-mail: su@pacer.cis.ufl.edu and hmchen@vnet.ibm.com

Abstract

There have been many recent research efforts on temporal databases for managing current and historical data and on active databases for monitoring real-world events as well as data conditions/constraints by rules and triggers. However, the specification and management of temporal rules in active OODBs has not been investigated. This paper deals with the specification and management of temporal requirements and constraints of real-world applications. We present a temporal knowledge model in which temporal rules are defined as part of the semantic specifications of object instances and object classes. We also present a temporal specification language which is characterized by its validity time specification, its trigger specification that involves time and system/user-defined operations, and the inclusion of temporal conditions and association patterns in temporal rules. Two general types of temporal rules are distinguished: constraint rules for specifying the legitimate or illegitimate states of a temporal knowledge base and deductive rules for deducing objects' data values and object associations which are not explicitly stored. Activations of temporal rules are controlled by triggers which specify the various times and conditions for rule evaluation. Rules can be updated resulting in historical rules. Rules can be inherited in a superclass-subclass hierarchy or a lattice as the inheritance of attributes and operations in the object-oriented paradigm. Temporal rules are modeled as first class objects and thus can be managed uniformly as temporal data by a temporal knowledge base management system. The methods for updating, retrieving, triggering, and evaluating temporal rules are also presented.

1 Introduction

There are two very important topics presently being investigated by researchers in the database community: temporal database management and active DBs.

---

*Acknowledgment: This research is supported by the National Science Foundation grant CCR-9200756. The implementation effort is supported by the Florida High Technology and Industry Council grant #UPN 90090708.

The advancement of both topics is essential for the development of sophisticated knowledge base management systems (KBMSs) for supporting future advanced applications. Research and development on temporal database management is motivated by the need to support decision-making based not only on current data but also on historical information. Efforts on temporal models, temporal languages, storage structures, and access methods for the implementation of temporal database systems have been reported in [LUM84, SNO85, SEG87, LOR88, NAV89, ELM90a, ELM90b, SU91, JEN92]. Research on active databases is motivated by the need for a database management system to automatically monitor and react to real-world (or external) events as well as database states and constraints. Research efforts on this subject have been reported in [MOR83, STO85, DIT86, HSU88, DAY88a, DAY88b, CHA90, BEE91]. It is natural and important to consider the merging of these two areas of efforts and investigate the problem of the specification and management of temporal rules in an active knowledge base management system. To the authors' knowledge and as pointed out in [SNO90], this problem has not been investigated, particularly in the context of object-oriented knowledge base management.

Knowledge rule has been the most common form of knowledge representation among a number of knowledge representation paradigms [NEW80, BAR81, CER83, WOO83, MYL84, LEV87]. The use of knowledge rules provides an effective mechanism for an intelligent system to predict changes over time, to take different actions under various conditions, and to deduce answers based on observable things and events stored in a knowledge base. Complex application requirements, semantic constraints, and rules for reasoning and logical deduction can all be expressed in forms of knowledge rules. In knowledge-based systems that incorporate knowledge rules as part of the semantic description of an application world, a rule may make reference to some temporal data conditions in both the condition part and the consequence part of the rule. The trigger associated with a rule may also make reference to temporal conditions under which the rule is to be evaluated. Furthermore, the applicability of rules, like data, may depend on the time these rules are applied. A rule that is meaningful at one time may not be applicable at another time. Similar to data, rules may be updated. Updated rules become historical rules which are applicable only to historical data. We shall call these updatable knowledge rules that make reference to temporal data conditions *temporal rules.*

An advanced knowledge base management system should provide users (knowledge base designers and end users) with the language facility for defining temporal rules associated with objects of concern in an application. It should also be capable of managing and enforcing these temporal rules. In this paper, we present the temporal rule specification component of an object-oriented semantic association model and the technique for managing temporal rules. It is the follow-up work reported in [SU91] in which the modeling and querying of temporal databases were presented. In Section 2, the use of temporal rules as part of the object-oriented knowledge base definition is presented. In Section 3, a temporal specification language is described with examples to illustrate two types of temporal rules. Section 4 presents the techniques for modeling and processing temporal rules. A conclusion is given in Section 5.

2 Temporal Rules as Part of O-O Knowledge Base Specification

The temporal knowledge model OSAM*/T [SU91] is an extension of OSAM* [SU89] which includes the temporal aspect of real-world objects to capture the objects' histories. It inherits from OSAM* most of the modeling features which provide a conceptual basis for uniformly capturing the semantics and interrelationships among objects of an application world. All things of interest in an application world, i.e., physical objects, events, processes, functions, etc., are uniformly modeled as objects in OSAM*/T and are grouped into object classes based on some common semantic properties. An object class, thus, captures the structural and behavioral semantics common to a set of objects. Object classes and their associated objects are interrelated through various association types, each of which represents a set of operational rules governing the manipulation of objects of the associated classes. Five system predefined association types (aggregation, generalization, interaction, composition, and crossproduct) are provided in OSAM*/T. Additional user-defined association types or subtypes of the existing association types are possible since association types are modeled as classes in the implementation model of a KBMS to be shown later.

In OSAM*/T, object histories are recorded by time-interval stamps using an object instance time-stamping technique: whenever the state of an object instance is changed (i.e., any of its attributes or association is modified, deleted, etc.), a new version of the object instance is created with a new time stamp. Since association types are also modeled as object classes in our system-level implementation model, each association instance of any type is conceptually treated as an object. Therefore, an association object also has history which can be derived from the histories of the associated object instances. A historical version of an object instance in a temporal knowledge base can be uniquely identified by a TIID (temporal IID) which consists of a valid time interval and an IID (or instance id) associated with the historical object instance. The two general time tags of the valid time notion, Start-time and End-time, are the only time notions used in OSAM*/T for recording the histories of object instances because we have observed that most of the real-world applications only concern about the valid time of data and that some other time notions are applicable only to some specific data in a specific application. The semantics of the other time notions are expressed by knowledge rules. Using knowledge rules to capture extra time notions for some particular applications has the advantages of achieving storage-saving, flexibility in introducing extra time notions, and easier retention of the closure property in database operations.

2.1 Object Class Definition

Temporal rules in OSAM*/T are treated as part of the object class definition. In OSAM*/T, an object class consists of three parts: (1) a specification part which defines the structural properties of the class (i.e., its descriptive attributes and associations with other classes), the meaningful operations (signatures) that can be performed on its object instances, and the temporal rules that are applicable to its instances, (2) an implementation part which contains the methods or program code for carrying out the specified operations, and (3) an extension part which contains the set of object instances belonging to the class. Object instances (similar to relational tuples) are the representations of objects in a class. An object has a system-assigned unique OID and an instance also has a unique instance identification or IID which is the concatenation of a class ID and OID. OSAM*/T allows an object to be a member of more than one class, thus having multiple instances. Temporal rules in OSAM*/T define the temporal constraints that objects of a class should always satisfy or obey. Temporal rules that are applicable to objects in multiple classes are defined in a superclass having these classes as its subclasses. These rules are their common semantic properties, thus are inheritable by their object instances in a manner similar to the inheritance of common attributes and operations (see Section 2.3 for more details.) This category of rules is called *class rule*. Different temporal rules can also be defined specifically for individual instances of an object class. This is achieved by storing these rules as values of a common attribute whose data type is **Rule**. This category of rules is called *instance rule*. Thus, a temporal rule can be associated with an individual object instance or with a class (if it is applicable to all the instances of the class.)

The template of a class definition is shown below.

```
Class_type <class name>
{Associations:
    Association-type = Association_type_1;
        {association_name_1: domain;
         association_name_2: domain;
         ············ }
    Association-type = Association_type_2;
        {············}
Operations:
    {operation_1(); operation_2(); ··· }
Temporal _Rule:
    {temporal_rule_1;
     temporal_rule_2;
     ············ }
}
```

In OSAM*/T, the structural properties of an object class are defined in terms of its associations with other related classes. As shown in the template, the association section specifies the different system/user-defined association types that an object class has with some other classes. The operation section specifies the operations which are applicable to the instances of the object class. These operations are defined by function and/or procedure declarations (i.e., the signatures) and their methods or program code. The temporal rule section specifies a set of temporal class rules which are applicable to all of its instances.

In the following, we give an example of a class definition and a class rule based on a schema diagram (or S-diagram used to graphically represent a database schema in OSAM*/T) shown in Figure 1. Additionally, we also define an attribute **Erule** of type **Rule** (i.e., an aggregation association between classes **Employee** and **Rule**) in this class definition for a later explanation of instance rule following this example.

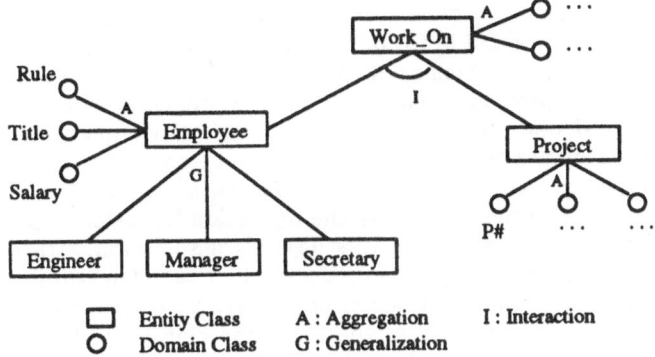

Figure 1: Semantic Diagram (or S-diagram) of a Database

Example of an object class definition and a class rule

In this example, we define the **Employee** class and a temporal rule with a *RID 00001* as follows:

```
ENTITY_CLASS Employee
{
ASSOCIATION_SECTION:
     AGGREGATION OF
     {salary: Salary;
      title: Title;
      Erule: Rule }
     GENERALIZATION OF
     {Engineer, Manager, Secretary}
     END ASSOCIATION_SECTION
OPERATION_SECTION:
     {TCOUNT(); AVERAGE(); TransferEmployee() }
END OPERATION_SECTION
TEMPORAL_RULE_SECTION:
     { Rule 00001
       Valid_T [11,−]
       triggered   (before TransferEmployee())
       condition   (exist this in this ∗ Work_On ∗ Project[P#=P2]) ∧
                   (exist this in WHEN T[3,5]
                            this ∗ Work_On ∗ Project[P#=P1])

     action      abort
     END /* end of class rule */
     }
END TEMPORAL_RULE_SECTION
} /* end of class Employee */
```

Rule 00001 was defined at time 11 and is still valid (this fact is represented by the valid time interval expression *Valid_T* [11,−], where *Valid_T* is a reserved keyword and "−" of the valid time interval stands for an infinite time point). This rule is applicable to all the instances of the **Employee** class and prevents those employees who are working on project P2 and ever worked on project P1 during the period of T[3,5] from being transferred. In this rule, the current and temporal conditions which need to be tested for an employee before she/he is transferred are expressed in two quantified expressions which are connected by a logical *AND* operator (represented by ∧). Each quantified expression in the *condition* clause is delimited by a pair of parentheses for clarity. In these two quantified expressions, **this** is a keyword which refers to the object (i.e., employee) to be operated on by the operation TransferEmployee(). Each expression checks the existence of this object's association with a **Work_On** object and a **Project** object having a specific P#. The time constraint of the first expression is *now* and the time constraint of the second expression is T[3,5][1] If the two expressions in the *condition* clause are both evaluated to True, the *condition* clause is evaluated to True; otherwise, the *condition* clause is evaluated to False. When the *condition* clause is True, i.e, the employee being transferred is working on P2 and worked on P1 during T[3,5], **this** employee should not be transferred and the **abort** specified in the action-clause will prevent the execution of the operation TransferEmployee(). The expression **this * Work_On * Project[P#=P2]** is an association pattern specification used in our implemented O-O query language OQL [ALA89]. It returns all the objects of **Work_On** class and those **Project** objects having P#=P2 which are associated with the object identified by **this** as specified by the associate operator. Further explanation of the rule format is provided in Section 3.

Example of instance rule

Since **Employee** class has an attribute Erule, every instance of the class can be associated with a different instance rule. In OSAM*/T, the data type **Rule** is modeled by a class called **Rule**. An instance rule associated with an employee instance is an instance of the **Rule** class and the value of Erule of the employee instance is the IID of this rule instance. An instance rule for employee John is given below:

```
Rule 00002
Valid_T [15,−]
triggered      (before RetrieveSalary())
condition      (INTERVAL(this)= T[3,6])
action         derived_value (this.Salary, this.Salary * 1.2)
END /* end of instance rule */
```

This rule specifies the formula used to reflect John's actual Salary during the period T[3,6]. This instance rule identified by *00002* was defined at time 15 for the object instance John of the **Employee** class and is still valid (represented by the *Valid_T* [15,−]). It captures the application of retroactive update on John's salary during the period T[3,6] and will be triggered before a retrieval of John's salary during this period. Other operations will not cause it to be verified. *Rule 00002* says that John's actual salary of the period T[3,6] should be 20% more

---

[1] In our implementation of the **K** knowledge base programming language (KBPL) [ARR92, SHY91], the usage of the existing quantifier **exist** follows the syntax: "exist variable(s) in context expression [suchthat boolean expression]", where **in** and **suchthat** are keywords; the keyword (or instance variable) **this** is used to identify the object instance to which an operation (i.e., TransferEmployee() in this example) is being applied.

than the recorded salary and this retroactive update is valid since time 15. In this example, if the valid time interval of John's historical instance is T[3,6] (specified by the expression "INTERVAL(**this**)= T[3,6]", where INTERVAL() is a function used to retrieve the valid time interval of the historical object instance), the action "Derived_value (**this**.Salary, **this**.Salary $*$ 1.2)" specified in the *action* clause of this rule will be executed to reflect John's retroactive salary. However, the computation caused by the method Derived($\cdots$) does not change the content of the database. From the above two examples, it is obvious that both instance rules and class rules have the same format. They can be handled uniformly by the same rule processing mechanism of a KBMS.

2.2   Object Instance Time-stamping

Object instance time-stamping is the technique employed to record the historical data in OSAM*/T [SU91]: every object instance in each class is time-stamped with a valid time interval [Start-time, End-time]. Start-time and End-time of the valid time are the two time notions used in OSAM*/T to uniquely characterize each historical object instance. The Start-time is the time when the information represented by an object becomes valid and the End-time is one time unit before the information becomes invalid. When an object instance is initially created, the Start-time is set to the instance creation time and the End-time is set to infinity represented by "-". As the object instance evolves (i.e., a change in the attributes of the object instance is observed), the current object instance will have a new Start-time which is the time when the object instance is modified and an End-time of infinity. The old version then becomes history and its End-time is set to one time unit before the Start-time of the new version. The old version is shifted into the historical area. An example of object instance time-stamping is given below. In this example, object instance Mary of the **Employee** class was created on 12-15-85 with IID 04 and had an infinity as its End-time. When Mary's salary was raised from $20K to $30K on 12-15-88, the End-time of the old version was set to 12-14-88 before it was shifted into the historical area; and the new version has a Start-time of 12-15-88 and an End-time of infinity. Here, a "day" is assumed to be the time unit. Any other time unit (second, minute, hour, month, year, etc.) can be used instead to suit an application domain.

(1) Initial creation of object Mary on 12-15-85:

IID	Name	Title	Salary	Start-time	End-time		
< 04	Mary	Secretary	$20K	12-15-85	—	>	$\cdots$ Current

(2) Update of object Mary on 12-15-88:

IID	Name	Title	Salary	Start-time	End-time		
< 04	Mary	Secretary	$30K	12-15-88	—	>	$\cdots$ Current
< 04	Mary	Secretary	$20K	12-15-85	12-14-88	>	$\cdots$ Historical

2.3   Inheritance of Structures, Operations and Rules

The structural and behavioral properties of a superclass are inherited by its subclasses so that these properties do not have to be defined in the subclasses repeatedly. Inheritance is implied by the *generalization* association in OSAM*/T.

For example, the attributes Salary and Title, the operations, and the temporal rules of the **Employee** class defined in Section 2.1 can be inherited by all its subclasses Engineer, Manager, and Secretary.

In some applications, a temporal rule may be applicable to instances of many object classes which do not have a generalization association among them. One approach is to define the rules in all these classes. However, this approach will result in rule redundancies. Another approach is to treat all rules to be global and thus applicable to all classes. This approach would require that a potentially large number of rules be searched to find the ones applicable to some objects in processing. An alternative approach used in OSAM*/T is to treat the rule as part of the semantic properties of a superclass which has these classes as its subclasses and the rule is made available to them through inheritance. For example, in Figure 2, Graduate_Student can be defined as a superclass of two pre-existing classes **TA** and **RA**.

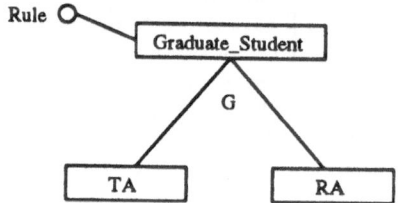

Figure 2: Rule Inheritance through Generalization Association

A rule such as "if a graduate student is either a **TA** or an **RA**, then only the academic advisor has the authority to see his (or her) GPA" can be defined in **Graduate_Student** and be inherited by **TA** and **RA**. Since rules are the semantic properties of objects just like attributes and operations, they are also inheritable by objects of subclasses. Thus, knowledge rules applicable to objects of different classes are naturally distributed among these classes and are readily accessible when their objects are being processed.

3 Temporal Rule Specification Language

The general format of a temporal rule in OSAM*/T is given below:

Rule rule-id
Valid_T [A, B] /* valid time interval */
triggered (trigger-time, trigger-operation)
Rule Body
      condition condition-clause
      action action-clause
      otherwise otherwise-clause
End

In this format, *rule-id* is the rule identification (RID). A rule is valid during *Valid_T* [A,B] which is a reserved keyword representing a valid time interval between Start-time A and End-time B; the Start-time is the time when a rule is valid to the temporal KBMS while the End-time is one time unit before a rule terminates its validity. In place of an explicit specification of a valid time interval for a rule, an interval function can also be used to drive the valid time interval based on either some database condition(s) or the occurrence of some event(s). The clause *triggered* (Trigger-time, trigger-operation) specifies the situation (or events) in which the temporal rule will be triggered. The **trigger-time** is drawn from four possible situations: *before, after, immediate-after, parallel*; the **trigger-operation** specifies either system-defined or user-defined operations such as InsertInstance(), InsertObject(), DeleteInstance(), TransferEmployee(), etc. The trigger time specifies the time for evaluating the rule relative to the time for carrying out the trigger operation. For example, the *after* delays the processing of the rule body until the end of the transaction of the specified operation. The trigger time of a rule is also the mechanism used in our implementation model for the coupling/decoupling between the original transaction and the spawned transactions from fired rules to achieve modularity as suggested in [DAY88b].

Rule Body is expressed by a *condition* clause, an optional *action* clause and an optional *otherwise* clause. The *condition* clause specifies the conditions in terms of logical expressions which are evaluated to True or False when a rule is triggered; the *action* clause and the *otherwise* clause (one of them can be optional) specify the alternative knowledge base states to be maintained or operations to be performed by the system if the *condition* clause is evaluated to True or False, respectively. In addition to logical expressions that contain logical AND and/or OR operators, the *condition* clause of a temporal rule can be specified in a guarded expression consisting of a string of expressions of the format "exp1, exp2, ..., exp$N$-1 | exp$N$", in which exp1 to exp$N$-1 serve as the guards for exp$N$. The result of evaluating a guarded expression will be one of the following values: True, False, or Skip. In its evaluation, the first N-1 expressions are evaluated sequentially. If they are all true and the Nth expression is also true, the guarded expression (and thus the *condition* clause) is True and the *action* clause of the rule will be taken. If they are all true except the Nth expression, the guarded expression (and thus the *condition* clause) is False and the *otherwise* clause of the rule will be taken. If any of the first N-1 expressions is false, the *condition* clause is evaluated to Skip, and the *action* clause and the *otherwise* clause will be skipped (i.e., the rule will not be fired). The mechanism of a guarded expression allows the interdependency relationship among the guards to be explicitly specified. Also, it allows the skipping of the entire rule if any of the guards is false. We note that the semantics of the sequential evaluation of the guards and the skipping of the entire rule if any one of them is evaluated to false are quite different from logically ANDing the expressions. This is because, due to the optimization of evaluating expressions, the conjunction of these guards do not guarantee their sequential evaluation in a proper order. We also note that, although the semantics of a guarded expression can be specified by a nested if-then-else expression, the former is a simpler and more declarative way of specifying a string of ordered conditions.

3.1 Types of Temporal Rules

Temporal rules in OSAM*/T are classified into two general types: temporal constraint rules and temporal deductive rules [ALA90, SU91]. Temporal constraint rules are used to specify legitimate or illegitimate states of a temporal knowledge base and take alternative actions depending on the true and false conditions of the temporal states. The operation specified in a constraint rule can either alter the state of a knowledge base by a system-defined or user-defined operation or cause an external event to occur such as triggering alarm, outputing message to a monitor, etc. by a user-defined operation. Both constraint and operational rules are used to verify and maintain the correct state of a knowledge base according to some application constraints. Temporal deductive rules, on the other hand, are used to deduce objects' data values and object associations which are not explicitly stored in the knowledge base.

We adopt from our own implementation of K the concept and technique of "object instance binding" in the specifications of temporal rules. If multiple occurrences of one class name in a temporal rule are intended to be bound to the same object instance(s), an instance variable will be defined for the first occurrence of this class name. For example, the expression e:Employee will assign the set of object instances of the Employee class to the instance variable e. Each of the succeeding occurrences of the bound class Employee can then be represented simply by the instance variable e. However, if a binding restriction is not intended among the multiple occurrences of a class, each occurrence represents a different scan of the set of instances of the class.

3.2 Temporal Constraint Rules

A temporal rule in OSAM*/T represents a user-defined semantic constraint. It states how the knowledge base activities should be constrained by the past, present and/or future activities to ensure semantic consistency and correctness of a knowledge base. A temporal constraint rule usually involves the verification of more than one knowledge base state which are associated with one or more than one knowledge base activity. The knowledge base states to be verified can be expressed in either guarded or simple logical expressions.

When a knowledge base evolves due to an update, insert, or delete operation, the state of the knowledge base changes. The change will trigger relevant temporal constraint rules to verify the consistency and correctness of the knowledge base. If any violation against the triggered temporal constraint rules is detected, the system will abort the operation to avoid the inconsistency or take compensation actions to correct the inconsistency. The users can therefore be relieved from writing tedious application programs to enforce the constraints. A temporal constraint rule defined in the Employee class is given in Example 1.

Example 1: *Those employees whose salaries are greater than $60K, who are working on project P7, and who worked for the Toy Department during the period T[2,4] should also work for the Sales Department.*

```
Rule 00004
Valid_T [7,−]
triggered        (after UpdateEmployee())
condition        (this.salary > $60K),
                 (exist this in  this * Work_On * Project[P#=P7]),
                 (exist this in  WHEN T[2,4]
                            this * Department[Name="Toy"]) |
```

```
                     (exist this in  this * Department[Name="Sales"])
otherwise            abort
END
```

This rule specifies a knowledge base constraint on current employees based on the conditions of their current salaries, current activities, and past activities during the time period T[2,4]. These conditions are specified by a logical expression consisting of three guards and one guarded expression. This rule was defined at time 7 with a user-defined *RID 00004* and has been valid ever since; the validity of the rule is represented by the valid time interval *Valid_T* [7,−]. It will be triggered after an employee is updated. The triggering condition in the *triggered* clause specifies that after an employee's record is updated (e.g., updating the salary with 10% increase), the rule should be triggered to check whether the updated record of the employee instance satisfies the conditions stated in the guards of the *condition* clause (i.e., whether the employee's salary is greater than $60K, the employee is working on P7 and the employee ever worked for the **Toy** department during T[2,4]). If so, we want to make sure that this employee also works for the Sales Department (which is expressed by the last expression) before the update transaction can be committed. If it is not true that this employee is also working for the **Sales** department, the transaction will be aborted because this update will result in a temporal state which violates the application constraint. Since we only need to check for the employee instance which is being updated, we use the existing quantifier **exist** and the keyword **this** to indicate that the evaluations of the expressions will be limited to the employee instance being updated.

3.3   Temporal Deductive Rules

A temporal deductive rule can be used by a KBMS to deduce/infer a data value for an object or an object association, which is not explicitly stored, based on some temporal information. In a temporal deductive rule, the temporal information which will be used to deduce a new fact is expressed in logical expressions in the *condition* clause; the deduced data value or object association is expressed in the *action* clause or *otherwise* clause. The statements in the *condition* and *action/otherwise* clauses of a temporal deductive rule are similar to the statements of the condition and consequence of a production rule in a conventional expert system. The effect of a temporal deductive rule can be on the past and/or the current state of a knowledge base. Temporal deductive rules for deducing an object's data value and object association are given in Example 2 and 3, respectively.

Example 2: *Those employees whose present salaries are greater than $60K and who ever participated in project P1 during T[4,12] must be a Senior Engineer.*

```
Rule 00005
Valid_T [18,−]
condition      (exist e in  e:Employee[Salary > $60K]) ∧
               (exist e in  WHEN T[4,12]
                            e * Work_On * Project[P#=P1])
action         derived_value (e.title, "Senior Engineer")
END
```

Example 3: *Those teachers who taught courses of the Computer Science Department during the period T[3,15] then must be affiliated with the Computer Science Department.*

```
Rule 00006
Valid_T [18,−]
condition        (exist t in   WHEN T[3,15]
                              t:Teacher * Teach * Course * Dept[Name= "CS"])
action           derived_association   (WHEN T[3,15]
                                       t * Dept[Name= "CS"])
END
```

Example 2 concludes that those employees whose present salaries are greater than $60K and who ever participated in project P1 during the period T[4,12] must have a (derived) title Senior Engineer. In this example, we assume that Title is a derived attribute which does not have an explicitly stored value; instead, its value can only be derived by triggering a temporal deductive rule. The temporal deductive rule of Example 2 will be triggered when a query makes reference to an employee's title.

Example 3 concludes that a teacher was associated with the CS Dept. during T[3,15] if the teacher taught courses offered by the CS Dept. In this example, we assume that there is no direct association between classes **Teacher** and **Department** in the schema. Their association can only be inferred from the associations among the object classes **Teacher, Teach, Course**, and **Department**. *Rule 00006* will be triggered when a query makes reference to the direct association between **Teacher** and **Department** classes which does not exist in a schema.

4   Managing Temporal Rules

Temporal rules are defined in class definitions in the database schema as explained in Section 2. Each rule can be parsed and stored in the form of a tree structure similar to a query tree using the same technique used in our earlier implementation of non-temporal knowledge rules. The information of the tree is then kept in a Rule Descriptor Table and a Rule Body Table of the data dictionary of the KBMS. The Rule Descriptor Table contains information of a rule such as the rule identification, the valid time, the trigger conditions, the pointer to the stored tree in the Rule Body Table, and the number of entries the tree occupies, etc. The Rule Body Table stores the trees of the parsed rules.

Temporal rules of a knowledge base may have conflicts and redundancies. The validation of temporal rules is essential to ensure the consistency and correctness of the knowledge base. As data are entered into the knowledge base, the validated temporal rules can be used to maintain the knowledge base. When a temporal rule is updated, the rule validation process needs to be performed again, and the existing data will have to be evaluated against this new rule. Rule validation is a non-trivial problem and is out of the scope of this paper. In this work, we assume that the rule base has been validated and shall concentrate on the management of temporal knowledge rules.

4.1 Modeling Rules as Objects

Temporal rules are meta-data or meta-knowledge of a knowledge base. They are part of the semantic properties of object instances and classes and are useful to the users of the knowledge base. For instance, a query such as "why could Ritter be a senior engineer and a sales manager at the same time five years ago ?" will require the processing of both the data and the rules of "five years ago" to obtain a correct answer. Therefore, it is important and necessary for a system to model and manage temporal rules so that they can be retrieved and processed just like application data for various purposes.

In our implementation of an O-O object manager based on C^{++}, temporal rules are modeled as first class objects [YAS91] which is similar to the approach taken in [DAY88b]. Figure 3 shows part of the meta-model of the system. The root of the class system is the class named OBJECT which contains all the objects of a knowledge base. E-CLASS_OBJECT and D-CLASS_OBJECT are the subclasses of the class OBJECT and are used to model system-named and self-named objects, respectively. The former models all objects of interest in an application domain whose identifiers are assigned by the system. The latter models objects named by their values which are used to describe or characterize E-CLASS and/or D-CLASS objects (e.g., integer 5, character string "John", etc.) Since the modeling constructs of OSAM*/T, such as temporal rules, classes, associations, and methods, are treated as system-named objects, they are modeled as subclasses of E-CLASS_OBJECT and named as TEMPORAL_RULE, CLASS, ASSOCIATION, and METHOD, respectively. The class named CLASS in the figure contains all the definitions of classes in the entire system. A class is defined by a class name, a set of temporal rules, a set of associations and a set of methods. The definitions of all the classes (entity and domain classes) shown in the figure, including the class CLASS itself, are instances of CLASS.

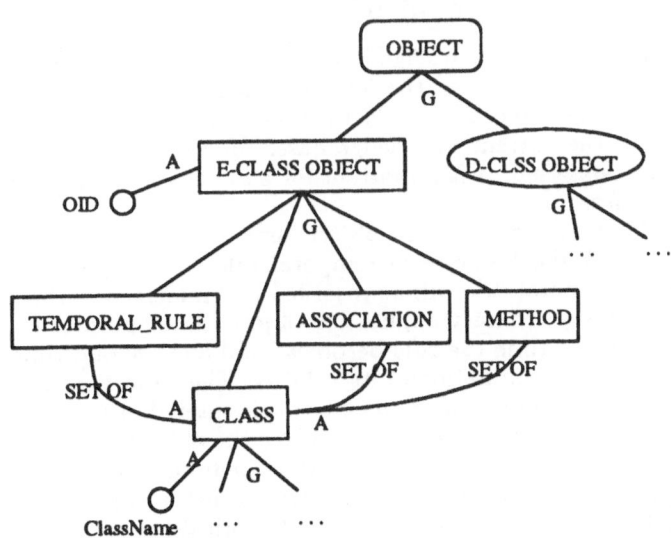

Figure 3: The Meta-model of the System

The class TEMPORAL_RULE in Figure 3 contains all the temporal rules used in the system as its instances. As object instances, they can be retrieved and processed as ordinary object instances. Each of these instances has a system-defined identifier (IID) and a user-defined rule identifier (RID) for unique identification when it is initially created. As illustrated in Figure 4, the components of a rule (e.g., RID, *triggered* clause, *condition* clause, *action* clause, etc.) are modeled as descriptive attributes of the class TEMPORAL_RULE.

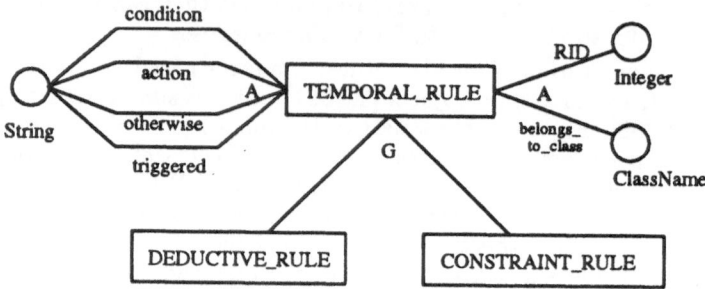

Figure 4: Temporal Rule Class Hierarchy in OSAM*/T

RID is a user-defined identifier, **belongs_to_class** specifies the class that a temporal rule belongs to, the *triggered* clause specifies the triggering condition of a temporal rule, the *condition* clause specifies the condition part of a temporal rule, the *action* clause and the *otherwise* clause specify the consequence part of a temporal rule. The two types of temporal rules described before (i.e., constraint rules and deductive rules) are modeled as subclasses of TEMPORAL_RULE and named as CONSTRAINT_RULE and DEDUCTIVE_RULE, respectively.

4.2 Uniform Treatment of Temporal Data and Rules

The temporal rules of a knowledge base can become out-of-date as the knowledge base evolves. In that case, the rules become invalid and need to be updated or deleted. The updated or deleted rules become historical rules and are no longer valid to the current knowledge base. However, they are still valid to some historical data and it is important for a system to maintain the histories of temporal rules.

In OSAM*/T, we use the same object instance time-stamping technique to model and record the histories of temporal rules. Using this technique, the evolution of a temporal rule will be recorded and managed in the same way as the evolution of any ordinary application object. A temporal rule has a Start-time to indicate the time the rule becomes valid and an End-time to indicate the time before the termination of its validity. The valid time interval can be user-specified or system-specified when a rule is entered or updated. Whenever a rule evolves, a new rule is created to replace the old rule which is shifted and stored in the historical area. It is the current temporal rules which affect and constrain the current knowledge base activities such as update, delete, insert, retrieve, and user-defined operations. The historical rules, on the other hand, are needed only when the historical data are referenced. In the following, we present examples of rule update, rule retrieval and rule evaluation.

4.2.1 Update of Temporal Rules

Updates to temporal rules are carried out by update transactions in the same manner as updating data because temporal rules are modeled as ordinary objects. An update transaction operated on a temporal rule would involve rule-modification, rule-parsing, and rule-validation before it can be committed. We use *Rule 00007* as an example to illustrate the update of a temporal rule. The update operation involves the modification of the *condition* clause and the *action* clause.

(a) An invalid rule to the current knowledge base.

```
Rule 00007
Valid_T [17,20]
triggered      (after InsertObject(Work_On))
condition      (exist this in  this AND (* that * Project[P#=P5],
                                         ! Work_On * Project[P#=P6]) ∧
               (exist this in  WHEN T[4,12]
                               this * Work_On * Project[P#=P1])
action         associate(this * Work_On * Project[P#=P6])
END
```

(b) A valid rule to the current knowledge base.

```
Rule 00007
Valid_T [21,−]
triggered      (after InsertObject(Work_On))
condition      (exist this in  this AND (* that * Project[P#=P5],
                                         ! Work_On * Project[P#=P7]) ∧
               (exist this in  WHEN T[4,12]
                               this * Work_On * Project[P#=P1])
action         associate(this * Work_On * Project[P#=P7])
END
```

In this example, *Rule 00007* defined at time 17 says that the employee (identified by **this**) who is assigned to project P5 by the currently inserted Work_On instance (identified by **that**) but does not work on project P6 and who participated in project P1 during the period T[4,12] should also join project P6. After the rule was defined for a while (i.e., 4 time units later), project P6 was completed and it is no longer meaningful to assign an employee to P6. Therefore, this rule was out-of-date and was updated at time 21 by changing P6 to P7.

4.2.2 Retrieval of Temporal Rules

Since temporal rules are modeled as ordinary objects, they can be retrieved in the same way as other ordinary data. For example, if a user needs to see the information of the *condition* clause of *Rule 00007* at time 28, this query can be expressed as follows:

```
Query:    AT 28
          CONTEXT r:Temporal_Rules [RID = 00005]
          Retrieve r.condition clause
```

4.2.3   Evaluation of Temporal Rules

Temporal rules are selected for evaluation based on whether their valid time intervals cover the time interval specified in a temporal query. The evaluation of temporal rules in OSAM*/T is based on the Match-Modify-Execute (MME) cycle proposed in [RAS88] and the nested transaction model proposed in [MOS85]. A first level database transaction (i.e., update, retrieve, insert, delete, etc.) is parsed into a query tree and is matched with the trigger conditions (i.e., trigger time and trigger operation) of the rules associated with the object(s) being operated on. If there is a match between the trigger operations of these rules and the operation in the transaction, then those rules would be selected for rule evaluation. Once the *match* is successful, the original transaction is *modified* to incorporate the processing of the triggered rules (i.e., both the evaluation of the *condition* and the execution of the *action*). The processing of the triggered rules then are treated as sub-transactions which are nested under the first level transaction. It is possible that a database transaction will go through several MME cycles (i.e., several layers of nested transaction) before it commits due to the continuous triggering of temporal rules (i.e., a triggered rule triggers another rule). More detailed descriptions of the implementation and evaluation of rules can be found in [RAS88, ARR92].

In the following, we explain the evaluation of temporal rules using the updated *Rule 00007* as an example. When the operation of inserting an object instance into the **Work_On** class is detected by the system (i.e., the application is assigning an employee to a project), the updated rule defined in **Employee** class will be triggered to evaluate the quantified expressions specified in the *condition* clause. In evaluating the expressions, the system will bind **that** to the inserted **Work_On** instance in the expression "**this** AND (∗ **that** ∗ **Project[P#=P5]**, ! **Work_On** ∗ **Project[P#=P7]**)". The employee who is being connected to P5 by the insertion of **that** instance is identified by the keyword **this**. The *condition* clause verifies if this employee instance falls in the association patterns specified. If so, the *action* clause is executed which associates this employee with project P7. For example, if the instance W1, which assigns employee John to project P5, is entered into **Work_On** class, the result of evaluating the *condition* clause of this rule will be True assuming that John is not involved in project P7 and worked on project P1 during T[4,12]. The associate() operation in the *action* clause will be executed and the result is the establishment of the association pattern **John** ∗ **W11** ∗ **P7** in the knowledge base.

5   Conclusion

In this paper, we have pointed out the importance of the specification of knowledge rules which make reference to temporal events and the management of histories of these rules in a knowledge base management system. A temporal knowledge model OSAM*/T which incorporates temporal rule specifications as part of object instance and object class definitions has been presented. Temporal rules associated with superclasses can thus be inherited by subclasses just like structural associations and operations. Temporal rules can also be defined for instances of a given class, thus allowing different rules to be operated on different instances. A temporal rule specification language has also been presented. The language is characterized by its validity time specification, the trigger specification which involves time and system/user-defined operations, and the inclusion of temporal conditions and association patterns in temporal rules. The last feature allows very complex patterns of object associations to be specified in a relatively simple way as the conditions and consequences of rules. Two general types of temporal rules are explained with examples. In this paper, we have also described the techniques of modeling and processing temporal rules as first class objects, thus the management of the histories of rules can be carried out in a uniform way as regular objects. The methods for updating, retrieving, triggering and evaluating temporal rules have also been presented.

References

[ALA89]   Alashqur A.M., Su S.Y.W. and Lam H., "OQL-An Object-oriented Query Language", Proc. of the Int'l Conf. on VLDB, 1989, pp. 433-442.

[ALA90]   Alashqur A.M., Su S.Y.W. and Lam H., "A Rule-based Language for Deductive Object-oriented Databases," Proc. of the sixth Int'l Conf. on Data Engineering, L.A., Calif., 1990, pp.58-67.

[ARR92]   Arroyo-Figueroa J., "The Design and Implementation of K.1: A Third Generation Database Programming Language," Master's Thesis, Electrical Eng. Dept., Univ. of Florida, 1992.

[BAR81]   Barr A. and Davidson J., "Representation of Knowledge" in Handbook of AI, Barr A. and Feigenbaum E., (eds), William Kaufman, Los Altos, CA, 1981.

[BEE91]   Beeri C. and Milo T., "A Model for Active Object-oriented Databases," Proc. of the Int'l Conf. on VLDB, 1991, pp. 337-349.

[CER83]   Cercone N. and McCalla G., "What Is Knowledge Representation?," Chapter 1 in The Knowledge Frontier: Essays in the Representation of Knowledge, Nick Cercone and Gordon McCalla (eds), Springer-Verlag, 1983.

[CHA90]   Charkravarthy U.S. and Nesson S., "Making an Object-oriented DBMS Active: Design, Implementation, and Evaluation of a Prototype," in Proc. of the Int'l Conf. on Extended Data Base Technology, March 1990.

[DAY88a]   Dayal U., Blaustein B., Buchmann A., Carey M., Charkravarthy U.S. et al., "Active Database Management System," Proc. of Int'l Conf. on Data and Knowledge Bases, 1988.

[DAY88b]   Dayal U., Buchmann A. and McCarthy D., "Rules are Objects Too: A Knowledge Model for an Active, Object-oriented Database Management System," Proc. 2nd Int'l Workshop on Object-oriented Database Systems, Sept 1988.

90

[DIT86]   Dittrich K.R., Kotz A.M. and Mulle J.A., "An Event/Trigger Mechanism to Enforce Complex Consistency Constraints in Design Databases," ACM SIGMOD Record 15, No. 3, 1986, pp. 22-36.

[ELM90a]   Elmasri R. and Wuu G.T.J., "A Temporal Model and Query Language for ER Databases, Proc. of the Int'l Conf. on Data Eng., 1990, pp. 76-83.

[ELM90b]   Elmasri R., El-Assal I. and Kouramajian V., "Semantics of Temporal Data in An Extended ER Model," Proc. of the ER Conf., 1990.

[HSU88]   Hsu M., Ladin R. and McCarthy D., "An Execution Model for Active Database Management Systems," Proc. of the Int'l Conf. on Data and Knowledge Bases, 1988, pp. 171-179.

[JEN92]   Jensen C.S. and Snodgrass R.T., "Temporal Specification," Proc. of the Int'l Conf. on Data Eng., Tempe, Arizona, 1992, pp.594-603.

[LEV87]   Levesque H.J., "A View of Knowledge Representation," in On Knowledge Base Management Systems, M.L. Brodie and J. Mylopoulos (eds), Springer-Verlag, 1987.

[LOR88]   Lorenitzos N.A. and Johnson R.G., "Extending Relational Algebra to Manipulate Temporal Data," Information Systems, Vol.13, No.3, 1988, pp.289-296.

[LUM84]   Lum V., Dadam P., Erbe R., Guenauer J. and Pistor P., "Designing DBMS Support for The Temporal Dimension," Proc. of the ACM SIGMOD Int'l Conf., 1984, pp.115-130.

[MAI86]   Maier D. and Stein J., "Development of an Object-oriented DBMS," Proc. of the OOPSLA Conf., 1986, pp. 472-482.

[MOR83]   Morgenstern M., "Active Databases as a Paradigm for Enhanced Computing Environments," Proc. of the Int'l Conf. on VLDB, 1983, pp. 34-42.

[MOS85]   Moss J.E.B., "Nested Transactions: An Approach to Reliable Distributed Computing," Ph.D. Dissertation, MIT, 1985.

[MYL84]   Mylopoulos J. and Levesque H., "An Overview of Knowledge Representation," in On Conceptual Modeling: Perspectives From Artificial Intelligence, Databases and Programming Languages, Brodie, M., Mylopoulos, J., and Schmidt, J. (eds), Springer-Verlag, 1984.

[NAV89]   Navathe S.B. and Ahmed R., "A Temporal Relational Model and A Query Language," An International Journal of Information Sciences, Vol.48, No.2, 1989, pp. 57-73.

[NEW80]   Newell A., "The Knowledge Level," Presidential Address, American Association for Artificial Intelligence, AAAI80, Stanford University, Stanford, CA (19 August 1980), in AI Magazine, Vol. 2, summer 1981, pp.1-20.

[RAS88]   Raschid L. and Su S.Y.W., "A Transaction-oriented Mechanism to Control Processing in a Knowledge Base Management System," Proc. of Int'l Conf. on Expert Database Systems, Tysen's Corner, VA., April 1988, pp. 353-373.

[ROS91]   Rose E. and Segev A., "TOODM - A Temporal Object-oriented Data Model with Temporal Constraints," Proc. of the ER Conf., 1991, pp. 205-229.

[SEG87]   Segev A. and Shoshani A., "Logical Modeling of Temporal Data," Proc. of the ACM SIGMOD Int'l Conf., 1987, pp. 454-466.

[SHY91]   Shyy Y.M. and Su S.Y.W., "K: A High-level Knowledge Base Programming Language for Advanced Database Applications," ACM SIGMOD, Denver, CO., May 1991, pp.338-347.

[SNO85]   Snodgrass R. and Ahn I., "A Taxonomy of Time in Database," Proc. of the ACM SIGMOD Int'l Conf., 1985, pp. 236-246.

[SNO86]   Snodgrass R., "Research Concerning Time in Databases: Project Summaries," ACM SIGMOD Record, Vol.15, No.4, 1986, pp. 19-39.

[SNO90]   Snodgrass R., "Temporal Databases Status and Research Directions," ACM SIGMOD Record, Vol.19, No. 4, Dec. 1990, pp.83-89.

[STO85]   Stonebraker M., "Triggers and Inference in Database Systems," in On Knowledge Base Management Systems (Brodie and Mylopoulos, eds) Springer-Verlag, 1985.

[SU89]   Su S.Y.W., Lam H. and Krishnamurthy V., "An Object-oriented Semantic Association Model (OSAM*)," Chapter 17 in Artificial Intelligence: Manufacturing Theory and Practice, edited by S.T. Kumara, A.L. Soyster, and R.L. Kashyap, Published by the Institute of Industrial Engineers, Industrial Engineering and Management Press, Norcross, GA, 1989.

[SU91]   Su S.Y.W. and Chen H.H.M., "A Temporal Knowledge Representation Model OSAM*/T And Its Query Language OQL/T," Proc. of the Int'l Conf. on VLDB, 1991.

[WOO83]   Woods W.A., "What's Important about Knowledge Representation?," IEEE Computer, Vol. 16, No. 10, October 1983, pp. 22-27.

[YAS91]   Yaseen R., Su S.Y.W. and Lam H., "An Extensible Kernel Object Management System," Proc. of the OOPSLA Conf., 1991.

Data Driven and Temporal Rules in PARDES

Opher Etzion

Technion- Israel Institute of Technology

Faculty of Industrial Engineering and Management Haifa, 32000, Israel

Avigdor Gal

Technion- Israel Institute of Technology

Faculty of Industrial Engineering and Management Haifa, 32000, Israel

Arie Segev

Haas School of Business, University of California and Information & Computing Sciences Division, Lawrence Berkeley Laboratory, Berkeley, CA 94720, USA

Abstract

Data driven rules is one of the important rule types that are used by database applications. This paper analyzes requirements for a programming paradigm appropriate for the support of data-driven rules, states the linguistic paradigm, discusses its supporting architecture and shows an extension of the model to support temporal functionalities, especially retroactive and proactive processing. The focus in this paper is on the software engineering aspects of the proposed model: ease of use through a high-level language and improving the verifiability of the rule language.

1 Introduction and motivation

The incorporation of rules in computerized applications evolved in the recent years into a major research area. Various research efforts deal with embedding of many types of rules in applications that interact with DBMS systems. The integration of rules and databases is beneficial to applications that involve constraints enforcement, expert systems, real time database systems, etc.

A *data driven rule* is a rule that should be activated as a result of modifications of certain data elements in a database.

A *temporal data driven rule* is a *data driven rule* supporting the use of the temporal dimension in rules, example: a retroactive activation of such a rule.

Throughout this paper we shall use the following example:

A newspaper distributing system in Old-Man city assigns subscribers to distributors based on the city map, the subscribers' addresses etc. Some data driven rules in this application are:

r1: A change in a distributor's load results in recalculation of the distributor's commission.

r2: A change in a distributor's load results in an integrity constraint's check verifying that the load does not exceed the upper bound for the distributor type.

r3: Any modification in a subscriber's address, activates a heuristic algorithm for a new distribution.

Data driven rules are useful for three types of activities:

Maintaining derived data: Derived data elements are generated from other data elements. The technological advances which made secondary storage relatively inexpensive, increased the utilization of derived data. In many applications derived data is required to be persistent, that is, to be physically stored in the database, due to either efficiency reasons (many retrieval operations vs. low update frequency) or effectiveness considerations (such as: real time constraints). Since the value of a derived data element is dependent on the values of the data elements used to derive it, rules whose action is contingent on the modification of data elements, are a natural implementation vehicle. The rule **r1** of the above example maintains a derived data element (commission).

Enforcing integrity constraints: Integrity constraints are logical assertions that a consistent database should satisfy. The assertions refer to values of data elements, thus a modification of such values may require re-evaluation of assertions. The enforcement of integrity constraints can be implemented by data driven rules that are contingent upon the modification of data elements that participate in the assertion. The rule **r2** is a rule enforcing an integrity constraint.

Triggering external operations: External operations are operations that are external to the rule system and invoke a routine whose logic is not captured by the rule system. The rule **r3** is a rule triggering the invocation of a heuristic procedure. Other examples are: broadcasting a message, activating an alerter [9] etc.

There are two useful observations about the *first two types* of data driven rules:

1. The knowledge about dependencies among data elements is sufficient to infer all the cases in which a rule has to be triggered. For example, the rule **r2** is triggered if either there is an increase in a distributor's load or a decrease in a load's upper bound; in the latter case, the constraint has to be checked for each distributor affiliated with this distributor type.

2. A family of rules that deal with the same data element can be generalized to a higher level rule using the knowledge about dependencies. For example, the rule **r1** stands for a group of rules such as:

   (a) When a subscriber is added to the distributor's area, increase the distributor commission.

   (b) When a subscriber is removed from the distributor's area, reduce the distributor commission.

   (c) When the commission per subscriber is changed, recalculate the distributor commission.

In the third type of rule, the logic of the rule cannot be inferred. However, its triggering conditions may be inferred by the same inference procedure that infers triggering conditions for the other two types of rules.

In this paper we devise a data driven rule model that exploits these observations to create a simple and concise language and supporting mechanism for expressing these rules. In the search for a programming language style we explored several contemporary styles and found that none of them meets the requirements of our desired functionality; the requirements and the comparison are shown in Section 2. Section 3 described the PARDES model for maintaining data driven rules. Section 4 discusses the temporal component, Section 5 concludes this paper.

2 The inadequacy of existing programming styles

2.1 Review of relevant programming styles

Existing database programming languages can be classified into four main programming styles: the imperative style, the active style, the deductive style and the script based style.

Imperative Style: Imperative languages are general purpose procedural languages. Originally, they did not contain database commands; thus database operations are embedded in a host language, or performed by calling auxiliary routines.

Persistent imperative language is a programming language that supports variables whose life-span are longer then the creating program's life-span, without a need for explicit or implicit physical data movement by the programmer [5]. Example of persistent languages are PS-ALGOL [3] and AMBER [10].

Embedded languages combine an imperative language with a query language such as SQL. The queries are combined with a host language and a pre-compiler is used to identify a query and to make an external call for the query language; examples of embedded languages are CODASYL interfaces to Cobol, PL/I and Fortran [4].

Active style: The programming style employed by most active database models (HiPAC [11], Ode [19], Starburst [24] etc.) follows the *E-C-A (Event-Condition-Action)* [25] architecture. Under this architecture a rule is composed of three components.

Event : either a database transition (when a distributor load is modified), or an external event such as a clock triggered event (each morning at 7:00 am).

Condition : a collection of queries.

Action : a user defined program.

Active database languages apply programming of a higher level relative to imperative languages in the control part of the application, that is, monitoring the decisions about rule activations. The "actions" are still written in an imperative language.

Deductive style: Deductive style programming languages are derivatives of logic programming. They are used in loose or tight coupling with database languages. The deductive style supports inferences that are phrased in a subset or an extension of first order logic using recursive database queries. Examples of languages associated with this programming style are DAT-ALOG [34] and KB2 [35].

Script style: In this programming style, rules are implemented as long term activities, using augmented petri nets [28] called *scripts*. A Script is a set of active entities, with an internal set of states that exchange messages. Examples of such languages are TAXIS [27] and Galileo [1].

2.2 Requirements of programming environment for data driven rules

Conventional programming languages migrated through several generations of programming environments: starting with assembly languages, moving through third generation languages (PL/I, Pascal, C etc.) and continuing to high level languages. In a similar way, the programming environment for rule languages that exists in many of the current models is analogues to an assembly language, supplying all the building blocks without any further abstractions. Example: in the imperative style, activation of a rule must be *hard coded* for any condition that might trigger this rule. In this Section, we employ several requirements that appear in the literature for high level languages. Using the analogy above, we modify these requirements to support a high level programming environment for data driven rules. Note that data driven rules have inherent semantic properties that make the use of high level languages both feasible and attractive.

Structural clarity: requires the ease of use of the language with respect to the tasks of writing, understanding and debugging [6].

The problems of using third generation languages are well documented [21]; the massive code and the low level of abstraction makes it difficult to write, understand and debug. In the **imperative style**, these problems are inherited from the host language.

In the **deductive style** rules are expressed in a formal language. Empirical studies [8] determined that the language of logic is clear and concise to logicians, however it cannot be effectively comprehended by an ordinary programmer.

In the **active style** and the **script style** there is a declarative component: the control model, deciding about the rule triggering. This feature improves the clarity relative to imperative languages. The "action" part of the rule is still specified using an imperative language, and thus inherits its clarity problems.

Uniformity: requires the homogeneity of the language in its syntax and logic [2]. A programming language should be uniform and self-contained, with minimal need for lower level external routines.

Persistent imperative languages are uniform due to the fact that the database commands are syntactically integrated. However, the embedded languages use at least two different languages (host and DB-related).

Some active models, such as Hipac [25], use two separate languages, one to define the control mechanism and the other to describe the actions. Other models, such as Postgres [32], unify all the operations in a single homogenous language.

A tightly coupled deductive languages, such as DATALOG [34], is a uniform language, while loosely coupled deductive languages employ at least two languages with different syntax (inference language and DB language).

Script languages are heterogenous; they employ several syntactic structures.

Abstraction level: the requirement is to support high level primitives embedded in the language syntax [20]. These primitives should include terms like "event", "trigger", "derivation", "exception handling mode" etc.

In imperative languages there are no high level abstractions of the desired type. In deductive languages terms such as "event" and "trigger" cannot be captured by first order logic but can be supported by more advanced logics, such as situational calculus [23]. In the active and script languages, abstractions that are common to all types of rules exist in most of the languages, but abstractions that are specific to data driven rules, such as "derivation" exists only in part of these models (Cactis [22]).

Extended data independence: requires the autonomy of the programmer from physical aspects in his programming. In addition to the traditional types of data independence [12] There are two extended types of required data independence [15]:

Situation independence: The dependencies are not situation oriented, that is, the programmer does not need to define and handle every single case in which a dependency can be realized, but general definition of the dependency is sufficient.

Referential independence: Reference connections (such as: match or join operations) are determined as much as possible by the system without involving the programmer.

Referential independence is not supported by any of the existing languages of all types. All languages require explicit reference in each case.

Situational independence is partially supported by deductive models (if the derivation is expressible in the language) and by some active models (Cactis). Other language types do not support situational independence.

Deterministic execution: requires a deterministic interpretation of update operations [16]. Deterministic models enable well-defined semantics for the execution process, thus permitting reasoning and verification of the execution process.

The imperative languages are deterministic, since programs are sequential by nature. Due to the low level programming, the semantics of the program is left to the programmer's discretion.

In deductive languages determinism exists in restricted forms of first order logic that do not include disjunction or existential quantifiers, example: Horn clauses.

In many of the active and script models, determinism is not guaranteed, due to either non deterministic selection of rules (example: Postgres) or non deterministic order of execution (example: HiPac).

Consistency maintenance mechanism: [26] requires the ability to define global constraints and enforce them in the database.

In imperative languages, consistency maintenance mechanisms is left to the programmer's control and cannot be guaranteed by the language.

In the active languages, rules can be defined for consistency enforcement. However, two major restrictions apply: an integrity constraint may not be phrased as a single rule which leads to a verification problem; exceptions to integrity constraints cannot be handled in a general way, exception handlers are expressed in imperative programs.

In the deductive languages, any expressible constraint can be stated as an assertion (a model axiom). In the script languages, integrity constraints must be hard coded by the programmer.

Update redundancy: [22] requires the existence of a control mechanism to eliminate redundant updates that may be created from interconnected dependencies.

In imperative and script languages, update redundancy mechanisms are left to the programmer's control and cannot be guaranteed by the language. Most of the active languages do not have a redundancy control mechanism; CACTIS is an exception to this.

In deductive languages, the update redundancy control is contingent upon the implementation of the deduction process.

2.3 Conclusion

Most of the requirements are not fully supported by any of these programming language styles. Figure 1 compares the programming styles with respect to the above discussed requirements. We use the following notation:

+ means that the particular style fully satisfies the requirement.

- means that it is not possible to fulfill the requirement using this style.

p means that a style partially meets the requirements.

s means that it is possible to satisfy the requirement using this programming style, but only some of the implementations do so.

Requirement	Imperative	Active	Deductive	Script
Structural clarity	-	p	-	p
Uniformity	persistent + embedded -	s	s	-
Abstraction level	-	p	p	p
Extended data independence				
Situation independence	-	p	p	-
Referential independence	-	-	-	-
Deterministic execution	p	s	s	-
Consistency maintenance	-	p	+	-
Updating redundancy	-	s	s	-

Figure 1: Requirement satisfaction comparison

3 The PARDES Model

The conclusion of Section 2, namely, the inadequacy of the existing programming styles, motivated the search for a new programming paradigm. In this section we present the PARDES paradigm using an **invariant language**. Section 3.1 presents the basic premises of this paradigm; Section 3.2 describes the PARDES architecture and components; Section 3.3 examines the PARDES model relative to the requirements presented in Section 2.

3.1 The PARDES Model - Basic Premises

The **programming-by-invariants** paradigm in data driven rules stems from the observation that in all *data-driven* rules there are explicit or implicit dependencies among the data elements. We use the term **PDI** (Persistent Derived Information) for a data element that is being updated by a derivation rule, and the term **deriver** for a data element that participates in a derivation or a constraint rule.

In the derivation case, a modification of any of the derivers' instances triggers (conditionally or unconditionally) an update operation to the relevant instances of the derived data-element. We refer to such a dependency as a *computational invariant*. In the integrity constraint case, a modification of any of the participants might trigger[1] the re-evaluation of the constraint. We refer to this type of invariants as *logical invariants*. The *data-driven* dependencies in an application are defined as **executable entities** using these types of invariants only, without involving any extra programming.

The premises of the invariant language and its supporting model are as follows:

Executability : The Invariant definition is directly executable. No extra programming is needed to maintain the invariant. The execution process guarantees **soundness** (all the invariants are maintained) and **completeness** (Each consistent state is reachable).

---

[1] An optimization mechanism may be applied to eliminate redundant triggerings.

Mutual Exclusiveness : An Invariant may include a conditional expression such as:

X:= Y, when Z > 0 ; 2*Y when Z ≤ 0.

The conditions must be mutually exclusive. The mutual exclusiveness is enforced by assuming that the order of a condition determines the relative priority. Thus, each condition is conjuncted with the negations of all the previous conditions. Example:

X:= Y, when Z > 0 ; 2*Y when W > 0

the second condition is interpreted as:

$W > 0 \land \neg (Z > 0)$

Uniqueness : Each derived data-element appears on the left hand side of exactly one invariant.

Non-Reflexiveness : An instance of any data-element may not be derived directly or indirectly from its own value. A derivation from the *old* value of a data-element (the value that existed prior to the transaction start) is allowed. Example:

Y := Y + 1 is not a valid assignment, while Y:= old (Y) + 1 is.

Since the value of old (Y) is not changed during the transaction, no infinite loop is generated.

Figure 2 is an example of schema and invariants definitions
Comments:

1. Each PDI has an associated unique invariant.

2. Reference matching among different classes is inferred where possible. Example: in the first derivation rule, there is a matching between Subscriber and Distributor based on the condition
Subscriber.Assigned-Distributor = Distributor. Distributor-Name.
See Section 3.2 for discussion.

3. The first two rules are derivation rules, the third rule is a constraint rule, the last rule applies an external rule whose logic cannot be captured by the system (this rules uses an external GIS system).

4. The last rule indicates that an external operation called Apply-Heuristic-Assignment is triggered whenever a change in any member of the derivers list (Zip-code, Expiration-Date) occurs. These types of rules will not be discussed in our analysis.

5. The Commission rule is conditioned. The conditions are mutually exclusive and priority is assumed according to the order.

3.2   The PARDES architecture

The main components of this architecture are:

1. An extended schema that includes a set of invariants.

2. A **Translator** that includes an **automatic matching** and creates a **dependency graph.**

```
Class =          Subscriber
Properties=      Subscriber-Number
                 Name
                 Address
                 Zip-code
                 Assigned-Distributor [PDI]
                 Expiration-Date

Class =          Distributor
Properties =     Distributor-Number
                 Name
                 Distributor-Type
                 Number-of-Subscribers [PDI]
                 Commission [PDI]

Class=           Distributor-Type
Properties =     Low-Commission-Rate
                 Medium-Commission-Rate
                 High-Commission-Rate
                 Medium-Lower-Bound
                 High-Lower-Bound
                 Subscribers-Limit
```

Number-of-Subscribers := count (Subscriber)

Commission   := Number-of-Subscribers * Low-Commission-Rate
                           when Number-of-Subscribers < Medium-Lower-Bound
                         Number-of-Subscribers * Medium-Commission-Rate
                           when Number-of-Subscribers < High-Lower-Bound
                         Number-of-Subscribers * High-Commission-Rate
                           otherwise

Number-of-Subscribers $\leq$ Subscribers-Limit

Assigned-Distributor := Apply-Heuristic-Assignment,
                        derivers = (Zip-code, Expiration-Date)

Figure 2: Schema and Invariants Definition

3. A **Situation interpreter** that interprets the **dependency graph** to determine which action should be taken when a given situation occurs.

4. A **Run-Time Controller** that controls the order of execution and eliminates redundant updates.

5. An **Exception-Handling Component** that determines the actions to be taken for any consistency violation.

6. A **Transaction Model** that determines the atomicity and synchronization of update operations.

A short description of these components follows:

Translator: A program that translates the schema and invariant definitions to a **dependency graph**. A novel feature of the **translator** is the **automatic matching** component.

Automatic Matching: Dependencies among properties of different entities may occur when a PDI belongs to a class, while a deriver of the same PDI belongs to another class. example:
Number-of-Subscribers := count (Subscribers)
There is a need to determine which instances of Subscriber affect the values of a certain instance of Distributor, or conversely: which instances of Distributor are affected by a change in a given instance of Subscriber. In conventional models this matching is done explicitly by designating the conditions for this match[2] or by using *path expressions*. The automatic matching protocol attempts to infer such a matching by using semantic equivalences (properties are semantically equivalent if they are mapped to the same set and have the same meaning). Automatic matching simplifies the language and makes it *matching independent*. Classes can be united or partitioned without the need to change the set of invariants.

Dependency Graph: The set of invariants is compiled (after resolving all the required matchings) to a dependency-graph, which models the *data-driven dependencies* among the various data-elements. This graph determines the transitive closure of an update operation and facilitates the reasoning about the update process including optimizations. A similar graph has been proposed in [31] in the context of transaction control.

Situation Interpreter: The **dependency graph** is used to infer the action that should be taken. Example: for the operation:

Commission:= Number-of-Subscribers * Low-Commission-Rate
            when Number-of-Subscribers < Medium-Lower-Bound
            Number-of-Subscribers * Medium-Commission-Rate
            when Number-of-Subscribers < High-Lower-Bound
            Number-of-Subscribers * High-Commission-Rate
            otherwise

the following actions are inferred:

---

[2] *Join* in relational algebra is a kind of "matching".

1. when a *Subscriber* is assigned to a *Distributor*: recalculate the *Commission* according to the appropriate value of *Number-of-Subscribers*.

2. when a *Subscriber* is removed from the *Distributor*'s assignment: recalculate the *Commission* according to the appropriate value of *Number-of-Subscribers*.

3. When a *Subscriber* is re-assigned to another *Distributor*: recalculate the *Commission* of both *Distributors*.

4. When *Low-Commission-Rate* is modified: modify the commission of all the relevant *Distributors* of the same *Distributor-Type*. The same applies for *Medium-Commission-Rate* and *High-Commission-Rate*.

5. When a *Medium-Lower-Bound* is modified: recalculate the commission of all the relevant *Distributors* of the same *Distributor-Type*. The same applies for *High-Lower-Bound*.

6. When the *Distributor-Type* of a *Distributor* is modified: recalculate the *Commission* according to the new *Distributor-Type* parameters.

The situation interpreter enables the PARDES model to support situation independence. In this case, the number of rules is drastically reduced in comparison to any other alternative.

Run-Time Controller: The Update Control mechanism is similar to the one in **Cactis** by the fact that the order of update operations is determined by using topological order on the dependency graph, to eliminate redundancy in update operations.

Exception Handling Component: All the models discussed above allow the specification of Exception-Handlers *only* in an *imperative* way, at the system designer's discretion. The PARDES model provides Exception-Handling abstractions as a part of the invariant language[13], as well as support of different types of null and defaults. The abstractions stand for generic strategies for handling exceptions in cases of: syntactic (range) violations, referential integrity violations, constraints violations and direct modifications of derived updates (bypassing the derivations).

Flexible Transaction Mechanism: There are two decision problems in the transaction model of an active database:

1. Should an operation to update a PDI instance be triggered by modifications of any of its derivers?

2. If the answer to the first decision is positive then:
   (a) Should the PDI be updated synchronously?
   (b) Is the system responsible to ensure consistency at all times with respect to the deriver's update operation?

The results of these two decisions determine the materialization strategy [30]. The topic and associated algorithms are discussed in [17]. The decision about assigning a consistency mode to a rule may be recommended by an optimization model that improves its own results by getting feedback based upon the application's behavior. This issue is discussed in [7].

This flexible mechanism becomes possible only due to existence of the dependency graph and the executability properties of the PARDES model.

3.3 Discussion - compatibility of the PARDES model with the requirements

In this section we analyze the PARDES model with respect to the requirements introduced in Section 2.

Structural clarity: The invariant language consists of declarative statements and contains only the minimal details needed for disambiguity. For example, the invariant
Number-of-Subscribers $\leq$ Subscribers-Limit
is easier to write then its formal interpretation:
$\forall$ *d $\in$ Distributor: [Number-of-Subscribers(d) $\leq$ Subscriber-Limit(t) | t=Distributor-Type(d)]*
or its equivalent path expression:
d.Number-of-Subscribers $\leq$ d.Distributor- Type.Subscribers-Limit.
We eliminate the variables *d* and *t* and the matching condition.

The language is unambiguous (ambiguities are resolved by prompting the system designer to choose among well-defined alternatives), yet not a formal one. This increases the ease of use of the language.

The situation independence property significantly reduces the size of the rule set, thus improves the manageability of the program.

Uniformity: The invariant language is an integral part of the schema definition language. There is a uniform language that contains the static schema, the update logic, exception handling definitions, transaction management parameters and retrieval operations. The same syntactic structure is kept in all these operations. An exception to that are external operations, in which the calling environment is consistent with the uniform syntax. The expressive power of the PARDES model supports most of the required operations, thus the need for use of external operations is limited.

Abstraction level: The PARDES language supports high level abstractions. In the schema definition it supports an extended set of semantic abstractions (classification, association, generalization, aggregation and partition). In the invariant level it supports "events", "derivations" and "constraints". In the exception handling component, the exception handling modes, which are high level abstractions, are supported. In the transaction management component, the materialization strategies supported are also high level abstractions.

Extended data independence: Situational independence is fully supported by the *situation interpreter*. Referential independence is supported in inferable cases by the *automatic matching* component of PARDES. In cases where automatic matching is impossible (due to ambiguity or lack of information) the user is addressed with a specific question. This mechanism helps naive users who have little knowledge about the programming environment.

Deterministic execution: Deterministic execution is enforced by combination of the following premises of PARDES: The **uniqueness** premise guarantees that there are no conflicting rules that update the same PDI and are triggered by the same operation. The **mutual exclusiveness** premise guarantees that within this unique rule there is at most one condition that applies to each case. Therefore, only deterministic updates can be generated.

Consistency maintenance mechanism: The PARDES model uses the invariant definitions as consistency assertions. It finds all the inconsistencies generated by a change in the database relative to these assertions. The consistency is enforced to the level required by the materialization strategy and the exception handling definitions without a need of any additional programming.

Update redundancy: The **run time controller** of PARDES coupled with the **non reflectiveness** premise that eliminates loops avoid update redundancies and guarantees minimal

number of update operations.

4 Temporal Data Driven Rules

In recent years the discipline of *temporal databases* [33] has been growing in scope. The objective of that research is to add support for the time dimension in the DBMS. Among other things, temporal databases view a database as a history and maintain different values for the same data-item for different time points. This Section surveys the need to augment the *data-driven rule* to support temporal features, especially proactive and retroactive processing, and discusses the types of such rules and their general logic.

4.1 Proactive and Retroactive Processing

A Retroactive (Proactive) Update is an update operation that modifies past (future) values of data elements.
A Retroactive (Proactive) Rule is a rule whose action includes a retroactive (proactive) update.
Retroactive (Proactive) Rule Activation is the application of a rule to past (future) states.

The above definitions indicate that rules can effect data *retroactively* in two main ways: due to retroactive rules, or due to retroactive activation of rules. The latter case can occur for two reasons:

1. a rule is introduced in the system with a valid time that includes past time interval(s).

Retroactive Update: On March 1993, it was decided that the *High-Lower-Bound* for *Distributor-Type* = 1 is modified from 150 to 130, and that this change is done retroactively to January 1993.

Proactive Update: On June 1993, it was decided that the *High-Commission-Rate* for all *Distributor-types* will be raised by 10 percent starting September 1993.

Retroactive Rule: On July 1993 it was decided that the *Low-Commission-Rate* for each *Distributor-Type* is dependent upon the *Medium-Commission-Rate* and is captured by the invariant
*Low-Commission-Rate := Medium-Commission-Rate * 0.8*
This rule is retroactively applied to April 1993.

Proactive Rule: On July 1993 it is decided on a new heuristic allocation routine that will be valid starting January 1994.

Figure 3: Temporal Operations

---

2. A retroactive update occurred, and the updated data element(s) trigger a rule which was valid at that past time. The same is true for *proactive* effects.

Retroactive processing has been mentioned in some works, e.g., [29], but no details of the execution model nor support for rules were given.

Figure 3 demonstrates examples of the temporal dimension effect:

4.2 Extensions to the data model

The support of the temporal component is carried out using an extension of the basic data model. In the basic model, an instance of each property is called a *variable* and has a *variable state* associated with it. To support temporal information, each *variable state* becomes a collection of *state elements*. A *state element* is a pair:
< *value, temporal extension* >.
A *temporal extension* is a triple $< t_x, t_d, t_v >$, where:

Transaction Time (t_x) - The commit time of the transaction which updated the variable state.

Decision Time (t_d) - The decision occurrence time in the real world.

Valid Time (t_v) - The time points in which the decision maker believes that this value reflects the object's value in the real world. t_v is expressed by a *temporal element* [18] which is a time-point or an interval $[t_s, t_e]$ or a collection of intervals and time-points. If t_v is an interval, it is believed that the object value is constant in this interval. Usually the starting point of the valid time interval (t_s) is well defined, however, the ending point of the interval (t_e) may be ∞ (unless it will be changed in the future) or frozen (the value cannot be changed). The valid time is not restricted to the data level. Meta-data entities also have valid time which limits their effect on the database. t_v values may be associated with:

objects, designating the object life-span and variables, designating the life-span of the existence of this variable within the object. t_v may also be applied to rules, generalizations, existence of properties in classes and classification of objects to classes.

4.3   Types of Temporal Rules

The effect of the temporal dimension on rules is manifested in several ways:

The applicability of rules: A rule is a meta-data object which is an instance of the "Rule" class. Properties of this class stand for assignments in the derivation case and assertions in the constraint case. If a rule is modified then the assignment variable of this rule has more than one state-elements, applicable in different time-points. For each update, a decision should be made, to select the rule or rules are applicable for the validity interval of this update.

Temporal Conditions: As discussed in Section 3, each rule may have several conditional assignments or assertions. The conditions may include operations that refer to any of the time perspectives, as well as to other temporal expressions.

Temporal actions: The action part of a rule might affect time points that are different than the one in which the rule is evaluated. In this case, the t_v itself is determined by the rule and not derived as a function of other t_v values. Direct update of the t_v may create conflict resolution problems, such as a state element with a t_v which exceeds the life span of its variable; two state elements created by the same transaction with overlapping t_v's, etc.

The principles of the temporal extension of PARDES are discussed in [14]. The implementation aspects are now in an early prototype phase.

5   Conclusion

The major contribution of this study is the construction of a high level language and a supporting mechanism to cope with data driven rules and temporal rules. Data driven rules have an important role in many applications that have to maintain complex relationships between data elements or inter dependencies between various parts of the database; yet, data driven rules are handled in contemporary models as part of the general rule language. The PARDES model improves the handling of data driven rules by using their inherent semantic properties, and it meets the requirements that were discussed in the literature for high level languages. The data driven rules are extended to support temporal processing of retroactive and proactive updates and rules, adding another novel feature to the PARDES model.

References:

[1]: Albano A., Luccam C., Rezno O. Galileo: A Strongly Typed Interactive Conceptual Language. *ACM TODS 10(2)*, 1985.

[2]: ARCADIA - Issues Encountered in Building a Flexible Software Environment; Lessons from the Arcadia Project - Proc. *ACM Sigsoft 1992*, pp 169-180

[3]: Atkinson M.P., Chisholm K.J., Cockshott W.P. PS-algol: An Algol with a persistent heap, *SIGPLAN Not. (ACM), 17(7)*, pp. 24-31, July 1981.

[4]: Atkinson M.P., Bailey P., Cockshott W.P., Chisholm K.J., Morrison R. Progress with Persistent Programming, *Cambridge University Press, Cambridge, England*, 1984.

[5]: Atkinson M.P., Buneman O.P. Types and Persistence in Data Base Programming Languages, *ACM Computing Surveys 19(2)*, June 1987.

[6]: Balzer R., Goodman N., Wile D. Informality in Program Specifications, *IEEE tran. on soft. Eng., 4(2)*, pp. 94-102, March 1978.

[7]: Botzer D. Optimization of Knowledge and Data Representation in Active Databases, *M.sc., Thesis, Technion- Israel Institute of Technology*, Sep 1992.

[8]: Braine M. On the Relation Between Natural Logic of Reasoning and Standard Logic, *Psychological Review*, 1978.

[9]: Buneman O.P., Clemons E. Efficiently Monitoring Relational Data Base, *ACM TODS 4(3)*, pp. 368-382, Sep 1979.

[10]: Cardelli L. Amber, *Technical Report AT&T Bell Labs, Murray Hill, N.J.*, 1984.

[11]: Chakravarthy S. et al. HiPAC: A research Project in Active, Time-Constrained Database Management, *Final Technical Report, XAIT-89-02*, July 1989.

[12]: Date C.J. An Introduction to Database Systems, *Addison Wesley*, 1986.

[13]: Etzion O. Active Handling of Incomplete or Exceptional Information Database Systems, *Proc WITS 91*, pp. 46-60.

[14]: Etzion O., Gal A., Segev A. Temporal Support in Active Databases, *Proc. WITS*, pp. 245-254, Dec 1992.

[15]: Etzion O. Active Interdatabase Dependencies, to appear in *Information Sciences*, 1993.

[16]: Etzion O. PARDES- A Data-Driven Oriented Active Database Model, *Sigmod Record*, March 1993.

[17]: Etzion O. Flexible Consistency Modes For Active Database Applications, to appear in *Information Systems*, 1993.

[18] : Gadia S.K., Yeung C.S. A Generalized Model for a Relational Temporal Databases, *Proc. of ACM SIGMOD 88*, pp. 251-259, June 1988.

[19]: Gehani N.H., Jagadish H.V. Ode as an Active Database: Constraints and Triggers, *Proc. VLDB 91*, pp. 226-327, 1991.

[20]: Hammer M., McLeod D. Data Base Description with SDM: a semantic Data Base Model, *ACM TODS, 6(3)*, 1981.

[21]: Horowitz E., Kamper A. Application Generators, *IEEE software 2(1)*, 1985.

[22]: Hudson S., King R. CACTIS: A Database System for Specification Functionally Defined Data, *proc. IEEE OOBDS Workshop*, 1986.

[23]: Kowalski R. Logic for Problem Solving. *North-Holland*, 1979.

[24]: Lohman G.M., Lindsay B., Pirahesh H., Schiefer K.B. Extensions to Starburst: Objects, Types, Functions and Rules, *cacm 34(10)*, pp. 94-109, Oct 1991.

[25]: McCarthy D., Dayal U. The Architecture of an Active Data Base Management System, *Proc. 1989 ACM SIGMOD International Conference*, pp. 215-224, June 1989.

[26]: Morgenstern M. Constraint Equations: Declarative Expression of Constraints with Automatic Enforcement, *Proc. VLDB*, pp. 291-300, 1984.

[27]: Mylopoulos J., Berenstein P., Wong H.K.T. A Language Facility for Designing Database Intensive Applications, *ACM TODS 5(2)*, Jun 1980.

[28]: Peterson J.L. Petri Net Theory and The Modeling of Systems, *Prentice-Hall, Englewood Cliffs, N.J. 07632*, 1981.

[29]: Sarda N.L. HSQL: Historical Query Language. *Chapter 5 in [33], pp 110-140*.

[30]: Segev A., Fang, W., Optimal Update Policies for Distributed Materialized Views. *Management Science*, Vol. 37, No. 7, July 1991.

[31]: Sheth A., Rusinkiewicz M., Karabaits G. Using Polytransactions to Manage Interdependent Data, Chapter 14 in: A. Elmagarmid (ed)- Transactions Models for Advanced Database Applications, *Morgan-Kaufmann*, 1992.

[32]: Stonebraker M., Hanson E., Potamianos S. The POSTGRES rules manager, *IEEE Tran. on soft. Eng*, pp. 897-907, July 1988.

[33]: Tansel A.U., Clifford J., Gadia S., Jajodia S., Segev A., Snodgrass R. Temporal Databases: Theory Design and Implementation. *The Benjamin/Cummings Publishing Co. Inc, Redwood City, Ca*, 1993.

[34]: Ullman J. Implementation of Logical Query Language for Data Bases, in: *Proceedings of the ACM-SIGMOD International Conference on Management of Data*, 1985

[35]: Wallace M. Kb2: A Knowledge Based System Embedded in Prolog, *Technical Report TR-KB-12, European Computer Industry Research Centre, Munich*, Aug. 1986.

Rules and Transactions

Rules in an Open System: The REACH Rule System

H. Branding, A. Buchmann, T, Kudrass, J. Zimmermann
Department of Computer Science, Technical University Darmstadt
64293 Darmstadt, Germany

Abstract

REACH is an active object system intended to control heterogeneous systems, possibly under timing constraints. When dealing with open systems in which the controlled system may execute irreversible actions, many notions of active databases must be revised and adapted to this situation. In this paper we draw the system boundaries between controlling and controlled system, present a rule system that includes events and actions both in the controlled and the controlling systems and analyze the effects of this open environment on the rule structure. We identify two new coupling modes, sequential causally dependent and exclusive causally dependent, which are necessary for handling irreversible actions in external systems and contingency plans, respectively.

1 Introduction

REACH (REal-time ACtive Heterogeneous system) is an active object system intended to control heterogeneous systems, possibly under real-time constraints. The external systems may range from database management systems to robot controllers or a variety of actuators. These external systems will be controlled through the execution of procedural rules that are triggered by events. Because of the heterogeneity of the external or controlled subsystem and the need to provide recoverability it is important to define carefully the boundaries of each system. Therefore, we start by defining the boundaries between controlling and controlled system. From the definition of these systems we can then derive the various events that need to be handled. Since events in REACH may be also temporal, we propose our time notion and discuss the problems that arise from the handling of temporal events. In addition to temporal events we must deal with rather complex events. This leads to issues of event composition and event consumption.

Rules may be applied internally to manage aspects of the active object system or they may be applied externally to the controlled system. We have considered a variety of rule classes and have organized them into a rule hierarchy. There are many different criteria along which rules may be organized. They may either be organized according to their application domain, to the nature of their triggering events or the nature of their actions and whether those are side-effect free or not. Depending on these properties, rules may behave differently, particularly under abnormal termination and timing constraints. We analyze rule classification and rule behavior from these points of view. As the application domains for rules we have considered consistency enforcement (which may be applied to external systems as well as the active object system itself), access control, transaction management, contingency plans, and the control of an external robot.

We are approaching the design and implementation of REACH first as a layered system, i.e., the rule classes are defined as classes in the object model of a conventional OODBMS. We describe our rule classes in the C++ based model of ObjectStore. This approach is intended as a testbed and as a mechanism for establishing the correctness of our approach. Later, we plan on implementing the critical functionality at lower levels within the object system. We are experimenting in parallel with other object models, in particular O2, but have encountered some problems in the closed nature of the O2 system. ObjectStore and O2 offer, in addition, quite different support for transactions, the former providing nested transactions while the latter only provides flat transactions.

The remainder of this paper discusses the system boundary definitions in Section 2. Section 3 introduces our rule structure and additional coupling modes needed for dealing with open systems and a hierarchy according to the application domain. Section 4 addresses events, their semantics and their management, condition evaluation and actions with side-effects. Section 5 touches briefly on rule execution strategies and Section 6 summarizes and discusses future work.

2 System Boundaries

Active object systems are intended as controlling systems that can react autonomously to events in the controlled system without user intervention. Because they can manage large amounts of information, they are also well-suited for controlling systems that must react to cumulative events or to trends in data over an extended period of time. We will illustrate the boundaries of the active system through the example of a moving robot.

The robot's task is to carry parts that are being worked on among stations. It moves around on the shop floor taking its bearings from fixed beacons and ceiling lights and is capable of avoiding obstacles. Even though the robot itself can act on real-world objects and can react autonomously to obstacles and avoid them, in the larger context of an active object system we will consider the robot as the controlled system that detects real-world situations and executes the actions mandated by the controlling system.

The robot's view of the real world is determined by its capacity to perceive data that describe its surroundings. Details of the surroundings are abstracted and detected through sensors. The perceived impulses are filtered and locally analyzed and then used either for local decisions or transmitted as signals to the controlling system. The structure of the signals is characterized by its type, value, spatial topology, and temporal topology (chronology).

The chronology of signals is of particular interest to us. Assuming the linearity of time, it is possible to determine through the temporal metric alone its topology. In the spatial case, it is necessary to determine both a metric and a topology to fully describe a signal sequence. Depending on the modelled reality, it may be necessary to describe not only the present state but the chain of events that led to the present state.

The controlling system must map the signal structure of the controlled system to an abstract model of the real world. The signals of the controlled system are mapped to events in the controlling system. The event abstraction considers the important properties of the signal structure (e.g. chronology) but eliminates unnecessary detail. The controlling system acts on the controlled system through the action part of an event-condition-action rule. The action part of the rule is expressed in the model of the controlling system and must be concretized, i.e. transformed into the proper signals understood by the controlled system. For example, the high-level command 'stop robot r1 at position x,y' in the model of the controlling system must first be converted into the necessary signals to activate at the proper time a switch to turn off the motor and another signal to start the braking procedure at the rate necessary to reach exactly position x,y.

Figure 1 illustrates the mapping of signals in the controlled system to events in the controlling system and the concretization of actions in the controlling system to signals for the controlled system.

Two possibilities exist for handling external events: to define the external events with the event detector directly, or to define all events as database-objects which must be updated/inserted and thus are converted to simple internal database events.

While for most systems of the real world that are described through signals, e.g. the robot, a linear time notion is sufficient, this is not the case for the controlling system. Active databases or object systems have been proposed for planning purposes or for control of multiple external systems under contingencies, i.e., depending on future states or events different actions are possible. The handling of "what-if-scenarios" and contingencies is, in fact, one of the strengths of active databases, since a variety of future actions can be considered, from which those that maximize the system's value are chosen. This requires, however, a branching notion of time. A branching time in turn requires a more complex temporal logic and a more elaborate description of temporal topology in the controlling system. We propose a linear history with branching futures as the temporal model for the controlling active object system.

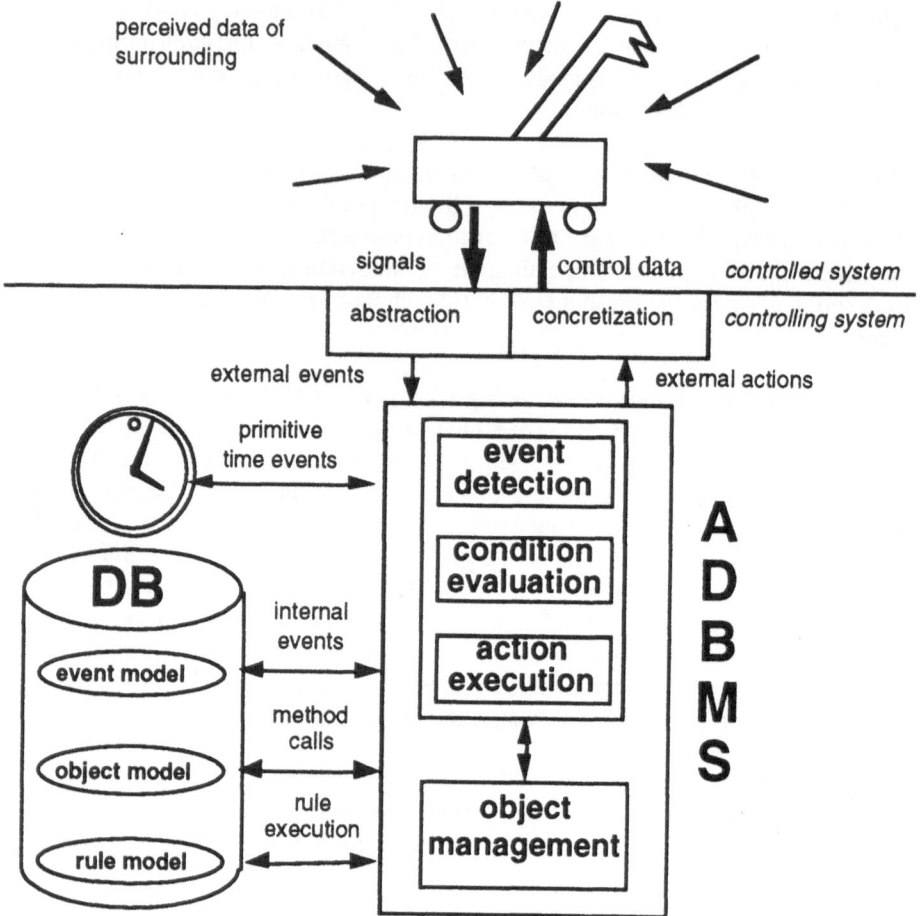

Figure 1: Mapping between controlling and controlled system

3 Rule Structure

The structure of the REACH rule system is based on the HiPAC rule structure [1] which distinguishes three parts: events, conditions and actions. From a conceptual point of view we treat all three parts as objects. Because of recoverability requirements, some events must be made persistent. Therefore, it makes sense to treat them as objects. Events may be primitive or composite and are composed according to an event algebra similar to SNOOP[2] and SAMOS[3]. A rule may be viewed as a complex object consisting of an event, a condition, and an action. Rules must have instantiated their event and action part while the condition part is optional. Rules without a condition are considered degenerate rules similar to [4].

3.1 Rule Classification

Rules may be organized into a class hierarchy. Subclasses inherit from the superclass RULE their structure, i.e. an event, a condition and an action with the possibility of defining a coupling mode between event and condition and between condition and action. Subclasses further inherit the basic methods of rules, such as create and delete, attach and detach, eval_cond, exec_action, etc.

Rules may be further subdivided according to an application domain. We have chosen as domains for our current research a mixture of internal and external domains, i.e., domains that are defined on the controlling system and/or the controlled system. These are access control, consistency enforcement, transaction /contingency management, and a CIM application. Accordingly, we organize our rule classes into access-control-rules, consistency-rules, flow-control-rules, and application-rules. Figure 2 shows an outline of the rule hierarchy.

Access control rules may again be subdivided into content-independent and content-dependent access-control-rules. The difference is twofold: content-independent rules need not access the objects themselves to determine whether access should be granted, while content-dependent access-control-rules do. Further, content-independent rules should be fired and executed before the command trying to access the data-object. Content-dependent rules are fired upon occurrence of the access event but are executed after the access or worked into the access query.

Consistency enforcement in an open system is more complex than in closed systems. Consistency rules in a closed system (e.g. the controlling system) may be executed in an immediate or a deferred mode, but always within the boundaries of the triggering transaction. Consistency in a closed system is also usually considered to be universal, i.e. to apply to all objects in the object space. In the case of open systems new consistency notions are required. The two main parameters that can be relaxed are the time of constraint enforcement and the extent. For the time being we are concentrating on relaxing the time of invocation of the consistency enforcement rules. This results in three subclasses, immediate consistency rules, deferred consistency rules, and user-invoked consistency rules.

Flow-control-rules are also of two types: transaction-rules and contingency-rules. As part of the REACH project we are exploring the possibility of defining complex transactions through rules and managing them using the infrastructure of a single rule system. The complex transaction model provides the capability of defining contingency transactions in case one of the original transactions cannot be successfully completed. The semantics of contingency transactions are detailed in [5]. The notion of contingencies is also intimately related to time-constrained processing. In this context a contingency transaction is invoked by the scheduler whenever an overload situation occurs and a task cannot be completed in time. In that case the original task is substituted by another task that is faster but may provide results of lower quality. The contingency rules we are defining can be used

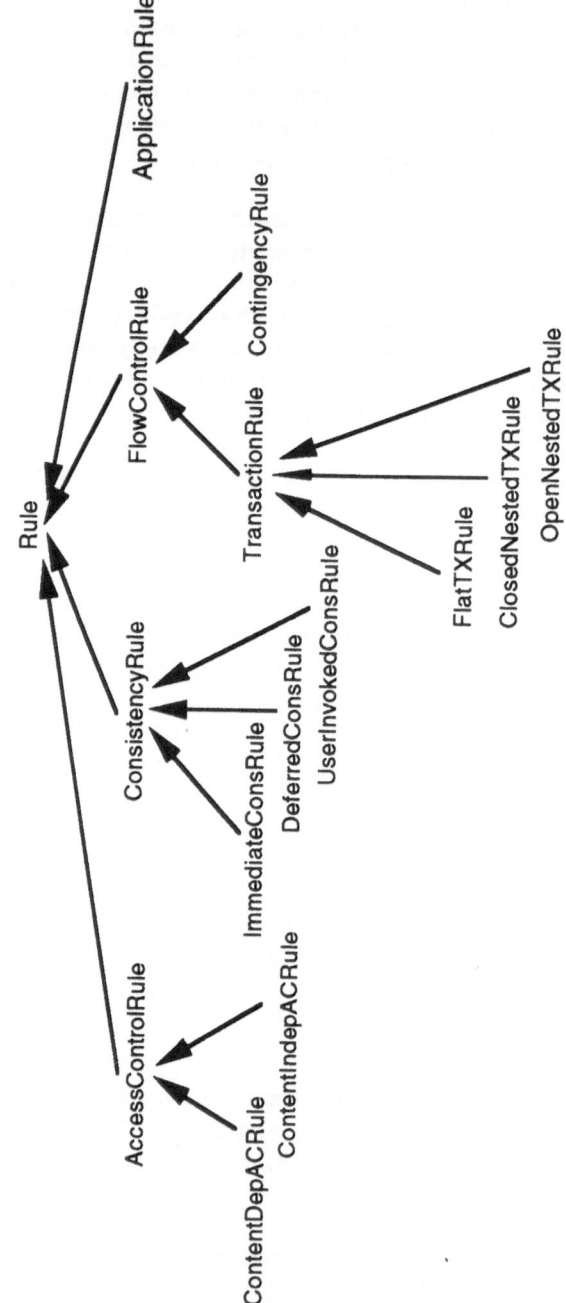

Figure 2: Rule Class Hierarchy

both to model the notion of a contingency transaction and for managing contingency plans in time-constrained environments. In both cases, the rules are used to change the flow of execution in a transaction by substituting alternate tasks. The contingency-rules are responsible for invoking the alternate task and guaranteeing that the original task is properly terminated and that necessary information is passed from the original task to the contingency task. The contingency rules need to interact closely with the transaction rules to obtain the necessary information. This means that contingency rules may receive special treatment with respect to the visibility sets of other transactions.

The application rules are a catch-all category at the current time and will be further spezialized according to more specific application domains such as robot control, control of power plants, and network management. The main intention behind calling them out as a separate class is that they refer to the controlled system only. To the best of our knowledge, extant active database prototypes do not address this type of rules. The actions of these rules have visible side-effects and must be treated with particular care since they are not recoverable in the conventional sense.

3.2 Rule Processing and Coupling Modes

When processing rules we distinguish between the firing of a rule and its execution. A rule is fired when the triggering event occurs. In the case of a composite event this happens when the event is completely composed. The effects of delays during event composition are discussed in the next section. Rule execution implies establishing the proper control structures, such as nested subtransactions or independent transactions in which the rules execute, and selecting the proper order of execution.

The necessary control structures for rule execution depend largely on the coupling between the triggering transaction and the components of a rule. All extant systems known to us use some subset of the coupling modes introduced in HiPAC [6]. These were introduced for characterization of the coupling of rules in a closed active database system, but are insufficient when dealing with external systems that may have side effects. In REACH we subsume the HiPAC coupling modes and introduce two additional coupling modes necessary when dealing with open systems that may have irreversible side-effects.

In HiPAC, the condition and action parts of rules are executed as subtransactions that may be individually coupled to the triggering transaction in one of four coupling modes: immediate, deferred, detached or detached but causally dependent. In the immediate case, a rule's condition or action is executed immediately after the event is detected (condition) or after the condition evaluation is completed (action). Upon completion of the rule execution, control returns to the point at which the event was detected. In deferred coupling mode, rule execution is delayed until the transaction completes and is inserted just before the commit. In detached coupling mode, a separate transaction is established for executing the rule with no dependencies between the triggering and the triggered transaction. In detached but causally dependent coupling mode, a separate transaction is created for rule execution. This transaction may begin with the execution but there exist a commit dependency and an abort dependency of the rule transaction on the triggering transaction, i.e., the rule transaction may begin processing in parallel with the triggering transaction but may not commit until the triggering transaction commits and must abort if the triggering transaction aborts. However, the causally dependent transaction does not commit through the triggering transaction but as an independent transaction at a later time. We shall call this coupling mode henceforth *parallel* causally dependent.

In REACH, because we are dealing with controlled systems in which the side effects of a rule's action may be irreversible, we have encountered the need to introduce two additional coupling modes. Both are variants of the detached but causally dependent coupling mode. The first is a *sequential causally dependent* coupling. In this coupling mode a rule is executed in a separate transaction from the triggering transaction but the triggered rule may only *begin* execution once the triggering transaction has committed. The second extension is an *exclusive causally dependent* coupling mode. In this case, the triggered rule is executed in a detached transaction in parallel with the triggering transaction, but the triggered transaction may commit only if the triggering transaction *failed*. This coupling mode is necessary to execute correctly the contingency rules. We expand on the need for additional coupling modes in Section 4.3. Figure 3 shows schematically the coupling modes available in REACH.

immediate coupling
deferred coupling
detached coupling
detached causally dependent
    parallel
    sequential
    exclusive

Figure 3: REACH Coupling Modes

4 Events, Conditions, Actions, and Recoverability

Conceptually, rules in REACH are complex objects. All rules have the same structure but may be built out of different events, conditions or actions. From these the rules derive their different behaviors.

4.1 Event Definition, Composition, and Recoverability

Lately, much emphasis has been given to precise event modeling and to the definition of algebras to carry out event composition. An early attempt at defining a simple event algebra was given in [1]. At present, the SNOOP and SAMOS event system and algebras [2,3] represent the state of the art. We based the event structure on the SNOOP system with some minor modifications [8]. Among the differences we observe that relative temporal events are composite events made up of another event and an increment operation on the timestamp of the reference event. Further, by treating transactions as objects, the transaction-specific events are subclasses of the CallMethod class. Our event hierarchy is not minimal at this time. The reason is that we are experimenting with various object models which support different primitive constructs. For example, the O2 model distinguishes between the access to attribute values and method calls. Figure 4 shows the event hierarchy.

We identify a particular type of relative temporal events, called milestones. Milestones are the triggering events of contingency rules for time-constrained transactions. A contingency transaction is invoked whenever a transaction cannot complete in time and an acceptable alternative transaction exists that could finish in time even if the results are of lower quality. Given the problems in predicting the execution time for transactions because of interference among transactions and variable workloads, we approach the problem in an incremental and pragmatic manner. During the execution of a time-constrained transaction milestones are checked to monitor the progress of a transaction relative to its ideal progress, i.e. the progress a transaction should have made to finish in time. If a transaction misses a milestone, a contingency transaction can be triggered. A milestone is therefore a relative temporal event that triggers a contingency rule at time $BOT+t_i$. Because the condition part of a contingency transaction requires information about the run-time behavior of the triggering transaction, the milestone passes this information.

The firing of a rule should be viewed as a point on the time axis. There is, however, a time between the occurrence of a primitive event e1 and the composition of a complex event e2 of which e1 is a part. A rule that is triggered by a complex event can only be fired once the complex event is composed. Another rule that is fired by the same primitive event e1 may be fired earlier, depending on how complex the event composition is allowed to become and how efficient the event handler works. In any case, the question arises whether a rule should fire and possibly begin execution as soon as the triggering event is available or if rules should fire in cycles, i.e., if a primitive event is detected, no rule fires until the event handler has determined what complex events are completed by the arriving primitive event. Only then are all rules fired at once. This approach has the advantage that possible precedence constraints or priorities among rules fired in a cycle can be enforced. It has the disadvantage that rule firings may be unnecessarily delayed while composition of complex events takes place. An alternative is to fire a rule as soon as the triggering event is available, thus giving priority to rules with primitive events. In favor of this latter approach speeks the fact that upon inclusion of temporal events the frequency with which these events may arise would create a back-log of rules triggered by primitive (temporal) events waiting for one rule that is fired by a complex event. This would make any assertion about the exact time of firing of a rule meaningless. In REACH we have tentatively opted for an immediate firing of rules as soon as an event is complete. This gives inherent priority to

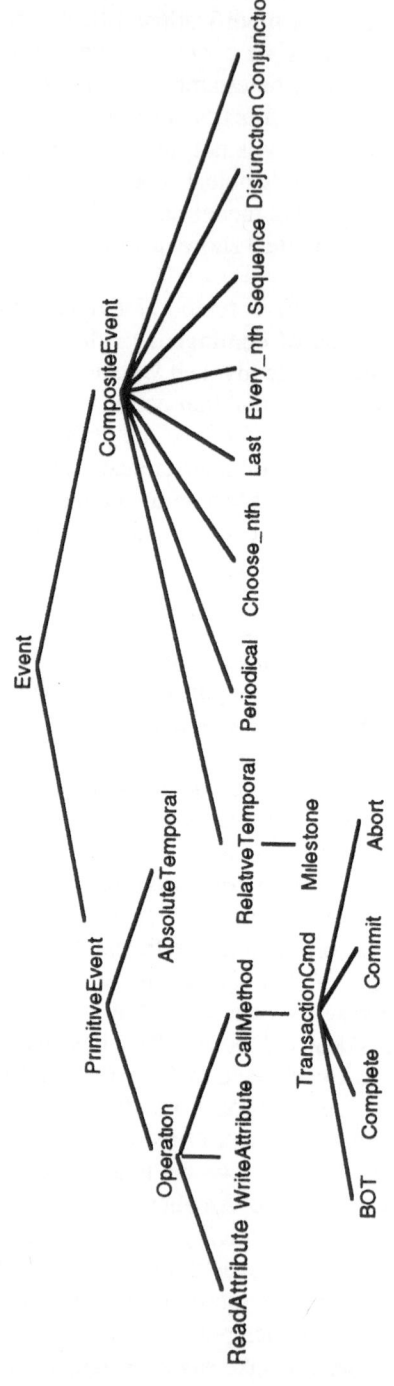

Figure 4: Event Hierarchy

simple events. It also implies that no rule triggered by a complex event can have precedence over rules triggered by primitive events that are part of the composite event.

The inclusion of temporal events raises some new questions when dealing with recovery in an active object system. In the literature mostly database operations are considered as the only possible events, thus ruling out problems with unrecoverability of events. Dealing with temporal events leads to problems with respect to rule recovery. This issue is briefly addressed in [7].

When rules that are fired by temporal events are aborted and reexecuted (perhaps because of a deadlock problem), it becomes necessary to ask about the meaning of reexecution. Absolute temporal events, e.g. *at* 5:00:00 may become meaningless under recovery, unless the semantics of the temporal event are unique. Does the event "at 5:00:00" mean exactly *at* 5 and not *after* nor *before*, or does it mean anytime after 5? If the former semantics is assumed, an absolute temporal event is not recoverable. The same problems arise with any relative temporal event that is defined relative to another event that originated in a committed transaction. We consider an event to be pinned, i.e. fixed on the timeline, if it is either an absolute temporal event, or if it is a relative temporal event that is defined relative to an event that has been committed as part of the transaction in which it was raised. Occurrences of pinned events cannot be undone.

Events may be combined with modifiers. For example, the modifier *before* and *after* placed on a database event signal the event immediately before and after the execution of the database operation, respectively. When modifiers are used on temporal events one must be particularly careful with the semantics. We discussed the implications of the semantics of the modifier *at* on recovery. A commonly used example in active databases is to say that consistency must be reestablished *by* time t. The user means that the action part should finish execution by time t. To accomplish this, the execution must start at $t - t_{exec}$. One should be careful not to define inadvertently a temporal constraint through the use of modifiers on the event.

It should be noted that events are strictly distinguished from temporal constraints on rules. A temporal event may trigger a rule and determines the point in time at which rule execution *begins*. Temporal constraints refer to the action part of a rule and specify the point in time at which execution must *complete*.

Another issue of interest when processing events is the "consumption" of events. Let's assume event of type E4 is defined as a composition of events of the types E1, E2, E3. If the instances of primitive events of type E1, E2 and E3 are produced in the sequence e1, e2, e2', e3, what are the correct semantics for composing e4? One possible semantics would be to use always the latest instance of an event in a composition. Another would be to use always the first primitive event of a type in a composition. This problem was recognized in [2] and approached through the definition of contexts. Specifying different event consumption semantics is complex and may introduce intolerable delays in the evaluation of events.

A possible alternative to complex event composition semantics is to use simple composition semantics for rule triggering and express any complex event semantics as conditions on the event history. Events are always composed by default taking the latest event of a type. Other event composition semantics are expressed as queries over the (persistent) event history. We propose this approach as the initial event composition/consumption semantics for REACH.

4.2 Conditions

Conditions are queries over the state of the objectbase at the moment the rule's condition part is executed. As such they are processed with the standard database tools. However, we established in Section 4.1 the need to make some events persist for recoverability purposes and for expressing complex composition semantics. If events are treated as objects in the object-space, they may also be queried, i.e., queries may be formulated over the event history.

Two possible approaches could be envisaged: one described above, in which event composition semantics are kept simple, but some event composition is still carried out by the event handler.

The second, more extreme, could be an alternative to the currently observable tendency towards ever more complex events. In the extreme case, one could allow only simple events to fire a rule. Complex events may be modeled as conditions over the event history. This approach would have the advantage of reducing the complexity of event monitoring, returning to the original idea of events as light and easy detectable units. However, the conceptual separation of event and condition would be blurred. The price for simplified event detection would be the firing of a rule whenever one of the component primitive events was detected, only to find that the rule could not be executed because one or more of the other primitive events was still missing. This overhead may be too heavy a price to pay. However, given the current state of the art and lack of solid knowledge about the complexity of events based on real applications this is an open issue worth of further exploration.

4.3 Actions and Recoverability

The action part of a rule determines to a large extent whether a rule is recoverable or not. A rule is recoverable in the traditional database sense, only if its action is internal to the controlling system and if its coupling mode is either immediate, deferred or detached but parallel causally dependent.

Rules whose actions have irreversible side effects, such as applying a welding-spot or opening a valve through which fluid escapes, are not recoverable. To guarantee a consistent behavior of the global system (controlled and controlling) it is important to make sure that rules with irreversible side effects are not executed in a coupling mode that may call for roll-back of the rule when the triggering transaction fails.

This means that rules with irreversible side effects may only be executed in a separate transaction and must include as part of the event definition the commit notification of the spawning transaction. We call this coupling *sequential causally dependent* to distinguish it from the *parallel* causally dependent coupling mode introduced in [6]. It is our contention that this coupling mode is of particular importance for systems that act on external objects and that it has been ignored before because extant systems have concentrated on internal rule processing and have neglected to a large extent recoverability issues.

Any rule that is fired and executed in a detached or sequential causally dependent mode, even if its effect is strictly internal to the controlling system, is not recoverable in the traditional sense. A rule that was executed in a detached but sequential causally dependent mode must be compensated, if a proper compensating transaction can be defined.

5 Execution Strategies

The firing and execution order of rules is a central issue in active databases. In the absence of specific application requirements, a variety of firing and execution strategies has been proposed [6, 1, 7, 9, 10, 11, 12] but no confirmed knowledge exists as to which execution strategy is best suited under what conditions.

The execution strategy of rules deals with the issue of ordering the execution of fired rules under the constraints of the available coupling modes. Assuming that rules are fired in parallel and join a pool of rules that are ready to be executed, then there is the issue of how to select the next rule for execution. Representative strategies are found in POSTGRES, STARBURST and HiPAC.

The first execution strategy is the strategy employed by POSTGRES [9]. In this approach, an event and conditions are not fully separated. An event/condition may cause several rules to fire, but based on priorities, only one is selected for execution in an immediate coupling mode and the others are discarded.

The original STARBURST approach [11] is essentially a sequential approach in which all the rules that are fired are kept in a pool of fired rules. One is selected from this pool, executed and may, through its action, possibly invalidate the condition part of another fired rule. In each cycle one rule is selected and applied. If a rule execution triggers additional rules, these join the pool of fired transactions and enter the competition for the next execution. This approach is simplified by the fact that in the version presented in [11] all rules are executed in a deferred mode, i.e., at the end of a transaction and before the commit.

The approach to rule execution presented in [7] allows for higher parallelism and assumes a distributed system. Therefore, it is theoretically feasible to execute many rules in parallel, possibly on different nodes and processors, However, many issues derived from the distribution of rules and the objects they act on are not considered.

Rules that are triggered and have an immediate coupling mode execute in parallel as sibling subtransactions of the spawning transaction. Rules that are to be executed in a deferred mode are all delayed until the end of the spawning transaction. At that point all the fired rules are executed in parallel. If they cause during their execution other rules to be fired, those that are immediate are executed as nested subtransactions, those that are themselves deferred are delayed until the original pool of deferred transactions was completely executed and then the new batch of deferred rules is executed in another cycle. Rules that have a detached coupling mode are executed as independent nested top transactions.

The distributed STARBURST approach [13] proposes strategies for partitioning the rule space and presents locking schemes and communication protocols to guarantee correct rule execution in closed environments with ACID transactions.

Of the above execution strategies, all exhibit some shortcoming when compared with the requirements of the rule classes we have defined. For example, the STARBURST approach is well suited for deferred consistency enforcement but unsuited for access control rules, both content dependent and content independent. On the other hand, the POSTGRES execution strategy is well-suited for content-dependent access rules and immediate consistency rules, but unsuited for deferred consistency, user-invoked consistency rules or flow-control rules. The HiPAC execution strategy is quite flexible but does not consider the coupling modes required for flow-control rules, particularly contingency rules, and processing of some of the application rules with external side-effects.

When dealing with open systems all the problems of distribution show up. To keep these problems to a minimum we assume the controlling system to be centralized. All rules and objects are assumed to be at a single site. Even for rules that act on the controlled system, there is always the corresponding placeholder object on the side of the controlling system to maintain control. We have chosen an execution strategy similar to HiPAC's with additional coupling modes and are experimenting with depth first execution of triggered rules. Depth first execution is necessary when dealing with rules that carry timing constraints.

6 Summary and Future Work

In this paper we addressed issues arising when dealing with open systems in which events and actions may not be recoverable. We started by defining the system boundaries and presented a rule hierarchy that includes rules for access control, consistency enforcement, flow-control and application domains. Each of these rule classes can be specialized to deal with a variety of aspects of each domain, both in the controlling and in the controlled system, i.e., they all aim at controlling an open system. This led to the definition of two additional coupling modes, sequential causally dependent and exclusive causally dependent.

We introduced temporal events and timing constraints and discussed some of the recoverability problems arising from it. We extended the discussion of recoverability to irreversible actions and motivated through it the inclusion of the sequential causally dependent coupling mode. We introduced flow-control rules that are subdivided into transaction management rules and contingency rules. The contingency rules can be used both for handling alternate transactions with and without timing constraints. Contingency rules motivated the inclusion of the exclusive causally dependent coupling mode.

Currently we are experimenting with a layered approach on top of ObjectStore. We chose ObjectStore because it offers a fair amount of flexibility and access to the dictionary and supports a nested transaction model that is compatible with the execution strategy we propose. Longterm, we plan to migrate to a platform that allows us to install active capabilities at lower system levels. The rule classes in the various domains are being developed and as we progress and experiment with them we hope to gain additional insight into the behavior of the various components of the rules.

Further ongoing work deals with the implementation of basic system components of the REACH rule system. Among them are an event detector and composer. An obvious need is to offer a high-level rule language with only few procedural features that can be mapped to C++ rule and event-classes. This is under development.

We are implementing an experimental contingency rule management exploring efficient and predictable alternative approaches. Efficient management is essential because time proceeds while invoking contingency rules. Predictable rule management is needed to control time behavior of overall contingency rule execution.

References

1. Dayal U., Buchmann A., McCarthy D.: Rules are Objects too: A Knowledge Model for an Active Object-Oriented Database System. In: Proc. of the 2nd Intl. Workshop on Object Oriented Database Systems, Bad Münster, Germany, 1988.
2. Chakravarthy S., Mishra D.: An Event Specification Language (SNOOP) for Active Databases and its Detection, UF-CIS TR-91-23. Sept. 1991.
3. Gatziu S., Dittrich K.R.: Events in an Active Object-Oriented Database System. In: Proceedings of the 1st Intl. Workshop on Rules In Database Systems, Edinburgh, 1993.
4. Kotz-Dittrich A.: Adding Active Functionality to an Object-Oriented Database System - a Layered Approach. In: Proc. of Datenbanksysteme Büro, Technik und Wissenschaft (BTW), Braunschweig, Germany 1993.

5. Buchmann A., Özsu M.T., Hornick M., Georgakopoulos D., Manola F.: A Transaction Model for Active Distributed Object Systems. In Elmagarmid A.K. (ed), Transaction Models for Advanced Database Applications, Morgan Kaufman Publishers, 1992.

6. Hsu M., Ladin R. McCarthy D.R.: An Execution Model for Active Database Management Systems. In: Proc 3rd Intl. Conf. on Data and Knowledge Bases, Jerusalem, 1988.

7. Dayal U., Hsu M., Ladin R.: Organizing Long-Running Activities with Triggers and Transactions. In: Proc. ACM SIGMOD Intl. Conf. on Management of Data, 1990.

8. Buchmann A., Branding H., Kudrass T., Zimmermann J.: REACH: a REaltime ACtive and Heterogeneous mediator system. Bulletin of the TC on Data Engineering, Vol.15, Dec. 1992.

9. Stonebraker M., Rowe L.: The Design of POSTGRES. In: Proc. of ACM SIGMOD, 1986.

10. Stonebraker M., Hanson E.N., Potamianos S.: On rules, procedures, caching and views in data base systems. In: Proc. of ACM SIGMOD, Atlantic City,1990.

11. Widom J., Finkelstein S.J.: Set-Oriented Production Rules in Relational Database Systems. In: Proc. of ACM SIGMOD, Atlantic City,1990.

12. Widom J., Cochrane R.J., Lindsay B.G.: Implementing Set-Oriented Production Rules as an Extension to Starburst. In: Proc. 17th Intl. Conf. on Very Large Databases, 1991, pp. 275-285.

13. Ceri S., Widom J.: Production Rules in Parallel and Distributed Database Environments. In: Proc. 17th Intl. Conf. on Very Large Databases, Vancouver, 1992.

Rule-Based Implementation of Transaction Model Specifications

Andreas Geppert
Klaus R. Dittrich
Institut für Informatik, Universität Zürich
Zürich, Switzerland

Abstract

We propose an active-mechanism based approach for the construction of database management systems (DBMS). We conceive a DBMS to be composed out of brokers (which realize subsystems), where a broker is defined by a set of production rules. In this setting, we show how specifications of transaction models can be realized. To that end, we apply a rule-based approach for the transformation of (logical) specification rules into production rules, which in turn describe the behaviour of the transaction management broker.

1 Introduction and Motivation

During the last decade, a significant number of database management systems (DBMSs) and persistent object systems have been realized for rather different application domains. Due to the diverging requirements of these application domains, no consensus exists —and most likely will never exist— for one, or even a small number, of DBMSs that are adequate for all these application domains. Based on this observation, we expect a variety of DBMSs to coexist·in the future.

As soon as more and more DBMSs have to be realized, the development of a *construction methodology* for DBMS becomes an urgent research issue. This is also the case with the development of toolkits and support tools for DBMS construction. The two most important characteristics of a successful construction methodology are:

- it covers all the relevant aspects of a DBMS, and
- it supports all the phases of DBMS construction.

While the major part of research in the field of extensible database systems [1] investigated support for the realization of data models, other aspects like transaction management, integrity enforcement, and so forth which are equally important are not addressed. Furthermore, extensible database systems concentrated on supporting *implementation*, while analysis and design are completely left to the user (i.e., the database system implementor, DBI).

Significant work has been done in the areas of specification and implementation of transaction management. For example, ACTA[1] [2] is useful for the specification of (extended) transaction models. Furthermore, toolkits are available for realizing transaction managers [3] (i.e., class libraries containing primitives for the implementation of transaction management). However, the work on ACTA does not address implementation so far, and toolkits alone do not support analysis and design very well. Hence, the (crucial) mapping from transaction model specifications to realizations is still an open problem.

In this paper, we address the problem of realizing ACTA specifications in the context of a DBMS construction method. In the KIDS[2] project [4], we investigate such a method based on large-scale reuse of software artifacts. In order to make reusability successful, the construction method makes (re)use of not only code, but also analysis and design information [5]. Roughly speaking, various *aspects* (e.g., data model, transaction model, integrity model) of a full-fledged DBMS are specified using aspect-specific languages. Based on these specifications, *subsystems* are realized by means of configuration/composition of reusable primitives, or by generation. These subsystems are plugged into an architecture skeleton (thereby making the DBMS architecture itself also subject to reuse).

As for transaction management, we conceive (sets of) ACTA-rules as constraints on correct histories, i.e., correct interleavings of operations issued by concurrently executing transactions. Operations are usually transaction events (like *commit*, *abort*) or database operations (e.g., insert, update, and so on). In order to ensure correctness, we translate ACTA-rules into (a simple form of) production rules (e.g., [6], [7]). In contrast to the majority of other work, however, production rules are applied as a construction and realization paradigm for *DBMS-internal* purposes. In other words, production rules are defined during the construction of a subsystem (of a DBMS) and are not necessarily visible to schema designers or end-users.

The remainder of this paper is organized as follows: in the following section, a short overview (as far as necessary for the understanding of this paper) of our understanding of a subsystem is given. Section 3 contains a short description of the ACTA framework. In section 4, we describe the transformation of ACTA specifications into production rules.

2 The Broker/Services Model

Our ultimate goal is to support the construction of database management systems (DBMSs) in such a manner that a DBMS implementor (DBI) is assisted throughout the analysis, design, and realization of (aspects of) a DBMS. Currently, we address three aspects: data models, transaction management, and integrity enforcement. Each of these aspects is realized by a *subsystem*. The *analysis* of one aspect results in a formal (requirements) specification, written in an aspect-specific language. *Design* refers to the development of the structure of the subsystem and its relationships to other subsystems, while during *realization*, classes and objects are determined that implement the subsystem's behaviour. In principle, realization can be done through the configuration or generation of components.

---

1. "Actions" in Latin
2. *K*ernel-machine based *I*mplementation of *D*atabase Management *S*ystems

For the construction of the various subsystems of a DBMS, we have the following requirements from an architectural point of view:

- While the independent and parallel development of various subsystems has to be supported, these are typically not completely independent from each other. Hence, we need a flexible model for interfacing subsystems. Especially, if (parts of) subsystems are generated, they will have to make assumptions on other subsystems, without knowledge of their concrete realization or of the principles guiding other generators.
- The stepwise realization of subsystems and control flow between subsystems has to be supported.
- A uniform model for the execution of DBMS services and the description of their semantics is necessary.

In order to satisfy these requirements, each subsystem is governed by a so-called *broker*, which is the only visible part of a subsystem. A broker is responsible for specific *services* and "knows" which actions to perform for requested services. At execution time, services are requested in that *events* are raised. These events are detected by the responsible broker, which then decides whether actions have to be performed and eventually executes them. One part of a reaction can be a *reply*, which is then caught by the object that raised the event. Other kind of reactions comprise propagation of events to subcomponents or the generation of additional events. At construction time, the designer specifies events which will be raised at execution time. Hence, in order to implement the control flow (between subsystems), we have to determine responsible brokers and to define how the respective broker reacts to the event. This process continues recursively if the (reacting) broker in turn raises events.

Brokers are defined by a set of ECA-rules (or equivalently, production rules) [6, 7], where each rule defines an event which the broker is responsible for, the corresponding reaction, and a condition that determines whether the reaction is performed or not. For our purposes, *simple events* (actually, *abstract events* [7]) are sufficient, whereas composite events are not necessary. However, events can have parameters which have to be supplied when the event is raised. Production rules have the following syntax:

> ON   event (arguments)
> IF   condition
> DO   action

where the condition can be omitted if it is assumed to be always true:

> ON   event(arguments)
> DO   action.

In this way, a broker offers a set of standard services; other components interacting with a broker only need to know the services, but not concrete interfaces or realization details. A broker, however, has to know (or to determine, during construction) how to realize a specific service. Hence, similar to the common object request broker architecture (CORBA [8]), a broker can be seen as a mediator between clients and servers.

In this paper, we focus on the realization of transaction management brokers, i.e., the mapping of a specification language for transaction models to (production) rules implemented by the transaction broker.

3 A Short Overview of ACTA

The intention of this section is to introduce ACTA, since a rough understanding of this specification framework is necessary for the comprehension of the translation approach explained below.

ACTA [2, 9] is a framework for the specification of extended transaction models based on first-order logic. Within this framework, *transaction types* can be specified, whereby a transaction type intensionally describes a set of transaction instances that share structure and behaviour. A transaction instance issues *events*, where the set of all event types can be further classified into *transaction events* (i.e., begin, commit, abort, split, join [10] and so forth), *object events* (i.e., data manipulation actions), and the like. The sequence of all occurred event instances forms a *history*, whereby the history up to a given point in time t is referred to as the *current history* H_{ct}. Two essential predicates are $e \in H$, where e is an event and H is a history (e is an element of history H), and $e_1 \rightarrow e_2$ (event e_1 precedes event e_2).

Typically, (parts of) the semantics of one transaction type depends on its relationships to other types. These relationships are captured by ACTA through the notion of *dependency*. Usually, a dependency is an implication that constrains the occurrence or order of events of two transactions (see Table 1). As an example, take an abort dependency between transactions t_1 and t_2: if t_1 aborts, t_2 has to abort as well, i.e., $\text{abort}(t_1) \in H_{ct} \Longrightarrow \text{abort}(t_2) \in H_{ct}$. Dependencies can arise due to structure (e.g., a subtransaction is weak-abort dependent on its parent transaction) or due to behaviour. In the latter case, dependencies can also be formed due to *object events* of the related transactions. For instance, if one transaction executes an operation on an (uncommitted) object, it is usually abort-dependent on the transaction that modified the object most recently.

Transactions perform operations (as defined by the data manipulation language) on objects. ACTA abstracts from both, the concrete set of operations and the notion of "object". However, we are interested in rules which constrain the access of transactions to objects and which define dependencies due to operations performed on objects on behalf of transactions. These rules typically use the definition of the following sets and functions:

- The *view set* of a transaction specifies which objects are visible (i.e., can be accessed and manipulated) to it. The view of a transaction can be defined in terms of the current history, other transactions, and existing dependencies.

- The *conflict set* of a transaction defines the operations that might conflict with the operations issued by the transaction. Like the view set, the conflict set of a transaction can be defined in terms of the current history, other transactions, and existing dependencies. If two operations p and q conflict (i.e., the respective return values depend on their execution order), the predicate conflict(p,q) is *true*. The definition of this predicate is assumed to be predefined for a given transaction

Name	Definition	Meaning
Strong-Commit: t_2 SCD t_1	$\text{commit}(t_1) \in H \Rightarrow \text{commit}(t_2) \in H$	if t_1 commits, t_2 commits as well
Abort: t_2 AD t_1	$\text{abort}(t_1) \in H \Rightarrow \text{abort}(t_2) \in H$	if t_1 aborts, t_2 aborts as well
Weak-Abort: t_1 WD t_2	$\text{abort}(t_2) \in H \Rightarrow (\neg(\text{commit}(t_1) \rightarrow \text{abort}(t_2)) \Rightarrow \text{abort}(t_1) \in H)$	if t_2 aborts and t_1 has not yet committed, t_1 aborts as well
Force-Commit-on-Abort: t_1 CMD t_2	$\text{abort}(t_2) \in H \Rightarrow \text{commit}(t_1) \in H$	if t_2 aborts, t_1 has to commit
Begin-on-Commit: t_2 BCD t_1	$\text{begin}(t_2) \in H \Rightarrow (\text{commit}(t_1) \rightarrow \text{begin}(t_2))$	t_2 can begin only after t_1 has committed
Begin-on-Abort: t_2 BAD t_1	$\text{begin}(t_2) \in H \Rightarrow (\text{abort}(t_1) \rightarrow \text{begin}(t_2))$	t_2 can begin only after t_1 has aborted
Weak-Begin-on-Commit: t_2 WCD t_1	$\text{begin}(t_2) \in H \Rightarrow (\text{commit}(t_1) \in H \Rightarrow (\text{commit}(t_1) \rightarrow \text{begin}(t_2))$	if t_2 has already started and t_1 has yet committed, then t_2 started after t_1 has committed

Table 1: Sample ACTA-Dependencies

model and an underlying data model. If two operations conflict and p_{t1} has been executed before q_{t2}, the predicate $C(t_1, t_2)$ evaluates to *true* (i.e., "t_1 is serialized before t_2"). C^+ is the transitive closure of C.

- The *access set* of a transaction identifies those operations for whose commit or abort the transaction is responsible. These responsibilities can be re-assigned to other transactions by means of *delegation*.

Given these constructs, a correctness criterion can be specified in that restrictions on transactions and objects are defined and in that dependencies are established. As an example for the first, a condition for a transaction to commit is $\neg C^+(t, t)$ (i.e., the absence of cycles in the serialization graph [11]), while an example for the second is an abort dependency (formed between t_1 and t_2) established when p_{t1} is executed before q_{t2} and both conflict.

4 Mapping ACTA Specifications Into Production Rules

In this section, we show how the rules of an ACTA specification can be mapped to production rules to be realized by a transaction broker.

4.1 Problems and General Solution

For realizing ACTA specifications, we are faced with two general problems:

1. ACTA-rules are based on logic (*deductive rules*), while the execution model is based on *production rules*.

2. Histories grow dynamically, while it is not feasible to wait until a history is complete and to decide then whether the complete history is correct.

As for the former, ACTA specifications restrict the set of correct histories (by means of rules). The problem here is that ACTA specifications do not tell us how to *ensure* correctness. They do neither specify *when* to check rules nor *how to react* in case of inconsistencies. The second, yet related problem is the sometimes underlying assumption that histories are complete, i.e., contain all the events issued by the transactions (including one termination event for each transaction). Again, naturally, it is not practical to reason only about complete histories, since in case of incorrect histories the entire history might need to be backed out. In fact, we have to detect (and avoid) inconsistent histories as soon as they occur, whereby the problem is that we have no knowledge about future events.

Similar to approaches for integrity enforcement, our solution translates deductive rules into production rules. This translation is again rule-based and is specified by *transformation rules*. Resulting production rules will ensure that the current history can be extended to a correct, complete history (in terms of transaction theory: the current history is a *prefix* of a correct history).

The general approach for transformation rules is to first rewrite ACTA-rules so that they obey a canonical form; namely, implications with a single ACTA event as antecedent (left hand side of the implication). In this way, we derive events of resulting production rules: namely, an event that lets the antecedent of the (ACTA) rule evaluate to *true*. In this case, we know that the consequent of the (ACTA) implication also has to be *true*. Hence, a reaction has to be performed whenever the consequent is *false*. In order to avoid this incorrect case, two reactions are possible: we can either avoid the antecedent to get *true* or enforce the consequent to become *true* as well. To that end, two strategies for reactions of production rules are possible:

- the preservation of the validity of (ACTA) rules can be *enforced* by raising or propagating events,

- validity of rules can be preserved by *rejecting* (i.e., ignoring) events.

Each of the alternatives already determines the kind of action to be performed upon the occurrence of events. In the first case, we ensure that a given ACTA rule evaluates to *true* since —by means of raising additional events— we guarantee that consequents of rules evaluate to *true*. As an example, in this case of abort dependencies, the consequent specifies that other (dependent) transactions also have to abort.

Hence, since they cannot come to a successful end, it is appropriate to abort them at the current point in time.

Nevertheless, it might not be possible to guarantee the preservation of the validity of some ACTA-rules (dependencies). For instance, assume the presence of a strong-commit dependency for compensating transactions. If the compensated transaction committed and the parent transaction aborts, the compensating transaction has to (execute and to) commit as well. However, it would not make sense to enforce the commitment of the compensating transaction (at the time the compensated transation commits), nor would it be adequate to disallow the compensated transaction to commit (since we cannot know whether the compensating transaction will ever execute). Hence, in this case we will generate production rules that fire on the *negation* of the required event and react adequately. In the example of commit dependencies, two rules can be generated: one that fires if an internal abort (e.g., due to deadlock) occurs and then restarts the compensating transaction as reaction, and one production rule that is triggered by an "external" abort (e.g., user intervention, semantic incorrectness in the sense of integrity violation) and reacts by starting a contingency transaction (alternative transaction) [12].

In the second case, we cannot preserve the validity of the rule by performing actions that would let the consequent evaluate to *true*. In rejecting the event, both parts of the implication evaluate to *false* and the rule is valid again. Hereby, *rejecting* an event means to act as if the event had never occurred. Consequently, the event is not an element of the current history. The event can be raised once more later on and can then be allowed if the corresponding rule is preserved. For example, assume a rule that specifies that nested transactions cannot commit until all their subtransactions have committed or aborted. If a nested transaction tries to commit while at least one of its subtransactions is still active, the commit request will be rejected (and we can imagine a corresponding notification to the application). Nevertheless, the nested transaction can try again (i.e., re-raise the event) at a later point in time.

Consequently, event occurrences are classified into two classes. Depending on the current history and the set of rules an event occurrence can be either *legal* or *illegal*. In the latter case, there is at least one rule that will reject that event. This distinction also implies a specific execution (or event handling) strategy: no rule is allowed to trigger upon the occurrence of an event until it is determined whether the event is legal at all. Additionally, as a prerequisite for realizing ACTA specifications, we classify ACTA dependencies as being either *enforcing* or *rejecting*. [3]

4.2 Assumptions

Without loss of generality, we make the following assumptions.

First, we assume that a *state* is attached to each transaction. Typically, any transaction is in one of the states *initialized*, *active*, *committed*, or *aborted*[4]. If we want to express that a transaction is no longer active, irrespective of whether it aborted or

---

3. This is in contrast to [13], where *events* are classified in rejectable, enforcible, and delayable ones.

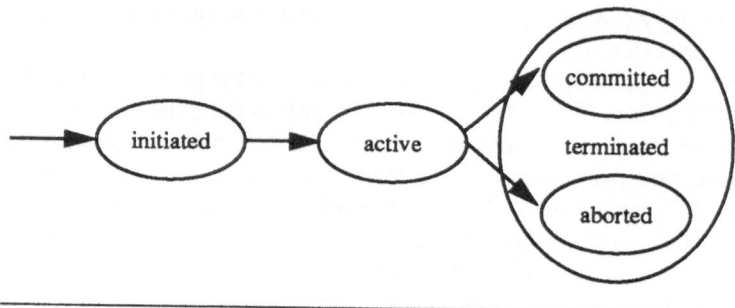

Figure 1 Transaction States

committed, we refer to the state as *terminated* (Figure 1). Likewise, *in-progress(t)* means that transaction *t* has not yet terminated. If a transaction *t* is in state *s*, the predicate *s(t)* evaluates to *true*. The state predicates later on will help to avoid the explicit representation of histories.

Further predicates and functions represent the structure of transactions. For instance, we have to formally represent parent/child-relationships of nested transactions, as well as the relationship between component transactions and compensating transactions in the Saga model [15]. Since the definitions of these functions are rather obvious, we omit them here for the sake of brevity. Also, we assume behaviour such as delegation, transaction rollback, commit of changes, and the like are implemented by various (transaction) classes.

Given these assumptions, the mapping of ACTA-rules into production rules is organized as follows:

1. The mapping of dependencies to production rules, and
2. The mapping of constraints on operations on objects to production rules.

The remainder of this section will be organized along these lines.

4.3 Realizing Transaction Dependencies Through Production Rules

Given the above distinction of rules, inter-transaction dependencies are generally realized in three steps:

- possibly rewrite ACTA-rules such that transformation rules can be applied,
- apply transformation rules which generate production rules for establishing dependencies,
- apply transformation rules generating production rules that fire when dependencies have to be preserved (for brevity, we say that "a dependency is triggered" in this case).

---

4. Additional states may be necessary, e.g., for distributed transactions or for realization of coupling modes in an active DBMS [14]. However, the aforementioned states are sufficient for now.

As examples for the latter two, assume an abort dependency as given in Table 1. Establishing the dependency for two specific transactions means simply recording the dependency. None of the aborts is actually performed at this point in time. However, the dependency is triggered as soon as the first transaction aborts and the abort has to be propagated to the second transaction.

4.3.1 Preparing ACTA-Rules for Transformation

Generally, we assume that both dependency-establishing rules as well as dependency-preserving rules are given as logical implications, and that the antecedent is a single event occurrence. In order to obtain this structure, ACTA-rules may need to be rewritten using well-known logical rules. For instance, assume an ACTA rule of the form $(e_1 \wedge e_2 \Rightarrow c)$, where c is a condition. This rule will be rewritten into two ACTA-rules as follows: $e_1 \Rightarrow (e_2 \Rightarrow c)$ and $e_2 \Rightarrow (e_1 \Rightarrow c)$. Later on, e_1 and e_2 will play the role of triggering events in the two resulting production rules, respectively. Additionally, ACTA events can still occur in consequents of rules, e.g., transaction events. These events will be replaced by predicates, e.g., on the state of the respective transaction. For instance, if the consequent contains $abort(t) \in H$, we will replace it by the state predicate aborted(t). By means of this replacement, we know that the specified event has occurred (and hence is an element of the history). Therefore, we do not have to represent (and check) the history explicitly.

4.3.2 Production Rules for Establishing Dependencies

In general, a transformation rule is a pair (i, r), where i is an implication (ACTA rule) and r is a production rule.

The general scheme for the transformation of dependency-establishing rules is as follows:

ACTA:	$post(e_1(t_1)) \Rightarrow ((t_1 \text{ DEP } t_2) \in DepSet_{ct})$
Production Rule:	ON $e_1(t_1)$ DO raise $(dep(DEP, t_1, t_2))$

Rule 1 Production Rule for Establishing Dependencies

The meaning of the ACTA rule is that after event e_1 has occurred, the dependency $(t_1 \text{ DEP } t_2)$ has to be in the set of current dependencies. The semantics of the production rule generated by (the transformation) Rule 1 are to establish the dependency as soon as the antecedent of the defining ACTA rule evaluates to *true*. At execution time, an event is raised and caught by the transaction broker, i.e., the predefined reaction of the event dep is to register the dependency (DEP). The notion of the current set of dependencies ($DepSet_{ct}$) is implicit and therefore does not have to occur in the production rule definition. Note that the ACTA rule is rather simple in this case, since its consequent is only a predicate. If the consequent in turn consists of an implication, we apply Rule 2 where c is a condition that might contain predicates over t_1 and t_2

ACTA: $post(\ e_1(t_1)) \Rightarrow (\ c \Rightarrow (t_1 \ DEP \ t_2) \in DepSet_{ct})$

Production Rule: ON $e_1(t_1)$
                   IF   c
                   DO   raise $(dep(DEP, t_1, t_2))$

Rule 2 Establishing Dependencies with Conditions

4.3.3 Production Rules for Triggering Dependencies

Once dependencies are registered, they trigger as soon as the corresponding event occurs. For each case we define separate transformation rules. The first case, where the preservation of the validity of the consequent can be enforced, is termed *enforcement*. The second case, where the consequent cannot be enforced and the triggering event has to be regarded as illegal, is referred to as *rejection*.

ACTA: $e_1(t_1) \in H \Rightarrow e_2(t_2) \in H$

Production Rule: ON $e_1(t_1)$
                   IF $\neg\ (e_2(t_2))$
                   DO   reject(e_1, t_1)

Rule 3 Triggering Dependencies (Rejection)

Rule 3 shows the general scheme for the transformation of ACTA dependencies into production rule definitions. Here, the ACTA rule specifies the semantics of a dependency. The resulting production rule will fire upon occurrence of event $e_1(t_1)$ if the dependency has been established (see Rule 1 and Rule 2). Again, the event will be caught by the transaction broker, which also has a predefined reaction reject. The negated predicate in the condition part should not be confused with a negative event in the sense of active database systems [7].

If the appropriate reaction is to enforce the consequent instead of rejecting the triggering event, Rule 4 is applied. Similar to Rule 2, if the corresponding ACTA rule has a more complex consequent, the resulting production rule will have a (more complex) condition as well.

ACTA: $e_1(t_1) \in H \Rightarrow e_2(t_2) \in H$

Production Rule: ON $e_1(t_1)$
                   DO   raise$(e_2(\ t_2))$

Rule 4 Triggering Dependencies (Enforcement)

4.4 Realizing Restrictions on Operations Through Production Rules

In order to preserve correct histories involving operation events (in the sequel referred to as data manipulation events, or DML-events, for short) it has to be determined whether such an event is allowed at the current time (at the actual "position" in the current history). Similar to transaction dependencies, it is not acceptable to require that the history is represented explicitly and to reason about this explicit representation.

In order to evaluate the correctness of DML-events on behalf of a specific transaction, we have to check whether the object to be manipulated is in the view of the transaction. Furthermore, we have to check for conflicts with other transactions. Note that view sets are typically much simpler than conflict sets. For example, in the ACTA specification of Sagas [9], the view set of a Saga is empty (i.e., a Saga itself cannot perform any DML-operations), while the view set of a Saga component transaction is the entire current history (i.e., a component is allowed to access an object without restrictions). In both cases, checking the visibility of objects is very simple (always *false* in the first case, and always *true* in the second). For more elaborate cases, we assume that both the view set as well as the conflict set, are defined in terms of access sets of other transactions. Production rules will have to be generated for the maintenance of the access sets of the transactions, for looking up these sets in order to ensure correct accesses, and for registering conflicts.

The general transformation rule for DML-events is given in Rule 5 where p is a DML-event (name), t is a transaction, o is an operation and args optionally are arguments of the operation. The event validateView is caught by the scheduler (broker). Its reaction is to check whether the object is in the view set of the transaction. Similarly, validateConfl is caught by the scheduler which checks for conflicts with other transactions. Finally, while the reaction to registerAccess typically will be the update of the transaction's access set, execute is caught by the object manager, which executes the DML-operation as specified.

ACTA:	p_t (o, args)
Production Rule:	ON p (t, o, args)
	DO raise (validateView(t, o))
	raise (validateConfl(p, t, o))
	raise (registerAccess(t, p, o))
	raise (execute(t, p, o, args))

Rule 5 Production Rules for DML-events

For the understanding of the first three events it is necessary to recall that we are addressing the *construction* of a transaction management subsystem. Essentially, in this phase of construction we will try to reuse existing primitives that are responsible for the events (e.g., a lock manager for validation). One problem is to find primitives that obey the specified semantics. Given our approach to describing and implementing brokers by means of production rules, it is straightforward to describe the semantics of primitives (partially) with production rules as well. As an example, the validateView event would be described as in Rule 6. The meaning of the ACTA rule is to make solely those objects visible to transactions where either the object is currently not accessed by any transaction, or any transaction responsible for the object is also an ancestor of the requesting transaction.

ACTA: $\quad\quad\quad\quad$ $View_t = \{p_{t'}(o) \mid (\neg\exists\, t' : p_{t'}(o) \in \text{access-set}(t')) \vee$
$\quad\quad\quad\quad\quad\quad\quad\quad\quad\quad (p_{t'}(o) \in \text{access-set}(t') \wedge \text{ancestor}(t, t'))\}$

Production Rule: $\quad$ ON $\quad$ validateView(t, o)
$\quad\quad\quad\quad\quad\quad\quad$ IF $\quad\; \neg\,(\forall\, t_2 : t_2 \in \text{accessingTAs}(o) \Rightarrow \text{ancestor}(t_2, t))$
$\quad\quad\quad\quad\quad\quad\quad$ DO $\quad$ reject(validateView)

Rule 6 Sample Production Rule for Validating View Set

The same approach is used for checking conflicts. Hereby, we assume that the conflict relation has been defined by the DBI. The resulting production rule defines the conflict check as the condition of the rule and also defines the reaction in case of conflict. We will next discuss additional strategies for the realization of conflict validation. First, some validation techniques (e.g., strict two-phase locking) would not simply allow or reject DML-events, instead they would try to re-order the current history attempting to preserve correctness. In this case, events or requests would be queued, and the scheduler made responsible for determining events to resume execution. This is supported by the operations defer and resume on events, which can be specified as reaction of production rules.

Furthermore, the simple transformation rule and the resulting production rule above (Rule 5) may need modifications in order to support the selection of components. Modifications are possible along the following lines:

- Additional events can be raised in the reaction part. For instance, *notification* events may be added in order to realize user notification upon the occurrence of specific events (e.g., changing design objects).

- The sequence of events raised in the reaction part can be modified, or some of these events can be assigned to other production rules. One criterion for classifying validation techniques is the *validation time*, the point in time DML-events are validated. For instance, if we would like to apply optimistic concurrency control, the validateConfl would not be raised in the reaction part of the DML-event, but would be assigned to a production rule triggered upon commit of responsible transactions.

- In order to optimize the execution of production rules, some events in the reaction part can be "merged". Depending on the chosen technique, validation of DML-events and registration can be done in one step.

4.5 The Saga Example

As an example, we show the production rules realizing dependencies for the Saga transaction type. We conceive a Saga [15] (in the example represented by the variable S) as a sequence of component transactions t_i. A compensating transaction ct_i is attached to each component. The dependencies as given in the left-most column in Table 2 are then specified for Sagas, component transactions, and compensating transactions [9]. For the semantics of dependencies, refer to Table 1. The second column identifies the applied transformation rule. The three columns on the right side specify events, conditions, and actions of generated production rules, respectively. These dependencies are recorded by production rules generated according to Rule 1. Due to space limitations, we omit these production rules here. The first three dependencies are established at the begin of the Saga, the second three at the begin of the respective component, the next two when a component commits, and the last one at the begin of the last component in the sequence.

As for one special case, consider the seventh dependency. Here we would have to ensure that the compensating transaction ct_i commits if the Saga aborts (which is impossible to ensure, see the discussion above). Hence, we defined a production rule that fires in one incorrect case (namely, rollback, i.e., internal abort due to deadlock or something alike). In this case, the reaction is to restart the compensating transaction.

The last row contains another noteworthy example. This dependency specifies that the Saga has to commit if the last component commits as well. While we typically would refrain from enforcing commits and apply the rejection rule, enforcement is safe in this context. Hence, both examples show the power of the rule-based transfor-

Dependency	Transf. Rule	Event	Condition	Action
t_i BCD t_{i-1}	3	begin(t_i)	$\neg$committed(t_{i-1})	reject
ct_i WCD ct_{i+1}	3	begin(ct_i)	active(ct_{i+1})	reject
ct_{n-1} BAD S	3	begin(ct_{n-1})	$\neg$aborted(S)	reject
t_i AD S	4	abort(S)	-	abort(t_i)
t_i WD S	4	abort(S)	$\neg$ committed(t_i)	abort(t_i)
ct_i BCD t_i	3	begin(ct_i)	$\neg$ committed(t_i)	reject
ct_i CMD S	4	rollback(ct_i)	aborted(S)	restart(ct_i)
ct_i BAD t_i	3	begin(ct_i)	$\neg$ aborted(S)	reject
S SCD t_n	4	commit(t_n)	-	commit(S)

Table 2: Dependencies for Sagas and Corresponding Production Rules

mation approach.The first example shows the necessity to let the DBI edit transformation rules or specify new ones, while in some cases like the second example the DBI can choose whether to follow the enforcement or the rejection policy for select dependencies.

5 Conclusion

While the vast majority of work in the field of active DBMS elaborates on support of active mechanisms for concrete database systems (e.g., as an implementation mechanism for concepts like integrity enforcement [16, 17, 18], for the realization of control flow for long-running activities [19], for access control, as a mechanism to control heterogeneous system components [12], and so forth), our work uses production rules for two purposes:

1. as an internal, unifying, and integrating concept for the design and realization of DBMS,
2. as a construction paradigm for specific functionalities in the context of a DBMS construction method.

For the first purpose, we have introduced a broker/subsystem model for the construction of DBMSs, where the behaviour of brokers is defined in terms of production rules. Additionally, the production-rule-based approach provides good support for the parallel development of different subsystems, as well as providing for the specification of control flows between and within subsystems (brokers).

In comparison with the work done in the field of extensible database management systems [1], our approach bridges the gap between the analysis and design phase on one hand and realization on the other, whereas the known extensible DBMSs only address the issue of realization and leave more implementation work to the DBI.

Second, we have described an approach for realizing ACTA specifications of transaction models based on the broker/subsystem approach. This approach is transformational since it translates (logical) ACTA-rules into production rules. The transformation in turn is rule-based, resulting in a high degree of flexibility. Due to the rule-based transformation, we can cope with new dependencies that might be defined within the ACTA framework. A similar approach based on transformation of specifications into production rules is followed for the integrity enforcement subsystem [21].

One of our ultimate goals (developing a construction method in general and supporting the construction of transaction management subsystems in particular) is to support the choice among a broad variety of techniques for transaction management (mainly, concurrency control). To that end, we will have to investigate in greater detail how the broker-based approach can support the selection of artifacts from a (DBMS) software information base.

Acknowledgements

The work of A. Geppert has been supported by the Commission for the Support of Scientific Research (KWF), Switzerland.

References

1. Carey M, Haas L. Extensible Database Management Systems. ACM SIGMOD Record 19:4, 1990, pp 54-60.

2. Chrysanthis PK. ACTA, A Framework For Modeling And Reasoning About Extended Transactions. PhD Thesis, Technical Report 91-26, Department of Computer Science, University of Pittsburgh, November 1991.

3. Unland R, Schlageter G. A Transaction Manager Development Facility For Non Standard Database Systems. In: Elmagarmid AK (ed) Database Transaction Models For Advanced Applications. Morgan Kaufmann Publishers, 1992, pp 399-466.

4. Dittrich KR, Geppert A, Goebel V, Nittel S, Scherrer S. KIDS: A Declarative Approach to DBMS Construction. In: Spaccapietra S (ed) Proc. SI-Conf. on Database Research in Switzerland, Lausanne, September 1991, pp 176-185.

5. Biggerstaff TJ, Richter C. Reusability Framework, Assessment, and Directions. IEEE Software, July 1987, pp 41-49.

6. Dayal U. Active Database Management Systems. Proc. 3rd Intl. Conf. on Data and Knowledge Bases, Jerusalem, 1988.

7. Gatziu S, Geppert A, Dittrich KR. Integrating Active Mechanisms into an Object-Oriented Database System. In: Kanellakis PC, Schmidt JW (eds) Proc. 3rd Intl. Workshop on Database Programming Languages (DBPL), Nafplion, Greece, August 1991, Morgan Kaufmann Publishers, pp 399-415.

8. *The Common Object Request Broker: Architecture and Specification.* OMG Document 91.12.1, Revision 1.1, Object Management Group and X/Open, 1992.

9. Chrysanthis PK, Ramamritham K. ACTA: The Saga Continues. In: Elmagarmid AK (ed.) Database Transaction Models For Advanced Applications. Morgan Kaufmann Publishers, 1992, pp 346-397.

10. Pu C, Kaiser GE, Hutchinson N. Split-Transaction for Open-Ended Activities. Proc. Intl. Conf. on Very Large Data Bases, 1988, pp 26-37.

11. Bernstein PA, Hadzilacos V, Goodman N. Concurrency Control and Recovery in Database Systems. Addison-Wesley, 1987.

12. Buchmann A, Oezsu MT, Hornick M, Georgakopoulos D, Manola FA. A Transaction Model For Active Distributed Object Systems. In: Elmagarmid AK (ed.) Database Transaction Models For Advanced Applications. Morgan Kaufmann Publishers, 1992, pp 123-158.

13. Attie PC, Singh MP, Sheth A,Rusinkiewicz M. Specifying and Enforcing Intertask Dependencies. Proc. Intl. Conf. on Very Large Data Bases, August 1993.

142

14. Buchmann AP, Branding H, Kudrass T, Zimmermann J. REACH: A REal-Time, ACtive and Heterogeneous Mediator System. Bulletin of the IEEE TC on Data Engineering 15:1-4, 1992, pp 44-47.

15. Garcia-Molina H, Salem K. Sagas. Proc. Intl. ACM-SIGMOD Conf. on Management of Data, 1987, pp 249-259.

16. Ceri S, Widom J. Deriving Production Rules for Constraint Maintenance. Proc. Intl. Conf. on Very Large Data Bases, 1990, pp 566-577.

17. Eswaran KP, Gray JN, Lorie RA, Traiger IL. The Notions of Consistency and Predicate Locks in a Database System. Communications of the ACM 19:11, 1976, pp 624-633.

18. Kotz AM, Dittrich KR, Mülle JA. Supporting Semantic Rules by a Generalized Event/Trigger Mechanism. Proc. Intl. Conf. on Extending Database Technology, Venice, 1988, pp 76-91.

19. Dayal U, Hsu M, Ladin R. Organizing Long-Running Activities with Triggers and Transactions. Proc. Intl. ACM-Conf. on Management of Data, 1990, pp 204-214.

20. Branding H, Buchmann A, Kudrass T, Zimmermann J. Rules in an Open System: The REACH Rule System. First Intl. Workshop on Rules in Database Systems, Edinburgh, August/September 1993.

21. Scherrer S, Dittrich KR. Towards an Integrity Model Specification Language. Technical Report 93.13, Institut für Informatik, Universität Zürich, April 1993.

Transaction Management to Support Rule Based Database Applications*

Christine Danner, Michael Ranft

Forschungszentrum Informatik (FZI)

Haid-und-Neu-Straße 10-14

D-76131 Karlsruhe, Germany

email: danner|ranft@fzi.de

Abstract

This article describes the design of a transaction management dedicated to database integrated rule systems. Especially, we look at an object management system which has to integrate several inference mechanisms. The transaction management of such a system has to support various integration architectures equally well with respect to *easy and effortless coupling* of database and rule system as well as *efficient rule evaluation*.

In the following we develop a classification of inference mechanisms and parallelism in database integrated production rule systems. Thereafter, we describe a transaction management which supports different rule systems that can be described by our classification scheme.

1 Introduction

In a design environment, the database system enables communication and cooperation of integrated tools via shared data. The integration of knowledge based tools puts additional new requirements on the database management. *Openness* and *extensibility* are major issues in this context, because new demands arise permanently. Extensibility with respect to the integration of rule based tools means especially that new rule types and new rule evaluation mechanisms can be defined. An open environment should not restrict the knowledge representation and inferencing strategies used by integrated tools.

Nevertheless, the integration of tools, of rule based systems in our case, should be supported explicitly by the system so that the implementation effort for the integration itself is bounded on an acceptable level. Therefore, the system JOKER[1] ([6]) is being developed. As part of a data handling component for CAx frameworks it is easily extensible by different inference mechanisms. The integration effort will be reduced, because basic generic mechanisms are

---

*This work was supported by the EC and the German BMFT. The work of the first author has been funded by the EC within the ESPRIT project 7364 JESSI-Common-Frame. The second author was supported by BMFT grant No. 01 IS 104 A/7

[1] JCF Object oriented Knowledge Representation and Management Component

provided which can be used by a broad range of rule systems (namely production rule systems) to implement their specific needs. We therefore call our approach an extensible KBMS toolkit.

This paper describes the design of a critical component of JOKER, the transaction facility. The transaction management deals with concurrency control (also called synchronization) and recovery. In the following we will concentrate on synchronization which serves for the isolation of concurrent applications of a database system such that multiple applications can run in parallel without creating inconsistent states in the database (e.g., by overwriting each others data).

When developing a transaction manager for a system like the one we outlined above, two main goals have to be achieved:

- **Easy Integration**: it has to offer sufficient and adequate functionality to ensure semantic correctness and to provide flexible means for inference control to support an easy coupling with the database system

- **Efficiency:** it has to be efficient, because the synchronization mechanisms of the database system have a strong influence on the performance

By integrating different rule systems[2] with the database management system (DBMS), we face the problem that these systems vary very much and therefore have distinct requirements with respect to synchronization, basically because of two main reasons:

- Different degrees of integration.

  For example since some rule systems were developed independently from the DBMS while others are implemented using the DBMS, integration of the latter ones will probably be more tight. In a loosely coupled system the inference takes place outside of the database system, which only serves as storage component for a persistent management of the knowledge base. In this case, the inference mechanism can be seen as an application transaction like any other application transaction. Of course, it can put requirements on the transaction management comparable to other non standard applications, derived from a long duration or the processing of very large amounts of data (like e.g. the requirement for intermediate savepoints to save partial results while suspending an expert system consultation).

  In tightly coupled systems the rule system is an integral part of the database system. The inference mechanisms operate directly on data structures which are managed by the DBMS. The notion of tight coupling comprises again different coupling architectures. The decisive point for us is that an interface to the internal functions of the inference mechanism is available, so that smaller working units of the inference can be mapped onto transactions. A consequence thereof is that not only synchronization with other applications is required but also rule system internal concurrency control can be implemented by the database transaction management.

---

[2]For a description of various production systems see e.g. [4].

- Application of different inference mechanisms by the rule system.

  Among others, the inference strategy being used in a rule system depends on the task of the system. For example, depending on the kind of problem and the complexity to solve it, various search strategies including heuristics could be applied and efficiency requirements could suggest a parallel processing of certain evaluation steps.

  In a tightly coupled rule/database system we expect that the transaction management is aware of the inference mechanisms and provides adequate support for this extended database service.

Therefore, the synchronization component not just has to be comfortable and efficient but also has to be flexible enough to reach these goals for all the integrated rule systems simultaneously. To solve the problem it is necessary to develop a schematic description of the rule systems to be integrated with the DBMS, to classify their requirements with respect to the rule transaction model, according to which the best suited transaction mechanisms can be determined. Since there is no work done in this direction, as far as we know, we will propose such a classification scheme for production rule systems where we classify rule inference mechanisms according to their requirements on synchronization. We will then discuss the appropriateness of well understood existing synchronization mechanisms to meet these requirements.

Based on this knowledge we can design a synchronization component which should meet all the requirements of production rule systems and therefore supports the integration of different systems according to our initial goals of an easy integration and run time efficiency.

The rest of the paper is organized as follows: The next section discusses other relevant work. In section 3 the basic production system model will be described. Section 4 contains our classification of database integrated production systems with respect to transaction relevant issues. Besides giving a short introduction to transaction management, we discuss in section 5 the mapping of rule execution to transaction models and develop the design of a flexible transaction management supporting various rule systems. Section 6 summarizes the results and provides an outlook on future work.

2 Related Work

The topic of rule execution within database transactions has recently been dealt with in the area of active database systems and other database integrated production rule systems. In active database systems this integrated rule system processes so called event condition action (ECA) rules which are triggered by data base internal or external events. In [30, 14], and [23] triggered actions form a linear extension of the triggering (user) transaction, whereas in most active database systems single rules are executed in transactions ([15, 17, 10, 5]). Such a rule transaction can be a nested subtransaction of the triggering transaction or an independent top level transaction. A sophisticated execution model with several coupling modes between triggering and triggered (trans)action was developed for the HiPAC active database system ([15]).

Rule transactions are also used in database integrated production rule systems to implement a concurrent rule execution for efficiency reasons. In the work of [27] and [28] the semantics of a sequential production system with a syntactic conflict resolution strategy is used as the correctness criterion for concurrent rule execution. Both approaches propose a locking mechanism for synchronization.

Another solution to the synchronization problem of concurrent rule transactions was proposed in the context of a rule based design environment in [2]. A combination of static pre-analysis of rule interferences and dynamic semantic based concurrency control ensures correctness in this approach.

It is common to all previous work that each transaction model has been developed for a certain rule system. The proposed transaction managers ensure correctness of a specific rule system, but would likely be insufficient if other semantics of rule systems should be implemented. For example, none of the rule transaction models we know respects all causal dependencies which are possible between rule transactions. Whereas active database systems focus on the relationships between triggering and triggered (trans)action, work on parallel rule transaction execution emphasizes the aspect of semantic correctness through serializability.

Further aspects of duration and structure of inference processes in database transactions have not been taken into consideration so far.

Additionally, we found that there was no systematic discussion of synchronization aspects in rule transaction models. Beneath giving such a systematic mapping of inference strategies to transaction mechanisms, our work aims at a combination and extension of existing rule transaction models to develop a transaction management which is suitable to support several rule execution models with different semantics at the same time.

3 Production Systems

In this chapter we will give a short introduction to the general production system model which describes the execution model of all rule systems to be integrated in our environment. We base this model on the descriptions of production systems in [19, 25]. A production system consists of a set of (production) rules, a data base, and a control system. A production rule is of the form:

if condition then action

The control system implements algorithms (also called strategies) for the selection of rules, to control their applicability according to their conditions, and for the execution of rules according to their action parts. We shall distinguish several varieties of production systems, which differ in the kinds of control systems they use, in the next section.

The basic algorithm for problem solving of a production system operates in a three phased cycle, named **recognize act cycle**, consisting of a match, select, and execute phase. This cycle is executed until the database fulfills a certain termination condition.

The task of the **match phase** is to determine all applicable rules, i.e. the procedure

match ({rules}, {facts}, {events})

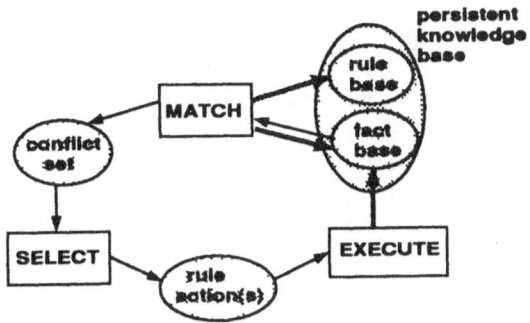

Figure 1: Recognize Act Cycle of a database integrated production system

returns as result the

$conflict - set =$

$\{< r, \{f\} > \mid$ condition of rule r is fulfilled by the set of facts $\{f\}\}$.

The set $\{Events\}$ describes those events that trigger the match process. In active systems these can be arbitrary database operations as well as external events. With incremental match algorithms in forward chaining systems (e.g.,[9]) these are just the modifications on fact objects done by executed rule actions. Incremental match algorithms store results of the matching process (e.g., partial matches of facts and rule conditions) across cycles so that they only have to process the actual modifications in each cycle. Those *state-saving* algorithms are more efficient than *non-state-saving* algorithms which have to implement a complete comparison of all patterns of all rules against the whole fact base in each cycle.

One of these rule instantiations is then selected for execution in the **select phase**, whereby different conflict resolution strategies can be applied to determine the sequence of rule execution. Without further knowledge, rules can be selected arbitrarily or following a first-in/first-out or last-in/first-out strategy, thereby implementing a breadth-first, respectively depth-first search.

In the **execute phase** a selected rule, i.e. its instantiated action, is applied, leading eventually to modifications of the data base.

Figure 1 shows the way a production rule system works in a database environment. Access to the knowledge base happens during match and execute phase (light arrows), whereby the match accesses are read-only. The dark arrows represent the data and control flow in the recognize act cycle.

The semantics of rule programs can be described by an execution graph (see figure 2) which shows all possible rule executions, starting from an initial state (the root node). One selected execution is then represented by a root-originating path to a leaf node (see the marked nodes in figure 2). In this representation, different leaf nodes do not necessarily stand for different states[3].

Production rules can be applied in two directions, forward and backward. If the goal of a problem is described as the termination condition and descriptions

---

[3] In a confluent system, all leaf nodes would have to represent the same result.

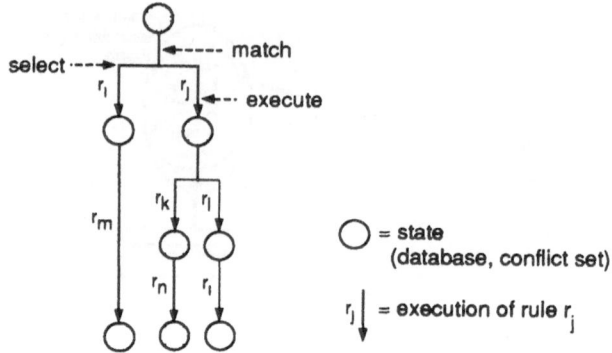

Figure 2: Rule execution graph with a marked selected execution sequence

of states are employed as the production system data base, the system works in a forward chaining manner. If, instead, the problem goal descriptions are employed as the production system data base, this is called backward chaining. Combinations of forward and backward chaining either allow changing the directions during evaluation (like e.g. the rule system of the expert system shell KEE [16] or the POSTGRES rule manager [26]) or transform the rules like the magic set transformation [29] to combine the advantages of both strategies.

4 Classification of Database Integrated Inference Mechanisms

For a general description and classification of inference strategies in production systems see for example [19]. Here, we concentrate on two criteria which are of special relevance to the transaction management: search strategies and parallelism in production systems. Within these two classes, **revocable search strategies**, respectively **sequential systems**, are of greatest importance for the design of the transaction component.

4.1 Search Strategies

The behavior of the control system of a production system during rule selection can be regarded as a search process ([19]). If one rule is selected in a state and the system does never return to this state, this is called an **irrevocable search strategy** ([19]). Irrevocable strategies are adequate for the evaluation of commutative rule sets, where the result is independent of the rule application order.

In contrast, **revocable search strategies** allow the return to a former state and the application of further rules, i.e. a tentative rule selection. Revocable strategies can be further subdivided in:

1. Backtracking Algorithms:

State and alternatively applicable rules are put in a stack (like e.g. in PROLOG interpreters)[4]

2. Graph Search Algorithms:
   (sometimes extensive) investigations are made about the consequences of applicable rules and knowledge about erroneous paths is explicitly stored

Going beyond simple depth first or breadth first searches graph algorithms can also incorporate heuristic information in form of evaluation functions for the alternatives to reduce the search space.

4.2 Parallelism

The basic production model of section 3 describes the semantics of sequential rule evaluation, i.e. in each cycle only one rule is selected for execution.

To increase efficiency the implementation of production systems can use parallel algorithms ([13]) and set oriented constructs in database rule languages ([12]). The correctness of a concurrent rule execution is then determined by the semantics of the sequential system. We call all production systems with this semantics **sequential**, independently of parallelism in the implementation. A definition of the correctness in concurrent rule systems through the equivalence of paths in the execution graph with a sequential execution is given in [1] and [28].

Non-sequential systems employ conceptual concurrency, i.e. they execute consciously several (or all) applicable rules and define their own correctness criteria for concurrent rule execution. Non-sequential systems are adequate for decomposable problems where e.g. evaluation can be done on several partitions of the initial database in parallel. Their execution model divides the execution process in concurrent and independent (or possibly loosely cooperating) processes, where each of them realizes its own recognize act cycle. Examples are also demons and triggers in active systems which process their actions independently, i.e. for each triggering event an execution process is started. Gupta calls this kind of parallelism between cooperating or alternatively investigating production systems *application parallelism* ([13]).

Sequential systems employ concurrency to increase efficiency. Various possibilities for parallelism in sequential systems are shown schematically in Fig. 3. We distinguish between *intra phase parallelism* (within a phase of the recognize act cycle) and *inter phase parallelism* (across phases).

- **intra phase parallelism**

  Since the amount of work done in the select phase is rather small (about 5 % of the whole execution time [13]) there is no indication to parallelize the selection.

  According to the parameters of the match procedure (see section 3) we can differentiate parallelism within the **match phase** in three aspects:

---

[4]Because of this last-in-first-out strategy the term backtracking is sometimes used as a synonym to depth first search.

150

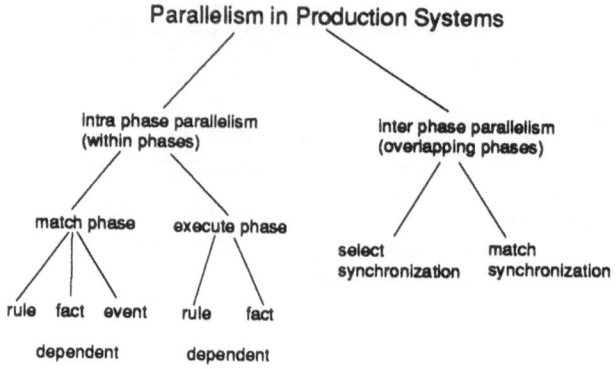

Figure 3: Survey of Possibilities for Parallelism

1. rule dependent: parallel matching for several partitions of the rule base (up to single rules) (this is called *production parallelism* in [13])

2. fact dependent: parallel matching for several partitions of the fact base (e.g., *culprit rules* in [20])

3. event dependent: parallel matching for triggering events or fact base modifications (*action parallelism* in [13])

All three kinds of parallelism can be combined.

In the **execute phase** selected rule instantiations of the conflict set are executed. According to the elements of the conflict set we find two criteria for differentiation:

1. rule dependent: parallel execution of several rule actions (called *inter production concurrency* in [27]); we want to emphasize the special case where several rules are instantiated by the same combination of facts which is equivalent to simultaneous triggering of different actions by the same event in active systems and call this *event concurrency*.

2. fact dependent: if there exist several instantiations of one rule their actions are executed concurrently (which is called *intra production concurrency* in [27]); this kind of parallelism is supported by set oriented language constructs ([12]).

Both aspects of parallelism can again be combined.

- **inter phase parallelism**

is reached by dropping synchronization points within the basic execution model. We speak of *select synchronization* if there is a synchronization at the beginning of the select phase, i.e. the selection takes place only after all the matches of this cycle are terminated. If the beginning of the match phase is synchronized, i.e. possible parallel match processes are started concurrently only after the execute phase of the previous cycle is terminated, we call this a *match synchronization*. A system which does neither select nor match synchronization is called *asynchronous*.

5 Transactions

This section gives a short introduction to the notion of transactions in database systems and to the extensions of conventional transaction mechanisms which are most relevant for rule systems. For an exhaustive discussion of transaction management issues see for example [3]. We also will discuss the mapping of rule execution onto transactions, regarding the previously described inference strategies. And we describe the design of the JOKER transaction management with respect to the developed mapping.

In general, transactions allow to write database application programs neglecting system crashes and concurrent applications, while they guarantee that results of completely processed applications are retained and that the database is in a consistent state. These characteristics have been described as the ACID property of transactions. ACID stands for *Atomicity, Consistency, Isolation,* and *Durability*. We concentrate in the following on the isolation property, which ensures that transactions only work with results of successfully completed transactions, because only their results are respected consistent. Data objects which are accessed by not yet completed transactions have therefore to be protected against concurrent accesses of other transactions. This is achieved by the synchronization mechanisms of a transaction management.

In our scenario, the synchronization component ensures that the evaluation of rule programs concurrently with other (rule based) applications leads to correct results, and enables a high performance and semantically correct behavior of rule systems exploiting concurrency internally.

5.1 Synchronization Mechanisms

The most popular mechanism to achieve isolation is *locking*. Each application has to lock the data it accesses. Usually, a distinction is made between *read* and *write locks*. Read locks allow parallel access of multiple reading applications, whereas write locks reserve a data item exclusively for one application. In general the so-called strict two-phase-locking protocol (2PL) is used. It means that locks can be acquired during transaction processing and will not be released until the transactions end[5]. For applications of long duration, isolation by locking causes long waiting times for other blocked applications.

This is avoided by the *optimistic concurrency control* (OCC) [18], where all applications arbitrarily access their (local copies of) data and in a validation phase at the transaction's end have to check whether there is an access conflict with another concurrently executing transaction. If so, one of the two conflicting transactions must be aborted. If lots of work has been done in a transaction aborting it may not be desirable, but if a backtracking strategy is used rollbacks are frequent and OCC can be of good aid.

---

[5] In the rest of this paper we mean strict two-phase-locking when we say locking.

152

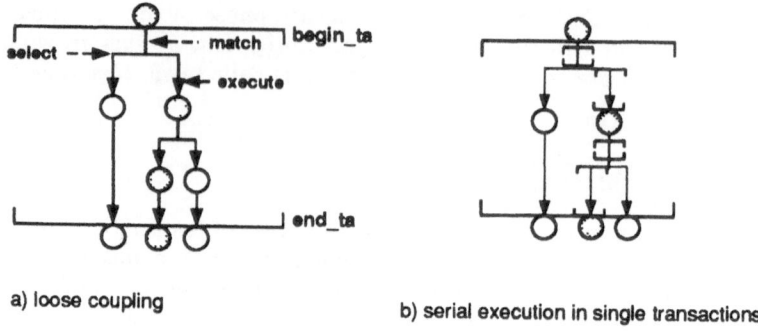

a) loose coupling

b) serial execution in single transactions

Figure 4: Rule execution in transactions

5.2 Extensions

To achieve transaction structuring and to support parallel processing within a transaction, the concept of *nested transactions* has been developed. Within one transaction (*parent transaction*) further transactions (*subtransactions*) can be started, which may run in parallel. It is distinguished between *closed* nesting, where the results of the subtransaction are inherited by the parent transaction, and *open* nesting, where the results are public to other transactions, once the subtransaction has committed. In case of locking as synchronization mechanism this means the locks will be inherited by the parent transaction (closed nesting) or released (open nesting). Because of our isolation requirements we consider in the following only the case of closed nesting.

5.3 Mapping Rule Execution on Transactions

Following the classification given in section 4 we will now demonstrate how different coupling and inference strategies of database integrated rule systems can be related to transactions and what kinds of problems arise.

Starting point is the execution of a whole application within one single flat (but maybe long lasting) transaction, like it would be done in a loosely coupled system (Fig. 4a).

In a more tightly coupled system this transaction would be divided in several transactions, e.g. for single phases of the recognize act cycle. If there are multiple applications running on the database which we assume to be the usual case, it has to be ensured that the rule evaluation as a whole is one atomic unit. A simple way to achieve this is to model the complete application as a nested transaction where the single phases form subtransactions (Fig. 4b).

In the following we describe the transactional support for the inference strategies described above and distinguish again between search strategies and parallelism in rule evaluation.

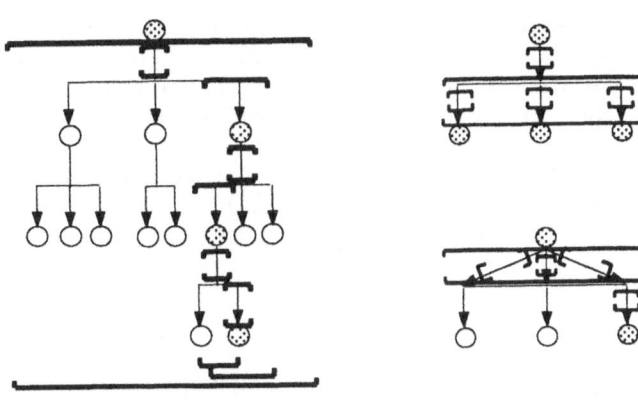

| a) Backtracking with nested transactions: reset by abort | b) Intra phase parallelism in the execute and match phase |

Figure 5: Rule execution in nested transactions

5.3.1 Search strategies

Whereas irrevocable search strategies do not impose further requirements on transactional support, the implementation of revocable search strategies can be supported well by the transaction management. It is advantageous to let the transaction management carry out the reset: the rule system does not need to maintain the reset information and in the case of system failures consistent database states are guaranteed. This could be achieved using nested transactions or transaction internal save points.

With *nested transactions* the execution path is encapsulated in a subtransaction and the rollback to previous states is done by aborting the appropriate subtransactions (see Fig. 5a).

With *save points* within transactions each branch of the rule execution tree is marked by a save point to which the system may return.

Being implemented with nested transactions, revocable strategies can also process alternative execution paths in parallel within sibling subtransactions, e.g. to search for alternative solutions.

JOKER Transaction Management

Since nested transactions support backtracking and - as will be seen in the following - also concurrency of and within the rule processing phases, nesting is an essential feature of the JOKER transaction manager.

5.3.2 Concurrent Rule Execution

We will not consider the application parallelism of *non-sequential systems* in the following, because their semantics is defined individually and a model of cooperating expert systems is out of the scope of this paper.

The correctness criterion for concurrent rule execution in *sequential systems* can be mapped straight-forward to the serializability property of transactions, if each single rule execution is modeled as one transaction ([28, 22]). A more flexibel rule transaction model would allow for various mappings of rules to transactions. In the following transaction models for different parallelization strategies will be discussed, referring to the description of the recognize act cycle in section 3. The select phase will not be considered any further, since a parallel select would only make sense if extremely large conflict sets are to be treated with.

5.3.3 Intra Phase Parallelism

The intuitive approach to ensure atomicity of the single phases is to model them individually in one transaction.

Activities within a single phase can be parallelized by distributing the parallel branches in sibling *subtransactions* (Fig. 5b). Thereby a parallel execution is achieved and at the same time atomicity of the whole phase is ensured by means of the enclosing parent transaction.

With respect to the match phase there are no problems with phase internal parallelism, because all accesses are read only, i.e. there are no conflicts between match transactions. In the contrary, concurrent modifying accesses during the execution phase have to be synchronized. This can be reached with the help of 2PL, but this method is very restrictive and restrains therefore the possible parallelism ([28]).

Furthermore, even with 2PL there is the problem with concurrent action execution that the modifications of a transaction could invalidate the condition corresponding to a concurrently executing rule action, because the condition evaluation was already performed in the previously terminated match phase and the locks were released at the end of the match phase.

For example, if there are two rules R1 and R2 in the conflict set with their conditions C1 and C2 as well as actions A1 and A2, and A1 invalidates condition C2, then A2 must not be executed any more. Valid execution sequences are only A2 A1 or A1, resp. A2 alone. The synchronization of both (trans)actions has to avoid that A2 is performed after A1.

This can be realized by locking the data. Thereby, all data used in the condition are locked, which prevents all actions from changing the data concurrently. Checking the condition immediately before the action takes place also reveals an already happened invalidation of the condition. The combination of condition check and action processing in one transaction is common for systems with match synchronization (for example see [28]). If match and execute phases are processed in sequence or select synchronization is used, it leads to additional overhead. In [22] only the rule's action is implemented in a transaction, in which the first step is to lock all relevant data objects during a kind of re-evaluation of the rule's condition.

Beneath the fact that 2PL is restrictive with respect to the possible concurrency and the problem of additional overhead due to doubled condition evaluations, another problem with locking is, that the rule system cannot influence the rules chosen to succeed. The rule that happens to lock a data item first will succeed. Rule systems using heuristics on the other hand need to have influence on rule ordering.

A synchronization method which could offer this influence is the *optimistic concurrency control* (OCC) method. Using OCC, the condition has to be rechecked before the action, too, if not match synchronization is used. During the validation phase of the OCC transaction it checks whether there are conflicts with concurrently executed, already finished transactions (e.g. because the data used in its condition has changed). In this case it will be aborted.

Besides this *backward-oriented concurrency control*, a *forward-oriented concurrency control* where not only finished but also still running rules are checked for conflicts is also possible. For conflicts with active rules, in contrast to [22], we have the choice which rule to abort[6].

The enhanced influence offered by optimistic concurrency has to be paid with lower system performance if conflicts between concurrently processed rules are common. In this case, a lot of processing power is spent on rules that will be aborted later on while in low conflict environments OCC offers better performance than 2PL as is shown in [7]. Also, OCC needs all accessed data to be copied, to allow parallel accesses without interference.

JOKER Transaction Management

The choice for one or the other method has to be done with respect to the used search strategy and the expected number of conflicts: rule processing which encounters many conflicts or is biased to a "broad" search strategy will use locking since conflicting operations are only blocked and can be processed later. Additionally, due to the high conflict rate, a better performance than with OCC can be expected. Rule systems that use "depth-first" or graph search strategies and expect low conflict rates will prefer OCC which offers more influence and better performance under these circumstances.

Since we want to support a broad variety of rule systems, the JOKER transaction management should offer *both* synchronization methods (strict 2PL and OCC) to cope with the above described problem of invalidation of concurrently execute productions as well as with flexibility requirements of rule selection and performance requirements. Each single rule system can then choose its most appropriate solution. Therefore, the methods have to be integrated, which is shown in [21].

5.3.4 Inter Phase Parallelism

Inter phase parallelism withdraws the division of the execute and match phase into two independent sequential transactions. Instead, there is a flow of information between these two phases, which cannot be dealt with within conventional transactions because of their isolation property. Therefore, the transaction has to be extended to spawn the match execute pair.

On the other side, the match phase is often accomplished by state saving algorithms (see section 3), which store relevant information across cycles. This means, that a database integrated match process using a two phase locking protocol would probably lock its data for possibly long times and thereby block all modifying operations (namely the executes). In this case, a decoupling of match and execute operations should be possible even in the case of inter phase parallelism.

---

[6]For example, by providing each rule with a priority and aborting the least important rule.

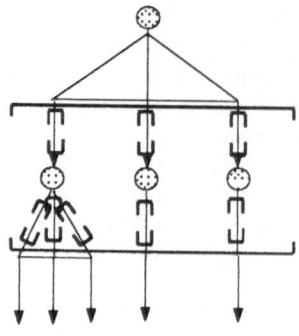
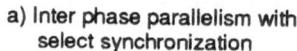
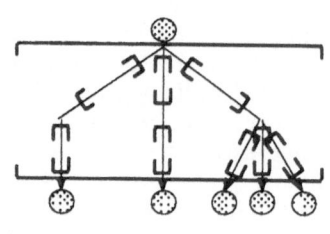

a) Inter phase parallelism with
select synchronization

a) Inter phase parallelism with
match synchronization

Figure 6: rule execution with inter phase parallelism

JOKER Transaction Management

A possibility which was also employed in the HiPAC and DOM rule transaction models ([15, 5]) is to introduce a so-called *Abort-Dependency* between the triggering and the triggered operation (transaction). An abort dependency forces a dependent transaction to abort if the transaction it depends on aborts. This kind of transaction management is depicted in Fig. 6. Abort-Dependencies have the disadvantage of higher overhead due to the dependency management and the more complex commit and abort processing.

Using dependencies the phases of the RAC can be decoupled. Therefore, dependency relations will be offered in JOKER. These relations can be realized using the Saga model of Garcia-Molina [11] or the ConTract model of Reuter [24].

5.3.5 Variations of Inter Phase Parallelism

As described above, there are several possibilities to overlap match and execute phase where the beginning of the select phase or the beginning of the match phase serves as synchronization point.

Select Synchronization In a system with merely select synchronization concurrently performed execute operations trigger match operations. This leads to an overlapping of the execute phase with the match phase of the succeeding cycle (Fig. 6a)). Thereby, two problems arise to gain a correct rule evaluation, i.e. an execution equivalent to a sequential execution:

- match operations which have been triggered by a not yet terminated execute operation could be invalidated by a later abort of this execute operation

- match operations which have been triggered by successfully terminated execute operations could be invalidated by still active parallel execute operations

Match synchronization   With this kind of overlapping phases the synchronization at the end of the match phase is dropped and match operations cause directly the execution of the instantiated actions (Fig. 6b)). That means a parallelization of match and execute phase within one cycle. It is obvious that the same problems as with the select synchronization occur.

Asynchronous systems   In asynchronous rule systems there is neither select nor match synchronization. The problems of both parallelization strategies described above with respect to invalidation, resp. hindering of match and execute operations, occur.

JOKER Transaction Management

The subsequent invalidation of a match is already known from the intra phase parallelism and can be solved by the methods described there (combination of locking and optimistic cc). The invalidation of match operations by an abort of the triggering execute operation can be solved using nested transactions, which are also employed for the revocable search strategies. Using nesting, a triggered operation is processed as subtransaction of the triggering operation. Another possibility is to use the before mentioned abort dependencies between the triggering and the triggered transaction.

Concluding, the JOKER transaction manager will offer nested transactions that can use locking or optimistic cc as the synchronization strategy. The transaction manager will also provide means for defining dependencies between transactions. The mechanisms together will enable the JOKER system to support differing rule systems appropriately.

6   Summary and Future Work

In this paper we have provided a description of rule systems which are to be integrated into an open design environment with help of the JOKER system. Thereby, we collected classifying properties of database integrated production rule systems which are relevant for a transaction management to support rule execution. This classification then served as a basis for deriving requirements and identifying problems which have to be solved by the transaction management. A first design for an adequate transaction management has been given.

This design includes the combination of optimistic and pessimistic synchronization protocols to support different search strategies. It also comprises extensions of flat transactions by nesting and by relationships between transactions. Thus, single rule evaluation phases can be decoupled and more concurrency achieved. The hypothesis that thereby a reasonable performance upgrade will be achieved will be proved by means of an analytic model.

So far we based the definition of access conflicts for synchronization between rule transactions on simple read and write conflicts. But this seems to be very restrictive, because not every modifying operation does necessarily invalidate the conditions of other rules which relate to the modified object. For example, to increase a number value of an attribute does surely not invalidate a greater-than-condition. An approach to increase concurrency here can be the employment of conflict definitions which know about the semantics of operations. For operations on relational databases this idea was already employed in [22]. Methods in object oriented database systems provide further possibilities due to their semantic richness.

We criticize previous work in the area of concurrent database integrated production systems in that they make simplifying assumptions about selection strategies. With the argument that most systems use a syntactic conflict resolution strategy (which is true for elder systems like OPS5 [4]) and therefore do not prevent a certain rule sequence entirely, the concurrent execution is defined as correct as long as its result is the same as any of the possible sequential results. This ignores the consequences of the fact that there are sequential results which will never or with a very low probability be gained in the concurrent system. For example, with a conventional locking mechanism and match synchronization those rules will be given advantage to, which have a relatively short match phase and get their locks first.

A second disadvantage of locking models is that the incorporation of heuristics for search is difficult if not impossible. Therefore, we provide this possibility also in concurrent production systems using optimistic mechanisms with forward-oriented concurrency control.

Currently, we are implementing the proposed transaction manager, using a multi-level architecture and we are preparing a simulation model to study further the influence of different transaction management solutions on rule processing.

Acknowledgements

The authors would like to thank their colleagues within the database research group at FZI and the unknown referees for their valuable comments on former versions of this paper.

References

[1] Aiken, A.; Widom,J.; Hellerstein, J.M. *Behavior of Database Production Rules: Termination, Confluence, and Observable Determinism* Proc. ACM SIGMOD, June 1992, San Diego, CA, pp.59-68

[2] Barghouti, N.S.; Kaiser, G.E. *Modelling Concurrency in Rule-Based Development Environments* IEEE Expert, Dec. 1990, pp.15-27

[3] Bernstein, P.A.; Hadzilacos, V.; Goodman, N. Concurrency Control and Recovery in Database Systems Addison-Wesley Reading MA, 1987

[4] Brownston, L.; Farrell, R.; Kant, E.; Martin, N. *Programming Expert Systems in OPS5 - An Introduction to Rule-Based Programming* Addison-Wesley Series in Artificial Intelligence, 1986

[5] Buchmann, A.; Özsu, M.T.; Hornick, M.; Georgakopoulos, D.; Manola, F.A. *A Transaction Model for Active Distributed Object Systems* in [8]

[6] Boss, B.; v. Bültzingsloewen, G.; Danner, C. *Integrating Rule Based Systems with JOKER* Proc. IDS-92, International Workshop on Data Base System Intellectualization, Kaliningrad, May 92, published in: System and Machines 5/6 1992

[7] Carey, M.J.; Muhanna, W.A. *The Performance of Multiversion Concurrency Control Algorithms* ACM Transactions on Computer Systems, 4(4), Nov. 1986, pp.338-378

[8] Elmagarmid, A. K. *Database Transaction Models for Advanced Applications* Morgan Kaufmann Series in Data Management Systems, San Marco, CA, 1992

[9] Forgy, C.L. *Rete: A Fast Algoritm for the Many Pattern/ Many Object Pattern Match Problem* Artificial Intelligence, 19-1, 1982, pp.17-37

[10] Gatziu, S.; Geppert, A.; Dittrich, K.R. *Integrating Active Concepts into an Object-Oriented Database System* Proc. 3rd Int. Workshop on Database Programming Languages (DBPL), Greece August 1991

[11] Garcia-Molina, H.; Salem, K. *Sagas* Proc. ACM SIGMOD Int. Conf. on Man. of Data, 1987, pp.249-259

[12] Gordin,D.N.; Pasik,A.J. *Set-Oriented Constructs: From Rete Rule Bases to Database Systems* Proc. ACM SIGMOD Int. Conf. on Man. of Data, 1991, pp.60-67

[13] Gupta, Anoop *Parallelism in Production Systems* Morgan Kaufmann, Research Notes in Artificial Intelligence, 1987

[14] Hanson,E.N. *An Initial Report on The Design of Ariel: A DBMS With an Integrated Production Rule System* SIGMOD RECORD, 18-3, Sept.1989, pp.12-19

[15] Hsu, M.; Ladin, R.; McCarthy, D.R. *An Execution Model for Active Data Base Management Systems* Proc. 3rd Int. Conf. on Data and Knowledge Bases, Israel 1988, pp.171-179

[16] *KEE Version 3.0* Technical Manuals, Intellicorp 1986

[17] Kotz, A. *Triggermechanismen in Datenbanksystemen* Informatik-Fachberichte, Bd. 201, 1989

[18] Kung, H.T.; Robinson, J.T. *On Optimistic Methods for Concurrency Control* ACM Transactions on Database Systems 6(2), 1981, pp.213-226

[19] Nilsson, N.J. *Priciples of Artificial Intelligence* Springer Verlag Berlin-Heidelberg-New York 1982

[20] Pasik, Alexander J. *A Source-to-Source Transformation for Increasing Rule-Based System Parallelism* IEEE Trans. on Knowledge and Data Engineering, 4-4, Aug.1992, pp.336-343

[21] Ranft, M. *Integrating Multiple Concurrency Control Algorithms* In Proc. Workshop on Next Generation Information Technologies and Systems (NGITS'93), Haifa, Israel, June 1993

[22] Raschid, L.; Sellis, T.; Delis, A. *On the Concurrent Execution of Production Rules in A Database Implementation* Technical Report UMIACS-TR-91-125, University of Maryland, September 1991

[23] Raschid,L.; Su,S.Y.W. *A Transaction Oriented Mechanism to Control Processing in a Knowledge Base Management System* Proc. 2nd Int. Conf. on Expert Database Systems, Vienna, 1988, pp.353-373

[24] Reuter, A.; Wächter, H. *The ConTract Model* IEEE Data Engineering Bulletin 14(1), 1991, pp.39-43

[25] Rich,E. *Artificial Intelligence* McGraw-Hill Series in Artificial Intelligence, 1983

[26] Stonebraker,M.; Jhingram,A.; Goh,J.; Potamianos,S. *On Rules, Procedures, Caching and Views in Data Base Systems* Proc. ACM SIGMOD Int. Conf. on Man. of Data, 1990, pp.281-290

[27] Sellis,T.; Lin,C.-C.; Raschid,L. *Data Intensive Production Systems: The DIPS Approach* SIGMOD RECORD, 18-3, Sept.1989, pp.52-58

[28] Srivastava,J.; Hwang, K.-W.; Tan, J.S.E. *Parallelism in Database Production Systems* Proc. 6th Int. Conf. on Data Engineering, LA, Febr. 90, pp.121-128

[29] Ullman, J.D. *Principles of Database and Knowledge-Base Systems, Vol.II* Computer Science Press 1989

[30] Widom, J; Finkelstein, S.J. *A Syntax and Semantics for Set-Oriented Production Rules in Relational Database Systems* SIGMOD RECORD, 18-3, Sept.1989, pp.36-45

Analysis and Debugging of Active Rules

Better Termination Analysis for Active Databases

Elena Baralis
Politecnico di Torino
Torino, Italy

Stefano Ceri
Politecnico di Milano
Milano, Italy

Jennifer Widom
IBM Almaden Research Center
San Jose, CA, USA

Abstract

An important problem for the usability of active databases is to determine by syntactic analysis whether a given set of rules is guaranteed to terminate. Rule processing in active databases does not terminate when rules activate each other indefinitely. Previous approaches to termination analysis in active databases use very conservative algorithms to determine when rules may activate each other. In this paper we introduce an algebraic model for a class of active database rules and we present a theory by which we can determine, much less conservatively, when rules may activate each other. Hence our theory forms the basis of better termination analysis for active databases.

1 Introduction

Active databases provide a facility for defining rules which are activated when certain triggering events take place or certain conditions are met, and which perform actions that may change the database. Active database rules are available in a number of recent research prototypes and some commercial systems, e.g. [2, 7, 8, 11, 12, 13, 15, 17]. An important problem for the usability of active databases is to determine, when a set of rules is installed, that the rules always are guaranteed to terminate [1]. Termination is ensured when any database changes that activate rules yield rule processing that cannot execute forever, i.e. rules cannot continue to activate each other indefinitely.

In the context of production rules for expert systems, which are similar to active database rules, the termination problem is of less concern. The target of these systems is to perform inferencing and draw conclusions. Rule processing may last for hours, and the user may terminate an endless computation by interrupting the running program. The same behaviour is obviously unacceptable for active database systems, which usually support on-line query and transaction processing for multiple users.

Many active database systems "solve" the termination problem by limiting, at run-time, the number of rules that may be activated during one phase of rule processing [13, 17]. Unfortunately, there always might exist situations in which rule processing may exceed this limit even when it will eventually terminate, thus causing erroneous interruption. Hence, a compile-time approach to this problem is very useful, even though the general problem is undecidable. Previous compile-time approaches to the termination problem, e.g. [1], propose conservative analysis techniques that detect all the groups of rules that can potentially activate each other forever. The approach in [1] is very conservative, as only the type of the rule's action is used to infer information on activation, without taking into account any detailed semantics of rule conditions and actions. Using this approach, in practice the key role for the analysis is played by the rule programmer, who evaluates each group of rules potentially leading to infinite rule processing, exploiting his knowledge of the rule semantics to determine whether infinite execution really is possible.

In this paper we propose analysis techniques that are based on semantic properties of rules and hence are considerably stronger than those in [1]. Similar to [1], we build an *activation graph*, where cycles in the graph indicate rules that may activate each other indefinitely. However, the graphs built by our methods are much less conservative than those in [1], so cycles in our graphs are more likely to indicate a real possibility of nontermination.

For the description of active database rules we use an extension of relational algebra; the generality of this algebraic representation makes our results applicable to all relational active database rule systems regardless of their base language (which can be, e.g., SQL [17] or Quel [8, 14]). Rule conditions are expressed as queries, while rule actions contain algebraic descriptions of the operations performed on the database.

2 Active database rules

Active database rule languages can be grouped into languages in which the rules are *condition-based*, *event-based*, or both [9]. In condition-based rules, if the rule condition is true, then the rule is activated and is eligible for execution. In event-based rules, a set of events is specified that activate the rule; once activated, the rule also may include a condition which must be true if the rule is to be eligible for execution. In this work we propose a model and analysis techniques for the condition-based class of rules, but we plan to extend the approach to event-based rules.

The general structure of a condition-based rule can be written as:

condition → *actions*

In active databases, rule conditions usually are queries over the database, and rule actions usually are modifications on the database. Hence, in our rule model conditions and actions are both represented using relational algebra expressions. In the first part of the remainder of this section we describe the extensions to relational algebra which are required to represent rule conditions and actions. Then we describe the syntax and semantics of our rule model using this algebra. Finally, we give examples of how our rule model relates to existing active database rule languages.

2.1 Algebraic operations

Queries in SQL or Quel can be translated into relational algebra through the set of operations presented in the following, with the exception of the han-

op	description
π_A	projection over attributes A
σ_p	selection with predicate p
$\times$	cartesian product
$\cup$	union
$-$	difference
$\alpha_{A,B}$	attribute rename

Table 1: Basic operations

op	description
$\bowtie_p$	join with join predicate p
$\ltimes_p$	semi-join with join predicate p
$\ltimes_{\exists p}$	semi-join with non-existential predicate p
$FN[A' = a(A); B]$	tuple extension and aggregate function evaluation
$TE[A' = f(t)]$	tuple extension and arithmetic function evaluation

Table 2: Derived operations

dling of duplicates and ordering conditions (see [5, 10]); these features are not influential on the termination problem and will be disregarded in this paper. The introduction of the tuple extension operation (described below) allows us to represent SQL and Quel data modification statements (insert, delete and update).

The five basic operations of relational algebra [16] are presented in Table 1. In this table, A and B are attribute lists, p is a predicate built as a boolean expression of simple predicates, and α renames attributes A as B. Table 2 presents derived operations. In this table, A and A' denote attributes, B denotes an attribute list, a is an aggregate function, and f is a tuple function. Note that $R \bowtie_p S = \sigma_p(R \times S)$ and $R\ltimes_p S = \pi_{Schema(R)}(R \bowtie_p S)$. We discuss the other derived operations in more detail, then we present the modification operations.

2.1.1 Not-exists semi-join

The *not-exists semi-join* operation, $\ltimes_{\exists p}$, is introduced to model negative subqueries, which are frequent in rule definitions. This operation is defined as:

$$E_1 \ltimes_{\exists p} E_2 = E_1 - \pi_{attr(E_1)}(E_1 \bowtie_p E_2)$$

Note that relation difference can be written as a particular case of $\ltimes_{\exists p}$, imposing equality on all the attributes: $R - S = R\ltimes_{\exists schema(R)=schema(S)} S$. Therefore, difference will not be considered in the remainder of the paper.

2.1.2 Aggregate and tuple functions

The tuple extension operation allows us to extend a relation R with a new attribute. We have:

- The FN operation, which computes aggregate functions (such as **max**, **min**, **avg**, **sum**, **count**) over partitions of R

- The TE operation, which computes arithmetic expressions applied to each individual tuple of R

The FN operation is a unary operation applied to a relation R with a given schema $schema(R)$; it produces a new relation with schema $schema(R) \cup A'$, defined as follows (see also [5]):

$$FN[A' = a(A); B]R = \bigcup_{\forall t \in R} a(A, \sigma_{B = t\,B} R)$$

where B is the set of attributes on which the relation R is partitioned; each group in the partition contains all the tuples with the same B value. a is an aggregate function which is applied to the (multiset of) values contained in the projection of each partition on attribute A, yielding one value for each partition; this value is entered into the attribute A' and added to each tuple of the partition. The attribute B in the specification of FN is optional; when it is omitted, no grouping is performed, and the aggregate function a is applied to the entire relation R, yielding one value; that value is entered into the attribute A' and added to each tuple of the relation.

The TE operation is a unary operation applied to a relation R with a given schema $schema(R)$; it produces a new relation with schema $schema(R) \cup A'$, defined as follows (similar to [4]):

$$TE[A' = f(A)]R = \bigcup_{\forall t \in R} f(A, t)$$

where f is a function which is applied to each tuple t of R (a conventional arithmetic function over attributes of t and constants), yielding one value for each tuple; this value is entered into the attribute A' and added to each tuple of R.

Often the result R' of the application of a TE operation to a relation R is made compatible in schema with R, by projecting A out of R' and then renaming A' to A, as follows: $\alpha_{A', A} \pi_{schema(R') - A} R'$. Such expression can be shortened by using A instead of A' in the TE operation: $TE[A = f(A)]R$.

2.1.3 Insert, delete, update operations

We represent data modification operations in relational algebra by characterizing operations in terms of the database state that they produce. Table 3 presents inserts, deletes, and updates by indicating the algebraic expressions that correspond to them and the way in which these expressions are applied to a relation R to produce a new value for R. We assume that each relation contains a primary key that cannot be updated. In Table 3, k denotes the primary key of R, p_k is an equi-join predicate on k, A_u is the schema of E_u and includes k and the updated attributes, and $A_r = (schema(R) - A_u) \cup k$ includes k and the attributes which are not updated.

Operation	Algebraic expression	New database state
insert	E_{ins}	$R \cup E_{ins}$
delete	E_{del}	$R \triangleright\!\!\!\triangleleft_{\overline{\exists}p_k} E_{del}$
update	$E_{upd} = < E_c, E_u >$	$R \triangleright\!\!\!\triangleleft_{\overline{\exists}p_k} E_c \cup (\pi_{A_r} R \triangleright\!\!\!\triangleleft_{p_k} E_c) \bowtie_{p_k} E_u$

Table 3: Algebraic description of insert, delete, and update operations

Insert operation. An insert operation is denoted by the expression E_{ins} that defines the tuples be inserted (either a set of constant tuples or the result of an algebraic expression). The schema of E_{ins} must coincide with the schema of R.

Delete operation. A delete operation is denoted by the expression E_{del} that defines the tuples be deleted; the schema of E_{del} must coincide with the schema of R.

Update operation. The pair $< E_c, E_u >$ represents an update operation, where E_c and E_u are algebraic expressions representing the selection condition and updated tuples respectively. We denote the pair as E_{upd}. The expression that describes the new state of R after an update operation contains two terms:

1. The first term $R \triangleright\!\!\!\triangleleft_{\overline{\exists}p_k} E_c$ includes in the result all tuples in R that are not modified by the update operation.

2. The second term $(\pi_{A_r} R \triangleright\!\!\!\triangleleft_{p_k} E_c) \bowtie_{p_k} E_u$ includes in the result the tuples that are modified by the update operation.

2.2 Rule syntax and semantics

A condition-based rule is defined as a couple:

$$\textbf{if} \quad E_{cond}$$
$$\textbf{then} \quad [A_i]$$

where:

- E_{cond} expresses the rule's condition as a relational algebra query on a set of relations.

- $[A_i]$ expresses the rule's sequence of actions; each action is a data modification statement modeled by relational algebra operations (i.e. using the expressions for E_{ins}, E_{del}, and E_{upd} given in Table 3).

When the rule is evaluated, the condition E_{cond} is true if and only if $E_{cond} - E_{cond}^{old} \neq \emptyset$, where E_{cond}^{old} denotes the result of E_{cond} the last time the rule was executed. If the rule has not previously been executed during rule processing, then $E_{cond}^{old} = \emptyset$. That is, the condition is true whenever the query produces tuples that have not previously been produced by that query. This is very similar to the interpretation of conditions in the *pattern-based* rules of Ariel [8]; it also is similar to the way many event-based rules are programmed in practice [6].

Rule processing occurs after some set of user modifications to the database. (The "granularity" of the user modifications with respect to rule processing, although an important issue [9], is irrelevant to the termination problem.) Rule processing is an iterative loop in which, in each iteration, a rule with a true condition is selected and that rule's actions are executed. (In this paper, we do not consider the effect of a *conflict resolution* policy for selecting among multiple activated rules [9]; we intend to consider this as an extension to our methods.) Rule processing terminates if and when there are no rules with true conditions.

2.3 Examples

Example 2.1 Consider the relations emp(eno,salary,dno,jno), dept(dno,

name), and job(jno,title). This example is expressed first in the Ariel rule language and is taken from [8]. The example rule behaves as follows: if a clerk's salary exceeds 30000, then the clerk's information is inserted in relation salaryWatch and the clerk's salary is reduced according to the department to which the clerk belongs.

```
if    emp.sal > 30000
and   emp.jno=job.jno
and   job.title = "Clerk"
then  append to salaryWatch(emp.all);
      replace emp (sal=30000)
        where emp.dno = dept.dno
          and dept.name = "Sales";
      replace emp (sal=25000)
        where emp.dno = dept.dno
          and dept.name != "Sales";
```

Rule actions in Ariel are implicitly bound to the data selected by the condition [8], so in our model the predicate of the condition must be added to the selection predicate of rule actions. Using our model, the above rule is represented as:

$$\textbf{if} \quad E_{cond}$$
$$\textbf{then} \quad [E_{ins}, E_{upd1}, E_{upd2}]$$

where (recall that $E_{upd1} = <E_{c1}, E_{u1}>$ and $E_{upd2} = <E_{c2}, E_{u2}>$):

$$
\begin{aligned}
E_{cond} &= \sigma_{sal>30000}\text{emp} \bowtie_{jno} \sigma_{title="Clerk"}\text{job} \\
E_{ins} &= E_{cond} \\
E_{c1} &= E_{cond} \bowtie_{dno} \sigma_{name="Sales"}\text{dept} \\
E_{u1} &= \pi_{eno,sal}\text{TE}[sal = 30000]\text{emp} \\
E_{c2} &= E_{cond} \bowtie_{dno} \sigma_{name'="Sales"}\text{dept} \\
E_{u2} &= \pi_{eno,sal}\text{TE}[sal = 25000]\text{emp}
\end{aligned}
$$

Example 2.2 Consider the relations `wire(wire-id,fr,to,type,voltage,power)` and `tube(tube-id,fr,to,type)`. This example is taken from [6], where the Starburst rule language is used for constraint maintenance. [1] This example rule behaves as follows: if any wires are not contained in a corresponding tube, then if tubes have been deleted by a preceding action the rule deletes the corresponding wires, and if wires have been newly inserted the rule inserts tubes for the wires.

For convenience we use `W` for `wire`, `T` for `tube`, and `del_T` for `deleted tube`. `del_T` is a *transition table* [18] containing deleted tubes. In our analysis we treat transition tables exactly as any other table in the database.

```
if    exists T: (select * from W
                    where not exists (select * from T
                                        where <fr,to> = W.<fr,to>))
then /* delete wires whose tubes were deleted */
      delete from W
      where wire-id in (select wire-id from T)
        and <fr,to> in (select <fr,to> from del_T)
      /* assign tubes to remaining wires */
      insert into T
      (select new-tube-id(), X.f, X.t, default-tube-type
       from X(f,t):(select distinct fr, to from T)
```

Using our model, the above rule is represented as:

$$\textbf{if} \quad E_{cond}$$
$$\textbf{then} \quad [E_{del}, E_{ins}]$$

where

$$
\begin{aligned}
E_{cond} &= \text{W} \bowtie_p \text{T} \\
E_{del} &= \text{del\_T} \bowtie_{\text{del\_T} <fr,to>=\text{W} <fr,to>} (\text{W} \bowtie_p \text{T}) \\
E_{ins} &= TE[\text{default}](\text{W} \bowtie_p \text{T}) \bowtie_{\not\exists \text{W} <fr,to>=\text{del\_T} <fr,to>} \text{del\_T}
\end{aligned}
$$

and p is given by:

$$p : \not\exists \text{W}. < \texttt{fr}, \texttt{to} > = \text{T}. < \texttt{fr}, \texttt{to} >$$

3 Termination analysis

Recall from Section 2.2 that rule processing is an iterative loop in which, in each iteration, a rule with a true condition is selected and that rule's actions are executed. Thus, termination for a rule set is guaranteed if rule processing always reaches a state in which no rules will have true conditions. Recall also from Section 2.2 that, for each rule, after the first execution of that rule, its condition is true iff new data satisfies it. Hence, rule processing does not terminate iff rules provide new data to each other indefinitely.

---

[1] The Starburst rule language is actually event-based, but the constraints in [6] are defined only in terms of conditions and actions.

We analyze termination by building an *activation graph* such that a cycle in the graph indicates that rules may provide new data to each other indefinitely. In the graph, nodes represent rules, and directed edges indicate that one rule may provide new data to ("may activate") the other. Hence, the core of the method is determining if a rule may activate another rule. To make this decision, we consider the algebraic structure of conditions and actions, thus our approach is far less conservative than [1]. Given a rule pair $< r_i, r_j >$, we "propagate" r_i's actions through r_j's condition to see if r_i's actions can produce new data for r_j's condition. When the answer is yes, we conclude that r_i may activate r_j, and we add the edge connecting r_i to r_j to the activation graph.

In Section 3.1 a formal definition of the activation graph is given and the termination property is defined. In Section 3.2 we provide an intuitive description of the propagation method. In Section 3.3 the propagation formulas are presented.

3.1 The termination property

We now formally define activation graphs and termination.

Definition 3.1 An Activation Graph AG is a pair $< R, E >$ where R is a finite set of nodes, representing rules, and $E : R \to R$ is a set of directed edges. A directed edge E_{ij} connects node r_i to node r_j if the action performed by rule r_i may cause new data to satisfy r_j's condition. $\square$

Given the above definition of the activation graph, we can state the following theorem:

Theorem 3.1 Let AG be the activation graph for a rule set R. If no cycles are present in AG then processing of the rules in R always terminates.

Proof. The proof is similar to that given in [1] and is a proof by contradiction. Suppose that rule processing does not terminate. Since there are only finitely many rules, some rule r_1 must be executed infinitely many times. Then, owing to the rule execution semantics and the fact that there are no cycles in AG, there must exist a rule r_2 that provides new data to r_1's condition infinitely many times. Hence r_2 must be executed infinitely many times. Therefore there must exist a rule r_3 that provides new data to r_2's condition infinitely many times, etc. This implies there are infinitely many rules, a contradiction. $\square$

3.2 Intuition for our method

To build the activation graph, we analyze every rule pair $<r_i, r_j>$ in the rule set. If the intersection between the set of relations affected by r_i's action and the set of relations over which r_j's condition is expressed is empty, it is trivially verified that rule r_i's action cannot cause new data to satisfy r_j's condition, hence an edge connecting r_i to r_j is not added to the graph. Otherwise, to determine whether an edge should be added, r_i's actions are propagated through a query tree representing r_j's condition. If rule r_i contains a sequence of actions, then they are propagated one at a time.

The leaves of the query tree representing r_j's condition are relations. One of these leaves corresponds to the relation R that is affected by r_i's action. (If

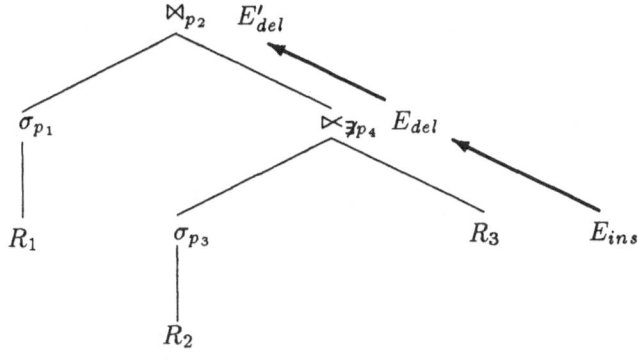

Figure 1: Propagation of E_{ins} action

no relation in the tree is affected, we fall into the trivial case described above. We assume there are not multiple references to R in the condition, although our method can easily be extended to handle this case.) Rule r_i's action is propagated from the affected relation up the query tree; it is transformed into one or more different actions during the propagation process. To describe the propagation, in Section 3.3 we give formal rules to propagate arbitrary actions through arbitrary nodes of the tree. These rules are iteratively applied until the root of the query tree is reached. At each point during the propagation, the actions associated with a node N of the tree indicate actions that occur to N's subtree as a result of performing r_i's original action.

If, at the root of the tree, the propagation process yields an *insert* or *update* action that is "consistent" (explained below), then r_j's condition will be satisfied: the insert or update corresponds to new data satisfying r_j's condition. Thus, r_i may activate r_j and the edge connecting r_i to r_j is added to the graph. If any other action or no action is obtained at the end of the propagation process, then r_i cannot cause r_j's condition to be satisfied, thus the edge is not added to the graph.

An insert or update action produced by the propagation process is consistent when the algebraic expression that describes it does not contain contradictions, that is, it is satisfiable. Satisfiability of relational expressions is undecidable in its generality, thus we can give sufficient but not necessary conditions for rule activation. However, in most of the practical cases arising in the area of active databases, it is possible to verify the satisfiability of expressions using the tableaux method described in [16]. The interested reader can refer to [3], where the soundness and completeness of this method are discussed.

Figure 1 illustrates the propagation of an insert action (described by the expression E_{ins}) on relation R_3 through the nodes of the query tree representing the condition $E_{cond} = (\sigma_{p_1} R_1) \bowtie_{p_2} (\sigma_{p_3} R_2 \bowtie_{\exists p_4} R_3)$. The bold line represents the propagation path of the E_{ins} action: The E_{ins} action is substituted for the affected relation R_3. Then, starting from the $\bowtie_{\exists p_4}$ node, for each node

Node	Applicability condition	Propagated action: $E^{in}_{ins} \to E^{out}_{action}$ Resulting expression	
π_{A_m}		$E^{out}_{ins} =$	$\pi_{A_m} E^{in}_{ins}$
σ_p		$E^{out}_{ins} =$	$\sigma_p E^{in}_{ins}$
$\bowtie_p$		$E^{out}_{ins} =$	$E^{in}_{ins} \bowtie_p E_2$
$\ltimes_p$		$E^{out}_{ins} =$	$E^{in}_{ins} \ltimes_p E_2$
$\ltimes_{\exists p}$	insert into E_1	$E^{out}_{ins} =$	$E^{in}_{ins} \ltimes_{\exists p} E_2$
	insert into E_2	$E^{out}_{del} =$	$E_1 \ltimes_p E^{in}_{ins}$
$\cup$		$E^{out}_{ins} =$	E^{in}_{ins}
$\times$		$E^{out}_{ins} =$	$E^{in}_{ins} \times E_2$
TE		$E^{out}_{ins} =$	$TE[A' = f(A)]E^{in}_{ins}$
FN	$B = \emptyset$	$E^{out}_{ins} =$ $E^{out}_{upd} =$	$(FN[f(A)](E \cup E^{in}_{ins})) \ltimes_{\exists key} E$ $(FN[f(A)](E \cup E^{in}_{ins})) \bowtie_{key}$ $(\pi_{f(A)} FN[f(A)]E)$
	$B \neq \emptyset$	$E^{out}_{ins} =$ $E^{out}_{upd} =$	$(FN[f(A); B](E \cup E^{in}_{ins})) \ltimes_{\exists key} E$ $(FN[f(A); B](E \cup E^{in}_{ins})) \ltimes_B E^{in}_{ins})) \bowtie_{key}$ $(\pi_{f(A)} FN[f(A); B]E)$

Table 4: Insert action propagation

whose operand is affected by the E_{ins} action, the corresponding propagated expression is computed. At the end of the propagation process a delete action E'_{del} is obtained. As the reader may verify, an insert operation on R_3 may only cause data satisfying E_{cond} to be deleted.

3.3 Propagation rules

The rules for propagation are given in tables, one for each kind of action (insert, delete and update in Tables 4, 5 and 6). Each row of the table contains the propagated action, E^{out}, as a function of the previous action, E^{in}, and the the relational operation in the query tree. The column labeled Applicability condition specifies when different propagation rules are used for different cases. In the tables: A_m denotes an attribute list, A_p denotes the list of attributes in predicate p, A_u denotes the list of updated attributes, and A^{bef} and A^{aft} denote the attributes in A_u before and after the update action, respectively.

The following theorem and proof sketch outline the correctness of our method. For a rigorous treatment of correctness see [3].

Theorem 3.2 Let Q be the query tree corresponding to a rule condition E_{cond} and let A be an action performed on a relation in Q. Let E^{out} be the actions produced at the root of Q by application of the propagation rules in Tables 4–6. E^{out} describes the actions that are performed on expression E_{cond} as a result of executing the original action A.

Proof sketch. The proof is given by induction on the depth of Q. *Base case:* Q is a single node representing the modified relation. Then $E^{out} = A$. The correctness in this case is evident. *Induction step:* Let the root of Q

Node	Applicability condition	Propagated action: $E_{del}^{in} \to E_{action}^{out}$ Resulting expression
π_{A_m}		$E_{del}^{out} = \pi_{A_m} E_{del}^{in}$
σ_p		$E_{del}^{out} = \sigma_p E_{del}^{in}$
$\bowtie_p$		$E_{del}^{out} = E_{del}^{in} \bowtie_p E_1$
$\ltimes_p$		$E_{del}^{out} = E_{del}^{in} \ltimes_p E_1$
$\ltimes_{\exists p}$	delete from E_1	$E_{del}^{out} = E_{del}^{in} \ltimes_{\exists p} E_2$
	delete from E_2	$E_{ins}^{out} = E_1 \ltimes_p E_{del}^{in}$
$\cup$		$E_{del}^{out} = E_{del}^{in}$
$\times$		$E_{del}^{out} = E_{del}^{in} \times E_1$
TE		$E_{del}^{out} = TE[A_i' = f(A_i)] E_{del}^{in}$
FN		$E_{del}^{out} = E_{del}^{in}$
	$B = \emptyset$	$E_{upd}^{out} = ((FN[f(A)]E) \ltimes_{\exists key} E_{del}^{in}) \bowtie_{key,A} (FN[f(A)](E \ltimes_{\exists key} E_{del}^{in}))$
	$B \neq \emptyset$	$E_{upd}^{out} = (((FN[f(A);B]E) \ltimes_{\exists key} E_{del}^{in}) \bowtie_B E_{del}^{in}) \bowtie_{key,A,B} (FN[f(A);B](E \ltimes_{\exists key} E_{del}^{in}))$

Table 5: Delete action propagation

be a relational operator op over a subtree S with incoming action E^{in}. By the induction hypothesis, we assume that E^{in} describes the actions that are performed on the expression rooted in S as a result of executing the original action A. We must show that, if we apply the appropriate propagation rule for op to obtain E^{out} from E^{in}, then E^{out} describes the actions that are performed on the expression rooted in Q as a result of executing the original action A. Hence, the proof proceeds step-by-step for each propagation rule given in Tables 4, 5, 6.

As an example, let op be a selection σ_p performed over a generic subtree S and consider an update action E_{upd}^{in} associated with S. Applying our propagation rules from the fourth line of Table 6, we obtain a triple $< E_{ins}^{out}, E_{upd}^{out}, E_{del}^{out} >$, corresponding to tuples added to, deleted from, and updated in the result of $Q = \sigma_p S$. It can be seen that $E_{ins}^{out} = (\sigma_p \pi_{A^{aft}} E_{upd}^{in}) \ltimes_{\exists key} (\sigma_p \pi_{A^{bef}} E_{upd}^{in})$ describes tuples that now satisfy the selection predicate as a result of E_{upd}^{in}, hence they are added to the result of Q. Analogously, it can be seen that $E_{del}^{out} = (\sigma_p \pi_{A^{bef}} E_{upd}^{in}) \ltimes_{\exists key} (\sigma_p \pi_{A^{aft}} E_{upd}^{in})$ describes tuples that now do not satisfy the selection predicate as a result of E_{upd}^{in}, hence they are deleted from the result of Q. Finally, $E_{upd}^{out} = (\sigma_p \pi_{A^{bef}} E_{upd}^{in}) \bowtie_{key} (\sigma_p \pi_{A^{aft}} E_{upd}^{in})$ describes the tuples that satisfy the selection predicate before and after E_{upd}^{in} but with different values, hence they are updated in the result of Q. Hence this propagation rule is correct. The other propagation rules are verified similarly. □

The formulas given in Table 6 don't take into account the structure of selection predicates and update expressions. In the case of simple predicates (comparisons between an attribute and a constant) and simple arithmetic update expressions (addition or subtraction of constants to an attribute), in many

Node	Applicability condition	Propagated action: $E^{in}_{upd} \rightarrow E^{out}_{action}$ Resulting expression
π_{A_m}	$A_u \cap A_m = \emptyset$	$\emptyset$
	$A_u \cap A_m \neq \emptyset$	$E^{out}_{upd} = \pi_{A_m} E^{in}_{upd}$
σ_p	$A_u \cap A_p = \emptyset$	$E^{out}_{upd} = \sigma_p E^{in}_{upd}$
	$A_u \cap A_p \neq \emptyset$	$E^{out}_{ins} = (\sigma_p \pi_{Aaft} E^{in}_{upd}) \ltimes_{\exists key} (\sigma_p \pi_{Abef} E^{in}_{upd})$ $E^{out}_{del} = (\sigma_p \pi_{Abef} E^{in}_{upd}) \ltimes_{\exists key} (\sigma_p \pi_{Aaft} E^{in}_{upd})$ $E^{out}_{upd} = (\sigma_p \pi_{Abef} E^{in}_{upd}) \bowtie_{key} (\sigma_p \pi_{Aaft} E^{in}_{upd})$
$\bowtie_p$	$A_u \cap A_p = \emptyset$	$E^{out}_{upd} = E^{in}_{upd} \bowtie_p E_1$
	$A_u \cap A_p \neq \emptyset$	$E^{out}_{ins} = ((\pi_{Aaft} E^{in}_{upd}) \bowtie_p E_2) \ltimes_{\exists key} ((\pi_{Abef} E^{in}_{upd}) \bowtie_p E_2)$ $E^{out}_{del} = ((\pi_{Abef} E^{in}_{upd}) \bowtie_p E_2) \ltimes_{\exists key} ((\pi_{Aaft} E^{in}_{upd}) \bowtie_p E_2)$ $E^{out}_{upd} = ((\pi_{Abef} E^{in}_{upd}) \bowtie_p E_2) \bowtie_{key} ((\pi_{Aaft} E^{in}_{upd}) \bowtie_p E_2)$
$\ltimes_p$	update E_1, $A_u \cap A_p = \emptyset$	$E^{out}_{upd} = E^{in}_{upd} \ltimes_p E_1$
	update E_1, $A_u \cap A_p \neq \emptyset$	$E^{out}_{ins} = ((\pi_{Aaft} E^{in}_{upd}) \ltimes_p E_2) \ltimes_{\exists key} ((\pi_{Abef} E^{in}_{upd}) \ltimes_p E_2)$ $E^{out}_{del} = ((\pi_{Abef} E^{in}_{upd}) \ltimes_p E_2) \ltimes_{\exists key} ((\pi_{Aaft} E^{in}_{upd}) \ltimes_p E_2)$ $E^{out}_{upd} = ((\pi_{Abef} E^{in}_{upd}) \ltimes_p E_2) \bowtie_{key} ((\pi_{Aaft} E^{in}_{upd}) \ltimes_p E_2)$
	update E_2, $A_u \cap A_p = \emptyset$	$\emptyset$
	update E_2, $A_u \cap A_p \neq \emptyset$	$E^{out}_{ins} = (E_1 \ltimes_p (\pi_{Aaft} E^{in}_{upd})) \ltimes_{\exists key} (E_1 \ltimes_p (\pi_{Abef} E^{in}_{upd}))$ $E^{out}_{del} = (E_1 \ltimes_p (\pi_{Abef} E^{in}_{upd})) \ltimes_{\exists key} ((\pi_{Aaft} E_1 \ltimes_p E^{in}_{upd}))$
$\ltimes_{\exists p}$	update E_1	see expressions for $\ltimes_p$
	update E_2, $A_u \cap A_p = \emptyset$	$\emptyset$
	update E_2, $A_u \cap A_p \neq \emptyset$	$E^{out}_{ins} = (E_1 \ltimes_{\exists p} (\pi_{Aaft} E^{in}_{upd})) \ltimes_{\exists key}$ $\quad (E_1 \ltimes_{\exists p} (\pi_{Abef} E^{in}_{upd}))$ $E^{out}_{del} = (E_1 \ltimes_{\exists p} (\pi_{Abef} E^{in}_{upd})) \ltimes_{\exists key}$ $\quad (E_1 \ltimes_{\exists p} (\pi_{Aaft} E^{in}_{upd}))$
$\cup$		$E^{out}_{upd} = E^{in}_{upd}$
$\times$		$E^{out}_{upd} = E^{in}_{upd} \times E_2$
TE		$E^{out}_{upd} = TE[A'^{aft} = f(A^{aft}), A'^{bef} = f(A^{bef})] E^{in}_{upd}$
FN	$B = \emptyset$, $A_u \cap A = \emptyset$	$E^{out}_{upd} = E^{in}_{upd}$
	$B = \emptyset$, $A_u \cap A \neq \emptyset$	$E^{out}_{upd} = FN[f(A')]FN[f(A)]((((TE[A' = A]E) \ltimes_{\exists key}$ $\quad E^{in}_{upd}) \cup E^{in}_{upd})$
	$B \neq \emptyset$, $A_u \cap A = \emptyset$, $A_u \cap B = \emptyset$	$E^{out}_{upd} = E^{in}_{upd}$
	$B \neq \emptyset$, $A_u \cap A \neq \emptyset$, $A_u \cap B = \emptyset$	$E^{out}_{upd} = FN[f(A');B]FN[f(A);B]((((TE[A' = A]E)$ $\quad \ltimes_{\exists key} E^{in}_{upd}) \bowtie_B (\pi_B E^{in}_{upd})) \cup E^{in}_{upd})$
	$B \neq \emptyset$, $A_u \cap B \neq \emptyset$	$E^{out}_{upd} = (FN[f(A), B'](((E \ltimes_{\exists key} E^{in}_{upd}) \bowtie_{B=B'}$ $\quad \pi_{B'} E^{in}_{upd}) \cup E^{in}_{upd})) \bowtie_{key}$ $\quad (\pi_{B, f(A)} FN[f(A), B]E)$

Table 6: Update action propagation

predicate	Arithmetic update expression		
	addition	subtraction	generic
$A_u = k$	E_{upd}	E_{upd}	E_{upd}
$A_u > k$	E_{del}	E_{ins}	—
$A_u < k$	E_{ins}	E_{del}	—

Table 7: Eliminated actions

cases it is possible to eliminate some of the propagated actions. For example, consider the propagation of a simple arithmetic update over an attribute A_u through the σ_p operation, where p is a simple predicate. Table 7 shows the actions that can be eliminated. In the table, *generic* indicates a more general arithmetic update expression, which in the restricted case of an equality predicate, still allows an action to be eliminated.

4   Examples

We apply our analysis techniques to pairs of rules taken from the PDDS case study [6]. This case study, inspired by a joint effort between the Politecnico di Milano and the Italian Agency for Electrical Energy (ENEL), considers constraints over a database supporting the design of power distribution networks. A power network connects a collection of plants to a collection of users, possibly through intermediate nodes. For the purposes of our analysis we consider the placement of wires (relation **wire**) connecting any two points in the network and of tubes (relation **tube**) containing the wires. In many cases, techniques for termination analysis in [1, 6] erroneously (conservatively) say that rules may not terminate, while our analysis correctly detects that in fact the rules do terminate. Subsequently we refer to the schema of relations **wire** and **tube** and use the shorthand notation described in Example 2.2.

Example 4.1   Two rules r_1 and r_2 are defined to enforce the following two constraints: there are no tubes without wires (r_1), and every wire is enclosed in a tube (r_2). All the wires defined in the **wire** table must be contained in tubes defined in the **tube** table. If a new wire is inserted, the corresponding tube must be inserted; if a wire is deleted, the corresponding tube must be deleted. In [6] the rule pair created an activation graph cycle. However, we will show that r_1's action will never cause new data to satisfy r_2's condition, thus the cycle will not be present in our activation graph.

In our model, rule r_1 is represented as:

$$\textbf{if} \quad E_{cond1}$$
$$\textbf{then} \quad [E_{del1}]$$

where

$$E_{cond1} = \text{T} \bowtie_{\not\exists} \text{T} \, \texttt{<fr,to>=W} \, \texttt{<fr,to>}^{\text{W}}$$
$$E_{del1} = E_{cond1}$$

Recall from Example 2.2 the representation of rule r_2:

$$\begin{array}{ll} \textbf{if} & E_{cond2} \\ \textbf{then} & [E_{del2}, E_{ins2}] \end{array}$$

where

$$\begin{aligned} E_{cond2} &= \texttt{W} \bowtie_p \texttt{T} \\ E_{del2} &= \texttt{del\_T} \bowtie_{\texttt{del\_T} <\texttt{fr,to}>=\texttt{W} <\texttt{fr,to}>} (\texttt{W} \bowtie_p \texttt{T}) \\ E_{ins2} &= TE[\texttt{default}](\texttt{W} \bowtie_p \texttt{T}) \bowtie_{\not\exists \texttt{W} <\texttt{fr,to}>=\texttt{del\_T} <\texttt{fr,to}>} \texttt{del\_T} \end{aligned}$$

and p is given by:

$$p : \not\exists \texttt{W}. <\texttt{fr,to}> = \texttt{T}. <\texttt{fr,to}>$$

When we analyze the effect of the action performed by r_1 on r_2's condition, the propagation of the E_{del1} action through the $\bowtie_{\not\exists}$ operation in E_{cond2} causes the transformation of the *delete* operation in an *insert* operation (see Table 5):

$$E_{ins}^{out} = \texttt{W} \bowtie_{\texttt{W} <\texttt{fr,to}>=E_{del1} <\texttt{fr,to}>} E_{del1}$$

This expression is satisfiable only if the following two predicates are non-contradictory:

$$\begin{aligned} \texttt{T}. <\texttt{fr,to}> &\neq \texttt{W}. <\texttt{fr,to}> \\ \texttt{W}. <\texttt{fr,to}> &= \texttt{T}. <\texttt{fr,to}> \end{aligned}$$

Since the predicates are contradictory, the expression is not satisfiable, therefore r_1 will not activate r_2.

Example 4.2   Two rules r_1 and r_2 are defined to enforce the following two constraints: each wire's voltage must not exceed the maximum for its wire type (r_1), and each wire's power must not exceed the maximum for its wire type (r_2). These constraints use an additional table `wire-type(type,cross-section, max-voltage,max-power)`, which we denote WT. Note that we consider the second version of r_1 from [6]. We perform again the analysis on the pair $< r_1, r_2 >$, showing that r_1 cannot activate r_2 and termination is guaranteed. Again, this is not detected by the conservative methods of [1, 6].

Rule r_1 is represented as:

$$\begin{array}{ll} \textbf{if} & E_{cond1} \\ \textbf{then} & [E_{del1}, E_{upd1}] \end{array}$$

where

$$\begin{aligned} E_{cond1} &= \texttt{W} \bowtie_{\texttt{W type=WT type} \wedge \texttt{W voltage>WT max-voltage}} \texttt{WT} \\ E_{del1} &= \texttt{W} \bowtie_p FN[\max(\texttt{max-voltage}), \max(\texttt{max-power})]\texttt{WT} \\ E_{upd1} &= E_{c1} \bowtie_{\texttt{W-id}} E_{u1} \end{aligned}$$

$$E_{c1} = \texttt{W} \bowtie_{p_1} FN[\max(\texttt{max-voltage})]\texttt{WT}$$
$$E_{u1} = \pi_{\texttt{W.w-id,WT type}} \sigma_{p_2} FN[\min(\texttt{WT.max-voltage}); \texttt{W.w-id}](\texttt{W} \bowtie_{p_3} \texttt{WT})$$

and p, p_1, p_2, p_3 are given by:

p : $\quad$ W.voltage $>$ max(WT.max-voltage) $\wedge$ W.power $>$ max(WT.max-power)

p_1 : $\quad$ W.type $=$ WT.type $\wedge$ W.voltage $>$ WT.max-voltage$\wedge$
$\qquad$ W.voltage $<$ max(WT.max-voltage)

p_2 : $\quad$ WT.max-voltage $=$ min(WT.max-voltage)

p_3 : $\quad$ WT.max-voltage $>$ W.voltage $\wedge$ WT.max-power $>$ W.power

Rule r_2 has the same structure of rule r_1:

$$\textbf{if} \quad E_{cond2}$$
$$\textbf{then} \quad [E_{del2}, E_{upd2}]$$

where:

$$E_{cond2} \;=\; \text{W} \bowtie_{\text{W type=WT type}\wedge\text{W power>WT max-power}} \text{WT}$$
$$E_{del2} \;=\; \text{W} \bowtie_{\text{W power>max(WT max-power)}} FN[\max(\text{max-power})]\text{WT}$$
$$E_{upd2} \;=\; E_{c2} \bowtie_{\text{w-id}} E_{u2}$$

$$E_{c2} \;=\; \text{W} \bowtie_{p_1} FN[\max(\text{max-power})]\text{WT}$$
$$E_{u2} \;=\; \pi_{\text{W w-id,WT type}}\sigma_{p_2} FN[\min(\text{WT.max-power}); \text{W.w-id}](\text{W} \bowtie_{p_3} \text{WT})$$

and p_1, p_2, p_3 are given by:

p_1 : $\quad$ W.type $=$ WT.type $\wedge$ W.power $>$ WT.max-power$\wedge$
$\qquad$ W.power $<$ max(WT.max-power)

p_2 : $\quad$ WT.max-power $=$ min(WT.max-power)

p_3 : $\quad$ WT.max-power $>$ W.power

We propagate the actions contained in rule r_1 through the query tree representing rule r_2's condition. By propagating the update action through the join operation contained in E_{cond2}, we obtain the three actions: *insert*, *delete*, and *update*. Since attribute w-id is the primary key of table wire, we have:

$$E_{ins}^{out} \;=\; ((\pi_{A_{aft}} E_{upd}^{in}) \bowtie_p \text{WT}) \bowtie_{\overline{\exists}\text{w-id}}((\pi_{A_{bef}} E_{upd}^{in}) \bowtie_p \text{WT})$$
$$E_{del}^{out} \;=\; ((\pi_{A_{bef}} E_{upd}^{in}) \bowtie_p \text{WT}) \bowtie_{\overline{\exists}\text{w-id}}((\pi_{A_{aft}} E_{upd}^{in}) \bowtie_p \text{WT})$$
$$E_{upd}^{out} \;=\; ((\pi_{A_{bef}} E_{upd}^{in}) \bowtie_p \text{WT}) \bowtie_{\text{w-id}} ((\pi_{A_{aft}} E_{upd}^{in}) \bowtie_p \text{WT})$$

where p is given by:

p : W.type $=$ WT.type $\wedge$ W.power $>$ WT.max-power

We consider satisfiability of the E_{ins}^{out} expression; E_{upd}^{out} is identical. E_{ins}^{out} is satisfiable only if the following predicates are non-contradictory:

W.type $=$ WT.type	(1)
W.power $>$ WT.max-power	(2)
W.voltage $>$ WT.max-voltage	(3)
W.voltage $<$ max(WT.max-voltage)	(4)
WT.max $-$ voltage $=$ min(WT.max-voltage)	(5)
WT.max-voltage $>$ W.voltage	(6)
WT.max-power $>$ W.power	(7)

where predicates (1) and (2) come from p, predicates (1), (3) and (4) come from E_{c1}, predicates (5), (6) and (7) come from E_{u1}. As predicates (2) and (7) are in conflict, the expression is not satisfiable.

We must also determine if r_1's E_{del1} action may activate rule r_2. As the E_{del1} action propagates through the $\bowtie_p$ operation in E_{cond2} as a delete action, it produces only a delete action at the root of E_{cond2}. We conclude that r_1's actions can never produce new data for r_2's condition, i.e. r_1 cannot activate r_2.

5 Conclusions and future work

We have defined a relational algebra representation of active database rules; based on this model, we have described a technique to prove termination for sets of condition-based rules. Our technique improves upon the approach in [1], as it allows us to exploit the semantics of conditions and actions to analyze the interaction between rule pairs. As in [1], our analysis technique identifies the responsible rules when termination is not guaranteed, so it can be used as a part of an interactive development tool to help the user define rules that are guaranteed to terminate.

This approach can be improved and extended in a number of directions. In particular:

- We plan to extend the rule model and analysis techniques to handle event-based rules. As an initial step, we will identify a class of event-based rules that behave in the same way as the condition-based rules considered here. (It is our feeling that event-based rules often are used this way in practice, e.g. [6].) For these rules, the methods given here should be applicable with only minor modifications. We then plan to extend our methods for arbitrary event-based rules.

- We plan to incorporate a notion of rule priorities and conflict resolution into our model. Priorities restrict the possible executions of rules, therefore termination analysis is more difficult but can be more precise.

- In [1], *confluence* also is analyzed, i.e. methods are given for determining whether rules are guaranteed to produce a unique final state. Confluence analysis in [1] is based on a conservative notion of rule *commutativity*. It is clear that the methods given here for termination analysis can be similarly applied for confluence, by determining less conservatively when rules are commutative.

- Our algebraic model for rules and our methods for analyzing the interactions of rule conditions and actions may be used as the basis for both compile-time and run-time optimizations to rule processing.

Acknowledgements

We would like to thank Filippo Cacace for all the useful discussions.

References

[1] Aiken A., Widom J., Hellerstein J.M. Behavior of database production rules: termination, confluence, and observable determinism. **Proc. of the ACM SIGMOD Int. Conf. on Management of Data**, pp 59-68, San Diego, California, June 1992.

[2] ASK Computer Co. **INGRES/SQL Reference Manual**, Version 6.4, 1992.

[3] Baralis E. An Algebraic Approach to the Analysis and Optimization of Active Database Rules, **PhD thesis**, Politecnico di Torino, 1993.

[4] Ceri S., Crespi-Reghizzi S., Lamperti L., Lavazza L., Zicari R. Algres: An advanced database for complex applications. In **IEEE Software**, June 1990.

[5] Ceri S., Gottlob G. Translating SQL into relational algebra: Optimization, semantics, and equivalence of SQL Queries. In **IEEE Transactions on Software Engineering** 4(11):324-345, April 1985.

[6] Ceri S., Widom J. Deriving production rules for constraints maintenance. In **Proc. of the 16th Int. Conf. on Very Large Data Bases**, pp 566-577, Brisbane, Australia, August 1990.

[7] Digital Equipment Co. **Rdb/VMS - SQL Reference Manual**, November 1991.

[8] Hanson E.N. Rule condition testing and action execution in Ariel. In **Proc. of the ACM-SIGMOD Int. Conf. on Management of Data**, pp 49-58, San Diego, California, June 1992.

[9] Hanson E.N., Widom J. An overview of production rules in database systems. **IBM Research Report RJ 9023**, IBM Almaden Research Center, San Jose, California, October 1992.

[10] Klug A. Equivalence of relational algebra and relational calculus query languages having aggregate functions. In **Journal of the ACM**, 29(3):699-727, 1982.

[11] McCarthy D.R. Dayal U. The architecture of an active database management system. In **Proc. of the ACM-SIGMOD Int. Conf. on Management of Data**, pp 215-224, Portland, Oregon, May 1989.

[12] Simon E., Kiernan J., de Maindreville C. Implementing high level active rules on top of a relational DBMS. In **Proc. of the 18th Int. Conf. on Very Large Data Bases**, Vancouver, Canada, August 1992.

[13] Stonebraker M., Jhingran A., Goh J., Potamianos S. On rules, procedures, caching and views in data base systems. In **Proc. of the ACM-SIGMOD Int. Conf. on Management of Data**, pp. 281-290, Atlantic City, New Jersey, May 1990.

[14] Stonebraker M., Kemnitz G. The POSTGRES next-generation database management system. **Communications of the ACM**, 34(10):78-92, October 1991.

[15] Sybase, Inc. **Transact-SQL User's Guide**, 1987.

[16] Ullman J.D. **Principles of Databases and Knowledge-Base Systems**, volumes I-II Computer Science Press, Potomac, MD, 1988.

[17] Widom J., Cochrane R.J., Lindsay B.G. Implementing set-oriented production rules as an extension to Starburst. In **Proc. of the 17th Int. Conf. on Very Large Data Bases**, pp 275-285, Barcelona, Spain, September 1991.

[18] Widom J., Finkelstein S.J. Set-oriented production rules in relational database systems. In **Proc. of the ACM-SIGMOD Int. Conf. on Management of Data**, pp 259-270, Atlantic City, New Jersey, May 1990.

DEAR: a DEbugger for Active Rules in an object-oriented context

Oscar Díaz

Dpto. de Lenguajes y Sistemas Informáticos,
University of the Basque Country, San Sebastián (Spain)
e-mail: diaz@si.ehu.es

Arturo Jaime

Dpto. de Lenguajes y Sistemas Informáticos,
University of the Basque Country, San Sebastián (Spain)
e-mail: jipjaela@si.ehu.es

Norman Paton

Departament of Computing Science and Electrical Engineering,
Heriot-Watt University, Edinburgh (Scotland)
e-mail: norm@cee.hw.ac.uk

Abstract

Experience using active rules in database systems has shown that, while
such rules can be utilised beneficially in a range of applications, it is not
a straightforward task to implement, debug or maintain large rule bases.
It is thus important for active rule systems to provide debugging and explanation facilities for two reasons: to inform the user which active rules
have been fired during the execution of an operation thereby increasing the user's confidence and understanding of the system, and to help
the designer to refine and analyze interactions among rules at execution
time. The idiosyncrasies of the rule's flow of control, where the rules
to be fired cannot be known in advance, introduce some requirements
different from those found in debuggers for conventional programming
languages. This paper presents an approach to the design and implementation of a debugger for active rules in an object-oriented context.
Due to the event-based nature of active systems, special attention has
been paid to making explicit the context in which rules are fired, and
on providing mechanisms to focus attention during the debugging process. These ideas have been tested empirically in an implementation
of a rule debugger for the EXACT rule system of the object-oriented
DBMS ADAM.

1   Introduction

Active database management systems are a fast-growing area of research mainly
due to the large number of applications which can benefit from this active
dimension. Among the new questions possed by this new area, two challenges
have been identified in [8], namely:

- the provision of rule languages expressive enough to handle the diversity of possible applications. However, increasing expressiveness is often associated with increasing complexity. A solution could be to find appropriate *declarative* rule languages which allow detection of inconsistencies in the rule set at *compile time*. Although these languages are appropriate for specifying conditions over database states, some problems arise when trying to describe reactions declaratively. Hence, the expressiveness of the language can be limited to focus on a particular application (e.g. integrity constraints with restricted reactions to restore the database state once a violation occurs) [2]. This approach retains the advantage of having a declarative language while providing some way of declaring reactions. However, we still need a general-purpose rule language in which reactions can be easily defined. In this case, as the number of rules increases it becomes difficult for the database administrator to foresee the possible interactions among rules. A rule debugger will help in this task.

- the provision of an explanation mechanism which allows users 'to ascertain what rules are activated during the execution of any command' [8]. This is seen by Stonebraker as an urgent need. Since, by definition, rules are fired automatically without user intervention, the only way to make the user aware of the system's behaviour is through explanation. Otherwise, users will be reluctant to rely on a system in which 'unexpected' behaviour occurs. Notice that debugging and explanation facilities are closely related.

This is quite a novel area of research in which few proposal have been made. In [8], some of the desired capabilities of a rule explanation system are explored in the context of POSTGRES, a relational DBMS extended with an active mechanism. Two facilities are seen as necessary:

- making the user aware of whether the retrieved data is stored data or derived data. In the latter, the derivation rule rather than the data itself could be provided. The command *described* is proposed for this function.

- making the user aware of the rules that become activated as a result of a command execution. The keyword *trace* before a command 'would cause the corresponding command to be executed and the user to be notified of any rules which are awakened'. A cascading trace, i.e. when tracing is done not only of the rules fired directly by the command but any other rule awakened as a consequence of executing a rule's condition or action, could be achieved inserting *trace**. Finally, if instead of executing the command, the user wants to explore what would happen if the command were run, the keyword *explain* rather than *trace* could be used.

In this paper, a DEbugger for Active Rules in an object-oriented context (DEAR) is presented. DEAR has been implemented on EXACT [3], a rule manager which supports event-condition-action rules in ADAM [5], an object-oriented DBMS in Prolog. DEAR provides a friendly graphical interface which was built using EDEN, a user interface toolkit which has been fully integrated with ADAM [6]. The DEAR system is thus, implemented as a network of ADAM objects, some of which represents interaction components such as buttons, dialog-boxes and menus.

Unlike previous approaches where only rules are traced, DEAR keeps track of both rules and events. It is our opinion that tracing events gives important hints to the user – the interwined event-rule cycle allows the user to know not which rules fired, but also what caused these rules to be fired. And vice versa, when an event is awakened, such an interwined cycle permits detection of the context where the event arose.

This approachis complementary to that of [1, 7] who are investigating the analysis of rule sets to detect certain characteristics such as confluence and termination. This paper concentrates on facilities which allow database users to observe rule system functionality at runtime.

This paper is organised in four sections. First, a brief overview of EXACT is presented and then we turn to address the DEAR system. In the third section an example on the use of DEAR is given. Finally some conclusions are presented.

2 The EXACT rule manager

EXACT is a rule manager built using the primitives provided by the ADAM system. Active behaviour is supported by event-condition-action rules (hereafter ECA rules). The structure of a rule is mainly described by the *event* that triggers the rule, the *condition* to be checked and the *action* to be performed if the condition is satisfied. The condition is a set of queries which checks that the state of the database is appropriate for execution of the action. The action is a set of operations that make some suitable response to the event.

The features of EXACT which have influenced the debugger are:

- events and rules are two distinct and first-class objects: they have object identifiers, they are described by attributes, and they are manipulated through methods,

- the condition mode (i.e. the time when the condition is evaluated relative to the event which triggers the rule) and the action mode (i.e. the moment when the action is executed relative to the condition evaluation of the rule) are both immediate,

- events can be primitive or composite. The former can currently be: behaviour invocation (i.e. the event is raised by the execution of some user-defined operation), structure operation (i.e. the event is raised by an operation on some piece of the internal structure of the object) and clock events. As for composite events, so far only conjunction and disjunction of events are supported.

- EXACT supports different management strategies for rules. For integrity rules, the ones used to illustrate the debugger in this paper, the firing mode is as follows: awakened integrity rules are fired in turn until one fails, in which case the firing of rules ends and the update which caused the rules to be fired is rejected.

Among the events, behaviour invocation events play a core role in object-oriented systems since any interaction with an object has to be through message sending. In EXACT, such events are described through the following attributes: the *active_method* which indicates the method to be monitored, the *when* attribute which can be *after* or *before* method execution, the *active_class* which indicates the class of the objects for which the sending of the message has to be detected, and/or the *active_object* which contains the instances to which, when the message is sent, the event is triggered.

In this context, making checks at compile time is not straightforward. As an example, consider the case where several rules are attached to the following events:

```
(increasing_size,before,circle)
(increasing_size,before,square)
(increasing_size,before,rhombus)
```

where *circle*, *square* and *rhombus* are subclasses of a higher class *figure* where the method *increasing_size* is defined. The above events arise *before* the *increasing_-size* method is sent to an instance of *circle*, *square* and *rhombus* respectively. Let us suppose that the following instruction appears in the action part of a rule:

```
increasing_size(12) to Afigure
```

whereby the *size* of the object (*Obj*) instantiating the variable Afigure is increased by 12. The difficulty lies in ascertaining which of the previous events will be raised as a consequence of sending the above message. The events raised depend on the type of the object *Obj*. If *Obj* becomes instantiated with a *circle*, rules having *(increasing_size,before,circle)* as their event, will be fired. Likewise, if *Obj* becomes instantiated with a *square* or a *rhombus*, the corresponding event will be raised, and thus the attached rules fired. If *Obj* becomes instantiated with a different figure, none of the above events will happen. The problem is that the type of *Obj* will not be known till execution time (*late binding*), preventing some checking (e.g. of rule interactions) at compile time.

Thus late binding, a core feature of object-oriented systems, makes it even more complicated to detect conflicting interactions at compile time, and motivates the need for a debugger.

3 DEAR: A debugger for active rules

It is our opinion that a rule debugger should provide at least three kinds of mechanisms which :

- make explicit the context in which the active rule is fired,

- focus the search during the debugging process,

- automatically detect inconsistencies and potentially conflicting interactions among rules.

As for the former, the model of traditional debuggers cannot be totally migrated into the context of active rules. Conventional debuggers show *the sequence* in which the tracked units (e.g. instructions in COBOL or predicates in Prolog) are executed. Sequence is the only and fixed control that traditional programming languages can follow: instructions are executed in the sequence given by the programmer. If an unforeseen situation arises (e.g. an unexpected value) then the program fails. The control is *context-independent*, the context has to be understood by the programmer.

By contrast, active rules are executed automatically without user intervention. There is no way to know in advance which rules will be fired. Rules eligible for firing, *the conflict set*, depend on the events raised (internal or external to the DBMS). The conflict set is thus, *context-dependent*.

A similar problem is found in Expert Systems where production rules are used. Here, the next production to be exploited is not known *a priori* (there is not an algorithm) but is based on the available facts, i.e. on *the working memory*. The control is once again *context-dependent*, although, unlike ECA rules, the context is the state of the database rather than the events. It is worth noticing that in a standard production system (e.g. OPS5), only one production rule of the conflict set is exploited in each inference cycle, and that there is re-evaluation of the conflict set each time a rule is executed. By contrast, most of the active mechanisms in DBMS fire all the ECA rules in the conflict set.

Therefore, to show the sequence in which rules are fired would be of little help here. A more meaningful way of keeping track of ECA rules is to show not only the rules but also the context in which these rules are fired. The context can be understood as the rule's event and the conflict rule set. Although events can easily be obtained from the rule [1], making the event explicit at debugging time enables the user to follow the chaining of rules. A second drawback with showing only the sequence is that, for a given rule, the user ignores whether this rule had to compete with other rules or not.

DEAR attempts to face this problem by:

- showing the interwined cycle of rules and events. Hence, the user can ascertain not only which rules are awakened, but also what caused these rules to be fired. And vice versa, when an event is raised, such a cycle permits detection of the context where the event took place.

  Figure 1 shows such an event-rule cycle. The representation is a tree where the root is artificially created (the corresponding node is labelled with *root*) and its direct descendents are the first events to be raised. Nodes can represent either events or rules, where event nodes alternate with rule nodes. An arc form an event node to a rule node means that the event awakens the rule. An arc form a rule node to an event node means that the event was produced by the rule. As execution proceeds, the event/rule tree is constructed depth-first. In figure 1, event *(put_projects,before,2#manager)* happens before event *(modify_method, before,2#manager)* and the leftmost occurrence of rule *12#integrity_rule* before the leftmost occurrence of rule *14#integrity_rule*.

---

[1] This is not always so easy. For example, for disjunctive events, if only the sequence of rules is shown the user will be unaware of which of the events appearing in the disjunction arose.

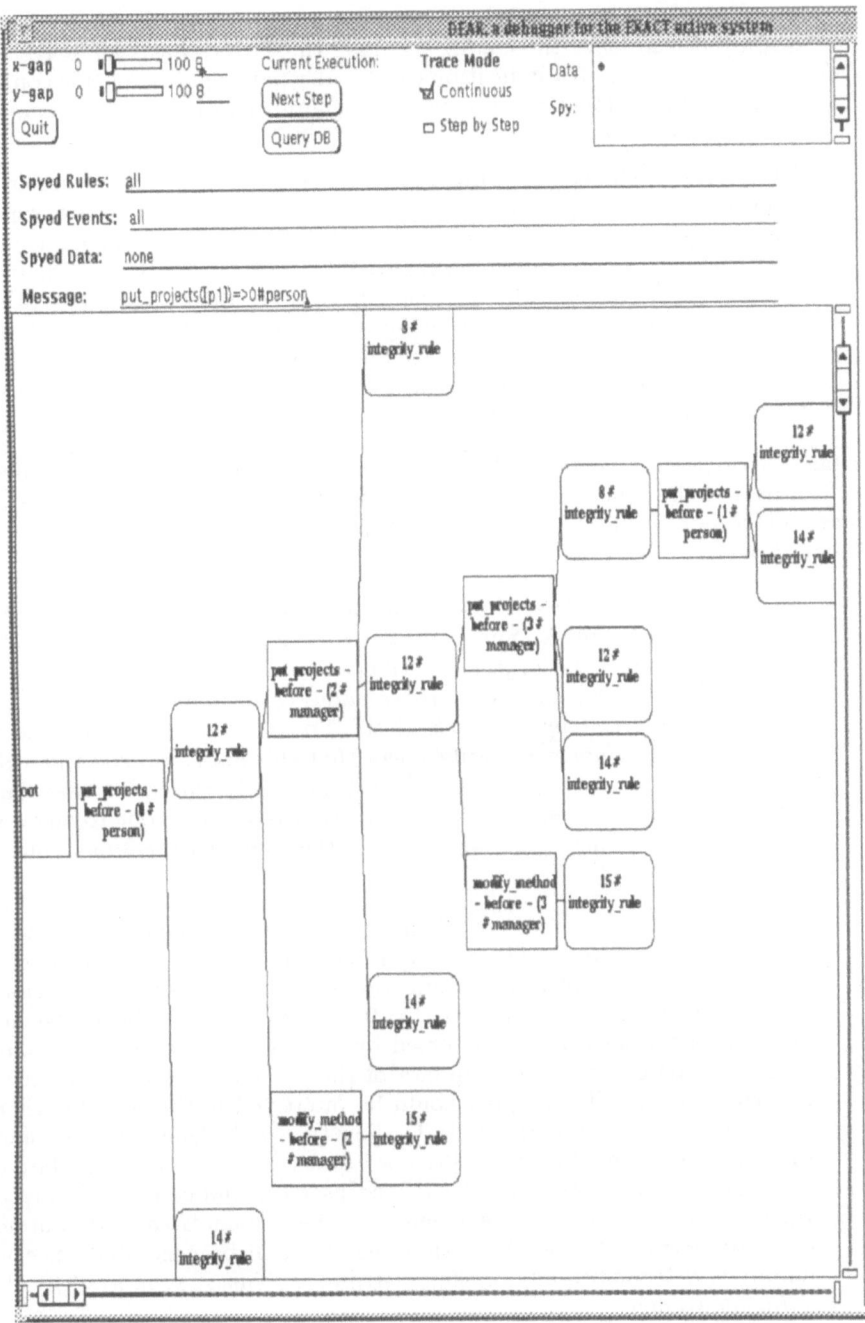

Figure 1: An interwined event-rule cycle.

- making explicit the conflict set of simultaneously triggered rules in the displayed tree, once the conflicts among those rules has been solved by the rule manager. An indication of the rules participating in this conflict set is useful for focusing on a restricted number of rules where complex interactions can occur.

  Since a rule is eligible for firing if its event is awaked, a conflict set can be intensionally defined by a set of events. This set represents events which arose *simultaneously*. This is shown by a link between event nodes. As an example, consider the following events: E1, E1 & E2, E1 or E3. If E2 has already occurred and the event E1 is raised, rules having any of the previous events are eligible for firing. Graphically, rules linked with any of the nodes representing these events are part of the conflict set, and thus they could have been fired in a different order. The user can then focus on this set and change priorities if required.

So far, all rules and events produced are shown by the debugger. However, this can lead to the generation of large trees which are cumbersome to analyze. To provide a more focused tracking, DEAR provides two ways of 'pruning' the debugger tree:

- debugging can be restricted to certain rules and/or events by the *spy_rule* and *spy_event* facilities. Since events and rules are objects in EXACT, the user provides the object identifiers of the events and rules to be traced. The tree will show only those nodes corresponding to any of the spy points specified by the user. Here, an arc from an event node to a rule node does not necessarily mean that this event awaked this rule, but that as a consequence of the event, and likely through a cascading process, this rule was fired. Likewise, an arc from a rule node to an event node means that the event was raised in the context (direct or induced) of this rule.

- allowing the designer to trace when some situation changes, rather than by following certain events and/or rules. As an example, consider a database for CAD/CAM. A modification in a given component can cause other changes to be propagated to its versions or its subcomponents. Such propagations can be supported by ECA rules. Among the modifications, some can cause the update of the estimated cost of producing this component. The designer could be interested in the context where the estimated cost were updated. To show the whole debugging tree since the very first event, forces the designer to ascertain when the update of the cost was produced. In DEAR, the user can indicate the debugger which attributes should be watched (e.g. the *estimated_cost* attribute of the *13#component* object), so that the tree will be generated once an update is detected on any of these attributes. This is supported by the *data_spy* window.

Finally, for detection of inconsistencies and conflict interaction, DEAR so far only detects potential cycles. This is pointed out by the system when an event is awaked twice in the same branch of the debugger tree. In this case, the system stops and the branch is underlined.

4   An Example

Let *manager* be a subclass of *person* where the attribute *projects* is defined. Suppose that managers can be *assisted_by* persons, and that person can be *led_by* managers. Consider a constraint similar to the one proposed in [4] which enforces the constraint that the *projects* which a *manager* has a responsibility for are to be the same as the set of *projects* his assistants work on.

This constraint can be violated (among other things) by updates in the number of projects or assistants of a given person. When the constraint is violated, several reactions can follow to restore consistency, namely:

- if a *project* is added to an assistant, it is also added to the corresponding manager

- if a *project* is added to a manager, it is also added to at least one of his/her assistants

The validation of this constraint together with the reaction counterpart, can be supported using ECA rules. For example, the next two rules can be defined:

1. object_identifier: 12#integrity_rule

   event:
   'before' sending 'put_projects' to a 'person'.
   The awakening of this event is shown by the debugger with
   the triple: (put_projects,before,OID of the person)

   condition:
   if the person's manager does not have this project

   action:
   insert the project to the person's manager

2. object_identifier: 8#integrity_rule

   event:
   'before' sending 'put_projects' to a 'manager'.
   The awakening of this event is shown by the debugger with
   the triple: (put_projects,before,OID of the manager)

   condition:
   if the manager's assistants do not have this project

   action:
   insert the project to the manager's assistants

The process of preserving this constraint can be quite complex. Consider the examples shown in figure 2. Notice that a *manager* can have several assistants,

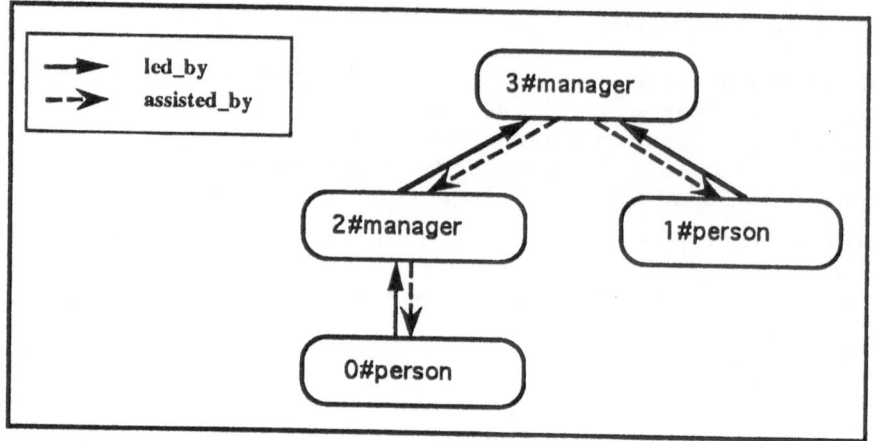

Figure 2: An example of constraint maintenance.

and at the same time be *led_by* a more senior *manager*. Consequently, if a new *project* (e.g. *p1*) is added to a *manager* (e.g. *2#manager*), the constraint has to be preserved in both of the roles played by a *manager*: as a supervisor, the *project* has to be added to his assistants (e.g. *0#person*); as one who is supervised, the *project* has to be added to his leader (e.g. *3#manager*). The former role is preserved by *8#integrity_rule*, whereas the second is maintained by *12#integrity_rule*.

Moreover, let us consider two more rules:

3. object_identifier: 14#integrity_rule

   event:
   'before' sending 'put_projects' to a 'person'.
   The awakening of this event is shown by the debugger with
   the triple: (put_projects,before,OID of the person)

   condition:
   if the number of projects assigned to this person is
   already 3

   action:
   prevent the method 'put_project' from proceeding

4. object_identifier: 15#integrity_rule

   event:
   'before' updating the structure of a 'manager'.
   The awakening of this event is shown by the debugger with
   the triple: (modify_method,before,OID of the manager)

```
condition:
    true

action:
    notify manager of the modification
```

It is worth noticing that these rules could be defined by different people. A user could introduce a new rule without being aware or previously existing rules.

Consider that the state of the database is the one shown in figure 2, where a new project is inserted (e.g. *p1*) to the person with object identifier *0#person*. This is achieved through the message *put_projects([p1]) => 0#person*. The debugger tree displayed from this message is shown in figure 1. The window which appears besides the tree is a conventional method tracer where methods are displayed as they are executed.

The event *(put_projects,before,0#person)* is awakened and the attached rules are fired, i.e. *12#integrity_rule* and *14#integrity_rule* The former propagates the update to the *manager* of the *0#person*, whereas the second rule checks that the number of *projects* of this person does not exceed three.

As a result of firing the first rule, a cascading process occurs which awakens two events: *(put_projects,before,2#manager)* and *(modify_method,before,2#-manager)*. The former in turn causes rules *8#integrity_rule, 12#integrity_rule* and *14#integrity_rule* to fire. *8#integrity_rule* would propagate the change from the manager to his/her assistant, but this is prevented from happening since the modification comes from this direction. The other two rules repeat a similar process to the one from *0#person*, but now with the corresponding manager. Furthermore, the event *(modify_method,before,2#manager)* causes the *15#integrity_rule* to be fired.

The rest of the debugger tree is generated from the cascading effect which materialises the propagation of the insertion of the project: *2#manager* propagates the update to his manager (i.e. *3#manager*), which in turn propagates this updates to his assistants (i.e. *1#person*).

In the previous example, the message ends successfully since none of the persons involved already has three projects. Thus, the rule *14#integrity_rule* which maintains this constraint does not verify its condition.

Suppose however, that the number of projects of the very first person, *0#person*, is already three. When the system attempts to assign the new project to the very last person *at the end of the propagation process*, the *14#integrity_rule* is fired and the update prevented from taking place.

Since the rule which maintains the number of projects at three is fired *once* the propagation process has completed, *it is not till the end of all the propagation that the system becomes aware of the violation of the above constraint and then blocks the update*. This situation is shown in figure 3. Notice that the tree

190

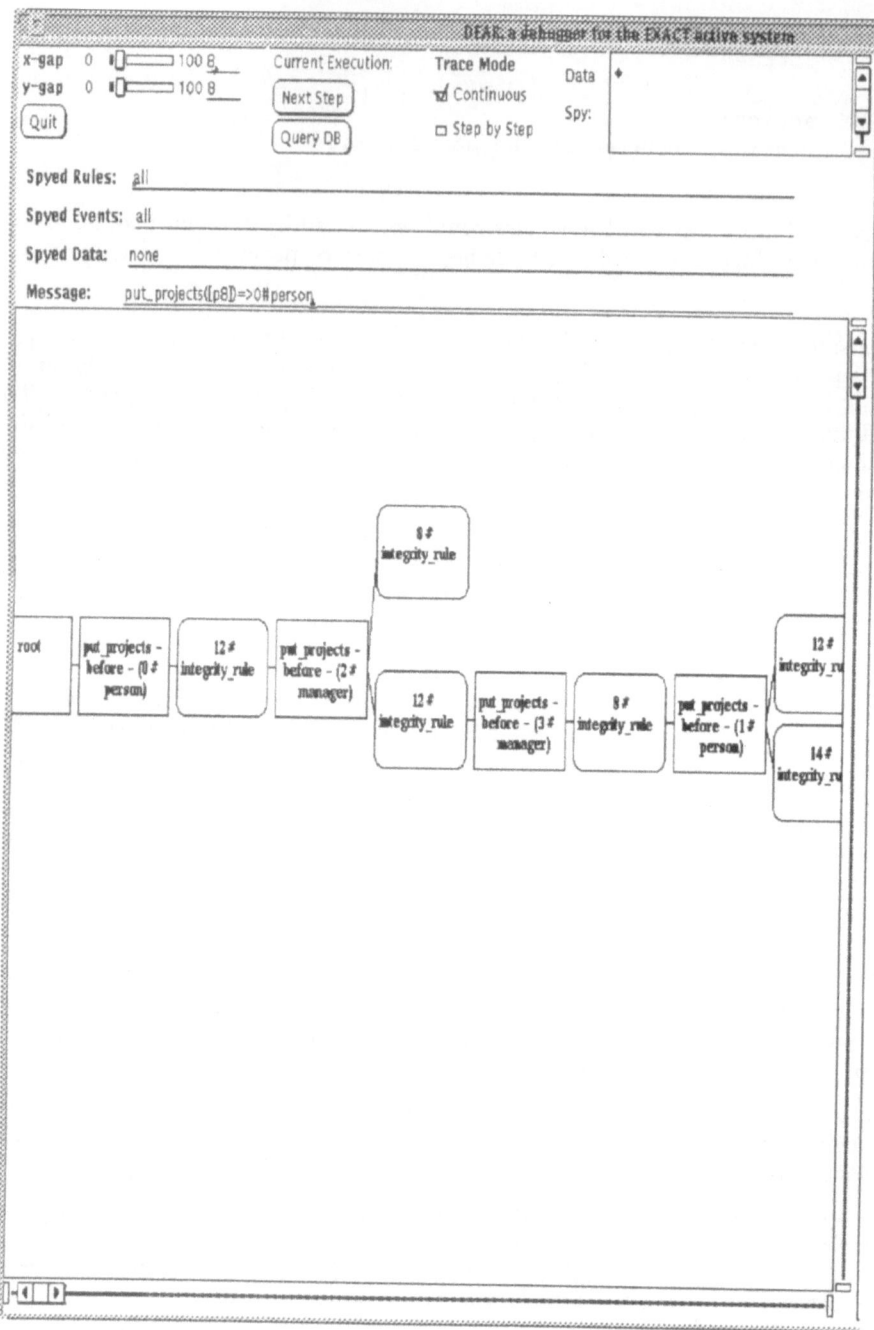

Figure 3: The debugger tree when the *no-more-than-three-project* rule is satisfied.

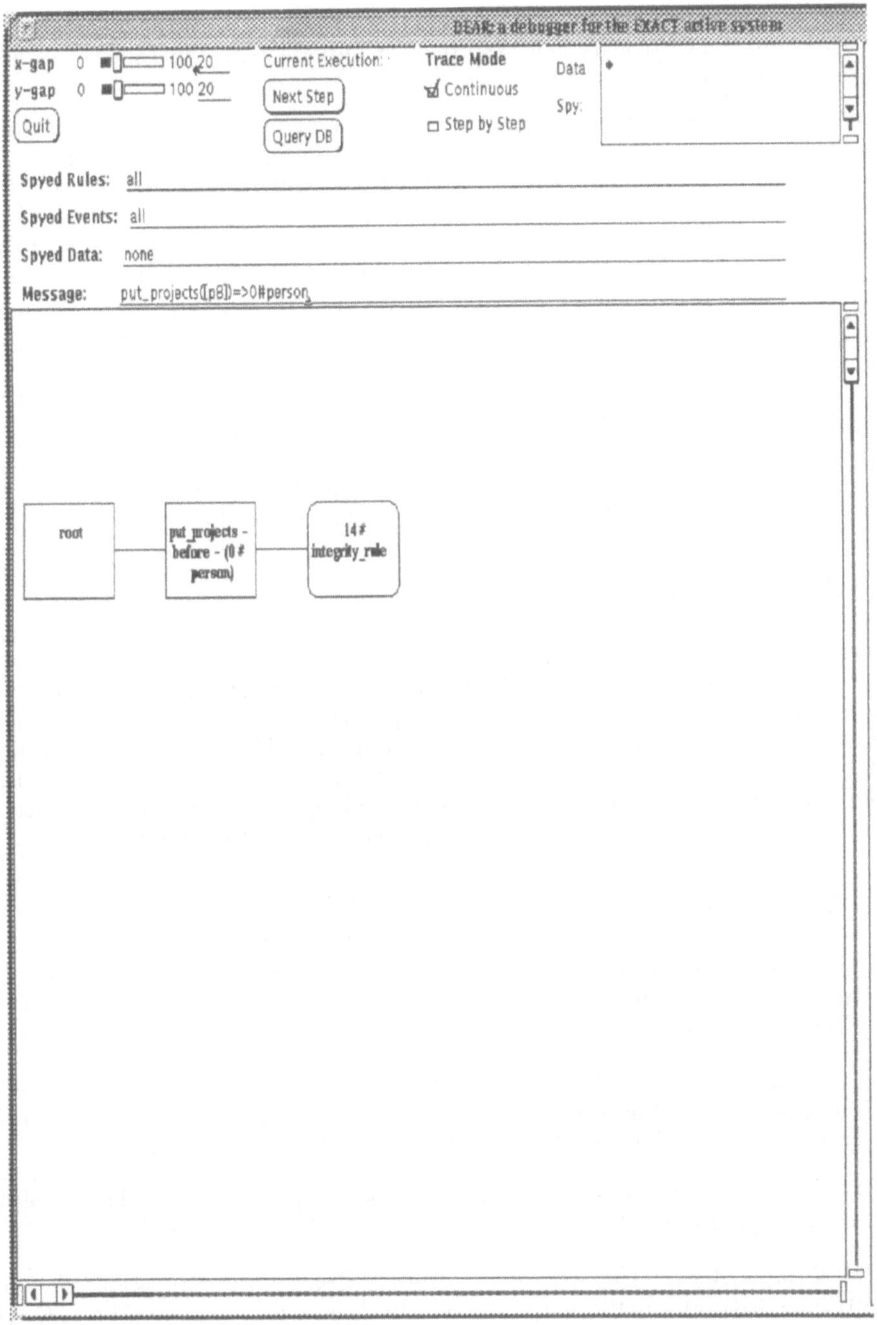

Figure 4: The debugger tree when the *no-more-than-three-project* rule is satisfied and its priority changed.

is 'pruned': neither is the event *(modify_method, before, a manager)* awakened, nor is the rule *14#integrity_rule* fired (except only once for the *1#person* where the inconsistency is detected).

The rule designer has then become aware of this process, and decides to check the number of projects before the beginning of the propagation process. This can be achieved by changing the rules' priorities. This situation is shown in figure 4. The database state is the same as in the previous figure except that here, the priority of the *no-more-than-three-projects* rule is higher than the *propagation* rules. In this case, the inconsistency is detected at the very beginning and only one rule is fired. The performance of the process is improved.

These examples illustrate how DEAR can help the designer to debug the rule set. In this case only performance gains have been achieved, but experience has shown that the order of rules influence other paramenters, even the final database state. This approach is complementary with rule analysis at compile time to detect certain features such as confluence and termination in rule sets. As shown by the previous example, to prove that the execution of the rule set will end does not imply that rules will fire in the appropriate order.

5 Conclusions

The complexity of a rule's action and the automatic execution of rules without user intervention, makes it necessary to provide a debugger/explanation toolkit for active DBMSs. In this paper, an approach has been presented for the EXACT system. Special emphasis has been put on making the context in which rules are fired explicit, and on providing a focusing mechanism to direct the debugging process. Conflicting interactions among rules have been restricted to the detection of cycles, and further research is needed in this area.

References

[1] A. Aitken, J. Widom, and J.M. Hellerstein. Behaviour of Database Production Rules: Termination, Confluence, and Observable Determinism *ACM SIGMOD Conference*, 59–68, 1992.

[2] O. Diaz and S.M. Embury. Generating active rules from high-level specifications. In R. Lucas P.M.D. Gray, editor, *Advanced Database Systems: Proc. BNCOD 10*, pages 227–243. Springer-Verlag LNCS series, 1992.

[3] O. Diaz and A. Jaime. EXACT: an EXtensible approach to ACTive object-oriented databases. *Submitted for publication*, 1993.

[4] M. Morgenstern. Constraint equations: Declarative expression of constraints with automatic enforcement. In *Proc. Intl. Conf. on Very Large Data Bases*, pages 153–299. Morgan Kaufmann, 1984.

[5] N.W. Paton. *ADAM: An Object-Oriented Database Implemented in Prolog. Proc 7th British National Conference on Databases*, M.H. Williams, editor, pages 147–162, CUP, 1989.

[6] N.W. Paton, G. al Qaimari, O. Diaz, and A. Jaime. On interface objects in object-oriented databases. In *Submitted for publication*, 1993.

[7] A. Siebes, M. Van der Voort, L. Kersten Towards a Design Theory for Database Triggers. In *Proc. Intl. Conf. on Database and Expert Systems Applications (DEXA)*, A.M. Tjoa, I. Ramos, editors, pages 338–344. Springer-Verlag, 1992.

[8] M. Stonebraker. The Integration of Rule Systems and Database Systems. *IEEE Trans. on Knowledge and Data Engineering*, 4(5):415–423, 1992.

Enforcing Confluence of Rule Execution

Leonie van der Voort
CWI
Amsterdam
The Netherlands

Arno Siebes
CWI
Amsterdam
The Netherlands

Abstract

Rules provide the functionality for constraint enforcement and view maintenance. A provably correct implementation of both issues based on rules, requires confluent and terminating behaviour of the rule set. In [15], we introduced a design theory for the static detection of these properties. The detection of confluence is based on commutativity of rule execution, called independence. In this article, we discuss the enforcement of confluence for terminating, dependent rule sets.

For a clear view on the cause of dependence, we identify a conflict set. This set is characterised by a set of dependent rules together with conditions that describe on which part of the database the rules are actually dependent. For the enforcement of confluence without re-definition of dependent rules, we define an ordering mechanism. Finally, a transformation of dependent rules into independent rules is given.

1 Introduction

A DBMS becomes active through the addition of rules or triggers. Rules allow specification of data manipulation operations that are executed automatically when certain conditions are met. They offer a flexible, unifying mechanism for common database management tasks, like constraint enforcement and view maintenance. As a consequence, a number of proposals for incorporating rules into DBMS's appeared recently [18, 5, 7, 4, 11, 2, 6, 3, 12, 13].

The correct implementation of constraint enforcement and view maintenance based on rules requires that the set is confluent and terminates [17]. A rule set terminates if its execution terminates on all database states. A terminating rule set is confluent if for each initial database state db_i the order of rule execution does not influence the final database state db_f. That is, db_f is uniquely determined by db_i and the rule set. Confluency of rule sets is thus similar to confluency of rewrite systems [9] in that the execution order is immaterial. The difference, however, is that a rule sets behaviour is affected by the underlying database state, and a rule set is confluent if it is confluent on all database states.

Whether a rule set is confluent or terminates depends, of course, on the rule execution semantics. There are two pre-dominant models in the literature: set and instance based semantics [12]. Set based semantics means processing all qualifying objects at a time, while instance based semantics means processing one qualifying object at a time. The choice between either one is mainly based on the computational model of the underlying DBMS and on the functionality of anticipated applications.

Rule interaction can be quite intricate. For example, rules may mutually activate or deactivate each other. This complicates static detection of properties such as termination and confluency. It is therefore necessary to develop a design theory which simplifies their analysis at design time. The relevance of such a theory is also endorsed by [1, 3, 6, 10, 14]. Work on rule analysis is described in [17, 19, 8, 12, 15].

The static detection of termination and confluence under both execution semantics is, amongst others, discussed in [15]. We introduced a design theory for rules in the context of an object oriented data model. The design theory is focussed on two predicates, i.e. *Terminate(n)* which guarantees termination in n steps and *Independent* which guarantees pairwise commutativity of rule execution. Together they enforce termination and confluence. The prime result of [15] is that recognition of Terminate(n) and Independent is decidable for both execution semantics.

Now suppose, a rule set is recognized to be terminating but it may be non-confluent. In this article, we describe three strategies for dealing with such a set. First, we give a characterisation of its conflict set. That is, the dependent rules together with that part of the database on which they actually are dependent are described. For example, a rule which paints red or yellow cells orange is dependent with a rule which paints red or blue cells green. They have a conflict for red cells. This characterisation is made with the use of *typical database states* (tdb). A tdb is a database state such that whenever a condition holds after rule execution in tdb, it holds in every database state after rule execution.

The characterisation may point to ill-defined rules. If a re-definition of these ill-defined rules does not help to establish confluence or if there are no ill-defined rules, confluence can be established by ordering the execution of rules. For this, the sequential composition of rules is defined. For example, to establish confluence for a rule which paints red cells yellow and a rule which paints yellow cells blue, a composed rule which first paints red cells and thereafter yellow cells can be defined.

The last strategy is a combination of the previous ones. Given two dependent rules, a characterisation of their conflict set, and an order between the rules, three independent new rules are defined. Two of them are like the old ones but are restricted to execute on the database minus the conflict set only. The other executes on the conflict set only, and is the ordered composition of the old ones. For example, the rule which paint red or yellow cells together with the rule which paints red or blue cells can be transformed into three rules. One which paints yellow cells, one which paints blue cells, and one which paints red cells.

Related work

Some work on the enforcement of confluence has been published in [17, 19]. Zhou and Hsu [19] describe a trigger (= rule) definition language and give it semantics such that conflicts in trigger execution results in an execution-abort. That is, confluence is partly enforced by execution abort in case of runtime conflicts. Aiken, Widom, and Hellerstein [17] formulate a sufficient condition for confluence based on commutativity of set based rule execution. For rule sets that are possibly non-confluent they identify a conflict set that hinders the detection of confluency. Confluence is enforced by the definition of a partial order between the rules of the conflict set.

We aim at the static enforcement of confluence to guarantee well-behaved execution under set as well as instance based semantics. In our opinion this excludes execution-aborts. In this respect we differ from [19]. Similar to [17], we identify a conflict set. However, our conflict set is not only characterised by a set of non-commutative rules but also by a subset of the database, specified by a condition, on which these rules are non-commutative. Furthermore, for the enforcement of confluence ordered composition of rules is defined.

Outline

Section 2 introduces a simple object oriented data model together with our rule model. The definition of termination and confluence is given in Section 3. Furthermore, to sketch the context of our work, Section 3 also contains a summary of results concerning termination and confluence. More details appear in [15]. Section 4 characterizes the conflict set of a set of non-confluent rules and describes an ordering mechanism for rules to enforce confluence. Given the characterisation of the conflict set and an ordering between rules, a new set of confluent rules can automatically be derived. Finally, in Section 5 we conclude and discuss future work.

2   Data and rule model

This section provides a brief overview of the simple object oriented data model and rule language through some examples; for a full report see [16]. The data model is not meant to be yet another object oriented data model, it is just a reflection of the common concepts in this area.

Data model

A **Class** definition describes the properties and behaviour of its objects through **Attributes** and **Methods**. The attributes consist of a name and a type. Each class induces a simple type and these can be combined inductively with tuple and set constructors to obtain complex types. The methods are of a simple nature; they assign new values to attributes of an object. An example is the class *cell* defined by:

>**Class** cell
>**Attributes**
>>no: Integer
>>color: String
>>neighbors: (left: cell, right: cell)
>>position: (x: Integer, y: Integer)
>
>**Methods**
>>paint_cell(new_color: String) = **self except** color := new_color
>>move_cell(new_position: (x: Integer, y: Integer)) =

          self except position := new_position
Endclass

As usual, a hierarchy is a set of classes, defined directly or through (multiple) inheritance. A database state is a set of objects. Each object belongs to one or more classes. Membership of object o of class C is denoted by $o \in C$. In this paper, we assume some fixed hierarchy. The universe of its database states is denoted by DB, with typical elements $db, db_0, db_1, db_2, \cdots$.

Queries are formulated through the definition of query classes. A query class is a class, derived from a superclass using a selection condition. This condition identifies the objects from the superclass that are member of the query class.

An example of a query is *neighbor*, which selects cells with equal colored neighbors.

      Qclass neighbor **isa** cell
      Where
          color = color ∘ neighbors.left ∧ color = color ∘ neighbors.right
      Endqclass

The selection condition is defined using a simple functional language, generated with the following grammar:

$$Expr = basic\_expr \mid Expr \circ Expr \mid (l_1 = Expr, \cdots, l_n = Expr) \mid$$
$$Expr.l \mid \{Expr\} \mid Expr \cap Expr \mid Expr \cup Expr$$

Basic expressions are the (polymorphic) identity function *id*, the class attributes, and constants. The constants are objects in basic classes such as *Int* and *String*. The ∘ denotes function-composition, i.e., $e_1 \circ e_2(x) = e_1(e_2(x))$. This slightly unconventional notation is chosen because it simplifies the reasoning later in this paper. *e.l* denotes the projection of a tuple-type expression e on it's l component. And finally, $\{e_1\}$ denotes a set with element e_1. Both ∩ and ∪ have their usual set-theoretic interpretation.

F_expr is the set of well-typed expressions generated with *Expr*, with the obvious typing rules [16]. Some examples are: *color, neighbors.left, (left_color = color ∘ neighbors.left, right_color = color ∘ neighbors.right)*, and *{color ∘ neighbors.left} ∪ {color ∘ neighbors.right}*.

The selection condition C_Q of a query Q is of the form $\bigwedge_i \bigvee_j (e \omega f)_{ij}$ with $\omega \in \{=, \neq, \subset, \not\subset, \in, \notin\}$, $e, f \in F\_expr$, and $(e \omega f)_{ij}$ well-typed. Furthermore, $C_Q(o, db)$ means that the condition C_Q holds for object o in database state db. The select set, $S_{db}(Q)$ of the query Q in database state db is defined by $\{o \in db | C_Q(o, db)\}$.

Let m be a method from a class C with header $m(l_1 : \tau_1, \cdots, l_n : \tau_n)$. A method-call for m is an expression of the form: $m(l_1 = e_1, \cdots, l_n = e_n)$ with each $e_i \in F\_expr$ and e_i is of type $C \to \tau_i$. The execution of a method-call m by an object o is denoted by $o(m)$.

For the characterisation of a conflict set, we need the notions of constants used in conditions and rules, the length of a condition, and the length of a method-call. For this, we postulate the function *constants* which returns the set of constants used in a condition or a rule. The constants of a conditions are the constants used in its expressions and the constants of a rule are the constants used in the selection condition and the derived attributes of its query together with the constants used for the assignments of its action. The length of conditions and methods are defined using the length of a functional expression, which is the depth of its parse tree. For example, $length(color) = 1$ and $length(neighbors.left) = 2$. Then:

1. $length(\bigwedge_i \bigvee_j (e \,\omega\, f)_{ij}) = max(\{max(length(e), length(f))\}_{ij})$

2. $length(m(l_1 = e_1, \cdots l_n = e_n)) = max(\{length(e_1), \cdots, length(e_n)\})$

Rule model

A rule is a (query, method_call) pair where the query selects the objects that have to execute the method-call. The method has, of course, to be one of the methods of the class underlying the query-class. The syntax for rule definition is:

Rule rule_name = (query, method_call)

An example of a rule is the **Rule** $paint\_red = (red, paint\_cell(new\_color=orange))$ where the query red is defined by **Qclass** red **isa** cell **Where** color = red **Enqclass**. [7]

The execution of a rule $R = (Q, M)$ in a database db is represented by $execute(R, db, set)$ or $execute(R, db, instance)$ depending under what semantics R is executed. Under set semantics the execution of R results in the execution of M by all objects that satisfy the selection condition of R in database db. With the provision that first the select set is determined, then for each object that satisfies the query the method-header is evaluated, and then the objects execute the method_call. This provision guarantees that the resulting state does not depend on a particular order. So, it is defined by:

$execute(R, db, set) = \{$
    forall $o \in S_{db}(Q)$ **do**
        $evaluate(o(M))$ **od**
    forall $o \in S_{db}(Q)$ **do**
        $db := db \setminus \{o\} \cup \{o(M)\}$ **od**
    $return\ db$ $\}$

Under instance semantics the execution of R results the execution of M by one randomly chosen object that satisfies the selection condition of R in database db. This is defined by:

$execute(R, db, instance) = \{$
    if $S_{db}(Q) \neq \emptyset$ **then**
        $o := choose(S_{db}(Q))$
        $db := db \setminus \{o\} \cup \{o(M)\}$
    fi
    $return\ db$ $\}$

We will sometimes use the, auxiliary, notation $execute(R(o), db, instance)$. It denotes the execution of rule R with subject o under instance semantics. If o is in the select set of R in db, it results in the execution of M by o otherwise it is a no-operation.

Rules are meant to respond automatical to interesting database states. As we only consider rule sets in isolation, i.e. there are no other queries or transactions, this behaviour can be represented by a repeating execution cycle, which executes a random selected, activated rule. A rule R is activated in database db if $S_{db}(Q_R) \neq \emptyset$ holds. The cycle stops when there are no more activated rules. The execution, denoted by $E(Rules, db, sem)$, of a rule set $Rules$ on a database db under semantics sem is thus defined by:

$E(Rules, db, sem) = \{$
    while $\exists R \in Rules : activated(R, db)$ **do**
        $R := choose(\{R | R \in Rules \wedge activated(R, db)\})$
        $db := execute(R, db, sem)$
    od
    return db $\}$

Given an initial database db, a set of rules $Rules$ and a semantics sem, the execution $E(Rules, db, sem)$ induces the set $Seq(Rules, db, sem)$ of *execution sequences*. Under set semantics, such an execution sequence registers which rule was chosen by the *choose* command. That is, an execution sequence is a, possibly infinite, list of rules, $Sq = [R_5, R_1, R_3, \cdots]$. Sq_i denotes the rule on the i-th position in the execution sequence.

Under instance semantics, an execution sequence not only registers which rule was chosen, but also which object was chosen to execute the method. So, in this case, an execution sequence is a, possibly infinite, list of the form $Sq = [R_5(o_1), R_1(o_4), \cdots]$. The object of the i-th position is denoted by o_i.

The predicate $finite(Sq)$ returns true if Sq is a finite list. So, if for $Sq \in Seq(Rules, db, sem)$ $finite(Sq)$ holds, the execution of the rule set on the database terminates in a stable database state. This final state will be denoted by $Ex(Sq, db, sem)$.

3   Termination and Confluence

As mentioned in the introduction, termination and confluence are important properties for rule sets that are used for constraint enforcement or view maintenance. These properties are formally defined as follows:

Definition 1: Let $Rules$ be a rule set and let sem denote either set or instance semantics:

1) $Terminate(Rules, sem) \stackrel{\text{def}}{=}$
    $\forall db \in DB \; \forall Sq \in Seq(Rules, db, sem) : finite(Sq)$

2) $Confluent(Rules, sem) \stackrel{\text{def}}{=}$
    $Terminate(Rules, sem) \wedge$
    $\forall db \in DB \; \forall Sq_1, Sq_2 \in Seq(Rules, db, sem) :$
        $Ex(Sq_1, db, sem) = Ex(Sq_2, db, sem)$

The detection of termination is restricted to the detection of termination in n steps. The most obvious definition of which would be to restrict the length of all execution sequences to n. Under instance semantics, however, this implies that no *non-trivial* rule terminates in n steps, as n puts a limit on the size of the database state.

Therefore, under set semantics n denotes the number of times a rule may execute and under instance semantics, it denotes the number of times a rule may execute on a particular object:

Definition 2: Let *Rules* be a rule set:

1) $Terminate(n,\ Rules,\ set) \overset{\text{def}}{=}$
   $\forall db \in DB\ \forall Sq \in Seq(Rules, db, set)\ \forall R \in Rules : |\{i \mid Sq_i = R\}| \le n$
2) $Terminate(n,\ Rules,\ instance) \overset{\text{def}}{=}$
   $\forall db \in DB\ \forall o \in db\ \forall Sq \in Seq(Rules, db, instance)\ \forall R \in Rules :$
   $|\{i \mid Sq_i = R \wedge o_i = o\}| \le n$

Because all rule sets and all databases are finite, both $Terminate(n,\ Rules,\ set)$ and $Terminate(n,\ Rules,\ instance)$ imply that all execution sequences are finite. That is, they imply termination of the rule-sets.

Our detection mechanism for confluency is like that of [17] based on commutativity of rule execution, which is called *Independent*:

Definition 3: Let *Rules* be a rule set:

1) $Independent(Rules,\ set) \overset{\text{def}}{=}$
   $\forall R_i, R_j \in Rules\ \forall db \in DB :$
   $execute(R_i, execute(R_j, db, set), set) =$
   $execute(R_j, execute(R_i, db, set), set)$
2) $Independent(Rules,\ instance) \overset{\text{def}}{=}$
   $\forall R_i, R_j \in Rules\ \forall db \in DB\ \forall o_k, o_l \in db :$
   $execute(R_i(o_k), execute(R_j(o_l), db, instance), instance) =$
   $execute(R_j(o_l), execute(R_i(o_k), db, instance), instance)$

So, to prove independence, it is sufficient to prove pair-wise independence. In particular, that a rule is independent of itself. Under set based semantics, this is obvious. Under instance semantics it is not.

Definition 4: Let R be a rule,

$Self\text{-}independent(R) \overset{\text{def}}{=} \forall db \in DB : \forall o_i, o_j \in db :$
$execute(R(o_i), execute(R(o_j), db, instance), instance) =$
$execute(R(o_j), execute(R(o_i), db, instance), instance)$

Under both kinds of semantics, independence implies the re-arrangability of execution sequences. This re-arrangability is a strong property. First, it enables a straight-forward proof that independence implies confluency for terminating rule sets (see also [17]). Secondly, re-arrangability allows for a characterisation of a class of rule sets for which set and instance based semantics coincide, viz., those rule sets which are independent and terminate under both semantics.

An important result concerning termination and confluence is the decidability of the predicates Terminate(n) and Independent for both execution semantics (see [15]). The decidability proofs are based on *typical database states* (*tdb*) as defined in Section 4. By constructing a tdb and executing rules upon it the required post-conditions for the predicates can be checked.

4 Enforcing confluence for terminating rule sets

The algorithms mentioned in the previous section detect for a given rule set whether it is confluent and terminates. Suppose the rule set terminates but is not confluent. Is it possible to enforce confluence? For this, we look at the cause of divergence. It can be due to intra-dependencies of rules (self dependence) and to inter-dependencies of rules. One strategy to deal with these dependencies is to guide the user in the re-definition of rules by giving a precise characterisation of that part of the database on which the rules are dependent. Another strategy is based on ordering the execution of rules, thereby enforcing confluency. This can only be used to resolve inter-dependencies of rules. Therefore, for rule ordering we assume the rules to be self independent. These strategies are discussed in the following two subsections. A combination of them is discussed in the last subsection.

Characterisation of the conflict set

For the characterisation of conflict sets of rules, one need to describe the effect of rule execution. This effect is described by the conditions satisfied by database objects before and after rule execution. A database state in which each possible pre- post-condition pair for a rule set is represented by an object is called a typical database state (tdb) for this rule set and it can be used to check the effect of rule execution. A tdb can be compared to the minimal models of logic programming. In contrast with minimal models, however, $tdbs$ are parameterized by L_c, L_m and $Const$ which constraint the conditions and methods (and thus rules) for which the tdb is typical. L_c and L_m constraint respectively conditions and methods by length and $Const$ constraints conditions and methods by allowed constants. Thus they restrict the conditions and rules for which the tdb is typical. The reason for this restriction is that L_c, L_m, and $Const$ determine a strictly increasing lowerbound on the number of objects in the typical database state. Because neither conditions nor method-calls are restricted in length and by used constants, no finite database state can be typical for *all* conditions and rules. The formal definition is as follows:

Definition 5: Let tdb be a database state, let $\mathcal{R}$ be the set of all possible rules, and let *sem* denote either set or instance based semantics. Then tdb is a typical database state for conditions of length L_c and methods of length L_m both based on constants in $Const$ only if

$\forall C_1, C_2 \in \{C \mid length(C) \leq L_c \land constants(C) \subset Const\}:$
$\forall R \in \{R = (Q, M) \in \mathcal{R} \mid length(C_Q) \leq L_c \land length(M) \leq L_m \land$
$\quad constants(R) \subset Const\}:$
$\forall db \in DB:$
$\quad ([\forall o \in tdb : C_1(o, tdb) \rightarrow C_2(o, execute(R, tdb, sem))]$
$\quad \rightarrow$
$\quad [\forall o \in db : C_1(o, db) \rightarrow C_2(o, execute(R, db, sem))])$

This definition is obviously non-constructive. The first result of this section is that there exists a constructive characterisation of typical database states. That is, there exists an effective algorithm for the construction of typical database states. The algorithm is only sketched in this paper, a full description can be found in [16].

The construction of typical database states is based on three observations. The first observation is that a condition induces an equivalence relation on a database state. Consider for example the rule *paint-red*, with selection condition *color = red*. For this rule, the actual color of an object is immaterial. All one needs to describe the effect of its execution is the distinction between *color = red* and *color ≠ red*. So, a database with only two objects, one whose color is red and the other whose color is not, is typical for this particular problem.

The second observation is that the truth of a post-condition depends on the truth of a, related, pre-condition. Consider for example the rule (*red, paint-cell(color = color ∘ neighbor.left)*), which gives red cells the color of their left neighbor. The evaluation of the condition *color = red* for an object *o after* execution of the rule equals the evaluation of *color ∘ neighbor.left = red* for that same object *o before* execution of the rule.

The final observation is that consistency is decidable for our class of conditions. That is, given a condition C it is possible to determine whether there exists a database state *db* with an object *o*, such that $C(o, db)$ holds. In fact, if the condition is consistent, the algorithm returns such a pair (o, db), otherwise it fails. The pair (o, db) is called a witness for C.

The consistency check goes roughly as follows. First the condition C is reordered according to some suitable order (basically in ascending complexity). Then one starts building a witness database state around an object *o*, using the elementary conditions of C in order. If at any point the construction of the state cannot be continued C is inconsistent, otherwise it is consistent.

With these three observations the construction of the typical database is roughly as follows:

1. Generate all consistent conditions of length $L_c \times L_m$ using only constants from the set *Const*, together with their witnesses.

2. Merge the witness database states into a final database state.

This final database state is typical for conditions of length L_c, methods of length L_m, and constants *Const*.

Theorem 1: There exists an effective algorithm for the construction of a typical database for conditions of length L_c, methods of length L_m, and constants *Const*

Now that typical database states can be constructed, it is relatively straightforward to characterize that part of a database state which causes dependence between two rules R_1 and R_2. For example, under set semantics the algorithm is as follows. First create a *tdb*, copy it, and execute R_1 followed by R_2 upon one of them and R_2 followed by R_1 upon the other. Subsequently, compare the resulting database states and collect the objects which differ in these states. This set causes the dependency between the rules. It is characterized by the disjunction of the conditions satisfied before rule execution by the objects in it.

Theorem 2: Let R_1 and R_2 be two rules for the classes C_{R_1} and C_{R_2} respectively. Then there exists an effective algorithm to construct conditions C_1 and C_2 such that

$\forall db \in DB$:
$$(\forall o \in C_{R_1} : C_1(o, db) \wedge \forall o \in C_{R_2} : C_2(o, db)) \leftrightarrow$$
$$(Ex([R_1, R_2], db, set) = Ex([R_2, R_1], db, set))$$

and there exists an effective algorithm to construct conditions C_1 and C_2 such that

$\forall db \in DB \; \forall o_1 \in C_{R_1} \; \forall o_2 \in C_{R_2}$:
$$(C_1(o_1, db) \wedge C_2(o_2, db)) \leftrightarrow$$
$$(Ex([R_1(o_1), R_2(o_2)], db, instance) = Ex([R_2(o_2), R_1(o_1)], db, instance))$$

Thus, the conflict set is characterized by the conditions $\neg C_1$ and $\neg C_2$. These conditions precisely indicate the database area in which the rules are independent and therefore helps the user to detect options for redefinition of rules to prevent dependencies. Note that the conflict set for self-independence can be characterised by setting $R_1 = R_2$ in theorem 2.

Ordering rules

A non-confluent, terminating rule set can, obviously, be made confluent by ordering the execution of dependent rules. For this, we introduce the sequence operator denoted by ;. To order the execution of a set of rules, R, a new rule composed of the sequence operator and the rules of R has to be defined. Let $R_1, \cdots, R_n$ be rules as defined in Section 2, then the syntax for composed rule definition is:

Rule rule_name $= (R_1 ; \cdots ; R_n)$

An example of such a rule is **Rule** move_paint_red $= (move\_red ; paint\_red)$ where *move_red* moves red cells to the right side of their board. Thus the rule *move_paint_red* moves red cells first and thereafter paints them orange.

A composed rule is activated whenever one of its components is activated. Its execution is described in terms of execution of these components. Let rule $R \equiv (R_1; \cdots; R_n)$ be a composed rule. Executing R under set semantics results in the sequential consideration of R_i for execution.

```
execute(R, db, set) = {
    for i := 1 to n do
        db := execute(R_i, db, set)
    od
    return db }
```

Under instance semantics the execution of R also results in the sequential consideration of R_i for execution. However, the difference with set semantics is that whenever a rule R_i is considered for execution it may execute as long as it is activated. This in order to make the ; operator suitable for confluence enforcement. If the instance semantics would have been to consider each R_i in sequence but only let it execute once, it would not have been suitable for this task. For example, to enforce confluence for the dependent rules R_1 and R_2 the execution sequences should not only be limited to sequences of the form $[R_1, R_2, R_1, R_2, \cdots]$ as then both the sequence $[R_1(o_1), R_2(o_2), R_1(o_3), R_2(o_3), \cdots]$ and the sequence $[R_1(o_3), R_2(o_3), R_1(o_1), R_2(o_2), \cdots]$ could occur and they do not necessarily result in the same database state. Thus sequences should be further restricted to the form $[R_1(o_1), R_1(o_3), \cdots, R_2(o_2), R_2(o_3), \cdots]$.

As the rules sets considered in this section are terminating, we know that the execution of rule R under this depicted instance semantics terminates too.

```
execute(R, db, instance) = {
    for i := 1 to n do
        while activated(Rᵢ, db) do
            db := execute(Rᵢ, db, instance)
        od
    od
    return db }
```

With these semantics, confluence of a rule set can indeed be enforced by ordering the dependent rules of the set.

Composed rules can be used for the definition of a total order. For example, if R_1, R_2, and R_3 terminate in n steps the order $R_1 > R_2 > R_3$ is defined by $R = (((R_1^n; R_2)^n; R_3)^n)$ where R^n means the sequence of n $R's$.

Theorem 3: Let *Rules* be a rule set, let $\mathcal{O}$ be a total order on *Rules*, and let *sem* denote either set or instance semantics. Then, *terminate(n, Rules, sem)* implies the existence of a rule R composed of rules in *Rules* such that the execution of R equals the execution of *Rules* while considering the order $\mathcal{O}$.

A combination

Characterisation of conflict sets together with ordering of rule execution can be used to transform two dependent rules into three independent ones. If R_1 and R_2 are two dependent rules they are transformed into two rules R_1' and R_2', which are like R_1 and R_2 restricted to the database minus the conflict set, and into a rule R_{12} which is the ordered composition of R_1 and R_2 restricted to the conflict set. In order for the transformed rules to be independent, R_1' and R_2' have to be independent of each other and they have to be independent of R_{12}. The latter requires R_1' to be independent from the R_1 and the R_2 part of R_{12} and the same holds for R_2'. Obviously, due to their definition, R_1' and R_2' are independent of each other. To guarantee the other requirements, the original rules and their (extended) conflict set have to satisfy an extra condition.

Independence of $R_1'(R_2')$ with the $R_2(R_1)$ part of R_{12} is guaranteed by self independence. Thus, the extra condition is that *Self_independent*(R_1) and *Self_independent*(R_2) should hold.

In [15], we formulated a sufficient condition for independence. It is based on stability of select sets and updates. This idea will be used to guarantee independence of R_1' and R_2' with the R_2 and R_1 part of R_{12}. For this, we extend the notion of conflict set. Not only objects for which the execution order of R_1 and R_2 matters are a member of the conflict set but also objects which are due to this are a member of the conflict set. The extended set is incrementally constructed as follows: First create a typical database, copy it, and execute $R_1; R_2$ upon one of them and $R_2; R_1$ upon the other. Compare the resulting databases and collect the objects which differ in them. This set of objects is the initial conflict set. In each following step, objects that might influence the objects in the conflict set are added to the set. An object o_1 influences an object o_2 if the update of o_1 affects the update of o_2. That is, if

o_1 is related to o_2 through an update expression, o_1 might influence the update of o_2. For example, if $a_1(o_2) = o_1$ and $a_3 := a_2 \circ a_1$ is an assignment executed by o_2 then o_1 might influence o_2. The construction of the conflict set is completed if there are no more objects to be added to it. This extended conflict set is characterized by the disjunction of the conditions satisfied before rule execution by the objects in it. Whenever the conflict set is invariant under the execution of R_1 and R_2 both the updates and the select sets of the transformed rules are stable. And thus the transformed rules are independent.

Theorem 4: Let $R_1 = (Q_1(C_1), M_1)$ and $R_2 = (Q_2(C_2), M_2)$ be two rules dependent of each other but independent of theirselves. Then there exists an effective algorithm to construct an extended, invariant conflict set characterised by the conditions C^1 and C^2 such that the rule set $\{R_1', R_2', R_{12}\}$ with the rules defined by

$$
\begin{aligned}
R_1' &= (Q_1(C_1 \wedge \neg C^1), M_1) \\
R_2' &= (Q_2(C_2 \wedge \neg C^2), M_2) \\
R_{12} &= (Q_1(C_1 \wedge C^1), M_1); (Q_2(C_2 \wedge C^2), M_2))
\end{aligned}
$$

is independent.

5 Conclusions and future work

We have described three strategies to establish confluence for terminating rule sets. First, a precise characterisation of the conflict set of dependent rules is given such that the user easily sees why rules are dependent and what can be done about it. Second, an ordering mechanism more expressive than a partial ordering is defined. By explicit ordering rule execution confluence is enforced. And finally, the characterisation of conflict sets and ordering of execution are combined for the generation of an independent rule set out of a dependent one.

The most important extension we are planning is to consider a more expressive rule language. For example, the incorporation of history in our data model such that rules not only react on interesting database states but also on interesting database state changes.

References

[1] S. Ceri and J. Widom. Deriving production rules for incremental view maintenance. In *Proceedings of the 17th International Conference on VLDB*, pages 577–589, 1991.

[2] S. Chakravarthy. Rule management and evaluation: An active dbms perspective. In *SIGMOD RECORD*, volume 18, pages 20–28, 1989.

[3] U. Dayal, A. Buchmann, and D.R. McCarthy. Rules are objects too: a knowledge model for an active object oriented dbms. In *Proceedings of the Second International Workshop on Object-Oriented Database Systems*, pages 129–143, 1988.

[4] O. Diaz, N. Paton, and P. Gray. Rule management in object oriented databases a uniform approach. In *Proceedings of the 17th International Conference on VLDB*, pages 317–326, 1991.

[5] S. Gatziu, A. Geppert, and K.R. Dittrich. Integrating active concepts into an object-oriented database system. In *Proceedings of the 3th International Workshop on DBPL*, pages 341–357, 1991.

[6] E.N. Hanson. An initial report on the design of ariel: A dbms with an integrated production rule system. In *SIGMOD RECORD*, volume 18, pages 12–19, 1989.

[7] R. Hull and D. Jacobs. Language constructs for programming active databases. In *Proceedings of the 17th International Conference on VLDB*, pages 455–467, 1991.

[8] Y.E. Ioannidis and T.K. Sellis. Conflict resolution of rules assigning values to virtual attributes. In *SIGMOD RECORD*, volume 18, pages 205–214, 1989.

[9] J.W. Klop. Term rewriting systems: A tutorial. In *Bull. European Assoc. Theoretical Computer Science*, volume 32, pages 143–183, 1987.

[10] A.M. Kotz, K.R. Dittrich, and J.A. Mulle. Supporting semantics rules by a generalized event/trigger mechanism. In *Advances in Database Technology: EDBT 90, LNCS 416*, pages 76–91, 1990.

[11] U. Schreier, H. Pirahesh, R. Agrawal, and C. Mohan. Alert, an architecture for transforming a passive dbms into an active dbms. In *Proceedings of the 17th International Conference on VLDB*, pages 469–478, 1991.

[12] E. Simon and C. deMaindreville. Deciding whether a production rule is relational computable. In *Proceedings of the ICDT 88, LNCS 326*, pages 205–222, 1988.

[13] M. Stonebraker, E. Hanson, and C.H. Hong. The design of the postgres rule system. In *Readings in Database Systems, eds. M. Stonebraker*, pages 556–565, 1988.

[14] M. Stonebraker, A. Jhingran, J. Goh, and S. Potamianos. On rules, procedures, caching and views in database systems. In *Proceedings of the ACM SIGMOD conference*, pages 281–290, 1990.

[15] M.H. van der Voort and A.P.J.M. Siebes. Termination and confluence of rule execution. In *To be published in the proceedings of the second international conference on Information and Knowledge Management*.

[16] M.H. van der Voort and A.P.J.M. Siebes. A design theory for active objects. Technical report, CWI, 1993.

[17] A. Aiken J. Widom and J.M. Hellerstein. Behavior of database production rules: Termination, confluence, and observable determinism. In *SIGMOD RECORD*, volume 21, pages 59–68, 1992.

[18] J. Widom and S.J. Finkelstein. Set-oriented production rules in relational database systems. In *Proceedings of the ACM SIGMOD conference*, pages 259–270, 1990.

[19] Y. Zhou and M. Hsu. A theory for rule triggering systems. In *Advances in Database Technology: EDBT 90, LNCS 416*, pages 407–422, 1990.

Integrating Graphs/Objects with Deduction

Merging Graph Based and Rule Based Computation*

J. Paredaens   P. Peelman

Dept. Wiskunde en Informatica[†]
University of Antwerp (UIA)
Antwerp, Belgium

L. Tanca

Dipartimento di Elettronica[‡]
Politecnico di Milano
Milan, Italy

Abstract

In this paper we propose the merging of two different computation paradigms: the fixpoint computation for deductive databases and the pattern matching computation for graph based languages. These paradigms are nicely combined in the declarative, graph based, database query language G-Log. A natural algorithm to compute general G-Log programs turns out to be very inefficient. We therefore present a more efficient backtracking fixpoint algorithm for Generative G-Log, a syntactical sublanguage of G-Log that, like G-Log, is non-deterministic complete. This algorithm reduces to the standard fixpoint computation for a sublanguage of Generative G-Log that is the graphical equivalent of Datalog. The paper further studies some interesting properties like satisfiability and triviality, that in general are undecidable for full G-Log and turn out to be decidable for sufficiently general classes of Generative G-Log programs.

Keywords: Deductive Databases, Graph Based Databases, Database Theory, Database Algorithms, Data Models, Complex Objects.

1   Introduction

Deductive databases provide a very interesting paradigm for extending the expressive power of database languages. Query languages such as Datalog [1, 2], which increase the expressiveness of the traditional query languages by the recursion mechanism, have already become widespread in the research community. Subsequently, extensions of Datalog incorporating features like

*This work was partially supported by the project LOGIDATA+ of the National Research Council of Italy (CNR) and by the "impulsprogramma informatietechnologie" of the "Diensten voor Programmatie van het Wetenschapsbeleid", nr. IT/IF/13.

[†]Address: Universiteitsplein 1, B-2610 Antwerpen, Belgium. Tel: 32.3/820.24.18. E-mail: peelman@wins.uia.ac.be.

[‡]Address: Piazza Leonardo Da Vinci 32, I-20133 Milano, Italy. Tel: 39.2/23.99.36.24. E-mail: tanca@ipmel2.elet.polimi.it.

negation, complex objects and aggregate functions have been developed [3, 4]. However, there are still fundamental shortcomings of logic bases, for instance the poor representation of objects with identity, and graph-like structures.

In this direction, research has gone towards the introduction of object-orientation in the field of database theory [5, 6]. Object-oriented data models offer a very natural way to represent very complicated data structures like networks, hypertext, pictorial information and even sound. However, such a high modeling power has to be presented to the user in a comprehensible, easy-to-manipulate fashion.

Nowadays, we have sufficient hardware to build graphical and graph-oriented interfaces for most of the software we use. Recently, a few products have been designed that use a "two-dimensional" interface. Query-by-Example was the first example of such an interface [7], while more recently OSF/Motif, AT&T/Open Look, Windows 3.1 and NextStep have been developed. On the other hand, graphical query languages such as PICASSO, ISIS, SNAP, OOQBE, GOOD and GraphLog have been designed [8, 9, 10, 11, 12, 13]. The fundamental data structure behind all these languages is graphs. The scheme, as well as the instances of a database, are represented by graphs, and the idea of most of the languages considered is to transform these graphs in such a way that the resulting graph represents the result of a query or update, or a constraint.

Readability is a major reason for preferring graphs to the classical linear form of logic. Graphs also have an important advantage: they can keep all the information about an entity at a single node and show related information by arcs connected to that node. Systems based on graphs take advantage of this in algorithms for scanning the graphs to generate language or perform inferences. By contrast, linear notations scatter related pieces of information all through a formula, thus making analysis and comprehension much more complex. Therefore, we propose a graph based data model combined with a rule based query language, which facilitates working with the end-user interface, but still offers strong expressive and modeling power.

In this paper we study a number of features of such an integrated language, *G-Log* [14, 15], which has proved to be very powerful. G-Log is non-deterministic complete, i.e. it can express any non-deterministic database query. The language can also be used to express database constraints. However, its rich syntax also makes it unhandy for efficient computation and prevents the decidability of many properties. Thus, we propose *Generative G-Log*, a syntactical restriction of G-Log, that is shown to have the same expressive power. A number of interesting properties that affect computation become decidable for a significant class of Generative G-Log programs.

Moreover, the algorithm that computes Generative G-Log programs is more efficient than the naive G-Log computation algorithm. Since it is always possible to translate a G-Log program into Generative G-Log, we obtain a different evaluation algorithm that reduces to standard fixpoint computation on the segment of Generative G-Log that is equivalent to classical Datalog.

This paper is organized as follows. In Section 2 we summarize the language of G-Log from [14, 16]. This section is included to make the paper self-contained and gives some examples of possible applications of the G-Log formalism. Subsection 2.7 is original, and presents the Naive Evaluation Algorithm for G-Log programs, which turns out to be quite inefficient. In Section 3 we study the decidability of triviality, satisfiability, identicality and emptyness, four properties that are related to the computation of programs.

Generative G-Log is presented in Section 4, together with the translation of a G-Log program into an equivalent Generative G-Log program. Subsection 4.2 contains the algorithm for the computation of Generative G-Log programs, that is a generalization of the standard fixpoint computation for Datalog programs. In Section 5, we show that the properties of Section 3 become decidable for Generative G-Log sets. Here we also discuss termination for Generative G-Log programs. Finally, in Section 6, we draw the conclusions of this discussion. Due to space limitation, all the proofs of the theorems are omitted; they can be found in [17], which is the unpublished report version of this paper.

2   The G-Log Language

In this section we informally present the data model and the language of G-Log. The formal definitions and more examples can be found in [14, 16].

In G-Log, *directed labeled graphs* are used as the formalism to specify and represent database schemes, instances, queries and constraints. The *nodes* of the graphs stand for objects and the *edges* indicate relationships between objects. We distinguish two kinds of nodes: *printable nodes*, depicted as ellipses, indicate objects with a representable value; *non-printable nodes*, depicted as rectangles, indicate abstract objects.

2.1   Data Model

The (database) *scheme* contains information about the structure of the database. This includes the (types of) objects that are allowed in the database, how they can be related and what values they can take. A scheme contains four sets: a set $NPOL$ of *non-printable object labels*, a set POL of *printable object labels*, a set EL of *edge labels* and a set $\mathcal{P}$ of *productions*.

The productions dictate the structure of G-Log instances; they are triples representing the types of the edges in the instance graphs. The first component of a production always belongs to $NPOL$ since only non-printable objects can be related to other objects. The second component is an edge label and the third component is a printable or non-printable object label. A database scheme can be represented as a directed labeled graph by taking $NPOL \cup POL$ as nodes and $\mathcal{P}$ as edges. Finally, we assume a function π associating to each printable object label a set of *constants*, which is its domain.

Figure 1 contains a scheme for a database about molecules. Molecules have a name and contain atoms. Atoms have a symbol and an atom number, and can be bound to other atoms of the molecule.

A (database) *instance* over a scheme S contains the actual information that is stored in the database. It is a directed labeled graph $I = (N, E)$.

N is a set of labeled nodes. Each node represents an object whose type is specified by its label. The label $\lambda(n)$ of a node n of N belongs to $NPOL$ or to POL. In the first case, n is called a non-printable node; otherwise n is printable. If n is printable, it has an additional label $print(n)$, called the *print label*, which must be a constant in $\pi(\lambda(n))$.

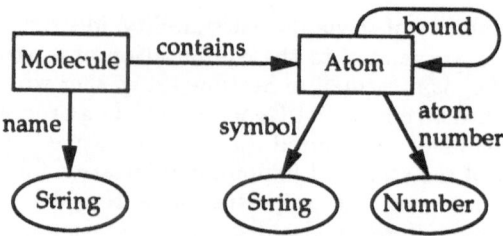

Figure 1: A database scheme for molecule representations.

E is a set of directed labeled edges. An edge e of E going from node n to n' is denoted (n, α, n'). α is the label of e and belongs to EL. The edges must also conform to the productions of the scheme, so $(\lambda(n), \alpha, \lambda(n'))$ must belong to $\mathcal{P}$. Besides these edges, we also assume an implicit equality edge (an edge with an equality sign as label) going from each node of the instance to itself.

Figure 2 contains an instance over the scheme of Figure 1. It represents a molecule with atom structure H_2O.

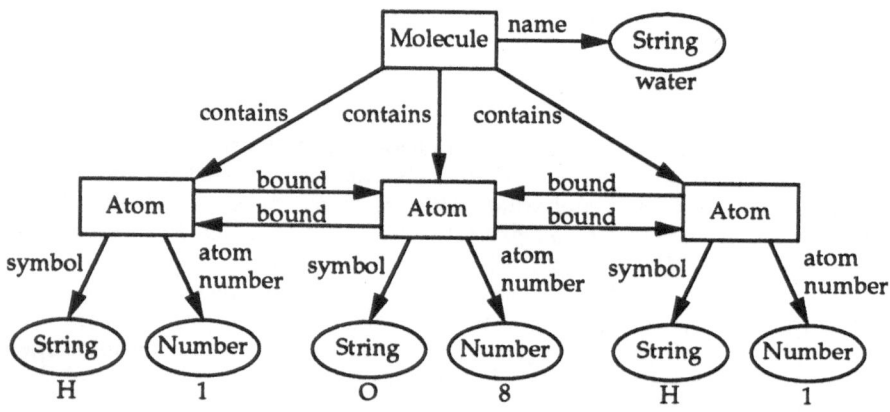

Figure 2: An instance of the molecules database.

2.2 An Introductory Example

G-Log queries over a database instance are expressed by *programs*, which consist of *rules*. These rules are also represented as graphs. Like Horn clauses, rules in G-Log represent implications. To distinguish the body of the rule from the head in the graph P representing the rule, the part of P that corresponds to the body is colored red, and the part that corresponds to the head is green. Since this paper is in black and white, we use thin lines for red nodes and edges and thick lines for green ones.

Figure 3 contains a G-Log rule over the database scheme of Figure 1. It expresses the query: *Give all molecules containing an oxygen atom.* To indicate all such molecules, we link them to a **Result**-node by an **in**-edge.

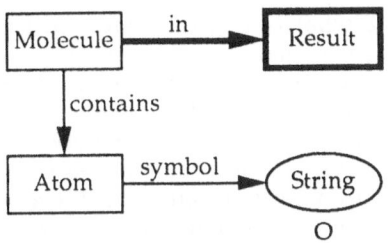

Figure 3: A G-Log rule.

An instance satisfies a rule if every matching of the red part of the rule in the instance, can be extended to a matching of whole rule in the instance. The matchings of (parts of) rules in instances are called embeddings. For example, the instance I of Figure 2 does not satisfy the rule r of Figure 3. In fact, there is one possible embedding i of the red part of r in I, since I contains only one **Molecule**-node that contains an oxygen atom: the water molecule. Hence, the **Molecule**-node of I must be connected to a **Result**-node and this is not the case.

Because I does not satisfy r, I is extended in a minimal way such that it satisfies r. In this case, the effect is that a **Result**-node is created and is linked to the **Molecule**-node by an **in**-edge. Now the instance satisfies the rule, and no smaller superinstance of I does, so this is the result of the query specified by the rule.

Rules in G-Log can also contain negation, both in the body and in the head. Therefore we use solid lines to represent positive information and dashed lines to represent negative information. So a G-Log rule can contain four colors: red solid (RS), red dashed (RD), green solid (GS) and green dashed (GD). The rule of Figure 4 contains no GD part and expresses: *Give all molecules containing an oxygen atom and no carbon atoms.*

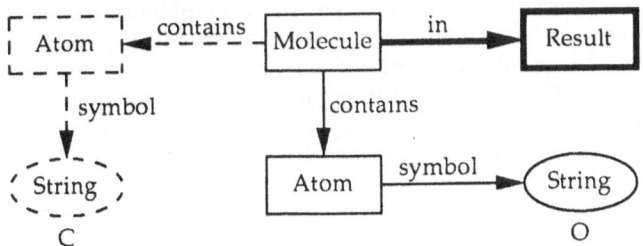

Figure 4: A G-Log rule involving negation.

The instance I of Figure 2 also does not satisfy this rule. The one possible embedding i of the RS part of r in I is a valid one since it cannot be extended to an embedding of the RS and the RD part of r in I. Hence, the **Molecule**-node of I must be connected to a **Result**-node (to extend i to an embedding of the RS and the GS part of r in I), and this is not the case.

2.3 G-Log Rules and Sets

We now formally define what G-Log rules are and when an instance satisfies such a rule, or a set of such rules.

G-Log rules are constructed from patterns. A *pattern* over a database scheme is similar to an instance over that scheme. There are two minor differences: in a pattern equality edges may occur between different nodes, having the same label, and in a pattern printable nodes may have no print label. A pattern denotes a graph that has to be embedded in an instance, i.e. matched to a part of that instance. An equality edge between two different nodes indicates that they must be mapped to the same node of an instance.

A *colored pattern* over a scheme is a pattern of which every node and edge is assigned one of the colors RS, RD, GS or GD. If P is a colored pattern, we indicate by P_{RS} the red solid part of P, by $P_{RS,RD}$ the whole red part of P, by $P_{RS,GS}$ the solid part of P and by $P_{RS,GS,GD}$ the whole pattern without the red dashed part. In general these parts will not be patterns, since they can contain dangling edges. However, for P to be a G-Log rule, we require that these four subparts of P are patterns.

Formally, a *G-Log rule* r consists of two schemes S_1 and S_2, and a graph P. S_1 is called the *source* (scheme) of r. S_2 is a superscheme[1] of S_1, and is referred to as the *target* (scheme) of r. P must be a colored pattern over S_2 such that P_{RS}, $P_{RS,RD}$, $P_{RS,GS}$ and $P_{RS,GS,GD}$ are patterns over S_2. Figure 3 contains the colored pattern P of a rule, that has as source the scheme of Figure 1, and as target the same scheme, to which a **Result**-node and an **in**-edge are added.

To define when an instance satisfies a rule, we need the notion of embedding. An *embedding* i of a pattern $P = (N_P, E_P)$ in an instance $I = (N_I, E_I)$ is a total mapping $i : N_P \rightarrow N_I$, such that for every node n in N_P holds that $\lambda(i(n)) = \lambda(n)$ and that if n has a print label, then $print(i(n)) = print(n)$. Also, if (n, α, n') is an edge in E_P, then $(i(n), \alpha, i(n'))$ must be an edge in E_I.

Let $P = (N, E)$ be a subpattern of the pattern P' and let I be an instance. An embedding j of P' in I is an *extension* of an embedding i of P in I if $i = j|N$. An embedding i of P in I is *constrained* by P' if P' equals P or if there is no possible extension of i to an embedding of P' in I. We use the notion of "constrained" to express negation: an embedding is constrained by a pattern if it *cannot* be extended to an embedding of that pattern.

Let r be a G-Log rule with colored pattern P and target S_2. An instance I over S_2 *satisfies* r if every embedding P_{RS} in I that is constrained by $P_{RS,RD}$, can be extended to an embedding $P_{RS,GS}$ in I that is constrained by $P_{RS,GS,GD}$.

As we informally mentioned before, the instance of Figure 2 does not satisfy the rule of Figure 4. The only embedding i of P_{RS} in I is constrained by $P_{RS,RD}$ (because it cannot be extended to an embedding of $P_{RS,RD}$ in I), and cannot be extended to an embedding of $P_{RS,GS}$ in I.

To express queries in G-Log, we can combine several rules that have the same source S_1 and target S_2 in one *G-Log set*. So, a G-Log set A is a finite set

---

[1]Sub- and superscheme, sub- and superinstance, and sub- and superpattern are defined with respect to set inclusion.

of G-Log rules that work on the same schemes. S_1 is called the *source* (scheme) of A and S_2 is its *target* (scheme). The generalization of satisfaction to the case of G-Log sets is straightforward. Let A be a G-Log set with target S. An instance I over S *satisfies* A if I satisfies every rule of A.

In G-Log is also possible to use goals. A *goal* over a scheme S is a subscheme of S, and is used to select information of the database. Normally, a goal is combined with a query to remove uninteresting information from the resulting instance.

The effect of applying a goal G over a scheme to an instance I over the same scheme is called I *restricted to* G (notation: $I|G$) and is the maximal subinstance of I that is an instance over G. The definition of satisfaction of a G-Log set is easily extended to sets with goals. If A is a G-Log set with target S_2, then an instance I over G *satisfies* A *with goal* G if there exists an instance I' over S_2 such that I' satisfies A and $I'|G = I$.

2.4   G-Log and First Order Predicate Calculus

There is a strong connection between G-Log and first order predicate calculus. In [18] we introduced the mapping τ_I, that transforms an instance over a G-Log scheme S into an interpretation over the many sorted first order language that corresponds to S. The following result holds ([18]):

Theorem 1   For every closed formula Φ of the binary many-sorted predicate calculus with equality, it is possible to construct a set of G-Log rules A and a goal G, such that an instance I satisfies A with G if and only if Φ is true in $\tau_I(I)$.   □

The previous result means that for every formula on a binary many sorted first order language there is an effective procedure that transforms it into an "equivalent" set of G-Log rules and a goal. Hence in this way, G-Log can be seen as a graphical counterpart of logic.

Based on this similarity, other applications besides the ones suggested by the previous example come to the mind. For example, expressing database constraints is very easy. Suppose we want to express that a molecule that contains no carbon atoms, must contain an oxygen atom that is not bound to any hydrogen atoms. This is naturally expressed in Figure 5. Note that the instance of Figure 2 does not satisfy this constraint.

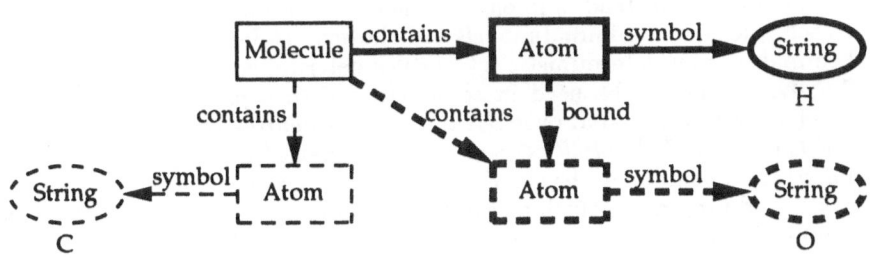

Figure 5: A constraint expressed in G-Log

Note that, even though the transformation of first order formulas into G-Log is completely algorithmic, there are simple formulas (for example $\forall x \; (A(x) \lor B(x) \lor C(x))$), which are not easily expressed in G-Log. However, we believe that the immediateness of the graph based notation, that for instance highlights links between objects very clearly, accounts for the increased difficulty of expression encountered in some special cases. Recall that even in Datalog it is not possible to express the example formula by means of only one rule.

2.5 G-Log Programs

In the previous section we defined when an instance satisfies a G-Log set. Since we also want to use G-Log as a database language, we need to define its effect, i.e. the way it acts on instances to produce other instances. The *semantics* of a G-Log set A with source S_1 and target S_2 is a binary relation over instances defined by:

$Sem(A) = \{(I, J) \mid$ 1. I is an instance over S_1 and J is an instance over S_2,
2. J satisfies A,
3. $J|S_1 = I$,
4. No subinstance of J satisfies conditions 1. to 3.

Item 3 expresses the requirement that in G-Log we only allow *queries*, and no updates. If a G-Log rule contains a red dashed and a green solid part, then it can be satisfied either by adding the red dashed part to an instance or by adding the green solid part. Because of item 3, the source scheme can be chosen is such a way that only one (or even none) of the two extensions is allowed. In this way the semantics of the rule also depends on its source scheme. Item 4 expresses minimality. In general there will be more than one minimal result of applying a G-Log set to an instance, which corresponds to the fact that G-Log is non-deterministic and *Sem* is a relation and not a function.

In G-Log, it is allowed to sequence sets of rules. A *G-Log program* P is a finite list of G-Log sets such that the target scheme of each set of P equals the source scheme of the next set in the program. The source scheme of the first set is the *source* (scheme) of P, and the target scheme of the last set is the *target* (scheme) of P.

The *semantics* $Sem(P)$ of a G-Log program $P = \langle A_1, \ldots, A_n \rangle$ is the set of pairs of instances (I_1, I_{n+1}), such that there is a chain of instances $I_2, \ldots, I_n$ for which (I_j, I_{j+1}) belongs to $Sem(A_j)$, for all j. If a number of G-Log rules are put in sequence instead of in one set, then, because minimization is applied after each rule, fewer minimal models are allowed. In fact, sequencing can be used to make a non-deterministic set of rules deterministic.

Finally, a goal can be used in conjunction with a program. If S_2 is the target of P and G is a goal over S_2, then the *semantics* of P with *goal* G is: $Sem(P, G) = \{ (I, J) \mid \exists (I, J') \in Sem(P) \text{ such that } J'|G = J \}$.

There are 3 complexity levels of constructions to express queries in G-Log: rules, sets and programs, which all three can be used in conjunction with a goal. This results in the six cases stated in the table of Figure 6. To avoid confusion, we will always use the notation of that table, so when we speak about a G-Log rule, we mean a G-Log rule without a set.

As an example, suppose we are given a binary relation B on a finite domain and we want to find all the (x, y)-pairs for which there is no "B-path" from x

	without goal	with goal
rule	G-Log rule	G-Log rule + goal
set of rules	G-Log set	G-Log set + goal
sequence of sets of rules	G-Log program	G-Log program + goal

Figure 6: The complexity levels of G-Log queries.

to y. In other words, we want all the (x, y)-pairs that are not in the transitive closure of B.

An easy and natural way to solve this query is to compute the transitive closure TC of B, and then take the complement CTC of that relation. The G-Log program + goal of Figure 7 solves this problem. It is a sequence of two sets of rules. The first set, which consists of two rules, adds tc-edges between all nodes that are linked by a B-path. The second set has only one rule and takes the complement of the transitive closure by adding a ctc-edge if there is no tc-edge. Finally, the goal removes the auxiliary tc-edges.

2.6 Expressive Power

If S_2 is a superscheme of S_1, then $Inst(S_1, S_2) = \{ (I_1, I_2) \mid I_1 \text{ is an instance over } S_1, I_2 \text{ is an instance over } S_2 \text{ and } I_1 \subseteq I_2 \}$.

A *non-deterministic database query* (from S_1 to S_2) is a subset of $Inst(S_1, S_2)$ which is recursively enumerable and C-generic, for some finite set C of constants [19]. C-genericity means that, except for the constants of C, the actual value of a constant has no effect on the transformation from instances over S_1 to instances over S_2. We say that a database query language is *non-deterministic complete* iff it defines precisely the set of non-deterministic database queries.

Every G-Log program P defines a non-deterministic database query, because it is recursively enumerable and C-generic, where C is the set of constants occurring in P. On the other hand, in [16] we showed:

Theorem 2   For every non-deterministic database query δ, there exist a G-Log set A and a goal G, such that $Sem(A, G) = \delta$. $\square$

Hence, G-Log is non-deterministic complete. Note that sequencing of G-Log sets is not required to reach the full expressive power of the language.

2.7 Naive Computation

We now show how to compute the result of a G-Log query. We do this by informally presenting an algorithm, the *Naive Instance Generation Algorithm*, that given a G-Log set A with source S_1 and target S_2, and a finite instance I over S_1, produces all finite instances J such that $(I, J) \in Sem(A)$, and does not terminate on infinite instances.

Once one knows how to compute the result of a G-Log set, it is easy to compute the result of a G-Log program: just use the output of the computation for the first set as input for the computation of the second set, and so on. Also the computation for a G-Log program + goal is straightforward: first compute

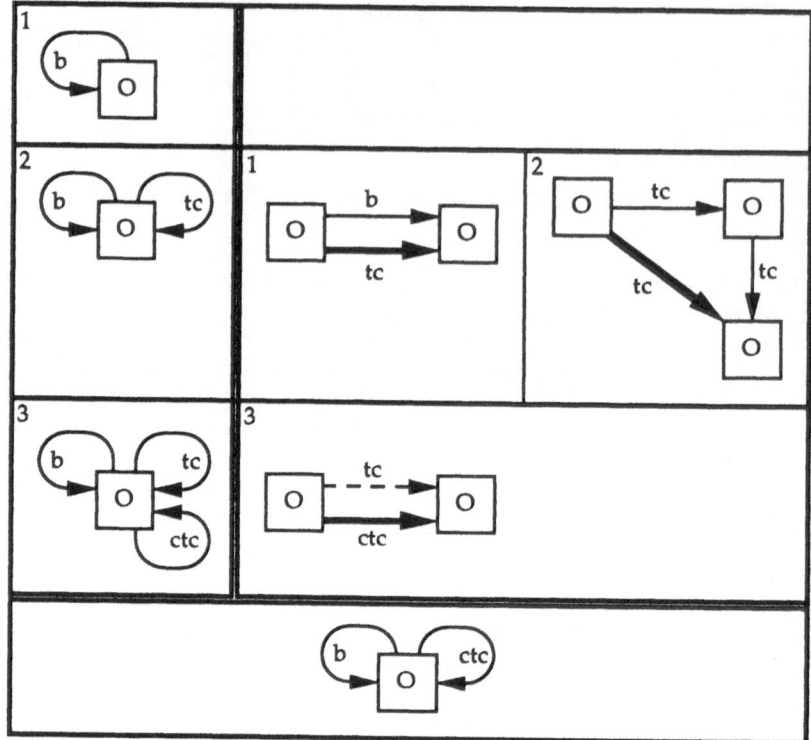

Figure 7: The complement of the transitive closure.

the result(s) of the program and then remove the nodes and edges not belonging to the goal.

Naive Instance Generation Algorithm

The input of the algorithm is a G-Log set A with source S_1 and target S_2, and an instance I over S_1. The algorithm consists of a loop, which iteratively constructs two sets of instances: *SuperInst* and *Result*. When the algorithm starts, *SuperInst* contains I and *Result* is empty (it is assumed that I does not satisfy A).

At each iteration step, *SuperInst* is enlarged by adding to it, for every instance J' that belonged to *SuperInst* at the previous iteration step, all possible superinstances J of J' such that:

1. J is an instance over S_2;

2. $J|S_1 = I$;

3. $|J| = |J'| + 1$.

($|J|$ equals the number of nodes and edges of J.) At each iteration step, all instances J of *SuperInst* that satisfy A and that are not a superinstance of any instance in *Result*, are added to *Result* and are presented as output of the algorithm. □

So, at iteration step n, *SuperInst* contains all superinstances J of I, such that $|J| \leq |I| + n$, and that satisfy Conditions 1 and 2. *Result* is a subset of *SuperInst* and contains all superinstances J of I, such $(I, J) \in Sem(A)$.

Note that this algorithm will never end, and keep producing minimal superinstances of I that satisfy A. Let $Comp(A)$ be the set of all the pairs of instances (I, J), such that J is an output of the algorithm, for input I.

In [17], we prove the soundness of the Naive Instance Generation Algorithm. Of course, we cannot show that it is complete, because $Sem(A)$ can contain infinite instances and no algorithm will produce an infinite result. Therefore we introduce the notion of *finite semantics* of a G-Log set. $FSem(A)$ is the set of pairs of instances (I, J) of $Sem(A)$ for which $|J|$ is finite. We say that the algorithm is *finitely complete* if $FSem(A)$ is contained in $Comp(A)$.

Theorem 3 The Naive Instance Generation Algorithm is sound and finitely complete: $Comp(A) = FSem(A)$, for every G-Log set A. □

Note that finite completeness is not a limitation since for the user it is not important whether there is an infinite answer to his query or there is no answer at all. Thus we can conclude that for every G-Log set A, the finite semantics of A is a semi-computable relation, and G-Log is "finitely semi-computable".

3 Decidability Results of G-Log

In this section, we introduce four properties in the context of G-Log. These properties are important since they can have an impact on the computation of G-Log queries. We then investigate the decidability of these properties. At the end of each subsection, we summarize the decidability results obtained w.r.t. all complexity levels of G-Log queries (Figure 6). Our most prominent result is that triviality is undecidable for G-Log rules. This is most unfortunate, since we cannot decide the property even on the simplest type of query. However, Section 5 will show the corresponding, more comforting results for the sublanguage Generative G-Log.

3.1 Decidability of Instance Related Properties

We introduce the notions of triviality and satisfiability, which are only based on the notion of the satisfaction of an instance to a G-Log set, and are well-known properties in logic. We say that a G-Log set A with target S_2 is:

- *trivial* iff every instance over S_2 satisfies A;

- *satisfiable* iff there exists an instance over S_2, satisfying A.

This definition can also be stated for G-Log rules, for G-Log rules + goals, and for G-Log sets + goals. It makes no sense to define these properties for G-Log programs because on this level a G-Log program is identical to the set of all rules of the program. The difference between a G-Log set and a G-Log program becomes important only when the model minimality is used (so in the semantics relation).

Note that knowing, for a given G-Log set (or rule), that it is trivial or unsatisfiable, allows us to skip the computation on any input instance I. Indeed, in the case of triviality, the result of the computation is always I itself, while in the case of unsatisfiability, there is no output for the computation, for any input I. Observe also that these considerations hold independently of the source scheme.

A simplification of the notion of G-Log rule and set is obtained by automatically deriving the target scheme from the rule patterns. Suppose A is a G-Log set with target S_2, and that S_2 contains a non-printable node $\mathbf{B}$, but that no rule of A contains a node with label $\mathbf{B}$ (a $\mathbf{B}$-node). Then it is irrelevant for the satisfaction of A whether or not an instance over S_2 contains $\mathbf{B}$-nodes. Hence, in the sequel of this paper, we will always assume that the target scheme of a G-Log set A is the *minimal* scheme over which the rules of A are patterns.

In the light of the previous discussion, we see that triviality and satisfiability are two scheme independent properties. So, a G-Log set A is trivial iff it is satisfied by any instance over any scheme, and A is satisfiable iff it is satisfied by some instance over some scheme. We now investigate the decidability of these properties for G-Log rules and sets, both with and without goals.

Theorem 4   The table of Figure 8 gives the decidability results in G-Log for triviality and satisfiability.

G-Log	Triviality	Satisfiability
Rule	U	D
Rule + Goal	U	D
Set	U	U
Set + Goal	U	U

Figure 8: Decidability of triviality and satisfiability.

Sketch of proof   In [17] we reduce the decidability of triviality for G-Log rules to the implication problem for string productions, which is known to be undecidable [20]. Since triviality is already undecidable for G-Log rules, it surely is undecidable for G-Log sets, for G-Log rules + goals and for G-Log sets + goals.

An embedding of a pattern $P = (N, E)$ into a subpattern $P' = (N', E')$ of P is a total mapping $k : N \rightarrow N'$, that is the identity on N', and such that for every node n in N holds that $\lambda(k(n)) = \lambda(n)$ and that if n has a print label, then $print(k(n)) = print(n)$. Also in this case, if (n, α, n') is an edge in E, then $(i(n), \alpha, i(n'))$ must be an edge in E'.

It can be proved [17] that a rule with pattern P is satisfiable iff $P_{RS,RD}$ is non-empty, or if P_{GD} is empty or if there is no embedding of $P_{RS,GS,GD}$ in $P_{RS,GS}$. Hence, satisfiability of G-Log rules is a decidable property. Since satisfiability is undecidable for formulas of the first order predicate calculus with equality [21], and any such formula can be expressed by a G-Log set and a goal, it follows that satisfiability for G-Log sets + goals is undecidable.

Further, because an instance I satisfies a G-Log set A with a goal G iff there is an instance J that satisfies A and such that $I = J|G$, it follows that a goal does not influence the decidability of satisfiability. So, this property is decidable for G-Log rules + goals, and undecidable for G-Log sets. $\square$

3.2 Decidability of Transformation Related Properties

In this section we investigate the notions of identicality and emptyness. These properties depend on the semantics of G-Log programs, as defined in Section 2.5 and therefore also apply to G-Log programs. A G-Log program P with source S_1 and target S_2 is:

- *identical* iff for every instance I over S_1 holds that $(I, I) \in Sem(P)$;

- *empty* iff $Sem(P) = \phi$.

This definition can easily be restated for the other 5 complexity levels of G-Log queries.

Again, observe that the results on identicality and emptyness give interesting hints about the results of computations. If a program with source S_1 is identical, we know in advance that the result of any computation on an instance I over S_1 will be I. Consider now a program P that is empty: we directly know that no result will be produced by applying P to an instance over S_1.

Let A be a G-Log set. One can show [16] that A is unsatisfiable iff there exists a scheme S_1 such that A with source S_1 is empty. This theorem implies that for G-Log sets unsatisfiability and emptyness are two equivalent properties.

Theorem 5 The table of Figure 9 gives the decidability results in G-Log for identicality and emptyness.

G-Log	Identicality	Emptyness
Rule	U	D
Rule + Goal	U	D
Set	U	U
Set + Goal	U	U
Program	U	U
Program + Goal	U	U

Figure 9: Decidability of identicality and emptyness.

Sketch of proof The notion of identicality is strongly connected to triviality. Not surprisingly, we can show that identicality for G-Log rules is undecidable. The proof of this theorem relies on the fact that a rule is trivial iff it is identical when its source and target scheme are equal. As a consequence, identicality is also undecidable for the 5 more complex types of G-Log queries.

Since for G-Log sets emptyness is equivalent to unsatisfiability, we immediately find that it is decidable for G-Log rules and undecidable for G-Log sets. This implies that emptyness is decidable for G-Log rules + goals, and undecidable for G-Log programs, for G-Log sets + goals and for G-Log programs + goals. $\square$

4 Generative G-Log

We now introduce *Generative G-Log*, a restriction of G-Log obtained by not allowing rules with a green dashed part. This simple restriction entails a number of interesting consequences, that are investigated in this section and in the next one. The absence of green dashed elements corresponds to the absence of negative information in the head of rules. In particular, this allows a much simpler computation method, where there is no need to control at every step that the added elements respect the restriction imposed by the green dashed part. The structure of Generative G-Log programs is the same as the structure of G-Log programs: they are sequences of sets of rules, and can be used together with a goal. Also the semantics is defined in the same way as for G-Log.

The ease of computation and the syntactical restriction do not limit the expressive power of Generative G-Log: we show that any G-Log program can be translated into an equivalent one without green dashed elements. As a consequence we obtain that, like G-Log, Generative G-Log is non-deterministic complete. However, it turns out that in order to simulate one G-Log set, a sequence of two Generative G-Log sets and a goal are needed. So, in contrast to G-Log, sequencing is really needed to obtain the required expressive power. We conclude that there exists a trade-off between the use of green dashed and the use of sequencing. Also the role of the goal is very important: it filters out the auxiliary nodes and edges that are used in the simulation.

4.1 Translation of G-Log into Generative G-Log

Rather than describing how G-Log rules, sets and programs can be translated into an equivalent Generative G-Log program with a goal, we give an indicative example that shows how the construction works.

Consider the G-Log rule r of Figure 10. r expresses that an instance must contain an **A**-node that is not connected to any **B**-node by a **1**-edge. Because the source S_1 and the target S_2 are equal, an input instance cannot be changed to satisfy r, so r only accepts or rejects instances. Hence, $Sem(r)$ consists of all pairs of instances (I, I), such that I contains an **A**-node that is not connected to any **B**-node of I by a **1**-edge.

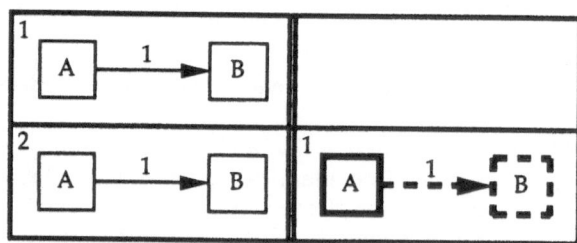

Figure 10: A rule r with a green dashed part.

We simulate r by a program P that is a sequence of two Generative G-Log sets (Figure 11). The first set, A_1, contains one trivial rule, r_1, that says that there must be an **Imp**-node in the instance, if there is an **Imp**-node in the instance. The only use of this rule is to transform S_1 to a scheme S_1', but not to change any instance. Therefore, we know that although S_1' contains a class **Imp** of non-printable nodes, the application of r_1 to any instance I over S_1 does not add an **Imp**-node to I.

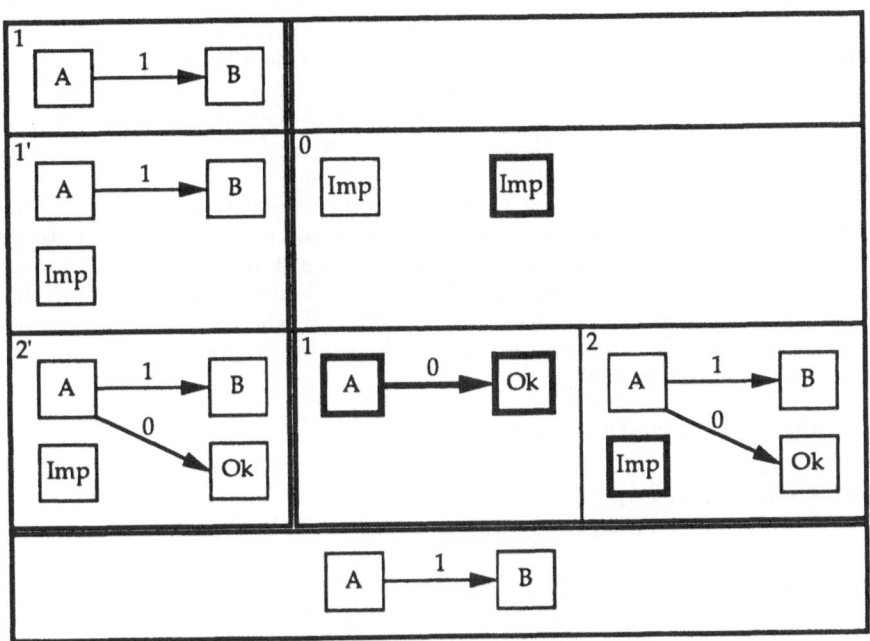

Figure 11: The translation of r.

The second Generative G-Log set, A_2, contains two rules r_2 and r_3. Rule r_2 tags some **A**-node by connecting it to an **Ok**-node with a 0-edge. However, rule r_3 expresses that a tagged **A**-node cannot be connected to a **B**-node. Otherwise there has to be an **Imp**-node in the instance. But, by definition of semantics, it is not allowed to add nodes and edges represented by S_1' to I, so it is not allowed to add an **Imp**-node to I.

So, if every **A**-node of the instance is connected to a **B**-node, then r_2 and r_3 cannot be satisfied both, and the instance is rejected. If there are **A**-nodes that are not connected to a **B**-node, then one of them (which one is non-deterministically chosen) is tagged in the result instance. After the execution of P, the tag is removed by the goal $G = S_2$ over the target S_2' of P. Hence, the instance is unchanged by the whole operation and is accepted.

In [17], we provide a general construction that, given a G-Log program and a goal, transforms it into a Generative G-Log program and a goal. Then we prove:

Theorem 6 For every G-Log program P_1 and goal G_1, there exists a Generative G-Log program P_2 and a goal G_2, such that $Sem(P_1, G_1) = Sem(P_2, G_2)$.

226 □

We conclude that Generative G-Log can express exactly the same transformations as G-Log, thus is just as expressive.

4.2 Efficiency of Evaluation in Generative G-Log

We now present the *FastComp* algorithm, that computes the result of a Generative G-Log set by using a kind of backtracking fixpoint technique. Note that this algorithm cannot be applied to a full G-Log program, since it lacks the control on the restrictions imposed by the green dashed part.

Suppose we are given a set of rules $A = \{r_1, \ldots, r_k\}$ with source S_1 and target S_2, and a finite instance I over S_1. The procedure *FastComp* will try to extend I to an instance J, in such a way that $(I, J) \in FSem(A)$. If this is impossible, it will print the message: "No solution".

FastComp calls the function *Extend*, which recursively adds elements to J until J satisfies A, or until J cannot be extended anymore to satisfy A. In this last case, the function backtracks to points where it made a choice among a number of minimal extensions and continues with the next possible minimal choice. If the function backtracks to its first call, then there is no solution. In this sense, *FastComp* reminds the "backtracking fixpoint" procedure that computes stable models [22].

Procedure *FastComp*(I, A, S_1, S_2)
$J = I$;
if $(Extend(J, A, S_1, S_2))$
{
   minimize(J);
   output(J);
}
else
   output("No solution");

Function *Extend*(**var** J, A, S_1, S_2))
for $(l = 1, \ldots, k)$
  for (every embedding i of $P_{l,RS}$ in J)
   if (J does not satisfy r_l due to i)
   {
     $SetExt = \phi$;
     if $(P_{l,RD} \neq \phi)$
       for (every legal, minimal RD extension Ext of J)
        $SetExt = SetExt \cup \{Ext\}$;
     for (every legal, minimal GS extension Ext of J)
       $SetExt = SetExt \cup \{Ext\}$;
     while $(SetExt \neq \phi)$
     {
       select Ext from $SetExt$;
       add Ext to J;
       if $(Extend(J, A, S_1, S_2))$

```
            return (True);
        else
            remove Ext from J;
            SetExt = SetExt\{ Ext };
    }
        return (False);
    }
return (True);
```

The algorithm uses the notion of "legal, minimal extension" of an instance. By *legal*, we mean that the extension may only contain nodes and edges not belonging to S_1. *Minimal* indicates that no subpart of the extension is already sufficient to make the embedding under consideration extendible.

Like for naive computation of G-Log, we denote by $FastComp(A)$ the set of all the pairs of instances (I, J), such that J is an output of the *FastComp* algorithm, for inputs I and A.

Theorem 7 The *FastComp* algorithm is sound and finitely complete: $FastComp(A) = FSem(A)$, for every Generative G-Log set A. □

Note that because we can simulate G-Log in Generative G-Log, given an input G-Log program, we can translate it into the equivalent Generative G-Log program and then use *FastComp* to compute the result. Another important remark is that *FastComp* reduces to the standard fixpoint computation for those G-Log programs that are the graphical counterpart of Datalog, i.e. programs containing rules that consist of a red solid part and one green solid edge.

We are now going to compare the *FastComp* algorithm with the Naive Instance Generation algorithm. Of course, both algorithms are exponential, since they are able to compute exponential queries, like for example the power set. Even worse, there exist queries for which there are only infinite answers (and this problem is undecidable), so it is even impossible to devise an algorithm for G-Log that gives an answer if there is one. Therefore, we will compare *Naive* and *FastComp* by means of a few examples.

Suppose we are given an instance containing three nodes that are linked by two edges (node 1 is linked to node 2 which is linked to node 3). Consider a program that computes the transitive closure (like the first set of the program of Figure 7). *FastComp* takes 3 steps to compute the result. *Naive* will generate all superinstances of the input instance, containing 3 transitive closure edges, before finding the answer. This results in a set of 252 instances.

As a second example, consider a instance containing three isolated **A**-nodes, and the program that says: "if there is an **A**-node, then it must be linked to a **B**-node by a 1-edge". *FastComp* again takes three steps to find one of the results. *Naive* finds the first solution after three steps, when it has generated 15 instances, and the last solution after six steps, when it has generated 291 instances.

5   Decidability Results of Generative G-Log

The fact that Generative G-Log is as expressive as G-Log is already a strong result. However, in this section we show results on the decidability of properties for Generative G-Log rules, sets and sets with goals, that make the use of Generative G-Log really preferable to that of the full G-Log.

It will become clear that trivial, satisfiable, identical and empty rules and sets are immediately recognizable by a simple inspection of the form of the rules. Especially the case of sets, where the distinction between G-Log and Generative G-Log is most pronounced – all four properties are undecidable for G-Log sets but decidable for Generative G-Log sets – is very important. Indeed, sets form the core of the computation of queries, as we explained in Section 2.7. This is also a concrete argument in favor of the representation power of graph-based languages.

At the end of this section, we discuss termination for Generative G-Log computations. This is undecidable in the general case, but we can easily single out interesting classes of rules and give an answer to the question: *does the computation of programs formed by such rules terminate?*

One of the first properties that Generative G-Log rules have, and that do not hold for full G-Log is the similarity between red dashed and green solid. Let r_1 be a Generative G-Log rule with a non-empty red dashed and green solid part. If r_2 is the rule obtained by switching the colors red dashed and green solid of r_1, then *the semantics of r_1 equals the semantics of r_2* [16]. This property will be fully exploited in the process of investigating termination for classes of Generative G-Log rules.

5.1   Decidability of Instance Related Properties

We now study the decidability of triviality and satisfiability in Generative G-Log.

Theorem 8   The table of Figure 12 gives the decidability results in Generative G-Log for triviality and satisfiability.

Generative G-Log	Triviality	Satisfiability
Rule	D	D
Rule + Goal	D	D
Set	D	D
Set + Goal	U	D

Figure 12: Decidability in Generative G-Log.

Sketch of proof   One can show that a Generative G-Log rule r with ground pattern P is trivial iff

- $P_{RS,RD}$ can be embedded in P_{RS} and P_{RD} is non-empty;

- or $P_{RS,GS}$ can be embedded in P_{RS}.

This implies that triviality is decidable for Generative G-Log rules.

Since a G-Log set A is trivial iff every rule of A is trivial, triviality is also decidable for Generative G-Log sets. To study triviality for rules and sets in conjunction with goals, we need to introduce the notion of a rule, restricted to a goal. Let r be a (Generative) G-Log rule with pattern P, source S_1 and target S_2 and let G be a goal over S_2. The restriction of r to G (denoted $r|G$), is the rule obtained by restricting the pattern and both schemes of r to G. The restriction of a scheme to another scheme is just the intersection of both schemes. Note that the target of $r|G$ is G itself.

It holds that a rule r with goal G is trivial iff

- $r|G$ is trivial;

- or P_{RS} is not a pattern over G.

Hence, triviality is decidable for Generative G-Log rules + goals.

If r is G-Log rule with a non-empty green dashed part, then Generative G-Log program P (and goal G) that expresses r, consists of two sets: A_1 and A_2. It can be shown that r is trivial iff A_2 with goal G is trivial. Since triviality is undecidable for G-Log rules, it is hence also undecidable for Generative G-Log sets + goals.

Satisfiability is decidable for Generative G-Log sets, since one can show that a Generative G-Log set is always satisfiable. Because a goal does not influence the satisfiability, we also find that this property is decidable for Generative G-Log sets + goals. Since satisfiability for G-Log rules and for G-Log rules + goals, is already decidable in the full G-Log, it is surely decidable in Generative G-Log. $\qquad\square$

5.2 Decidability of Transformation Related Properties

Theorem 9 The table of Figure 13 gives the decidability results in Generative G-Log for identicality and emptyness.

Generative G-Log	Identicality	Emptyness
Rule	D	D
Rule + Goal	D	D
Set	D	D
Set + Goal	U	D
Program	D	U
Program + Goal	U	U

Figure 13: Decidability in Generative G-Log.

Sketch of proof It is possible to show that a Generative G-Log rule r with source S_1 and ground pattern P is identical iff

- r is trivial;

- or P_{RS} is no pattern over S_1.

We also proved that a G-Log set is identical iff every rule of the set is identical, and that a G-Log program is identical iff every set of the program is identical.

So, we find that identicality is decidable for Generative G-Log rules, sets and programs.

On the other hand, since identicality is undecidable for G-Log rules, and a G-Log rule can be simulated by a Generative G-Log program with a goal, it follows that identicality is undecidable for Generative G-Log programs + goals. So in this case, the use of goals makes a decidable property undecidable. We now investigate whether a goal has the same effect on the decidability of identicality for Generative G-Log sets and rules.

Let r be a Generative G-Log rule with ground pattern P, source S_1 and target S_2, and let G be a goal over S_2. Take S_1' as S_1 restricted to G, and r' as r restricted to the smallest superscheme of S_1 and G. Then r with goal G is identical iff

- r' is trivial;

- or $P_{RS}|S_1' \neq P_{RS}$.

Hence, identicality is decidable for Generative G-Log rules + goals.

Let A be a Generative G-Log set and let G be a goal over the target of A. Construct A' as A but with source G. Then A with goal G is trivial iff A' with goal G is identical. This implies that for Generative G-Log sets + goals identicality is undecidable.

For G-Log sets and rules, emptyness is equivalent to unsatisfiability. Hence also for Generative G-Log sets and rules this is the case, so for them emptyness is decidable. Like for satisfiability, the use of goals has no influence on emptyness. Hence, emptyness is also decidable for Generative G-Log rules + goal and for Generative G-Log sets + goals. Finally, since emptyness is undecidable for G-Log sets, and a G-Log set can be simulated by a Generative G-Log program with a goal, emptyness is undecidable for Generative G-Log programs and for Generative G-Log programs + goals. □

5.3 Termination

As we mentioned before, there exist G-Log sets and finite instances such that the application of the set to the instance yields infinite results. Even in Generative G-Log there exist sets and finite instances such that the application of the set to the instance yields only infinite results (we will give an example of such a set and an instance at the end of this section).

In this section, we consider subclasses of Generative G-Log. A subclass of Generative G-Log is obtained by putting further restrictions on the allowed colors of nodes and edges. For example, the N(RS,GS);E(RS,RD)-class consists of rules with red and green solid nodes and with red solid and dashed edges; N(RS,RD,GS);E(RS,RD,GS) is Generative G-Log itself. Since there are three colors, there are eight possible color combinations for both the nodes and the edges, so there are 64 classes. 23 classes are syntactically impossible (for instance N();E(RS) is not allowed because P_{RS} is not a graph), so there remain 41 possible classes.

We say that a subclass C of Generative G-Log is *finite* if for every set of rules A of the class C holds that for every pair $(I, J) \in Sem(A)$ holds that if $|I|$ is finite, $|J|$ is finite too. We will now for each of the 41 classes determine whether or not it is finite. Of course, we will not examine all of them. Indeed, if we find out that a class is finite, then all subclasses of it are finite too, and if we find that a class is infinite, then all superclasses of it are infinite too. We have shown that the classes N(RS,RD);E(RS,RD), N(RS);E(RS,RD,GS), N(RS,RD,GS);E(RS), N(RD,GS);E(RD,GS) and N(RS,RD);E(RS,GS) are finite.

If we also consider the subclasses of these 5 classes, we already decided for 27 classes that they are finite. Because the colors red dashed and green solid can be switched, there are 7 subclasses of Generative G-Log that have an equivalent subclass. For example N(RS,RD);E(RS,GS) is equivalent to N(RS,GS);E(RS,RD). Because of this the total number of finite classes becomes 29, so there remain 12 classes.

Consider the set A of rules of the N(RS,GS);E(GS)-class C that is given in Figure 14. If I_ϕ is the empty instance and J is the instance at the bottom of Figure 14, thus an infinite chain of **B**-nodes, then $(I_\phi, J) \in Sem(A)$.

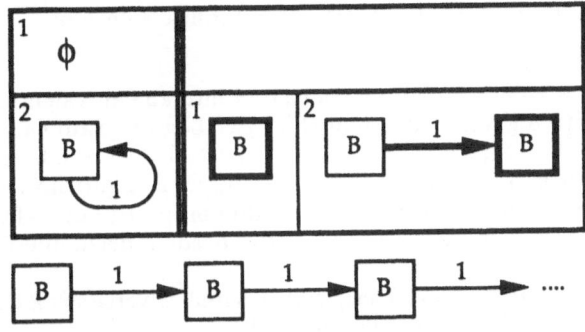

Figure 14: A set with infinite solutions.

There are 7 superclasses of C and the 4 remaining classes have an equivalent class among these 7, so we find that all 12 remaining classes are infinite.

The program of Figure 14 shows that there are sets that can have an infinite result for a given instance. However, there is always a finite result too. Figure 15 presents a set of rules that applied to the empty instance only yields an infinite result.

6   Conclusions

In this paper we discussed the merging of the fixpoint computation paradigm for rule based languages and the pattern matching computation paradigm for graph based languages on the example of the database query language G-Log. We first gave a quick overview of G-Log and introduced a very simple but inefficient algorithm to compute G-Log programs. Because of its generality, G-Log has many undecidable properties. On the other hand, being able to decide such properties would be of great help in the computation of a G-Log program.

Generative G-Log, a syntactical sublanguage of G-Log that, like full G-Log, is non-deterministic complete, is much easier to handle. We showed that any

232

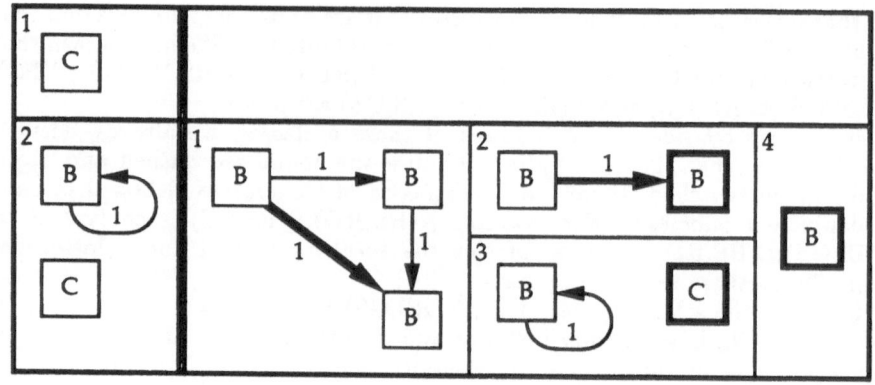

Figure 15: A set with only infinite solutions.

G-Log program with a goal can be translated into an equivalent Generative G-Log program with a goal. Because of this, a G-Log program can be translated into Generative G-Log, and then computed by the more efficient FastComp algorithm, which is a kind of backtracking fixpoint algorithm. Another conclusion of this paper is that many undecidable properties of G-Log sets, which form the core of the computation of queries, become decidable for Generative G-Log.

We wish to thank Stefano Ceri, who revised a version of this paper and provided a great number of useful comments.

References

[1] Ceri S, Gottlob G, Tanca L. Logic Programming and Databases. Springer Verlag, 1990

[2] Ullman JD. Principles of Databases and Knowledge-Base Systems, vol 1 and 2. Computer Science Press, Rockville, MD, 1989

[3] Abiteboul S, Grumbach S. COL: a Logic-based Language for Complex Objects. Proc 1988 EDBT

[4] Lambrichts E, Nees P, Paredaens J, Peelman P, Tanca L. Integration of functions in logic database systems. Data & Knowledge Engineering 1990; 5:207–226

[5] Abiteboul S, Kanellakis PC. Object Identity as a Query Language Primitive. Proc 1989 SIGMOD

[6] Atkinson M, Bancilhon F, De Witt D, Dittrich K, Maier D, Zdonik S. The Object-Oriented Database System Manifesto. Proc 1989 DOOD

[7] Zloof M. Query-by-Example: a Database Language. IBM Systems Journal 1977; 324–343

[8] Kim H, Korth H, Silberschatz A. PICASSO: A Graphical Query Language. Software Practice and Experience 1988; 169–203

[9] Goldman K, Goldman S, Kanellakis P, Zdonik S. ISIS: Interface for a Semantic Information System. Proc 1985 SIGMOD

[10] Bryce D, Hull R. SNAP: A Graphics-based Schema Manager. Proc. 1986 International Conference on Data Engineering

[11] Staes F, Tarantino L, Tiems A. A Graphical Query Language for Object Oriented Databases. Proc 1991 IEEE Workshop on Visual Languages

[12] Gyssens M, Paredaens J, Van Gucht D. A Graph-Oriented Object Model for Database End-User Interfaces. Proc 1990 SIGMOD

[13] Consens MP, Mendelzon AO. GraphLog: a Visual Formalism for Real Life Recursion. Proc 1990 PODS

[14] Paredaens J, Peelman P, Tanca L. G-Log: A Declarative Graphical Query Language. Proc 1991 DOOD

[15] Paredaens J, Peelman P, Tanca L. G-Log; A Graph Based Query Language. Politecnico di Milano Internal Report 92-013

[16] Paredaens J, Peelman P, Tanca L. G-Log: A Declarative Graphical Query Specification Language. University of Antwerp Internal Report 91-16

[17] Paredaens J, Peelman P, Tanca L. Merging Graph Based and Rule Based Computation. University of Antwerp Internal Report 92-07

[18] Paredaens J, Peelman P, Tanca L. G-Log and First Order Predicate Calculus. University of Antwerp Internal Report 91-53

[19] Abiteboul S, Vianu V. Datalog Extensions for Database Queries and Updates. INRIA Internal Report 900

[20] Hopcroft JE, Ullman JD. Introduction to Automata Theory, Languages and Computation. Addison-Wesley, 1979

[21] Dreben B, Goldfarb WB. The Decision Problem. Addison-Wesley, 1979

[22] Sacca D, Zaniolo C. Stable Models and Non-Determinism in Logic Programs with Negation. Proc 1990 PODS

A Logical Query Language for an Object-Oriented Data Model

Alvaro A.A. Fernandes, Norman W. Paton, M. Howard Williams

Department of Computing & Electrical Engineering

Heriot-Watt University

Edinburgh, UK

Abstract

We report on our experience in designing and prototyping ROLL, a logical query language under which object-oriented databases conforming to the model defined in [14, 15] can be seen as *deductive object-oriented databases*. The main contribution of ROLL is to demonstrate the possibility of pursuing for the object-oriented case the same research strategy used in the last decade to extend relation databases with deduction. This paper briefly describes the rationale behind our approach to the field and the DOOD project that is underway at Heriot-Watt. After an introduction to ROLL's underlying data model by means of a simple example, the paper focusses on the implementation of ROLL in a prototype which has been built to experiment with both the language and the model. Certain techniques used in the prototype are described, and ROLL is contrasted with some well-known proposals of deductive languages for object-oriented databases. An indication of future work is given with some conclusions.

1 Introduction

It has long been recognized that the principal benefits offered by deductive and by object-oriented technologies to database systems are distinct and complementary. Deductive databases offer declarative query expression and rule-based programming, and systems are underpinned by a theoretical framework developed from first-order logic. Object-oriented databases (OODBs) offer rich data modelling constructs, and integrate programs and data to provide an effective development platform for new application areas. Furthermore the weaknesses of deductive databases are exactly the strengths of their object-oriented counterparts, and vice-versa – deductive databases are normally associated with the relational model which lacks the expressiveness of the object-oriented models; object-oriented database systems are normally developed without much regard to a theoretical framework, and commonly provide limited support for queries or deductive rules. Any database system which smoothly integrates the two paradigms, without sacrificing the characteristic virtues of either, is likely to present significant opportunities for application-developers in both novel and conventional domains.

The deductive object-oriented database (DOOD) project at Heriot-Watt is developing a system which supports object-oriented and deductive facilities. The approach adopted in this project differs from alternative proposals [11] in using a formally defined object-oriented data model as the starting point for the development of a DOOD. The data model [14, 15], which is outlined briefly in Section 2, supports the mandatory data model features identified in [4], and has been significantly influenced by the structural abstractions supported by many semantic data models. This model has been used as the basis for the design of two languages – an imperative data manipulation language [5] which is used to describe complete applications and as the sole means of performing updates, and a logical query language, which is the subject of this paper. The architecture of the complete system is described in more detail in [13]. The management facilities which implement that data model and the manipulation language are collectively referred to as ROCK (Rule Object Computational Kernel). The logic language itself is referred to as ROLL (Rule Object Logic Language).

ROCK is currently in an advanced stage of implementation using the EXO-DUS extensible database system [20], with the implementation of ROLL soon to follow. ROLL has been prototyped using MegaLog [6]. This stand-alone, inter-active prototype uses the meta-interpretation technique described in Section 4 and has served two purposes – it has enabled experimentation with querying databases conforming to the data model described in Section 2 by means of a logical query language and it has assisted with the theoretical formulation of the logic language, providing a test ground for ideas. This paper describes the current syntax of the logic language under development at Heriot-Watt, and outlines how it has been prototyped using MegaLog.

The paper is structured as follows: Section 2 gives a flavour of the data model on which the logic language acts; the language is itself introduced in Section 3, and illustrated using a number of examples; Section 4 describes the prototype implementation; Section 5 contrasts this work with alternative ap-proaches to the development of query languages for DOODs; Section 6 outlines future directions, and presents some conclusions.

2   The Data Model

This section informally describes the main structural and behavioural con-structs used in the data model. *Primitive types* are domain-independent, and their instances, called *primary objects*, are named by *values*. For instance, string and integer are primitive types; "scotcars" and 18 are primary ob-jects. *Object types* are domain-dependent, and can be user-defined if their in-stances are named by (proper) object identifiers, otherwise their instances are named by values, e.g. company and companyName are object types; !1 is an object identifier naming an instance of company; "scotcars" is a value naming an instance of companyName. (The use of '!' to syntactically mark an object identifier is arbitrary.)

A hardware and software environment implies the existence and the well-typedness of primary objects, i.e. they are assumed to conform to an adequate structural and behavioural representation. Users assign a secondary object to one or more object types, whereby it acquires a structure and a behaviour to conform to. Object identity is strictly supported, detaching the existence of an object from its contingent *state*.

The state of an object consists only of the *references* it makes to other objects. References are of two kinds: the first models *properties*; the other, *construction*. Property references are stipulated through an abstraction mechanism called *attribution*; conceptually, they appear in an object's state as a type-heterogeneous type-indexed collection of object-names. Construction references characterize the object as *complex* and are stipulated by one of three abstraction mechanisms: *association* (stipulating that an object's state will contain a type-homogeneous non-indexed collection of object-names, a set of object identifiers in short); *sequentiation* (in this case, a type-homogeneous $\mathcal{N}$-indexed collection, somewhat like a list if $\mathcal{N}$ is the set of natural numbers); and *aggregation* (in this case, a type-heterogeneous type-indexed collection, somewhat like a record). Attribution and aggregation become distinct by the account they are given in the presence of multiple inheritance, aggregation being the more restrictive.

The *behaviour* of objects is determined by the *interfaces* of the object types they have been assigned to. An interface declares *operations* by associating *operation names* with *operation signatures*. Operation names can be *overloaded* by being declared on two or more distinct object types. The notion of *object class* is introduced, in one-to-one relationship with object types, to detach an interface from the *operation implementation*, called *method*, that realizes it. Users are only concerned with operation interfaces, whereas it is up to designers to write the methods which implement the interfaces using the language components the database is provided with, viz. ROCK & ROLL. This detachment protects users from changes designers may need to make in the implementation. Also, the state of an object is *encapsulated*, i.e. users can only manipulate it by invoking operations contained in the interface of the types it is assigned to. In this paper, only access operations, i.e. queries, are considered. A more comprehensive overview is found in [13].

Both structural and behavioural (multiple) *inheritance* are supported, potential conflicts being ruled out by well-formedness conditions on the schema. Inheritance can be presented as either *specialization*, *generalization* or *partition*, the latter differing from generalization by implicitly implying a non-intersection constraint on the extension of the types involved. Aspects are also catered for: an object type t' is thought of as an aspect of some object type t if t is best modelled by a distinct, typically unrelated, interface even though the structural characterization t' is best modelled as identical to that of t. The presence of inheritance and overloading of operations requires support for *overriding* and *late-binding*.

The schema in Figure 1 is used in examples throughout the paper. The notation used in the diagram is briefly described as follows. A *circle* represents the source from which names of instances of object types are drawn. (In Figure 1, not all arrows into circles are drawn.) A *horizontal oval* represents an object type whose instances are named by values; a *full-line rectangle* one whose instances are named by proper object-identifiers; a *dashed-line rectangle* represents an aspect; a *round-cornered rectangle* represents an operation. A *labelled directed edge* has as label one out of seven symbols: ○ for *attribution*, ⊡ for *generalization*, ⊙ for *partition*, △ for *specialization*, ⊗ for *aggregation*, ✳ for *association*, and ◎ for *sequentiation*. The last three abstraction mechanisms may be specified in a *cohesive* version (not used in Figure 1) by enclosing the characteristic symbol within a square, rather than a circle. The semantic import of cohesion is to define an existence dependency between an object and the object it refers to, i.e. deleting the referred object may imply the deletion of the referring one. An *unlabelled directed edge* drawn as a *full-line* leads from

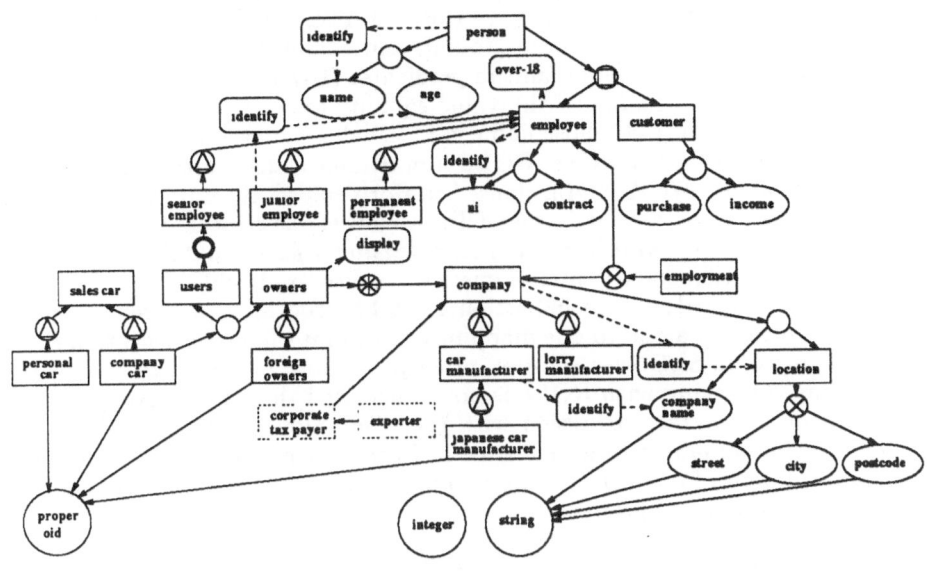

Figure 1: Company Schema Diagram

an object type to the source of its objects' names; drawn as a *dashed-line* it
leads from/to object types that are arguments/results of operations. Finally, in
edges labelled with association, sequentiation or aggregation symbols, a *double-
headed full-line arrow* stipulates the constraint that each instance of the type
being pointed to must be referenced by, possibly many, instances of the type
where the arrow comes from; a *single-headed full-line arrow* the constraint that
each instance must be referenced and at most once. Versions of the latter two
not occurring in the diagram use dashed lines to drop the mandatory aspect of
the reference.

3   The Logic Language

This section introduces ROLL, a logical query language for databases conforming to the model overviewed in Section 2. The ROLL syntax presented here is
reminiscent of [16]. Syntactic sugar will be used to integrate it with ROCK [13].

A ROLL **term** is either a variable, a constant or a keyword (denoting built-
in operations, as clarified later). The alphabet contains no function symbols,
therefore a term is *ground* iff it is a constant or a keyword. The set of all terms
is $Term = Cons \cup Kwords \cup Var$. The set of all ground terms, called the
Herbrand universe, is denoted by H_U. Since $Cons$ and $Kwords$ are finite, so
is H_U. A ROLL **atom** has the following general structure $\alpha[\beta(\gamma)=>\delta]$. The
Greek letters are place-holders: α is filled by an object-denoting ROLL term;
β is filled by a ROLL term denoting an operation in the interface to a class of
α; γ is filled by a comma-separated sequence (of object-denoting ROLL terms)
denoting the argument-tuple of β; δ is filled by a ROLL term denoting the result

238

of applying the operation β with arguments γ to the object α. When β takes no arguments or returns no results, (γ) or $=>\delta$, respectively, can be dropped. An atom is *ground* iff α and β are ground, and γ and δ are either ground or missing. Note that a number of built-in predicates (BIPs) exist that are written in infix notation. For instance, the value-equality operation is '=='. Thus !1 == !2 is true iff the object whose name is !1 is value-equal to the object whose name is !2. From ROLL atoms, ROLL literals and clauses are defined as for deductive databases [7]. A ROLL clause is a Horn clause. Again, **ROLL facts, rules and goals** are special forms of Horn clauses, as expected. The usual characterization of an *intensional* and an *extensional part* of databases and the logical interpretation to variables in queries are also applicable.

In the prototype described in Section 4, ROLL programs are given an operational semantics by a one-to-one mapping onto an internal representation that is then input to an SLDNF-resolution proof procedure, extended to cope with late binding. Querying with ROLL is now illustrated through excerpts from a transcript of an interactive session with the stand-alone prototype ROLL interpreter. The domain is that of Figure 1. Note that proper object identifiers (constant symbols of the form !n) would not appear explicitly in ROLL queries embedded in ROCK programs.

3.1 Schema-Level and Instance-Level Queries

First, a wide-ranging example of schema-level querying in ROLL. In the schema-level queries below all operations invoked are built-in, and their axiomatic semantics is captured at the level of the data model [15]. Intuitively, sending **ipo** to an object type t returns the object types t' which aggregate t, sending **has** to an object type t returns the object types t' that are attributes of t. Sending **isa** to an object type t returns the supertypes t' of t. Finally, sending **ici** to an object type t returns the object types t' which associate or sequentiate t. The query then reads: *which object types* X, *which aggregate* city, *are a property of subtypes* Y *of* company, *such that object types* Z *associate* Y?

```
roll ?- city[ipo => X], Y[has => X], Y[isa => company], Y[ici => Z].
[X = location, Y = carManufacturer, Z = owners]
another? ;
[X = location, Y = carManufacturer, Z = foreignOwners]
another? ;
[X = location, Y = company, Z = owners]
...
```

Using an **isa** atom with the addressee- and result-position free, and a interpreter-directive **all** to collect all answers and return them at once, it is simple to retrieve, as a set of <Sub,Super> pairs, the entire is-a hierarchy:

```
roll ?- all Sub[isa => Super].
...
[Sub = japaneseCarManufacturer, Super = japaneseCarManufacturer]
[Sub = japaneseCarManufacturer, Super = carManufacturer]
[Sub = japaneseCarManufacturer, Super = company]
[Sub = juniorEmployee, Super = juniorEmployee]
[Sub = juniorEmployee, Super = employee]
[Sub = juniorEmployee, Super = person]
```

...

Now, some examples of instance-level querying in ROLL. Again, most operations are built-in. Intuitively, sending iof to an object i returns the object types t it has been assigned to. Sending .t (a shorthand for get(t)) to an object i returns the object i' referred to by i as its t-property. The first query reads: *what is the name of employees* E *who are older than people named Mary?*

```
roll ?- E[.name => Ename], E[.age => Eage],
        Mary[.name => "mary"], Mary[.age => Maryage],
        Eage :> Maryage.
[E = !3, Ename = john, Eage = 30, Mary = !4, Maryage = 25]
another? ;
[E = !3, Ename = john, Eage = 30, Mary = !19, Maryage = 25]
...
```

Note the import of object identity in the fact that two distinct objects, !4 and !19, with the same name and age, "mary" and 25, respectively, play a part in answering the query. In the next example, sending ..t (a shorthand for ith(t)) to an object i returns the object i' referred to by i as its t-coordinate. Sending iin to an object i returns the objects i' which refer to i as an association element. The query reads: *what is the name of companies* C *located in* edinburgh *that are owners?*

```
roll ?- C[.companyName => Name],C[iof => company], C[.location => L],
        L[..city => "edinburgh"], O[iof => owners], C[iin => O].
...
[C = !21, Name = scotplanes, L = !14, O = !16]
...
```

Finally, to retrieve all property-value pairs of all objects:

```
roll ?- all Object[.Property => Value].
[Object = !1, Property = companyName, Value = scotcars]
[Object = !1, Property = location, Value = !2]
[Object = !3, Property = age, Value = 30]
[Object = !3, Property = income, Value = 67890]
[Object = !3, Property = name, Value = john]
[Object = !3, Property = purchase, Value = 0]
...
```

The conciseness achieved in retrieving all subtype-supertype and all property-value pairs illustrates well the usefulness of logical variables in queries.

3.2 Overloading, Overriding and Late-Binding Methods

From the point of view of users, the features known as overloading, overriding and late-binding are among the most distinctive of the object-oriented paradigm. Currently, many well-known proposals for deductive object-oriented databases run into problems in their handling of the three features by being simplistic, or even wholly dismissive, as discussed in Section 5. The way ROLL accounts for all three features is intuitive from both the logic-programming and the object-oriented points of view, and gives ROLL querying a truly object-oriented look-and-feel. To illustrate the three features, consider the following query: *what are the identification Id and class C of the objects O ?*

```
roll ?- O[identify => Id], O[iof => C].
...
[O = !1, Id = scotcars, C = company]
another? ;
[O = !3, Id = john, C = customer]
...
[O = !4, Id = 12345, C = seniorEmployee]
...
```

From Figure 1 it can be seen that **identify** is a domain-dependent user-defined operation. That it is overloaded can be seen from the excerpt above, where it is answered by objects belonging to three different types. Since operations are inherited and Figure 1 shows that **customer** and **seniorEmployee** lie along an inheritance path, overriding takes place: a **customer**, like **!3**, being identified by **name**; a **seniorEmployee**, like **!4**, by ni, the national-insurance number. The method available in the object's most specific class is the one selected by default, and there is one and only one such method by a well-formedness property imposed on the schema.

ROLL handles methods as an integral part of a domain definition, i.e. database designers include in the intensional part of the database a method definition to implement each domain-dependent operation. Such implementations are, if ROLL is the chosen language, ROLL programs. Given an operation μ and an object type t, assigning a ROLL program to the pair $<\mu, t>$ defines a method in the necessary way for overloading, overriding and late-binding to be catered for. Because of inheritance, methods assigned to other classes may be available at any single class. For instance, as depicted in Figure 1, the operation name is distinctly defined on five different classes, viz. **company**, **carManufacturer**, **person**, **employee**, **juniorEmployee**, and is available through inheritance on yet others, e.g. **permanentEmployee**. The three (of a total five) different implementations of **identify** used in the last example query are as follows:

```
method(identify,person,
     {X as person[identify => Y] <- X[.name => Y]}).

method(identify,employee,
     {X as employee[identify => Y] <- X[.ni => Y]}).

method(identify,company,
     {X as company[identify => Y] <- X[.companyName => Y]}).
```

In the above, the ROLL program implementing each method lies between the pair of curly brackets. Note that the *role* in which the object should respond to message is explicitly stated using the syntactic marker **as**. The way ROLL uses the *role* annotation in queries is addressed later. To late-bind methods to messages (ROLL goal-atoms, in the present case), it is necessary to extend the proof procedure to select the most adequate implementation taking into account the classes of the addressee. In ROLL's underlying model 'most adequate' is stipulated to mean 'most specific', of which there is one and only one, as previously pointed out. From this stipulation and the fact that **employee** is a more specific class than **person**, objects that happen to be instances of both **person** and **employee** respond to messages using the method defined in the latter class, as the last example query has shown.

Static type checking was not implemented in the prototype described in this paper. The result types of **identify** in the three excerpted answers above are **name**, **ni**, and **companyName**. The data model leaves it to designers to stipulate a common supertype, e.g. **identification**, for types requiring a guaranteed comparability. This requirement may propagate upwards till the definition of a *unique* most general class than any other, e.g. **objects**.

ROLL also allows for user-defined binding through the annotation of the addressee with a role. The next query shows how the outcome varies accordingly:

```
roll ?- X[identify => Y], X as person[identify => Z].
...
[X = !4, Y = 12345, Z = mary]
...
```

3.3 Recursion

As pointed out in [21], support for object identity introduces certain problems for DOODs, especially relating to the creation of objects by the proof procedure. However, the magnitude of this problem has sometimes been overestimated, as discussed in [11], and this section briefly presents a solution which is supported in ROLL.

To set the scene, note that in a Prolog procedure, such as **display/1** below, the intermediate arguments with which the procedure is recursively invoked have one and the same nature under the data model, viz. value-based tuples.

```
display([]).
display([H|T]):- write(H),nl,display(T).
```

However, under an object-oriented data model the intermediate argument with which the procedure is recursively called must be an identity-based object whose state is that resulting from the recursion step in which the call takes place. Thus a naive implementation of a **display** method in a DOOD will create a new (potentially persistent) object, whose state is to contain the remainder of the collection, every time a call is made to the recursive clause of **display**.

In ROLL such objects are given *volatile identities* which, intuitively, have an existence that is terminated at the end of the proof within which they were created. The particular value defined for these volatile identities is a unary Skolem function **void** (for volatile oid) on the identifier of the object from which the volatile one is derived in the recursion step. The implementation of recursion is discussed in Section 4. Two BIPs correspond to 'first' and 'rest' functions on type-homogeneous collections, i.e. on associations and sequentiations (in the former case, the 'first' element is chosen at random). They are written as >-> and >==>, respectively. In what follows, assume that object !16 is built by association, and contains references to objects !18 and !21 in the construction part of its state. The following queries illustrate the use of these two BIPs:

```
roll ?- !16 >=> Rest, Rest >-> First, First[.Prop => Value].
[Rest = void(!16), First = !21, Prop = companyName, Value = scotplanes]
another? ;
[Rest = void(!16), First = !21, Prop = location, Value = !14]
another? ;
no
roll ?- !16 >=> R, R >=> RestOfR, RestOfR >=> RestOfRestOfR.
no
```

The first query shows that remaindering the object named !16 creates an object named **void(!16)** in whose construction the first object is named !21, the properties of which can be retrieved in the normal way. The second query shows that applying >=> three times to !16 fails, because the cardinality of its construction is only 2.

The ROLL equivalent to Prolog's **display/1** makes use of the above BIPs. In the case of the example domain, **display** is implemented as a method assigned to class **owners**, whose instances are built as associations of **company** objects.

```
method(display,owners,
    {   X as owners[display] <- ~(X >-> H)
    #   X as owners[display] <-   X >-> H, H[write], X >=> T,
                                    T as owners[display] }).
```

Within the definition of **display**, the operator # is used to separate ROLL clauses in the program which implements it in the class **owners**. The built-in unary predicate ˜ implements negation, as described further in Section 4. The BIP **write** prints out at top level the (name of the) object to which it is sent. Sending the query !16[display], where !16 is an instance of **owners** results in observable behaviour that is equivalent to the Prolog version.

4   Prototype

A prototype has been built on top of MegaLog [6] whose purpose is twofold:

Implementing the data model of [11] - Given a schema definition, a set of objects and a set of methods, the prototype provides facilities for storing and checking the schema for well-formedness and well-definedness, for storing and checking each object for well-typedness under the schema, taking into account each type the object is assigned to, and for compiling each method (as described further down in this section) and storing it with the other data. Schemas and objects are given a concrete representation that closely resembles the abstract set-theoretic notation of [11], while rules and methods are input as sets of ROLL clauses, the latter bound to the pair <operation, type> which identifies a particular implementation. Internally, all the above database elements are represented as first-order terms, and the database thus generated is made to persist using the secondary storage provided by MegaLog.

Implementing an interpreter for ROLL - A mapping was defined that, given a database element, returns an *image* of that element in the form of a set of CROLL clauses (CROLL, as explained below, is an extremely trimmed-down subset of pure Prolog). Based on this, the prototype acts as a user-level front-end which accepts ROLL goals, compiles them into CROLL goals, and, by means of a meta-interpreter, resolves them against the union of the *image* database (i.e. the database transformed into a set of CROLL clauses by the mapping previously alluded to) with the methods and rules previously compiled into CROLL. Here, both the image database and the methods and rules, are stored as clauses which, from the point of view of the meta-interpreter, comprise the stored program against which goals are evaluated.

The rationale behind this approach is consistent with our belief that the data model must be independently defined. Note that the two stages above are distinct. They are conceptually bound by an explicit mapping to effect the logical reconstruction of a database as a logic program. This makes it less important which concrete syntax and internal representation is chosen for either, because within reasonable bounds one syntax can be translated into the other and syntactic sugar can be easily added.

Some interesting features of the prototype are the static approach to inheritance (i.e. all propagation of properties and operations from super- to subtypes is computed at schema-installation time) and to the extension of semantic relationships (i.e. all semantic relationships have their closures computed and their entire extensions stored at schema-installation time). This approach has the main advantage that it eliminates the need for the prototype to handle properties of semantic relationships by means of inference rules. In other words, once the semantic relationships have had their closures computed and stored, a great number of goals that would otherwise require special consideration or the invocation of specific inference rules, can be solved in a single resolution step against the ground facts in the image database.

We now briefly describe how a database can be mapped into a set of clauses in a Horn language (precise details are found in [12].) The mapping amounts to a logical reconstruction of our model along the lines first suggested by Reiter [19] in the relational case. As mentioned before, due to the relative ease with which parsers and meta-interpreters can be written in Prolog, it was decided to recast a database as a set of clauses in a language referred to as *CROLL* (Compiled ROLL). Essentially, CROLL is a very restricted subset of pure Prolog. The alphabet which determines the language has the following main features:

- No function symbols, as usual in the database field.

- Constant symbols are those introduced by the schema and by the set of objects plus a number of *keywords*, some of them interpreted by the semantic relationships defined by the data model (e.g. **isa**, **iof**, **has**, etc.), others interpreted as BIPs (e.g. **equals**, which is the CROLL equivalent of the Prolog **is**).

- There is only one 4-ary predicate symbol **m** (for **message**).

The notions of term, literal, clause, fact, rule and goal are as in Prolog. CROLL atoms have the general form $m(\alpha, \beta', \gamma, \delta)$ corresponding to a ROLL atom of the form $\alpha[\beta(\gamma)=>\delta]$, as defined in Section 3. The nature of β' and its relationship with β can be explained as follows.

If β is a keyword, then β' has a one-to-one correspondence with β, and either identifies the invocation of a BIP (e.g. $\beta' = $ **equals**) which the meta-interpreter has support for, or else it acts as a discriminator between sets of clauses in the image database (i.e. a role similar to that of predicate symbols in determining the definition of a procedure by the sharing of a symbol in the heads of clauses). For instance, if $\beta = \beta' = $ isa, then the CROLL atom expresses a fact about the structural subsumption relationship. The mapping which yields the image database places identifying keywords at β' according to the kind of fact expressed by the corresponding clause as described in detail in [12]. Some instances of schema-level CROLL facts:

```
m(carManufacturer, isa, [], [carManufacturer]).
m(carManufacturer, isa, [], [company]).
```

If β is an operation name μ, then β' is a pair $<\mu, \theta>$, where θ is the type in which the method implementing μ is applicable. Note that, in a ROLL query, if the user refrains from specifying the desired binding, θ remains free after compilation into CROLL, and it is up to the meta-interpreter to provide the late-binding of θ to the most specific class of α for which μ is defined. For instance, (arigeq identifies the arithmetic greater-or-equal BIP) the method over_18

```
method(over_18,employee,
    {   X as employee[over_18] <- X[.age => Y],
                                  Y :>= 18 }).
```

is compiled into

```
m(X1, over_18 - employee, [], []) <-
    m(X1, iof, [], [employee]),
    m(X1, get, [age], [X4]),
    m(X4, arigeq, [18], []).
```

The mapping, informally and in broad terms, takes advantage of the fact that the extension of semantic relationships is stored by making each tuple[1] in a relationship correspond one-to-one with a CROLL fact. This captures as CROLL facts practically all the schema-level information. Similarly, at the instance level, each object is translated into a ground theory, i.e. a set of CROLL facts, each of which is distinguishable by keywords that correspond to the kinds of reference an object makes to other objects or to types. These correspond to the semantic relationships holding between an object and its assigned types, and between an object and the objects it references as a value of some property or as a component in its construction. The end result of this mapping is referred to as the *image* database. The image database is a subset of the CROLL Herbrand base, i.e. the extensional database over which the meta-interpreter is to act. As an example, consider the ground theory corresponding to the object !2 of type location, with no properties and a construction with three coordinates street, city, postcode:

```
m('!2', iof, [], [location]).
m('!2', abst, [], [aggregation]).
m('!2', cohe, [], [nonc]).
m('!2', ith, [street], ["grassmarket"]).
m('!2', ith, [city], ["edinburgh"]).
m('!2', ith, [postcode], ["eh12hj"]).
```

---

[1] This is set-theoretic, not relational database, terminology

The intensional database comprises the set of compiled methods previously mentioned, as well as deductive rules used to characterize derived data and to define integrity constraints not directly captured by the modelling formalism. Note that deductive rules, like methods, are input as ROLL programs and undergo compilation into CROLL before being stored. The basic meta-interpreter is:

```
roll_solve(true).
roll_solve((A,B)):-
    roll_solve(A),
    roll_solve(B).
roll_solve(m(A,X,AL,RL)):-
    late_bind(m(A,X,AL,RL),m(A,Y,AL,RL)),  % ROLL extension
    croll(m(A,Y,AL,RL),C),
    roll_solve(C).
```

The extended features occur in the third clause, where `croll/2` is equivalent to Prolog's `clause/2`, i.e. it is used to retrieve CROLL clauses from Mega-Log relations (this interaction with MegaLog uses a slightly different syntax). Recall that X may be a pair $<\mu, \theta>$. In this case, if θ is free then the call to `late_bind/2` results in the binding of θ, in Y, to the most specific class of which A is an instance that has μ defined for it. The call also ascertains that the arguments AL and the result RL are well-typed. If θ is bound then the call only serves to perform type-checking.

The basic meta-interpreter is extended to handle collected multiple-answers, BIPs and (Prolog-style) negation-as-failure, by the inclusion of the following as third, fourth and fifth clauses of the meta-interpreter:

```
roll_solve(findall(Vars,A,Answers)):-
    findall(Vars,roll_solve(A),Answers).      % collect multiple-answers
roll_solve(A):-
    roll_built_in(A).                          % handling of BIPs
roll_solve((not A)):-
    not roll_solve(A).                         % negation as failure
```

where example of clauses belonging to the definition of `roll_built_in/1` are:

```
roll_built_in(m(X,write,[],[]))             :- write(X),nl.
roll_built_in(m(Answer,equals,[Expression],[])) :- Answer is Expression.
```

which handle the output of ROLL terms and evaluation of arithmetic expressions, respectively. Note that the definition of `roll_built_in/1` essentially uses the host language (in this case, MegaLog Prolog) to implement the BIPs of the user-level language.

The last extension to the meta-interpreter is needed to handle recursion as described in Section 3. It requires that `roll_solve/1` and `roll_built_in/1` have their arity increased to 3. The two additional argument places are lists of CROLL clauses, corresponding to the volatile objects created during the proof by the use of the *first* and *rest* BIPs. The second argument of `roll_solve/3` comes instantiated with the volatile objects created thus far, while the third argument exits with the previous volatile objects plus any others created by the current proof step. The complete meta-interpreter with additional arguments and an additional sixth clause is:

```
roll_solve(true,U,U).
roll_solve((A,B),U,W):-
    roll_solve(A,U,V),
    roll_solve(B,V,W).
roll_solve(findall(Vars,A,Answers),U,V):-
    findall(Vars,roll_solve(A,U,V),Answers).
roll_solve(A,U,V):-
    roll_built_in(A,U,V).
roll_solve((not A),U,V):-
    not roll_solve(A,U,V).
roll_solve(A,U,U):-
    memberchk(croll(A,true),U).              % try volatile facts
roll_solve(m(A,X,AL,RL),U,V):-
    late_bind(m(A,X,AL,RL),m(A,Y,AL,RL),U),
    croll(m(A,Y,AL,RL),C),
    roll_solve(C,U,V).
```

i.e. an additional way of proving a CROLL goal is to resolve it against a fact about volatile objects created thus far in the proof.

5 Related Work

In this section our approach to deductive object-oriented languages is compared with some selected alternative proposals. First, note that the problem of integrating object-orientation and logic programming can be tackled either by extending an object-oriented system with some form of deduction, or by extending logic-programming languages with object-oriented concepts. All the proposals discussed here adopt the latter viewpoint. Further, one can bias the work towards programming-language issues or towards databases issues. Again, the present proposal as well as those discussed below are mainly concerned with the latter. Three main approaches can be used to develop a DOOD language against the background of previous research into deductive relational databases (DRDBs):

1. *extending the deductive language* - this characterizes work such as the COL/IQL/IQL+ family of languages [1, 2, 3], in which DATALOG [7], seen as the logic-programming language underlying DRDBs, is progressively extended with complex typed-terms, object identity, inheritance and so on.

2. *redesigning the deductive language* - this characterizes the work that resulted in the family composed of the C-/O-/F-logic languages [8, 16, 17]. Here, no data model is assumed in the background, rather there is the intention of expressing directly at the logic-language level all the features deemed necessary to model a domain in an object-oriented style.

3. *redesigning the data model* - this characterizes our work [13, 11]. Here, the underlying data model is defined independently, in a deliberate attempt to retrace, for the object-oriented case, the development path that led from the relational model to DATALOG. The idea is to obtain for classes, objects, and methods on one hand and clauses of a logic language on the

other, the same sort of structural similarity that holds between relations and DATALOG clauses. This also has the advantage that imperative features can be handled by a separate language component, which can be seamlessly integrated with the logic language by virtue of their sharing a single type system.

The remainder of this section focusses on IQL+ and F-logic (as the latest members in their respective families) and contrasts these approaches with ROLL. However, it should be stressed that ROLL is but one part of a three-component architecture [13], while most other proposals for DOOD are based on single-component architectures.

IQL+ was proposed as a stand-alone language, powerful enough to tackle small-scale application development and resorting to external functions to extend its capabilities. Its data modelling constructs are less comprehensive than those available in our model (e.g. it does not cater for multiple inheritance; also, it has no means of expressing existence dependences required to inform update propagation of composite objects), but they satisfy usual requirements. One point of contrast with both ROLL and F-logic is that schema expressions in IQL+ are not part of the logic language, and hence they cannot be queried. IQL+ has a number of control structures to drive the computation of fixpoints. In certain respects, IQL+ resembles more a production-rule system than a logic programming one. No declarative semantics has been proposed to characterize the meaning of an IQL+ program.

F-logic is, in a different way, a more complex proposal. Its avoidance of data modelling issues is, we believe, a serious obstacle to its acceptance as a DOOD language. While ROLL is strongly influenced by semantic data-modelling research, with its emphasis on the precise characterization of abstraction mechanisms to model data, F-logic conflates the schema- and instance-levels by using the same linguistic construct to express the membership relationship between an individual and its class and the inclusion relationship between a sub- and a superclass. Since all three languages are semantically first-order, all are similarly bound to interpret constants in the language as individuals in the world, which may imply some form of reification of types, for example. However, in both ROLL and IQL+ one is not short of means for distinguishing membership from inclusion. The F-logic proposal is closer to ours in its provision of a declarative and a procedural semantics for the language. F-logic also has no control mechanisms and does not handle updates. The proposal of F-logic comes with a proof procedure for the monotonic part of the language and a unification algorithm for F-terms. Both the unification algorithm (which has to handle set unification and a higher-order syntax) and the proof procedure (which uses a number of additional inference rules to handle inheritance and typing issues) pose non-trivial problems for efficient implementation.

There is a close analogy between ROLL and DATALOG, in that several desirable properties of DATALOG programs (e.g. concerning termination) hold for ROLL also. It can be seen from the meta-interpreter presented in Section 4 that giving a procedural semantics to ROLL programs based on an extended SLDNF proof procedure is straightforward. In general, the semantics of ROLL programs is as intuitive as those of DATALOG programs, a characteristic which, we believe, makes it very attractive as a query language for end-users. This is only possible because critical issues of control and updates are handled by a separate language component.

Neither IQL+ nor ROLL should present particular difficulties for implementation, although the style used for that task in each case would be probably different. An implementor for ROLL is able to benefit directly from the large body of work carried out in recent years in implementing DRDBs and, more generally, Horn-clause languages. In contrast, F-logic proposes implementation problems of its own to handle the more complex unification algorithm and proof procedure, unless a compilation approach similar to the one described in Section 4 is used, reducing the burden on the proof procedure.

The most important point of contrast between the three proposals, however, concerns the account for those core notions that characterize the object-oriented paradigm. Unless these notions are clearly and convincingly accounted for, doubts will always be cast on whether the end-result qualifies as *object-oriented*. Object identity and inheritance are well-catered for by most proposals. The two crucial areas of difference are *encapsulation* and the *overriding/overloading/-late-binding* trio.

F-logic considers methods to be essentially properties of objects. This leads to an account of encapsulation that resembles that of private views, i.e. programs are specialized to users according to their signatures for each class object. This is ingenious, but in no way a very faithful account of how encapsulation is construed in object-oriented systems. It conflates structural and behavioural inheritance and preempts the issue of late-binding by not acknowledging the existence of separate implementations (i.e. programs). IQL+ uses modules to account for encapsulation and treats overloading of methods as a non-monotonic feature, and, similarly to F-logic, also preempts the issue of late-binding.

The approach to giving a semantics to ROLL, viz. by rewriting ROLL into Horn clauses, has a close similarity to the one used for OIL [22] and OOLP+ [10] (OIL acquires a semantics by a rewriting into $\mathcal{LDL}$ and OOLP+ by a rewriting into Prolog), but otherwise both proposals are very different from ROLL, not least in their treatment of object as terms, as opposed to objects as theories as is the case with ROLL.

In contrast to all above proposals, ROLL is quite faithful to the object-oriented approach. It supports strict encapsulation by a clear-cut distinction between structure and behaviour: encapsulated access to the state of objects can be enforced simply by restricting legal queries to those that use operation names *only*. As for overriding, overloading and late-binding, we have given examples and explained the technique used to account for them in a way that is true to both paradigms.

6 Future Directions and Conclusions

ROLL has been completely formalized in [15], a task that involved defining the language from its foundations in the data model of [11] and showing how it extends the class of Horn programs with accounts for semantic relationships, methods, encapsulation, overriding, overloading and late-binding.

The surface syntax of ROLL will be defined in consonance with the imperative database-programming language of [5]. Our goal is to obtain an integrated language which is free from impedance mismatches. The single underlying type-system is instrumental in that respect: objects retrieved by ROLL expressions within the imperative language are instances of types which the imperative language itself has defined. The other dimension of mismatch, namely, the computation paradigm, should not be a difficult issue as both languages rely on message-sending as the means to drive computation. Also, the rich control structures of the imperative language can accommodate a great variety of styles. As indicated in Section 1, the DOOD system will be built on top of EXODUS. After the surface syntax of the logic-language component has been defined, an interpreter for it will be implemented. This will naturally imply the choice of efficient techniques to evaluate ROLL queries both as a stand-alone language and as a component.

Our experience in prototyping an interpreter for ROLL has convinced us that there are important advantages in taking a model-based approach to the problem of extending OODBs with deduction. The lack of a widely-agreed formal model for OODBs has only made things look more forbidding, which has led some to try and accommodate within the relational model the necessary extensions, and others to skip the modelling issue altogether. As described in this paper, the main contribution of ROLL is to demonstrate that by formalizing OODBs in terms that are close to the roots of logic-programming theory, one is able to retrace for DOODs the simple extension path that proved so successful for DRDBs.

Acknowledgements   The work that resulted in this paper has been funded by the Science and Engineering Research Council through the IEATP programme, and their support is duly acknowledged. We would also like to thank our colleagues Maria Luisa Barja and Alia Abdelmoty, and Dr. Keith G. Jeffery of Rutherford Appleton Laboratory for useful discussions on the subject of this paper, and Dr. J.M.P. Quinn representing ICL and Mr Neil Smith of Ordnance Survey for their contribution as the industrial partners in the project.

References

[1] S. Abiteboul. Towards a Deductive Object-Oriented Database Language. *Data & Knowledge Engineering*, 5:263–287, 1990.

[2] S. Abiteboul and S. Grumbach. COL: A Logic-Based Language for Complex Objects. In F. Bancilhon and P. Buneman, eds., *Advances in Database Programming Languages*, Frontier Series, pp. 347–374. ACM Press/Addison-Wesley Publ. Co., 1990.

[3] S. Abiteboul and P.C. Kanellakis. Object Identity as a Query Language Primitive. In *[9]*, pp. 159–173. 1989.

[4] M. Atkinson, F. Bancilhon, D. DeWitt, K. Dittrich, D. Maier, and S.B. Zdonik. The Object-Oriented Database System Manifesto. In *[18]*, pp. 223–240. 1990.

[5] M.L. Barja, N.W. Paton, and M.H. Williams. Design of an Object-Oriented Database Programming Language for a DOOD. *Tech Report TR92016, Dept. Comp. and E. Engineering,*Heriot-Watt University, December 1992.

[6] J. Bocca. Megalog: A Platform for Developing Knowledge-Base Management Systems. In *Proc. International Symposium on Database Systems for Advanced Applications*, pp. 374–380, Tokyo, 1991.

[7] S. Ceri, G. Gottlob, and L. Tanca. *Logic Programming and Databases*. Springer-Verlag, Berlin, 1990.

[8] W. Chen and D.S. Warren. C-Logic of Complex Objects. In *Proc. 8th ACM SIGACT-SIGMOD-SIGART Symposium on Principles of Database Systems*, pp. 369–378, Philadelphia,PA, March 1989. ACM Press.

[9] J. Clifford, B. Lindsay, and D. Maier, eds. *Proc. 1989 ACM SIGMOD*, Portland,OR. ACM Press, 1989.

[10] M. Dalal and D. Gangopadhyay. OOLP: A Translation Approach to Object-Oriented Logic Programming. In *[18]*, pp. 593–606. 1990.

[11] A.A.A. Fernandes, N.W. Paton, M.H. Williams, and A. Bowles. Approaches to Deductive Object-Oriented Databases. *Information and Software Technology*, 34(12):787–803, December 1992.

[12] A.A.A. Fernandes. An Object-Oriented Logic by Examples. *Tech Report TR92015, Dept. Comp. and E. Engineering*, Heriot-Watt University, September 1992.

[13] A.A.A. Fernandes, M.L. Barja, N.W. Paton, and M.H. Williams. A Deductive Object-Oriented Database for Data Intensive Application Development. In *Advances in Databases: Proc. 11th British National Conference on Databases (BNCOD 11)*, LNCS 696, pp. 176–198, Keele, UK, July 1993. Springer-Verlag.

[14] A.A.A. Fernandes, M.H. Williams, and N.W. Paton. A Formal Abstract Definition of Objects as a Data Modelling Primitive. *Tech Report TR92003, Dept. Comp. and E. Engineering*, Heriot-Watt University, April 1992. (Revised June 1992).

[15] A.A.A. Fernandes, M.H. Williams, and N.W. Paton. An Axiomatic Approach to Deductive Object-Oriented Databases. *Tech Report TR93002, Dept. Comp. and E. Engineering*, Heriot-Watt University, April 1993 (Revised September 1993).

[16] M. Kifer and G. Lausen. F-logic: A Higher-Order Language for Reasoning about Objects, Inheritance and Scheme. In *[9]*, pp. 134–146. 1989.

[17] M. Kifer and J. Wu. A Logic for Object-Oriented Logic Programming (Maier's O-logic: Revisited). In *Proc. 8th ACM SIGACT-SIGMOD-SIGART Symposium on Principles of Database Systems*, pp. 379–383, Philadelphia,PA, March 1989. ACM Press.

[18] W. Kim, J-M. Nicolas, and S. Nishio, eds. *Deductive and Object-Oriented Databases (1st Int. Conf. DOOD'89, Kyoto)*. Elsevier Science Press (North-Holland), 1990.

[19] R. Reiter. Towards a Logical Reconstruction of Relational Database Theory. In M.L. Brodie, J. Mylopoulos, and J.W. Schmidt, eds., *On Conceptual Modelling: Perspectives from Artificial Intelligence, Databases, and Programming Languages*, pp. 191–233. Springer-Verlag (Topics in Information System Series), 1984.

[20] J.E. Richardson and M.J. Carey. Implementing Persistence in E. In J. Rosenberg and D. Koch, eds., *Persistent Object Systems: Proc. 3rd International Workshop*, pp. 175–199. Springer-Verlag, 1989.

[21] J.D. Ullman. A Comparison Between Deductive and Object-Oriented Database Systems. In C. Delobel, M. Kifer, and Y. Masunaga, eds. *Deductive and Object-Oriented Databases (2nd Int. Conf. DOOD'91, Munich)*. pp. 263–277. Springer-Verlag, 1991.

[22] C. Zaniolo. Object Identity and Inheritance in Deductive Databases – An Evolutionary Approach. In *[18]*, pp. 7–24. 1990.

Semi-Naive Evaluation for Hyperlog, a Graph-Based Language for Complex Objects

Kerima Benkerimi

Dept. of Computer Science, University College London,
Gower Street, London WC1E 6BT

Alexandra Poulovassilis

Dept. of Computer Science, King's College London,
Strand, London WC2R 2LS

Abstract

This paper is concerned with the evaluation of a graph-based declarative language called Hyperlog. Hyperlog is a query- and update-language for a graph-based data model called the Hypernode Model. The single data structure of this model is the *hypernode* - a graph whose nodes can themselves be graphs. A Hyperlog program is a set of rules whose bodies consist of templates to be matched against a database of graphs. The heads of rules are also templates and indicate the updates to the database to be undertaken for each match of the templates in the body. These updates may include the update of existing graphs or the generation of new graphs.

We first define the semantics of Hyperlog programs in terms of a bottom-up "naive" evaluation strategy. We then show the semi-naive evaluation algorithm developed for relational languages can be adapted for the more efficient evaluation of Hyperlog programs. This is achieved by partitioning the templates in the bodies of rules into those templates which cannot be affected by any updates to the database during the evaluation of the programs and those templates which may be affected by updates to the database. The former templates are the analogue of EDB predicates and the latter of IDB predicates in relational rules.

1   Introduction

Much recent database research has focussed on deductive and object-oriented databases and also on graph-based representation and manipulation of data. Following the general direction of these trends, a graph-based data model, called the Hypernode Model, has been developed which supports object identity, arbitrarily complex objects, and the derivation of implied information from factual information [1],[2],[3]. The Hypernode Model uses nested, possibly recursively defined, graphs termed *hypernodes*. Hypernodes have unique labels which serve as object identifiers.

Other models have also used graphs as their underlying data structure, for example [4], [5], [6], [7], [8]. However, a feature common to all these models is that the database consists of a single flat graph. This has the drawback that complex objects consisting of many inter-connected nodes are hard to represent in a clear way. In contrast, a hypernode database consists of a set of nested graphs. This unique feature of the model provides inherent support for data abstraction and the ability to represent each real-world object as a separate database graph.

The Hypernode Model comes equipped with a computationally- and update-complete language called Hyperlog. A Hyperlog program is a set of rules. The body of a rule consists of a number of graphs, called *templates*, which are matched against the database. The head of a rule is also a template and indicates the updates (if any) to the database to be undertaken for each match of the graphs in the body. The evaluation of a program comprises a repeated matching of its set of rules against the database until no more updates can be inferred.

The model and language were first described in [1]. In [2] that work was consolidated and expanded upon in several directions, including negation in rule heads (which may cause deletions from the database), extension of the model with types, an analysis of the efficiency of type checking and of inference, and a brief description of the 3-level architecture of a prototype DBMS which is currently being implemented. The lowest level of this architecture was addressed in [3] where the physical storage of hypernodes was described. Work on the highest level of the architecture (the graphical user interface) is still in progress and will be addressed in a future paper. The purpose of the present paper is thus to describe the implementation of the middle level of the architecture, namely the Hyperlog evaluator.

We restrict our discussion here to the version of Hyperlog described in [1], which is untyped and does not include negation in the heads of rules. More specifically, we first define the semantics of Hyperlog programs in terms of a bottom-up "naive" evaluation strategy for a single *graph* predicate (Section 2). We then present the main contribution of the paper, namely we show how the Hyperlog evaluator can utilise a modification of the semi-naive evaluation algorithm for relational languages [9] for the evaluation of Hyperlog programs (Section 3). Since we only have one *graph* predicate, this is achieved by syntactically partitioning the templates of rules into those templates which cannot be affected by any updates to the database during the evaluation of the program and those templates which may be affected by updates to the database. The former templates are the analogue of EDB predicates and the latter of IDB predicates in relational rules. After a brief discussion of query processing, we conclude the paper with directions of further research (Section 4).

2 Background

In this section we present the necessary background material for the rest of the paper: the definition of hypernodes and hypernode repositories (section 2.1), the Hyperlog language syntax (section 2.2), and the semantics of Hyperlog programs (section 2.3). In particular, we present the latter using a variant of bottom-up *naive evaluation* [9].

2.1 Hypernodes and Hypernode Repositories

For the purposes of defining hypernodes two disjoint sets of constants are required: a finite set of *primitive nodes*, **P**, and a countably infinite set of *labels*, **L**. The set **P** is assumed to include alphanumeric strings. Other elements of **P** are denoted by identifiers which start with a lowercase letter. Elements of **L** are denoted by identifiers which start with an uppercase letter.

The graphs of the Hypernode Model are defined by equations of the form
$$G = (N, E)$$
where $G \in \mathbf{L}$, $N \subset (\mathbf{P} \cup \mathbf{L})$ and $E \subseteq N \times N$. Such equations are termed *hypernode equations* (or simply *equations*). A node $n \in N$ is *isolated* if there is no edge (n, n') or $(n', n) \in E$.

From now on in this paper we assume that any set, S, of hypernode equations does not contain two equations with the same left hand side. We also assume the equation
$$G = (\{\}, \{\})$$
for any "dangling" label G i.e. for any label that appears in the right hand side of some equation of S but not on the left hand side of any equation.

A *hypernode repository* (or simply a *repository*) is a finite set of hypernode equations.

Since hypernode repositories are just sets of equations, they should have a unique solution for the indeterminates, i.e. for the labels $G \in \mathbf{L}$, in some well-defined domain. As discussed in [1], [2] a hypernode repository HR does indeed have a unique solution in the universe of non-well-founded sets [10] i.e. the universe of sets that may contain themselves. This solution assigns to each label G on the left hand side of an equation a non-well-founded set. This non-well-founded set is what is termed a *hypernode*.

We illustrate some hypernodes in Figures 1 - 3. In Figure 1 we show a hypernode labelled COUPLE-1 containing two nodes labelled PERSON-1 and PERSON-2 which are also hypernodes. They themselves contain further hypernodes labelled PERSON-3 and PERSON-4 which we show in Figure 2. In Figure 3 we illustrate two recursively defined hypernodes labelled PERSON-5 and PERSON-6.

2.2 Hyperlog

For the purposes of defining Hyperlog, a finite set of variables, **V**, is required. The elements of **V** are denoted by uppercase identifiers from the end of the alphabet. The set of variables **V** and the set of labels **L** are assumed disjoint.

A Hyperlog rule has a, possibly empty, set of graphs in its body and a single graph in its head. These graphs are termed templates. A template may have a variable as its label and may have variables in its node set. Also, its nodes and edges may be negated (meaning "absent", intuitively).

More formally, a *template* is an equation of the form
$$L = (N, E)$$
where $L \in \mathbf{L} \cup \mathbf{V}$ and (N, E) is a graph such that:

1. $N \subset (\mathbf{P} \cup \mathbf{L} \cup \mathbf{V})$.

2. N is the disjoint union of two sets, N^+ and N^-. N^+ contains "positive" nodes and N^- contains "negative" nodes.

3. E is the disjoint union of two sets, E^+ and E^-. E^+ contains "positive" edges and E^- contains "negative" edges.

4. $(n_1, n_2) \in E^+ \cup E^-$ implies that $n_1, n_2 \in N^+$.

Condition 4 restricts all edges to be between positive nodes. Clearly, a positive edge containing a negative node is impossible. Also, a negative edge containing a negative node is tautological.

A *rule* is an expression of the form
$$Q_0 \leftarrow Q_1, Q_2, ..., Q_n$$
where $n \geq 0$, $Q_0, Q_1, ..., Q_n$ are templates, and Q_0 contains no negative nodes or edges.

A *program* is a finite set of rules.

We illustrate some programs in Figures 4 - 7. The program in Figure 4 generates the descendants of all person "objects" and updates the objects accordingly. The program in Figure 5 guarantees that any object Y that is loved by some object X itself loves some object Z. The program in Figure 6 derives three "relations" labelled NAME, SURNAME and CHILD from the information in all person objects. Finally, the program in Figure 7 guarantees that any object X that contains an object Y in its node set is itself contained in the node set of some object Z.

2.3 Semantics of Hyperlog

The evaluation of a Hyperlog program comprises a repeated matching of its rules against the repository until no more updates can be inferred. The templates in the body of each rule R are matched against the equations in the repository, and the head of R, which is also a template, indicates the updates (if any) to be undertaken for each match of the body. In general, there may be variables appearing in the head of R that do not appear in its body - see for example the programs in Figures 5 and 7. In this case if the head of R does not match any existing equation in the repository, a new equation is generated for each such variable. The labels on the left hand sides of these new equations are hitherto unused in the repository and in the program and are chosen non-deterministically. Note that these label generation semantics differ from IQL's invention of object identities [11] in that Hyperlog generates new labels as a necessary consequence of new equations being inferred whereas in IQL the generation of an object identity and the assignment of a value to it are independent. Note also that as a result of this generation of new equations the computation of the fixpoint of a Hyperlog program might not terminate.

In [1] [2] the evaluation semantics of Hyperlog were formalised via a one-step inference operator. In this section we give an equivalent semantics for Hyperlog in terms of the naive bottom-up evaluation [9] of a single 3-ary predicate *graph*.

We first define a mapping μ which associates with every Hyperlog program a first-order theory called a *flat* Hyperlog program. This first-order theory has a single predicate, namely *graph*, and a special first-order term, called a *set term*, denoted by curly braces {}. The semantics of this term are that of a mathematical set.

Definition μ_E

Let Eqn be a hypernode equation of the form $G = (N, E)$. We define a mapping μ_E from hypernode equations to literals termed *flat equations* as follows:

$$\mu_E : Eqn \rightarrow graph(G, N, E).$$

Definition μ_Q

Let Q be a Hyperlog template of the form $L = (N^+ \cup N^-, E^+ \cup E^-)$. We define a mapping μ_Q from Hyperlog templates to literals termed *flat templates* as follows:

$$\mu_Q : Q \rightarrow graph(L, N^+, E^+), \neg graph(L, N^-, E^-).$$

In the case that $N^- = E^- = \{\}$, we simplify this to

$$\mu_Q : Q \rightarrow graph(L, N^+, E^+).$$

For any literal $graph(L, N, E)$ we denote by $VARS(graph(L, N, E))$ the set of variables appearing in the arguments L, N, E.

Definition μ_R

Let R be a Hyperlog rule of the form $Q_0 \leftarrow Q_1, \ldots, Q_n$. We define a mapping μ_R from the set of Hyperlog rules onto the set of *flat rules* as follows:

$$\mu_R : R \rightarrow \mu_Q(Q_0) \leftarrow \mu_Q(Q_1), \ldots, \mu_Q(Q_n).$$

Let P be a Hyperlog program consisting of the rules $R_1, \ldots, R_m$. The corresponding *flat Hyperlog program* is defined to be the set of flat rules, $\mu_R(R_1), \ldots, \mu_R(R_m)$.

From now on, we use the terms template, equation, rule and program to mean flat template, flat equation, flat rule and flat program, respectively. We are now ready to define the matching of a template in the body of a rule with respect to a set of equations. Before doing so we define the familiar notions of a substitution and an application thereof:

Definition Substitutions

A *substitution* is a set $\{X_1/t_1, \ldots, X_n/t_n\}$, where each X_i is a distinct variable and each t_i is a first-order term.

The *application* of a substitution $\theta = \{X_1/t_1, \ldots, X_n/t_n\}$ to an expression E is the expression $E\theta$ resulting from the simultaneous replacement of each variable X_i by the term t_i in E.

Definition Matching positive templates

Given a positive template $graph(L, N^+, E^+)$ such that

$$VARS(graph(L, N^+, E^+)) = \{X_1, \ldots, X_n\}$$

and a set of equations S, a *match* for the template with respect to S is a substitution $\theta = \{X_1/t_1, \ldots, X_n/t_n\}$ such that the t_i are distinct and there exists an equation $graph(L\theta, N, E) \in S$ satisfying the following two conditions:

1. $\forall\, n_1 \in N^+, \exists\, n_2 \in N$ such that $n_1\theta = n_2$.

2. $\forall\, e_1 \in E^+, \exists\, e_2 \in E$ such that $e_1\theta = e_2$.

We note that the all substitution terms t_i in a match are constants from **P** $\cup$ **L**. We denote the set of distinct matches for a positive template Q with respect to a set of equations S by $Matches(Q, S)$.

For example, if S is the set of equations illustrated in Figures 1 - 3 and Q is the template $graph(X, \{child, Y\}, \{(child, Y)\})$, then $Matches(Q, S) = \{\{X/\text{PERSON-1}, Y/\text{PERSON-3}\}, \{X/\text{PERSON-2}, Y/\text{PERSON-3}\}, \{X/\text{PERSON-2}, Y/\text{PERSON-4}\}\}$.

We now extend this matching to the sequence of positive templates that appear in the body of a rule. In particular, we need to define the *join* of sets of matches. This is the analogue of the natural join of relations and could indeed be implemented as such if sets of matches were stored as relations.

Definition Joining sets of matches

Given two sets of matches, $Matches(Q_1, S_1)$ and $Matches(Q_2, S_2)$, we define their *join*, $Matches(Q_1, S_1) \circ Matches(Q_2, S_2)$, as follows:
Let
$$VARS(Q_1) \cap VARS(Q_2) = \{Z_1, \ldots, Z_n\},$$
$$VARS(Q_1) - \{Z_1, \ldots, Z_n\} = \{X_1, \ldots, X_p\}$$
and
$$VARS(Q_2) - \{Z_1, \ldots, Z_n\} = \{Y_1, \ldots, Y_q\}.$$
Then every pair of substitutions
$$\{Z_1/t_1, \ldots, Z_n/t_n, X_1/t_{n+1}, \ldots, X_p/t_{n+p}\} \in Matches(Q_1, S_1)$$
and
$$\{Z_1/s_1, \ldots, Z_n/s_n, Y_1/s_{n+1}, \ldots, Y_q/s_{n+q}\} \in Matches(Q_2, S_2)$$
such that $t_i = s_i$ for all $1 \leq i \leq n$, gives rise to a substitution
$$\{Z_1/t_1, \ldots, Z_n/t_n, X_1/t_{n+1}, \ldots, X_p/t_{n+p}, Y_1/s_{n+1}, \ldots, Y_q/s_{n+q}\}$$
$\in Matches(Q_1, S_1) \circ Matches(Q_2, S_2)$.

We note that the join operator $\circ$ is associative i.e.
$(Matches(Q_1, S_1) \circ Matches(Q_2, S_2)) \circ Matches(Q_3, S_3) = Matches(Q_1, S_1) \circ (Matches(Q_2, S_2) \circ Matches(Q_3, S_3))$.

Lastly, we need to address the matching of the negative templates appearing in the body of a rule. For this, we make the usual assumption of *range restriction* of negative information [9] so that once matching of positive templates has occurred, negative templates become ground:

Definition Matching negative templates

Given a set of equations S, a negative template $\neg graph(L, N^-, E^-)$ and a substitution θ such that $graph(L\theta, N^-\theta, E^-\theta)$ is ground, we say that θ is a *match* for the template with respect to the set of equations if there is no equation $graph(L\theta, N, E) \in S$ that satisfies either condition 1 or condition 2 below (or both):

1. $\exists\, n \in N^-$ such that $n\theta \in N$.

2. $\exists\, e \in E^-$ such that $e\theta \in E$.

We now consider the updates to the repository that result from the heads of rules. Before doing so we need to define the semantics of the *label generation* that may be caused by variables appearing in the head of a rule but not in its body.

Definition Label generation

Given a set of equations S, a program P, a rule $R \in P$ with head Q and a substitution θ, let $VARS(Q\theta) = \{X_1, ..., X_n\}$. Then, we denote by $extend(\theta, HR, Q)$ an arbitrary match ϕ for the template $Q\theta$ with respect to HR if such a match exists, or otherwise the substitution $\theta\{X_1/G_1, ..., X_n/G_n\}$ where the G_i are arbitrary distinct labels drawn from **L** and hitherto unused in HR or P.

We recall from section 2.1 that the equation $graph(G, \{\}, \{\})$ will be assumed for any "dangling" label G arising from this label generation process.

Thus, for each match for the body of a rule, the head of the rule contributes an equation which must be merged into the repository while maintaining the uniqueness of labels. This is accomplished by the following operators:

Definition The operators $+$ and $merge$.

Given two sets of equations, S and S', $S + S'$ returns a triple of sets of equations $(Old, Updated, New)$ where

1. Old contains every equation $graph(G, N, E) \in S$ such that there is no equation $graph(G, N', E') \in S'$;

2. New contains every equation $graph(G, N', E') \in S'$ such that there is no equation $graph(G, N, E) \in S$;

3. for every pair of equations $graph(G, N, E) \in S$ and $graph(G, N', E') \in S'$, $Updated$ contains the equation $graph(G, N \cup N', E \cup E')$.

Given two sets of equations, S and S', $merge(S, S')$ returns the set of equations $Old \cup Updated \cup New$, where $(Old, Updated, New) = S + S'$.

We now define the semantics of a Hyperlog program P with respect to a hypernode repository HR in terms of its naive bottom-up evaluation - Algorithm 2.2 below. This algorithm calls the following auxiliary algorithm for computing the updates resulting from the matching of a single rule:

Algorithm 2.1 $EVALRULE(R, Matches_1, ..., Matches_n)$
Input: A rule R with head Q_0 and n positive templates in its body. A set of matches for each positive template in the body of R, $Matches_1, ..., Matches_n$.
Output: A set of equations S.

$S := \{\}$
for all $\theta \in Matches_1 \circ Matches_2 \circ ... \circ Matches_n$ **do**
    if θ is a match for every negative template of R w.r.t. HR **then**

$$\phi := extend(\theta, HR, Q_0)$$
$$S := merge(S, \{Q_0\phi\})$$

return S

Algorithm 2.2 Naive Evaluation
Input: A repository HR and a program P.
Output: The updated repository.

repeat

$\qquad OldHR := HR$
$\qquad$ **for all rules** $R_i \equiv Q_0 \leftarrow Q_1, ..., Q_n, \neg Q_{n+1}, ..., \neg Q_{n+r} \in P$ **do**
$\qquad\qquad (Old_i, Updated_i, New_i) := HR+$
$\qquad\qquad EVALRULE(R_i, Matches(Q_1, HR), ..., Matches(Q_n, HR))$
$\qquad$ **for all rules** $R_i \in P$ **do**
$\qquad\qquad HR := merge(HR, Updated_i \cup New_i)$

until $HR = OldHR$

We note that $EVALRULE$ can be executed in parallel for all the rules. We also note that Algorithm 2.2 may not terminate since variables are allowed to appear in the head of a rule without appearing in its body. For example, the algorithm will not terminate for the program in Figure 5 if there is initially some match for the body of the rule that requires a new equation to be generated for the variable Z in the head of the rule. Similarly, the algorithm will not terminate for the program in Figure 6 provided there does initially exist in the repository a hypernode X that has a non-empty node set. Note that Figure 7 successively nests hypernodes - [2] discusses how successive nesting can be used to count in Hyperlog.

3 Semi-Naive Evaluation

In this section we show how semi-naive evaluation [9] can be modified for the evaluation of Hyperlog programs. Since we do not have multiple EDB and IDB predicates but only one *graph* predicate, we achieve this by syntactically partitioning a program into those templates which will not be affected by any updates to the repository during the evaluation (which we term extensional templates) and those templates which may be affected by updates to the repository during the evaluation (which we term intentional templates). We do this by defining the notion of the *unification* of the heads of rules with the positive templates in the bodies of rules. If no head of a rule unifies with a template in the body of a rule, the set of matches for that template remains invariant throughout the evaluation and need not be recomputed at each inference step (such a template is the analogue of an EDB predicate). Conversely, if the head of some rule unifies with a template in the body of a rule, the set of matches for that template may increase (never decrease) during the evaluation and must be recomputed after each inference step with respect to the updated equations (such a template is the analogue of an IDB predicate). Since the sets of matches for intentional templates are monotonic increasing, we can adopt a semi-naive strategy for computing the joins of these sets.

3.1 Definitions

We first give the definitions of the *unification* of a template in the head of a rule with a template in the body of a rule, and for *intentional* and *extensional* templates. We then discuss the rationale behind the definition of unification.

Definition Unification

Let Q_h and Q_b be two positive templates $graph(L_h, N_h, E_h)$ and $graph(L_b, N_b, E_b)$ respectively, where Q_h occurs in the head of a rule and Q_b in the body of a rule. We say that Q_h *unifies with* Q_b if there is a substitution θ such that

1. $L_h\theta = L_b\theta$, and either

2. $\exists\, e_h \in E_h$ and $e_b \in E_b$ such that $e_h\theta = e_b\theta$, or

3. $\exists\, n_h \in N_h$ and isolated $n_b \in N_b$ such that $n_h\theta = n_b\theta$, or both.

Definition Extensional and intensional templates

Let P be a Hyperlog program and Q a positive template in the body of a rule in P. We say that Q is an *extensional* template if no template in the head of any rule of P unifies with Q. Otherwise, we say that Q is an *intensional* template.

The rationale behind our definition of unification is two-fold : firstly, the set of matches for an extensional template should remain invariant during the evaluation of the program, and secondly the property of unification should determine which rule heads may increase the set of matches for an intentional template. Given a template $graph(L_b, N_b, E_b)$ in the body of some rule, a rule head may contribute nodes or edges to an equation that could be matched by $graph(L_b, N_b, E_b)$ either by the addition of a new edge that an edge in E_b might match - whence clause 2 of the definition - or by the addition of a new node (not necessarily isolated) that an isolated node in N_b might match - whence clause 1 of the definition - or by both.

For example, consider the program P below which is the flat program corresponding to the Hyperlog program depicted in Figure 4:
$$graph(X, \{des, Y\}, \{(des, Y)\}) \leftarrow graph(X, \{child, Y\}, \{(child, Y)\})$$
$$graph(X, \{des, Z\}, \{(des, Z)\}) \leftarrow graph(X, \{des, Y\}, \{(des, Y)\}),$$
$$graph(Y, \{child, Z\}, \{(child, Z)\})$$
Then the set of extensional templates of P is
$$\{graph(X, \{child, Y\}, \{(child, Y)\})\}$$
for the first rule and
$$\{graph(Y, \{child, Z\}, \{(child, Z)\})\}$$
for the second rule; the remaining template is intentional and both rule heads unify with it. Similarly, we note that the template in the body of the rule of Figure 5 is intentional as is that of Figure 7 while all three templates in the rule bodies of Figure 6 are extensional.

The following two Lemmas state the correctness of our definition of intentional and extensional templates:

Lemma 3.1 *Given a repository HR, a program P and an intentional template Q of some rule R of P, the set $Matches(Q, HR)$ is increased during an iteration of the repeat loop in Algorithm 2.2 only by matches of Q with respect to the sets of equations $Updated_i \cup New_i$ such that the head of R_i unifies with Q.*

Lemma 3.2 *Given a repository HR, a program P and an extensional template Q of some rule R of P, the set $Matches(Q, HR)$ remains invariant during Algorithm 2.2.*

Note that it is safe to remove any rule R of P for which some extensional template of R has no match, obtaining a new program P':

Lemma 3.3 *The programs P and P' have the same meaning (up to re-naming of new labels).*

This follows since if for some rule R of P and extensional template Q of R we have $Matches(Q, HR) = \{\}$, then $EVALRULE$ of R will return an empty set of equations on the first iteration of the repeat loop of Algorithm 2.2. Furthermore, $EVALRULE$ of R will continue to return an empty set of equations on subsequent iterations since Q is an extensional template.

3.2 Algorithms

In this section we give the algorithm for the semi-naive evaluation of a Hyperlog program P with respect to a hypernode repository HR - Algorithm 3.2 below. This algorithm starts off by calling the following procedure *Partition* to determine the intentional and extensional templates and to remove any rule of P for which some extensional template in its body has no match.

Procedure $Partition(HR, P, \overline{IntQs}, \overline{Matches})$
Input: A Hypernode repository HR. A program P consisting of the rules $R_1, ..., R_m$.
Output: The intentional templates of each rule R_i, $IntQs_i$. The matches of the k-th positive template of the i-th rule Q_{ik} w.r.t. HR, $Matches_{ik}$. An updated program P.

for all rules $R_i \in P$ **do**
  $IntQs_i := \{\}$
  for all positive templates Q_{ik} in the body of R_i **do**
    $Matches_{ik} := Matches(Q_{ik}, HR)$
    if Q_{ik} is an intentional template **then**
      $IntQs_i := IntQs_i \cup \{Q_{ik}\}$
    else if $Matches_{ik} = \{\}$ **then**
      $P := P - R_i$

By Lemma 3.2 we do not need to recalculate the matches for extensional templates, but we do need to do so for intentional templates with respect to the updated or new graphs. Algorithm 3.1 below encapsulates the semi-naive evaluation of a single rule. The parameters $\overline{Matches}$ and $\overline{\Delta Matches}$ record the total matches and last round's matches, respectively, for each template with respect to the repository. They are the analogue of relations and their increments in conventional semi-naive evaluation.

Algorithm 3.1 $EVALRULEINCR(R_i, \overline{Matches}, \Delta Matches)$
Input: A rule R_i of a program P with head Q_{i0} and n positive templates in its body. The set of accumulated matches for each positive template of P, $\overline{Matches}$. The previous increments to these sets of matches, $\Delta Matches$.
Output: A set of equations S.

$S := \{\}$
for all $Q_{ik} \in IntQs_i$ **do**

    for all $\theta \in Matches_{i1} \text{ o } ... \text{ o } Matches_{i(k-1)} \text{ o } \Delta Matches_{ik} \text{ o } Matches_{i(k+1)} \text{ o } ... \text{ o } Matches_{in}$ **do**

        if θ is a match for every negative template of R_i w.r.t. HR **then**

            $\phi := extend(\theta, HR, Q_{i0}))$
            $S := merge(S, \{Q_{i0}\phi\})$

return S

The overall semi-naive evaluation algorithm is Algorithm 3.2 below. This first calls *Partition* to determine the extensional and intentional templates and to initialise the set of matches $Matches_{ik}$ for each template Q_{ik}. It then sets the increment $\Delta Matches_{ik}$ for each Q_{ik} to be the initial set of matches $Matches_{ik}$. Thereafter $EVALRULEINCR$ is repeatedly called for every rule with the previous round's increments, $Old\Delta Matches_{ik}$, and the total set of accumulated matches, $Matches_{ik}$, to obtain the new and updated equations. The new increments, $\Delta Matches_{ik}$, are calculated from these equations which are then merged into the repository.

We observe here a departure from conventional semi-naive evaluation in that, although extensional and intentional templates are the analogue of EDB and IDB predicates, two templates may match the same equation. So the new matches for an intentional template must be determined with respect to all the new or updated equations contributed by rule heads that unify with the template.

We also note that on the first iteration of the **repeat** loop of Algorithm 3.2 below, the call to $EVALRULEINCR$ could be replaced by a call to $EVALRULE$ which would be more efficient and have the same effect. On this assumption, Algorithms 2.2 and 3.2 have a similar first round. In subsequent rounds however Algorithm 3.2 has performance gains over Algorithm 2.2 in three main ways : firstly, only intentional templates are matched against equations, not all templates; secondly, a template is matched only with respect to the updated and new equations that arise in the current round from those rule heads that unify with the template, not with respect to the entire repository; and thirdly, only the current round's updated and new equations are merged into the repository, not all updated and new equations.

Algorithm 3.2 *Semi-NaiveEvaluation*
Input: A hypernode repository HR and a Hyperlog program consisting of the rules $R_1, \ldots, R_m$.
Output: The updated repository HR.

$Partition(HR, P, \overline{IntQs}, \overline{Matches})$
for all rules $R_i \in P$ **do**

> **for all** $Q_{ik} \in IntQs_i$ **do**
> > $\Delta Matches_{ik} := Matches_{ik}$

repeat

> **for all** intentional templates Q_{ik} **do**
> > $Old\Delta Matches_{ik} := \Delta Matches_{ik}$
> > $\Delta Matches_{ik} := \{\}$

> **for all** rules $R_i \in P$ **do**
> > $(Old_i, Updated_i, New_i) := HR+$
> > $EVALRULEINCR(R_i, \overline{Matches}, \overline{Old\Delta Matches})$
> > **for all** intentional templates Q_{jk} such that Q_{i0} unifies with Q_{jk} **do**
> > > $\Delta Matches_{jk} :=$
> > > $\Delta Matches_{jk} \cup Matches(Q_{jk}, Updated_i \cup New_i)$

> **for all** rules $R_i \in P$ **do**
> > $HR := merge(HR, Updated_i \cup New_i)$

> **for all** intentional templates Q_{ik} **do**
> > $\Delta Matches_{ik} := \Delta Matches_{ik} - Matches_{ik}$
> > $Matches_{ik} := Matches_{ik} \cup \Delta Matches_{ik}$

until $\Delta Matches_{ik} = \{\}$ for all intentional templates Q_{ik}

The following theorem states the correctness of Algorithm 3.2:

Theorem 3.4 *Each round of Algorithm 3.2 returns the same repository as the same round of Algorithm 2.2, up to the renaming of new labels.*

The theorem can be proved by induction on the current round number with the base case being round one, as in the proof of conventional semi-naive evaluation [9]. In our case we also need to appeal to Lemmas 3.1 and 3.3 for the correctness of *Partition*, and also to Lemma 3.2 for the correct inference of new matches for intentional templates.

3.3 Evaluation of queries

We now briefly consider queries in Hyperlog. We first define a Hyperlog *query* to be a rule without a head:

$\leftarrow Q_1, \ldots, Q_n, \neg Q_{n+1}, \ldots, \neg Q_{n+r}$

Up to now in this paper our programs have been "generation" programs that permanently update the repository. It is of course also possible to view

Hyperlog programs as "derivation" programs representing intentional information. In this case we are interested in the evaluation of a query with respect to a given hypernode repository HR and derivation program P.

Let HR' be the repository that would result from the fixpoint computation of P with respect to HR using Algorithm 2.2 or 3.2. We define the "answer" to the query to be the set of matches $\theta \in Matches(Q_1, HR')$ o ... o $Matches(Q_n, HR')$ which are also matches for every negative template $\neg Q_{n+1}, ..., \neg Q_{n+r}$.

However, the full evaluation of P with respect to HR will in general result in updates that contribute no matches to this answer. So we need to investigate syntactic techniques for rewriting P given Q (c.f. magic sets [12]).

4 Concluding Remarks

We have described a graph-based declarative database language called Hyperlog and have defined its semantics using a variant of bottom-up naive evaluation for a single *graph* predicate. Our main contribution has been to show how the semi-naive evaluation of [9] can be utilised for the more efficient evaluation of Hyperlog programs. This has been achieved by observing that the templates in the bodies of rules can be used to conceptually partition the database into multiple EDB and IDB "predicates" in the absence of true predicates.

We are currently considering the implications of allowing negation in the heads of rules (so that database updates are no longer monotonic increasing). We are also investigating the optimisation of query evaluation by a form of program rewriting akin to magic sets. Finally, the storage level [3] of our prototype DBMS needs to be extended with indexing that more effectively supports the matching of templates with respect to sets of equations that lies at the heart Hyperlog i.e. the operation $Matches(Q, S)$ for a template Q and set of equations S.

Hyperlog itself has application in a number of areas, for example as a very high level data manipulation language for non-graphical data models, and as a means of integrating declarative querying and navigation in graph-based databases such as hypertext and design databases.

Acknowledgements

We would like to thank our colleagues on the Hypernode Project, Mark Levene and Eran Tuv for many stimulating discussions. The Hypernode Project has been funded by the U.K. Science and Engineering Research Council (grant no. GR/G26662).

References

[1] M. Levene and A. Poulovassilis, The hypernode model and its associated query language, In Proceedings of the 5th Jerusalem Conference on Information Technology, IEEE Press, pp 520-530, 1990.

[2] A. Poulovassilis and M. Levene, A nested-graph model for the representation and manipulation of complex objects, ACM Transactions on Information Systems, 1993, in press.

[3] E. Tuv, A. Poulovassilis and M. Levene, A storage manager for the hypernode model, In Proceedings of the 10th British National Conference on Databases, Springer-Verlag, pp 59-77, 1992.

[4] M.P. Consens and A.O. Mendelzon, Graphlog: a visual formalism for real life recursion, In Proceedings of the ACM Symposium on Principles of Database Systems, Nashville, Tennessee, pp 404-416, 1990.

[5] M. Gyssens, J. Paredaens and D.V. Van Gucht, A graph-oriented object model for database end-user interfaces, In Proceedings of the ACM SIGMOD International Conference on the Management of Data, Atlantic City, New Jersey, pp 24-33, 1990.

[6] J. Paredaens, P. Peelman and L. Tanca, G-Log: A Declarative Graphical Query Language, In Proceedings of the 1st International Conference on Deductive and Object-Oriented Databases, pp 108-128, 1991.

[7] F.W. Tompa, A data model for flexible hypertext database systems, ACM Transactions on Information Systems, 7(1), pp 85-100, 1989.

[8] C. Watters and M.A. Shepherd, A transient hypergraph-based model for data access, ACM Transactions on Information Systems, 8(2), pp 77-102, 1990.

[9] J. D. Ullman, Principles of Database and Knowledge-Base Systems, Computer Science Press, Rockville, Maryland, 1988.

[10] P. Aczel, Non-well-founded Sets, Center for the Study of Language and Information (CSLI) Lecture notes no. 14, Stanford, California, 1988.

[11] S. Abiteboul and P.C. Kanellakis, Object identity as a query language primitive, In Proceedings of the ACM SIGMOD International Conference on the Management of Data, Portland, Oregon, pp 159-173, 1989.

[12] C. Beeri and R. Ramakrishnan, On the Power of Magic, In Proceedings of the ACM Symposium on Principles of Databases Systems, pp 269-283, 1987.

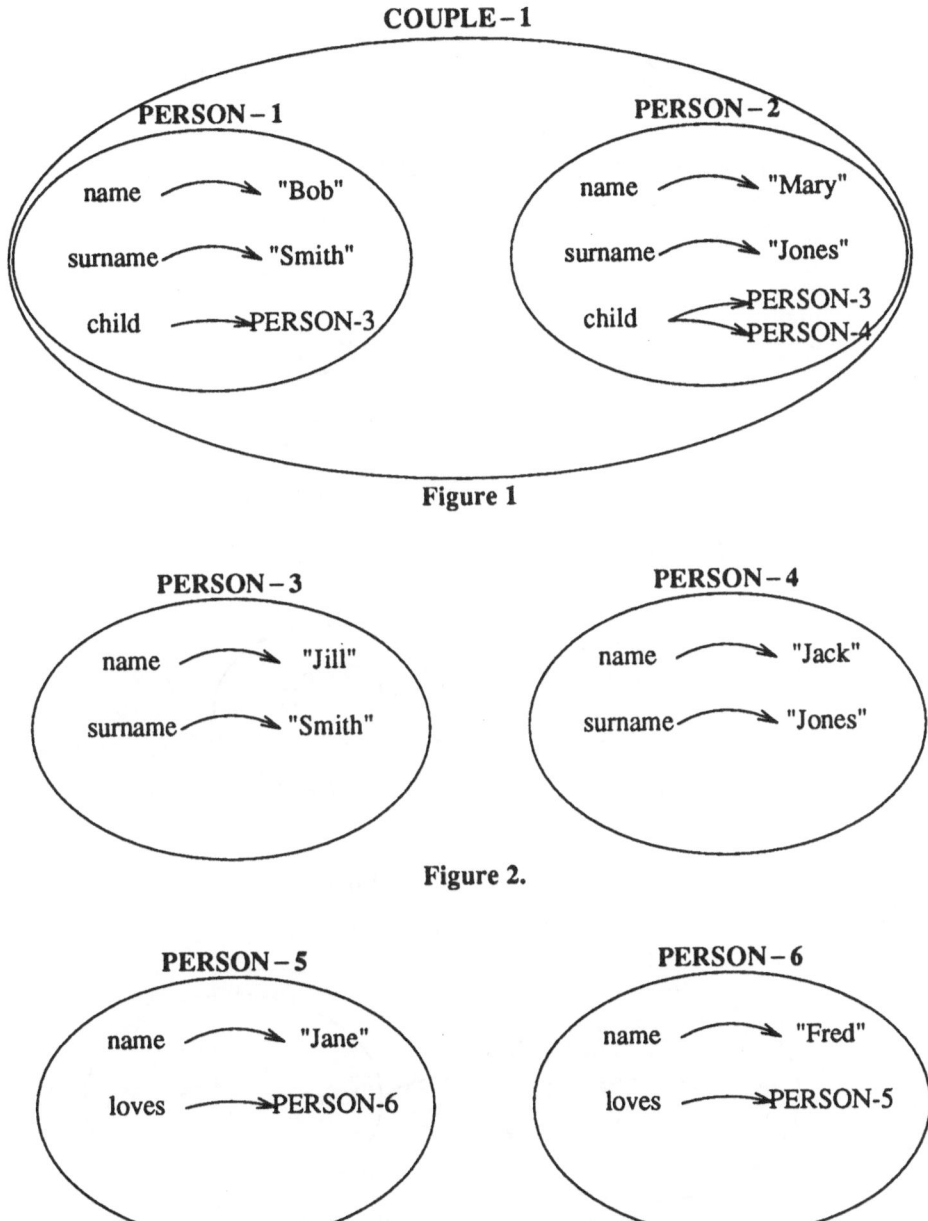

COUPLE-1

PERSON-1

name → "Bob"

surname → "Smith"

child → PERSON-3

PERSON-2

name → "Mary"

surname → "Jones"

child → PERSON-3
       → PERSON-4

Figure 1

PERSON-3

name → "Jill"

surname → "Smith"

PERSON-4

name → "Jack"

surname → "Jones"

Figure 2.

PERSON-5

name → "Jane"

loves → PERSON-6

PERSON-6

name → "Fred"

loves → PERSON-5

Figure 3.

266

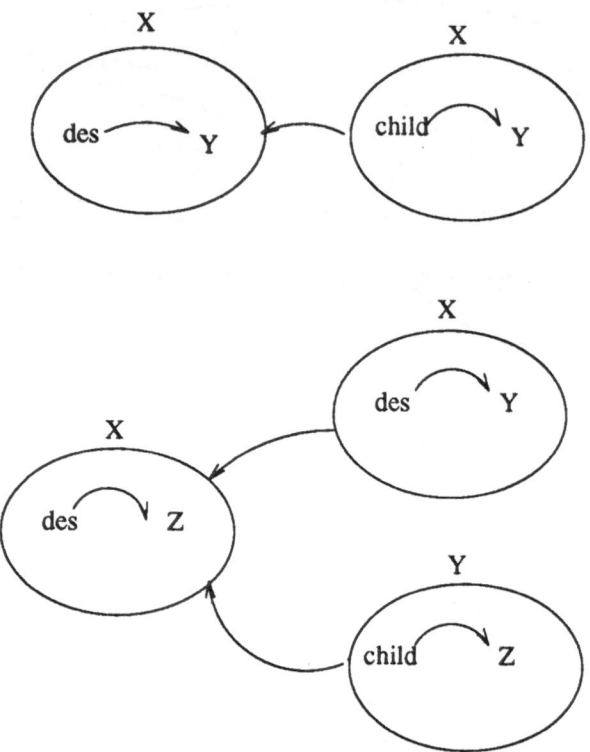

Figure 4.

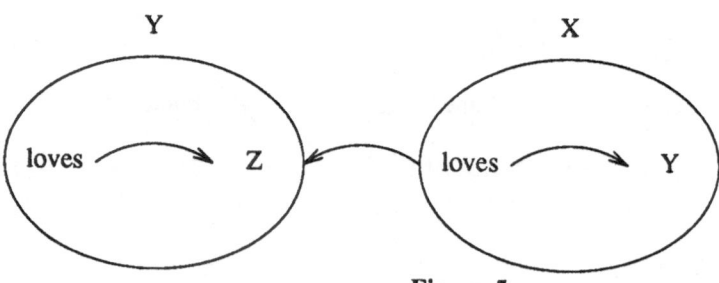

Figure 5.

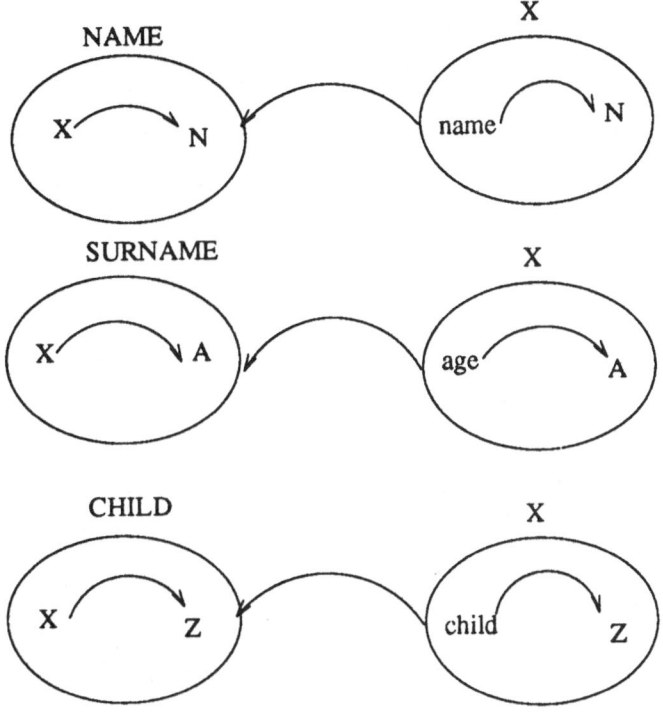

Figure 6.

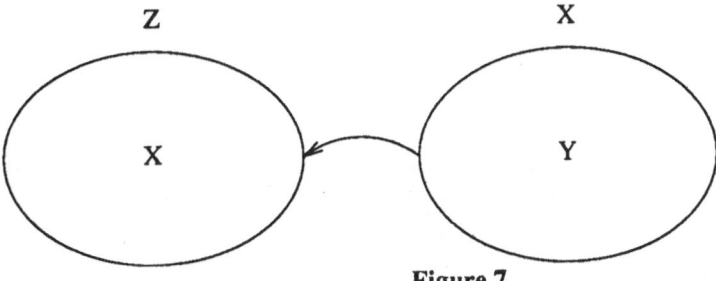

Figure 7.

Integrating Deductive and Active Rules

A Unified Semantics for Active and Deductive Databases

Carlo Zaniolo

Computer Science Department
University of California
Los Angeles, California U.S.A.
zaniolo@cs.ucla.edu

Abstract

These two rule-oriented paradigms of databases have been the focus of extensive research and are now coming of age in the commercial DBMS world. However, the systems developed so far support well only one of the two paradigms—thus limiting the effectiveness of such systems in many applications that require complete integration of both kinds of rules. In this paper, we discuss the technical problems that make such an integration difficult, and trace their roots to a lack of a unified underlying semantics. Then, we review recent advances in the semantics of non-monotonic logic and show that they can be used to unify the foundations of active databases and deductive databases. Finally, we outline the design a new rule language for databases that integrates a deductive system with a trigger-based DBMS.

1 Introduction

Rules provide the main paradigm for expressing computation in active databases and deductive databases. The unification of the two paradigms represents a research problem of obvious theoretical interest and many important applications could benefit from it; yet, there has been little formal work on the marrying these powerful paradigms. While cultural and historical biases share the blame for this chasm, the root of the problem is actually technical and can be traced to certain semantic inadequacies in the conceptual foundations of both approaches.

Several active database languages and systems have been proposed so far: a very incomplete list include [4, 8, 20, 21, 28]. However, there is is no unifying semantic theory for active databases: most of the work done so far has concentrated on explaining operational semantics of particular systems. On the contrary, not one but three equivalent formal semantics exist for Horn clauses that form the core of deductive database languages [29, 18]. Unfortunately, this elegant semantics is brittle and can not be generalized easily to deal with non-monotonic constructs, such as negation and updates. Similar non-monotonic reasoning problems have emerged in the areas of knowledge representation and of logic programming and remain the focus of intense research. While deductive databases encountered early successes in this problem area (e.g., with the introduction of the concept of stratified negation), recent progress has been very slow. No totally satisfactory semantics currently exist for programs which use non-monotonic constructs such as negation and aggregates in recursion—and the problem of updates in recursion is understood even less. Also, the problem of finding a logic for reasoning about actions and situations represents one of the classical challenge of AI [17].

Given this rather ominous background, the solution presented in this paper is surprisingly simple and general. We introduce the notion of XY-stratified programs that allow non-monotonic constructs in recursive rules. Then, we show that a formal semantics for updates and triggers in databases can be given using XY-stratified programs. The blueprints for the design of a unified rule language for active databases and deductive databases follow from such a solution.

2   Logic-Based Semantics

This area has benefited significantly from research in deductive databases. The adoption of the fixpoint-based bottom-up approach to define the declarative and constructive semantics of logic programs led almost immediately to the concept of stratified negation and stratified set aggregates [24]. This concept removes several of the limitations and problems of Prolog's negation-by-failure, and it is conductive to efficient implementation, as demonstrated by systems such as *Glue-Nail*, $\mathcal{LDL}$ and $CORAL$ [23, 5, 26]. However, experience gained with real-life applications [33] revealed that stratification is too restrictive and there remain many important applications where negation and set aggregates are needed: such applications, range from processing a Bill of Materials to finding the shortest path in a graph [33].

Therefore, during the last five years, a substantial research effort has been devoted to solving the non-stratification issue. This endeavor has produced significant progress on the theoretical front, with the introduction of concepts such as locally stratified programs, well-founded models [12], and the stable models[9], but it has not yet begotten a solution that is both general and practical. Indeed a practical solution must satisfy three difficult requirements, inasmuch as it must

- have a formal logic-based semantics,

- have a simple and intuitive constructive semantics,

- be amenable to efficient implementation.

Thus, in addition to requiring formal semantics and efficient implementation, any practical proposal must also stress the importance of having a simple concrete semantics: i.e., one that can be easily comprehended by the application programmer, without a need to understand abstract formalisms. For instance, a notion such as stratification can be mastered by a programmer, who can make full use of it without having to understand its formal perfect-model semantics. Furthermore, it is simple for a compiler to verify that stratification is satisfied, and then support stratified programs by an efficient bottom-up computation. However, an understanding of the logical formalism is required to understand notions such as well-founded models or stable models. Furthermore, no simple syntactic check exists for deciding whether a program has a well-founded model or a stable model; when such models exist their computation can be very expensive.

The notion of XY-stratified programs was recently proposed to overcome these difficulties [34]. This is a special subclass of locally stratified programs that is easy for a compiler to recognize and implement using the fixpoint-based computation of deductive DBs. It was shown in [34] that classical computational problems such as Floyd's shortest path algorithms, can be expressed naturally by programs in this class using non-stratified negation and aggregates. In this paper, we will build on such a semantics to provide a formal model of updates in deductive databases and triggers in active databases.

The problem of providing a formal semantics to updates in the context of logic also represents a difficult challenge. Several of the approaches proposed deal with the more general problem of modeling revisions of knowledge bases— i.e., including additions, deletions and modifications of rules [3, 6, 32, 13]. As a result, these theories are more complex and less conducive to efficiency than it is desirable in a practical semantics, according to the criteria discussed above. Therefore, we will restrict our attention to the problem of modifying the extensional database only [22]. Most of the work done in this more specific context is based on Dynamic Logic [7]. In particular, the approach given in [30, 19] uses dynamic logic to formalize a concrete semantics where the updates take place according to rule instances—a *tuple-at-a-time* semantics often leading to non-determinism. However, relational databases support a *set-at-a-time* update semantics, where all the applicable updates are fired at once, in parallel. A set-at-a-time semantics based on dynamic logic was adopted and efficiently implemented in $\mathcal{LDL}$ [25, 5]. While the $\mathcal{LDL}$ design has progressed further than other systems toward a complete integration of database-oriented updates into a logic-based language, several problems remain, such as multiple update rules sharing the same heads, and failing goals after update goals [15]. Furthermore, since dynamic logic is quite different from standard logic, the two do not mix well, and, as a result, updates are not allowed in recursive $\mathcal{LDL}$ rules; a special construct, called **forever** had to be introduced to express **do-while** iterations over updates [25]. A further illustration of the difficulties encountered by declarative logic-based languages in dealing with updates is provided by the design of the *Glue-Nail* system [23]. In this second-generation deductive database system, updates were banned from the core declarative language and relegated to the procedural shell that is tightly wrapped around the core [26].

Viewed against the tormented landscape of previous work, the model of updates and active databases proposed in this paper is surprisingly simple. Basically, we define rules with updates in their heads by simply re-writing them into equivalent update-free logic programs that are XY-stratified. The common semantics of active and deductive predicates, so obtained, is the basis for our unification of the active and deductive aspects of databases. This semantics is conducive to the design of a powerful language capable of expressing reasoning, triggers and detection of events as required by the next generation of intelligent database applications.

2.1 XY-Stratification

We begin with a simple example [1] that computes the nodes X of a graph g reachable from a given node a, and the minimum distance of X from this node:

Example 1 *Reachable nodes:*

r_0 : delta(nil, X, 1) ← g(a, X).

r_1 : delta(s(I), Y, D1) ← delta(I, X, D), g(X, Y),
¬all(I, Y, _), D1 = D + 1.

r_2 : all(s(I), Y, D) ← all(I, Y, D), delta(s(I), _, _).
r_3 : all(I, Y, D) ← delta(I, Y, D).

This program presents several unusual traits. A most obvious one is the presence of terms such as nil, I, s(I) in the first argument of the recursive predicates. These arguments will be called *stage arguments*, and their usage is for counting as in the recursive definition of integers: nil stands for zero and s(I) stands for I+1.

The intuitive meaning of the program of Example 11 is quite obvious: it implements a seminaive computation of a transitive closure [25], through the use of two predicates: delta contains the new values, and all is the union of all values computed so far. In rule r_1, all is used for checking that no previous (therefore shorter) path exists to this node.

The formal semantics of the program also supports its intuitive semantics. Because of its particular syntactic form, the program is locally stratified, where each stratum corresponds to a different value of the stage argument. The first stratum contains atoms of the form:

delta(nil, ...), all(nil, ...)

the next stratum consists of all atoms of the form:

delta(s(nil), ...), all(s(nil), ...)

and so on. The particular syntactic form of the recursive rules, w.r.t. the stage arguments, makes it simple for a compiler to recognize the presence of a *locally stratified program* (although local stratification is normally undecidable in the presence of function symbols).

Furthermore, this type of program can be implemented efficiently using a modified fixpoint computation. In general, the perfect model of such a program can only be obtained using a transfinite computation called iterated fixpoint [24]. This proceeds as follows: the least fixpoint is first computed for the first (bottom) stratum; then, once the least fixpoint is computed for the n-th stratum, the least fixpoint is computed for the $n + 1$-th stratum. The transfinite computation of perfect models simplifies dramatically for the program at

---

[1]We assume our reader familiar with the basic concepts pertaining to Datalog and logic rules including the concept of locally stratified programs and the *iterated fixpoint procedure* that computes the perfect model of these programs [24, 25]. Given a program P, a set of rules of P defining a maximal set of mutually recursive predicates will be called a *recursive clique* of P. The non-recursive rules in this set are called *exit* rules (r_0 is the only exit rule in Example 1).

hand. Assume, for now, that the stratification is determined by the values of stage arguments. The fixpoint at the bottom stratum is reached after firing rule r_0 followed by r_3. The fixpoint for the stratum $s(nil)$ is reached by firing rule r_1, followed by firing r_2 and r_3. Then, the higher strata are inductively generated by firing these three rules in the same order. Therefore, the general transfinite procedure to compute perfect models here reduces to the customary fixpoint iteration. Further improvements can be easily made to ensure that this computation executes quite efficiently. For instance, while rule r_2 seems to suggest that a complete copying of the old relation is needed at each step, no such operation is needed in reality. In fact, the only instances of rules that can produce new atoms are those instantiated with stage values from the current stratum: values from the old strata are not used and can be discarded. Thus, if we keep the values of the stage variable in a separate memory cell, all is needed to perform the copy operation is to increase the value of the integer in this cell by one.

Given a recursive clique, Q, the first arguments of recursive predicates of a rule r (of Q) will be called the *stage arguments* of r (of Q) [2] Then a recursive rule will be called an

- **X-rule** when all the stage arguments of r are equal to a simple variable, say J; furthermore, J does not appear anywhere else in r;

- **Y-rule** when (i) some positive goal of r has as stage argument a simple variable, say J, (ii) the head of r has stage argument $s(J)$, (iii) all the remaining stage arguments are either J or $s(J)$ and (iv) J does not appear anywhere else in r.

In Example 11, r_3 is an X-rule, while r_1 and r_2 are Y-rules. A recursive clique Q such that all its recursive rules are either X-rules or Y-rules, will be said to be a recursive XY-clique. We now introduce simple syntactic criteria for classes of non-stratified programs that are amenable to efficient implementation.
Priming: p'(...) will be called the primed version of an atom p(...). Given an XY-clique, Q, its primed version Q', is constructed by priming certain occurrences of recursive predicates in recursive rules as follows:

- X-rules: all occurrences of recursive predicates are primed,

- Y-rules: the head predicate is primed, and so is every goal with stage argument equal to that of the head.

The primed version of our example is as follows:

$r_0 : \text{delta}(nil, X, 1) \leftarrow \ \text{g}(a, X).$

$r_1 : \text{delta}'(s(I), Y, D1) \leftarrow \ \text{delta}(I, X, D), \text{g}(X, Y),$
$\qquad\qquad\qquad\qquad\qquad \neg\text{all}(I, Y, \_), D1 = D + 1.$

$r_2 : \text{all}'(s(I), Y, D) \leftarrow \ \text{all}(I, Y, D), \text{delta}'(s(I), \_, \_).$
$r_3 : \text{all}'(I, Y, D) \leftarrow \ \text{delta}'(I, Y, D).$

---

[2] This is only a matter of convention. Alternatively, we could let the last arguments of recursive predicates be our stage arguments.

Definition 1 *An XY-clique Q will be said to be* XY-stratified *when*

- *The primed version of Q is non-recursive*

- *All exit rules have as stage argument the same constant.*

□

A program will be said to be *XY-stratified* when every recursive rule that contains some negated recursive goal(s) in its body belongs to an XY-stratified clique.

The dependency graph for a primed clique provides a very simple syntactic test on whether a program is *XY*-stratified. Furthermore, these programs are amenable to efficient implementation as proven in the following discussion.

The primed version Q' of an XY-stratified clique defines a non-recursive program: i.e., the dependency graph of Q' contains no cycle. Therefore, there exists a topological sorting of the nodes of Q' which obeys stratification, and such that all unprimed predicate names precede the primed ones. For Example 1, for instance, the following

```
all < delta < delta' < all'
```

is such a topological sorting. The tail of such a sorting, restricted to the primed predicate names will be called a *primed sorting* of Q. For the previous example, we obtain the following primed sorting:

```
delta' < all'
```

Now, we can partition the atoms in Herbrand Base B_Q of the *original Q* into classes according to their predicate names and their stage arguments as follows:

- there is a distinct class, say σ_0, containing all instances of non-recursive predicates in Q—i.e., those without a stage argument.

- all atoms with the same recursive predicate name and the same number of function symbols **s** in the stage argument belong to same equivalence class $\sigma_{n,p}$ with n denoting the number of **s** function symbols in the stage argument of p. Thus, $all(s(nil), ...)$, and $all(s(a), ...$, belong to the same class (stratum) in our example.

The partition Σ of B_Q so constructed can be totally ordered, by letting σ_0 be the bottom stratum in Σ, and then letting $\sigma_{n,p} \prec \sigma_{m,q}$ if

- $n < m$, or

- if $n = m$ but p' precedes q' in the primed sorting of the clique.

The total ordered Σ so constructed will be called the *stage layering* of B_Q. For Example 1, let each of $C_1, C_2, ...$ range over the set $\{nil, a, 1\}$ and each $V_1, V_2, ...$ range over Q's Herbrand Universe; then Σ has the following form:

$$\{g(V_1, V_2)\} \prec$$
$$\{delta(C_1, V_3, V_4)\} \prec \{all(C_2, V_5, V_6\} \prec$$
$$\{delta(s(C_3), V_7, V_8)\} \prec \{all(s(C_4), V_9, V_{10})\} \prec ...$$

A locally stratified program p will be called *strictly* stratified when for every instance r of of a rule in P, the head of r belongs to a layer strictly higher than the layers for the goals of r. Then, we have the following theorem:

Theorem 1 *Each XY-stratified clique Q is strictly stratified according to a stage layering of B_Q.*

Proof: If g is an unprimed goal g for r then, the stage argument of the head of r, $h(r)$ contains one more **s** than g. If g is primed, then $h(r)$ is also primed and its name follows the name of g in the primed ordering. □

Since the stratification is strict, in computing the iterated fixpoint, *the saturation for each stratum is reached in one step.* Therefore, the compiler can resequence the rules according to the primed sorting of their head names. Then, once all atoms with stage value J have been computed, a *single pass through the rules of Q ordered according to the primed sorting* computes all the atoms with stage value $s(J)$. Therefore, if Q is an XY-stratified clique, then (i) Q is locally stratified, and (ii) its perfect model can be constructed by a fixpoint iteration to the first ordinal: the recursive rules in the clique are fired according to the topological layering. We thus obtain the following algorithm, which assumes that the stage arguments are projected out from the rules (the notation w.s.a. will denote a rule without its stage argument) [34]:

Perfect Model Computation for XY-stratified Cliques

Step 1. The stage variable is assigned the stage constant from the exit rules

Step 2. Fire the X-rules (w.s.a), once

Step 3. Fire the recursive rules (w.s.a.) sequentially.

Therefore, the stage argument is updated only once per cycle. XY-stratified programs can express every program expressible under inflationary fixpoint [34].

3 Syntactic Encapsulation

New syntactic constructs introduced to replace frequently used expressions of First Order Logic can yield dramatic benefits in terms of readability and efficient implementation. For instance, the simple idea of encapsulating disjunctive clauses, with no more than one non-negated literal, by the basic rule notation yields the improvements in readability and amenability to efficient implementation that are at root of the popularity of the logic programming paradigm. The same method has be used with remarkable success in other situations. For instance, the choice construct was defined in [11] to capture the notion of don't care non-determinism and encapsulate certain kinds of negative programs amenable to a polynomial-time computation. Two other such constructs are `if-then(-else)` and `min/max` predicates, both used in the XY-stratified program below. This expresses a linear version of Floyd algorithm for computing the shortest paths in a graph:

Example 2 *Floyd Algorithm.*

$$\text{delta}(\text{nil}, X, X, 0).$$
$$\text{delta}(s(J), X, Z, \min(< C >)) \leftarrow \quad \text{delta}(J, X, Y, C1),$$
$$g(Y, Z, C2), C = C1 + C2.$$

$$\text{all}(s(J), X, Z, C) \leftarrow \quad \text{all}(J, X, Z, C).$$
$$\text{all}(J, X, Z, C) \leftarrow \quad \text{delta}(J, X, Z, C),$$
$$\text{if}(\text{all}(J, X, Z, C3) \text{ then } C3 > C).$$

The **if-then** construct used in the last rule of Example 2, is a construct of $\mathcal{LDL}$ and $\mathcal{LDL}++$ whose formal semantics is defined by its re-writing into a negative program: our rule is equivalent to

$$\text{all}(J, X, Z, C) \leftarrow \quad \text{delta}(J, X, Z, C),$$
$$\text{all}(J, X, Z, C3), \ C3 > C.$$
$$\text{all}(J, X, Z, C) \leftarrow \quad \text{delta}(J, X, Z, C),$$
$$\neg \text{all}(J, X, Z, C3).$$

Thus, programs containing if-then-else constructs are X-Y stratified iff their expansion using negation is. Likewise, the notion of least elements in a set can be defined by the property that no lesser element exists. Take for instance the following rule from Example 2:

$$\text{delta}(s(J), X, Z, \min(< C >)) \leftarrow \quad \text{delta}(J, X, Y, C1),$$
$$g(Y, Z, C2), C = C1 + C2,$$

Here $< C >$ denotes the grouping of C values with respect to the other variables in the head; and **min** denotes the least of such values. The meaning of the previous rule can in fact be defined through the definition of set aggregates [34] or equivalently by its expansion using negation [10].

$$\text{delta}(s(J), X, Z, C) \leftarrow \quad \text{delta}(J, X, Y, C1), \ g(Y, Z, C2), C = C1 + C2,$$
$$\neg \text{lesser}(s(J), X, Z, C).$$
$$\text{lesser}(s(J), X, Z, C) \leftarrow \quad \text{delta}(s(J), X, Z, C'), \ g(Y, Z, C2), C' = C1 + C2,$$
$$C' < C.$$

The approach of establishing a one-to-one correspondence between certain syntactic constructs leading to efficient operational semantics and classes of non-monotonic programs with a formal semantics has far-reaching implications. For instance, in supporting a program such as that of Example 1, it is clear that rules r_2 and r_3 can be implemented efficiently via an imperative *append_to (insert)* operator. Conversely, database updates can often be viewed as a syntactic encapsulation for XY-stratified programs: we will expand on this approach in the next sections.

4   Semantics of Updates

Let us now consider a database language that, in addition to query requests, supports other commands, such as requests to add or delete some extensional facts. As shown in [27], the definition of the semantics of programs with updates need not make use of imperative constructs. Rather, defining the semantics of such a language tantamounts to defining the external behavior of programs written in this language. Neglecting for the moment integrity constraints, we see that the external response to an update command should basically be an acknowledgement of some sort (e.g., a carriage return). Thus, all it is left to do is to define the meaning of queries. However, there is a key difference with respect to standard framework of query-only logic-based semantics [18, 29]: here we must specify the answer to queries *after the database has been modified by a given sequence of updates*. Thus, in our formal model we have (i) a program P containing a set of rules and a schema describing the extensional database, (ii) a set of extensional facts D defining the initial database state (iii) a sequence of update requests R, and (iv) a query Q; then we must define the *meaning function* $M(P, D, R, Q)$. For instance, consider the following example

Example 3 *We assume that our program P contains the declaration of two database relations* std *and* grad *(describing the majors of students and the courses and grades they took) and the following rule*

$$\text{csst}(X, C) \leftarrow \text{std}(X, \text{cs}), \text{grad}(X, C, \_).$$

The initial database D contains the following facts:

std(ann, ee).   grad(ann, cs143, 3).
std(tom, cs).

R, the set of update requests, is:

req(1, add, std(marc, ee)).
req(2, del, std(ann, ee)).
req(2, add, std(ann, cs)).

The query Q is: ?csst(X, Y).

We have represented our sequence of update requests as a relation req; the first argument in req places the particular request in the proper time sequence. Successive requests are given successive integers by the system. However, several requests can be given the same sequence number, to ensure that they are processed in parallel. For instance, the last two entries in R correspond to a user-level request to modify the major of Ann from EE to CS.

Inasmuch as we only need to define the external behaviour of the system, the definition of our meaning function reduces to the specification of the response (answer) to any query such as ?csst(X, Y), given a certain initial database and an arbitrary sequence of updates. Since a query can inquire about the content of any relation after a sequence of such updates, we will have to model the notion of states the database goes through; however, we must avoid destructive assignments in order to remain declarative and obtain a logic-based semantics. Toward this goal, we use a distinguished predicate quevt that, basically, operates as a queue of events. For now, the quevt predicate can be thought of as performing a copy of the req predicate as follows:

Example 4 *A first attempt at* quevt

$$\text{quevt}(\text{N}, \text{ActionTyp}, \text{Atom}, \text{N}) \leftarrow \text{req}(\text{N}, \text{ActionTyp}, \text{Atom}).$$

The meaning of a program P with external updates is thus defined by generating an equivalent program P'. For each extensional predicate q/n (q is the name of the predicate and n is its arity) we now define a new intensional predicate q/n+1 (we assume without loss of generality that there is no q/n+1 in the original P.) These new predicates are defined recursively, by XY-stratified programs:

Example 5 *From extensional predicates to XY-stratified programs.*

$$\text{std}(0, \text{X1}, \text{X2}) \leftarrow \quad \text{std}(\text{X1}, \text{X2}).$$
$$\text{std}(\text{J} + 1, \text{X1}, \text{X2}) \leftarrow \quad \text{quevt}(\text{J} + 1, \_, \_, \_), \text{std}(\text{J}, \text{X1}, \text{X2}),$$
$$\neg \text{quevt}(\text{J} + 1, \text{del}, \text{std}(\text{X1}, \text{X2}), \_).$$
$$\text{std}(\text{J} + 1, \text{X1}, \text{X2}) \leftarrow \quad \text{std}(\text{J}, \_, \_), \text{quevt}(\text{J} + 1, \text{add}, \text{std}(\text{X1}, \text{X2}), \_).$$

$$\text{grad}(0, \text{X1}, \text{X2}, \text{X3}) \leftarrow \quad \text{grad}(\text{X1}, \text{X2}, \text{X3}).$$
$$\text{grad}(\text{J} + 1, \text{X1}, \text{X2}, \text{X3}) \leftarrow \quad \text{quevt}(\text{J} + 1, \_, \_, \_), \text{grad}(\text{J}, \text{X1}, \text{X}, \text{X3}),$$
$$\neg \text{quevt}(\text{J} + 1, \text{del}, \text{grad}(\text{X1}, \text{X2}, \text{X3}), \_).$$
$$\text{grad}(\text{J} + 1, \text{X1}, \text{X2}, \text{X3}) \leftarrow \quad \text{grad}(\text{J}, \_, \_), \text{quevt}(\text{J} + 1, \text{add}, \text{grad}(\text{X1}, \text{X2}, \text{X3}), \_).$$

Furthermore, the old rules of P are replaced with new ones, obtained from the old ones by adding a stage argument to every predicate in the rules:

Example 6 *Rewriting the original rules*

$$\text{csst}(\text{J}, \text{X}, \text{C}) \leftarrow \quad \text{std}(\text{J}, \text{X}, \text{cs}), \text{grad}(\text{J}, \text{X}, \text{C}, \_).$$

The query goal ?sst(S, C) is then modified in an obvious way. To find the proper answer to the query after the first request req(1, add, std(marc, ee)), we pose the query: ?csst(1, S, C). But, the correct answer to the same query after the next two requests have been serviced is produced by ?csst(2, S, C).

Thus, we replaced the old predicates with new ones containing an additional stage argument. For notational convenience we shall represent the stage as a superscript; thus instead of writing std(J, X, cs) we write $\text{std}^{\text{J}}(\text{X}, \text{cs})$. Thus a new program P' is constructed from the original one P by replacing the old rules of P with new ones where the predicates are stage-superscripted. Moreover, for each extensional predicate q of P, P' contains the following set of XY-stratified rules:

Example 7 *Updates modeled by rules*

$$r_1 : q^0(X) \leftarrow q(X).$$
$$r_2 : q^{J+1}(X) \leftarrow quevt^{J+1}(\_,\_,\_), \ q^J(X),$$
$$\neg quevt^{J+1}(\text{del}, q(X), \_).$$
$$r_3 : q^{J+1}(X) \leftarrow q^J(X), \ quevt^{J+1}(\text{add}, q(X), \_).$$

These three rules will be called, respectively as follows: r_1 the *base rule*, r_2 the *copy-delete rule*, and r_3 the *add rule*. Then, the deletion-copy rule copies the old relation into a new one, modulo any deletion that is currently pending on the event queue quevt. The insert rule services the add requests currently pending in quevt. The base rule defines a derived predicate with stage value of zero, for each extensional predicate.[3]

The resulting program P' is XY-stratified and defines the meaning of the original program P. The correct answer to query $?q(X)$ once all the req^J entries have been serviced is simply the answer to $?q^J(X)$. For instance, with P, D and R defined in Example 4, the perfect model of our modified program P' contains the following derived facts:

Example 8 *The perfect model for P' (derived facts only)*

$std^0(\text{tom}, cs)$	$grad^0(\text{ann}, cs143, 3)$	
$std^0(\text{ann}, ee)$		
$std^1(\text{tom}, cs)$	$grad^1(\text{ann}, cs143, 3)$	
$std^1(\text{ann}, ee)$		
$std^1(\text{marc}, ee)$		
$std^2(\text{tom}, cs)$	$grad^2(\text{ann}, cs143, 3)$	$csst^2(\text{ann}, cs143)$
$std^2(\text{marc}, ee)$		
$std^2(\text{ann}, cs)$		

A query, such as $?csst(S, C)$, is then changed into $?csst^2(S, C)$ and answered against such a perfect model.

This simple rendering of the semantics of updates captures one's intuitive understanding of these operations. It also is suggestive of efficient operational semantics. In fact, delete-copy rules can be implemented with the update-in-place policy, outlined for XY-programs, whereby records are simply added to, or deleted from, the current copy of the relation. The declarative semantics of these rules is, however, fully retained, as demonstrated by the fact that queries corresponding to update subsequences are also supported: it is also possible to pose queries such as $csst^0(S, G)$ or $csst^1(S, G)$.

Integrity constraints can also be treated in this framework. If the enforcement policy consists in rejecting any request that violates the constraint (e.g., rejecting a request for insertion of a new tuple violating a key constraint), then the proper checking conditions can be attached to the rule defining quevt. Policies where violations are corrected by additional actions (e.g., elimination of dangling foreign key references) can be supported using the condition-action rules or the event-action rules discussed next.

---

[3] We assume that initially our database relations are not empty. Otherwise, an additional exit rule, $p^0(\text{nil}) \leftarrow \neg p(X)$, can be added.

5   Condition-Action Rules

Say that we want to enforce a rule such as: If a student has taken both cs10 and cs20, then he or she is considered having CS as major. For that, we could write:

$$r_4 : \mathtt{add(std(S, cs))} \leftarrow \mathtt{grad(S, cs10, \_)}, \ \mathtt{grad(S, cs20, \_)}.$$

Another possible rule could enforce a deletion dependency whereby one will want to delete the classes taken by students that are not longer enrolled. This can be accomplished as follows:

$$r_5 : \mathtt{del(grad(S, C, G))} \leftarrow \mathtt{grad(S, C, G)}, \ \neg \mathtt{std(S, \_)}.$$

The urgency for a formal semantics to supplement intuition is obvious even in this simple example. In fact, assume that a request is placed to add a cs20 record and a cs10 record in **grad** for a new student **adam**, as follows:

```
req(3, add, grad(adam, cs10, 4)).
req(3, add, grad(adam, cs20, 3)).
```

Then, according to intuition alone, each of the following alternatives appears plausible: (i) the addition of two initial **grad** records followed by that of a new cs student in **std**; (ii) the insertion of the two initial records immediately followed by deletion of all the courses this student has taken; (iii) the addition of the initial **grad** records followed by the parallel insertion of a record for the new student and the deletion of course records for this student; (iv) no action; or (v) an infinite loop. After the introduction of a formal semantics, only one of these alternatives will be considered correct

The semantics we propose for active rules, views **del** and **add** as built-in derived predicates. Thus these two rules are simply re-written as any other rule:

$$r_4' : \mathtt{add}^J(\mathtt{std(S, cs)}) \leftarrow \mathtt{grad}^J(\mathtt{S, cs10, \_}), \ \mathtt{grad}^J(\mathtt{S, cs20, \_}).$$
$$r_5' : \mathtt{del}^J(\mathtt{grad(S, C, G)}) \leftarrow \mathtt{grad}^J(\mathtt{S, C, G}), \ \neg \mathtt{std}^J(\mathtt{S, \_}).$$

Furthermore, there is no change in the intensional update rules for the extensional predicates. However, the rules defining **quevt** must be extended to account for the **add** and **del** predicates as follows:

Example 9 *An improved definition for* **quevt**

$$\mathtt{quevt}^{J+1}(\mathtt{add, W, N}) \leftarrow \mathtt{quevt}^J(\_, \_, \mathtt{N}), \ \mathtt{add}^J(\mathtt{W}).$$
$$\mathtt{quevt}^{J+1}(\mathtt{del, W, N}) \leftarrow \mathtt{quevt}^J(\_, \_, \mathtt{N}), \ \mathtt{del}^J(\mathtt{W}).$$
$$\mathtt{quevt}^{J+1}(\mathtt{X, W, N+1}) \leftarrow \mathtt{quevt}^J(\_, \_, \mathtt{N}), \ \neg \mathtt{add}^J(\_), \neg \mathtt{del}^J(\_),$$
$$\mathtt{req}^{N+1}(\mathtt{X, W}).$$

Thus, active rules will add to the `quevt` table. Once these rules have stopped firing, then new external requests from `req` can further expand the table.

After a sequence of n requests, the correct answer to query $?q(\mathbf{X})$, is obtained by answering the following three goals

$$?\mathtt{quevt}^J(\_,\_,n), \neg\mathtt{quevt}^{J+1}(\_,\_,n), q^J(\mathbf{X})$$

The first two goals find the highest value J reached by the stage variable after servicing all requests with sequence number n; then the values for the correct answer are derived from $p^J(\mathbf{X})$.

For our previous example for instance, the request to add the cs10 and cs20 courses for adam (with respective grades 4 and 3) will generate the following "new" state:

$$\mathtt{std}^3(\mathtt{tom,cs}) \qquad \mathtt{grad}^3(\mathtt{ann,cs143,3}) \qquad \mathtt{csst}^3(\mathtt{ann,cs143})$$
$$\mathtt{std}^3(\mathtt{marc,ee}) \qquad \mathtt{grad}^3(\mathtt{adam,cs10,4})$$
$$\mathtt{std}^3(\mathtt{ann,cs}) \qquad \mathtt{grad}^3(\mathtt{adam,cs20,3})$$

Then, both rules r_4' and r_5' are activated in this situation resulting in the appearance of $\mathtt{std}^4(\mathtt{adam,cs})$ and the disappearance of adam's cs10a and cs20 records in the final state (basically option (iii) among the alternatives above).

Condition-action rules are very powerful, and can be used in several applications, including constraint maintenance or truth-maintenance support [2]. On the other hand, condition-action rules can be expensive to support since they require the recomputation of the body of each rule every time a new update occurs in the base relations defining such a rule. Thus, every database predicate appearing in the body of an active rule must be monitored for changes; for derived predicates, possibly recursive ones, the derivation tree (dependency graph) must be traced down to the database predicates involved. While differential methods, such as the semi-naive fixpoint, and truth-maintenance techniques, can be exploited in this context, it is also clear that condition-action rules tend to be complex and expensive to support. For these reasons, more recent proposals favor an alternative approach where the events that can trigger the firing of the rules are stated explicitly in the bodies of the rules. This is discussed next.

6 Event-Action Rules

In systems such as Postgres [28], the events upon which a rule fires are stated explicitly. These rules can be easily modeled in our framework. For instance, the previous active rules involving students and courses could be expressed as follows:

Example 10 *Event-driven rules*

$$\mathtt{add(std(S,cs))} \leftarrow \mathtt{add(grad(S,cs10,\_))}, \mathtt{grad(S,cs20,\_)}.$$
$$\mathtt{add(std(S,cs))} \leftarrow \mathtt{grad(S,cs10,\_)}, \mathtt{add(grad(S,cs20,\_))}.$$

$$\mathtt{del(grad(S,\_,\_))} \leftarrow \mathtt{del(std(S,\_))}.$$

These event-driven rules are easily supported in our framework. We basically interpret event-action rules as stating that, when add or del events are queued in the quevt relation, then, the add or del predicates are enabled (requested). Thus, the meaning of the previous rules is defined by the following re-writing:

Example 11 *Expansion of event-driven rules*

$$add^J(std(S, cs)) \leftarrow \quad quevt^J(add, grad(S, cs10, \_), \_), grad(S, cs20, \_).$$
$$add^J(std(S, cs)) \leftarrow \quad grad(S, cs10, \_)), quevt^J(add, grad(S, cs20, \_), \_).$$
$$del^J(grad(S, \_, \_)) \leftarrow \quad quevt^J(del, std(S, \_), \_).$$

By the definition of quevt, these add and del requests queued at stage J will be executed at stage $J + 1$.

Observe that since our event driven rules have been written to detect single events they will not be triggered by the contemporary request of inserting the two records cs10 and cs20 for adam. The final result therefore corresponds to alternative (i) out of those listed above.

7 Event-Based Programming

New events can be defined in addition to the basic add, del ones and used in various roles, including constraint management and application programming. As a (somewhat contrived) example, for instance, say that we want to raise the grades of Ann until her grades are all greater or equal to 4. This will be accomplished by the definition of a new **raise** event,

Example 12 *Raising the grades of students*

$$del(grad(S, C, G)) \leftarrow \quad evt(raise(S)), grad(S, C, G), G < 4.$$
$$add(grad(S, C, G')) \leftarrow \quad evt(raise(S)), grad(S, C, G), G < 4,$$
$$G' = G + 1.$$
$$evt(raise(S)) \leftarrow \quad evt(raise(S)), grad(S, C, G), G < 4.$$

followed by the request: evt(raise(ann)). These rules, with S = ann are now executed in parallel enabling the corresponding set of events. These are then enqueued by the following quevt rules:

Example 13 *The final definition of* quevt

$$quevt^{J+1}(add, W, N) \leftarrow \quad quevt^J(\_, \_, N), add^J(W).$$
$$quevt^{J+1}(del, W, N) \leftarrow \quad quevt^J(\_, \_, N), del^J(W).$$
$$quevt^{J+1}(ev, W, N) \leftarrow \quad quevt^J(\_, \_, N), ev^J(W).$$
$$quevt^{J+1}(X, W, N + 1) \leftarrow \quad quevt^J(\_, \_, N),$$
$$\neg add^J(\_), \neg del^J(\_), \neg evt^J(\_),$$
$$req^{N+1}(X, W).$$

Then, event-action rules can be re-written as follows:

Example 14 *Raising the grades of students*

$$\text{del}^J(\text{grad}(S,C,G)) \leftarrow \quad \text{quevt}^J(\text{evt},\text{raise}(S),\_),\text{grad}^J(S,C,G),G < 4.$$
$$\text{add}^J(\text{grad}(S,C,G')) \leftarrow \quad \text{quevt}^J(\text{evt},\text{raise}(S),\_),\text{grad}^J(S,C,G),G < 4,$$
$$G' = G + 1.$$
$$\text{evt}^J(\text{raise}(S)) \leftarrow \quad \text{quevt}^J(\text{evt},\text{raise}(S),\_),\text{grad}^J(S,C,G),G < 4.$$

The detection of an event condition evt(raise(S)) results in the checking of additional conditions and in the setting of a new event, including the re-setting of the old event evt(raise(S)), as illustrated by the last rule above. All applicable rules are fired in parallel; it is thus possible to perform recursive programming, whereby the same action is repeated while the body conditions remain true. The action performed at each step can be a basic update, or some other action, including the invocation of a query or the printing of some results.

8 Conclusion

The semantic framework here proposed yields the design of a rule-based language capable of addressing both the active and deductive aspects of programming. For deductive rules, one can keep the basic framework of Horn Clauses, with non-monotonic extensions, including negation and aggregates under the XY-stratification assumption. Active rules can be specified with the same syntax, provided that add, del, evt are built-in predicates. A uniform perfect-model semantics is ensured by the re-writing methods just discussed, which do not rely on meta-level or higher order constructs.

Building on this semantic bedrock, the language designer can consider further improvements and structuring of the language to improve the efficiency and clarity of programs. For instance, practical considerations might suggest that condition-action rules should be disallowed; in this case, the language will only support two kinds of rules. The first kind of rules are deductive ones without any event predicate. The other kind consists of event-action rules: these are defined as having an event predicate in their head, and one or more positive event goals in their bodies. Syntactic sugaring conventions might also be used to improve the expressivity of the language. A simple improvement would allow rules with multiple heads as a short-hand for several rules with similar bodies. The previous example, for instance, could be abbreviated as follows:

Example 15 *A multi-head rule.*

$$\text{del}(\text{grad}(\text{ann},C,G)),$$
$$\text{add}(\text{grad}(\text{ann},C,G1)),$$
$$\text{evt}(\text{raise}(S)) \leftarrow \quad \text{evt}(\text{raise}(S)),$$
$$\text{grad}(S,C,G),G < 4,G1 = G + 1.$$

Also observe that that within the power and uniformity provided by such a language, there will be specialized usages. For instance, a system administrator will be predominantly concerned with monitoring events such such as add and del. However, application programmers will be mostly interested in defining new event types that will be invoked by certain classes of users. Each such application is defined by an event that is invoked by a user request or triggered by other applications. Each application can call itself recursively, or can take various actions, including calling other applications.

A new rule-based language incorporating these principles is currently being designed at UCLA.

References

[1] S. Abiteboul and V. Vianu. Datalog extensions for database queries and updates. *Journal of Comp. and System Sc.*, 43(1):62–124, August 1991.

[2] Apt, K., and J.M. Pugin, "Maintenance of stratified databases viewed as a belief revision system", *ACM PODS*, 1987.

[3] Bry, F., Intensional updates: abduction via deduction, in: *Proc. 7th Int. Conf. on Logic Programming*, Jerusalem, 561-575, 1990.

[4] S. Ceri and J. Widom. Deriving production rules for constraint maintenance. *Sixteenth International Conference on Very Large Data Bases, Brisbane*, pages 566–577, 1990.

[5] Chimenti, D. et al., "The $\mathcal{LDL}$ System Prototype," *IEEE Journal on Data and Knowledge Engineering*, vol. 2, no. 1, pp. 76-90, March 1990.

[6] Fagin, R.., Kuper, G., D.Ullman and M.Y.Vardi, "Updating logical databases", *Advances in Comp.Res.*, vol.3, 1-18, JAI Press Inc., 1986.

[7] Harel, D., "Dynamic logic", in *Handbook of Philosophical Logic*, (Gabbay and Guenther, eds.), D.Reidel Publishers, 1983.

[8] N.H. Gehani and H.V. Jagadish. Ode as an active database: Constraints and triggers. *Seventeenth International Conference on Very Large Data Bases, Barcelona*, pages 327–336, 1991.

[9] M. Gelfond and V. Lifschitz. The stable model semantics of logic programming. *Proceedings of the Fifth Intern. Conference on Logic Programming*, pages 1070–1080, 1988.

[10] S. Ganguly, S. Greco, and C. Zaniolo. *Minimum and Maximum Predicates in Logic Programming. Proceedings of the Tenth ACM Symposium on Principles of Database Systems*, pp. 154–113, 1991.

[11] F. Giannotti, D. Pedreschi, D. Saccà, and C. Zaniolo. Nondeterminism in deductive databases. *Proc. 2nd Int. Conf. on Deductive and Object-Oriented Databases*, 1991.

[12] A. Van Gelder, K.A. Ross, and J.S. Schlipf. The well-founded semantics for general logic programs. *Journal of ACM*, 38(3):620–650, 1991.

[13] Katzuno, H. and A.O. Mendelzon, Propositional knowledgebase revision and minimal change, *Artificial Intelligence*, 52, 263-294, 1991.

[14] P.G. Kolaitis and C.H. Papadimitriou, Why not negation by fixpoint?, *JCSS*, 43(1), 125-144, 1991.

[15] Krishnamurthy, R., Naqvi, S. and C. Zaniolo, "Database Updates and Transactions in $\mathcal{LDL}$", *Procs. of 1989 North American Conference on Logic Programming*, MIT Press, 1989.

[16] Gelfond, M. and Lifschitz, V., "Representing Actions in Extended Logic Programming," *Proc. Joint Int. Conf-Symp on Logic Programming*, 1992, MIT Press, 1992.

[17] Lifschitz, V. "Formal Theories of Action" in: F.M. Brown, ed. *The Frame Problem in Artificial Intelligence*, Proc. 1987 Workshop, Morgan Kaufman, Los Altos, CA, 1987.

[18] Lloyd, J.W., *Foundations of Logic Programming,,* Springer Verlag, 1977.

[19] Manchanda, S. and D.S. Warren, "Towards a logical theory of database view updates", *Int. Worksh. on Foundations of Deductive databases and Logic Programming*, J.Minker ed., Aug. 1988.

[20] D. McCarty and U. Dayal. The architecture of an active database management system. In *ACM SIGMOD International Conf. on Management of Data*, pages 215–224, 1989.

[21] M. Morgenstern. Active databases as a paradigm for enhanced computing environments. In *Ninth International Conf. on Very Large Data Bases, Florence*, pages 34–42, 1983.

[22] L. Palopoli and R. Torlone. Specifying the dynamics of complex object databases. In *4th Int. Workshop on Foundations of Models and Languages for Data and Objects – Modeling Database Dynamics*, pp. 143–160. Springer-Verlag, 1992.

[23] Phipps, G., M.A., Derr and K. A. Ross, "Glue-Nail: a Deductive Database System," *Proc. 1991 ACM–SIGMOD Conference on Management of Data*, pp. 308-317 (1991).

[24] Przymusinski, T.C. "Every logic program has a natural stratification and an iterated fixed point model", in *PODS 1989*.

[25] S. A. Naqvi, S. Tsur *"A Logical Language for Data and Knowledge Bases"*, W. H. Freeman, 1989.

[26] Ramakrishan, R., Srivastava, D. and Sudarshan, S., *"CORAL: A Deductive Database Programming Language,"* Proc. VLDB'92 Int. Conf, pp. 238-250, 1992.

[27] Reiter, R., "On Formalizing Database Updates: Preliminary Report," in, *Advances in Database Technology–EDBT'92*, (Pirotte, Delobel, Gottlob, eds.), Springer Verlag, 1992

[28] M.L. Stonebraker, A. Jhingran, J. Goh, and S. Potamianos. On rules, procedure, caching and views in data base systems. In *ACM SIGMOD International Conf. on Management of Data*, pages 281–290, 1990.

[29] van Emden M.H. and R.A. Kowalski, "The Semantics of Predicate Logic as a Programming Language," *J.ACM 23*, 4 (Oct. 76), 67-75.

[30] Warren, D.S., Database Updates in Pure Prolog, *Proc. Int. Conf. on Fifth Generation Computer Systems*, 244-253, 1985.

[31] J. Widom and S. Finkelstein. Set-Oriented production rules in relational database systems. In *ACM SIGMOD International Conf. on Management of Data*, pages 259–270, 1990.

[32] M. Winslett, "A model-theoretic approach to updating logical databases", *ACM PODS*, 1986.

[33] Zaniolo, C., *Intelligent Databases: Old Challenges and New Opportunities*, Journal of Intelligent Information Systems, 1, 271-292 (1992).

[34] Zaniolo, C., N. Arni, K. Ong, "Negation and Aggregates in Recursive Rules: the $\mathcal{LDL}$++ Approach", *Proc. 3rd Int. Conference on Deductive and O-O DBs, DOOD-93*, Phoenix, AZ, Dec 6-8, 1993.

Integrating Active and Deductive Rules

John V. Harrison

Department of Computer Science, University of Queensland
Brisbane, QLD Australia

Suzanne W. Dietrich

Department of Computer Science and Engineering, Arizona State University
Tempe, AZ U.S.A.

Abstract

This paper describes how active and deductive rules can be integrated to form an expressive representation for declaring and reasoning about events and conditions. Specifically, this paper describes an extension and optimizations to the PF algorithm, which detects events, i.e. updates, that affect derived relations (or views), even when the derived relation is recursively defined. This capability improves the expressiveness of the *event-condition-action* (ECA) rules, which can then be used to detect more complex events and express conditions that reason with the updates to both stored and derived relations. The updates to the derived relations can be detected *without* having to materialize the derived relations. The *PF* algorithm can detect these updates when certain modifications to the definition of the derived relation are made. This approach has been implemented to form an event detector and condition evaluator for an *active deductive* database. These enhancements increase the sophistication of an active database since ECA rules can be defined that react to a larger scope of real-world situations.

1 Introduction

An *active* database management system (DBMS) automatically monitors user-defined situations and reacts when these situations are detected. Neither the monitoring of the pre-defined situations, nor the initiation of the various actions resulting from the detection of a situation, require user intervention. The services provided by an active database are often termed *active services*. Some support for active services is present in several commercial database systems, e.g., Oracle, Sybase, Ingres.

Active services include alerters, triggers and integrity constraints. An *alerter* notifies a user or process that a situation has been detected. If the situation associated with a *trigger* is detected then another database transaction may be created and executed. An *integrity constraint* aborts a transaction when a situation is detected that implies an integrity violation has occurred.

All three mechanisms can be represented uniformly using *active rules*, also referred to as *event-condition-action* (ECA) rules. An ECA rule is a declarative representation of the expression: *when event E occurs, check condition C, and if true, then execute action A*. When the event and condition component are unified into one expression, the expression is referred to as a *situation*.

A deductive database, which is based on the *Datalog* data model [23], extends a relational database by including inherent support for deductive rules with the power of recursion. Deductive databases provide a logic-based language, called *Datalog*, that can be utilized to declaratively express deductive rules along with all other system components such as data, queries, views and the data manipulation language. Datalog, when enhanced with support for stratified negation, is a strictly more expressive query language than relational algebra. This is due to the fact that Datalog can be used to directly express recursive queries and view definitions.

Many researchers in active databases consider updates to relations a fundamantal event type. However, some experimental active database systems restrict event detection to updates to stored relations [22], or to derived relations defined using only a subset of the relational operators [9]. Other approaches support event detection to derived relations defined using all of the relational operators but not recursion [3, 6, 11, 19, 21]. Active rules can be more expressive, hence capture more real-world situations, if events, i.e., updates, affecting derived relations defined using all of the relational operators, recursion and aggregation can be detected.

Consider the following example. Let the derived (IDB) relation *LINK*, which is defined by the Datalog predicate *link*, contain tuples that represent the reachability between source and destination stations on a network. The stored (EDB) data referenced in the definition of *LINK* is represented by a single relation, namely *DIRECT_LINK*. Let *link* be comprised of two deductive rules that represent a simple left-recursive transitive closure, which is given below:[1]

$$link(X,Y) \leftarrow direct\_link(X,Y).$$
$$link(X,Y) \leftarrow link(X,Z), direct\_link(Z,Y).$$

If the user is interested in detecting lost links in the network, both direct *and indirect*, the capability of detecting events affecting the derived relation *LINK* is required. The event detection algorithm described here can detect this type of complex event without incurring the cost of materializing the derived relation. Alternatively, the algorithm can be employed when the application requires materialization of the derived relation,

Let *V* be the definition of a derived relation, which can also be considered as a *view* definition. Let *R* be a stored relation that represents the materialization of *V*. If an event, e.g., an update, to *V* is detected, then the action component of the ECA rule can perform the update to *R* to maintain *R*'s validity.

Another reason for supporting ECA rules that detect events on derived relations is to increase the availability of active services where database security is a concern. Consider the case where a derived relation, i.e., view, has been defined for a user X to prohibit X from having access to the stored relations comprising V's definition. If X does not have the capability to detect events to V nor has permission to detect events to the stored relations because of a lack of access, X can not utilize active services.

If updates to derived relations can be detected, they can both be reasoned with during condition evaluation and available during action execution. Several experimental systems, along with the proposed SQL3 standard, allow for conditions to refer to both the *old* and *new* values of a tuple corresponding to an update event. If update events affecting derived relations can be detected, the conditions can then reason with the old and new values of the derived tuples as well. They can also access both states of derived relations to support additional expressiveness.

---

[1] The proposed standard for SQL3 supports such views defined using recursion, namely views defined by a SQL statement involving *recursive union*.

This paper describes how deductive and active rules were integrated to create an event detector for derived relations and to create a unified representation for both events and conditions. The updates to derived relations can be detected *without* materializing the (possibly recursive) derived relation regardless of whether the events result from updates to stored relations or modifications to the definition of the derived relation. The approach has been implemented to form an event detector and condition evaluator for an *active deductive* database.

In section 2, basic terminology is introduced. An overview of event detection in the presence of derived relations and its relationship to condition evaluation is given. In section 3, an algorithm is described that identifies events to derived relations when events occur to the stored relations. In section 4, the representation for conditions is presented and some examples are provided. In section 5, a series of optimizations that improve the efficiency of detecting the satisfaction of event-condition pairs are described. The paper concludes with a summary and a discussion of future research directions.

2 Basic Concepts

Situation monitoring in an active database differs from query processing since it involves reasoning with two database instances, i.e., the state before and after the updates, whereas query processing occurs in the context of a single database instance. The approach employed for situation monitoring must be more general than traditional integrity constraint checking algorithms. This is because a fundamental assumption of these algorithms, namely that every expression representing an IC is false before the algorithm is executed, cannot be made.

The approach for event detection and condition monitoring described in this paper relies on a procedure for computing the difference between two consecutive database states. This difference represents the changes that must be made to the initial database to obtain the updated database. The approach also relies on a procedure that reasons with the computed changes to detect condition satisfaction.

Let DB be a database formed by the union of a set of extensionally defined, i.e., stored relations (EDB) and a set of intensionally defined, i.e., derived relations (IDB). Let relation $R \in$ DB. Let $\mathcal{U}$ represent an update to the EDB.

The database state before $\mathcal{U}$ is performed is referred to as *old*. The database state after $\mathcal{U}$ is performed is referred to as *new*. Let the difference between R in the old state (R_{Old}) and R in the new state (R_{New}) be termed the "delta set" (abbreviated Δset) for R and be represented using the notation ΔR. A Δset consists of two distinct (possibly empty) subsets. The first, labeled ΔR_{add}, consists of tuples that must be added to the *old* relation to obtain the *new* relation. The second, labeled ΔR_{rem}, consists of tuples that must be removed from the *old* relation to obtain the *new* relation.

A Δset is defined for each updated relation, including both EDB and IDB relations. The Δset ΔE for an updated EDB relation E consists of ΔE_{add}, which are the additions to E appearing in $\mathcal{U}$, and ΔE_{rem}, which are the removals from E appearing in $\mathcal{U}$. The Δset ΔI for an updated IDB relation I consists of the changes in the IDB relation, which can be computed by the difference between the materialization of the IDB relation in the old state and the materialization of the same relation in the new state.

These concepts are formalized using the definitions below, which assume that the predicates that define the IDB relations are not updated. Let *materialize(IDB_Rels, DB_State)* denote the materialization of the set of IDB relations specified by *IDB_Rels* using the EDB indicated by *DB_State*.

Definition. Let EDB_{Old} refer to an arbitrary EDB before $\mathcal{U}$ is performed. Let EDB_{New} refer to the same EDB after $\mathcal{U}$ is performed. Let p denote a predicate representing an arbitrary IDB relation P.

$$DB_{Old} = EDB_{Old} \cup IDB(EDB_{Old})$$
$$DB_{New} = EDB_{New} \cup IDB(EDB_{New})$$
$$\Delta P_{rem} = materialize(p, Old) - materialize(p, New)$$
$$\Delta P_{add} = materialize(p, New) - materialize(p, Old)$$
$$\Delta P = \{\Delta P_{rem}, \Delta P_{add}\} \qquad \square$$

The event detection/condition evaluation process described in this paper is illustrated in Figure 1, which indicates that two tasks are performed when updates to the base relations are made. The first task is to identify the updates, i.e., Δsets, to the set of IDB relations that are referenced in the user-defined conditions. This step corresponds to detecting events that affect derived relations. The second task is to evaluate the user-defined conditions, which can contain references to the Δsets and each state of the database.

The first task could be accomplished using the straightforward definition above as an algorithm. However, this would result in a very inefficient implementation. A more efficient technique would compute the changes using an *incremental* approach. An update propagation algorithm can be used for this purpose and is the subject of the next section.

The second task involves reasoning with the computed changes to detect satisfied *event-condition* (E-C) pairs, which are implemented using additional Datalog rules. The body of these rules may include references to the Δsets computed during update propagation and also the database predicates, which the user designates to be evaluated over either the old or the new database state.

3   Detecting Update Events on Derived Data

This section describes an approach for detecting updates to derived data using an algorithm known as *Propagation/Filtration (PF)*. This algorithm performs update propagation to identify the events to derived relations that are defined using recursive Datalog with stratified negation[2]. A description of the basic algorithm, which supports stratified negation, appears in [13].[3] Here we describe an extension that detects updates to derived relations when there are modifications to the definition of the derived relations. A short review of the basic algorithm is given below to provide a basis for this material and material appearing in later sections.

The dependency graph [23] $\mathcal{DG}$ for a Datalog program $\mathcal{D}$ can be used to determine the IDB relations defined by $\mathcal{D}$ that may have been updated as a result of the updates to specific EDB relations. An IDB relation I may have been updated as a result of updates to the EDB relations if the predicate i defining I depends, directly

---

[2]The approach has been extended to support *group stratified reducible aggregates*[17] but is not described here due to space limitations. The extension is described in [14]

[3]A complete description, correctness proofs and performance measurements can be found in [10].

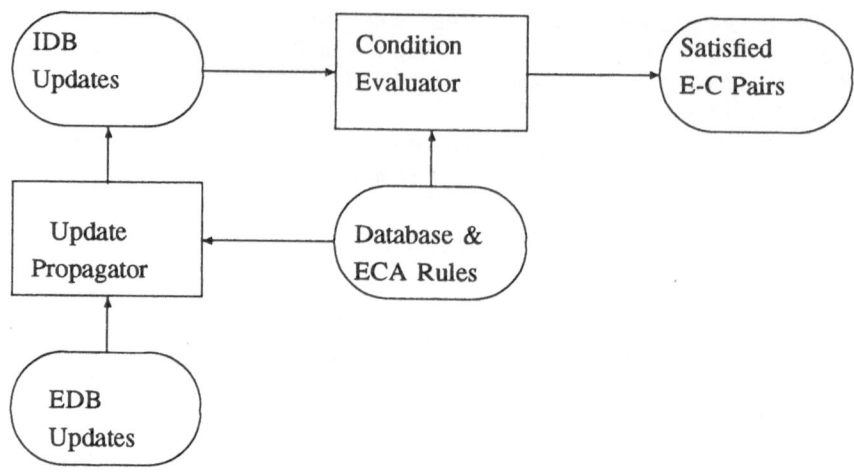

Figure 1: Event Detection and Condition Evaluation

or indirectly, on one or more of the set of updated EDB relations $\mathcal{E}_u$.

Definition. Let e_u represent the predicate defining an arbitrary EDB relation E_u where $E_u \in \mathcal{E}_u$. Let $p \Rightarrow q$ represent a path in $\mathcal{DG}$ from p to q. An IDB relation I, defined by the predicate i, is a *candidate* for update if:

$$e_u \Rightarrow i \in \mathcal{DG}$$

An IDB relation is *unaffected* if it is not a candidate. □

The objective of the update propagation algorithm is to compute the updates for all candidate relations. Since candidate relations may be defined by several rules, only those rules that depend on candidate relations or updated EDB relations need to be considered in the update propagation process.

Definition. Let *c-rule* represent a rule defining an arbitrary candidate predicate. If *c-rule* contains one or more literals in its rule body corresponding to either a candidate predicate or an updated EDB relation, then *c-rule* is a *candidate rule*.

The *PF* algorithm computes the updates for all candidate relations using the candidate rules. The candidate rules are processed by performing a *propagation* phase followed by a *filtration* phase. A high-level description of each phase is given below.

3.1 The Propagation Phase

During the propagation phase, candidate rules are evaluated when the relations that correspond to subgoals appearing in the body of the rule are updated. The evaluation is constrained using bindings taken from these updates. The result of the evaluation is a set of tuples representing possible updates to the candidate relation.

Definition. The set of tuples generated for an IDB relation as a result of a propagation phase is termed an *approximation*. Each tuple in the approximation is termed a *potential IDB update*.

To obtain an approximation from a candidate rule, a query consisting of the literals appearing in the rule body is invoked over either DB$_{Old}$ or DB$_{New}$. Consider a rule r defining an IDB relation P where both additions and removals have been identified for a relation L corresponding to a literal l appearing in the body of r. To propagate the additions to L to the IDB relation P, the rule body is evaluated using DB$_{New}$. The evaluation is constrained using bindings from ΔL_{add}. The result of this evaluation is a relation whose schema contains all of the variables that occur in the rule body. The relation is projected onto the set of attributes corresponding to the set of variables that appear in the head literal. A similar procedure is performed to process the removals, however, the rule body is evaluated using DB$_{Old}$ and the evaluation is constrained using bindings from ΔL_{rem}. The result of the projection is the approximation for P.

Note that for both additions and removals the subgoal representing the literal l can be removed from the query for efficiency, since the updates to L used to constrain the query bind all variables appearing in subgoal l. This forms a query that tests a tuple that has already been determined to be an actual IDB update and, therefore, represents redundant computation.

If the rule body contains several literals, each representing either a candidate relation or an updated base relation, then a separate query is issued for each literal. In addition, a separate query is issued for the additions to, and the removals from, each relation. In the worst case situation, where a rule defining a predicate p has k subgoals each corresponding to a relation where both addition and removal updates have been identified, $2k$ queries would be issued during the propagation phase to obtain all potential updates for p. In our implementation, a multiple query optimizer identifies common subexpressions in the queries, which all involve the same set of predicates, thereby significantly reducing the actual computation performed.

3.2 The Filtration Phase

The propagation phase propagates the changes to the extensional relations up through the rules and identifies potential changes to the derived relations. Potential changes are filtered to identify actual changes. For example, a potential addition represents a derivation of a tuple t. If t is provable in the database state before the updates, then the potential addition is filtered and is not reflected as an actual change to the database. Similarly, a potential removal represents the deletion of a derivation for a tuple t and if t is still provable in the database state after the updates, then the filter phase does not identify the potential removal as an actual removal.

Thus, the filtration phase of *PF* refines the approximation of potential updates to IDB relations identified during the propagation phase. Potential IDB updates that cannot be proven are removed from the approximation. Each potential addition is posed as a query to the database using DB$_{Old}$. Each potential removal is posed as a query to the database using DB$_{New}$. Tuples returned as a result of the query do not represent a change in the database state so they are deleted from the approximation.

Definition. A potential IDB removal is termed *disqualified* if it is provable in DB_{New}. A potential IDB addition is disqualified if it is provable in DB_{Old}. A potential IDB update that is not disqualified is termed an *actual IDB update*.

Actual IDB updates are saved in global Δsets and are available for use in subsequent invocations of the algorithm, including recursive ones. Note that duplicate elimination is easily performed when updates are tabled in a Δset. This also serves to reduce the size of subsequent approximations.

3.3 Event Detection and Deductive Rule Updates

In this section, we address event detection when the definition of the derived relation is modified. When the derived relation is defined using deductive rules, these modifications are in the form of *rule updates*. Rule updates are defined here as either the addition or removal of a rule from the database. This changes the definition of a derived relation. The derived relation can be viewed as being comprised of a n-way union where each rule defines one operand of the union. An update to the definition of a candidate IDB relation can result in the generation of actual IDB updates to the IDB relation that the rule defines.

Consider the case where a rule update is performed on a non-recursive IDB relation I. When a rule r defining I is added to the database, an unconstrained query consisting of the conjunction of literals representing the rule body is issued over DB_{New}. The result is an approximation that is filtered using DB_{Old}. Conversely, the body of a deleted rule is issued over DB_{Old} to obtain the approximation and DB_{New} is used for filtration.

The query issued over either state includes all literals from the rule body and there are no bindings to constrain computation. Actual IDB updates computed for P resulting from a rule update are propagated using the PF algorithm in the same manner as those resulting from base relation updates. The rule update algorithm can be applied to recursive IDB relations. There is a constraint, however, as to the order in which rules are removed. When removing rules defining a recursive predicate, the base rule must be removed last to avoid an ill-defined recursive specification. When adding rules defining a recursive predicate, the order of addition is inconsequential. The complete algorithm for rule updates can be found in [12].

4 Event-Condition Pairs as Deductive Rules

The previous section described how the PF algorithm is used to detect updates to derived relations. The Δsets correspond to the set of identified events. When satisfied, the E-C pairs trigger the action component of the ECA rule. A method for evaluating these E-C pairs is described. If evaluating a rule produces a non-null result then the E-C pair has been satisfied.

To represent the E-C pairs, a set of Datalog predicates called *ec-preds* are created. Each *ec-pred* is defined using one or more *ec-rules*. The body of an ec-rule may include special literals, termed Δset *literals*, that represent the Δsets produced during update propagation.

In addition to containing Δset literals, ec-rules can also include literals that represent both stored and derived relations. Since both states of each type of relation is accessible, the user must specify either the old or new state. The choice is indicated by a *state designator* that appears in the literal. The state designator directs the evaluator as to what database state that evaluation of the predicate is to occur. Also note that, like rules comprising IDB predicates, ec-rules may contain evaluable literals, e.g., $\leq, =, \geq$.

Consider the following example, which illustrates the concepts above. The ec-pred *connection_lost* represents an E-C pair that detects when any connection between two stations on a network is lost.

$$connection\_lost(X,Y) \leftarrow \Delta link_{rem}(X,Y).$$

It consists of one ec-rule that refers to the Δset computed for the IDB relation *LINK*. The E-C pair is satisfied once for each removal computed by the *PF* algorithm for *LINK*. In this example, the condition is null.

A second example involves a derived relation defining a high salaried employee as one whose annual salary and bonus equals or exceeds fifty thousand dollars. The definition appears below:

high_salaried_employee(E_Name,Tot_Salary) ←
    base_salary(E_Name, E_Salary), yearly_bonus(E_Name, E_Bonus),
    Tot_Salary = E_Salary + E_Bonus, Tot_Salary $\geq$ 50, 000.

Let the attribute *E_Name* uniquely identify an employee. Assume the manager wants to detect the situation where a high-salaried employee receives an increase in total salary that is greater than or equal to ten percent, regardless of the classification of the income. The following ec-pred *large_raise_given(E_Name)* defines the E-C pair. The Δset literals are used to detect the updates to the derived relation and the evaluable literal ($\geq$) represents the condition.

large_raise_given(E_Name) ←
    $\Delta high\_salaried\_employee_{rem}$*(E_Name,Old_sal),*
    $\Delta high\_salaried\_employee_{add}$*(E_Name,New_sal),*
    *New_sal $\geq$ Old_sal * 1.1.*

Consider an inventory management example. The ec-pred *inventory_shortage*, shown below, identifies parts that need to be reordered when the required amount to be maintained drops below the currently available amount for that part. Additions to the *part* relation, which may have been caused by either a decrease in the available amount or from the addition of a new part, are compared to the required amount, which may have also been updated requiring the reference to the new state.

inventory_shortage(Part) ←
    $\Delta part_{add}$*(Part,Avail_Amt), stock_required$_{New}$(Part,Req_Amt),*
    Avail_Amt $\leq$ Req_Amt.

The *PF* algorithm need only compute updates for candidate relations that are directly or indirectly referenced in Δset literals. This provides an initial opportunity to customize the *PF* algorithm for its use in derived relation event detection since the *PF* algorithm need only compute updates for these relevant candidate relations. The concept is formalized below.

Definition. A candidate relation is termed *relevant* if it is represented by a Δset literal appearing in an ec-pred. If R_{rel} is a relevant candidate relation and:

$$E \Rightarrow R_{rel} \in \mathcal{DG}$$

then E is a relevant candidate relation. A candidate rule that defines a relevant candidate relation is termed a *relevant* candidate rule.

Evaluating the Conditions After Event Detection

Tuples that are produced as a result of evaluating a ec-pred indicate the satisfaction of an E-C pair. All ec-preds representing situations of interest are evaluated after completion of the update propagation algorithm. The evaluation can be performed using a conventional recursive query evaluation strategy [1]. A minor modification would be made to allow the strategy to ignore removed facts when evaluating in the new state and to ignore new facts when evaluating in the old state.

5 Optimizing Complex Event Detection

In this section, optimizations are described that improve the efficiency of the event detector. The optimizations are motivated from deductive database query evaluation strategies but require adaptation for use in event detection.

5.1 Dependency Graph Analysis

The efficiency of the *PF* algorithm can be improved by reducing irrelevant computation. The computation of actual IDB updates that cannot contribute to the formation of ec-pred tuples can be identified and eliminated using the dependency graph.

The *PF* algorithm need only compute updates for candidate relations that are directly or indirectly referenced in Δset literals. All other updates represent irrelevant computation. The concept of a *relevant* candidate relation is formalized below.

Definition. A candidate relation is termed *relevant* if it is represented by a Δset literal appearing in an ec-pred. If R_{rel} is a relevant candidate relation and:

$$E \Rightarrow R_{rel} \in \mathcal{DG}$$

then E is a relevant candidate relation. A candidate rule that defines a relevant candidate relation is termed a *relevant* candidate rule.

In certain cases, updates to a relevant candidate relation can be identified as irrelevant with respect to the definition of the E-C pair that directly or indirectly references the relation.

Definition. An actual IDB update or an EDB update is *condition relevant* if it participates, directly or indirectly, in the formation of a ec-pred tuple. Conversely, actual IDB updates or EDB updates that do not participate, directly or indirectly, in the formation of a ec-pred tuple are *condition irrelevant*.

The optimization involves analyzing the program's dependency graph to identify paths that the *PF* algorithm would use to propagate condition irrelevant tuples. The objective of the optimization is to inform the *PF* algorithm to remove the paths from consideration.

Intuitively, the implementation of the optimization involves pushing the addition/removal specifier, which appears in Δset literals, down through the paths in the dependency graph towards the base relations. This will identify if either additions to, or removals from, a base relation are condition irrelevant.

If a Δset literal $\Delta p_{U type}$ appears in a condition, it indicates that the corresponding relation P is relevant candidate. The update type specification *Utype* indicates whether removals from, or additions to, the relevant candidate relation are of interest. The Δset tuples produced for a relation R that represent additions to R are of no consequence to the references in the ec-preds that refer to removals from R. Therefore, if all references to the ΔR that appear in the ec-preds indicate additions then certain base relation updates, namely those that result only in removals to R, need not be propagated. An equivalent relationship holds for Δset tuples produced for a relation R that represent additions.

After the completion of path analysis, the update types, i.e., additions or removals, for each relation that cannot contribute to the formation of a condition relevant tuple will have been identified. Any update classified as one of these types is ignored by the condition monitor and will not be propagated.

The optimization can reduce irrelevant computation in instances where negation is present. Since no significant cost is incurred at run-time, its application is advantageous in virtually all instances.

5.2   Optimizing Rule Evaluation

Both the propagation and filtration phases of the *PF* algorithm invoke queries to the database. Each query issued during the propagation phase consists of a subset of the literals that appear in a rule body. The *sideways information passing* strategy (SIP)[2] chosen for query evaluation has a direct effect on the efficiency of the algorithm. Informally, a sip implements the decision as to how bindings will be utilized during each step of query evaluation. In our prototype, which is implemented in Prolog, the different sip's are implemented by reordering the subgoals appearing in the Prolog queries.

The sip optimization dynamically computes an optimal sip for every query issued during both the propagation and filtration phases. The heuristic used to create the sips is the traditional "bound-is-easier" assumption [24]. This assumption implies that the more arguments that are bound in a call to a subgoal, the less expensive it will be to compute the result of the call.

Consider the non-linear recursion example shown in Figure 2. The predicate *sg* has a non-linear recursive definition but, for ease of comprehension, defines the traditional *same generation* relationship. Assume that updates were made to relation *PAR* and this has resulted in updates U to relation *SG*. Since the *PF* algorithm derives additional IDB updates from those already computed, the set U will be used for a subsequent propagation phase, which will now be examined in detail.

The second rule defining predicate *sg* contains subgoals representing *SG*. It must therefore be used for propagation. The body of the second rule is issued as a query three times, once for each occurrence of the *sg* literal in the rule. Each query will consist of the body of the rule less one of the three *sg* literals.

```
sg(X,Y)  :- par(X,P),par(Y,P).
sg(X,Y)  :- sg(X,X1),par(X1,XP),sg(XP,YP),par(Y1,YP),sg(Y1,Y).
```

Figure 2: A Non-linear Recursion

The first query, issued without the subgoal $sg(X,X1)$, is given below.

$$par^{bf}(X1, XP), sg^{bf}(XP, YP), par^{fb}(Y1, YP), sg^{bf}(Y1, Y)$$

Variables X and $X1$ will be bound using constants extracted from $\mathcal{U}$. The adornment of the call to each subgoal comprising the query is indicated by a superscript.

Note that both subgoals in the above query that refer to predicate sg are called with adornment bf. The rules below show the adornments associated with the subgoals when the query to subgoal sg^{bf} is made.

$sg^{bf}(X,Y) :- par^{bf}(X, P), par^{fb}(Y, P).$
$sg^{bf}(X,Y) :- sg^{bf}(X, X1), par^{bf}(X1, XP), sg^{bf}(XP, YP),$
$\qquad par^{fb}(Y1, YP), sg^{bb}(Y1, Y).$

Note that all of the calls to predicate sg that appear in the rule bodies will be at least partially constrained, i.e., a b appears in the adornment.

Now consider the second query where variables XP and YP are bound using $\mathcal{U}$. This query consists of the rule body without the literal $sg(XP,YP)$ and is given below. Again, note the adornment of the call to each subgoal representing predicate sg.

$$sg^{ff}(X, X1), par^{bb}(X1, XP), par^{fb}(Y1, YP), sg^{bf}(Y1, Y)$$

The first subgoal in the query is called with adornment ff. This introduces a gross inefficiency since this unconstrained call to predicate sg would result in the complete materialization of the predicate. This would dramatically raise the expense of computing the updates.

Subgoal reordering based on the "bound-is-easier" assumption can correct this inefficiency. The query below has the subgoals reordered. The adornments are updated to reflect the reordering.

$$par^{fb}(X1,XP), par^{fb}(Y1,YP), sg^{bf}(Y1,Y), sg^{fb}(X,X1)$$

Unfortunately, this first pass at optimizing the rule via subgoal reordering is not enough to avoid the inefficiency. Even though the adornment of the call to $sg(X,X1)$ has been restricted from ff to fb, the call to $sg^{fb}(X,X1)$ reintroduces the inefficiency. The rules below show the adornments associated with the subgoals when the query to subgoal sg^{fb} is made.

$sg^{fb}(X,Y) :- par^{ff}(X,P), par^{bb}(Y,P).$
$sg^{fb}(X,Y) :- sg^{ff}(X,X1), par^{bf}(X1,XP), sg^{bf}(XP,YP),$
$\qquad par^{fb}(Y1,YP), sg^{bb}(Y1,Y).$

Note that the ff adornment again appears; this time in the first subgoal of the second rule. However, the inefficiency can again be corrected by a second pass at reordering the subgoals. The rules for $sg^{fb}(X,Y)$, which have reordered subgoals so that no ff adornment appears, are given below:

$sg^{fb}(X,Y) :- par^{bf}(Y,P), par^{fb}(X,P).$
$sg^{fb}(X,Y) :- sg^{fb}(Y1,Y), par^{bf}(Y1,YP), sg^{fb}(XP,YP),$
$\qquad par^{fb}(X1,XP), sg^{fb}(X,X1).$

The solution to avoiding the inefficiency is to create optimized versions of certain predicates in the IDB. Each version has the subgoals of its rules ordered to correspond to the sip that allows for the most efficient evaluation with respect to a single adornment. To be consistent with the semantics of negation, negated subgoals are ordered such that their evaluation will be delayed until their arguments are fully bound. Evaluable predicates are also delayed until fully bound.

The subgoal reordering could be performed statically using an IDB preprocessor that would rewrite the rules of each predicate for as many possible adornments for which the predicate could be called. This is what is performed in the Magic Sets[1] approach to achieve the unique binding property. Unfortunately, significant rewriting is called for since a predicate with n arguments has 2^n possible adornments. This approach may be suboptimal since it is unlikely that all of these "sip-optimized" versions will be required during computation. The costs of computing and storing all of them may not be required.

One way to avoid the costs of statically creating the sip-optimized versions of every predicate in the database is to dynamically create only the versions required by the PF at execution time. This introduces overhead during execution of the condition monitoring instead of the preprocessing phase. In an implementation of the condition monitor designed for practical use, a more sophisticated rule-rewriter should be employed by the IDB preprocessor that analyzes both the IDB rules and the Δset literals and will only generate sip-optimized versions of predicates that are likely to be utilized.

The non-linear same-generation example was utilized to illustrate the potential benefit of the subgoal reordering optimization. As can be observed from the example, the reduction in cost of query evaluation as a result of subgoal reordering can be significant. Without the optimization, an unconstrained query is posed to the database. This unconstrained call increases the cost of computing the updates for the particular relation to that of the naive approach.

Since all sip-optimized predicates can be created before runtime, very little cost is incurred during update propagation as a result of this optimization. In this example, the predicate sg has only two arguments resulting in the creation of four sip-optimized versions. Unless the relations in the database are extremely small, the improved performance of the PF algorithm will generally outweigh the cost of storing the sip-optimized versions of the predicate. In addition, the sip-optimized rules can be used during query evaluation. The cost of creating and storing the sip-optimized rules is amortized over both event-condition monitoring and query evaluation.

5.3 Multiple Query Optimization

A database system that utilizes multiple query optimization (MQO) exploits similarities that may exist in a set of queries. When the system receives the query set it analyzes the queries to detect if any common subqueries exist. Evaluating common subqueries more than once represents redundant work. The heuristic that justifies MQO is that the queries will likely share subqueries and that overall query response time will decrease. Unfortunately, if no common subqueries exist, query response time may increase because time is spent analyzing the queries.

The *PF* algorithm may issue many queries to compute the Δsets. The queries are issued during both the propagation and filtration phases. The worst case situation for update propagation involves a rule that has n subgoals where each subgoal corresponds to a relation that has been updated as a result of both additions and removals. In this situation, $2n$ queries would need to be issued, where n queries would be issued in the *new* database state and n queries would be issued in the *old* database state. Each of these queries will involve essentially the same set of predicates hence the queries will be very similar. A call made to the same predicate by different queries represents a common subquery if the arguments of each query will unify with the arguments of the others. This behavior is consistent with the heuristic justifying MQO and motivates its use.

Depending on the database, it is possible that the call to a predicate resulting from one query subsumes one or more calls invoked by other queries. In this situation, result sharing is possible. The reduction in redundant computation can be dramatic if p_i is recursive.

The invocation of multiple related queries motivates the development of a multiple query optimization (MQO) algorithm to increase the efficiency of the *PF* algorithm. As indicated in [7], memoing inherently implements the MQO task of *common subexpression identification* [5, 20]. Each occurrence of a literal defining an IDB predicate represents the subexpressions defined by the conjunction of literals in the bodies of the rules defining the predicate.

Our prototype employs a top-down recursive query evaluation strategy known as $EQ^*\neg$[12]. This strategy, which is an optimized version of ET^* [7], utilizes memoing to insure completeness. This memoing feature facilitates the implementation of MQO. The $EQ^*\neg$ algorithm detects *completed* calls. A completed call has an extension, which has been computed by the $EQ^*\neg$ algorithm, that is complete. Completed calls that are detected by the algorithm are not recomputed. Instead, the answers for the call, which are retained in the extension table, are returned to the caller. If a call is made to a predicate that is not subsumed by an earlier call, the call is tagged complete after evaluation and the results are made available to subsequent callers.

The MQO optimization benefits both the propagation and filtration phases of the *PF* algorithm. Answers obtained from DB_{New} (DB_{Old}) when computing potential additions (removals) during a propagation phase are available to reduce the effort required to test potential removals (additions) in a subsequent filtration phase. Tuples stored in a memo table for unaffected predicates, obtained during a propagation or filtration phase, can be utilized regardless of the state in which the query is posed.

Four memo tables are maintained in the prototype. Two are used to record the *calls* made to both the initial and updated database states. Two more are used to record the *answers* computed in each database state resulting from the calls.

5.4 Partial Evaluation of Deductive Rules

Lakhotia and Sterling describe partial evaluation, as it applies to logic programming, as follows. Given a program $\mathcal{P}$ and a goal $\mathcal{G}$, the result of partially evaluating $\mathcal{P}$ with respect to the goal $\mathcal{G}$ is the program $\mathcal{P}'$ such that for any substitution θ, evaluating $\mathcal{G}\theta$ results in the same answers with respect to both $\mathcal{P}$ and $\mathcal{P}'$. The objective of partial evaluation is to produce a $\mathcal{P}'$ on which $\mathcal{G}\theta$ can be evaluated more efficiently than on $\mathcal{P}$ [16]. A theoretical foundation for partial evaluation is given in [18].

CP: *possible_vessel_failure(V) ← Δabnormal_vessel_condition_{add}(V).*

IDB: *abnormal_vessel_condition(V) ←*
        vessels_in_use(V), vessel_spec_violation(V).

        vessel_spec_violation(V) ← temp(V,Current_Temp),
        max_temps(V,Max_Temp), Current_Temp > Max_Temp.
        vessel_spec_violation(V) ← pressure(V,Current_Pres),
        max_pressure(V,Max_Pres), Current_Pres > Max_Pres.

Figure 3: Conditions and IDB before Partial Evaluation Optimization

Partial evaluation can be used to form optimized deductive rules that increase the efficiency of event detection in the case of derived relations. The optimization applies when constants appear as arguments in the Δliterals, which appear as ec-pred subgoals. A Δliteral for some predicate p serves as the goal $\mathcal{G}$. The Datalog definition of predicate p serves as the program $\mathcal{P}$. Condition relevant updates are computed more efficiently using the partially evaluated predicate p' than they are using p.

Informally, the partially evaluated predicate p' is created by pushing the constants appearing in the Δliteral down through the rules that directly or indirectly define the predicate p. The constants bind variables in the rules and are used to form new, restricted versions of the predicates. These new predicates are essentially copies of the initial database predicates. However, they are bound using the constants from the ec-preds and may have less arguments and even less subgoals.

The Δset literal $\Delta p'$, where p' represents the partially evaluated version of p, is substituted for Δp in the ec-pred. The IDB relation P is no longer *relevant candidate* with respect to the Δliteral being processed. If P is not referenced directly or indirectly by any other Δliteral then P will no longer be relevant candidate and will not require update propagation. Instead, the IDB relation P' is now *relevant candidate*. Updates will now be propagated using the definition of the partially evaluated predicate representing relation P'. The predicate P' is less expensive to monitor since it will not propagate irrelevant tuples. The result of this optimization is a reduction in computation performed by the *PF* algorithm as well as a reduction in the cost of evaluating the ec-preds during condition evaluation.

Example

The following simple example illustrates the partial evaluation concept. The condition states that a vessel V may have failed if its current condition is abnormal. An abnormal condition is defined as one where either the temperature is higher or internal pressure is lower than is considered normal. Figure 3 shows the condition and the IDB before the optimization.

Now, assume that the user is solely concerned with vessel $v5$ since it alone contains flammable chemicals. The constant $v5$ is substituted for the variable V in the ec-pred. The updated ec-pred appears below.

possible_vessel_failure(v5) ← Δabnormal_vessel_condition_{add}(v5).

Since a constant, namely *v5*, appears as an argument in the Δliteral:

$$\Delta abnormal\_vessel\_condition,$$

the partial evaluation optimization is applicable. Initially, a partially evaluated version of the predicate *abnormal_vessel_condition* is created. The predicate has one rule:

$$abnormal\_vessel\_condition\_v5 \leftarrow vessels\_in\_use(v5), vessel\_spec\_violation(v5).$$

Note that the arity of the new predicate is less than the original since there is no need to pass the constants that were used to form the partially evaluated version. Predicate *vessels_in_use* represents an EDB relation so no further partial evaluation is necessary. However, predicate *vessel_spec_violation* represents an IDB relation so partial evaluation can continue. The partially evaluated predicate *vessel_spec_violation_v5* is defined by the following two rules:

$vessel\_spec\_violation\_v5 \leftarrow temp(v5,Current\_Temp),$
    $max\_temps(v5,Max\_Temp), Current\_Temp > Max\_Temp.$
$vessel\_spec\_violation\_v5 \leftarrow pressure(v5,Current\_Pres),$
    $max\_pressure(v5,Max\_Pres), Current\_Pres > Max\_Pres.$

Using this revised definition, only updates that affect vessel *v5* are propagated. For example, updates to EDB relation *temp* that will not unify with *temp(v5,Current_Temp)* are identified as condition irrelevant and will not be propagated. The initial definitions of the IDB predicates remain in the database after the optimization but since they no longer define relevant candidate relations, they will not be utilized for update propagation.

When the partial evaluation optimization can be applied, a performance increase, in terms of speed is achieved. The optimization requires that additional rules be added to the database. A tradeoff exists between the costs of maintaining the additional rules and the increased speed of update propagation.

It is expected that in a practical application, speed would be the primary concern. The optimization can reduce irrelevant computation in instances where constants appear in the Δliterals. Since the costs of partial evaluation and rule rewriting are incurred at compile-time and the optimization can only improve the performance of the algorithm at run-time, the application of the optimization is justified.

5.5   Minimizing the Approximation

Potential IDB updates that have already been filtered and determined to be actual IDB updates need not be filtered again. In addition, potential IDB updates that have been disqualified during the filtering phase need not be filtered again. Memoing can be used to reduce the size of the approximation by identifying tuples that are known to be actual IDB updates or disqualified potential IDB updates. This reduces the computation that must be performed during any subsequent filtration phase and results in an efficiency improvement.

In order to ensure termination and to identify the events to the derived relations, the actual IDB updates computed by the *PF* algorithm are retained in the Δsets. A potential IDB update computed for an IDB relation *P* during a propagation phase that already occurs in ΔP as a result of prior computation need not be tested for disqualification. As evidenced by its occurrence in ΔP, it would pass the filtration phase, incurring the cost of filtering, but simply be discarded later as a duplicate. The Δset serves as a memo table to reduce the tuples tested during the filtration phase and therefore reduces redundant computation.

Potential IDB updates that have been disqualified as a result of previous invocations of the *PF* algorithm can also be used to prefilter the approximation. These disqualified updates can be used to identify disqualified tuples that appear in future approximations. Identified tuples are removed from the approximation to avoid unnecessary computation during the filtration phase.

6 Discussion

The sophistication of an active database system can be increased by allowing complex events to be detected and expressive conditions to be defined. This paper described how updates to derived relations could be detected using the *PF* algorithm. The updates can be detected without having to materialize the derived relations. In addition, the updates are detected even when the definition of the derived relation is modified via the addition or deletion of deductive rules. We describe how conditions can be defined that offer a unified representation for reasoning with derived relations, stored relations and evaluable predicates. These conditions can also reference both the old and new values of tuples representing updates to either stored or derived relations. The result is an expressive representation for events and conditions that can specify more complex situations.

Integrity constraint enforcement [26], computing the differences between database states [15], managing derived relations [4, 8] and performing change computation [25] can be directly supported using the *PF* algorithm. Performance improvements can be obtained by employing the optimizations described here.

For future work, a suitable execution model will be coupled with the event-condition monitor to form an *active deductive* DBMS. In addition, since the *PF* algorithm only queries the database, we are investigating whether parallelism can be used to improve the performance of the event detector thereby providing better support for real-time applications.

References

[1] Bancilhon, F., Maier, D., Sagiv, Y. and Ullman, J., "Magic Sets and Other S-trange Ways to Implement Logic Programs", *Proc. 5th ACM SIGMOD-SIGACT Symposium on Principles of Database Systems*, Washington, DC, 1986, pp. 1–15.

[2] Beeri, C. and Ramakrishnan, R., "On the Power of Magic", *Journal of Logic Programming*, October , 1991:10, pp. 255–299.

[3] Ceri, S. and Widom, J., "Deriving Production Rules for Incremental View Maintenance", *Proc. 17th Intl. Conf. on Very Large Database Systems*, Barcelona, September, 1991, pp. 577–589.

[4] Ceri, S. and Widom, J., "Deriving Incremental Production Rules for Deductive Data", IBM Research Report RJ 9071 (80884) November, 1992.

[5] Chakravarthy, U. S. and Minker, J., " Multiple Query Processing in Deductive Databases using Query Graphs", *Proc. of the 12th Intl. Conf. on Very Large Data Bases*, Kyoto, August 1986.

[6] Chakravarthy, S. and Garg, S., "Extended Relational Algebra (ERA): for Optimizing Situations in Active Databases", Technical Report UF-CIS TR-91-24, CIS Department, University of Florida, Gainesville, November 1991.

[7] Dietrich, S. W., "Extension Tables: Memo Relations in Logic Programming", *IEEE Symposium on Logic Programming*, San Francisco, CA, 1987, pp. 264–272.

[8] Gupta, A., Mumick, I. S. and Subrahmanian, V. S., "Maintaining Views Incrementally", *Proceedings of the 1993 ACM SIGMOD*, Washington, DC, May 1993.

[9] Hanson, E., Chaabouni, M., Kim, C. and Wang, Y., "Rule Condition Testing and Action Execution in Ariel", *Proceedings of the 1992 ACM SIGMOD International Conference of Management of Data*, San Diego, CA, June 1992, pp. 49–58.

[10] Harrison, J. V., and Dietrich, S. W., "Condition Monitoring using Update Propagation in an Active Deductive Database", Arizona State University Tech. Rep. TR-91-027 (Revised), December, 1991, To appear: *J. Info. Sys.*

[11] Harrison, J. V. and Dietrich, S. W., "Towards an Incremental Condition Evaluation Strategy for Active Deductive Databases", In Proceedings of Databases '92, Third Australian Database Conference, Melbourne, Australia, February 1992. pp. 81–95.

[12] Harrison, J. V., "Condition Monitoring in an Active Deductive Database", Ph.D. Dissertation, Arizona State University, July, 1992.

[13] Harrison, J. V. and Dietrich, S. W., "Maintaining Materialized Views in Deductive Databases: An Update Propagation Approach", Proceedings of the Deductive Database Workshop held in conjunction with the Joint International Conference and Symposium on Logic Programming, Washington, D.C., November, 1992, pp. 56–65.

[14] Harrison, J. V., "Monitoring Complex Events defined using Aggregates in an Active Deductive Database", University of Queensland Tech. Rep. 268, May, 1993 (revised).

[15] Kuchenhoff, V.,"On the efficient computation of the difference between consecutive database states", In *Proc. of the Second Intl. Conf. on Deductive and Object-Oriented Databases (DOOD)*, Munich, Germany, December 1991.

[16] Lakhotia, A. and Sterling, L., "ProMiX: a Prolog Partial Evaluation System", In *The Practice of Prolog*, Sterling, L. (eds), MIT Press, Cambridge, 1990, pp. 137–179.

[17] Lefebvre, A., "Towards an Efficient Evaluation of Recursive Aggregates in Deductive Databases", *Proc. of FGCS'92*.

[18] Lloyd, J. W. and Shepherdson, J. C., "Partial Evaluation in Logic Programming", *Journal of Logic Programming*, 11:217-242, 1991.

[19] Lohman, G., Lindsay, B., Pirahesh, H. and Schiefer, K. B.,"Extensions to Starburst: Objects, Types, Functions, and Rules", *Communications of the ACM*, Vol. 34, No. 10, October 1991, pp. 94–109.

[20] Park, J. and Segev, A., "Using Common Subexpressions to Optimize Multiple Queries", *Proc. of Seventh IEEE Conf. on Data Engineering*, 1988, pp. 311–319.

[21] Schreier, U., Pirahesh, H., Agrawal, R. and Mohan, C., "Alert: An Architecture for Transforming a Passive DBMS into an Active DBMS", *Proceedings of the 17th Intl. Conf. on Very Large Databases (VLDB)*, Barcelona, Spain, 1991, pp. 469–478.

[22] Stonebraker, M. and Kemnitz, G, "The Postgres Next-Generation Database Management System", *Communications of the ACM*, Vol. 34, No. 10, October 1991, pp. 78–92.

[23] Ullman, J., *Principles of Database and Knowledge-base Systems*, Vol. 1, Computer Science Press, Rockville, MD, 1988.

[24] Ullman, J., *Principles of Database and Knowledge-base Systems*, Vol. 2, Computer Science Press, Rockville, MD, 1989.

[25] Urpi', T. and Olive, A., "Events and Event rules in Active Databases", *Special Issue on Active Databases, Bulletin of the Technical Committee on Data Engineering*, December, 1992 Vol. 15, No. 1-4.

[26] Vieille, L., Bayer, P. and Kuchenhoff, V., "Integrity Checking and Materialized Views Handling by Update Propagation in the EKS-V1 System", ECRC Technical Report TR-KB-35, ECRC, Munich, Germany, June 1991.

Deductive and Active Databases: Two Paradigms or Ends of a Spectrum?

Jennifer Widom

IBM Almaden Research Center

San Jose, CA, USA

Abstract

This position paper considers several existing relational database rule languages with a focus on exploring the fundamental differences between deductive and active databases. We find that deductive and active databases do not form two discernible classes, but rather they delineate two ends of a spectrum of database rule languages. We claim that this spectrum also corresponds to a notion of abstraction level, with deductive rule languages at a higher level and active rule languages at a lower level.

1 Introduction

Research on incorporating rule processing into database systems historically has been divided into two distinct areas: *deductive* databases and *active* databases. In deductive databases, logic programming style rules are used to provide a more powerful user interface than that provided by most database query languages [3, 12]. In active databases, production style rules are used to provide automatic execution of database operations in response to certain events and/or conditions [5]. We claim that although some database rule languages are clearly classifiable as either deductive or active, there is no obvious delineation between the two types of languages.

We support our claim by considering six relational database rule languages prominent in the literature: *Datalog* [12], *RDL* [8], *A-RDL* [9], *Ariel* [6, 7], *Starburst* [13, 14], and *Postgres* [10]. We believe that these six rule languages form a spectrum along a "deductive to active axis", as shown in Figure 1. We also believe that the same spectrum describes the level of abstraction of these database rule languages, with deductive to active rule languages ranging accordingly from a higher level to a lower level.

In Section 2 we introduce a generic notation for database rules and a generic rule processing algorithm. In Sections 3–8 we expand these generic concepts to describe each of the six rule languages. We begin with Datalog, which we view as the "most deductive" language, and we end with Postgres, which we view as the "most active" language. It will be seen that the description of each language requires only small revisions to the description of the previous language, substantiating our claim that these languages form a spectrum rather than two distinct classes. Furthermore, as we move along the spectrum from deductive to active, we note that in general each rule language includes more constructs

DEDUCTIVE ...   ... ACTIVE
  higher level ...   ... *lower level*

|——|

  Datalog ... RDL ... A-RDL ... Ariel ... Starburst ... Postgres

Figure 1: Spectrum of Database Rule Languages

than the previous language but also requires more behavior to be specified explicitly by the rule programmer. This leads to our claim that deductive rule languages provide a higher level of abstraction than active rule languages.[1] In Section 9 we draw conclusions and discuss implications of our claims.

It is important to note that in considering the six database rule languages we focus only on the "essence" of each language. That is, we consider features that have a direct bearing on whether the language should be considered as deductive or active, i.e. features such as basic language constructs and rule processing semantics, while we ignore features that have little or no bearing on the deductive versus active question, i.e. features such as syntax, minor semantic restrictions, assignment to variables, rule ordering, relationship to database transactions, etc. Note also that we sidestep the issue of whether these languages should be considered as *declarative* or *procedural*.[2]

2   Generic Framework

In all rule languages, each rule consists of at least some form of *antecedent* and some form of *consequent*. In addition, rules in the database context sometimes include an *activator*. (We specifically avoid terms such as *head*, *body*, *event*, *condition*, *action*, *trigger*, etc., since these often are associated with a particular database rule language paradigm.) Hence, we use the following generic notation for database rules, where square brackets indicate optionality:

[*Activator* ⤳] *Antecedent* ⤳ *Consequent*

The generic interpretation of such a rule is: "[when the *Activator*] if the *Antecedent* then the *Consequent*", and a generic algorithm for processing a set of such rules is:

repeat until steps 1–2 can have no effect:
  1. find a rule r [that is activated] whose antecedent is true
  2. ensure r's consequent

---

[1] An analogy can be drawn with programming languages, where there are high-level languages with few constructs, such as Lisp, low-level languages with many constructs, such as assembly code, and "in-between" languages such as C.

[2] Actually, it is our belief that here too the languages form a spectrum—with "more declarative" towards the left of Figure 1 and "more procedural" towards the right—but the notions of declarative and procedural are fuzzy enough in this context that we prefer to avoid the issue.

We expand these generic concepts for our six database rule languages, considering the languages in left-to-right order along the spectrum of Figure 1.

3 Datalog

In Datalog, rules do not include activators. The antecedent of a Datalog rule corresponds to a query over the database that produces a set of tuples. The consequent of a Datalog rule states that the tuples produced by the antecedent are in a specified relation in the database. Thus, a Datalog rule has the form:

Query producing t's $\rightsquigarrow$ *t*'s are in relation R

The interpretation of a set of Datalog rules is based on a *fixpoint* semantics [12]; it can be described by the following variation on our generic rule processing algorithm:

repeat until steps 1–2 can have no effect:
1. find a rule r whose antecedent produces tuples
2. ensure that the tuples are present in r's consequent relation

(In the repeat clause, "no effect" here means that no rule produces tuples in step 1 or no executions of step 2 add tuples to the consequent relation.) In an actual implementation there are many alternatives and optimizations to this rule processing approach, but they do not affect the semantics of the language. Note that the relations in the consequents of Datalog rules often are not actually stored in the database (i.e. they are *intensional* or *virtual*), but this too is not an inherent property of the rule language.

4 RDL

RDL rules are identical to Datalog rules except that the consequent of an RDL rule is a sequence, where each element of the sequence specifies either that the tuples produced by the antecedent are in a specified relation or that the tuples produced by the antecedent are not in a specified relation. Thus, an RDL rule has the form:

Query producing t's $\rightsquigarrow$ *t*'s are in relation R_1
  t's are not in relation R_2
  . . .
  t's are in relation R_n

The processing of RDL rules is described using the following slight variation on the rule processing algorithm given for Datalog:

repeat until steps 1–2 can have no effect:
    1. find a rule r whose antecedent produces tuples
    2. for each element in r's consequent:
        ensure that the tuples are present or absent in the
        specified relation

Hence, we see that the only significant difference between RDL and Datalog is that RDL allows rule consequents to specify both the presence and absence of tuples.[3]

5 A-RDL

A-RDL is described as "an extension of RDL with active capabilities" (corroborating our claim that we are moving along the spectrum from deductive to active rule languages). The A-RDL language is identical to RDL except that queries in A-RDL rule antecedents may refer to *delta relations* in addition to normal database relations. There are three delta relations—**inserted**, **deleted**, and **updated**—associated with each database relation. Thus, an A-RDL rule has the form:

$Query_\Delta$ *producing t's* $\leadsto$ t's are in relation R_1
                                      t's are not in relation R_2
                                      ...
                                      t's are in relation R_n

where $Query_\Delta$ denotes that the *Query* may refer to delta relations. The rule processing algorithm for A-RDL is identical to that for RDL, except that rule processing occurs with respect to a previous database state S as well as the current state (intuitively, S corresponds to the database state preceding some set of modifications):

$S \leftarrow$ some previous database state
repeat until steps 1–2 can have no effect:
    1. find a rule r whose antecedent produces tuples according to S
    2. for each element in r's consequent:
        ensure that the tuples are present or absent in the
        specified relation

In step 1 rule antecedents may refer to delta relations; for each database relation, the three delta relations associated with it contain the tuples that have been inserted, deleted, and updated between previous state S and the current state.

Hence, we see that the only significant difference between A-RDL and RDL is that A-RDL rules are considered with respect to a database state transition along with the current database state and they may refer to this state transition in their antecedent.

---

[3] This is very similar to suggested extensions of Datalog as described in, e.g., [1].

6 Ariel

In Ariel there are two forms of rules: rules without activators, called *pattern-based* rules, and rules with activators, called *event-based* rules. For convenience, we refer to these two forms of rules as *Ariel-p* and *Ariel-e* respectively. Along our deductive-to-active axis, Ariel-p lies to the deductive (left) side of Ariel-e, so we consider Ariel-p first.

6.1 Ariel-p

Syntactically, the antecedent of an Ariel-p rule is a query over the database, as in Datalog and RDL. However, the interpretation of an Ariel-p antecedent is that the query produces tuples by systematically replacing each normal database relation referenced in the query by a combination of delta relations **inserted** and **updated**.[4] Ariel-p includes a mechanism whereby this feature can be circumvented, i.e. entire relations are used. Therefore, the antecedents of Ariel-p rules are very similar to the antecedents of A-RDL rules, except Ariel-p rules cannot refer to delta relation **deleted**.

The consequent of an Ariel-p rule is a sequence of set-oriented relational database modification commands (**insert**, **delete**, and **update**). The tuples produced by the antecedent may be referenced in these commands along with normal database relations. Thus, an Ariel-p rule has the form:

$$Query_\Delta \ producing \ t\text{'s} \ \leadsto \ DB\text{-}Mod_1(t\text{'s}) \ \cdots \ DB\text{-}Mod_n(t\text{'s})$$

where $DB\text{-}Mod(t\text{'s})$ denotes a database modification command that may reference the tuples produced by the antecedent.

The rule processing algorithm for Ariel-p is identical to that for A-RDL, except a different notion of previous state is used for evaluating delta relations, and more complex consequents are executed:

> $S \leftarrow$ some previous database state
> repeat until steps 1–2 can have no effect:
> > 1. find a rule r whose antecedent produces tuples according to previous state S'
> > 2. execute each command in r's consequent using the tuples from step 1

State S' in step 1 is S if it is the first time rule r is selected during rule processing; otherwise S' is the database state from the last time rule r was selected. (One additional slight difference in Ariel-p, as well as in the remaining languages discussed below, is that "no effect" in the repeat statement means only that no rule produces tuples in step 1, independent of step 2.)

---

[4] This interpretation ensures that the antecedent is satisfied if and only if it is satisfied by "new" data, similar to expert systems rule languages such as OPS5 [2].

Hence, we see that the most significant difference between Ariel-p and A-RDL is that the consequents in Ariel-p rules are more general. Less significant differences are that Ariel-p cannot reference **deleted**, and that the two languages use a different notion of previous state for delta relations.

6.2 Ariel-e

Rules in Ariel-e are identical to rules in Ariel-p except Ariel-e rules include activators. The activator in an Ariel-e rule is either $I(R)$, $D(R)$, or $U(R)$, corresponding to insertions, deletions, or updates on a relation R. Thus, an Ariel-e rule has the form:

$$I(R) \mid D(R) \mid U(R) \ \rightsquigarrow \ Query_\Delta \ producing \ t's \ \rightsquigarrow$$
$$DB\text{-}Mod_1(t's) \ \cdots \ DB\text{-}Mod_n(t's)$$

As in Ariel-p, delta relations are referenced implicitly in rule antecedents. However, in Ariel-e only references to relation R (from the activator) implicitly reference delta relations, and they implicitly reference only the delta relation corresponding to the activator's operation. For example, in the antecedent and consequent of a rule with activator $D(R)$, references to R implicitly reference delta relation **deleted** for R.

The rule processing algorithm for Ariel-e is a slight variation on the rule processing algorithm for Ariel-p, taking activation into account:

$S \leftarrow$ some previous database state
repeat until steps 1–2 can have no effect:
1. find a rule r that is activated according to previous state S' and whose antecedent produces tuples according to S'
2. execute each command in r's consequent using the tuples from step 1

State S' is the same in Ariel-e as in Ariel-p. In step 1, a rule is activated if and only if the delta relation corresponding to its activator is non-empty.

Hence, we see that the most significant difference between Ariel-e and Ariel-p is that Ariel-e has the additional requirement of activation based on non-empty delta relations. A less significant difference is that Ariel-e can implicitly reference **deleted**, while Ariel-p cannot.

7 Starburst

Starburst rules are very similar to Ariel-e, although there are several minor differences:[5] A Starburst rule may specify the disjunction of multiple activators. A Starburst rule references delta relations corresponding to the rule's activator(s) explicitly rather than implicitly, and its consequent may not reference antecedent tuples but may reference delta relations. A Starburst rule consequent may include database retrieval commands as well as database modification commands. Thus, a Starburst rule has the form:

---

[5]Some of these differences are particularly good examples of one language (Starburst) providing more constructs than the other (Ariel), but also requiring more behavior to be specified explicitly by the rule programmer.

$$[I(R)] \ [D(R)] \ [U(R)] \ \rightsquigarrow \ Query_\Delta \ \rightsquigarrow$$
$$DB\text{-}Command_\Delta^1 \ \cdots \ DB\text{-}Command_\Delta^n$$

where at least one activator is specified and $DB\text{-}Command_\Delta$ denotes a database retrieval or modification command that may reference delta relations. The rule processing algorithm for Starburst is a very slight variation on the rule processing algorithm for Ariel-e:

> $S \leftarrow$ some previous database state
> repeat until steps 1–2 can have no effect:
> 1. find a rule r that is activated according to previous state S' and whose antecedent produces tuples according to S'
> 2. execute each command in r's consequent according to previous state S'

State S' is the same in Starburst as in Ariel-e.

Hence, we see that there are no significant differences between Starburst and Ariel-e.

8 Postgres

Like Starburst and Ariel-e, Postgres rules have activators. The activator of a Postgres rule includes the same alternatives as Starburst and Ariel-e with the addition of $S(R)$, corresponding to data retrieval (or "Selection") on a relation R. Postgres rules do not include disjunction of activators as in Starburst. A Postgres antecedent is a query that may explicitly reference the delta relation corresponding to the rule's activator, and a Postgres consequent is a sequence of data modification and retrieval commands that also may explicitly reference this delta relation. A Postgres consequent may include "instead", indicating that the consequent commands should be executed from a previous database state rather than from the current state (see below). Thus, a Postgres rule has the form:

$$I(R) \mid D(R) \mid U(R) \mid S(R) \ \rightsquigarrow$$
$$Query_\Delta \ \rightsquigarrow \ [\text{ instead }] \ DB\text{-}Command_\Delta^1 \ \cdots \ DB\text{-}Command_\Delta^n$$

The rule processing algorithm for Postgres is a slight variation on the rule processing algorithm for Starburst:

> $S \leftarrow$ immediate previous database state
> repeat until steps 1–2 can have no effect:
> 1. find a rule r that is activated according to previous state S and whose antecedent produces tuples according to S
> 2. execute each command in r's consequent according to previous state S

Note that here S is defined specifically to be the "immediate previous state"—the state preceding the most recent (tuple-level) operation. One implication of this is that when commands are executed in step 2 the rule processing algorithm is called recursively rather than iteratively. We feel that the recursive versus iterative issue, although important, is orthogonal to the deductive versus active issue. Also note that in step 2, when a rule consequent includes "instead", the notion of executing commands according to previous state S also indicates executing the commands from state S.

Hence, we see that the only significant differences between Postgres and Starburst are that Postgres includes a data retrieval activator and that Postgres consequents may specify execution from a previous state.

9 Conclusions and Implications

In summary, using a generic framework we have described the essential features of six important database rule languages. Our descriptions began with Datalog, which is considered to be a typical deductive database rule language; by making only incremental changes in each step we proceeded to describe RDL, A-RDL, Ariel, Starburst, and finally Postgres, which is considered to be a typical active database rule language. The fact that we were able to traverse smoothly from Datalog to Postgres indicates that database rule languages form a spectrum rather than two distinct classes.

Through our rule language descriptions it can be observed that, in general, each language provides more features than the previous language. In particular, along the spectrum from deductive to active languages we see the addition of:

- A notion of database state transition, including the ability to reference state transitions in more and more complicated ways

- More and more powerful operations in rule consequents

- A notion of rule activator, with more and more complicated activators allowed

One feature that appears to be lost when moving from deductive to active rule languages is a notion of passing data from the antecedent to the consequent of rules. However, it can be seen that in the more active rule languages, although data from a rule's antecedent is not implicitly operated on by the rule's consequent, the same effect can be achieved by using the powerful rule consequents and delta relations provided by these languages. This is one (important) instance of our general observation that in the more deductive rule languages certain behavior is implicit while the same behavior must be specified explicitly in the more active rule languages, i.e. deductive rule languages provide a higher level of abstraction than active rule languages.

Given our claim that the more deductive rule languages (i.e. languages towards the left of the spectrum) are at a higher level than the more active rule languages (i.e. languages towards the right of the spectrum), it should be possible to translate rules in a language L into rules in a language L', where L' lies to the right of L on the spectrum. That is, it should be possible to use a lower-level rule language as the target language of a compiler for a higher-level rule language. By examining the descriptions in Sections 3–8 it is evident that, with the exception of a few fine points, such compilation is indeed possible. In fact, as a complete example of this, a compiler from Datalog to Starburst is described in [4].[6]

To conclude, in designing a database rule system we do not believe that a choice must be made between deductive and active paradigms, but rather a point must be chosen along a spectrum of database rule languages. The appropriate point depends on the desired level of abstraction and the desired suite of features provided by the rule language. We close by noting that we have considered relational database rule languages only; in an object-oriented setting the distinction between deductive and active database rule languages may be even fuzzier and more complex.

Acknowledgements

Thanks to Elena Baralis, Stefano Ceri, Bobbie Cochrane, and Eric Simon for helpful and varied reactions to an initial draft, and to the participants at the workshop for lively discussions on this topic.

References

[1] S. Abiteboul and E. Simon. Fundamental properties of deterministic and nondeterministic extensions of datalog. *Theoretical Computer Science*, 78:137–158, 1991.

[2] L. Brownston, R. Farrell, E. Kant, and N. Martin. *Programming Expert Systems in OPS5: An Introduction to Rule-Based Programming*. Addison-Wesley, Reading, Massachusetts, 1985.

[3] S. Ceri, G. Gottlob, and L. Tanca. *Logic Programming and Databases*. Springer-Verlag, Berlin, 1990.

[4] S. Ceri and J. Widom. Deriving incremental production rules for deductive data. IBM Research Report RJ 9071, IBM Almaden Research Center, November 1992.

[5] U. Dayal and J. Widom. Active database systems. In *ACM SIGMOD International Conference on Management of Data* (tutorial), San Diego, California, June 1992.

[6] E.N. Hanson. An initial report on the design of Ariel: A DBMS with an integrated production rule system. *SIGMOD Record, Special Issue on Rule Management and Processing in Expert Database Systems*, 18(3):12–19, September 1989.

[7] E.N. Hanson. Rule condition testing and action execution in Ariel. In *Proceedings of the ACM SIGMOD International Conference on Management of Data*, pages 49–58, San Diego, California, June 1992.

---

[6]It is interesting to note that a "reverse" compilation (from an active to a deductive rule language) is suggested in [11]; however, it is obvious that this translation is far less natural and requires significant capabilities in the deductive rule language.

[8] J. Kiernan, C. de Maindreville, and E. Simon. Making deductive databases a practical technology: A step forward. In *Proceedings of the ACM SIGMOD International Conference on Management of Data*, pages 237–246, Atlantic City, New Jersey, May 1990.

[9] E. Simon, J. Kiernan, and C. de Maindreville. Implementing high level active rules on top of a relational DBMS. In *Proceedings of the Eighteenth International Conference on Very Large Data Bases*, pages 315–326, Vancouver, British Columbia, August 1992.

[10] M. Stonebraker, A. Jhingran, J. Goh, and S. Potamianos. On rules, procedures, caching and views in data base systems. In *Proceedings of the ACM SIGMOD International Conference on Management of Data*, pages 281–290, Atlantic City, New Jersey, May 1990.

[11] L. Tanca. (Re-)Action in deductive databases. In *Proceedings of the Second International Workshop on Intelligent and Cooperative Information Systems*, pages 55–61, Como, Italy, October 1991.

[12] J.D. Ullman. *Principles of Database and Knowledge-Base Systems, Volumes I and II*. Computer Science Press, Rockville, Maryland, 1989.

[13] J. Widom, R.J. Cochrane, and B.G. Lindsay. Implementing set-oriented production rules as an extension to Starburst. In *Proceedings of the Seventeenth International Conference on Very Large Data Bases*, pages 275–285, Barcelona, Spain, September 1991.

[14] J. Widom and S.J. Finkelstein. Set-oriented production rules in relational database systems. In *Proceedings of the ACM SIGMOD International Conference on Management of Data*, pages 259–270, Atlantic City, New Jersey, May 1990.

A Framework for Supporting Triggers in Deductive Databases

Petra Bayer, Willem Jonker

European Computer-industry Research Centre

Arabellastrasse 17, D-81925 Munich, Germany

Abstract

In this paper we introduce a framework for supporting triggers in the context of deductive databases. The framework focusses on a precise definition of primitive and composite events, and of event occurrences. First we abstract from the actual representation of events, conditions and actions. Then we refine the framework in the context of deductive databases. In this context we also give a precise definition for the trigger processing. Finally we outline an architecture for implementing the framework[1].

1   Introduction

Active databases are an active area of research. The initial emphasis has been on the integration of triggers (also called active rules, production rules, or event-condition-action rules) with relational database systems ([16], [21]) or with object-oriented database systems ([4], [8]). For relational systems this resulted in systems like Postgres [18], Starburst [20], or Ariel [13], for object-oriented systems in HiPAC [17] or Ode [12].

Less research has been reported on how deductive databases can be extended with triggers. [5] describes how to combine triggers with a deductive object-oriented database, but emphasizes the development of a deductive object-oriented language and a logic for objects. In the RDL1 system ([15]) triggers, consisting of condition and action only, are used to implement a deductive database system.

The triggers reported in the literature are often tailored to a specific implementation (for a specific database system). This then leads to a rather informal treatment of triggers and especially of events. Some work in the direction of generalizing and formalizing the notion of triggers and events can be found in ([22], [12]).

In this paper we will introduce a framework for supporting triggers in the context of deductive databases. The framework focuses on a precise definition of events and event occurrences, considering composite events as well. It abstracts from the actual representation of events, conditions and actions, and is then applied to deductive databases. In this context we also give a precise definition for the trigger processing.

This paper is organized as follows. We first introduce a framework for event specifications, events and event occurrences in section 2. Then we show in

---

[1]This research was partly funded by the CEC under Esprit project 6333 IDEA.
This paper reflects the opinions of the authors and not necessarily those of the consortium.

section 3 how the framework can be applied to integrate triggers in deductive databases, and in 4 we give a precise definition for the trigger processing based on our framework. In section 5 we present an architecture for the implementation. Finally, we compare our approach to related work in section 6, and present some conclusions in section 7.

2 The Framework

A trigger is a general mechanism for automatically executing actions. Most kind of trigger specifications found in the literature consist of three parts, an event specification part, a condition specification part, and an action specification part. Sometimes either the event or the condition specification may be omitted.

In the event specification it is described which event occurrences will cause the trigger to be processed. The condition is a formula expressed in the database query language. The actions are restricted to those statements which are supported by the underlying database system and will be executed in case the event occurred and the condition was satisfied.

In the framework we first focus on the event specification part of the triggers. When placing the trigger definitions in the context of deductive databases, we will define the specific event, condition and action language (section 3), and the trigger processing (section 4) which uses the framework introduced so far.

2.1 Events and Triggers

Informally, an event is a happening of interest; it may come from different sources, e.g. the update of some data in a database system, the signaling of an alarm in a monitoring system, or a clock signal from a timer. Characteristic for an event is, that it happens at a point in time. This event occurrence relates a point in time to an event.

In the literature the term event itself is used rather informal; it is sometimes used to denote a set of happenings, sometimes a single happening, or even to refer to what we call an event occurrence.

We illustrate these three kinds of 'events' by examples in a database context:

> $+$ *employee(X)*[2] denotes a set of events, i.e. all those events that insert a tuple into the relation employee; $+$ *employee(john)* denotes a single concrete event; and $+$ *employee(john) at 12:15* denotes the occurrence of the concrete event $+$ *employee(john)* at time *12:15*.

In this paper we will use the term *event* to refer to a single concrete event. The term *abstract event*[3] will be used to refer to sets of concrete events. Finally, the term *event occurrence* will be used to refer to the occurrence of a concrete event at a point in time.

In the remainder we will formalize these notions. We start by introducing the notion of *abstract events*. Let E, be a set of events. We define the set AE of abstract events as the powerset of E: $AE = 2^E$.

---

[2] Here '+' denotes the insertion of data.

[3] Note that our notion of 'abstract event' differs from proposals where 'abstract events' describe events signaled by external systems.

So, an abstract event is a set of events. The abstract event $+employee(X)$ for example describes the set of events $E = \{+\text{employee}(X) \mid X \in D\}$ where D is a set of values (a domain). Given an event e, we can infer (by membership) to which abstract event ae it belongs.

For a given set of events, we want to allow only event specifications that specify elements of the corresponding set of abstract events. So, given a set E of events, let AE be the set of abstract events corresponding to E. A set ES of event specifications is said to *correspond to* E if there exists a mapping $I_{abs} : ES \rightarrow AE$.

Now we can define the notion of trigger. Given a set E of events, a set CS of condition specifications and a set AS of action specifications. Let ES be a set of corresponding event specifications, then we define a trigger[4] as a 3-tuple (es, cs, as), where $es \in ES$, $cs \in CS$ and $as \in AS$.

Note that in the context of the framework we abstract from the specific form of events, conditions and actions. We will just assume the existence of languages L_e, L_c and L_a to specify events, conditions and actions respectively. Further note that given a trigger specification (es, cs, as) we obtain the abstract event by applying I_{abs} to es.

2.2 Event Occurrences and Triggers

Whereas the above section deals with the 'static' part of trigger definition, this section deals with the 'dynamic' part of trigger processing. Trigger processing is concerned with the selection and 'firing' of relevant triggers based on the occurrence of events. Here 'firing' or 'activating' a trigger means executing the action of a trigger.

We will first introduce the notion of event occurrences, and then discuss the selection of triggers based on event occurrences.

2.2.1 Event Occurrences

Events 'happen' at a point in time. This is the event occurrence. An important aspect of event occurrences are that they are ordered due to the ordering of points in time.

Let E by a set of events and let T be a set with total order $<_T$[5]. Then, we define the set EO of event occurrences as $\{ e@t \mid e \in E, t \in T \}$.

Informally, event occurrences link events to points in time, and thus define an order on events. So, for example, an event occurrence $+employee(john)@t_1$ can be interpreted as: the event $+employee(john)$ happened at the discrete point in time t_1.

2.2.2 Relation between Triggers and Event Occurrences

For a given set of triggers and a set of event occurrences we want to define the set of triggers relevant to the event occurrences. Informally, a trigger and an event occurrence are related when the event occurrence is described by the event specification of that trigger.

---

[4]One might argue that we should use the term 'trigger specification', however we prefer to use the shorthand 'trigger'.

[5]Think of T as a chain of points in time.

An event occurrence $eo = e@t$ and a trigger $tr = (es, cs, as)$ are *related* iff $e \in I_{abs}(es)$. We write $rel(tr, eo)$.

So, given a set of triggers TR and a set of event occurrences EO, we define the set of related *event-occurrence trigger pairs* as

$Pairs_{EO,TR} = \{ (eo,tr) \mid eo \in EO, tr \in TR, rel(tr,eo)\}$.

2.3 Composing Events

The events introduced so far are called 'primitive' events. In order to extend the expressive power of event specifications we will now introduce 'composite' events, and extend our framework for these.

A composite event is defined as one of the following:

- if e is an event, than e is a composite event;

- if ce_1 and ce_2 are composite events, then $ce_1 \& ce_2$, $ce_1|ce_2$ and $ce_1 \lhd ce_2$ are composite events.

The event constructors $\&$, $|$, $\lhd$ stand for *and*, *or* and *before* respectively.

Let CE, be a set of composite events. Then, we define the set ACE of abstract composite events as the powerset of CE: $ACE = 2^{CE}$.

Let CE by a set of composite events and let T be a set with total order $<_T$. Then, we define the set of composite event occurrences as $\{ ce@t \mid ce \in CE, t \in T \}$.

We extend our trigger specification in order to allow composite event specifications. So a trigger is now (ces,cs,as), where *ces* is a composite event specification that has an interpretation (I_{cabs}) in terms of an abstract composite event.

Again we are interested how composite event occurrences and triggers are related. Since composite events are constructed from primitive events, the occurrence of composite events should be derived from the occurrence of primitive events. Intuitively, we define composite event occurrences as follows.

- The composite event $ce_1 \& ce_2$ occurred if both the composite events ce_1 and ce_2 occurred.

- The composite event $ce_1|ce_2$ occurred if either the composite event ce_1 or ce_2 occurred.

- The composite event $ce_1 \lhd ce_2$ occurred if the composite event $ce_1 \cdot$occurs before the composite event ce_2 occurred.

Let E be a set of events, CE a set of composite events based on E, EO a set of event occurrences based on E. Assume $ce, ce_1, ce_2 \in CE$, then we define the composite closure C^*_{EO} of EO as $\{ce@t \mid ce \in CE, EO \vdash ce@t\}$, where $\vdash$ is defined as

- $EO \vdash ce@t$ iff $ce@t \in EO$

- $EO \vdash ce_1 \& ce_2@max(t_1, t_2)$ iff $EO \vdash ce_1@t_1$ and $EO \vdash ce_2@t_2$

- $EO \vdash ce_1|ce_2@min(t_1, t_2)$ iff $EO \vdash ce_1@t_1$ and $EO \vdash ce_2@t_2$

- $EO \vdash ce_1|ce_2@t$ iff $EO \vdash ce_1@t$ or $EO \vdash ce_2@t$

- $EO \vdash ce_1 \lhd ce_2@t_2$ iff $EO \vdash ce_1@t_1$ and $EO \vdash ce_2@t_2$ and $t_1 <_T t_2$

Note that & and | are both commutative and associative, where $\lhd$ is not. That $\lhd$ is not associative is seen as follows. Let $t_1 < t_2 < t_3$, and let $EO = \{a@t_2, b@t_1, c@t_3\}$ be a set of event occurrences, then

- $(a@t_2 \lhd b@t_1) \lhd c@t_3 \notin C_{EO}^*$ since $(a@t_2 \lhd b@t_1) \notin C_{EO}^*$

- $a@t_2 \lhd (b@t_1 \lhd c@t_3) = a@t_2 \lhd (b \lhd c)@t_3 = (a \lhd (b \lhd c))@t_3 \in C_{EO}^*$

2.3.1 Relation between Triggers and Composite Event Occurrences

Extending triggers to deal with composite events, means that we replace the event specification by a composite event specification. For the composite event specification we again assume an interpretation in terms of an abstract composite event. As a result the relation between triggers and composite event occurrences is similar to that between triggers and primitive event occurrences.

A composite event occurrence $ceo = ce@t$ and a trigger $tr = (ces, cs, as)$ are related iff $ce \in I_{cabs}(ces)$. We write $rel(tr, ceo)$.

So, given a set of triggers TR and a set of composite event occurrences C_{EO}^*, we define the set of related *composite event-occurrence trigger pairs* as

$Pairs_{C_{EO}^*, TR} = \{ (ceo, tr) \mid ceo \in C_{EO}^*, tr \in TR, rel(tr, ceo) \}$.

Notice that C_{EO}^* is infinite, however for a specific finite set of triggers with finite composite operator applications, we will not construct C_{EO}^*, but use $\vdash$ on EO directly.

3 Triggers in Deductive Databases

So far, we considered only the event specification part of triggers and we abstracted from the actual events. Also, we abstracted from the condition and action specification part. In this section we apply the framework to deductive databases. We do this by taking a deductive database as a starting point and define conditions, events and actions based on this.

If p is a predicate symbol and c_i are constants, $p(c_1, ..., c_n)$ is a fact. We call a predicate defined by facts a *base predicate*, a predicate defined by rules (see 3.2) a *virtual predicate*. A *deductive database* DDB consists of a (finite) set of base predicates (the *extensional database*), and a (finite) set of virtual predicates, defined by rules (the *intensional database*). The language used to define the intensional database is also used to query the database. For a deductive database DDB a minimal model can be constructed as defined in [1].

We will use capital letters to denote variables, small letters to denote constants.

3.1 Events

For predicates p_i in our database update operations exist to add (resp. remove) facts to (resp. from) p_i. We will use $+$ to denote the addition operator, and $-$ to denote the deletion operator.

For a deductive database and a (finite) number of predicates p_i, $1 \leq i \leq n$, we now define an event specification as one of the following:

- The insertion operation on a predicate p_i: $+p_i(X_1, ..., X_k)$ where k denotes the number of arguments of predicate p_i. X_j, $1 \leq j \leq k$, may be a variable or a constant.

- The deletion operation on a predicate p_i: $-p_i(X_1, ..., X_k)$ where k denotes the number of arguments of predicate p_i, X_j, $1 \leq j \leq k$, a variable or a constant.

- The composition of the above (primitive) event specifications using the operators defined in section 2.3. Variables will range over the complete composite event specification of a trigger and are considered to be universally quantified.

Note that this event specification syntax may be extended in order to grasp system generated events, external events, and so on.

In order to link our event specifications to abstract events in the framework, we have to specify the set of events and the mapping I_{cabs}. For a deductive database with predicates $p_1, ..., p_n$ and a domain D, we give the following definitions.

The set of events E is defined as
$E = \{+p_i(V_1, ..., V_k), -p_i(V_1, ..., V_k) | V_j \in D, 1 \leq j \leq k\}$. For a (composite) event specification $CES(X_1, ..., X_l)$ where the $X_j, 1 \leq j \leq l$, denote the variables of the event specification, the interpretation I_{cabs} is defined as
$I_{cabs}(CES(X_1, ..., X_l)) = \{CES(V_1, ..., V_l) | V_j \in D, 1 \leq j \leq l\}$. To illustrate these definitions, assume a database with predicates emp/1 and student/1, and a domain D = {john, james, mary}. Then

> E = {+emp(john), +emp(james), +emp(mary), -emp(john), -emp(james),
> -emp(mary), +student(john), +student(james), +student(mary),
> -student(john), -student(james), -student(mary)}.

For an event specification $'+emp(X) \lhd -student(X)'$ I_{cabs} is defined as
$I_{cabs}(+emp(X) \lhd -student(X)) =$
> {+emp(john) $\lhd$ -student(john), +emp(james) $\lhd$ -student(james),
> +emp(mary) $\lhd$ -student(mary)}.

3.2 Condition

For the declarative specification of the condition we will use Datalog ([6]), a database query language based on the logic programming paradigm.

A Datalog rule is of the form $L \leftarrow L_1, ..., L_n$, n≥1, where L is an atom and each L_i is a literal (an atom or a negated atom) of the form $p_i(t_1, ..., t_k)$ where p_i are predicate symbols and the t_k are either constants or variables (terms). The left hand side is called the *head* of the rule, the right hand side the *body* of the rule.

Several extensions to Datalog exist; we restrict ourselves to Datalog extended with negation and built-in predicates for the comparison of terms. Definitions which are allowed for the body of a Datalog rule may be used for the definition of conditions of triggers. Thus, a *condition specification* is of the form: "$L_1, ..., L_n$" where each $L_k, 1 \leq k \leq n$, is a literal.

The evaluation of the condition against some database state results in 'true' and returns values satisfying the condition, or in 'false'. In order to guarantee that the number of facts which can be derived for a condition are finite, we impose the usual safety conditions: a) facts in the database have to be ground; b) variables which occur in the head of a rule also have to occur in the body of the rule in a positive literal; and c) variables which occur in negated literals have to occur at least once in a positive literal.

3.3 Actions

For the framework we also need to assume a language to specify actions, and an execution of actions against some database state. As we chose a deductive database environment, the actions allowed in this environment will also be allowed as actions of triggers, e.g. database operations like data definition and data manipulation commands, or the rollback command.

In our framework the *action specification* of a trigger consists of a list of actions A_i: "$[A_1, ..., A_n]$".

3.4 Syntax

So far we presented specific languages for event, condition and action specification, and assumed a trigger to be of the form (Event-Spec, Condition-Spec, Action-Spec). Now we are interested in the way these specifications can be linked, and in the way variables can be passed from one to the other. The scope of variables used within the event, condition or action specification is the full trigger. This allows to link the event, condition and action specification in terms of variables and is the basis for a unification of variables at run-time. In the remainder we will use a more readable syntax: *Trigger_name [,Priority]: ON Event-Spec*
IF Condition-Spec DO Action-Spec. *Trigger_name* is the name of the trigger. Optionally priorities can be assigned to triggers. *Priority* is a list with elements of the form $T_i > T_j$, where T_i and T_j are trigger names, indicating that trigger T_i has priority over trigger T_j. If no priorities are given, triggers are activated randomly.

4 Trigger Processing

While for trigger definition abstract and concrete events are relevant, for trigger processing event occurrences are important. Trigger processing determines how event occurrences, conditions, and actions interact. It determines when the condition is checked after the event occurred, and when the action is executed after the condition was checked. Processing may be invoked when just one or several events occur. Some systems invoke trigger processing after single events (*tuple-oriented trigger processing*), some after a set of events (*set-oriented trigger processing*). In this paper we will focus on set-oriented trigger processing.

Informally, a trigger is activated, if the event occurred, and the condition is satisfied. However, many variations are possible for trigger processing ([3]).

We divide trigger processing into two phases. In a first phase the composite event detection, the trigger selection and the condition check are performed. Composite event detection and trigger selection are based on the set of event occurrences, the given set of triggers, and the time interval of a transaction (see 4.1). For the selected event-occurrence trigger pairs the respective conditions are checked. In a second phase the trigger activation is performed, based on the priorities between triggers, and the values returned from the condition check. Trigger activation may produce further events which have to be processed again.

4.1   Transactions

Within database systems, operations may be grouped into transactions which are considered as atomic units, for concurrency and recovery purposes. Atomicity means that either all operations in a transaction are executed or none of them. Applying a transaction to a database state defines a new database state. Transactions can commit or abort, in the latter case this means undoing all its effects.

Trigger processing with respect to transactions varies across active database system proposals, and one can basically distinguish between:

- Immediate processing. Triggers are processed immediately after the event occurred (tuple-oriented);

- Deferred processing. Triggers are processed at the end of the transaction where the events occurred (set-oriented) and the transaction is extended by actions of triggers;

- Separate processing. Triggers are processed at the end of the transaction where the events occurred (set-oriented) and new transactions are started for actions of triggers.

Different modes can be chosen for the coupling between the occurrence of the event and the check of the condition (e.g. immediate: as soon as the event occurs the condition is checked), and for the coupling of the satisfaction of this condition and the execution of the respective action (e.g. separate: execute the action at the end of the current transaction in a separate transaction).

In the case of deferred trigger processing, trigger processing is linked to the time interval of a transaction. Starting with a database state s_0, a transaction t defines a database state s_1. Trigger processing starts at transaction commit time t_c of transaction t. Executing the actions of triggers may extend transaction t up to a time t_e, $t_e > t_c$, define a new database state s_2, and add further events which require trigger processing again. Trigger processing will terminate in a state s_n when no new events occur, or no more conditions are satisfied. Now transaction t can finally commit. The database state s_0 will be restored if one of the trigger actions is the rollback command in order to abort the transaction.

4.2   The Trigger Selection

In the framework trigger selection takes into account a set of event occurrences EO and a set of triggers TR. Now we also introduce a time interval I according to which the trigger selection should take place. Introducing the time interval implies that only events which 'happened' during this time interval will be taken into account, and only the corresponding triggers will be activated.

Then, for a time interval $I = [t_s, t_e]$, and set of event occurrences EO, the set EO_I of event occurrences restricted to that interval is { e@t | e@t $\in$ EO, $t_s \leq t \leq t_e$}. For a set of triggers TR, the trigger selection returns a *set of time-interval related event-occurrence trigger pairs*

$Pairs_{EO_I,TR} = \{$ (eo,tr) | eo $\in EO_I$, rel(tr,eo) $\}$.

Then for a transaction t from t_s to t_c the time interval to be considered is $I = [t_s, t_c]$. All the event occurrences are processed, one after the other, according to the above definition, to determine the relevant set of event-occurrence trigger pairs.

Note that the same trigger might be selected several times. First, due to the occurrence of the same event at several points in time during the interval, and second, due to the multiple selection of the same trigger from different events. In the framework both cases can be determined by the set $Pairs_{EO_I,TR}$.

For the first case, consider $e@t_i$ and $e@t_j$, $i \neq j$. If e is related to the event specification of a trigger tr, we will select both $(e@t_i, tr)$ and $(e@t_j, tr)$ in $Pairs_{EO_I,TR}$. If we choose to ignore occurrences of the same event, we may simply filter out these event occurrences from the set of event occurrences before determining $Pairs_{EO_I,TR}$. In the second case, we would have $(e@t_i, tr)$ and $(f@t_j, tr)$ in $Pairs_{EO_I,TR}$, for events e and f.

4.2.1 Composite Events and Trigger Selection

Based on the set of (primitive) event occurrences EO, the set of triggers TR, and the time interval, the set of composite event occurrences has to be determined as well. Therefore, if composite event specifications are given for trigger definitions, the respective composite event occurrences C_{EO}^* are determined according to the definitions in 2.3.

Then, given the set of composite event occurrences C_{EO}^*, the set of triggers TR, and a time interval $I = [t_s, t_e]$, we define the *set of time-interval related composite event-occurrence trigger pairs* as

$Pairs_{C_{EO_I}^*,TR} = \{$ (ce@t,tr) | ce@t $\in C_{EO_I}^*$, tr $\in$ TR, rel(tr,ce@t) $\}$.

4.3 The Condition Check

For the triggers selected in the trigger selection, we perform a (partial) instantiation of the respective conditions by unifying variables of the condition specification with the respective values according to the event occurrence. Recall that an event specification is an expression using variables, and that the scope of a variable is the full trigger. An event is a ground instance which provides bindings for the condition and action specification.

Trigger selection returns a set of time-interval related event-occurrence trigger pairs $Pairs_{EO_I,TR}$. Assume a trigger $T \in$ TR is of the form
$T :$ ON $E(X_1, ..., X_m)$ IF $C(X_1, ..., X_k, Y_1, ..., Y_n)$ DO $A(X_j, ..., X_l, Y_1, ..., Y_n)$.
Where $1 \leq i \leq k \leq j \leq l \leq m$, and E, C, and A represent the event, condition, and action specification, and $X_1, ..., X_m$ the set of variables occurring

in the event specification[6], and $Y_1, ..., Y_n$ the set of variables occurring in the condition specification but not in the event specification.

Then the partial instantiation which is performed by taking the event occurrence eo from an event-occurrence trigger pair (eo, T) and unifying variables in condition (and potentially action) specification returns a trigger of the form

$$T : \text{ON } E(v_1, ..., v_m) \text{ IF } C(v_1, ..., v_k, Y_1, ..., Y_n) \text{ DO } A(v_j, ..., v_l, Y_1, ..., Y_n)$$

with $v_1, ..., v_m$ constants.

Now the condition is passed to the evaluator which returns either $TRUE$, together with values satisfying the condition, or $FALSE$:

$$eval(C(v_1, ..., v_k, Y_1, ..., Y_n)) = (\{(TRUE, (w_{j1}, ..., w_{jn}))\} \vee FALSE).$$

Where $1 \leq j \leq s$, and s indicates the (finite) number of solution tuples which were found.

We are interested only in those conditions (and the respective triggers) which are satisfied, i.e. where the evaluation returned $TRUE$, together with values $w_{j1}, ..., w_{jn}$. Thus, for each event-occurrence trigger pair the condition check returns a set of tuples $\{(TRUE, (w_{j1}, ..., w_{jn}))\}$, j=1 to s. Each of the tuples satisfies the condition. This leads for an event-occurrence trigger pair (eo, T) to a (finite) set of to 3-tuples

$$\{(eo, T, (TRUE, (w_{11}, ..., w_{1n}))), ..., (eo, T, (TRUE, (w_{s1}, ..., w_{sn})))\}$$

where each $w_{j1}, ..., w_{jn}$, j=1 to s, satisfies the condition of T in the current database state.

4.4 The Trigger Activation

Informally, we take the answers produced in the condition check, instantiate the action part, and execute the actions. Formally, each 3-tuple $(eo, T, (T, (w_{g1}, ..., w_{gn})))$, $1 \leq g \leq s$, leads to the execution of the respective actions for T. Taking the answers produced in the condition check, we can now fully instantiate the trigger to:

$$T_i : \text{ON } E(v_1, ..., v_m) \text{ IF } C(v_i, ..., v_k, w_1, ..., w_n) \text{ DO } A(v_j, ..., v_l, w_{g1}, ..., w_{gn}).$$

The list of actions specified in A can be executed for the set of values which satisfied the condition.

Note that we execute in this stage for all the trigger whose conditions are satisfied, the respective actions, by taking into account the priorities between triggers, and that each (list of) action(s) of a trigger is executed for each set of values satisfying the respective condition.

4.5 A Simple Example

Assume a set of triggers TR

$T_1, [T_1 > T_3]$:
ON + emp(Name)
IF responsibility(Name, Project), works_on(Project, Emp)
DO [+ manages(Name, Emp, Project)].
T_2: ON - room(301, 'Miller')[7] IF ... DO ...

---

[6]Note that not all the variables of the event specification need to occur both in condition and action specification.

[7]Note that within the event specification of a trigger, also concrete events may be specified, in order to grasp a particular event.

T_3:
ON + emp(Name) $\lhd$ -student(Name)
IF job(Name, permanent) DO [roll_back].

From this we deduce the set of events E being:
{+emp(X),-emp(X),+student(X),-student(X),+room(X,Y),-room(X,Y) | X $\in$
NAME, Y $\in$ ROOM }, where NAME is {'Moore','Jones',...} and ROOM is
{301,...}.

Further, assume a set of event occurrences
EO = { $+emp('Moore')@t_1, +emp('Jones')@t_6, -student('Jones')@t_7$ }
and a transaction with related time interval $I = [t_2, t_8]$.

So EO_I is { $+emp('Jones')@t_6, -student('Jones')@t_7$ }

Based on E and EO_I we determine $C^*_{EO_I}$:

$\{+emp('Jones')@t_6, -student('Jones')@t_7,$
$\quad +emp('Jones')\& -student('Jones')@t_7, ...$
$\quad +emp('Jones')| -student('Jones')@t_6, ...$
$\quad +emp('Jones') \lhd -student('Jones')@t_7, ...\}$

Trigger selection is performed, for the time interval $I = [t_2, t_8]$, $C^*_{EO_I}$, and
the set of triggers TR. This results in the following event-occurrence trigger
pairs: $Pairs_{C^*_{EO_I}, TR} =$

{ $(+emp('Jones')@t_6, T_1), ((+emp('Jones') \lhd -student('Jones'))@t_7, T_3)$ }.

Thus trigger selection returns trigger T_1 and T_3.

The condition check has to be performed for each condition related to an
event-occurrence trigger pair, leading to the evaluation of
$responsibility('Jones', Project), works\_on(Project, Emp)$, and
$job('Jones', permanent)$.

Assume the results to be $\{(TRUE, (databases, 'Miller')),$
$(TRUE, (databases, 'Small')), (TRUE, (databases, 'King'))\}$,
$\{(TRUE, \emptyset)\}$, i.e. the 3-tuples

$(+emp('Jones')@t_6, T_1, (T, (databases, 'Miller'))),$
$(+emp('Jones')@t_6, T_1, (T, (databases, 'Small'))),$
$(+emp('Jones')@t_6, T_1, (T, (databases, 'King'))),$
$((+emp('Jones') \lhd -student('Jones'))@t_7, T_3, (T, \emptyset)).$

Then the actions to be executed are:

+ manages('Jones', 'Miller', databases).
+ manages('Jones', 'Small', databases).
+ manages('Jones', 'King', databases).
roll_back

5 Architecture

In this section we outline the architectural components corresponding to our
framework. We distinguish a trigger manager, an event detector, a condition
evaluator, a trigger compiler, and a transaction manager.

The **transaction manager** is supposed to be part of the underlying deductive database system, responsible for transaction management, but also for the

execution of statements within a transaction. The transaction manager also acts as an event generator and reports events to the event detector.

The **trigger manager** is responsible for the processing of the triggers, after a set of event occurrences, and the time interval of a transaction. Therefore it interacts with the event detector, the condition evaluator and the transaction handler. The main tasks of the trigger manager are the trigger selection (based on primitive and composite event occurrences) and the determination of the set of event-occurrence trigger pairs, the scheduling of the condition check and the trigger activation.

At trigger definition time the trigger manager interacts with the event detector and the trigger compiler.

At run-time the trigger manager is informed by the transaction manager when to start trigger processing. The trigger manager consults the event detector for event occurrences and performs the trigger selection. For each of the selected event-occurrence trigger pairs the respective trigger condition is (partially) instantiated, the condition evaluator is called, and the result is stored. Finally the trigger manager schedules trigger activation for each 3-tuple (event-occurrence, trigger, values). The trigger with the highest priority is activated first (by passing the compiled code of the actions to the transaction manager). Then the next trigger is activated, until none is left.

The **event detector** is informed by the trigger manager about the event specification (at trigger definition time). This enables the event detector to filter out, at run-time, event occurrences which are not relevant for trigger processing. In order to detect composite event occurrences finite automata ([11]) and Petri Nets ([10]) were proposed.

At run-time the transaction manager (acting as event generator) reports event occurrences to the event detector. The event detector records relevant events (temporarily).

The **condition evaluator** is called by the trigger manager, to evaluate a set of conditions (perform the 'condition check'). The task of the condition evaluator is to determine which conditions are satisfied, and to return the respective values. The condition evaluator is the standard rule evaluator of the underlying deductive database system, as the condition is expressed declaratively in safe (recursive) Datalog, which is also the query language of the deductive database system. In order to efficiently check conditions a number of dedicated methods exist. In HiPAC incremental relational operators are proposed [7], in Ariel an optimization of the Rete network ([9]) is adapted for the database context ([13]).

The task of the **trigger compiler** is to compile the condition of a trigger to a form which can be executed by the rule evaluator, and to compile the action of a trigger to a form which can be executed by the transaction manager. It is called from the trigger manager.

6 Related Work

As has been mentioned in the introduction, a lot of specific active database systems have been developed, however, less effort has been taken in coming up with a precise framework for event and trigger processing.

However, in terms of formalizing event processing, [12] and [11] propose a language for specifying basic and composite events. They also present how to detect (composite) events using finite automata, but do not consider conditions and actions of triggers. Their notion of event history is similar to our notion of a set of event occurrences. However, while they formalize the detection of events, we formalize the trigger processing as well. They present an elaborate event language, while we restrict ourselves first to three constructors for composite events.

Also [14] propose a framework for supporting triggers in the context of object-oriented databases, and present a categorization of events into database access events and external events. Database access events are further distinguished according whether they involve a tuple, a relation, several relations, or the entire database. Based on this categorization performance estimations are given, but they do not formalize event and trigger processing as we do. Further, they consider an object-oriented database while we are in a deductive database environment.

In terms of a precise definition of trigger processing, [17] and [7] (HiPAC) present an execution model that is based on the assignment of transactions for the condition check and the execution of actions. A variety of coupling modes allow to specify how condition check and action execution are embedded into database transaction handling. Again an event algebra is proposed and a classification of events into primitive and composite events. They also have the notion of an event detector which is responsible for detecting a predefined class of events. However, while they precise trigger processing for an object-oriented database, we are in a deductive database environment. While their execution model is based on a nested transaction model, and an assignment of condition check and action execution to transactions (based on the user-defined coupling modes), we base trigger processing on the variable passing between event, condition and action.

7   Conclusions and Future Work

In this paper we presented a precise framework for event and trigger processing, and used it to support triggers in a deductive database environment. In this context we also presented an architecture, to guide the implementation. The motivation for this work was twofold. First we felt that we should investigate in a precise framework to support triggers, instead of offering yet another active database system only. Second we felt that the support of triggers in the context of a deductive database could benefit from the expressiveness deductive databases offer for the declarative definition of the trigger condition, in terms of base as well as virtual predicates. Further the combination of declarativity (in the condition specification) and procedurality (in the action specification) within a trigger might open new application areas for deductive databases.

However, our framework can also be used for an integration of triggers into a relational database system, as we abstracted from specific languages.

We also intend to investigate in the application of this framework to a deductive and object-oriented database (DOOD), integrating the concept of objects, classes and inheritance. We have to investigate in how far the framework has to be extended to fulfill this purpose. For example, in the event specification we have to take into account method invocations, the creation of objects, and so on. We also have to formalize the inheritance of events.

Another extension we have in mind is the support of implicit events, i.e. to allow the specification of triggers without explicitly giving an event specification (see RDL1 [15] , Ariel [13]) . This frees the user from thinking about events and event specifications, and allows to concentrate on the declarative condition which has to be satisfied, in order to make the action be executed. Triggers consisting only of condition and action specification seem more suitable for the integration into a deductive database, as they make events implicit, just as a declarative database query language makes database navigation implicit. The events would then be derived implicitly by the system; then the same processing is applied as for explicitly specified events, and our framework can be adopted again. For the derivation of implicit events, we think of using a technology developed for integrity checking and materialized view maintenance in the context of the EKS deductive database system ([19], [2]).

Another topic which requires further investigation are time events. If we take time events into account we have to apply an immediate mode for trigger processing, to guarantee (some kind of) real-time response.

References

[1] K.R. Apt, H.A. Blair, and A. Walker. *Towards a Theory of Declarative Knowledge*, pages 89–148. Morgan Kaufmann Pub.Inc., 1988.

[2] P. Bayer. Update Propagation for Integrity Checking, Materialized View Maintenance and Production Rule Triggering. TR-92-10, ECRC, February 1992.

[3] P. Bayer State-Of-The-Art Report on Reactive Processing in Databases and Artificial Intelligence. *The Knowledge Engineering Review*, 8(2), 1993.

[4] C. Beeri and T. Milo. A Model for Active Object Oriented Database. In Camps Lohman, Sernadas, editor, *Proc. of the 17th VLDB Conference*, pages 337–349, Barcelona, September 1991.

[5] Y. Caseau. An Object-Oriented Deductive Language. *Annals of Mathematics and Artificial Intelligence*, 3, 1991.

[6] S. Ceri, G. Gottlob, and L. Tanca. What You Always Wanted to Know About Datalog (And Never Dared to Ask). *IEEE Transactions on Knowledge and Data Engineering*, 1(1):146–166, March 1989.

[7] S. Chakravarthy. Rule Management and Evaluation: An Active DBMS Perspective. *SIGMOD REC., Special issue on Rule Management and Processing in Expert Database Systems*, 18(3), September 1989.

[8] O. Diaz, N. Paton, and P. Gray. Rule Management in Object Oriented Databases: A Uniform Approach. In Camps Lohman, Sernadas, editor, *Proc. of the 17th VLDB Conference*, pages 317–326, Barcelona, September 1991.

[9] C.L. Forgy. Rete: A Fast Algorithm for the Many Pattern/Many Object Pattern Match Problem. *Artificial Intelligence (19)*, 1982.

[10] S. Gatziu and K.R. Dittrich. SAMOS: An Active Object-Oriented Database System. *Special Issue On Active Databases, Bulletin of the Technical Committee on Data Engineering*, 15(1-4), 1992.

[11] N.H. Gehani, H.V. Jagadish, and O. Shmueli. Composite Event Specification in Active Databases: Model and Implementation. In *Proc. of the 18th Int. Conf. on Very Large Databases*, Vancouver, Canada, August 1992.

[12] N.H. Gehani, H.V. Jagadish, and O. Shmueli. Event Specification in an Active Object-Oriented Database. In *Proc. of the ACM SIGMOD Int. Conf. on Management of Data*, San Diego, California, June 1992.

[13] E.N. Hanson. Rule Condition Testing and Action Execution in Ariel. In *Proc. of the ACM SIGMOD Int. Conf. on Management of Data*, San Diego, California, June 1992.

[14] W. Kim, Y. Lee, and J. Seo. A Framework For Supporting Triggers in Object-Oriented Database Systems. *Int. Journal of Intelligent and Cooperative Information Systems*, 1(1):127–143, 1992.

[15] G. Kiernan, C. Maindreville, and E. Simon. Making Deductive Database a Practical Technology: a step forward. In H. Garcia-Molina and H.V. Jagadish, editors, *Proc. of the ACM Conference on the Management of Data (SIGMOD)*, pages 237–246, Atlantic City, May 1990.

[16] C. Lin, T. Sellis, and L. Raschid. Implementing Large Production Systems in a DBMS Environment: Concepts and Algorithms. In H. Larson H. Boral, editor, *Int. Conf. on Management of Data*, pages 404–412, Chicago, June 1988.

[17] D. R. McCarthy and U. Dayal. The Architecture Of An Active Data Base Management System. In *Proc. of the ACM SIGMOD Conference on Management of Data*, pages 215–224, Portland, Oregon, June 1989.

[18] M. Stonebraker and A. Jhingran. On Rules, Procedures, Caching and Views in Data Base Systems. In H. Garcia-Molina and H.V. Jagadish, editors, *Proc. of the ACM Conference on the Management of Data (SIGMOD)*, pages 281–290, Atlantic City, May 1990.

[19] L. Vieille, P. Bayer, V. Küchenhoff, and A. Lefebvre. EKS-V1: A User Guide. TR-KB-33, revised, ECRC, September 1991.

[20] J. Widom, R. J. Cochrane, and B. G. Lindsay. Implementing Set-Oriented Production Rules as an Extension to Starburst. In Camps Lohman, Sernadas, editor, *Proc. of the 17th VLDB Conference*, pages 275–285, Barcelona, September 1991.

[21] J. Widom and S.J. Finkelstein. Set-Oriented Production Rules in Relational Database Systems. *ACM Transactions on Database Systems*, pages 259–270, 1990.

[22] Y. Zhou and M. Hsu. A Theory for Rule Triggering Systems. In F. Bancilhon C. Thanos and Tsichritzis, editors, *Proceedings of the 2nd International Conference on Extending Database Technology (EDBT 90)*, pages 407–421, Venice, Italy, March 1990.

Integrity Constraints

A Review of Repairing Techniques for Integrity Maintenance

Piero Fraternali, Stefano Paraboschi

Dipartimento di Elettronica e Informazione

Politecnico di Milano

P.zza Leonardo da Vinci 32

20133 Milano - Italy

e-mail: {fraterna,parabosc}@ipmel2.elet.polimi.it *

Abstract

In this paper we review the research on integrity enforcement in database systems. Integrity enforcement is the task of ensuring that a user transaction applied to a legal database state leads to a new state which is also legal. The common rationale of the research in this area is to centralize the management of data integrity, by extracting this task from application programs and by bringing it into an ad-hoc component, which may be incorporated into the DBMS.

1 Introduction

Integrity constraints are a declarative specification of the conditions that a database state (or a sequence of states) must satisfy in order to be legal.

Today's DBMS technology offers a limited support to the automated verification of constraint satisfaction and their enforcement. Typically, only a limited class of constraints, like keys and referential integrity, are dealt with by DBMSs. The remaining ones must be managed directly by application programs, so that the integrity criteria become scattered and difficult to maintain. Also the response given by DBMSs to constraint violations, i.e., rollback of the transaction, is unsatisfactory; there may be cases in which the violation can be safely repaired and the transaction committed.

Very recently, a novel discipline has emerged in the area of database research, that aims at developing appropriate technological support to integrity constraint maintenance.

This discipline is rooted in the research about database dependencies and constraint verification, but has its major focus on guaranteeing that faulty user's transactions can be corrected to produce a final state that is consistent and respects the intended semantics of the original transaction.

*This work has been partially supported by ESPRIT Project n. 6333 IDEA and by Progetto Finalizzato LOGIDATA+ of C.N.R. (Italian National Research Institute)

This goal requires the capability of *enforcing* constraints, either by modifying the original transaction or by post-processing it.

In this paper we review the research effort in this area and compare different approaches to integrity enforcement. Although the contributions may differ in many aspects, e.g., in the underlying data model or in the repair technique, they exhibit the common rationale of providing an ad-hoc support to the task of integrity maintenance, so that transaction designers may separate application logic from data integrity.

The structure of the paper is the following: in Section 2, we introduce the problem of integrity enforcement in general; Section 3 illustrates the cultural roots of the research in this field, by relating it to other areas of database research; in Section 4 we describe several recent contributions to integrity enforcement, and compare them with respect to a number of characterizing features.

2   Problem Statement

The general problem considered in this paper is represented in Fig. 1.

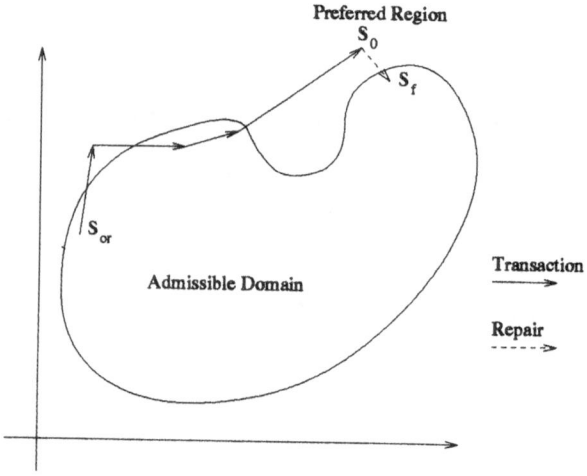

Figure 1: A pictorial view of the integrity enforcement problem

We represent a database state as a point in an n-dimensional space; integrity constraints partition the space of possible states into two distinct regions, an "admissible" region (in which all constraints hold) and a "forbidden" region (in which one or more constraints are violated). All transactions apply to an initial legal state; faulty transactions lead to a forbidden state.

The traditional response of a DBMS to this event is to rollback the transaction; an alternative approach is that of substituting the original transaction T with a new transaction T', which is "consistent" with T and brings the database into a correct state.

T' may be the result of a compile-time modification of T or the result of a run-time activity performed by the DBMS to extend T. In any case, we call the difference between T' and T *repairing action*.

An additional requirement is that the final state reached by repairing a faulty transaction be chosen within a subspace of states as compliant as possible to the original intention of the transaction supplier. The state resulting from the composition of the transaction and the repairing action should therefore belong to the intersection of the admissible region and the region describing the preferences of the transaction supplier.

3   Related Work

Integrity constraint enforcement has been recently recognized as an autonomous discipline; its cultural roots can be traced back to at least three areas of database research, namely the works on dependencies, active databases and view updating.

Database dependencies are declarative expressions used to convey additional semantics of a database schema [1]. Integrity constraints are a particular case of dependencies that prescribe conditions for a database instance to be admissible. Most constraint languages are derived by formal notations, such as *tuple calculus* or *logic programming* [1, 2, 3, 4, 5, 6, 7]. A major distinction in the expressive power of constraints concerns their *static* or *dynamic* nature. Static constraints specify conditions that must be satisfied by a single database state [3, 5, 6, 7, 8, 9, 10, 11, 12]. Dynamic constraints allow expressing condition over time-ordered sequences of states [13]. A particular case is that of *transition* constraints [2, 14, 15, 16], that impose restrictions on pairs of states, the *before* and *after* state of a transaction.

A fundamental issue about integrity constraints is their verification; the purpose of constraint checking is to determine in advance database updating operations or transactions that are likely to violate constraints [6, 8, 11, 12] or to assess a database state to discover violations [2, 3, 13, 14, 17].

An application of constraints close to integrity enforcement is in transaction design systems [6, 11], where constraints are used to validate the design of database transactions, possibly by including into them additional code for constraint verification (pre- and post- conditions to transaction execution).

The technology of active databases provides a natural framework for implementing integrity enforcement through "reactive" repairing actions [8, 18]. Active databases couple data storing facilities and rule-based programming [19, 20, 21]. The predominant paradigm for active databases is that of ECA (*event-condition-action*) rules: rules are triggered by an event and their action is executed only if a condition is met [22]. Research in the field of active databases addresses the problems of giving database production systems a precise semantics [23] and formally investigates properties like termination, correctness and determinism of the computation [18, 24], which are also relevant in the context of rule-based integrity enforcement.

Another related issue is the so-called *view update problem*, i.e., the selection of a *translator* for insertion, deletion, or replacement operations performed on a view. A translator maps a view update to the base tables mentioned in the view definition [25, 26, 27, 28]. In general, such translation is not unique; when multiple translations are possible, the view update is semantically ambiguous. Classes of translators for different types of views and updating operations have been characterized in the literature according to their structural properties [25, 26, 27].

The integrity enforcement problem can be considered a special case of the view update problem, since constraints can be regarded as particular views over the database schema that must be kept empty. Thus, enforcing a constraint is analogous to deleting entries from a view, and translation techniques carry over from one problem to the other. The main difference is that, while semantic ambiguity is an undesired feature in the case of view updates, the existence of multiple choices for repairing constraints adds alternative solutions to the problem and is not necessarily bad.

4   Approaches to Integrity Enforcement

While the number of contributions in the areas of database dependencies and integrity checking is significant, far less work has been done on the specific topic of automatic repair of constraint violations [2, 3, 5, 7, 8, 16, 29, 30].

The described works, though aiming at the same goal, differ in a number of features:

- *Data model*: relational, deductive, object-oriented and deductive object-oriented (DOO) data models are all represented.

- *Constraint language*: the languages employed differ in the style and expressive power: SQL-like languages, full or restricted forms of first-order logic languages. Another distinction is among languages for static or transition constraints. In general, the more expressive the language, the less automated the support to integrity enforcement.

- *Repairing action language*: in principle, repairing actions are written in the same update language as user's transactions. In practice, besides the case in which repairing action design is completely manual, only elementary operations are supported, namely tuple or object insertion and deletion. Some contributions handle also finer granularity repairing actions that update tuples or objects.

- *Repair technique*: repairs can be performed by rewriting the original transaction at compile-time, by extending at run-time the faulty transaction with additional operations, by generating an independent transaction to be submitted after the faulty one, or by firing the execution of a set of autonomous production rules of an active database.

- *Time of repair*: repairs may be performed completely at run-time, completely at compile-time, or partly at run-time and partly at compile-time.

- *Alternative repairing actions*: for a faulty transaction there may be either a unique repairing action or a set of alternative repairs; in the latter case, techniques for evaluating the various solutions may be given.

- *Constraint and repairing action analysis*: the repair of one constraint may cause the violation of another constraint; in the worst case, conflicts among repairing actions may lead to non-termination or failure of repair. Different techniques to discover and/or prevent such situations are proposed.

In the following we first present the approaches based on the active database paradigm; then, we introduce other contributions that rely on different techniques.

Table 1 summarizes the reviewed works and their features.

4.1 Active rule-based repairing techniques

4.1.1 The approach of Ceri-Widom [8] and Ceri-Garzotto-Gottlob [2]

The work in [8] is a pioneering approach to the repair of faulty transactions in (active) relational databases, based on the generation of *repairing production rules*.

The main contribution is a technique for generating at compile-time Starburst production rules [21, 23] from the declarative specification of constraints.

Constraints are expressed through a declarative language, whose syntax extends SQL. Advanced features like aggregate functions and recursively defined constraints are allowed.

Once constraints have been declared, they can be translated into a set of ECA rules [22] that enforce them. Only one rule per constraint is permitted. Each rule has:

- An event part, containing a so-called *transition predicate*, that lists all the data manipulations potentially violating the constraint.

- A precondition: an arbitrary predicate which is true whenever the constraint is violated.

- An action: an arbitrary list of SQL statements whose execution may correct the constraint's violation.

A rule is triggered when any of its transition predicates is verified by some database modification occurred since the last firing of the rule; in addition, the rule's precondition must evaluate to true, denoting the existence of some actual constraint violation. In this case, the rule is executed, provided that no other rule with higher priority is also ready to fire.

Rule generation and analysis in [8] are only partially automated:

- Only the event and precondition part of rules are generated (in the form of *rule templates*); the action part of rules has to be added manually by the user.

- A lexical analysis of rules determines potential sequences of rules which can trigger each other indefinitely and cause non-termination. This information is embodied in a graph, called *Triggering Graph*: a directed cycle in the graph represents the potential for infinite triggering. Then, the user is responsible for taking appropriate actions to resolve cycles, e.g., by modifying the involved rules.

Ref(s)	Data Model	Constraint Type	Constraint Language	Repairing Action Language	Repairing Technique	Repair Time	Multiple Repairing Actions	Analysis	Worst Case Behavior
CW90 [8]	Relational	Static / Transition	Extended SQL	Extended SQL	ECA Rules	C/R time	No	Triggering graph	Manual correction of bad rules
CGG92 [2]	Relational	Static / Transition	Restricted 1st order (modal) logic	Insert / Delete	Run-time extension	C/R time	Yes	Not addressed	Not addressed
UKN92 [30]	DOO	Static	Restricted 1st order logic	Rich object update language	ECA Rules	C/R time	Yes	Triggering graph	Transaction abort
CFPT92 [29]	Relational	Static	Restricted domain relational calculus	Insert / Delete / Update	ECA Rules	C/R time	Yes	Triggering hypergraph + Problem solver	Transaction abort
STSW92 [16]	OO	Static / Transition	Function free 1st order logic	Insert / Delete / Update	Rewriting	Compile time	No	Not supported	C. A. = $fail$
Wu93 [7]	Deductive	Static	Function free 1st order logic	Insert / Delete	Rewriting	Run time	No	Not supported	Realization Failure
ML91 [3]	Deductive	Static	Function free 1st order logic	Insert / Delete	Run-time extension	Run time	Yes	Simulation of alternative C.A.	Transact. undo

Table 1: Comparison between the different approaches

Although the actual repair is done at run-time, most of the work to generate the appropriate repairing actions and to assess their termination is done at compile-time, which reduces the execution overhead of the repair.

A related work is that of [2], which is a preliminary attempt to perform constraint repair in a fully automated way, though in a limited context. Constraints are expressed in a logical language, similar to Domain Relational Calculus (with the addition of transition constraints expressed through the modal operators *insert* and *delete*). Transactions are defined in terms of a *Transaction Schema*, i.e., a sequence of operations described by their signature. The main contribution of this approach is to identify the subset of constraints potentially affected by a transaction schema. These are called *relevant constraints*. Then, a compile-time resolution technique is presented to obtain a simplified version of the relevant constraints that can be used both for constraint checking, i.e., to see if an actual transaction does produce violations, and for suggesting repairing actions.

At run-time, the identified repairing actions are instantiated based on the actual transaction and database state. The repair process is driven by constraint violations: repairing actions are executed to eliminate one violation at a time in an arbitrary order; if the repair of one constraint violates an already enforced one, the process fails and the user's transaction is rolled-back. However, the analysis of constraints and repairing actions to achieve an order of repair that prevents failure is not addressed.

4.1.2 The approach of Urban et al. [30]

The works in [6, 30, 31] delineate a framework for constraint analysis and enforcement in deductive, object-oriented databases (DOOD).

As in [8], the core issue is the transformation of a set of declaratively expressed constraints into a set of production rules, called Integrity Maintenance Production Rules (IMPRs), that are executed by an active DBMS to repair possible constraint violations before committing a user's transaction.

Constraints are conceptually divided into two classes: *inherent* constraints and *explicit* constraints: the former express restrictions due to the semantics of the data model, like inverse properties and disjoint restrictions; the latter are arbitrary properties to be satisfied by the database instance, that cannot be captured by schema restrictions.

Both kinds of constraints are expressed as clausal formulas of a first order logic language.

Repairing actions are encoded as ECA rules with a particular format: several condition-action pairs may be associated to a single triggering event.

Triggering events correspond to the elementary operations on objects: object creation and deletion, single-valued/multi-valued property modification and class migration. The same operations can be used in the action side of a rule, which may also contain composite operations and I/O operations.

The generation of IMPRs from constraints is supported by a tool called CONTEXT [32]: the generation is completely automated for simple inherent constraints and requires the user's assistance for more complex, explicit constraints. The tool presents the available repairs to the user, who keeps the responsibility to decide which IMPRs to generate. Multiple repairing actions for a single constraint are allowed.

The execution model of repair is the following: all updates executed by the user's transaction are logged; before committing the transaction, the log file is passed to the Integrity Maintenance Subsystem, which detects the violated constraints. If there is a violated constraint without repair, the user transaction is aborted. Otherwise, IMPR execution is started. If this terminates successfully, an extended transaction comprising the user's updates and the modification performed by IMPRs is committed.

The success of IMPR's computation can be hampered for two reasons: infinite triggering, as in [8], and conflicting updates. The latter is due to contradictory operations within the sequence of updates performed by the user's transaction and the IMPRs, e.g., the creation of an object followed by its deletion.

A variant of the Triggering Graph introduced in [8] is used to assess a set of IMPRs to see if they may cause contradicting updates and infinite triggering.

In addition to nodes representing rules, the graph contains a node for every possible elementary operation. Two kinds of arcs are defined: *propagation* arcs that connect an operation or a rule to another rule, iff the former can generate the triggering event of the latter; *conflict* arcs that link a rule to another rule or to an operation, iff the action of the former contradicts the latter. Direct cycles comprising only propagation arcs denote potential infinite triggering, while cycles containing at least one conflict arc show the possibility of conflicting updates.

Cycles are *essential* if they always generate anomalous IMPR behavior, *inessential* if it can be demonstrated, based on IMPR's semantics, that infinite triggering or conflicting updates do not arise at run-time; *instance-based* if the occurrence of anomalies depends on the actual transaction and database instance.

The goal of IMPR analysis is that of identifying inessential cycles and to provide information to the run-time executor of IMPRs, to reduce the probability of repair failure. This requires a problem-solving tool which is planned in the prosecution of the research.

4.1.3   The approach of Ceri-Fraternali-Paraboschi-Tanca [29]

The approach [29, 33] aims at defining the architecture of an Integrity Maintenance System, based on the active database paradigm. A relational data model is used and the constraint language is a subset of Domain Relational Calculus. The expressive power is augmented with the possibility to use non-recursive views in the definition of constraints.

Repairing actions, in the form of ECA-rules, are automatically generated from constraints.

The repairing operations supported are tuple insertion, deletion and single attribute update; the latter permits a finer granularity of the repairing actions. An automatic generation algorithm permits alternative repairing actions for each constraint; the system exploits this redundancy to obtain a rule system that terminates and respects as much as possible user's intentions.

The generation algorithm is formally specified and it is demonstrated to be sound and complete, i.e., only correct rules are generated and all the repairing actions expressible through the permitted database updating operations are detected, up to rule subsumption.

The problem of correctness and termination is explicitly addressed and compile-time analysis tools are provided.

Since each rule is correct with respect to the constraint it enforces, the problem reduces to that of guaranteeing termination. For this purpose, a tool called *Triggering Hypergraph* (THG) is introduced, which is a further extension of the Triggering Graph used in [8]. A THG is a directed labeled hypergraph; nodes represent constraints and hyperarcs represent rules so that a hyperarc from C_1 to C_2 and C_3, labeled r_1, indicates that rule r_1 repairs constraint C_1 but may violate constraints C_2 and C_3. Rule analysis is then formulated as a combinatorial problem: determine the "optimal" set of hyperarcs to be removed from a THG, so that it is reduced to a directed acyclic hypergraph (DAHG) such that the rules in DAHG satisfy the "maximal" number of constraints. The problem has been demonstrated to be NP-complete and polynomial heuristic techniques have been developed [34].

The run-time system post-processes user's transactions by using the rules in the DAHG and possibly others, when some constraint has been left without repairing actions in the DAHG by the compile time analysis.

If the run-time system comprises only rules in the DAHG, then termination is guaranteed a priori. Otherwise, rules not in the DAHG are monitored: if they violate an already enforced constraint, rollback of the user's transaction is produced.

One of the novelties of the approach of [29, 33] is the explicit treatment of the semantic adequacy of alternative repairing actions for a constraint. The adequacy of rules is embodied in a rule's *weight*, that is used to direct the heuristic algorithm for DAHG computation. In the actual prototype, such weight is automatically computed and can be overridden by the user.

An interesting enhancement would be that of associating to the definition of constraints the repairing strategy preferred by the user selected from a pre-defined set identified through a classification of constraint typologies.

Experiments with a complete prototype of the Integrity Maintenance System confirmed the adequacy of the approach, when automatic solution of a test case were compared with manual ones.

4.2   Other Techniques

4.2.1   The approach of Schewe-Thalheim-Schmidt-Wetzel [16]

In [16], the integrity enforcement problem is addressed in the context of Object-Oriented Databases (OODBs). Static and transition constraints, expressed in a function-free first-order logical language, may be imposed on the classes of the OODB schema.

The approach adopted is that of modifying a user's transaction, by replacing the (basic) methods that update objects with rewritten ones, which satisfy the established constraints.

Such rewritten methods constitute the *Greatest Consistent Specialization (GCS)* of database updating operations.

A GCS is defined as a derived operation that augments the original one to make it compliant to a single constraint. A GCS can add to the original operation extra updates—similar to repairing actions—provided that they do not contradict the original operation; in addition, the distance between the original and the augmented operation must be minimal; this means that any other consistent specialization of the original operation must be "more specific", i.e., less liberal, than the GCS. The GCS of a generic update operation of a class with respect to a single static or transition constraint is shown to exist and to be unique, up to semantic equivalence. The minimality requirement causes all alternative, non-minimal repairs of an update operation to be discarded. However, a GCS of a deterministic operation may contain choices and thus be non-deterministic.

Multiple constraints can also be treated, since the result of deriving the GCS with respect to a constraint C_2 of the GCS of an operation S with respect to a constraint C_1 is demonstrated to be semantically equivalent to deriving the GCS of the original operation with respect to the conjunction of C_1 and C_2.

The notion of repair failure is also present: when it is impossible to derive a consistent specialization of the original operation that respects the constraints, the GCS is conventionally set to a *fail* operation. This happens, for example, when the repairing action needed to enforce the integrity constraints contradicts the original operation (e.g., it updates an object created by the original operation).

Constructive results are only given under particular circumstances: GCSs can be built for canonical operations (insertion, deletion and update) of particular classes, for a distinguished set of constraints (comprising functional, uniqueness, inclusion/exclusion and object generating constraints). A negative result shows that the constructive approach does not scale up trivially: it is not possible to build GCSs of arbitrary methods or transactions by simply "assembling" GCSs of elementary operations. Also, building GCSs for multiple constraints is a problem, since GCSs for a single constraint usually are not elementary operations.

4.2.2 The approach of Wüthrich [7]

The work in [7] addresses the problem of performing updates in knowledge bases with integrity constraints. Updates and (static) constraints are expressed as arbitrary, allowed, function-free first-order formulas. They may also contain intentionally defined predicates, specified by recursive clauses, comprising negation in the body. Performing an update means making the corresponding formula true in the database, by adding and/or deleting a minimal set of facts. Consistency requires, in addition, that the execution of an update generates a database state in which all the defined constraints are satisfied. Since constraint formulas can themselves be seen as particular updates, the approach generalizes to that of enforcing the truth of a violated constraint.

The main contribution is a technique to define a so-called "realization" of an update. This is a derived formula obtained by means of an "unfolding procedure", that takes the original update and *all* the constraints and produces a unique new update that contains only extensional predicates.

A realization is "executed" by means of a procedure that, if possible, returns the set of facts to be added and deleted from the database, in order to achieve a new state in which the original update holds and all the constraints are respected. The output of the procedure reflects the actions to be taken to perform the update plus the repairing actions needed to enforce the constraints.

If the procedure fails, it is not possible to repair the original update in order to respect the constraints. Failure occurs when the execution of a realization attempts to assert a fact and its negation at the same time (with an approach similar to that of [18]).

The procedure to execute a realization is in general non-deterministic, but only one solution is computed: the user must choose among alternative deletions and insertions that implement the same realization. This choice is critical since it may produce an execution failure. There is no provision for the explicit analysis of conflicts among repairing actions, for example, by contrasting different sets of facts to insert or delete to avoid failure.

Also, the execution procedure requires run-time access to the database. However, the access is restricted to a minimum and is done in a set-oriented fashion, to enhance efficiency.

4.2.3 The approach of Moerkotte and Lockemann [3]

A comparable contribution is [3], which proposes an architecture for dealing with constraint checking and enforcing in deductive databases. Constraints are defined as closed range-restricted formulas of a first-order function-free language and a transaction is a (non-contradictory) sequence of insert and delete operations.

The goal is to check, at transaction commit time, if any constraint is violated and to suggest possible repairing actions.

Integrity checking is performed at two levels: at the "symptom" level, constraint checking takes into account both stored and inferred facts (called symptoms); at the extension level, violations are regarded as produced only by extensional facts (called causes).

Orthogonally, causes and symptoms are defined to be potential, if their removal restores a single constraint (possibly violating other ones); definite, if their removal does not violate any of the defined constraints. Then, a (potential/definite) repair is defined as a (minimal) transaction which eliminates the causes of a constraint violation.

The main contribution is a technique to check what constraints are violated in the database state produced by a given transaction, to extract the symptoms of such violations, to look for their causes and to use these causes to define a repairing transaction.

Constraint checking is done at run-time (it needs to know the after state of the transaction), and works by keeping a trace of what facts contribute to make a constraint violated. Differently from [7], all alternative sets of (potential) symptoms are collected. Then, each potential symptom is processed to obtain the set of stored facts that violate the constraint.

Since constraint checking is done for each constraint separately, the identified causes cannot be simply eliminated, since there is the possibility that removing the cause of the violation of one constraint makes another constraint violated.

Thus, an iterative algorithm is given, which tries and concatenates to the original transaction different combinations of repairing actions, until a sequence of operations is found that does not violate any constraint. This requires that each tentative transaction be simulated and the database state be checked for new violations.

The algorithm is combinatorial and every possible sequence can be generated: if the constraints are non-contradictory, the algorithm is assured to find a solution, at least the inverse of the original transaction. The output of the algorithm is a set of alternative sequences of repairing actions to be added at the end of the user's transaction. The main limitation of this approach is that a repairing transaction is constructed by generating tentative sequences of repairing actions, with no indication on the order to follow in the repair. In addition, the paper provides only few general criteria for the semantic ranking of alternative repairing transactions.

5 Conclusions

We have presented a review of the major approaches to integrity maintenance through repairing actions. In several application domains, repair offers advantages with respect to executing a rollback whenever a violation occurs. Commercial DBMSs are beginning to provide these mechanisms, but limited to restricted families of constraints. The common goal of the described approaches is to extend repairs to more general constraints and to provide a higher level and more powerful support. This leads to the definition of an Integrity Maintenance System, a dedicated component that extends traditional DBMSs. This idea has recently received considerable attention, as is demonstrated by the different approaches illustrated and compared. We also propose a classification schema, which evaluates the illustrated contributions with respect to a number of characterizing features.

An important role in the development of Integrity Maintenance Systems will be played by the active database paradigm, which seems to be the more adequate technological support to this task.

References

[1] B. Thalheim "Dependencies in relational databases", B. G. Teubner Verlgsgesellshaft, Stuttgart, 1991

[2] S. Ceri, F. Garzotto, G. Gottlob "Specification and management of database integrity constraint through logic programming techniques", to be published as Tech. Rep. Laboratorio di Calcolatori, Dipartimento di Elettronica, Politecnico di Milano

[3] G. Moerkotte, P. C. Lockemann, "Reactive Consistency Control In Deductive Databases" ACM TODS, Vol. 16 No. 4, Dec. 1991, pp. 670-702

[4] J. M. Nicolas, K. Yazdanian "Integrity checking in deductive databases", in Logic and Databases, H. Gallaire and J. Minker Eds., Plenum, New York, 1978, pp. 325-344

[5] J. A. Pastor, "Deriving Consistency-preserving Transaction Specification for (View-)Updates in Relational Databases", Proc. 3rd Int. Workshop on the Deductive Approach to Information Systems and Databases, Roses - Costa Brava (Catalonia), Sept. 1992, pp. 275-300

[6] S. Urban, L. Delcambre "Constraint analysis: a design process for specifying operations on objects", IEEE Trans. on Knowledge and Data Engineering, Vol. 2 No. 4, Dec. 1990, pp. 391-400

[7] B. Wüthrich "On Update and Inconsistency Repairing in Knowledge Bases", Proc. 9th IEEE Int. Conference on Data Engineering, Vienna, Austria, Apr. 1993, pp. 608-615

[8] S. Ceri, J. Widom "Deriving Production Rules for Constraint Maintenance", Proc. 16th VLDB, Brisbane, Australia, Aug. 1990, pp. 566-577

[9] M. A. Casanova, L. Tuckerman, A. L. Furtado "Enforcing inclusion dependencies and referential integrity", Proc. 14th VLDB, Los Angeles, California, Aug. 1988, pp. 38-49

[10] P. Fraternali, S. Paraboschi, L. Tanca "Automatic rule generation for correction of constraint violations in active databases", Proc. 4th Int. Workshop on Foundations of Models and Languages for Data and Objects, Volkse, Germany, Oct. 1992, pp. 93-112

[11] D. Stemple, S. Mazumdar, T. Sheard "On the modes and meaning of feedback to transaction designer", Proc. of ACM-SIGMOD, San Francisco, California, May 1987, pp. 374-386

[12] T. Sheard, D. Stemple "Automatic Verification of Database Transaction Safety", ACM TODS, Vol. 14 No. 3, Sept. 1989, pp. 322-368

[13] J. Chomicki "History-less Checking of Dynamic Integrity Constraints", Proc. 8th IEEE Int. Conf. on Data Engineering, Phoenix, Arizona, Feb. 1992, pp. 557-564

[14] S. Ceri, F. Garzotto "Specification and management of database integrity constraint through logic programming", Tech. Rep. n. 88-025, Laboratorio di Calcolatori, Dipartimento di Elettronica, Politecnico di Milano, 1988

[15] M. Gertz, U. W. Lipeck "Deriving Integrity Maintaining Triggers from Transitions Graphs", Proc. 9th IEEE Int. Conf. on Data Engineering, Vienna, Austria, Apr. 1993, pp. 22-29

[16] K. D. Schewe, B. Thalheim, J. W. Schmidt, I. Wetzel "Integrity Enforcement in Object-Oriented Databases", Proc. 4th Int. Workshop on Foundations of Models and Languages for Data and Objects, Oct. 1992, Volkse, Germany, pp. 181-206

[17] F. Bry, H. Decker, R. Manthey "A Uniform Approach to Constraint Satisfaction and Constraint Satisfiability in Deductive Databases", in Proc. EDBT 88, LNCS 303, Venice, Italy, pp.489-505

[18] Y. Zhou, M. Hsu "A theory for rule triggering systems", in Proc. of EDBT '90, LNCS 416, Springer-Verlag, Berlin, March 1990, pp. 407-421

[19] S. Chakravarthy "Rule management and evaluation: an active DBMS perspective", ACM SIGMOD Record Vol. 18 No.3, Sept. 1989, pp. 20-28

[20] M. Stonebraker, A. Juingran, J. Goh, S. Potamianos "On rules, procedures, caching and views in database systems", Proc. of ACM-SIGMOD, May 1990, pp. 281-290

[21] J. Widom, S. J. Finkelstein "Set-oriented production rules in relational database systems", Proc. of ACM-SIGMOD, May 1990, pp. 259-270

[22] U. Dayal et al. "The HiPAC Project: combining active databases and timing constraints", ACM SIGMOD Record Vol. 17 No. 1, Mar. 1988, pp. 51-70

[23] J. Widom "A denotational semantics for the Starbust production rule language", SIGMOD Record, Vol 21 No. 3, Sept. 92, pp. 4-9

[24] A. Aiken, J. Widom, J. M. Hellerstein "Behavior of database production rules: termination, confluence and observable determinism", Research Report RJ 8562 (77200), IBM Research Division, Almaden Research Center, San Jose, California, Jan. 1992

[25] F. Bancilhon N. Spyratos "Update Semantics of Relational Views" ACM TODS Vol. 6 No. 4, Dec. 1981, pp. 557-575

[26] A. M. Keller "Choosing a View Update Translator by Dialog at view Definition Time" Proc. 12th VLDB, Kyoto, Japan, Aug. 1986, pp. 467-474

[27] G. Gottlob, P. Paolini, R. Zicari "Properties and Update Semantics of Consistent Views" ACM TODS Vol. 13 No. 4, Dec. 1988, pp 486-524

[28] J. A. Larson, A. S. Sheth " Updating Relational Views Using Knowledge at View Definition and View Update Time" Information Systems, Vol. 16 No. 2, 1991, pp. 145-168

[29] S. Ceri, P. Fraternali, S. Paraboschi, L. Tanca "Automatic Generation of Production rules for Integrity Maintenance", Tech. Rep. n. 92-054, Laboratorio di Calcolatori, Dipartimento di Elettronica, Politecnico di Milano, 1992 (submitted for publication)

[30] S. D. Urban, A. P. Karadimce, R. B. Nannapaneni "The Implementation and Evaluation of Integrity Maintenance Rules in an Object-Oriented Database", Proc. 8th Int. Conf. on Data Engineering, Feb. 1992, Phoenix, Arizona, pp. 565-572

[31] A. P. Karadimce, S. D. Urban "Diagnosing Anomalous Rule Behavior in Databases with Integrity Maintenance Production Rules", Proc. 3th Int. Workshop on Foundations of Models and Languages for Data and Objects, Aigen, Austria, Sept. 1991, pp. 77-102

[32] S. D. Urban, M. Desiderio "CONTEXT: A CONstrainT EXplanation Tool" Data & Knowledge Engineering, Vol. 8 (1992), pp. 153-183

[33] S. Ceri, P. Fraternali, S. Paraboschi, L. Tanca "Constraint Enforcement through Production Rules: Putting Active Databases to Work", Data Engineering, Vol. 15 No. 1-4, Dec. 1992, pp. 10-14

[34] P. Fraternali, S. Paraboschi "Selecting Rules for Constraint Maintenance: Complexity and Heuristic Solution", Tech. Rep. n. 92-057, Laboratorio di Calcolatori, Dipartimento di Elettronica, Politecnico di Milano, 1992 (submitted for publication)

Implementing Relationships and Constraints in an Object-Oriented Database Using a Monitor Construct

Michael Doherty *

Dept. of Computer Science, University of Colorado at Boulder
Boulder, CO, USA 80309

Joan Peckham †

Dept. of Computer Science and Statistics, University of Rhode Island
Kingston, RI, USA 02881

Victor Fay Wolfe

Dept. of Computer Science and Statistics, University of Rhode Island
Kingston, RI, USA 02881

Abstract

Semantic models have shown the utility of arbitrary user-defined relationships for defining the semantics of database information, while object-oriented models have developed a strong paradigm for the expression of individual database entities. The SORAC project merges the strengths of these two models by extending the object-oriented model through the addition of active semantic relationships. These active relationships express and enforce the constraints imposed on an object by the participation of the object in some group of related objects. The SORAC system is supported by the data definition language OIL (Object Interaction Language), which automatically maps schema specifications to a database implementation supported by the ONTOS Object Database Management System. By providing an automatic mapping from the semantic data model to the object-oriented database, the SORAC system provides a consistent semantic and structural view of the data.

1   Introduction

The meaning of information stored in a database is expressed in the semantics of the data objects as well as the relationships between those objects. Current applications require tools for modeling both complex objects and complex inter-object relationships. The development of semantic data models [1, 2] has shown the utility of relationships for capturing the semantics of the interaction between database objects. Semantic models have, however, been viewed as design tools and not implementation tools, resulting in an imperfect correspondence between database design and the realized database. Object-oriented

---

*Work done while attending the University of Rhode Island

†Partially supported by URI Proposal Development Grant #537116, and NUWC IPA #535373, Navel Underwater Warfare Center, Newport, RI

data models [3, 4] are based on a strong, well-defined paradigm for the definition and implementation of complex objects. Object-oriented models lack support for complex and arbitrary relationships, since support for relationships is restricted to a small number of well-defined relationships, such as inheritance and composition.

The SORAC project (Semantic Objects, Relationships and Constraints) combines the two models by enhancing the object-oriented model with relationship semantics through which object interaction is expressed and implemented. The SORAC system provides a data definition language called OIL (Object Interaction Language) which supports the semantics of arbitrary objects and active relationships. The database schema defined in OIL is automatically translated into a pure object-oriented model, specifically the C++ based model provided by the Ontos object database management system [5, 6].

1.1 Relationships as Semantic Constructs

Although the importance of the relationships between objects is recognized in object-oriented analysis and design [7, 4], few object-oriented systems directly support the implementation of the relationships. In most object-oriented systems, the implementation of the relationships is buried in the implementation of the participating objects. This design limits the flexibility of the relationship, violates the principle of encapsulation [8], and reduces the relationship to a second-class construct [9]. Rumbaugh [9] points out that the primary reason that object-oriented programming has become important is that it provides a way of thinking about the decomposition of a problem. Since the programming language directly supports the constituent constructs of the problem, the programmer can operate in the same paradigm for both design and implementation. However, since relationships are not directly expressible, this strength of the object-oriented paradigm is severely limited in domains where the relationships between objects are of prime importance.

This mismatch in the paradigms used in the design and implementation phases of a system also causes a problem in assessing the correctness of an implementation. If there is a not a direct correlation between the constructs used to specify the requirements of the system and the constructs presented to users of the system, verifying that the system correctly implements the design cannot be assured except by ad hoc techniques.

In addition to the practical benefits of providing constructs for the implementation of relationships, it is often required that queries be performed over the relationships between objects. If the relationships are buried in the implementation of the participating objects, querying over relationships can be difficult, if not impossible. For this reason it is important that relationships be implemented as first-class constructs.

In semantic data models, *integrity constraints* describe the restrictions placed on an object as a result of the relationships in which that object participates. To implement the database, constraints must be translated to *enforcement rules* which define how the constraints will be maintained. Since these constraints are properties of the relationships between objects, the enforcement rules should be implemented as part of relationship constructs. One significant problem with this view of constraints is that they are inherently non-local since they define restrictions on objects other than the one on which they are defined. However, if the constraints and corresponding update rules are regarded as behavioral constraints, and are defined in terms of the interaction between objects, rather than the internal state of the objects, enforcement rules can be defined on the relationship between objects without violating the encapsulation of the objects. The propagator construct [8] illustrates how this can be done in the context of object-oriented programming languages.

Since our interest was a design to support the implementation of semantic relationships, the terminology and examples presented here reflect our view of relationships as active objects. The implementation, however, does not restrict active behavior to relationship objects; such behavior may be freely defined for any database object.

1.2   SORAC – Semantic Objects, Relationships and Constraints

The SORAC project has developed a prototype database system which is designed to aid the database designer in ensuring the correctness of a database schema through the analysis of relationship constraints. The system provides the designer with the ability to select from built-in relationships and to define new arbitrary relationships. A formalism for analyzing the global semantics of the constraints is given in [10] and will be used to develop a schema checking system. Two separate design systems have been developed. The first is used to support the design of architectural databases, as a new generation of the ArchObjects system [11, 12]. The second supports a graphical user interface for the design and specification of abstract relationships [13].

This paper describes the SORAC system, the schema definition language OIL (Object Interaction Language), and the implementation of the generated database using the Ontos object database management system [14]. Section 2 describes the SORAC data model and how it supports relationships and active semantics. Section 3 gives an overview of the OIL language and section 4 describes the implementation of the system. The final section evaluates the current status of the SORAC system and describes work in progress as well as some unresolved questions.

2   The SORAC Data Model

2.1   Design Considerations

The following criteria influenced the design of the SORAC data model.

- Relationships are available as modeling constructs and are implemented by corresponding objects in the database.

- Objects need not be designed with prior knowledge of the relationships in which they may participate.

- The implementation of constraints should not violate object encapsulation.

- Enforcement rules must be explicitly supported by the data definition language.

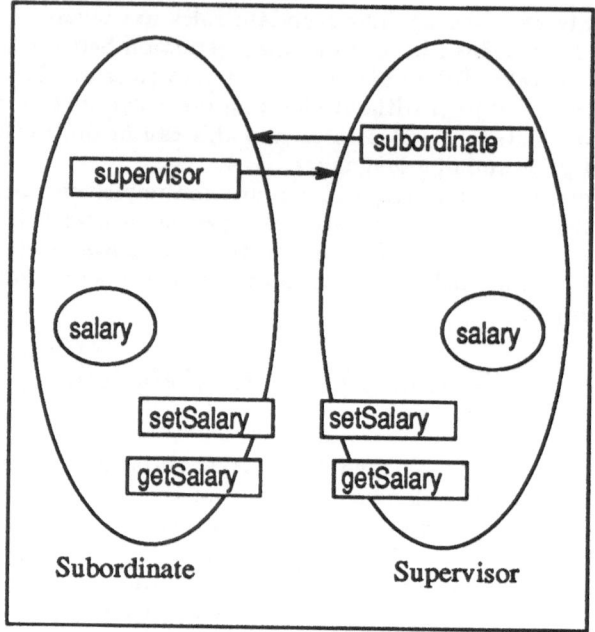

Figure 1: Object References

- The semantics of common application-oriented relationships and unique user-defined relationships must be equally supported.

The first three criteria imply that assertions and enforcement rules are often properties of the relationships among objects and not necessarily properties of the objects themselves. From this it follows that assertions, enforcement rules and the events which trigger them are not local to the affected objects. To support such non-local behavior, the SORAC data model provides **monitors** which implement the active behavior of relationships. Monitors operate by reacting to the messages received by the related objects and thus conform to object-oriented encapsulation.

The last two requirements are included to support user-defined abstract relationships. Since the SORAC system is intended to support a diverse range of applications, it is insufficient to supply a set of system-defined relationships from which the database designer must choose.

2.2   An Example Schema

Figures 1 – 3 illustrate how the SORAC data model supports objects and relationships. Consider the relationship between a supervisor and her subordinate. The semantics of the relationship are defined by the following constraint:

> The salary of a subordinate must be no more than the salary of his or her supervisor.

351

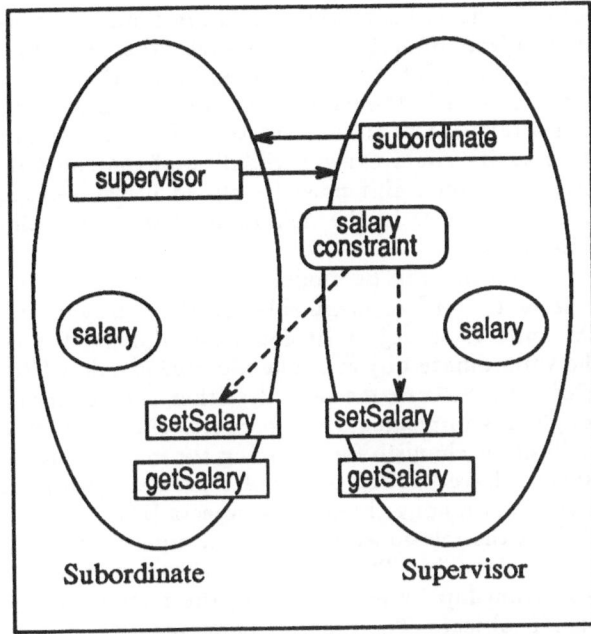

Figure 2: Interacting Objects

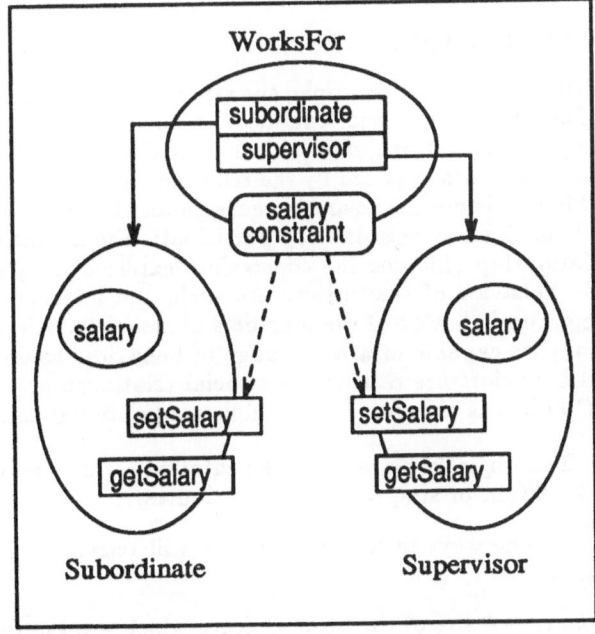

Figure 3: Interactive Object

A typical object-oriented solution is shown in Figure 1. Here the supervisor and subordinate objects directly reference each other, and there is no distinct object representing the relationship. Consequently, there is no mechanism to enforce the inverse nature of the relationship, and no obvious place to define the enforcement rules required to implement the salary constraint. Since a modification to either salary could cause a violation of the constraint, enforcement rules to maintain the constraint must be placed in the setSalary method of both objects. Any changes in the definition of the constraint would require changes to both objects.

The same relationship can be modeled by adding active behavior as shown in Figure 2. Here the enforcement rule for the salary is implemented as a monitor on the supervisor object (it could be implemented equally well as a monitor on the subordinate object). The monitor is defined to be triggered by the reception of a setSalary message by either the supervisor or the subordinate. Although this implementation properly encapsulates the enforcement rule, there is still no mechanism for enforcing the inverse nature of the relationship. Other authors have pointed out similar problems with the distribution of relationship semantics among the related objects [15].

Figure 3 defines the relationship between a supervisor and subordinate as a separate active relationship. The WorksFor relationship maintains the inverse nature of the relationship by encapsulating the references to the participants in the relationship object. The monitor enforcing the relationship constraint is naturally placed on the relationship. Note that this monitor is virtually the same as the monitor in the previous example, but its implementation now adheres to the semantics of the relationship.

2.3   SORAC Objects

As illustrated by the previous example, the separation of the internal and external aspects of an object's behavior enhances object-oriented design by allowing the data storage considerations of an object to be designed without considering the additional constraints imposed by the relationships in which the object may participate. Thus, it is not necessary to redesign an object in order to create an object whose behavior is constrained by participation in a relationship. Rather, the active relationship enforces the constraints externally, by monitoring and restricting the behavior of the object. As such, the interaction of objects is similar to the group behavior of the members of a society. Although a member of a society may be capable of a wide range of behaviors as an individual, the allowed social behaviors are restricted by social relationships.

A SORAC object is composed of the following optional components:

- State – The object's private implementation, which may be a complex object definition or simply a list of attributes.

- Methods – The ways in which an object will respond to the messages it receives.

- Participants – A list of the other objects which are known by an object.

- Monitors – The means by which an object monitors the activities of participants to enforce assertions and enforcement rules.

It is the addition of a list of participants and associated monitors which distinguishs a relationship object from a data object, by defining the relationship object's ability to be interactive. There are no distinctions made between relationship and data objects, and the definition of participants and monitors is unrestricted. This design allows relationships to be queried and manipulated as first-class objects. A relationship object monitors the messages received by the participating objects and takes appropriate actions to maintain the integrity of the relationship. A relationship object can enforce an assertion on a participating object by causing it to reject a message which would violate the assertion. Active semantics are maintained by enforcement rules which cause a relationship to propagate the effects of a message received by an object to other related objects.

The concept of an interactive object is more general than that of a relationship. It is possible to define the interaction between two objects directly in the public interface of the objects (as illustrated by Figure 2). However, since the application domain addressed by the SORAC project is database modeling, only the use of interactive objects to explicitly express relationships will be discussed here.

2.4   Monitors – Implementing Interobject Constraints

The semantics of relationships are implemented through the use of *monitors*. A monitor gives an object the ability to react to messages received by related objects and to take appropriate actions to maintain the integrity of the relationship. The monitor construct is derived from the propagator [8], which implements encapsulated constraints in an object-oriented language (Procol). A propagator implements a constraint by specifying an action to be taken in response to a message received by some object. Monitors differ from propagators in the following ways:

- The triggering method of a propagator may be defined at any arbitrary object. The triggering methods of monitors are limited to the objects that are listed as participants in the relationship which defines the monitor. In this way, the possible effects of a monitor are better defined than those of a propagator, making the analysis of the global semantics defined by the relationships more tractable.

- To more naturally express the semantics of constraints (as defined below) monitors add a boolean guard condition to be checked before any action is taken in response to a triggering method; propagators have no such feature.

- Monitors can utilize the native Ontos transaction control to undo the effects of operations which violate constraints for which no corrective action is specified. Propagators can only attempt to correct violations, not undo them.

For the purpose of schema checking and validation, assertions and enforcement rules are defined in terms of operations on objects. The following formalism is described in [16].

Assertions:

$$OP(O:OT) - (C) - (R) \rightarrow ()$$

Update rules:

$$OP(O:OT) - (C) - (R) \rightarrow OP2(O2:OT2)$$

The first rule states that an operation of type OP on an object of type OT which participates in the relationship R should be rejected unless condition C is true. An assertion is therefore a declaration that the condition C must remain true. The second rule defines the conditional propagation of an operation across a relationship. It states that if an operation of type OP is performed on an object of type OT and condition C is true, then operation $OP2$ should be performed on all objects of type $OT2$ which participate in the same relationship R as object O.

The monitor construct generalizes these definitions by replacing operations with message reception, and by allowing arbitrary behavior in place of the enforcement rule operation $OP2$. It is left to the schema designer, or the design interface to determine if the enforcement rule conforms to the above definition.

A monitor is triggered at a relationship by the reception of a message by a participating object. The monitor may define an arbitrary number of assertions and enforcement rules. Assertions are defined by stating the asserted condition as a boolean expression, and update rules are defined by a guard condition and a procedure to be executed if the guard condition is true.

3 OIL – Object Interaction Language

OIL is the SORAC data definition language. Low level OIL constructs, such as statements and expressions, are a subset of C++, while high level constructs are designed to reflect the nature of objects and relationships in the SORAC data model. A SORAC schema is defined entirely as OIL object declarations. Each OIL object type definition consists of a block of object components corresponding to the state, participants, methods and monitors which define the SORAC data model.

3.1 Data Objects

A data object is defined by its private implementation and the methods that define its public interface. An implementation of an Employee object is given in Figure 4. The private part of the object is simply the attribute salary, although arbitrary C++ objects could be used to implement the state.

The syntax of a public method includes two lists of parameters, the first parameter list defines the inputs to the method (the contents of the message) and the second parameter list defines the outputs of the method (the response to the message). The return value is also part of the response to the message, but is separated to allow function call syntax in the body of the object sending the message.

```
object Employee
{
    state
    {
        float salary;
    }
    void setSalary(float new_salary)()
    {
        salary = new_salary;
    }
    float getSalary()()
    {
        return salary;
    }
}
```

Figure 4: An Employee Object

3.2 Relationship Objects

Relationship objects extend data objects by the addition of monitors, that encode the constraints and enforcement rules defined by the relationship, and a list of objects that may participate in the relationship. Relationships may also have state and methods, although the example relationship shown here does not.

Figure 5 shows the definition of a Works_For relationship between two employees. The relationship consists of a single monitor, which will be triggered by a change in salary to either employee. The keyword monitor is followed by a list of triggers, which specify the actions that invoke the monitor. These actions are defined in terms of messages which may be received by participants in the relationship. Each trigger is defined by *participant.message* where *participant* is the local name for a participating object and *message* is the name of the message to the participating object which triggers the monitor.

The constraint that the supervisor's salary must be at least that of the subordinate is implemented as an assertion. The semantics of the monitor specify that if either the supervisor or subordinate receive a message to change their salary, and the new salary violates the assertion, then the transaction which initiated the salary change should be aborted.

The constraint can also be enforced by active semantics through the use of enforcement rules. Figure 6 shows the Works_For relationship reimplemented so that a message to change the subordinate's salary that would violate the constraint is replaced by a message that will not violate the constraint. In this case, the new salary of the subordinate is simply restricted to be the same as that of his supervisor. The same assertion is still used to implement the inverse constraint.

Monitors can also be used to cause the propagation of operations across a relationship. A deletion constraint may be used to force propagation of a deletion message across a relationship. This is illustrated in Figure 7, where

```
object Works-For
{
    participants
    {
        object Employee subordinate;
        object Employee supervisor;
    }
    monitor (subordinate.setSalary,
             supervisor.setSalary)
    {
        assert (subordinate.getSalary()() <=
                supervisor.getSalary()())
    }
}
```

Figure 5: An Assertion Constraint

```
object Works-For
{
    participants
    {
        object Employee subordinate;
        object Employee supervisor;
    }
    monitor (subordinate.setSalary)
    {
        updateif (subordinate.getSalary()() >
                  supervisor.getSalary()())
        {
            subordinate.setSalary
                (supervisor.getSalary()())();
        }
    }
    monitor (supervisor.setSalary)
    {
        assert (subordinate.getSalary()() <=
                supervisor.getSalary()())
    }
}
```

Figure 6: An Enforcement Rule

```
object Works-For
{
    participants
    {
        object Employee subordinate;
        object Employee supervisor;
    }
    monitor (supervisor.Delete)
    {
        updateif (true)
        {
            subordinate.Delete()();
            self.Delete()();
        }
    }
}
```

Figure 7: A Deletion Constraint

the Works-For relationship forces a subordinate to be deleted if his *superior* is deleted. In addition, the Works-For relationship then deletes itself. (Delete is a system defined message supported by all objects.)

4 Implementation

4.1 System Overview

The SORAC database management system (SDBMS) is implemented using the Ontos object database management system [6, 5] on a SUN Sparc architecture. The Ontos system accepts database schema defined in C++, and as such provides exceptional support for the definition of complex object types. As with most object-oriented systems, Ontos provides little support for abstract relationships between objects. Through the implementation of the monitor construct, the SDBMS adds support for user-defined abstract relationships while maintaining the object implementation capabilities of Ontos. This design allows an object's private implementation to be arbitrarily complex, constrained only by the underlying database management system.

An overview of the system is shown in Figure 8. The system adds two extensions to the Ontos system, the OIL compiler and the SORAC class library. The OIL compiler allows the schema to be defined using the OIL constructs described in the previous section, while the SORAC extensions of the Ontos library provide the required interactive behavior to support the constraints defined by monitors. Ontos cplus preprocesses the source code and utilizes the native C++ compiler to compile the methods that define object behavior. Ontos classify processes the C++ class definitions to generate the Ontos class objects that define the database schema.

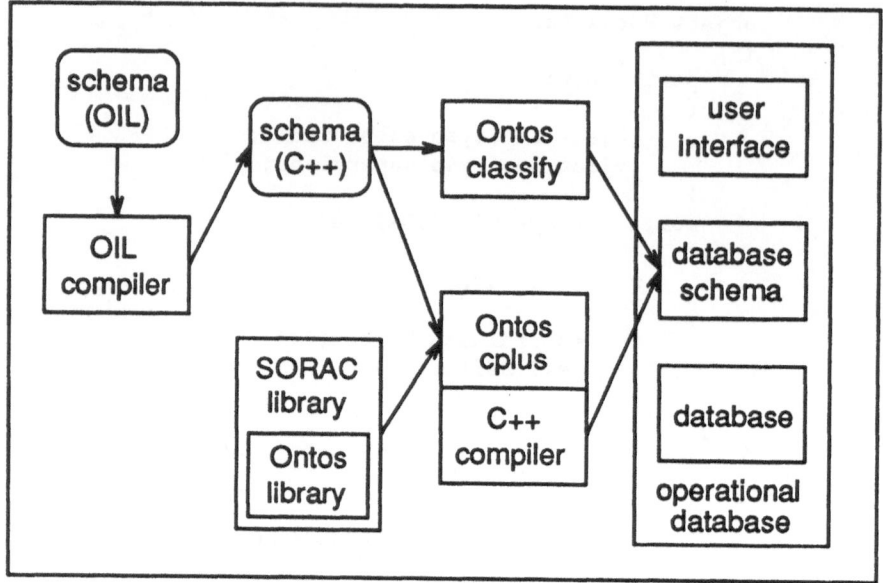

Figure 8: System Overview

4.2 The OIL Compiler

The OIL compiler accepts SORAC object definitions and generates C++ code which is compatible with the Ontos system and the extended class library described below. Each OIL object is translated into two C++ class definitions, one defining the object class, and the other defining the object instances.

In addition to supporting the semantic constructs, the use of the OIL compiler frees the schema designer from considering the generic behavior of the objects. All code to support Ontos functions, such as transaction control, as well as the generic behavior of SORAC objects is automatically inserted into the resulting SORAC schema.

4.3 The SORAC Class Library

The SORAC class library provides the following features:

- The data definition language is raised to a higher level of abstraction. The object type definitions of an Ontos schema must encode the persistence and transaction related behavior of objects. Such implementation detail, which is not of interest to the schema designer is abstracted away by the OIL language.

- Objects have the ability to monitor and react to the messages received by related objects. The SDBMS adds a message passing layer and listeners to implement active behavior.

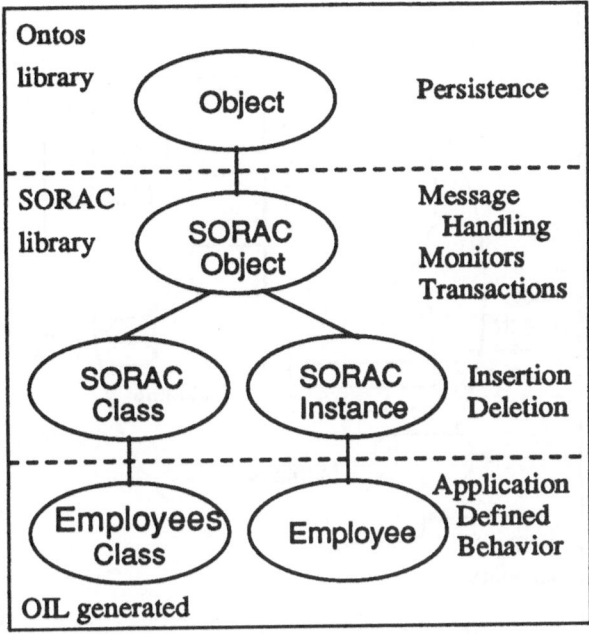

Figure 9: SORAC Class Hierarchy

- The effects of messages which cause the violation of constraints can be undone. The native Ontos transaction control is used to remove the effects of offending messages.

The SDBMS class hierarchy is shown in Figure 9. The SORAC library extends the Ontos library by defining subclasses of the Ontos Object class, which is the base class for all persistent objects and which provides standard database behavior. All objects in a SORAC schema are derived from class SORAC_Object through two subclasses SORAC_Class and SORAC_Instance. The code produced by the OIL compiler consists entirely of class definitions of subclasses of SORAC_Class and SORAC_Instance.

- Object – The root class for all persistent objects is provided by the Ontos library. It provides the default behavior for all database objects.

- SORAC_Object – All behavior required of all SORAC objects, including message handling, monitors, constraints and relationship instantiation.

- SORAC_Class – Class based operations, to support the insertion and selection of instances of the class.

- SORAC_Instance – The required behavior of all instances, in particular, support for deletion.

- OIL generated classes – Application specific behavior is defined by the OIL generated classes.

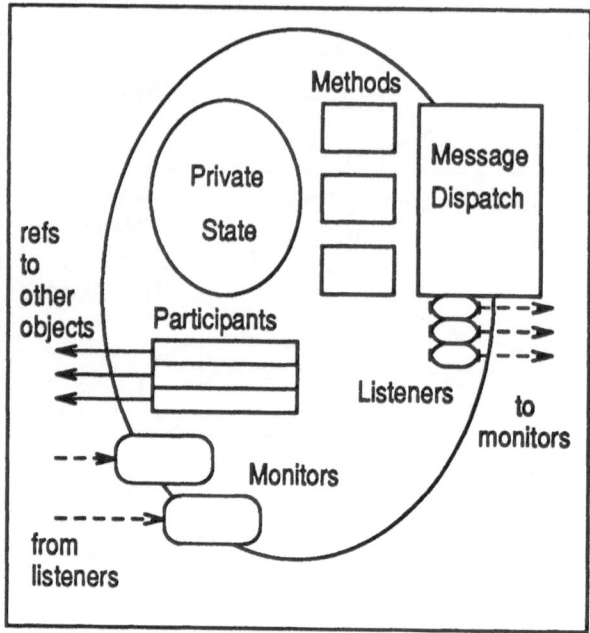

Figure 10: A SORAC Object

4.4 Object Implementation

The generic implementation of all SORAC objects is shown in Figure 10. To support the interactive nature of the non-local enforcement rules, it is necessary for an interactive object to be able to monitor the operations applied to the objects that are connected as participants to that object. Since the Ontos ODBMS is based on C++, operations are applied to objects through statically linked calls to member functions. Although this implementation of the object's public interface supports object-oriented design and coding of the objects, the static nature of the function calls means that an object is unaware that it has been modified, unless additional functionality is coded into each public function to cause the object to react to the changes. The SORAC DBMS adds a message dispatch unit through which all messages received by an object must pass. This provides a single location from which an object can inform any relationships in which it participates of any messages which it receives.

Rather than actively monitoring all the messages received by all participant objects, an interactive object inserts *listeners* into the objects when they are connected as participants. A listener is created for each trigger defined by a monitor, and contains the identification of the monitoring object and the name of the message which is being monitored.

After an object has executed the method specified by a message, the object's message dispatch checks the method name against all listeners. For each listener that matches the message name, a request to validate the message is sent to the object that inserted the listener. The monitoring object responds with a flag value which indicates if the message should be accepted or rejected. All listeners must agree to accept the message, to ensure that no immediate constraints have been violated. If any listener rejects the message, then the rejection flag in the message packet is set. When propagation occurs as the result of an update rule, the entire sequence of propagated messages must be approved or the initiating transaction is rejected.

The affected object first performs the method corresponding to the received message, and then informs any relationships in which it participates that it has acted on the message. The system then uses a two-phase commit protocol to verify that all immediate constraints resulting from the propagation of the initial message from the user interface have been resolved. If no immediate constraints have been violated, then the transaction is committed, otherwise it is aborted. (In the prototype implementation, a transaction is defined by a single user-initiated operation.)

When an object is asked to validate a message as a result of a listener at another object, it executes all immediate enforcement rules associated with all triggered monitors. If an enforcement rule is an assertion, the assertion expression is evaluated. If it is false, then the constraint which it enforces has been violated and the enforcement rule returns **reject**. Update rules consist of a guard expression and the rule to be executed. If the guard expression evaluates to false, then the rule is not executed and the enforcement rule returns **accept**. If the guard expression evaluates to false, then the rule is executed. The enforcement rule returns **accept** if all messages sent by the execution of the rule are accepted, otherwise the enforcement rule returns **reject**. As with methods, the execution of a **reject** statement by an update rule will cause the enforcement rule to return **reject**.

The SDBMS uses Ontos transactions to undo the effects of denied operations. For an enforcement rule to work, the triggering message must be accepted by the receiving object, and the appropriate method must be executed before the monitoring object can execute the enforcement rule. If the enforcement rule requires that the operation be denied, then the effects of that operation must be undone.

The atomic unit of a transaction is a message sent from the user interface. The monitoring activity described above is applied recursively to all messages resulting from a message sent by the database user. If any of these messages causes a constraint violation, the entire transaction is aborted.

5 Conclusion

The SORAC DBMS bridges the gap between semantic data modeling and object-oriented database implementation. Giving objects active behavior, in addition to the traditional passive behavior, provides a simple mechanism for the implementation of relationship based constraints. Since relationships can be supported by first-class objects, semantic data models can be implemented on the SORAC system while retaining the uniform design space of an object-oriented database.

The SORAC system has been implemented using the ONTOS ODBMS [14]. Two separate semantic design interfaces have been constructed using the OIL data definition language. These design interfaces demonstrate the ability of the SORAC system to support both specific applications such as architecture [11] and general semantics [13].

Rather than supporting predefined semantics for relationships and constraints, active objects can be used for programming arbitrary user-defined constraints. The structure of the enforcement rules for maintaining constraints is given in [16]. The sufficiency of these enforcement rules for the definition of application specific schema is being investigated [11, 13].

The automatic generation of the schema from the OIL design code, and the direct correspondence between design entities and relationships and the database objects allows for a direct analysis of schema correctness. A system for the correctness analysis of SORAC schema is planned.

The system is a prototype, and no performance analysis has been performed on the OIL interface or resulting databases. In the test cases run, the OIL compiler operates significantly faster than the subsequent ONTOS compiler, and therefore does not significantly impact the database development process. Although the message passing and monitoring facilities add a real-time cost proportional to the number of messages sent, our current hypothesis is that the use of the relationship construct to limit the conditions which must be checked for constraint enforcement will reduce the time necessary to carry out database actions and result in improved performance.

References

[1] J. Peckham and F. Maryanski, "Semantic data models," *ACM Computing Surveys*, vol. 20, pp. 153–189, Sept. 1988.

[2] R. Hull and R. King, "Semantic database modeling: Survey, applications, and research issues," *ACM Computing Surveys*, vol. 19, pp. 201–260, Sept. 1987.

[3] S. B. Zdonik and D. Maier, eds., *Readings in Object-Oriented Database Systems*. San Mateo, CA: Morgan Kaufmann Publishers, Inc., 1990.

[4] G. Booch, *Object-Oriented Design*. Redwood City, CA: The Benjamin/Cummings Publishing Company, Inc., 1991.

[5] Ontologic, Inc., Burlington, MA, *ONTOS Developer's Guide:*, 1991.

[6] T. Andrews and K. Sinkel, "ONTOS: A persistent database for C++," in *Object-Oriented Databases with Applications to CASE, Networks, and VLSI CAD* (R. Gupta and E. Horowitz, eds.), pp. 387–406, Englewoods Cliffs, NJ: Prentice Hall, 1991.

[7] T. Korson and J. D. McGregor, "Understanding object-oriented: A unifying paradigm," *Communications of the ACM*, vol. 33, pp. 40–60, Sept. 1990.

[8] C. Laffra and J. van den Bos, "Propagators and concurrent constraints," *OOPS Messenger*, vol. 2, pp. 68–72, Apr. 1991.

[9] J. Rumbaugh, "Relations as semantic constructs in an object-oriented language," in *OOPSLA '87*, pp. 466–481, ACM Press, Oct. 1987.

[10] J. Peckham, F. Maryanski, and S. Demurjian, "The correctness and consistency of update semantics in semantic database schema." Submitted IEEE TDKE, Oct. 1990.

[11] F. Vora, "Data modeling interface for architectural design systems," Tech. Rep. TR93-223, The University of Rhode Island, Department of Computer Science and Statistics, Aug. 1992.

[12] B. MacKellar and F. Ozel, "ArchObjects: Design codes as constraints in an object-oriented KBMS," in *Proceedings of the First International Conference on Artificial Intelligence in Design, Edinburgh, Scotland*, p. 115, June 1991.

[13] Z. H. Dong, "A user interface for database schema design and analysis," Tech. Rep. TR93-224, The University of Rhode Island, Department of Computer Science and Statistics, Dec. 1992.

[14] M. Doherty, "Implementing relationships in an object-oriented database," Tech. Rep. TR93-222, The University of Rhode Island, Department of Computer Science and Statistics, Aug. 1992.

[15] O. Diaz and P. M. D. Gray, "Semantic-rich user defined relationship as a main constructor in object oriented database," in *Object-Oriented Databases: Analysis, Design & Construction (DS-4)* (R. A. Meersman, W. Kent, and S. Khosla, eds.), Elsevier Science Publishers B.V. (North-Holland), 1991.

[16] J. Peckham and B. MacKellar, "SORAC: Modeling dynamic database semantics, extended abstract," Tech. Rep. TR92-210, The University of Rhode Island, Department of Computer Science and Statistics, Apr. 1992.

Constraint Maintenance using Generated Methods in the P/FDM Object-Oriented Database

Suzanne M. Embury, Peter M.D. Gray and Nick D. Bassiliades[1]
Department of Computing Science, University of Aberdeen
Aberdeen, Scotland, AB9 2UE

Abstract

We discuss the use of code-generated methods in Prolog as a flexible and efficient way to implement complex semantic constraints in an OODB. We introduce a high-level constraint language CoLan, based on functions and sets and including range quantifiers, from which fragments of code are generated to check the constraints. These fragments are attached to slots in class descriptors, and are also inherited (constraints cannot be overridden). Thus many fragments can come from one constraint and one slot may have attached fragments from many constraints. Constraints can be selectively disabled or removed which causes inhibition or disabling of corresponding fragments. This overcomes many objections to implementing constraints through methods. We have prototyped it by using the metaclass facilities of ADAM to initiate code generation. We are now re-implementing it in P/FDM, using changes to metadata (P/FDM does not have full metaclasses). This will incorporate a transaction mechanism and also provide queries on constraints. This approach opens a number of interesting future directions.

1 Introduction

This paper concerns the implementation of a particular kind of rule in an object-oriented database, namely one to support a complex semantic integrity check. We have devised a high-level language CoLan [?] to express semantic constraints. The constraint checking is implemented by code-generating fragments of Prolog attached to class descriptors in the ADAM OODB [?, ?]. These fragments check that the constraint is not violated by a particular state change; they can be inherited and are triggered on update. This is different from a programmer embedding checks in hand-written code in two ways. Firstly, the original declarative form of the constraint is stored in the database and can be used for explanation and in other ways. Secondly, the constraint can be selectively deleted, in which case the system will selectively remove the appropriate code fragments, without interfering with other constraints enforced on the same class or classes.

Our prototype implementation uses ADAM's metaclass facilities. Metaclasses are very powerful for experimental prototyping but the ADAM system

---

[1] Current address: Digital Systems and Computers Lab., Dept. of Physics, Aristotle University of Thessaloniki, 54006 Thessaloniki,

is heavily interpreted and therefore slow. Having tested the value of our design within ADAM, however, we are now re-implementing CoLan in another Prolog-based object-oriented database, P/FDM. P/FDM [9, 8] supports the high-level functional database language Daplex, and provides alternative object storage strategies. It is used to search and maintain data on large numbers of protein structures and can be used to explore alternative hypotheses about the structure of a particular protein. We wish to explore the use of constraints in the protein modelling process and also possible uses in other applications in scientific and engineering databases.

Unlike ADAM, P/FDM is not extensible through the use of metaclasses, but its architecture has been designed to allow system programmers to be able to extend the behaviour relatively easily. This approach provides less security and flexibility than the metaclass approach of ADAM, but does not incur the same efficiency costs.

The design philosophy of the implementation of CoLan has been to reconcile two conflicting arguments about the implementation of constraints. The former [5] says that constraints should be separate objects with their own structure, and the class descriptor should only refer to them through their object identifiers. The latter says that the former is too slow when implemented, so it handles constraints as methods attached to the class descriptor and it refers to them using their code translation. The latter is easier to implement and it performs better but the former is more general and flexible as it allows more control of constraint behaviour.

An intermediate approach has been adopted in our ADAM implementation, which is to handle constraints as distinct objects for maintenance purposes but to cache code that ensures constraint checking inside the class to which it applies. To be more specific, when a CoLan expression is inserted in the schema, its high level description along with other properties of the constraint are stored as separate objects, as instances of the class *constraint*. The generated code fragments are stored within the classes to which they apply and are retrieved by the *check-constraints* routine at run-time. When moving to P/FDM we have followed almost the same philosophy. The class descriptors are represented by system metadata clauses [6], and we are able to extend them with references to constraints, which are allocated unique identifiers and also held as metadata clauses. This has the advantage that they can be queried using the Daplex query language, just as for the main data.

Our approach has some similar points to the approach used in ABEL system [5], where constraints are stored separately and treated as first class objects. The main difference is that in ABEL the constraint expression is translated into an active rule [4] and the rule is stored and treated as a separate object, not the constraint itself. For CoLan this does not hold, as the translation (i.e. the Prolog code) is not treated as a separate object, but is stored in the classes involved, while the original constraint expression is treated like a first class object. Another difference is that, in ABEL, active rules are separate objects both virtually (from the user's point of view) and pragmatically (from the system's point of view), while in CoLan constraints are objects only from the system's point of view. The user in CoLan does not realise that constraints are not really stored in a different object, other than the class it is defined on, but he/she *understands* the constraint just as a simple property of a class.

The outline of this paper is as follows: Section 2 describes the CoLan language and restrictions on it, while Section 3 discusses related work including the use of active rules. Section 4 describes our general approach to constraint checking and discusses its implementation in both the ADAM and P/FDM databases. Section 5 discusses plans for future directions, including a transaction mechanism not available in ADAM, and Section 6 concludes.

2   The CoLan Language

The CoLan language is based on a semantic data model. Its significance lies not in its syntactic form (although we like its readability and generality) but in the underlying implementation which allows one to express constraints declaratively, and even to retract constraints, whilst taking advantage of an efficient implementation technique which uses methods triggered by an update. Thus it has the speed advantage of code embedded in a method, but since it is generated from a declarative form stored in a database, then it can always be altered and regenerated. Furthermore, constraints are shared and inherited in a way that avoids multiple copies, and their formal specification is readable and can be referenced by way of explanation or used by a query optimiser. This overcomes almost all the objections made in [18], which argues strongly against embedding constraints in unintelligible method code. Instead, CoLan uses constraint methods which are effectively cached with each class and inherited by subclasses.

CoLan uses a functional style, instead of the inference rule style used by the ALICE language [20]. This is because we are looking for readability. It is strongly influenced by the syntax of Daplex [17], which we use in one of the databases for which CoLan is designed. However, it has a similar underlying view of data to many semantic data models, including that used by ALICE. Thus, property definitions are viewed as functions defined over entity classes. The functions may be single or multi-valued (i.e. return a set or sequence). They may range over basic atomic types or else over entity types, and thus be used to represent relationships between entities. The functions may represent a stored relationship, such as suppliers(drug), but they may instead be implemented by calculation using a stored procedure (or method). The entity classes can form part of a sub-type hierarchy, in which case all properties and methods on the superclass are inherited by each subclass.

This similarity in basis makes CoLan portable to a range of data models. In another paper [2] we describe in detail how it has been implemented in ADAM, where it effectively provides ADAM with a declarative front end and thus saves the user from writing many separate complex pieces of method code. Instead, it code-generates pieces of Prolog which are activated by messages sent to class descriptors. It also uses the powerful metaclass descriptors of ADAM to ensure that constraints on superclasses cannot be over-ridden by more specialised constraints — these can only be added in conjunction.

CoLan is designed for the expression of semantic integrity constraints rather than structural constraints, which will usually be enforced by the underlying data model. These semantic constraints are specified as Boolean-valued expressions involving sets and functions, which must evaluate to true for any change in the number or to the state of instances of a given entity class (or classes). Note that the functions used in constraint expressions may either be based on stored relationships or on method code. In the latter case, dynamic binding means that we use the most recent definition of a particular method for constraint checking, and are not restricted to the definition that was current at the time of constraint code generation.

2.1 CoLan Syntax

A typical constraint expressed in CoLan consists of two parts: the quantification part, where the variables that are going to be used are given a domain and are quantified over that domain, and the second part, which consists of zero, one or more predicates that should be satisfied by the instances described by the quantification part. A constraint about the permissible range of ages for a lecturer, for example, is expressed as follows in CoLan:

```
forall l in lecturer
    age of l > 24 and age of l < 66
```

Although the quantification part is mandatory, the predicate part is optional for a CoLan expression. Some CoLan expressions quantify only the number of instances in a given domain regardless of their properties, so they act more like structural constraints than semantical ones. An example of such a constraint is the following:

```
exist at most 30 s in staff,
```

which constrains the cardinality of the object warehouse of a class, or:

```
exist at most 3 r in research_assistant of lecturer
```

which constrains the cardinality of a set attribute.

More complex constraints are the ones that relate the object that received the update message with the other objects in its class. For example, the constraint:

```
exist at least 1 s in staff
    such that job of s = ''secretary''
```

restricts the minimum number of instances of class staff that satisfy the predicate section of the constraint. To evaluate the validity of such a constraint in the context of a certain update, we must not only search for data locally (i.e. instance variables of the recipient object), but also globally (i.e. instance variables of other instances of the same class).

CoLan constraints can also relate the instances of two classes (not necessarily distinct), as illustrated by the following example:

```
forall l in lecturer
    not exists s in staff
        such that phone of l = phone of s
```

The above constraint guarantees the uniqueness of the phone numbers of lecturers. It combines search among the instances of two classes, *lecturer* and *staff*. These two classes are related through an "is-a" link, so an instance of the class *lecturer* is also an instance of the class *staff*. That means that an additional condition (l <> s) is understood.

So far, we have demonstrated CoLan expressions concerning only simple attributes, i.e. attributes whose values are simple objects, like integers, strings, etc. Complex attributes are the ones that "point" to other objects by storing their object identifier (henceforth OID). Constraints that compare complex attributes are called navigational, because they are defined on one class but they really constrain the values that attributes of other classes can have. We can use function composition to follow these chains of instances, linked by binary relationships. The following constraint illustrates this:

```
forall l in lecturer
    age of research_assistant of l < 35
```

The *host* class of the above constraint is *lecturer*, but the constraint itself inhibits values for the class *ra*, because the slot *research_assistant* contains OIDs of instances of class *ra*. Therefore, the constraint is really about the *age* slot of the instances of the class *ra*, but is only applicable to those that are related to instances of class *lecturer* through the relationship *research_assistant*.

We can also use complex attributes in the quantification part of the constraint, as is illustrated in the following constraint:

```
forall l in lecturer
    forall r in research_assistant of l
        research_interests of l =
            research_interests of tutor of r
```

This constraint is recursive, since it relates the class *lecturer* with itself, through the class *ra* and the complex attributes *research_assistant* of *lecturer* and *tutor* of *ra*.

Of course, all these features can be combined to express even more complex constraints. It is also possible to make use of mathematical operations and functions to compute the values that are to be constrained. The constraints shown above are intended to give a flavour of CoLan, and a fuller range of examples, plus details of how the Prolog rules are compiled from the CoLan constraints, can be found in [1, 2]. The full syntax for the CoLan language is given in BNF format in the Appendix.

3 Related Work

It has been suggested [13] that constraints should be expressed in pure logic and held in deductive databases, so that the constraints can be proved correct by some kind of mechanised proof technique. However, semantic constraints on explicit data are relatively straightforward and deterministic to check. They apply to specific instances and have to be checked individually. Thus there is no particular advantage to a logic representation for CoLan, and indeed we claim that the functional form is easier to read. However, it would be useful to have a logic-based checker to show that a new constraint being inserted was not inconsistent with existing constraints, nor was it subsumed by any of them. This would improve performance but it is really part of constraint design and analysis, and we do not consider this issue further here. Work such as [3] has shown how to use Prolog fragments to enforce constraints with a relational or deductive database. This showed how to compile relevant rules, but had no concept of fragment re-use and inheritance in an object-oriented context.

Kulkarni and Atkinson [1986] describe a syntax for constraint definitions in their implementation of Daplex (EFDM). Constraints are expressed on property values thus :-

```
constraint c1 on cname(person), sname(person) -> unique;
constraint c2 on sex(person) -> total;
constraint c3 on student,staff -> disjoint;
constraint c4 on grade(student,course) ->
        some c in courses(student) has c = course
```

Of these, c2 and c3 are structural constraints, c1 is a structural constraint but expressible in CoLan, and c4 is a predicate constraint of the kind which CoLan is designed to express. One weakness of EFDM constraints is that they are expressed in terms of restricting the values of specific properties on specific entity types. Instead, CoLan expresses the constraint on the entity class rather than the property, and although stored with this class it is cross-referenced from all the update-methods for properties mentioned in the constraint. Thus one CoLan constraint stands for several constraints in EFDM.

The CoLan equivalent of constraint c1 is:

```
forall p1 in person
    not exists p2 in person
        such that cname of p2 = cname of p1 and
                  sname of p2 = sname of p1
```

Note that CoLan implicitly requires that a second variable over the same entity class does not have the same value as the first (i.e. p1 <> p2). We can express c4 in CoLan by introducing an enrollment entity with properties student, course and grade:

```
forall e in enrollment
    exists c in courses of student of e
        such that c = course of e
```

CoLan generalises the EFDM syntax in that it quantifies over instance identifiers and not over property values. It also generalises the notion of *fixed* value by using the comparator *"exactly"*, and implements numerical quantifiers, such as "at most 3", which appear in EFDM syntax but not in any published examples of EFDM constraints.

Urban [1987, 1989] discusses many types of constraint. As noted in [9] most of these are enforced by the FDM as structural constraints, apart from the unique constraint discussed above and a covering constraint for subtypes. The ALICE language is used by [20, 21] to write constraints in a predicate logic style. The original use of ALICE was for "constraint analysis", in conjunction with tools which allowed a user to foresee interactions between constraints and to specify actions to recover from violations. Thus there was no system to enforce the constraints, but in [21] a system is described for constraint enforcement through active rules. This system generates methods ("state-altering database operations") which trigger active rules generated from ALICE constraints. This is an impressive system. Its aims are similar to ours in that it code-generate rules from declarative specifications. The main difference is that it uses an active-rule interpreter, with a forward chaining mechanism instead of a recursive Prolog goal-driven mechanism.

Their system attempts to use rules to recover from integrity violation by triggering other updates. This can run into cycles or "anomalous rule behaviour". By contrast, we are concerned only with rejecting invalid transitions, which is an easier problem to solve. The other main difference is that the declarative rules in ALICE use logic instead of a functional form. The functional form makes it natural to call out to functions which compute derived values, for example using methods declared on object classes. There are no examples of constraints incorporating derived values in [21]. Thus we feel that the functional form for constraints fits better with an object-oriented approach.

A recent paper on ADAM by Paton, Diaz and Barja [1993] argues strongly for using a combination of metaclasses and active rules in ADAM to represent object semantics. They are sceptical of the value of enforcing constraints through methods. In particular, they are worried about having specialisations of methods accidentally overriding important constraints. They are also worried about unforeseen interactions between constraints inherited from methods defined independently on various superclasses. They propose to solve this by triggering active rules from the methods and passing the problems to an active rule interpreter, for it to resolve the interactions. We believe we can overcome their objection by code-generating all constraints in a way that cannot be overridden. Thus we insist that constraints are defined in a high-level language which is easier to check at compile time and in a single consistent regime, which makes it easier to recognise and deal with interactions.

4   Implementation Strategy

The behaviour we propose for integrity maintenance is essentially very simple. At compile-time, we take a high-level declarative specification of a constraint and generate several fragments of code that will check for violation of that constraint by various updates. Both the declarative text of the constraint and the code fragments are stored in the metadata in such a way that the link between the constraint and its associated code is maintained, and that facilitates run-time retrieval of individual code fragments.

The run-time behaviour is specified as a guard to each database update operation. This guard uses the metadata and the details of the current update to decide which constraints (including inherited constraints) may be violated by the update, and consequently which code fragments must be executed. These fragments are extracted from the metadata and executed in the context of the current update. If the update passes all the checks then it is allowed to succeed.

The important point here is that the guard (i.e. the constraint checker) decides which code fragments must be executed independently of any other system binding mechanism (such as method binding), at run-time. This means that constraints may be added to or deleted from the schema without requiring any recompilation of methods, and also that we can specialise the inheritance strategy for constraints according to the semantics we require. Constraints are a kind of definitional property attached to classes and therefore cannot be overridden [5]. Thus, they require a completely different inheritance strategy from methods, which can be overridden and/or cancelled completely by more specialised versions. Our approach gains us these advantages without incurring the overhead of a general-purpose rule manager.

This approach to constraint maintenance can be implemented in any system which has the following:

1. a schema description language into which a high-level constraint language can be introduced,

2. the ability to store constraint information and fragments of code as meta-data at run-time,

3. some mechanism for guarding update operations with constraint checking code,

4. and, most importantly, the ability to retrieve, manipulate and execute fragments of code at run-time.

To illustrate how this approach works in practice, we now give descriptions of our two implementations.

4.1   Implementation in ADAM

4.1.1   Maintenance of Constraint Metadata

A new constraint is added to the ADAM system by sending the message *put_constraint*, with the constraint text as a string-valued argument, to the class on which the constraint is defined. This method is responsible for calling the parser, the code generator, the optimiser and the storer in order to translate the constraint into Prolog code and store it in the database. The generated code fragments are stored in set-valued slots inside the decsriptor of the classes to which they refer. There are five such slots per class, one for each type of update: *new_constraints*, *delete_constraints*, *put_constraints*, *update_constraints* and *delete_slot_constraints*.

This arrangement facilitates fast and accurate retrieval of the code, because it uses a two-place index for locating the relevant fragment repository, and the search within the repository is then linear. The two parts to the index are the recipient class and the update type, so that if we are searching for constraint code for checking the method *new* defined on the class *lecturer*, we should send the message *get_new_constraints* to *lecturer*.

The actual constraints are stored not as simple strings but as distinct objects that are instances of the class *constraints*. The code storer is responsible for storing the identifier of a constraint instance with the code fragments that have been generated from it. This helps the constraint maintenance system to locate the code attached to a constraint more easily, for constraint deletion, and to locate the constraint to which a piece of code is attached, for generation of meaningful error messages upon constraint violation.

The system of using code attached to update methods (triggers) depends on the assumption that the database is already consistent with the constraints, and that one is only checking the constraint incrementally on the changes. Thus, when a new constraint is to be inserted, the system first checks that all existing instances in the database satisfy it. If not, a warning message is printed and the constraint is not inserted. If the user wishes to know which instances fail then it is a simple matter to query the database and find them, before deciding on appropriate updates.

When a constraint is deleted, the system uses a stored relationship between each constraint object and the classes and slots which have attached code fragments in order to locate and remove the fragments. It also removes the stored textual form of the constraint. This is where the representation makes easy something almost impossible with hand-written method code.

4.1.2   Constraint Checking and Inheritance

In ADAM, inheritance of more general method definitions is implemented by delegating the message received by an instance of a class to its superclass. Thus, if the user does not include a call to the superclass, when specialising a method, then the default behaviour is lost/overridden. For constraints, however, we want inclusion inheritance and not the cancellation inheritance of methods. Hence, in CoLan, inheritance and checking of all the constraints is carried out by a special predicate called *check_constraints*, as follows. When an update message is received by an instance of a class, a call to *check_constraints* is made, which works out what constraints need to be checked. Inheritance proceeds in a top-down fashion, i.e. first constraints defined in the root class are checked and then constraints defined in the immediate subclasses, etc. In fact, what is inherited is not the high level description of the constraint but the appropriate fragment of generated code that ensures the validity of the corresponding constraint. When the piece of code is obtained, whether from the target class or one of its superclasses, it is applied in the context of the current update and the recipient object. If the fragment of Prolog code succeeds, i.e. the update does not violate the constraint, then the algorithm backtracks to get another piece of code that corresponds to another constraint. If all constraints are inherited and checked successfully, the update is accepted and the default method that responds to the update message is executed. If one of the constraints is violated, then no further constraints will be checked, because the update is invalid anyway. In this case the update is rejected and the default method is not invoked. An informative error message is displayed and the original call fails.

4.1.3   Expressing Constraints in ADAM

Constraints can be expressed and checked in ADAM by altering the default method definitions. This approach makes it very awkward for a user to hand-implement constraints, because one has to translate the semantics of the constraint into Prolog and then replace the method definitions for updates and modifications inside all the relevant classes and metaclasses. Fortunately, we are able to use Prolog to work out what code is needed where automatically.

To demonstrate the complexity of hand-generating constraint checking in ADAM, we translate an earlier example:

"Lecturers may not share a phone with any other members of staff".

We need to check this constraint whenever a phone number is inserted into *phone* slot of an instance of class *lecturer*, and so we override the default method *put_phone* in class *lecturer* with the following call:

```
:- put_method([
      (put_phone(global,[],[integer],[],[Phone]) :-
          (get_by_phone([Phone],_) => staff ->
                write('There cannot be two lecturers with
                                the same phone number!'), nl,
              fail
        ;
              put_phone([Phone]) => super
```

```
        )
    )]) => lecturer.
```

However, this is not the only piece of code to create to ensure the consistency of the database. Methods *update_phone* and *new* must also be altered to exclude every potential modification of the database that would lead to an inconsistency. Code must be generated for the corresponding methods of class *staff*, too, to inhibit a staff instance from violating the constraint. A single constraint here affects at least six methods!

The code fragment generated by the CoLan system to check this constraint when new phone numbers are added, takes a more general approach to checking the constraint, as is to be expected with automatically generated code:

```
put_phone(global,[],[integer],[],[Phone]) :-
    message_recipient(Id),
    findall(Inst, (
            get(Inst) => staff,
            get_phone(PhoneStaff) => Inst,
            Inst \== Id,
            Phone == PhoneStaff
    ), List),
    length(Length, List),
    (not (Length < 1) ->
            error_message(...), fail
    ;
            true
    ).
```

The system would generate similar fragments for each of the updates that may violate the constraint. We make two points here. The first is the use of "findall" to collect the set of things that satisfy the criteria of the constraint. This approach provides uniformity, because every constraint has a similar structure, however, this may prove inefficient, since for constraints with a small upper limit in the quantification part, only a minimal check would suffice and save time as well. Thus, in the P/FDM implementation we plan to store counts and replace findall by specialised predicates for efficiency. The second point to note is that, depending on the constraint, we may need to check it only for methods creating new instances (e.g. when checking against a maximum limit) or only on methods deleting or changing instances. The general technique for this is described in [2], along with other significant optimisations. These are being carried across to P/FDM, where appropriate.

4.2 Implementation in P/FDM

4.2.1 Maintenance of Constraint Metadata

P/FDM has a rather different design brief to ADAM's and consequently a rather different architecture (despite the common implementation language). ADAM is an extensible system that allows the prototyping of new data model elements while P/FDM concentrates on providing efficient access to a simple but expressive data model. P/FDM has no concept of metaclasses and the metadata for classes and functions is stored in special Prolog terms. We have been able to design these terms so that we have efficient access to metadata, which is an important prerequisite for efficient access to data. We have also provided a special interface to these metadata clauses that allows them to be queried as if they were true database objects [6]. While this gives general *read* access to metadata, only system programmers and specially provided primitive operations are allowed to update it.

To store constraint information in P/FDM, then, we have introduced some new Prolog metadata terms. We have a *constraint descriptor* term, which stores general information about each constraint, such as its system identifier, its enabled flag and, for numerically quantified constraints, a count of the number of instances currently satisfying the constraint. The term also stores the specification of the constraint as a string suitable for displaying to the user, and the internal form of the constraint, as a sort of quantified set expression. We store this parse tree (which is really the intermediate format generated by the compiler) as it can be queried and manipulated more easily than either the CoLan string or the generated Prolog code. It is also very close to the intermediate format used when compiling ordinary Daplex queries and we hope that this will facilitate the incorporation of constraint information into other queries.

As with the ADAM implementation, it is necessary to maintain a two-way relationship between constraints and the code fragments which check their validity. Since we do not allow slots to be defined on class descriptors in P/FDM, we must maintain these links as three relations, represented as Prolog term structures (or clauses). Two of these relations are called *constraint index* terms, because they provide an associative index to constraint identifiers, one from classes and the other from functions (i.e. attributes):

```
class_to_constraint(ClassName, ConstraintId).
```

```
function_to_constraint(FunName, FirstArgType, ConstraintId).
```

Note that we do not index inherited constraints in the constraint index terms as we wish to hide the details of the actual inheritance process within the `check_constraints` method. If we later find that the performance of the constraint checking is not adequate, we can consider sacrificing the flexibility this gives us and embedding the inheritance strategy into these indexes.

We must also provide a link to the Prolog code fragments that implement the constraint checks. As with the ADAM implementation, in P/FDM we generate fragments of code that check that consistency is maintained for each of the basic update operations: creating a new instance, deleting an instance, adding a new function (i.e. attribute) value, deleting a function value and updating (changing) a function value. Again, since we cannot attach these directly to the class and function metadata, we must represent them as a set of related clauses. This is the third relation, which we call the *fragment index terms*:

```
constraint_to_code(ConstraintId, Class/FunctionId,
    UpdateType, ArgumentsToUpdate, HeadOfFragment).
```

This relation allows us to retrieve the code head for the fragment that checks the given update for the given class or function. We use this two-stage lookup process (i.e. metadata identifier to constraint, constraint and metadata identifier to code fragment) because this simplifies the handling of inherited constraints.

Although, as we have said, metadata for P/FDM is stored in specially designed Prolog terms, it is possible to query metadata as if it were stored in an ordinary database using either the Prolog primitives or the Daplex query language. This gives both the user and the system programmer very flexible access to information about the current set of constraints. We might, for instance, want to find out which constraints are currently disabled:

```
for each c in constraintmeta such that enabled(c) = ''no''
print(text(c));
```

or list all constraints which involve the "student" class:

```
for the e in entitymeta such that oname(e) = ''student''
    for each c in constraints_on(e)
print(text(c));
```

We expect this facility to be particularly useful for applications which make use of constraint information other than for integrity maintenance.

4.2.2 Constraint Checking and Inheritance

Another difference between ADAM and P/FDM is the handling of methods. When a new ADAM class is created, the system automatically generates the methods required to manipulate instances of the class and their slots. The class *staff* has, for example, its own **get** method for retrieving staff members, and its own **new** method for creating them. The interface to P/FDM databases, on the other hand, consists of a set of primitives which operate on all classes or attributes; instances of any class are retrieved by the **getentity/3** primitive and created by the **newentity/3** primitive, for example. In fact, P/FDM does allow different definitions for these primitives so that different storage systems can be supported, but they are all accessed via a single *driver* primitive that hides the process of binding to the correct definition.

Rather than placing the call to the constraint checker within individual methods, as in the ADAM implementation, in P/FDM we place the call inside these driver primitives, before the code which binds to and executes the actual definition of the primitive (the *internal* primitive):

```
newentity(Class, KeyValues, NewInstId) :-
    check_constraints(Class, KeyValues),
    class_name_to_module_type(Class, ModType), !,
    internal_newentity(ModType, Class, KeyValues, NewInstId).
```

This illustrates the need for the two indexes relating class and function names to constraints. In the ADAM implementation, we get automatic indexing on class because constraint fragments are stored with the class to which the update method is sent. In P/FDM, however, a single primitive routine deals with all classes, and so we must make the link from the class to the constraint explicit. This strategy does have the advantage of allowing us to index from a function to a constraint as well, which the ADAM implementation does not currently do.

To check the constraints relevant to a particular update in the P/FDM implementation we use the metadata about the class inheritance hierarchy and the constraint indexes to find all constraints that are relevant to the class or function being updated (whether directly or by inheritance). We then use the fragment index terms to retrieve the heads of the code fragments that must be executed, with their arguments instantiated with details of the update that is to be made. Unlike the ADAM implementation, in P/FDM we retrieve all the code heads at once, and then execute them together in the form of a negated disjunction. The reason for this is that we generate code fragments that *succeed* when the constraint is violated, on the grounds that it is potentially more efficient to search for a single set of values that violate a constraint than to test that all combinations satisfy it. We check that all the constraints are satisfied, then, by checking that $\bar{A} \wedge \bar{B} \wedge \bar{C}$ succeeds (where A, B and C represent code fragments) or, in other words, that $A \vee B \vee C$ fails.

4.2.3 Expressing Constraint Checks in P/FDM

To illustrate the advantages of generating code fragments that succeed on constraint violation, consider the following (simplified) Prolog routine that checks for violation of the constraint on staff phone numbers given earlier by the addition of a new lecturer's phone number:

```
constraint1_addfnval1([Lecturer], Phone) :-
    getentity(staff, Staff),
    \+ relative(staff, Lecturer, Staff),
    getfnval(phone, [Staff], Phone),
    error_message(...).
```

The checking process begins by enumerating an instance of the class *staff* (using the `getentity/3` call), and then checking that it is distinct from the *lecturer* instance that is being updated (using the `relative/3` primitive). We then retrieve the phone number of this staff member (if any) and, if it is equal to the new phone number, then the constraint has been violated and we can display the error message and succeed. Otherwise, the call to `getfnval/3` fails, causing the retrieval of the next *staff* instance.

There are two advantages to this style of constraint checking. The first, as we have said, is that it is potentially more efficient than a check for non-violation of a constraint. The second advantage is that it simplifies code generation. It is very easy to generate the code for a weak translation of CoLan constraints in this way, because the non-existence of any value involved in the constraint (e.g. when a staff member has not been allocated a phone number) is signalled in the same way as constraint satisfaction — i.e. with failure. Also, we do not have to generate concluding if-then-else constructs in order to ensure that the code fragment succeeds.

5 Future Plans for Constraints in P/FDM

A declarative constraint language is generally considered to be easier for people to write (in their capacity as database designers) and to understand (in their capacity as domain experts). In fact, declarative specifications are not only easier for humans to understand and analyse but they are also easier for programs to manipulate, and this opens up the possibility for more intelligent data handling by database management systems. The potential uses of constraint information in query optimisation has long been recognised [10] but more ambitious projects, such as the use of constraint specifications in suggesting corrective updates when integrity is violated [12, 21], have also been tackled. Here we outline two potential uses for constraint information in the P/FDM system.

5.1 Constraints and Backtrackable Updates

We have recently extended the Daplex language with a new loop construct that allows the user to describe the creation of database objects declaratively in terms of the properties that they must have, rather than the exact details of their attribute values [7]. Such programs are translated into recursive Prolog routines that use backtracking and special undo-able database updates (called *backtrackable updates*) to find a combination of attribute values that meets the given criteria. In effect, backtrackable updates work like a special kind of transaction, where we accept limitations on the updates that may be performed in return for the ability to undo updates up to an arbitrary point (i.e. not necessarily to the beginning of the transaction). We would like to examine the potential for optimising this search process by incorporating appropriate constraints into the program to restrict the search space as much as possible. It was with this possibility in mind that we stressed the importance of two features of our representation of constraint metadata:

1. the similarity between the internal formats for constraints and ordinary Daplex programs, which should ease the process of incorporating constraints into pieces of Daplex at compile-time.

2. the flexible querying facilities on constraint metadata, which should allow us to locate the constraints which might reduce the search space under consideration.

5.2 Constraints and Transactions

We have also implemented a simple transaction mechanism for P/FDM, that operates rather like a differential file. Within a transaction, updates are stored in two in-memory database modules — one storing the newly created objects and function values, and the other containing the deletions. The contents of these two modules are managed so that, at any one time, they represent the minimal set of database updates that would be needed to reproduce the effect of the transaction so far. This means that it is possible to find out what the net effect of a transaction is by using the ordinary database querying primitives (which is not so simple in other systems, such as Starburst [22], which compute the net effect of a transaction from the log of changes at commit-time).

Transaction mechanisms are often found alongside constraints in database systems as they provide a neat solution to the problem of "composite updates", i.e. the problem of sequences of updates that collectively do not violate integrity but which individually do. An ordinary constraint maintenance system (such as either of the two implementations described here) would prevent any of the individual updates from being made and therefore prevent the whole, perfectly legal update from going ahead! With a transaction mechanism, though, we can suspend the checking of integrity constraints until transactions are committed, by which time integrity ought to have been restored.

Our differential representation of the state of a transaction provides a concise description of the updates that must be checked by the constraint mechanism, and cuts down on the number of redundant checks that must be made (as opposed to, say, a transaction mechanism that works by logging updates). If we consider the numerically quantified constraints, for example, we can count the number of instances in the transaction modules which satisfy the constraint condition (transaction count = addition count − deletion count) and can then combine this total with the count stored in the constraint metadata to decide whether the constraint has been violated or not.

We would like to investigate possible ways of helping the user to recover database integrity when constraints are found to have been violated at the end of a transaction. The simplest action is to exit the commit with the user still within the transaction, so that they can take remedial action and attempt to commit again, but we feel that the DBMS ought to be able to take a more active role in helping the user. The great advantage of our approach over an active-rule based approach, in this respect, is that we are able to examine all the updates that have been made during a transaction, and our field of vision is not limited to the update (or, possibly, the sequence of updates if complex events are allowed) that fired the current rule. This ought to allow us to be able to present the user with a set of alternative actions, from which they may select the most suitable option for restoring integrity.

6 Conclusion

The integration of integrity constraints and databases has been a long-term goal of database research. Simple constraints can be enforced by type checks and range checks in the interpreter for the update language, but we are concerned with the more complex semantic integrity constraints which require a significant amount of computation and navigation. These can only be represented by procedural code, stored and shared in the database. However, we do not wish to store it in the same way as methods, nor do we wish to hand-code it as part of a method, because

1. we want users to be able to write clear declarative code which they can easily check, instead of multiple code fragments which they easily get wrong.

2. we wish to share code fragments between various classes

3. we do not wish constraints to be overridden

4. we wish to be able to selectively disable or delete individual constraints without knowing how they are implemented.

The design given above fulfils all these aims. It has been proved in ADAM but it does not require a language with metaclasses; thus we can re-implement it in P/FDM which uses clauses as class descriptors. Basically this is because only system programmers are able to use Prolog in P/FDM and thus to change the slots and metadata, whereas in ADAM this is open to all but controlled through metaclasses.

One advantage of P/FDM is that it allows us to use constraints with our existing scientific data, and also to use Daplex as a query language on the constraints themselves, as on other metadata. Another advantage is that we have been able to make use of a new transaction mechanism developed for P/FDM so as to delay tests on constraints until a trial version of the database (represented by a kind of differential file) has been updated. This is necessary where any single update on a slot would break attached constraints unless one (or more) other updates are performed. This shows the weakness of relying on triggers attached to slots to check integrity constraints.

In ABEL [5], for example, active rules change the state of the database to restore consistency, usually via an action initiating a dialogue with the user. Effectively the system "jumps the gun" in checking after the first update, instead of waiting to be told about other compensating updates! Although an active rule system can be helpful in prompting and suggesting extra updates required to restore consistency, we feel this may annoy some users (or even a remote program) carrying out a complicated pre-planned update. Thus we are exploring the more usual transaction scheme, but adapting it to use delayed constraints expressed in Prolog. This approach resembles some other active systems, such as [21, 22], which support transactions and are able to delay rule-firing until commit-time.

Appendix: CoLan Syntax

```
<constraint>              ::= <quantification> [such that] [<predicates>]
<quantification>          ::= <quantified_expr> [<quantification>]
<quantified_expr>         ::= <quantified_var> [such that]
                              [<predicates>] | <constraint>]
<quantified_var>          ::= <quantifier> <var> in <compound_class>
<quantifier>              ::= forall | [not] exists |
                              exist <numerical_quantifier>
<numerical_quantifier>    ::= <numerical_expression> <number>
<numerical_expression>    ::= <numerical_symbol> | <numerical_words>
<numerical_symbol>        ::= = | > | >= | < | =<
<numerical_words>         ::= only | exactly | more than | no less than
                              at least | less than | no more than | at most
<compound_class>          ::= <slot> of <compound_class> |
                              <class>
<predicates>              ::= <conjunction> [or <predicates>]
<conjunction>             ::= <predicate> [and <conjunction>]
<predicate>               ::= <multi_operand> <relational_connector>
                              <multi_operand>
<multi_operand>           ::= <operand> | <complex_operand>
<operand>                 ::= <slot_operand> | <constant>
<slot_operand>            ::= [<slot> of] <var> |
                              <slot> of <slot_operand>
<complex_operand>         ::= <operand> <operation> <operand>
<operation>               ::= + | - | * | \
<relational_connector>    ::= = | <> | > | < | >= | =< | is in | not in
```

where:

```
<var>       ::=   atom        % denoting a variable
<slot>      ::=   atom        % denoting a slot
<class>     ::=   atom        % denoting a class
<constant>  ::=   integer | string | prolog
<number>    ::=   integer
```

References

[1] N.D. Bassiliades
"Constraint Description in ADAM", MSc. Thesis, University of Aberdeen.

[2] N.D. Bassiliades and P.M.D. Gray
"CoLan: a Functional Constraint Language and its Implementation", in
preparation.

[3] F. Bry, H. Decker and R. Manthey
"A Uniform Approach to Constraint Satisfaction and Constraint Satisfiability in Deductive Databases", in Advances in Database Technology - EDBT
'88, J.W. Schmidt, S. Ceri and M. Missikoff (eds.), Springer-Verlag, pp.
488–505.

[4] O. Diaz and N.W. Paton
"Sharing Behaviour in an Object-Oriented Database using a Rule-Based
Mechanism", in Aspects of Databases – Proc. 9th BNCOD, Butterworth,
1991, pp. 17–37.

[5] O. Diaz, N.W. Paton and P.M.D. Gray
"Rule Management in Object-Oriented Databases: a Uniform Approach",
in F. Saltor (ed.), Proc. 17th VLDB, Barcelona, 1991, pp. 317–326.

[6] S.M. Embury, Z. Jiao and P.M.D. Gray
"Using Prolog to Provide Access to Metadata in an Object-Oriented
Database", in Proc. 1st Practical Application of Prolog Conf., Applied
Workstations Ltd.

[7] S.M. Embury and P.M.D. Gray
"Compiling Daplex into Backtrackable Updates", in preparation.

[8] P.M.D. Gray, D.S. Moffat and N.W. Paton
"A Prolog Interface to a Functional Data Model Database", in Advances in
Database Technology - EDBT '88, J.W. Schmidt, S. Ceri and M. Missikoff
(eds.), Springer-Verlag, pp. 34–48.

[9] P.M.D. Gray, K.G. Kulkarni and N.W. Paton
Object-Oriented Databases, A Semantic Data Model Approach, Prentice
Hall, 1992.

[10] J.J. King
Query Optimisation by Semantic Reasoning, UMI Research Press.

[11] K.G. Kulkarni and M.P. Atkinson
"EFDM:extended functional data model", The Computer Journal (29),
1986, pp 38–46.

[12] M. Morgenstern
"Constraint Equations: Declarative Expression of Constraints with Automatic Enforcement", Proc. 10th VLDB, pp. 291–300.

[13] J.M. Nicolas
"Logic for Improving Integrity Checking in Relational Databases", in Acta Informatica, no. 18, Springer-Verlag, 1982, pp. 227–253.

[14] G.M. Nijssen, "Modelling in Data Base Management Systems" in Proc. Euro IFIP 79, London, ed. P.A. Samet, North-Holland, 1979, pp 39–52.

[15] N.W. Paton
"ADAM: An object-oriented database system implemented in Prolog", in Proc. 7th BNCOD, ed. Williams, CUP, 1989, pp. 147–161.

[16] N.W. Paton, O. Diaz and M.L. Barja
"Combining Active Rules and Metaclasses for enhanced extensibility in Object-Oriented Systems", Data and Knowledge Eng., 10, pp. 45–63.

[17] D.W. Shipman
"The functional data model and the data language DAPLEX", ACM TODS 6, 1981, pp 140–173.

[18] M.L. Stonebraker et al.
"Third-Generation Database System Manifesto" in "Object-Oriented Databases: Analysis, Design and Construction (DS-4)", eds. R.A. Meersman, W.Kent and S. Khosla, North-Holland, 1992, pp 495–511.

[19] S.D. Urban
"Constraint Analysis for the Design of Semantic Database Update Operations", PhD Dissertation, University of Southwestern La., September 1987.

[20] S.D. Urban
"ALICE: An Assertion Language for Integrity Constraint Expression", in Proc. of Computer Software Applications Conf., Orlando, September 1989.

[21] S.D. Urban, A.P. Karadimce and R.B. Nannapaneni,
"The Implementation and Evaluation of Integrity Maintenance Rules in an Object-Oriented Database", in Data Engineering, 1992.

[22] J. Widom, R.J. Cochrane and B.G. Lindsay,
"Implementing Set-Oriented Production Rules as an Extension to Starburst", in F. Saltor (ed.), Proc. 17th VLDB, Barcelona, 1991, pp. 275–285.

Deductive Databases

A Heuristic for Rule Allocation in Distributed Deductive Database Systems

Mukesh K. Mohania

Department of Computer Science & Engg.

Indian Institute of Technology

Bombay, INDIA

mukesh@cse.iitb.ernet.in

N. L. Sarda

Department of Computer Science & Engg.

Indian Institute of Technology

Bombay, INDIA

nls@cse.iitb.ernet.in

Abstract

Allocation of rules to sites in a distributed deductive database system is an important and challenging task especially for a large knowledge base. We identify communication cost in rule execution to be the primary basis for decomposing a global knowledge base into clusters for their allocation to sites. It has been shown that the problem of optimal allocation is a 0-1 quadratic programming problem, which has prohibitive execution times for large knowledge bases. We propose an efficient heuristic algorithm for rule allocation and study its performance experimentally. We represent a knowledge base as a hierarchy of rules. These rules are then allocated in a bottom-up fashion w.r.t. the hierarchy. The experimental results of the heuristic algorithm on random hierarchies as well as on hierarchies with varying heights are seen to be close to the optimal solution.

1 Introduction

The development of database technology has currently reached the stage of Deductive Database Systems (DedDBSs) [3], which not only manage a large database but also provide for deduction [7] from the given database and rulebase. They use horn clauses for defining relations (for storing database), rulebase as well as user queries. A Distributed Deductive Database System (DDed-DBS) consists of many autonomous deductive database systems connected by a computer network to facilitate sharing of both database and rules. Efforts are being focused on defining an architecture for such systems [2, 12, 15]. In this paper, we consider one important aspect of the problem of designing a distributed deductive database system, namely, allocation of rules to sites. Henceforth, we will use the term "Knowledge Base (KB)" for the rulebase.

Designing an application for DDedDBMS differs from the conventional non-distributed deductive database systems in that it requires design of distribution of both the database and knowledge base. Distribution of data in a Distributed Database Management System (DDBMS) has already received considerable attention [4], while partitioning and allocation of the knowledge base and optimization of deductive queries in a DDedDBMS have not yet been addressed adequately.

In this paper, we focus our attention to the problem of partitioning and allocation of a knowledge base. Given (i) a set of sites (a site is a physical location/address of a database system), (ii) a (possibly replicated) allocation of relations to the various sites, and (iii) the global knowledge base consisting of Datalog rules [3], the objective is to partition the global knowledge base into what we term as 'clusters' so that they can be assigned to the sites. Our approach assumes that the problems of distribution of data and knowledge base can be treated separately. Further, we assume that the former has already been done based on the dominant database queries (including updates) and that the latter needs to be done based on the database usage and interrelationships between the rules, which are the potential knowledge base queries.

Since a rule may refer to another rule or data stored at another site, the individual DedDBS must cooperate during the execution of that rule. This cooperation consists of resolution and/or database access and transmitting data from one site to another. Minimizing communication cost is one important goal in partitioning and allocation of knowledge base.

The problem of optimal rule allocation is shown in [14] as a 0-1 quadratic programming problem which is NP-complete [8] and has prohibitive execution times for large knowledge bases. We propose and evaluate a heuristic algorithm to solve this problem and also compare the results of our heuristic with the exhaustive enumeration algorithm that produces allocations of rules with minimal communication cost.

The general problem of clustering comes up in various contexts in computer-based systems. In a multiprocessor or a distributed computing system, tasks to be processed may have to be clustered onto a set of processors so that interprocessor communication cost can be reduced [13]. Stone [17] has used a graph-theoretical approach to model intermodule communications in a program and adapted the maximum flow algorithm to find an optimal partitioning of a modular program in a two processor system. In distributed DBMS [4], the relations of a database can be fragmented in three ways, namely, horizontal, vertical, and mixed fragments. Each fragment is a cluster of data which are predominantly used together by applications. Many object oriented DBMSs [1, 11] have been designed using different clustering schemes which are static in nature. Objects are clustered based on their inter-relationships and/or their simultaneous access potential. A dynamic reclustering scheme of objects has been discussed in [5]. A number of data clustering algorithms have also been developed in application areas such as statistics and pattern classification and analysis which address the problem of grouping or clustering data using various criteria. The most commonly used partitioning/clustering strategy is based on the square-error criterion [10]. Kemal Oflazer [16] addressed the problem of production rulebase partitioning in OPS5 production systems. The problem of partitioning productions in a production system for parallel execution, which is NP-complete [8], is shown in [6] as a 0-1 integer programming with a quadratic objective function. The objective in [6] is to assign compatible rules to different clusters so that maximum parallelism can be achieved, whereas we wish to allocate the rules based on their usage of data stored in each database system. Cost due to indirect dependencies has not been considered in production partitioning problem formulation. We have, perhaps for the first time, studied the problem of clustering and distributing rules of a given global knowledge base across a set of interconnected relational database systems in order to convert them into a cooperative deductive database system [15].

In section 2, we outline the need and basis for clustering a knowledge base. Section 3 describes input and output matrices of the rule allocation problem. Section 4 describes representation of knowledge base as a hierarchy and presents a 'bottom-up' heuristic algorithm for allocation of rules to sites. The experimental results for measuring effectiveness of our efficient algorithm in finding near-optimal solutions are given in section 5. It also contains some characterizations of real-world knowledge bases, and shows satisfactory performance of our algorithm for knowledge bases satisfying these characteristics. Finally, section 6 contains our conclusions and future plans.

2   Preliminaries

2.1   Definitions

A Datalog rule has the form
$$P_0(X_0) : -P_1(X_1), \ldots, P_n(X_n)$$
where P_i is a predicate name, X_i is a vector of terms and each term involves a variable or a constant. Each $P_i(X_i)$ is called a literal. The left hand side of a rule is the head of rule. It is a derived predicate. The right hand side of the rule is the body. It contains either derived predicates or base predicates or both. A base predicate corresponds to a relation in the database. A rule with an empty body and a constant term vector is a fact. A query is a rule without a head. A rule is recursive if the definition in the body may depend on the head predicate, either directly by reference or transitively through a predicate referenced in the body. The transitive dependence is called indirect dependence. P and Q are mutually recursive if they belong to the same cycle of indirect dependence relationship.

A cluster is a collection of rules. It represents a partition of the global knowledge base. As rules in a cluster will have same site allocation, the clusters can also be viewed as units for allocation. In practice, we expect a cluster to represent closely interrelated knowledge, where rules mostly refer to either other rules in the same cluster or the database available at that site. The clusters can be suitably labeled, e.g., as *production-scheduling rulebase*, *design rulebase*, etc. Often, the cluster and the database at a site will serve some well-defined functional area of the application. Within a cluster, rules are distinguished by their unique head predicates. The cluster containing definition of a rule is its home cluster.

A rule of one cluster may refer to a rule of another cluster in its body as well as to the databases stored elsewhere. In order to execute queries efficiently, we require in our architecture [15] that references to non-local (i.e. remote) literals in the body of a rule be preceded by the identifier of the cluster containing definition of that predicate.

2.2 Need for Clustering

Let us briefly characterize the application scenarios of DDedDBMSs envisaged by us. A DDedDBMS may serve a single large organization, or multiple organizations may wish to share their data and knowledge bases for cooperative processing or profit. Assume a set of sites in these cases, each with a database. Either these database systems already exist as autonomous units (the 'bottom-up' approach) or the data has been distributed across sites to meet their operational needs (the 'top-down' approach). A Global Knowledge Base (GKB) is now given to be stored appropriately at the sites for efficient querying by the users.

It has been recognized that many centralized knowledge based systems utilize a large number of rules and is used in many applications, including engineering processes, manufacturing and communication. For example, the Boeing connection assembly specification expert system and the expert system for VLSI design [9] contain more than 10,000 rules each. We are also interested in applications where GKB may contain hundreds of thousands of rules to be shared by users at tens or hundreds of sites. GKB may be partitioned into one/more clusters and stored at sites with or without replication. As with distributed database systems, availability and local accessibility will be among the criteria for partitioning and allocation. Although the definitions of rules in GKB are expected to be much less time invariant than the data in databases, full replication of GKB is not realistic for reasons of administration of GKB.

The clustering and distribution of GKB has significant impact on overall system performance. To understand the benefits, assume that a rule executes at the site it is stored (this is desirable as it is stored at the site from where it maximally uses the rulebase and database). The following benefits can be identified:

- **reduced search space:** knowledge base must be searched during resolution (i.e. query compilation) to locate the definitions of predicates occurring in the body of a rule. Confining this search to a smaller cluster rather than GKB reduces the search time.

- **reduced communication:** by executing the rule at the site where relevant rules and database are stored, we will need to move only the results of rule to the query site.

We can formulate our strategies for allocation of rules to sites from the above considerations. A rule that uses data and/or rules from only one site is best stored at that site. However, if a rule uses databases or knowledge bases at multiple sites must be stored to that site so as to maximize the above benefits. Of these, the communication cost is the most dominating, and to minimize it we need to consider some application specific data such as frequencies of executions, expected volume of results, etc.

2.3 Normalization of Rules

Before rule allocation, we normalize the rules of GKB for achieving the following objectives:

(i) Rules with the same head predicate are assigned to the same cluster.

To meet this objective, we replace multiple definitions of a rule by a single 'disjunctive' rule with body as disjunction of earlier bodies.

(ii) Rules involved in a dependency cycle are assigned to the same cluster.

To achieve this, we replace all the rules of a cycle by a single 'compiled recursive' rule.

After allocation of the rules of a rulebase, the compiled recursive rules and disjunctive rules can be replaced back by the rules merged in their definitions.

Example

Consider the following database systems and a global KB.

Library database schema:
  Book(Book_no,Title,Author,Area).
  Issue_status(Book_no,Emp_no,Issue_Date,Due_Date).
  Emp(Emp_no,E_name,Rank,Ph_no).

R&D Department database schema:
  Emp(Emp_no,E_name,Rank,Ph_no).
  Research_Int(Emp_no,E_name,Area).
  Paper_Pub(Emp_no,E_name,P_Title,Area,Kind_of_Pub,Year).

Global Knowledge Base:
  Issue_Class(B#,E#,En,DD) :- Emp(E#,En,R,Ph#), Issue_status(B#,E#,ID,DD).
  Co_worker(E#,En,R,Ph#,A) :- Emp(E#,En,R,Ph#), Research_Int(E#,En,A).
  Overdue_Book(B#,T,E#,DD) :- Book(B#,T,Au,A), Issue_status(B#,E#,ID,DD).
  Expert_in_Area(Au,A) :- Paper_Pub(E#,Au,T,A,K,Yr).
  Expert_in_Area(Au,A) :- Book(B#,T,Au,A).
  Expert_Colleague(E#,En,R,A) :- Expert_in_Area(En,A), Co_worker(E#,En,R,A).

We will use this as a running example to illustrate clustering techniques. Note that the two Expert_in_area definitions will be replaced by the following disjunctive definition :
Expert_in_area(Au,A) :- Book(B#,T,Au,A) ∨ Paper_pub(E#,Au,T,A,K,Yr). ∎

3   Rule Allocation Problem

We wish to allocate the rules of a knowledge base to sites based on their usage of data stored in each database system and rule execution information pertaining to transmission cost. The mapping of rules to sites can be performed in two ways: statically or dynamically. In static mapping, rules are mapped to sites based on their usage of database at various sites, and this mapping does not change during execution. In dynamic mapping, the mapping decisions are based on the site of rule execution. In this paper, we will consider static clustering only because we expect the knowledge base and database definitions as well as the pattern of their usage to be fairly stable, and also the dynamic mapping involves some overheads at execution time and is not guaranteed to be cost-effective.

We propose the partitioning of a global rulebase into as many clusters as there are sites. If there are m sites, then there will be m clusters. It means that if a rule r_i is placed in cluster k, then it is mapped to site k.

3.1 Inputs

Let n be the number of rules, m be the number of sites and l be the total number of relations stored at various sites. We will use the following index variables:

i, i'	:	for rules
j, j'	:	for relations
k, k', y, x	:	for sites or clusters

A rule-rule dependency matrix, $P=\{p_{ii'}\}$ for $1 \leq i, i' \leq n$, is defined as

$$p_{ii'} = \begin{cases} 1 & \text{if rule } i \text{ is dependent on rule } i' \\ 0 & \text{Otherwise} \end{cases}$$

A relation-site allocation matrix, $A=\{a_{jk}\}$ for $1 \leq j \leq l$, and $1 \leq k \leq m$, is defined as

$$a_{jk} = \begin{cases} 1 & \text{if relation } j \text{ is present at site } k \\ 0 & \text{Otherwise} \end{cases}$$

Each rule r_i is associated with a relative execution frequency f_{ik}, which gives how frequently r_i is executed at site k. The frequency matrix F is defined as

$$F = \{f_{ik} \mid 1 \leq i \leq n \text{ and } 1 \leq k \leq m\}$$

We assume that frequencies are measured over a suitable time frame.

A rule-relation cost matrix T is defined as

$$T = \{t_{ij} \mid 1 \leq i \leq n \text{ and } 1 \leq j \leq l\}$$

where t_{ij} is the average volume of data contributed by relation j to rule i (if rule i uses relation j in its definition; otherwise t_{ij} is zero). The result size cost matrix, Z is defined as

$$Z = \{z_i \mid 1 \leq i \leq n\}$$

where z_i is the average answer size returned by execution of rule i.

The matrices T and Z will be used for computing communication costs, which, we assume, is directly proportional to the amount of data transferred from one site to another (and not on how the sites are connected by the topology).

Example

The matrices given below give input values for our example. Note that, rules 4 & 5 are replaced by a disjunctive rule because they have same head predicate and it corresponds to 4th row of matrices P, T, F, and Z.

$$P = \begin{bmatrix} 0 & 0 & 0 & 0 & 0 \\ 0 & 0 & 0 & 0 & 0 \\ 0 & 0 & 0 & 0 & 0 \\ 0 & 0 & 0 & 0 & 0 \\ 0 & 1 & 0 & 1 & 0 \end{bmatrix} \quad T = \begin{bmatrix} 0 & 4 & 1.5 & 0 & 0 \\ 0 & 0 & 4 & 2.2 & 0 \\ 8 & 1.5 & 0 & 0 & 0 \\ 2.4 & 0 & 0 & 0 & 1.4 \\ 0 & 0 & 0 & 0 & 0 \end{bmatrix}$$

$$A = \begin{bmatrix} 1 & 0 \\ 1 & 0 \\ 1 & 1 \\ 0 & 1 \\ 0 & 1 \end{bmatrix} \quad F = \begin{bmatrix} 3 & 1 \\ 0 & 1 \\ 1 & 0 \\ 1 & 1 \\ 1 & 3 \end{bmatrix} \quad Z = \begin{bmatrix} 1.2 \\ 1.0 \\ 0.8 \\ 0.6 \\ 1.6 \end{bmatrix}$$

3.2 Output

Each rule should be assigned to only one cluster. The clustering problem is essentially to generate a system configuration specified by matrix $X = \{x_{ik}\}$, where x_{ik} for $1 \leq i \leq n$ and $1 \leq k \leq m$ as defined below.

$$x_{ik} = \begin{cases} 1 & \text{if rule } r_i \text{ is assigned to cluster } k \\ 0 & \text{Otherwise} \end{cases}$$

4 A Heuristic Algorithm for Clustering

The optimal allocation problem, as shown in [14], is a 0-1 quadratic programming problem. For large knowledge bases, its execution speed becomes prohibitive. In this section, we propose an efficient heuristic algorithm which can be used for allocation of thousands or millions of rules to sites. The proposed clustering approach is based on coloring the nodes of a dependency graph which is modeled from the input matrices defined in section 3.1. A dependency graph is a directed graph which is composed of a set of nodes representing rules and relations, and a set of directed edges representing dependencies between the nodes. A unique color is assigned to each site and relations stored at this site have the same color. Since relations may be replicated, they may have more than one color. In the dependency graph, initially the colored nodes correspond to relations and uncolored nodes correspond to rules. The objective is to color all the uncolored nodes such that total cost is minimized.

4.1 Representation of KB as a Dependency Graph

We construct a dependency graph $G = \langle V, E \rangle$ of a KB using input matrices P, A, T, and Z defined in section 3.1. The graph in figure 1 is the dependency graph for our example. Here, the relation nodes are shown by rectangles on the right with its allocation site alongside them. The rule nodes are represented by small circle on the left along with their weights in parentheses.

The same dependency graph can be redrawn as in figure 2 as a hierarchy, where relation nodes are at leaf level. We associate distance d with each rule node computed as

$$\text{max (distance of descendents)} +1$$

with d=0 for leaf nodes. All nodes with same d are drawn at same level. We define height h of the hierarchy as maximum d of any node. There are two advantages in representing the hierarchy in this fashion: we allocate rules to sites level-by-level, and addition of new rules does not affect level of a node. All edges are directed downwards, hence arrows are omitted.

A triplet, say $L_i = <d, Q, k>$ is associated with each rule node i, where

$L_i.d$ attribute denotes distance of node i from leaf level,

$L_i.Q$ attribute denotes communication cost of executing rule i once, and

$L_i.k$ attribute denotes site allocated to rule i .

The values of attributes $L_i.d$ and $L_i.Q$ are intermediate values of our algorithm and $L_i.k$ is the final result. figure 2 shows these triplets for our example.

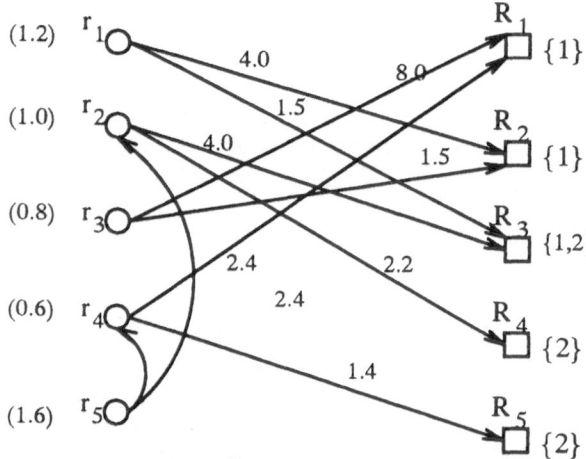

Figure 1: A dependency graph

4.2 A Heuristic Algorithm for Rule Allocation

We now present an efficient heuristic algorithm for rule allocation to the sites. For exposition purpose, we present it in terms of coloring of rule nodes in the dependency graph. Our objective is to color all uncolored rule nodes in such a way that overall communication cost is minimized. Our algorithm is characterized by the following heuristics:

- allocate rule to a site based on sites allocated to its descendent nodes,

- choose the site which gives minimum communication cost for this rule,

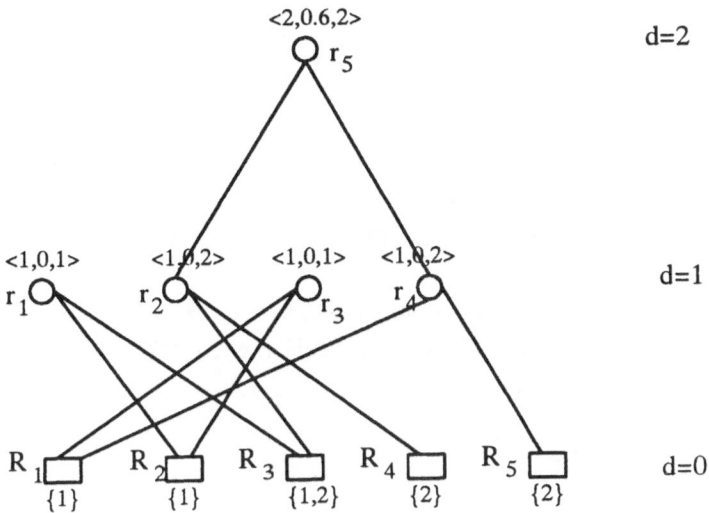

Figure 2: A dependency graph with hierarchy

- subsequent allocations do not affect allocation of this rule, and

- a site which does not share its rulebase and/or database with a rule need not be considered for allocation to that rule.

As a consequence of the above heuristics, the algorithm may not produce a globally optimum solution. In section 5, we will analyze its effectiveness on sample knowledge bases. The algorithm proceeds as follows:

(i) Determine distance d of each node; this is easily done using matrix P (basically implementing a depth-first search algorithm).

(ii) Allocate colors to rule nodes in bottom-up fashion, going up in increasing order of distance d. It is now always possible to allocate color when we visit a rule node, since its descendents by then would have been colored.

(iii) To choose a color for a node, say i, we first compute set $X = \{X_1\} \cup \{X_2\}$ of colors of its descendents, where X_1 is a set of colors of the descendent relation nodes and X_2 is a set of colors of the descendent rule nodes. The set X gives possible choices, and for each choice we compute the communication cost using the input matrices.

We define matrix B as

$$B = T * \bar{A} = \{b_{ix} \mid 1 \leq i \leq n \text{ and } 1 \leq x \leq m\}$$

where b_{ix} is volume of data (due to descendent relations) accessed from remote sites if rule i is assigned to site x. $\bar{A}$ is obtained by taking the complement (i.e., switching between 0 and 1) of the entry in A.

For each color $x \in X$, the cost consists of the following terms:

(a) Cost of accessing relations from remote sites

$$C_d = \left(\sum_{y \in X} f_{iy} \right) \cdot b_{ix}.$$ (1)

(b) Cost of using its subordinate rules

$$C_r = \left[\left(\sum_{y \in X} f_{iy} \right) \cdot \sum_{i'=1, i \neq i'}^{n} \left(\begin{cases} z_{i'} + L_{i'}.Q & \text{if } p_{ii'} = 1 \text{ and } L_{i'}.k \neq x \\ L_{i'}.Q & \text{if } p_{ii'} = 1 \text{ and } L_{i'}.k = x \\ 0 & \text{if } p_{ii'} \neq 1 \end{cases} \right) \right]$$ (2)

where $L_{i'}.Q$ represents communication cost of executing rule i' once.

(c) Cost of sending results of executing rule i when it is invoked from other sites is

$$C_s = \left(\sum_{y \in X, \, y \neq x} f_{iy} \right) \cdot z_i.$$ (3)

(iv) The value of $L_i.Q$ can be calculated from the following equation

$$L_i.Q = \sum_{i'=1, \, i \neq i'}^{n} \left(\begin{cases} z_{i'} + L_{i'}.Q & \text{if } p_{ii'} = 1 \text{ and } L_i.k \neq L_{i'}.k \\ L_{i'}.Q & \text{if } p_{ii'} = 1 \text{ and } L_i.k = L_{i'}.k \\ 0 & \text{if } p_{ii'} \neq 1 \end{cases} \right) + b_{iL_i.k}.$$ (4)

Recall that $L_i.Q$ represents single execution cost of rule i. The second term of this equation is due to remote relations accessed by rule i.

(v) Net communication cost for executing rule i over all sites at specified frequencies is

$$Val_i = \left(\sum_{k=1}^{m} f_{ik} \cdot L_i.Q \right) + \left(\sum_{k=1, \, k \neq L_i.k}^{m} f_{ik} \cdot z_i \right).$$ (5)

The algorithm **KB_clustering** is described in figure 3.

Lemma: The heuristic algorithm **KB_clustering** has a time complexity $O(me)$, where m is the number of sites (colors) and e is the number of dependency edges in the hierarchy graph.

Proof: An uncolored node can have a choice of at most m colors. We calculate the cost for each edge incident at the uncolored node. There are at most e edges. Assume that the cost of computation for a single edge is unity. Therefore, the total cost of computation is $O(me)$. ∎

Example

In figure 2, either color 1 or color 2 can be assigned to rule r_1 because they are adjacent colors to it. If color 1 is assigned, then the cost will be

$$C_1 = C_d + C_r + C_s$$
$$C_1 = 0 + 0 + 1 * 1.2 = 1.2.$$

If color 2 is assigned to rule r_1, then the cost will be

$$C_2 = C_d + C_r + C_s$$
$$C_2 = 4*4+0+3*1.2 = 19.6.$$

$C_{t_1} = \text{Min}(1.2, 19.6) = 1.2$, which corresponds to color 1. Hence, color 1 is assigned to rule r_1. Likewise, we find the color of all rules. These are shown by the third attribute of the triplets. The total communication cost for clustering the knowledge base in the example is 6.4. This turned out to be equal to the optimal value found by the Exhaustive Enumeration (EE) algorithm. ∎

```
global data:
    input matrices: P, A, F, T, Z ;
    output array: L (of triplets);
    computed matrix B = T * Ā;
    computed matrix S = T * A;

procedure KB_clustering();
    total_cost=0;
    for d = 1 to h do
        for each node i having distance d do
            {
            allocate_color(i, d: in; Val_i: out);
            total_cost = total_cost + Val_i;
            }
        endfor
    endfor
    print total_cost;
end_KB_clustering.

procedure allocate_color(i, d: in; Val_i: out);
    compute the adjacent colors of node i;
    X_1 = {y | s_iy ≠ 0, y = 1 ··· m};
    X_2 = {L_i'.k | p_ii' = 1, i' = 1 ··· n};
    X = {X_1} ∪ {X_2};
    C_t_i = Min {∀_x∈X [C_d + C_r + C_s]} where C_d, C_r, and C_s are computed
                    as per equations 1, 2, and 3 respectively;
    L_i.k = x corresponding to the minimum cost C_t_i;
    L_i.d = d;
    compute L_i.Q using equation 4;
    compute Val_i using equation 5;
end_allocate_color.
```

Figure 3: Algorithm for knowledge base clustering

5 Empirical Results

We have carried out a number of experiments to measure the performance of the proposed heuristic algorithm. The algorithm has been designed for carrying out

Rules and Sites	Comm. cost of heuristic solution	Comm. cost of optimal solution
12 rules, 2 sites	71.84	66.52
37 rules, 3 sites	93.04	91.60
20 rules, 4 sites	54.25	54.25
70 rules, 5 sites	218.16	203.10
100 rules, 6 sites	208.26	189.54
137 rules, 7 sites	164.43	153.67
200 rules, 8 sites	324.46	-
340 rules, 9 sites	283.57	-
638 rules, 10 sites	302.62	-

Table 1: Comparison between communication costs

the allocation efficiently in situations involving hundreds or thousands of rules and tens of sites. The running time of Exhaustive Enumeration (EE) algorithm in such situations is expected to be unacceptable even though it produces an optimal allocation. This is due to the fact that number of permutations are exponential in nature. The second objective in conducting our experiments was to measure the quality of the results given by our heuristic algorithm as compared to the optimal algorithm. In this section, we report our experimental results for both these algorithms. They were coded in C and executed on the SPARC based ICL/ICIM DRS 6000 machine.

5.1 Random KB Hierarchies

The performances of the two algorithms for a set of randomly chosen KB hierarchies is given in Tables 1 and 2. In each example, we decided on the number of rules and sites, but inter-relationships between the rules as well as between rules and relations were chosen randomly. We found that going beyond the 137 rules and 7 sites case resulted in very high execution times for exhaustive enumeration algorithm and '-' in the tables indicate that we could not obtain the value because of very high execution time. Table 1 compares communication costs for allocations produced by the two algorithms. The results indicate that the heuristic solutions are close to the optimal solutions. It is, of course, difficult to generalize from these limited results on random examples. Table 2 compares running speeds of these two algorithms. It confirms that our algorithm is indeed very efficient and can be used for clustering large knowledge bases.

5.2 Effect of Height

A knowledge base may be large horizontally or vertically with reference to its hierarchical representation. That is, the KB may be 'broad' or 'deep' (as shown in figure 4) or something in between. Intuitively, one feels that real-world knowledge bases will have many more nodes at lower levels (i.e., at lower distances d), and the heights of KB hierarchies will be quite limited. We were

Rules and Sites	Running time of heuristic algorithm (milliseconds)	Running time of exhaustive enumeration algorithm (milliseconds)
12 rules, 2 sites	10	18
37 rules, 3 sites	40	3.6×10^3
20 rules, 4 sites	16	470
70 rules, 5 sites	61	2.3×10^5
100 rules, 6 sites	88	7.9×10^6
137 rules, 7 sites	124	1.3×10^7
200 rules, 8 sites	324	-
340 rules, 9 sites	283	-
638 rules, 10 sites	302	-

Table 2: Comparison of execution times

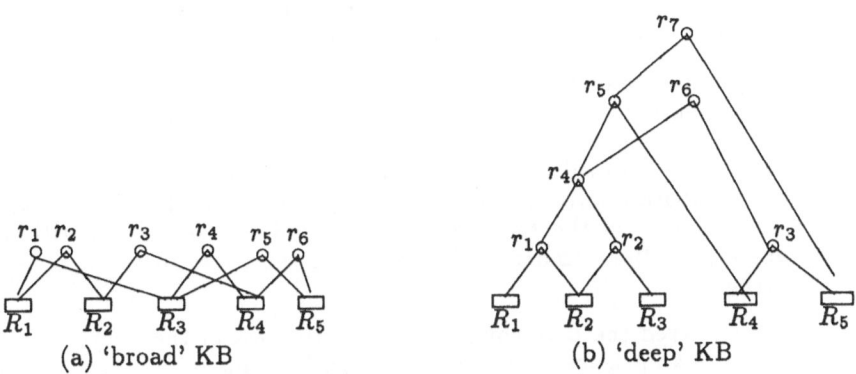

(a) 'broad' KB   (b) 'deep' KB

Figure 4: KB characterization on height

interested in observing the performance of our heuristic algorithm for knowledge bases of different heights. It is simple to show that for h=1, the heuristic algorithm gives the optimal result. The algorithm may deviate from optimum as height increases, since it may not consider certain coloring alternatives. This is confirmed by our results in Table 3, which compares communication costs of allocations obtained by the two algorithms for a knowledge base for 120 rules, 3 sites and 142 edges, arranged in hierarchies of heights 1 to 7. For lower heights, heuristic results are same as the optimal. As h increases, the heuristic results are suboptimal, but are well within 20% of the optimal results for the observed cases.

6   Conclusions

This paper has addressed the problem of allocating rules in a distributed deductive database system, where knowledge base (a collection of rules) and database are shared across autonomous sites. The problem is relevant and challenging

Height (h)	Comm. cost of heuristic solution	Comm. cost of optimal solution
1	40.8	40.8
2	67.7	66.7
3	70.8	69.1
4	97.6	89.5
5	105.2	99.3
6	123.0	101.5
7	128.3	119.9

Table 3: Comparison of Costs for different h

in applications involving large knowledge bases. We have identified communication cost as the primary consideration in allocation of rules.

We have proposed an efficient heuristic algorithm for decomposing a knowledge base into non-redundant clusters so that a cluster can be allocated to a single site. We represent the knowledge base as a directed hierarchy with relations as leaf nodes and rules as non-leaf nodes, and edges representing usage of rules and database relations. The proposed algorithm performs allocations in bottom-up fashion in the hierarchy. The complexity of the algorithm is $O(me)$, where m is the number of sites and e is the edges in the knowledge base hierarchy.

We have analyzed the performance and effectiveness of the heuristic algorithm for a set of knowledge bases, characterized in terms of number of nodes, sites and edges. We found that allocations produced by it had total communication costs well within 20% of the optimal.

For performance analysis, we have attempted a characterization of large knowledge bases. Our characterizations are based on the premises that real-world knowledge bases will be more 'broad' than 'deep', and that they will contain some natural clusters covering majority of the rules, with only a relatively smaller number of rules which 'span' across these clusters. we have defined these characterizations with respect to the hierarchical structure of a knowledge base. We then studied performance of the algorithm for knowledge base hierarchies of varying heights. We found the heuristic algorithm to give solutions which are reasonably close to the optimal solutions.

For further work, we plan to characterize the real-world knowledge bases in greater depth. In our experimental performance evaluations, we were constrained by our inability to obtain optimal results for large knowledge bases using the exhaustive enumeration algorithm for comparing effectiveness of our heuristic algorithm, since the running time of the optimal algorithm was prohibitive. We wish to explore these experiments further in future. We also propose to investigate other approaches such as dynamic programming and genetic algorithm, and compare them with the heuristic algorithm proposed here.

Acknowledgment

We thank S. Seshadri for his helpful comments. We are extremely grateful to Daniel Chan (Computing Science Department, Glasgow University, U.K.) for presenting our paper at the conference and for his suggestions.

References

[1] J. Banarjee, W. Kim, S.J. Kim, and J.F. Garra. Clustering a DAG for CAD databases. *IEEE Transactions on Software Engineering*, 14(11):1684–1699, Nov. 1988.

[2] D.A. Carlson and S. Ram. An architecture for distributed knowledge base systems. *DATA BASE*, 22(1):11–21, 1991.

[3] S. Ceri, G. Gottlob, and L. Tanca. *Logic Programming and Databases*. Springer-Verlag Berlin Heidelberg New York, 1990.

[4] S. Ceri and G. Pelagatti. *Distributed Databases: Principles and Systems*. McGraw-Hill Book Co., 1986.

[5] J.R. Chang and A.R. Hurson. Effective clustering of complex objects in OODB. In *Proc. ACM SIGMOD Int. Conf. on Management of Data*, pages 22–31, May 1991.

[6] V.V. Dixit and D.I. Moldovan. The allocation problem in parallel production systems. *Journal of Parallel and Distributed Computing*, 8:20–29, 1990.

[7] M. Gallaire, J. Minker, and J. Nicolas. Logic and database: A deductive approach. *ACM Computing Survey*, 16(2):153–185, 1984.

[8] M.R. Garey and D.S Johnson. *Computers and Intractability: A Guide to the theory of NP-Completeness*. W.H. Freeman and Company New York, 1979.

[9] M.A. Jabri. A prolog knowledge based systems shell for vlsi cad. In *27th Design Automation Conference, IEEE CS Press*, pages 272–277, June 1990.

[10] Anil K. Jain and R.C. Dubes. *Algorithms for Clustering Data*. Prentice Hall Advanced References Series, 1988.

[11] W. Kim, H.T. Chou, and J. Banerjee. Operations and implementation of complex objects. In *Proc. 3rd Int. Conf. on Data Engg.*, pages 626–633, 1987.

[12] Y.P. Li. DKM: A distributed knowledge representation framework. In *Proc. 2nd Int. Conf. on Expert Database*, pages 313–331, 1988.

[13] P. Markenscoff and W. Liaw. Task allocation problems in distributed computer systems. In *Proc. Int. Conf. on Parallel Processing*, pages 953–960, 1986.

[14] M.K. Mohania. Decomposition of a knowledge base for a distributed deductive database system. In *4th Int. Conf. on Management of Data, Bangalore India*, pages 94–106, Dec. 1992.

[15] M.K. Mohania and N.L. Sarda. An architecture for a distributed deductive database system. *Appearing in IEEE TENCON'93*, Bezing, China, 1993.

[16] K. Oflazer. Partitioning in parallel processing of production systems. In *Proc. Int. Conf. on Parallel Processing*, pages 92–100, 1984.

[17] H.S. Stone. Multiprocessor scheduling with the aid of network flow algorithms. *IEEE Transactions on Software Engineering*, 3(1):85–93, Jan. 1977.

Bottom-Up Evaluation of DataHiLog

Peter T. Wood*

Department of Computer Science, University of Cape Town
Rondebosch 7700, South Africa

Abstract

Many queries which may be useful in applications such as "data mining" and knowledge acquisition in databases cannot be expressed in traditional query languages such as SQL or Datalog because they lack the ability to query information regarding the schema of the database. We study the language DataHiLog introduced by Ross as a restriction of the language HiLog developed by Chen, Kifer and Warren. DataHiLog is still able to mix schema-level and instance-level queries, while avoiding the problem of infinite answers which can arise in HiLog. We show how the standard techniques for Datalog can be extended to provide a bottom-up evaluation mechanism for DataHiLog, and consider whether Datalog optimization techniques can also be extended to DataHiLog.

1 Introduction

Most declarative query languages for relational databases have been based on first-order predicate calculus or Horn clauses. While these languages are powerful, there are still useful queries which can not be expressed in them, as well as ways of structuring data which are excluded by them.

Example 1 Consider a database representing people and the relationships among them. The relations *mother* and *father* are stored explicitly in the database, while other relationships are defined by means of rules in the language Datalog [16]:

$$parent(X, Y) \leftarrow mother(X, Y).$$
$$parent(X, Y) \leftarrow father(X, Y).$$
$$ancestor(X, Y) \leftarrow parent(X, Y).$$
$$ancestor(X, Y) \leftarrow parent(X, Z), ancestor(Z, Y).$$

We adopt the convention of using uppercase letters for variables, and lowercase letters for constants. Assume that the tuples $(sally, jill)$ and $(jill, john)$ are in the *mother* relation. We may wish to establish in what ways *jill* and *john* are related. This requires a "schema-level" query of the form $? - X(jill, john)$. which would not be permitted in Datalog. The answers we would expect are *mother*, *parent* and *ancestor*. For the query $? - X(sally, john)$. we would expect the single answer *ancestor*. □

Example 2 As an example of structuring information, consider a simplification of the method for representing a generic hierarchy over vehicles proposed by Smith and Smith shown in Figure 1 [15].

---

*Part of this work was performed while the author was visiting the Computer Systems Research Institute, University of Toronto, Toronto, Ont. M5S 1A4, Canada.

vehicle:

identity number	manufacturer	medium category	propulsion category
V1	Mazda	land vehicle	motorized vehicle
V2	Schwin	land vehicle	man powered vehicle
V3	Boeing	air vehicle	motorized vehicle
V4	Aqua Co	water vehicle	wind propelled vehicle
V5	Gyro Inc	air vehicle	motorized vehicle

motorized vehicle:

identity number	horsepower	motor category
V1	150	rotary
V3	9600	jet
V5	1500	rotary

air vehicle:

identity number	maximum altitude	lift category
V3	30	plane
V5	5.6	helicopter

Figure 1: Relations representing a generic hierarchy.

This requires the ability to store relation names as values in other relations. a characteristic not permitted by first-order languages. To retrieve all information regarding the various vehicles, we would like to be able to express a rule of the form:

$$v(U, V, W, X, Y, Z) \leftarrow vehicle(U, V, W, X), W(U, Y, \_), X(U, Z, \_).$$

Once again, there is a need to have variables ranging over predicate names. □

The languages HiLog [3, 4], DataHiLog [13], and relational HiLog [14] have been developed to address the above deficiencies, among others. The initial motivation for the development of HiLog was to provide a clean syntax and sound semantics for some of the ad-hoc higher-order features of Prolog [3]. Another use for the language is as an implementation language for a number of object logics which have been proposed [4, 5, 7, 8].

From a database perspective, HiLog can be viewed as a more powerful version of Datalog, allowing, for example, the mixing of queries of database instances with those about the schema. Queries of this form, such as "what relations contain value x?", may also be useful in the areas of "data mining" and knowledge acquisition from databases.

Example 3 One of the classic examples of the power of HiLog is the following pair of rules which define a generic transitive closure predicate.

$$tc(R)(X, Y) \leftarrow R(X, Y).$$
$$tc(R)(X, Y) \leftarrow R(X, Z), tc(R)(Z, Y).$$

By specifying a query of the form $? - tc(r)(X, Y)$., one can compute the transitive closure of any given relation r. A problem, however, occurs if the query is of the form $? - tc(R)(a, b)$, where one might be trying to establish in what ways a and b are related. Now, assuming there is a relation r in the database, R can be bound to each of r, $tc(r)$, $tc(tc(r))$, and so on. $\square$

In the following we consider a restriction of the language HiLog to the language DataHiLog [13]. In fact, in this paper we restrict DataHiLog further by requiring that no negative literals appear in the body of any rule. There are two principle motivations for this restriction. On the one hand, DataHiLog is still more powerful than (function-free, negation-free) Datalog, being able to express both of the queries mentioned in Examples 1 and 2 above; on the other, efficient evaluation methods may be available for DataHiLog but not for HiLog in general. Since it is easy to recognise whether a given HiLog program is in fact a DataHiLog program, such special purpose evaluation techniques can be applied when appropriate.

The problem identified in Example 3 above does not occur with the simplified language DataHiLog. Although the above example could not be expressed as neatly in DataHiLog, it can be written as follows.

$$tc(R, X, Y) \leftarrow R(X, Y).$$
$$tc(R, X, Y) \leftarrow R(X, Z), tc(R, Z, Y).$$

Although this program is not strictly equivalent to that of Example 3, the answers to it are guaranteed to be finite, no matter what query is posed. This is because variables can be bound only to constants, not arbitrary terms, in DataHiLog.

In this paper, we develop a bottom-up evaluation procedure for DataHiLog. Using the additional relational algebra operators defined in [14], this is a relatively straightforward modification of the bottom-up evaluation for Datalog [16]. Ross gave an overview of the bottom-up evaluation of full HiLog using the magic sets rewriting method in [13], but he imposes a condition of range-restrictedness on programs which is more strict than the conditions we propose. Ross also shows, in principle, how relational HiLog queries can be evaluated in [14]. However, relational HiLog does not permit the formulation of recursive queries, and hence does not require the specification of a fixpoint evaluation mechanism. We give a detailed presentation of how DataHiLog queries might be evaluated with reasonable efficiency.

The outline of the paper is as follows. In the next section, we provide background information in terms of definitions of the languages and algebraic operators we will be studying. Section 3 is devoted to a comparison of various restrictions placed on DataHiLog programs in order to ensure that the answers to queries are always finite. The description of the bottom-up evaluation procedure for DataHiLog is divided between Sections 4 and 5. In Section 4 we consider the problem of computing a relation representing the body of a DataHiLog rule, this being used in Section 5 in a method to evaluate complete DataHiLog programs. Section 6 provides some thoughts on how to improve the efficiency of the proposed evaluation procedure, as well as how Datalog optimization techniques might or might not be able to be extended to DataHiLog.

2   Background

We shall assume that the reader is familiar with the language Datalog, as well as with the techniques for its bottom-up evaluation as described, for example, in Ullman's books [16, 17].

The syntax and semantics of HiLog, as well many examples of its elegance both as a logic programming language and a database query language. were introduced by Chen, Kifer and Warren in [3, 4]. Subsequently, Ross proposed a stable model semantics and a well-founded model semantics for HiLog programs with negative literals in the bodies of rules [13]. In so doing, he also introduced the restriction of HiLog to *Datahilog* in order to characterise a class of programs for which evaluation is guaranteed to terminate.

The language DataHiLog we study is identical to that of Ross. except that we do not allow negative literals in the bodies of rules. The language is defined as follows.

Definition 1 A DataHiLog *term* is either a variable or a constant symbol. If t. $t_1, \ldots, t_n$ are DataHiLog terms, where $n \geq 1$, then $t(t_1, \ldots, t_n)$ is a DataHiLog atom[1]. A DataHiLog *rule* is a logical rule of the form

$$A \leftarrow A_1, \ldots, A_n.$$

where $n \geq 0$, and A and each A_i is a DataHiLog atom. A DataHiLog *program* is a finite set of DataHiLog rules. $\square$

We will also refer to the atoms in the body of a DataHiLog rule as subgoals. Subgoals with constant predicate symbols, such as $p(X, Y)$, will be termed *ordinary* subgoals, while those with variable predicate symbols, such as $X(Y, Z)$, will be called *variable* subgoals.

In fact, we shall usually call rules for which $n = 0$ *facts*, and assume that a DataHiLog program is a set of rules other than facts   As we shall see in the next section, we will also consider only facts which are ground, allowing us to view such facts as being stored in a database as relations. This is similar to Datalog, where the set of facts is called the EDB (extensional database), while the set of relations computed by the given program is called the IDB (intensional database). The EDB and IDB are usually assumed to be disjoint.

In DataHiLog, however, we can no longer distinguish the EDB and IDB, since the EDB may be modified during evaluation of a program. In addition. we cannot always tell by inspection of the program what "IDB" relations will be produced. Instead of referring to the EDB, we will call the set of facts stored in the database before execution of a given program the *initial* database.

Example 4 Assume we have as initial database the single fact $e(e, c)$. The program P:

$$X(Y, Z) \leftarrow e(X, Y), e(Z, Y).$$

both adds a new tuple (c, e) to relation e, and produces a new relation c not mentioned (explicitly) in P. $\square$

---

[1] Since relations must have at least one attribute, 0-ary atoms are not allowed.

Assume we have a set of facts F stored as relations, and consider the evaluation of a program P in which the complete set of arities of predicate variables is $\{i_1, \ldots, i_k\}$. Then we can assume the initial database I comprises a relation r^{i_j}, $1 \leq j \leq k$, for each constant symbol r mentioned in F or in P. That is, each constant can be interpreted either as itself or as a number of relations of differing arities. Of course, only the relations corresponding to facts in F are nonempty in I.

Ross has also defined a relational calculus based on HiLog, called *relational* HiLog [14]. The terms of relational HiLog are identical to those of DataHiLog; the difference is in the formulas which are allowed in the two languages.

Definition 2 [14] A relational HiLog *term* is either a variable or a constant symbol. If $t, t_1, \ldots, t_n$ are relational HiLog terms, where $n \geq 1$, then $t(t_1, \ldots, t_n)$ is a relational HiLog *atom*. Relational HiLog *formulas* can be built from relational HiLog atoms in the usual way using the connectives $\vee$, $\wedge$, $\neg$, the quantifiers $\forall$, $\exists$, and parentheses. $\square$

In order to prove equivalences between various forms of relational HiLog and relational algebra, Ross introduced two classes of relational operators, in addition to the standard relational algebra. The first operator is called an *expansion* operator, denoted by α^k, $k \geq 1$, which expands a set of relation names into the union of relation extensions of arity k.

Definition 3 Let R be a relational expression with one component (or attribute). Then $\alpha^k(R)$ denotes the relation of arity $k+1$ defined by

$$\bigcup_{r \in R}(\{r\} \times r(X_1, \ldots, X_k)).$$

$\square$

The second class of new relational operators are the *totality* operators. For each $k \geq 1$, there is a totality operator ρ_k which holds for all relation names whose extensions at arity k are nonempty. It is often convenient to view each ρ_k as a unary relation.

We will use the above operators in Section 4 when compiling an expression for evaluating the body of a DataHiLog rule. Before doing so, we consider various restrictions on DataHiLog rules in order to ensure that answers to queries are finite.

3 Levels of Safety for DataHiLog

We now define what it means for a DataHiLog rule to be range-restricted or strongly range-restricted. These definitions are natural modifications of the corresponding ones in [13], where additional conditions are imposed because of the presence of negative subgoals. The differences between the following two definitions are highlighted in italics.

Definition 4 We say that a DataHiLog rule r is *range-restricted* if

1. every variable appearing in an argument in the head of r also appears as an argument in the body of r, and

2. there exists an ordering $A_1, \ldots, A_n$ of the atoms in the body of r such that if a variable X appears in the predicate name of A_j, then either X appears as an argument in A_k, for some $k < j$, or X appears in the predicate name in the head of r.

If every rule in a DataHiLog program P is range-restricted, then we say that P is range-restricted. We also have to ensure that predicate names are ground in queries to range-restricted programs. This can be achieved by requiring that the rule

$$answer(X_1, \ldots, X_n) \leftarrow Q(X_1, \ldots, X_n).$$

is range-restricted, where $Q(X_1, \ldots, X_n)$ is the conjunction of literals in the query. $\square$

Definition 5 We say that a DataHiLog rule r is *strongly range-restricted* if

1. every variable appearing in an argument *or in the name* in the head of r also appears as an argument in the body of r, and

2. there exists an ordering $A_1, \ldots, A_n$ of the atoms in the body of r such that if a variable X appears in the predicate name of A_j, then X appears as an argument in A_k, for some $k < j$.

If every rule in a DataHiLog program P is strongly range-restricted, then we say that P is strongly range-restricted. There is no need to restrict the queries to strongly range-restricted programs. $\square$

We now introduce a third definition of safety for DataHiLog. In essence, it is the same as the definition for safe Datalog programs.

Definition 6 We say that a DataHiLog rule r is *safe* if every variable appearing in an argument or in the name in the head of r also appears in the body of r. Program P is safe if every rule in P is safe. $\square$

Example 5 The following DataHiLog rules are strongly range-restricted:

$$p(X) \leftarrow X(a), q(X).$$
$$tc(G, X, Y) \leftarrow graph(G), G(X, Y).$$
$$Medium(Name) \leftarrow vehicle(Medium, Name).$$

The following DataHiLog rules are range-restricted, but not strongly range-restricted:

$$X(Y) \leftarrow p(Y, Z), X(Z).$$
$$X(a).$$
$$X(Z) \leftarrow X(Y), Y(X, Z).$$

The first and third rules above are also safe, while the second is not. On the other hand, the following DataHiLog rule is safe but not range-restricted:

$$p(Z) \leftarrow X(Y), Y(X, Z).$$

Thus while all strongly range-restricted rules are range-restricted and safe, the classes of range-restricted rules and safe rules are incomparable. $\square$

Since range-restricted rules allow for nonground facts (as indicated in the above example), we do not consider them further in this paper.

4 Evaluating Rule Bodies

We begin our discussion of evaluating DataHiLog programs by considering techniques for evaluating the body of a single rule. In this respect, we follow Ullman's approach [16]. Methods for evaluating an entire program are presented in the next section.

Assume we are given the following strongly range-restricted DataHiLog rule:

$$p(X, Z) \leftarrow q(X, Y), r(X), X(Y), Y(Z).$$

where we have already computed relations Q and R for subgoals q and r, respectively. Values for the predicate variable X can be obtained from either the first argument of q or the first argument of r, while values for Y can be obtained from either the second argument of q or the first argument of X.

In order to reduce the number of potential bindings for X, we should join $Q(X, Y)$ and $R(X)$ before passing any bindings to $X(Y)$. Let

$$S(X, Y) := Q(X, Y) \bowtie R(X)$$

where S is a new temporary relation. We can now evaluate either $X(Y)$ or $Y(Z)$. Let $T(X, Y)$ and $U(Y, Z)$ be the temporary relations for $X(Y)$ and $Y(Z)$, respectively. Then we have

$$T(X, Y) := \alpha^1(\pi_{\$1}(S(X, Y)))$$
$$U(Y, Z) := \alpha^1(\pi_{\$2}(S(X, Y)))$$

Alternatively, having computed T, we could compute U as follows:

$$U(Y, Z) := \alpha^1(\pi_{\$2}(T(X, Y)))$$

Now we simply join the three temporary relations to obtain a relation over X, Y and Z representing the body of the rule:

$$S(X, Y) \bowtie T(X, Y) \bowtie U(Y, Z)$$

Rather than making the production of relation S part of the evaluation process, one might be tempted to perform a rewriting of the program as follows:

$$s(X, Y) \leftarrow q(X, Y), r(X).$$
$$p(X, Z) \leftarrow s(X, Y), X(Y), Y(Z).$$

where s appears nowhere else in the program. This is similar to the use of supplementary predicates in the magic sets transformation [17]. This will work if the program is strongly range-restricted and we assume that s does not appear in any of the initial relations. However, if the program is not strongly range-restricted, there may be an atom of the form $X(Y, Z)$ in the body of some other rule in the program which will match $s(X, Y)$, possibly producing results different from those of the original program.

Now consider evaluating a rule which is not strongly range-restricted but is safe, for example:

$$p(X, Z) \leftarrow X(Y, W), W(Z).$$

Let $Q(X, Y, W)$ and $R(W, Z)$ be the temporary relations for $X(Y, W)$ and $W(Z)$, respectively. Since X does not appear as an argument of any subgoal, we will have to use the totality operator to produce Q. We could, of course, also use the totality operator to evaluate $W(Z)$ but choose not to do so. The relations Q and R are computed as follows:

$$Q(X, Y, W) := \alpha^2(\rho_2)$$
$$R(W, Z) := \alpha^1(\pi_{\$3}(Q(X, Y, W)))$$

The relation R computed in this way can be no larger than that for $W(Z)$ obtained using the totality operator, hence our preference for avoiding the totality operator whenever possible. As before, the relation for the body is obtained by joining Q and R. The general algorithm is given below.

Algorithm 1: Computing the relation for a DataHiLog rule body.

INPUT: The body of a DataHiLog rule r, which we shall assume consists of subgoals $S_1, \ldots, S_n$ involving variables $X_1, \ldots, X_m$. For each ordinary subgoal S_i, a relation R_i of the same arity has already been computed.

OUTPUT: An expression of relational algebra computing $R(X_1, \ldots, X_m)$, a relation comprising exactly the set of tuples $(a_1, \ldots, a_m)$ such that, when we substitute a_i for X_i, $1 \leq i \leq m$, all the subgoals $S_1, \ldots, S_n$ are made true.

METHOD: The expression is constructed in the following stages.

1. Construct a "predicate binding" graph G as follows: there is a node v_i for each subgoal S_i in r, and an edge from v_i to v_j if S_i contains the predicate variable of S_j as an argument. Thus S_i provides a set of bindings for the predicate variable of S_j.

2. Partition the subgoals into two sets: the set C of ordinary subgoals, and the set V of variable subgoals. No node in G corresponding to a subgoal in C can have an incoming edge.

3. Collapse all nodes in G corresponding to subgoals in C into a single node c. If r is strongly range-restricted, then every node is reachable from c. We now construct expressions for relations corresponding to subgoals in r according to an ordering given by a topological sort of G starting at c, which, whenever possible, chooses as the next node, one from which an incident edge was just deleted, rather than one which had no incoming edges in the original graph. Since G may be cyclic, this process may terminate without having deleted all nodes in G. If this occurs, the cycle is broken by choosing a node with maximal outdegree, deleting all its incoming edges, and continuing.

4. Relational expressions are computed in three different ways: one for the special node c, one for nodes without incoming edges, and one for nodes with an incoming edge.

(a) The relation for node c is computed as follows. Let the variables which appear in C as well as either in V or in the head of r be $X_{i_1}, \ldots, X_{i_k}$. Compute an expression for the relation $T(X_{i_1}, \ldots, X_{i_k})$ using Algorithm 3.1 in [16].

(b) Let v_i be a node (other than c) which had no incoming edges in G, and assume that S_i has j arguments. Then R_i is the expression

$$\pi_{V_i}(\sigma_{F_i}(\alpha^j(\rho_j))).$$

That is, we find all relations of arity j and expand them. As in [16], F_i is used to cater for constants and repeated variables, while V_i ensures only a single component of those which share variables in S_i appears in the relation.

(c) All other nodes v_j in G will be reached through the deletion of an edge, say from v_i to v_j. In R_i, there is a unique component in which the predicate variable of S_j appears. Assume that this is the k'th component of R_i, and that S_j has l components. Then R_j is the expression

$$\pi_{V_j}(\sigma_{F_j}(\alpha^l(\pi_{\$k}(R_i)))).$$

That is, we expand all relation names of arity l found in the k'th component of R_i, where F_j and V_j are as in (b) above.

5. The final expression is given by the natural join of all expressions computed in (4) above.

5 Evaluating DataHiLog Programs

In this section, we consider bottom-up evaluation techniques for complete DataHiLog programs, given the method of the previous section for evaluating the body of a DataHiLog rule. Once again, we follow the standard techniques for evaluating Datalog programs, namely, a fixpoint computation based on the naive or semi-naive algorithm [16].

In Datalog, rather than applying the fixpoint computation to the entire program which would be inefficient, the program is partitioned into mutually recursive rule components to which the fixpoint computation is applied. We would like to adopt the same technique for DataHiLog. However, while the detection of mutually recursive rules is simple in Datalog, such detection is more subtle and complicated in DataHiLog.

The following two examples demonstrate recursive single-rule programs, the first with a predicate variable in the body, the second with a predicate variable in the head. We will write the initial values of all (nonempty) relations in the database as facts in the Prolog style. Program P_1 is as follows:

$$e(a, b).$$
$$e(b, a).$$
$$p(X, Y) \leftarrow e(X, Z), W(Y, Z).$$

Since p is initially empty, the first round of the fixpoint computation yields $p(a, a)$ and $p(b, b)$. Now $W(Y, Z)$ matches $p(a, a)$ and $p(b, b)$, so that $p(a, b)$ and

$p(b, a)$ are produced in the second round. Thus, p is dependent on itself by virtue of the variable subgoal in the body.

We have already seen program P_2 which is as follows:

$$e(e, c).$$
$$X(Y, Z) \leftarrow e(X, Y), e(Z, Y).$$

The first iteration produces only $e(c, e)$, while the second iteration yields $c(e, c)$ in addition. Thus e is dependent on itself by virtue of the variable head.

Once again, we modify Datalog techniques for use with DataHiLog. Given a program P, we use a (modified) dependency graph G to detect mutually recursive rules in P, as well as to determine the order in which the rules of P should be evaluated.

The nodes of G are the predicate names (along with their arities) appearing in P. For example, if $p(X, Y)$ appears in P, then $p/2$ is a node in G. On the other hand, if $X(Y, Z)$ appears in rule i of P, then $i/2$ is a node in G (we assume that predicate names are disjoint from the integers).

There is an edge labelled i from each node representing a subgoal of rule i to the node representing the head of rule i. If X/n appears in the body of rule i, then there is an edge labelled i from each n-ary predicate in G to the node i/n. If X/n appears in the head of rule i, then there is an edge labelled i from node i/n to each n-ary predicate in G.

It is necessary to represent variable subgoals explicitly, rather than simply including edges to all appropriate predicates, in order to classify correctly rules of the form

$$X(Y, Z) \leftarrow Z(X, Y).$$

In addition, if one does not have distinct nodes in G for variable subgoals appearing in different rules, it is possible to classify certain nonrecursive rules incorrectly as recursive. The following program provides such an example:

1. $p(Y, Z) \leftarrow e(X, Y), e(Z, Y).$
2. $X(Y, Z) \leftarrow r(X, Y, Z).$
3. $q(X, Y, Z) \leftarrow X(Y, Z).$

If $X(Y, Z)$ in both rules 2 and 3 was represented by a single node v, there would be an edge from v to $e/2$ because $X(Y, Z)$ appears in the head of rule 2, and from $e/2$ to v because $X(Y, Z)$ appears in the body of rule 3. However, rules 2 and 3 are not mutually recursive.

Note that, in general, X/n in the body of a rule will also (potentially) match (nonempty) relations in the initial database. However, we do not depict this fact in G since it does not affect the detection of recursion among the rules of the program.

Example 6 Consider the following program P:

1. $X(Y, Z) \leftarrow p(X, Y), q(Z, Y).$
2. $s(X, Y) \leftarrow r(X, Y).$
3. $p(X, Y) \leftarrow t(X, Y, Z).$
4. $p(X, Y) \leftarrow u(X, Y).$

The dependency graph for P is depicted in Figure 2. $\square$

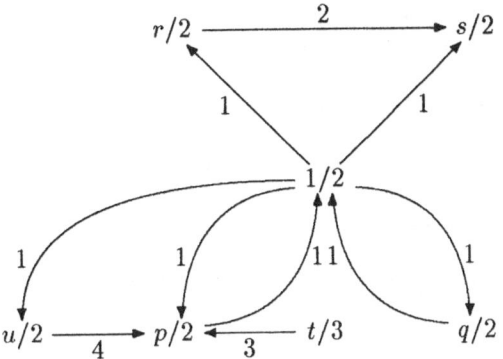

Figure 2: Dependency graph for Example 6.

As in Datalog, a predicate is recursive if it appears on some cycle in G. The strongly connected components (SCC's) of G indicate the sets of mutually recursive rules in P. Thus rules 1 and 4 in the above example are mutually recursive. If we form the acyclic condensation of G by collapsing SCC's to single nodes, we obtain a (partial) ordering for evaluating a program. In the above example, we would evaluate rule 3 first, followed by a fixpoint evaluation of rules 1 and 4, after which rule 2 would be evaluated.

Note that if $u(X, Y)$ in rule 4 had been $U(X, Y)$, $u/2$ in G would have become $4/2$ and there would have been additional edges in G from p, q, r and s to $4/2$, making rules 1, 2 and 4 mutually recursive.

We have not stated yet how to evaluate the head of a rule given an expression for its body. When the head contains a predicate variable, we need an operation which is effectively the inverse of the expansion operator. In any event, since we do not assume that the heads of rules are rectified [16], we need to take repeated variables and constants into account.

Assume, for example, we have an expression $T(X, Y, Z, W)$ for the body of a rule whose head is $Z(X, X, a)$. The operation we need to perform to evaluate the head is as follows: for each $r \in \pi_{\$3}(T)$,

$$r := r \cup (\pi_{\$1, \$1}(\sigma_{\$3='r'}(T)) \times \{a\})$$

For a constant predicate name, such as in $p(X, X, a)$, the operation is simpler, namely,

$$p := p \cup (\pi_{\$1, \$1}(T) \times \{a\})$$

Since all relations other than those representing facts in the initial database are assumed to be empty and rules are assumed to be safe, these operations have the desired effect.

Because of space limitations, we do not present the general algorithm here, but rely on the above examples to indicate the approach needed. We denote the evaluation of rule r with initial relations $R_1, \ldots, R_k$ for the ordinary subgoals of r by $\text{EVAL}(r, R_1, \ldots, R_k)$.

Finally, we present the naive algorithm for computing the fixpoint of an SCC of a DataHiLog program. A semi-naive algorithm can be defined similarly. The principal difference from the algorithm for Datalog given in [16] is that we have to take into account new relations generated during the computation.

Algorithm 2: Evaluation of a DataHiLog SCC.

INPUT: An SCC and an initial set N of constant predicate names appearing in the SCC, along with, for each predicate $p \in N$, a relation P (possibly empty) representing its initial value.

OUTPUT: A set of relations representing the least fixpoint of the rules in the SCC.

METHOD:

> **repeat**
>   **for each** $p \in N$ **do**
> $old\_P := P$
> $old\_N := N$
>   **for each** rule r in SCC **do**
>   EVAL($r, old\_P_1, \ldots, old\_P_k$), where $N = \{p_1, \ldots, p_k\}$
> $M :=$ predicate names generated by EVAL
> $N := N \cup M$
> **until** $old\_N = N$ **and** $old\_P = P$ for all $p \in old\_N$
> output P for each $p \in N$

6 Conclusion

The language DataHiLog provides a more powerful query capability than that offered by (negation- and function-free) Datalog. Nevertheless, we have seen that the basic approach to the bottom-up evaluation of Datalog programs can be extended to DataHiLog programs. The presence of predicate variables, however, would seem to have a negative effect of the efficiency of query evaluation Below, we present preliminary thoughts on how evaluation efficiency might be improved, firstly in terms of reducing the size of the sets of mutually recursive predicates (the SCCs), and secondly in terms of making use of constants in queries.

Since, with predicate variables, we expect larger SCCs in DataHiLog programs than in Datalog programs, the rule ordering techniques presented by Ramakrishnan *et al.* in [12] are particularly appropriate to DataHiLog. In certain circumstances it is also possible to reduce the size of an SCC. For example, it is not hard to show that if a program P is strongly range-restricted and no constant predicate symbol p/n which appears in the head of a rule in P appears either in any initial relation or as an argument in any rule head of P, then no predicate variable X can ever be instantiated to p. This means that, in Figure 2, we can delete the edges from $1/2$ to both $p/2$ and $s/2$. Although this does not remove the mutual recursion in this case, it would in the following program:

$$X(Y, Z) \leftarrow p(X, Y), q(Z).$$
$$p(X, Y) \leftarrow e(X, Y, Z).$$

If we have schema information which includes type constraints on the attributes of relations, we might be able to detect additional optimisations. For example, disjointness constraints between attributes might allow us to classify rules which would otherwise be potentially recursive as nonrecursive. Consider the rule

$$X(Y) \leftarrow e(X, Z, W), Z(Y).$$

and assume that we know that X and Z are disjoint. This might be because X represents "medium category" while Z represents "propulsion category" from Example 2. Then the above rule is clearly nonrecursive, while our procedure would classify it as recursive. This is also related to the problem of detecting bounded recursion in Datalog programs, as studied, for example, in [11, 19].

It does not seem to be trivial matter to extend techniques which make use of constants in queries, such as magic sets [1, 2] and factoring [9, 10, 18], to DataHiLog programs. For example, assume we are given the following strongly range-restricted program P:

$$sub(X, Y) \leftarrow cat(X), X(Y).$$
$$sub(X, Y) \leftarrow sub(X, Z), Z(Y).$$

which computes the transitive closure of a hierarchy of categories (for example, ACM CR categories). With query $? - sub(h, Y).$, this can be rewritten using factoring as

$$f\_sub(Y) \leftarrow cat(h), h(Y).$$
$$f\_sub(Y) \leftarrow f\_sub(Z), Z(Y).$$
$$sub(h, Y) \leftarrow f\_sub(Y).$$

This query is still strongly range-restricted and can presumably be evaluated as least as efficiently as the original. With query $? - sub(X, h.2.1).$, P can be rewritten as

$$f\_sub(X) \leftarrow cat(X), X(h.2.1).$$
$$f\_sub(X) \leftarrow f\_sub(Y), X(Y).$$
$$sub(X, h.2.1) \leftarrow f\_sub(X).$$

However, this program is no longer strongly range-restricted and it is not clear whether its evaluation will be more or less efficient than that of P. While in P the complete transitive closure is computed, in the above program unrestricted retrievals from all unary relations in the database are performed on each iteration of the evaluation procedure. The same problem would be encountered with the magic sets transformation, unless we insist on preserving an ordering of subgoals for the recursive rule which satisfies the definition of strongly range-restrictedness.

While magic sets and factoring can transform a program which is strongly range-restricted into one that is not (and therefore potentially less efficient to evaluate), the converse is also true. Consider the following program P

$$X(Y, Z) \leftarrow X(W, Z), e(Y, W).$$

with query $? - a(Y, Z)$. Although P is not strongly range-restricted (it happens to be range-restricted), after transforming it with the magic sets transformation we get

$$m\_2(a).$$
$$X(Y,Z) \leftarrow m\_2(X), X(W,Z), e(Y,W).$$

which is strongly range-restricted.

We plan to address the above issues in a subsequent paper, while also considering the implications of adding negation to DataHiLog. Since we have a bottom-up procedure for evaluating DataHiLog programs, computing the well-founded semantics of a DataHiLog program with negation as defined in [13] should be possible using the algorithm described by Kemp *et al.* in [6].

Acknowledgements

The author would like to thank Andrew Luppnow and the referees for comments which helped improve the paper.

References

[1] F. Bancilhon, D. Maier, Y. Sagiv, and J. Ullman. Magic sets and other strange ways to implement logic programs. In *Proc. Fifth ACM SIGACT-SIGMOD Symp. on Principles of Databases Systems*, pages 1–15, 1986.

[2] C. Beeri and R. Ramakrishnan. On the power of magic. In *Proc. Sixth ACM SIGACT-SIGMOD-SIGART Symp. on Principles of Databases Systems*, pages 269–283, 1987.

[3] W. Chen, M. Kifer, and D. S. Warren. HiLog: A first-order semantics of higher-order logic programming constructs. In *Proc. North American Conf. on Logic Programming*, pages 1090–1114, 1989.

[4] W. Chen, M. Kifer, and D. S. Warren. HiLog as a platform for database languages. In R. Hull, R. Morrison, and D. Stemple, editors, *Proc. 2nd Int. Workshop on Database Programming Languages*, pages 315–329. Morgan Kaufmann, 1989.

[5] W. Chen and D. S. Warren. C-Logic for complex objects. In *Proc. Eighth ACM SIGACT-SIGMOD-SIGART Symp. on Principles of Databases Systems*, pages 369–378, 1989.

[6] D. B. Kemp, D. Srivastava, and P. J. Stuckey. Magic sets and bottom-up evaluation of well-founded models. In V. Saraswat and K. Ueda, editors, *Logic Programming, Proceedings of the 1991 International Symposium*, pages 337–354, San Diego, USA, 1991. The MIT Press.

[7] M. Kifer and G. Lausen. F-Logic: A higher order language for reasoning about objects, inheritance and scheme. In *Proc. of the ACM SIGMOD Conf. on Management of Data*, pages 134–146, 1989.

[8] M. Kifer and J. Wu. A logic for object-oriented logic programming (Maier's O-Logic revisited). In *Proc. Eighth ACM SIGACT-SIGMOD-SIGART Symp. on Principles of Databases Systems*, pages 379–393, 1989.

[9] J. F. Naughton, R. Ramakrishnan, Y. Sagiv, and J. D. Ullman. Argument reduction by factoring. In *Proc. 15th Int. Conf. on Very Large Data Bases*, pages 173–182, 1989.

[10] J. F. Naughton, R. Ramakrishnan, Y. Sagiv, and J. D. Ullman. Efficient evaluation of right-, left-, and combined-linear rules. In *Proc. ACM SIG-MOD Conf. on Management of Data*, pages 235–242, 1989.

[11] J. F. Naughton and Y. Sagiv. A decidable class of bounded recursions. In *Proc. Sixth ACM SIGACT-SIGMOD-SIGART Symp. on Principles of Databases Systems*, pages 227–236, 1987.

[12] R. Ramakrishnan, D. Srivastava, and S. Sudarshan. Rule ordering in bottom-up fixpoint evaluation of logic programs. In *Proc. 16th Int. Conf. on Very Large Data Bases*, pages 359–371, 1990.

[13] K. A. Ross. On negation in HiLog. In *Proc. Tenth ACM SIGACT-SIGMOD-SIGART Symp. on Principles of Databases Systems*, pages 206–215, 1991.

[14] K. A. Ross. Relations with relation names as arguments: Algebra and calculus. In *Proc. Eleventh ACM SIGACT-SIGMOD-SIGART Symp. on Principles of Databases Systems*, pages 346–353, 1992.

[15] J. M. Smith and D. C. Smith. Database abstractions: Aggregation and generalization. *ACM Trans. Database Syst.*, 2(2):105–133, June 1977.

[16] J. D. Ullman. *Principles of Database and Knowledge-Base Systems*, volume 1. Computer Science Press, Rockville, Maryland, 1988.

[17] J. D. Ullman. *Principles of Database and Knowledge-Base Systems*, volume 2. Computer Science Press, Rockville, Maryland, 1989.

[18] P. T. Wood. Factoring augmented regular chain programs. In *Proc. 16th Int. Conf. on Very Large Data Bases*, pages 255–263, 1990.

[19] P. T. Wood. Syntactic characterizations of 1-bounded datalog programs. In *Proc. 2nd Int. Conf. on Deductive and Object-Oriented Databases*, pages 208–225, 1991.

Author Index

Published in 1990–92

Building Interactive Systems: Architectures and Tools
Philip Gray and Roger Took (Eds)

Functional Programming, Glasgow 1991
Proceedings of the 1991 Glasgow Workshop on Functional Programming, Portree, Isle of Skye, 12–14 August 1991
Rogardt Heldal, Carsten Kehler Holst and Philip Wadler (Eds.)

Object Orientation in Z
Susan Stepney, Rosalind Barden and David Cooper (Eds)

Code Generation – Concepts, Tools, Techniques
Proceedings of the International Workshop on Code Generation, Dagstuhl, Germany, 20–24 May 1991
Robert Giegerich and Susan L Graham (Eds)

Z User Workshop, York 1991, Proceedings of the Sixth Annual Z User Meeting, York, 16–17 December 1991
J E Nicholls (Ed)

Formal Aspects of Measurement
Proceedings of the BCS-FACS Workshop on Formal Aspects of Measurement, South Bank University, London, 5 May 1991
Tim Denvir, Ros Herman and R W Whitty (Eds)

AI and Cognitive Science '91
University College, Cork, 19–20 September 1991
Humphrey Sorensen (Ed)

5th Refinement Workshop, Proceedings of the 5th Refinement Workshop, organised by BCS-FACS, London, 8–10 January 1992
Cliff B Jones, Roger C Shaw and Tim Denvir (Eds)

Algebraic Methodology and Software Technology (AMAST'91)
Proceedings of the Second International Conference on Algebraic Methodology and Software Technology, Iowa City, USA, 22–25 May 1991
M Nivat, C. Rattray, T Rus and G. Scollo (Eds)